Communicating Today

Second Edition

Raymond Zeuschner

California Polytechnic State University
San Luis Obispo

Allyn and Bacon

Boston   London   Toronto   Sydney   Tokyo   Singapore

Series Editor: Carla F. Daves
Vice President, Humanities: Joseph Opiela
Editorial Assistant: Andrea Geanacopoulos
Marketing Manager: Karon Bowers
Sr. Editorial Production Administrator: Susan McIntyre
Editorial Production Service: Ruttle, Shaw & Wetherill, Inc.
Interior Text Design: Glenna Collett
Composition Buyer: Linda Cox
Manufacturing Buyer: Megan Cochran
Cover Administrator: Linda Knowles
Photo Research: Laurie Frankenthaler

Copyright © 1997, 1993 by Allyn & Bacon
A Viacom Company
160 Gould Street
Needham Heights, MA 02194
Internet: www.abacon.com
America Online: Keyword: College Online

Library of Congress Cataloging-in-Publication Data

Zeuschner, Raymond F.
    Communicating today/Raymond Zeuschner, — 2nd ed.
        p.   cm.
    Includes bibliographical references and index.
    ISBN 0-205-20042-7
    1. Public speaking.   2. Communication.   I. Title.
    PN4121.Z46   1997
    302.2—dc20

96-25917
CIP

PHOTO CREDITS
p. 7, M & E Bernheim/Woodfin Camp & Associates; p. 10, 14, North Wind Picture Archives; p. 23,
Library of Congress; p. 28, North Wind Picture Archives; p. 32, Will Faller; p. 48, Tom McCarthy/
The Picture Cube; p. 51, Brian Smith; p. 58, Will Hart; p. 64, North Wind Picture Archives; p. 76,
Karsh/Woodfin Camp & Associates; p. 82, Stephen Marks; p. 85, Robert Harbison; p. 91, Robert
Azzi/Woodfin Camp & Associates; p. 108, Will Hart; p. 113, Will Faller; p. 122, Corbis-Bettmann;
p. 128, John Coletti; p. 140, Bob Daemmrich/The Image Works; p. 143, 152, Will Hart; p. 165,
176, John Coletti; p. 199, UPI/Corbis-Bettmann; p. 224, Don Farber/Woodfin Camp & Associates;
p. 235, Elizabeth Crews/Stock, Boston; p. 236, F. Pedrick/The Image Works; p. 242, Robert
Harbison; p. 244, Lawrence Migdale/Stock, Boston; p. 268, Jeff Greenberg/The Picture Cube;
p. 278, John Coletti; p. 287, The Image Works Archives; p. 292, UPI/Corbis-Bettmann; p. 303, Bob
Daemmrich/The Image Works; p. 312, Bob Daemmrich/Stock, Boston; p. 321, Paula Lerner/The
Picture Cube; p. 322, Robert Harbison; p. 339, Will Hart; p. 342, John Coletti; p. 343, Joseph
Nettis/Stock, Boston; p. 353, Robert Harbison; p. 354, David Burnett/Contact Press Images/
Woodfin Camp & Associates; p. 368, Michael Grecco/Stock, Boston; p. 372, Joseph Nettis/Stock,
Boston; p. 385, Robert Harbison; p. 398, Cary Wolinsky/Stock, Boston; p. 399, Bob Daemmrich/
The Image Works; p. 410, North Wind Picture Archives; p. 411, Swesrey/Gamma Liaison; p. 417,
Nathan Benn/Woodfin Camp & Associates; p. 418, Pamela Price/The Picture Cube; p. 420, Will
Hart; p. 424, AP/Wide World Photos; p. 425, North Wind Picture Archives.

Printed in the United States of America

10   9   8   7   6   5   4   3   2   1   02   01   00   99   98   97   96

Brief Contents

Contents

3 WHAT WE KNOW ABOUT LISTENING *37*

4 WHAT WE KNOW ABOUT CRITICAL THINKING *57*

5 WHAT WE KNOW ABOUT NONVERBAL COMMUNICATION *79*

6 WHAT WE KNOW ABOUT VERBAL COMMUNICATION *95*

 7 INTRAPERSONAL COMMUNICATION *117*

 8 INTERPERSONAL COMMUNICATION *135*

INTERVIEWING   *161*

 SMALL-GROUP COMMUNICATION   *181*

 PREPARING SPEECHES   *209*

19   DIVERSITY IN COMMUNICATION   *383*

20   COMMUNICATION AND TECHNOLOGY   *405*

Preface

We are nearly at the end of the twentieth century. The role of communication as a central force in our lives is reaffirmed in every area of human activity. The desire to communicate ideas and feelings remains important to people, and their concerns, fears, hopes, desires, questions, and answers are still the subject matter for their communication. With a wider array of communication methods available, people around the world are linked together ever more closely. Given the tremendous technological advances that have occurred over the past century and the dangers and risks that accompany these developments, it seems that improved competence in communication will play a pivotal role in determining the positive direction of future decisions. *Communicating Today* is designed to build your knowledge of communication and improve your ability to be an effective communicator. Although few of us will have the opportunity to influence major world events directly, we can all use communication to better our daily lives and interactions. In these small events, the larger fabric of social progress can develop.

Themes of the Book

This text is built on several premises that reflect the author's point of view concerning communication. As you read *Communicating Today,* you will find these themes:

- **Understanding Communication Principles.** The communication principles relate to you the results of many years of communication knowledge development. It is important to build a strong foundation on the principles which guide human communication. Although only major trends in human communication theory development are covered in the introduction, this theme appears throughout the book, showing you how and where communication principles evolved.

- **Development of Communication Competencies.** Application of skills makes the theory directly relevant and useful to you. Your class may offer some opportunities for practice, or you may need to work on these skills independently. Either way, you will see opportunities in every chapter to take the knowledge and theory developed by scholars over the years and put it to use in your daily activities.

- **Diversity in Communication.** It is true that we all possess the ability and desire to communicate. It is also true that we communicate in a variety of ways. We develop various languages, cultures, rules, norms, values, and expectations in our communication behavior, and these differences can be viewed as both a barrier to effective communication and a diversity to be celebrated and enjoyed. Diversity issues are addressed as a theme throughout the text, and Chapter 19 is focused on diversity as a unique communication perspective.

- **Influence of Technology.** Part of the story of civilization is the effect of new technologies on our communication. This theme is woven throughout the text and is featured in its own special box in each chapter. The final chapter in the book is devoted to this topic.

Features

The purposes and themes of the book are addressed in a variety of features and pedagogy that are designed to reinforce, clarify, or give added depth or application. You will notice these features in every chapter, and by making use of them from the outset, you can enhance your success in mastering the content and developing your abilities.

- **The Story of Communication Boxes.** In every chapter, the history and development of communication unfold as part of the story of our civilization. The communication boxes offer stories about people and events that illustrate the importance of communication throughout the development of civilization. These stories are designed to emphasize that the study of communication has a human face in addition to the studies, statistics, and advice that make up much of our knowledge.

- **Critical Thinking in Communication Boxes.** At every point in the study of communication, you will be asked to think carefully about concepts or applications. Although an entire chapter is devoted to specific aspects of critical thinking, it is not an event to be learned in isolation, but a process that can be applied in every communication situation. These boxes are designed to illustrate that point.

- **Diversity in Communication Boxes.** Diversity issues are relevant to almost every communication context. These boxes are designed to help us appreciate the function that diversity plays in our lives. Sometimes the examples are celebrations, and sometimes they are sad reminders of how far we still have to go.

- **Improving Competency Boxes.** Being a competent communicator is a major theme of the book, and each chapter has a boxed feature to challenge you to develop or apply a communication competency. Some of these challenges are meant to be taken immediately—take a break from your reading and try them out. Others are intended for daily application or for raising your awareness of a skill or application.

- **Technology in Communication Boxes.** Understanding the part technology has played in developing our communication and how it has influenced our ideas and concepts about communication is the purpose of these features. These boxes are designed to remind you of the pervasive influence of technology on your life.

Pedagogy

Every chapter also contains features that are designed to clarify the material and to assist you in mastering and reviewing information.

- **Chapter Objectives.** Each chapter begins with a statement of goals presented to help you see clearly the purpose of the material. It's a good idea to return to the objectives once you have finished reading the chapter to see whether those objectives have been met.
- **Chapter Summaries.** At the end of each chapter, a brief summary gives you a start on reviewing the themes presented in the chapter.
- **Key Terms.** Each chapter highlights vocabulary concerning key ideas and terms that are explained in the chapter. These terms can be used as study aid to help you focus on the themes and goals of the text.
- **Exercises.** Each chapter concludes with a set of exercises. Your instructor may assign some of these to you, or you may try some on your own. Some are quick and fun; others may involve starting a long-term project that lasts through the entire course.

Plan of the Book

There are many ways to present ideas about communication. This text takes a chronological approach. The first six chapters look at the past and the perspectives developed about communication study up to this point. Chapter 1 discusses how we arrived at this point in history and shows the link between the development of communication and the development of civilization. Communication principles (Chapter 2) summarizes scholarship in the field. Listening (Chapter 3), critical thinking (Chapter 4), nonverbal communication (Chapter 5), and verbal communication (Chapter 6) take the communication principles and provide you with an introduction to the development of knowledge in these specific areas.

Chapters 7–10 move from the past to the present and show how to apply many of the principles from the earlier chapters to personal communication situations. You will learn about intrapersonal communication (Chapter 7), interpersonal communication (Chapter 8), interviewing (Chapter 9), and small-group communication (Chapter 10).

Chapters 11–15 apply communication principles in a more public way. These five chapters detail the core of public speaking, both in preparing and presenting your own speeches and in analyzing the public communication of others (Chapters 11 and 12). The research that has led to the development of the information in these chapters is included. Informing other people (Chapter 13) and persuading others (Chapter 14) have both practical and ethical dimensions; the role of attitudes and values is also discussed. Applications to special settings (Chapter 15) ends this section with a discussion of situations you may find now in school and looks to applications beyond the classroom.

The last five chapters address the future of your communication applications and interests. Although some of you may already have careers (Chapter 16) and families (Chapter 17), these chapters point to ways you can apply your knowledge and skills of communication in new and effective ways. We all are

influenced by mass media communication (Chapter 18), so some of the principles that are discussed are important to us every day as we move to a future that
is increasingly dominated by media. The future of a diverse society is previewed
(Chapter 19) by discussing culture, gender, and health as three major areas in
which diversity and communication will continue to grow in importance.
Finally, the way technology influences our daily communication is explored
(Chapter 20). The past, present, and future effects are discussed by context.

ACKNOWLEDGMENTS

No one ever writes a book like this one alone. There have been dozens of people who have made contributions. Most directly, the energetic staff at Allyn and
Bacon: Carla Daves, Editor for Communication, whose continued enthusiasm
for this project has nurtured it to production; Andrea Geanacopoulos, Editorial
Assistant, whose positive communication skills have made each step of production easier for me. Special thanks go to my student, teacher, and friend, Steve
Mandel of Mandel Communications in Soquel, California, for sharing many
humorous and insightful examples of communication in action, some of which I
now pass along to the readers of this text. My colleagues at Cal Poly, especially
B. Christine Shea, Michael Fahs, and Steve McDermott, who were helpful, supportive, and willing listeners. The former dean of the School of Liberal Arts,
Sidney Ribeau, deserves thanks for supporting my request for a time grant at an
important juncture in my writing. I am certain there is no way to acknowledge
the many hours I took from my wife, Linda, and our children, Lisa and James,
during the writing of this work, but I shall try anyway in a more personal setting
than this paragraph.

Finally, I would like to acknowledge the debt owed to the reviewers of vari-
ous parts and stages of the manuscript as their comments were seriously read
and their suggestions were responded to in order to create a book for you, our
students. My appreciation to my colleagues: Ruth Aurelius, Des Moines Area
Community College; Edward Brown, Abeline Christian University; Robert
Dixon, St. Louis Community College; Kenneth Frandsen, University of New
Mexico; Carol Jablonski, Wake Forest University; Lee Polk, Baylor University;
Beth Waggenspack, Virginia Polytechnic Institute and State University.

In addition to those mentioned above, the second edition owes a debt of
gratitude to Michele Hunkele, Margaret Lant, James Howland, and Doug Smith,
colleagues at Cal Poly, and to the careful work and many suggestions provided by
users and reviewers to this text. I wish to thank Michael Hecht, Arizona State
University; Thomas M. Rapne, Northern Virginia Community College; John
Pauley, Saint Mary's College; Nan Peck, Northern Virginia Community College;
Lorraine Jackson, California Polytechnic State University; Kenneth D. Frandsen,
University of New Mexico; Leonard Wurthman, California State University; Mary
Bozik, University of Northern Iowa; Bobbie R. Klopp, Kirkwood Community
College; Donna Halper, Emerson College; Deanna D. Sellnow, North Dakota
State University; Robert Dixon, St. Louis Community College at Meramec; Judith
K. Bowker, Oregon State University.

How We Got Here: Communication Study in the Past

After reading this chapter, you should be able to:

- Describe the historical development of communication study in human societies.

- Understand the relationship between communication systems and political systems.

- Show how communication influenced the early development of our country, its traditions, and its institutions.

- Feel connected to a 5,000-year tradition of studying and applying communication principles and skills.

- Realize that the modern field of speech communication evolved as our knowledge grew and that it continues to expand its concerns and methods.

nthropologists are fairly certain that as ancient peoples of the north-central part of eastern Africa began to gather in groups, they used patterns of verbal and nonverbal signs to communicate. As these groups began to remain in stable clusters, the signs also stabilized and were taught to children by the group and then sometimes shared by others living near. Some signs probably imitated the sounds of nature or gestures that mimicked the complete action they indicated, and thus a vocabulary developed for each group. The story of the Tower of Babel is probably a good analogy for early language. As the groups interacted, languages were developed. When groups in an area interacted and combined, their languages also merged. Although we cannot pinpoint exactly the emergence of languages as we know them today, scholars generally agree that a somewhat common language emerged in Mesopotamia, centered on the modern nations of Iran and Iraq. They call this language **Indo-European,** but it was probably not a real language spoken consistently by any single group. It does, however, permit us to see a link between many modern Western languages, and often a word in English has a common root with a similar word in Farsi, Greek, Norwegian, or Coptic.

As people developed civilizations, they also created ways in which to record spoken sounds. Writing followed speech as a way to remember, transmit, or express spoken ideas. The early forms of both cuneiform (which eventually grew into systems of lettering) and hieroglyphics (which used pictures to symbolize words or sound) were found in the ancient Middle East. In Asia, the Chinese were developing a pictographically based writing system that survives today in many forms in modern China, Korea, and Japan.

One thing in these developments is very clear. When people began to write and record ideas that were meaningful to them, some of their earliest writings were about the importance of communication education.

EARLY EDUCATION

As civilization advanced, the training of young people to continue the ways of the culture began to take on regular, if informal, patterns. Children were usually taught at home and during local community events—meetings, meals, rituals, festivities, and religious activities. All of these events served to educate upcom-

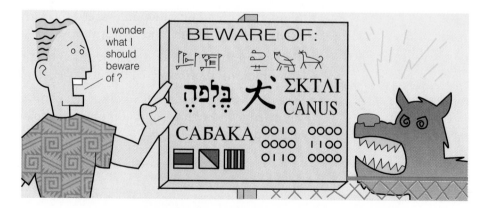

Writing became a way to remember spoken ideas.

ing generations about the group, and this method of education depended on oral language. Often, the most important person in the group was the one who presided over these events and communicated to the whole group. In other words, the best public speaker was an important person—then as now.

Western Approaches

When we turn to more formal training, we look back especially in this chapter to our roots in Western civilization and find that communication skills were an important part of early Egypt, Greece, and Rome.

Egypt.   The earliest fragments of writing we have in human civilizations come from Egypt. However, the hieroglyphic inscriptions remained indecipherable for nearly 2,000 years until 1799 with the discovery of the **Rosetta Stone** in Egypt. This stone, which is on display today in the British Museum of Natural History, carried an identical message inscribed in three languages, including Greek and hieroglyphics. In the 1800s, scholars in Europe were able to translate the ancient writings of these ancient Africans. Among those writings was a part of a lesson from the Egyptian Ptah-Hotep, who advised speakers to be clear, to talk to the concerns of the listeners, and to be careful to have good delivery, clear and loud. His advice, although over 3,000 years old, is still good for speakers of today. Egypt, however, was ruled by priests and pharaohs, who depended on religious authority and a divinely based dictatorial style of government. Other than for ceremony and discussion among themselves, they had little need for effective public speaking to the masses. Although they certainly had discussions and paid attention to nonverbal elements, they did not indicate that these communication areas were formally studied. We find that when our roots grew out of Africa and reached Greece, especially in the period 500–300 B.C., public speaking moved to a prominent position in education.

Greece.   About 2,600 years ago, the Greeks developed a city-state form of government in which citizens (generally, male property owners) gathered in public meetings to debate and decide matters of policy and to elect leaders. Although this system was a good beginning to democracy (our word is based on the Greek terms meaning "people" and "rule"), these meetings usually involved only a small fraction of the population. In Athens, for example, around the time of Socrates, there were only about 12,000 citizens in a population of about 120,000.

Because these meetings were both legislative and judicial, a citizen had to be able to speak well. We know of the first public speaking textbook: *Techne*, written about 465 B.C. by Corax, a Greek teacher from Sicily, which is concerned with teaching the art of public speaking, especially persuasion (Ryan, 1992). Small-group discussion was certainly a part of daily life in Greece, and the **Socratic method** of teaching by question-and-answer dialogue was certainly done best in small groups. However, the Greeks made major decisions in public meetings and therefore focused their communication training on that setting. This focus guided communication education in the West until modern times and has only recently been challenged by emerging lines of scholarship.

The ancient Greeks engaged in some practices of what we would now call *mass communication* in the form of declarations and announcements, but there was no press. Often, a courier would run with a written message from one place to another, and stories are told that if the news he brought was bad, the receivers would kill the messenger. These first attempts to be critics of mass communication were certainly hard on the couriers. Nevertheless, we can still see people reacting the same way when they say, "Hey, don't blame me, I'm just relaying the message!"

Many early Greek scholars devoted their teaching and writing to the study of communication, especially public speaking. While the first Greek academies usually taught four general subjects—rhetoric, mathematics, music and gymnastics—it was the study of the first, rhetoric, that included much of what we study today. To learn rhetoric, one also needed to be familiar with history, philosophy, grammar, and human nature. This sounds a lot like modern college requirements in general education! One of these teachers, Isocrates, wrote about the place of good public speaking in society, which is as true today as it was then:

TECHNOLOGY IN COMMUNICATION

From Papyrus to Microchips

The development of papyrus and vellum to replace clay tablets as writing surfaces profoundly affected the development of communication. Easier to store and easier to transport, sheepskin and especially paper made it possible to send letters over great distances and store large volumes of writing in small spaces. Early couriers paved the way for modern postal systems, and you can still visit the library at Ephesus, where Saint Paul stopped on his famous journey to Asia Minor. These technologies meant that the receiver needed to be able to read and understand the sender's writing and thus helped to foster standardized forms of language: grammars and vocabularies. These in turn promoted commerce, culture, and trade. Speed and the ability to store more information—the same two features helped to invent paper along the Nile Valley and the microchip in Silicon Valley.

> Because there has been implanted in us the power to persuade each other and to make clear to each other whatever we desire, not only have we escaped the life of wild beasts, but we have come together and founded cities and make laws and invented arts; and, generally speaking there is no institution devised by man which the power of speech has not helped to establish (Isocrates, 1929).

Probably the most influential book ever written about speech communication is *Rhetoric* by **Aristotle.** Building on ideas from Socrates and Plato, Aristotle added his own keen observation and insight into the topics of finding a subject and supporting materials, organizing them, using an appropriate level in the style of expression, delivering the speech so that it has clarity and impact, and using the speaker and listener's memory of events to make the speech appealing. Because he covered his material soundly and carefully, Aristotle is read widely today in translation and sometimes in the original. *Rhetoric* continues to teach new generations of students at the end of the twentieth century because of the care and depth of its explanation and applications (Cooper, 1932; Solmsen, 1954).

Although ancient Greece had many colorful, dramatic speakers, there was not complete freedom of speech, even for the privileged citizens. Socrates was fond of asking questions and instilled the same habit in his students. Sometimes the questions turned toward existing morals and values as well as the way those in power were behaving. Eventually, Socrates was convicted of corrupting the youth of Athens and was sentenced to death. His thoughts and teachings survive through the writings of his star pupil, Plato.

Teachers of public speaking found a wide and ready market for their classes and were termed **sophists,** which originally meant simply "wise man" or "teacher." As time went on and the opportunity for profit in this profession became evident, other teachers also set up shop, teaching clever or tricky ways to persuade, and the term *sophist* took on a negative connotation. Much the same fate has happened to the subject they taught—**rhetoric.** Originally, educated people knew rhetoric to be the study of creating, organizing, supporting, and presenting messages. It applied to written and spoken forms and was at the heart of curriculum then, as it is today. Your teachers in the speech, communication, and English departments still use the term in its traditional denotation. However, the popular use of the term has come to mean an empty display of superficial, emotional, or exaggerated words. Aristotle (like the teachers of rhetorical principles today) took great care to instill in students the importance of substance, ethics, support, and honesty in communication. So the term, **rhetoric** has had a complete reversal in connotation. Even after Rome conquered Greece and made it a part of the Roman empire, the influence of these Greek rhetoricians continued to be felt.

Rome.   The Roman armies did more than just conquer territory. They were good at exporting treasures from their new domains back to Rome. When they added Greece to their empire, they added the products of advanced culture and civilization. In early Rome, as in all of the Western world, knowing how to read, write, and speak Greek was the mark of an intelligent and well-educated person. The Roman armies sent back to Rome hundreds of Greek slaves, many of whom were well educated and were used as tutors in the most prominent families. It was a status symbol to have a Greek tutor in one's home. In Latin, these teachers were known by the term *rhetor.* Of course, these tutors taught what they knew best, and that included the rhetorical principles of the sophists.

The Roman forum, or marketplace, gives its name to the current practice of exchanging ideas and debating important issues in public. Over time, Roman writers created their own systems for teaching communication skills. Especially notable in this regard were Cicero and Quintillian. The Romans were excellent at organizing and systematizing everything, from roads and taxes to commerce, trade, and rhetoric. The rhetorical system they established is still used today. It divides the study and practice of rhetoric into five major headings which the Romans termed **canons,** meaning "laws."

Today, the first of these, **invention,** concerns the discovery of ideas and materials for a speech. When you brainstorm for topics, when you do research in a library, when you try to think up good explanations, you are dealing with invention. You need to consider your opinions, your audience, your analysis of the topic, and the ideas and opinions of your potential listeners. You must also consider your strengths and weaknesses. How might they affect the willingness of others to believe what you say?

The second major canon, **organization,** is based on the Latin term *disposition*. This canon is easiest to see in speech and English outlines. A variety of organizational formats is available to put ideas and information into a sensible pattern that you can go through and that your audience can follow. Any decisions you make about arranging material in a speech or an essay involves the principles of organization.

Style, the third canon, refers to the use of language. Are your sentences simple or complex or a variety? Do you use simple vocabulary or challenging terms, or do you lose your listeners by using too much jargon? You need to consider yourself, your subject, and your audience when making decisions about style. The Roman term for this concern was *elocution*.

The fourth, **memory,** refers to a speaker's ability to read and remember enormous amounts of material. In Greece and Rome, most major speeches were delivered from memory by people who depended on their memory to bring up facts, stories, previous cases, and other references. With the advent of libraries, manuscripts, notes, overhead projectors, flipcharts, data banks, and recordings, memory no longer serves the same purpose. However, when you are asked to respond in class to a teacher's question, to explain a complex idea spontaneously, or to write a clear and compelling essay on a test, you are working in the domain of memory. You may someday have an opportunity to give impromptu speeches, and memory is all that you will have.

The last Roman canon was **delivery,** which concerned the same things then as now—voice, articulation, volume, nonverbal cues, and gestures, all of which help listeners understand and appreciate the intellectual and emotional content of your message. The choices you make regarding the use of notes, your speaking volume, use of a microphone, where you look, and so on are all based on your sense of delivery.

The Romans' contributions were dominant for over 1,000 years of academic study in Western Europe; and because our educational and cultural traditions are so strongly tied to that heritage, they continue to be the perspective of this and other texts in the field. The continued use of these traditions has been called a **Eurocentric perspective,** meaning that we have largely underused ideas and concepts in our education and research from outside this Greco-Roman-European point of view. Some chapters of this book are direct descendants of the Greek and Roman systems and cover the five canons outlined above. There were, however, other communication traditions in non-Western civilizations. Recently, more and more of these traditions are being studied, appreciated, and incorporated into modern communication study.

Non-Western Approaches

Writings from Asian cultures indicate that some training in public speaking and in communication skills in general were also historically important in those cultures. With the invention of paper in China around A.D. 105, writing on paper replaced writing on silk and bamboo, both of which were less satisfactory, owing to their expense or weight. Block printing emerged in China in the T'ang

Dynasty period (618–906) and, when combined with paper, gave rise to an increased output of recorded information from that time (Carter, 1991). We have fairly extensive written records from Chinese and Japanese civilizations that include advice from Lao-Tzu in China and from Shotetsu Mongatari in Japan, whose book *Zoku Gunsho Ruiju* gave instruction on how to create beautiful and effective communication (deBarry, 1958, 1960). Writing around the year 1405, the Japanese critic Seami told his readers about the important goal of speaking in public: "the *yugen* (ultimate goal) of discourse lies in a grace of language and complete mastery of the speech of the nobility and gentry, so that even the most casual utterance will be graceful" (deBarry, 1958:280).

Other than the Egyptians and Ethiopians, most early African, Pacific Island, and Native American societies did not leave written records of their ancient history. The Incas developed a recording system of knotted string collections *(quipu)*, which registered events and accounting data for goods, production, and census information (Ascher and Ascher, 1981) and thus created an alternative to writing. The strong oral traditions of these cultures point out the prominent place of the **storyteller,** who acted as a sort of living history book. Through the use of memory and delivery, these key members of societies created the very fabric of culture. The most important member of a group was often neither the warrior nor the healer, but the storyteller. In these cultures, people spent much of their time in family or tribal clusters, and instead of libraries as we think of them today, they turned to a revered elder to relate the history and traditions of that group. In his important work *The Power of Myth,* Joseph Campbell tells us how cultures have developed in every part of the world largely through the myths they developed through their storytelling experiences (Campbell, 1988). In these cultures, many legends, songs, and chants developed into living libraries of information that members of the group passed on to successive generations. In modern times, storytelling still has an active role. Many colleges offer courses in storytelling. Each year, numerous storytelling festivals are held in the United States. The most prominent are those in the

The storyteller is a living library.

Southern Mountain region, where the tradition of storytelling, especially among African American families, remains strong. Some say that the powerful speaking style of leaders such as Martin Luther King, Jr. was founded on the strong oral traditions of the black community.

Showing those of us with Eurocentric traditions how important the storytelling skill is, Ray Bradbury, in his novel *Fahrenheit 451*, describes a world in which all the books have been burned by the government. A small band of rebels gathers, and each one "becomes" a book from the culture, learning it word for word and reciting it to keep it alive. The storytelling tradition of the past is used here as the vehicle to save literature for future generations in much the same way as traditional cultures passed on their past. Even today, strong social events center on Native American gatherings where storytellers continue the tradition, and in African American communities, you will still find some of the best of modern storytellers (Sawyer, 1962).

COMMUNICATION IN THE MIDDLE AGES AND RENAISSANCE EUROPE

The time between A.D. 500 and 1300 was an often chaotic and troubled time for Europe. Many small nations grew and fell around prominent leaders, and some of these groups spent their energies crisscrossing Europe as bands of destructive armies.

Preservation of Knowledge

Education, culture, literature, and history were kept mostly by the early Christian Church in European monasteries; by the great libraries and universities of the Arab world in North Africa and Spain; and by hundreds of Jewish settlements spread widely from the Mediterranean throughout northern and eastern Europe and possibly India and China. Each of these groups made important contributions to preserving the study of communication. For example, the early Christian Church, with its Roman/Latin base, preserved and expanded on the writings of Cicero and Quintillian.

The Beginnings of Mass Communication

Saint Augustine reminded his church that teaching the masses was part of its mission, and that could be done best by effective preaching—public speaking. Literacy was limited, and the only way most of the population would get access to the Bible was through someone else's reading it aloud. Saint Isidore of Seville lived in Spain in the early 600s and wrote about many topics, including the importance of language and speech (Brehart, 1912). In the Arab world of this period, great libraries were kept in North Africa and Spain and included many of the early Greek and Latin writings, such as Aristotle's *Rhetoric* and Cicero's *De Oratore*. Jewish civilization was intermixed throughout this area, and Jewish teachers (rabbis) were thought to have preserved and passed on principles of clear organization and effective style. History tells us that the beginnings of mass communication were evident in these times, and other factors, such as nonverbal communication, small-group discussion, and interpersonal communication, must have been evident. For example, the town crier was a person who presented announcements and read important information or related current events as a sort of radio broadcaster without the radio. Many councils must have used small-group communication, and interpersonal influence certainly affected everyday communication. However, because the formal emphasis was still on one expert or authoritative person speaking to and teaching others, the skills of public speaking for a privileged and elite few continued to occupy the study of communication.

 ## THINKING, SPEAKING, AND LEARNING

With the resurgence of culture and education, beginning in the early 1300s in Italy, the study of communication skills returned to the public area from its sheltered existence in the church, library, or rabbinical school.

Early Renaissance Schools

Early Italian schools followed much the same model as the first Greek academies; they were places for the male children of the wealthy to learn important skills and improve their thinking. Business and trade areas were discussed, especially since the great seaport cities of Italy were opening up the trade routes to the Middle East and Asia. Literacy expanded with trade and commerce, and more and more of the general population learned about communication in the forms of thinking, speaking, and writing. Universities taught their subjects through a method called *disputations,* which were public debates assigned by the professor. These debates called for students who were skilled in thinking and researching as well as in giving clear and compelling presentations. As the Renaissance moved northward, interest and training in communication skills moved with it.

CRITICAL THINKING IN COMMUNICATION

The Debate Method

The debate method of teaching thinking and speaking was a strong form. The famous question "How many angels can dance on the head of a pin?" might have been a topic for two students to dispute. The process of defining the arguments and then making them plausible depended to a large extent on the skills of logic. Aristotle used the syllogism, especially the shortened form called an *enthymeme,* to teach reasoning skills. Medieval debaters followed this tradition by training themselves in clear, critical, logical thinking.

Gutenberg's press helped to spread literacy.

The Impact of Printing

When printing began in Europe around 1450, books became available to many people for the first time in human history. With books and debating skills available to them, people began to ask many new questions—about life, business, government, and religion. While there had been freethinking people throughout history, their numbers now increased, and they communicated with each other and with the public through printed words that had not been available previously. Other people who could now read and write could also check ideas and opinions against other written works and debate and discuss their value and impact. Scholarship still remained largely within the church but was expanded to make it possible for the writings and philosophies of people such as Martin Luther to be widely read, discussed, and debated.

All of these factors increased communication. Through trade with many different cultures; through the education of a variety of populations; through discussions, arguments, and debates; and through interaction across cultures and national borders, communication helped to shape the Protestant Reformation and changed the way the Christian religion was practiced.

COMMUNICATION AND POLITICAL CHANGES

For many subsequent political leaders, such as Henry VIII, who ruled England from 1509–1547, the changes in religion were potentially dangerous to their survival. After all, most rulers used religion to justify their powers and positions.

Therefore questions and debates about religion led to similar examinations of the monarchy. Henry, the first truly modern monarch from the point of view of his education and insight, joined in questioning the established religion, broke with the existing church, and actually gained power from the momentum of the Protestant Reformation.

The Birth of Parliament

The English tradition of a monarch's sharing power with a limited group was already well established by Henry VIII's reign. One of his ancestors, King John (the same one from the tales of *Robin Hood)*, was forced by a group of nobles to sign the **Magna Carta** in 1215. This document was the basis for setting up a consultative form of government in England. That form of government then developed into England's **Parliament**—a term derived from the French word *parler,* meaning "to speak." Speaking is exactly what government representatives do in Parliament.

The Parliamentary Tradition

Much like the Greeks and Romans, members of Parliaments debated at great length about the policies of their governments. Especially in the British Parliament, on which we base our model of government, speaking freely developed into a protected and expected behavior over several hundred years.

For the most part, however, those who became members of Parliament were the same kind of people as those who always spoke in governmental affairs—wealthy, male property owners. They spoke to each other out of a common experience and educational background and out of concern for the protection of the privileged. In 1275, Edward I began the practice of inviting representatives of the merchant class and the towns' middle class to sit with Parliament. In turn, Parliament began the custom of voting the king some regular revenues from the trade and export business to run the government. Eventually, two houses, or sections, of Parliament, grew out of this practice, and they are still known today as the House of Commons and the House of Lords. This bicameral system is the forerunner of the U.S. Senate and House of Representatives.

Because it held the power of the purse, Parliament became the center of governmental authority. Although its power rose and fell over the next four hundred years, it always grew stronger in the long run.

Government of the People

It took the English revolution of 1645–1660 to give people other than the nobility a substantial role in government. As common people were elected to the government, and as its influence grew over the centuries, Parliament became the center of government, replacing the monarchy as the locus of power (Smith, 1957). To this day, the Prime Minister of England must be a member of Parliament. The Prime Minister usually has to climb the seniority ranks before becoming a party leader and then becomes the Prime Minister when that party is elected to a majority.

THE STORY OF COMMUNICATION

British Debate

There are dozens of famous speakers from the British Parliament, where wit, humor, and even clever insults developed into a fine art. In recent times, it is perhaps Winston Churchill who stands out among them. One of his most antagonistic opponents was Lady Astor, and their exchanges have become legendary. As the story goes, one time when Churchill had had a little too much to drink, he encountered Lady Astor and remarked, "Madame, you are exceedingly ugly." She responded, "And you, sir, are exceedingly drunk!" Churchill took a deep breath and replied, "That may be true, madame, but in the morning, *I* shall be sober." Infuriated, Lady Astor exclaimed, "Sir, if you were my husband, I would give you poison!" Churchill looked right at her and said, "Madame, if I were your husband, I would *take* poison!"

Free, robust, and eloquent speech became identified with the best of these leaders. A member of Parliament could be cross-examined by the opposition for hours and be expected to have witty answers ready in reply. If you have C-SPAN available, you can watch "Question Time" directly from London and experience the parliamentary tradition at its source. It is not surprising that the study of public speaking includes many outstanding orators who spoke in the British Parliament over the past four hundred years.

As Britain's influence spread around the world during the period 1600–1900, so, too, did its parliamentary model of government. After the loss of the American colonies during 1776–1782, the British began to institute local Parliaments in their other colonies, so much of the world is now governed on this model, from India to Canada and from Australia to the Bahamas. In addition, many modern nations have adopted a similar system, some only after long periods under an autocratic or discordant government. As history shows, protracted, authoritarian governments usually end in revolution. The dramatic changes in Eastern Europe and the former Soviet Union are a continuing step in the long march of people toward the freedom to speak in order to govern themselves.

THE REVOLUTIONARY TRADITION

In addition to using public speaking in a formal meeting such as Parliament, speakers also used their abilities to address large crowds and advocate the overthrow of some established group—religious or governmental.

Power in Words

Stories of attempts at revolution in several countries generally focus on one or two prominent speakers who stood before crowds and urged them to action. The celebrated oratory of Patrick Henry or that of the impassioned Vladimir Lenin gives us a revolutionary image instantly.

Because literacy was still not widespread in the eighteenth century, the tradition of an effective speaker continued to be an important means of transmitting information. Speaking to the masses has always served the cause of those who want to overthrow the established order. Whole volumes have been written about the Irish speakers who have urged rebellion against England for centuries. Latin American history is filled with examples of people who were able to rally the population to revolt against a powerful ruling group, from Juárez in Mexico in the last century to Castro in Cuba in this century.

Peace or Violence

The ability of a powerful speaker to cause ordinary citizens to rise up against an existing government—be it Napoleon in 1800 or Hitler in 1932—is amply demonstrated across time, countries, and cultures. This revolutionary tradition is an alternative to the parliamentary tradition. One tradition says that the power of speech must be used to incite the violent overthrow of a system; the other says that the power of speech must be used within a system so that it will change through rational, persuasive discourse.

The United States has some of each heritage—methods of debate from the British Parliament and methods of revolution to establish a forum for change. Most of the revolutionaries of 1776 would have stopped their rebellious activities if the British Parliament had simply given meaningful representation to the colonies in the governmental decision-making process. In other words, when a governmental structure does not allow free speech and government becomes oppressive, then the revolutionary use of speech will prevail. If, on the other hand, a governmental structure includes a method whereby free speech can influence decisions and create change, then the parliamentary tradition is likely to emerge. However, even with setbacks, the eventual emergence of free expression is inevitable. The dramatic events of the late 1980s and early 1990s in Eastern Europe and the former Soviet Union are built on a premise of free expression of ideas. Former rubber-stamp Parliaments in those countries changed from quiet, docile meetings to arenas of robust comment and dissent.

COMMUNICATION IN U.S. LIFE

It is not surprising, given the heritage of the United States as well as the care and vision of its founders, that one of the first important steps in the establishment of a new country was to guarantee the freedom of expression. At first, this freedom meant that the reasoned discourse of an educated lawmaker was protected. Antigovernment, inflammatory, or personal attack was still frowned upon and not permitted.

Free Speech, Free People

U.S. history has seen a steady expansion of the right to free expression, but it has not been a smooth one. Originally, the free-speech clause of the First Amendment applied primarily to spoken words and somewhat less to printed

Patrick Henry represents America's revolutionary tradition of speaking.

words, and it was still subject to much regulation. The expression of unpopular ideas had to be permitted—that much was recognized.

In the early days, freedom of expression was protected as long as it stayed within the bounds of prevailing taste and moral codes. During periods of great national stress—the Civil War, for example—the mood in the country and the courts was such that there was a tightening up on these limits. In times of ease and prosperity, the boundaries of free expression seemed to expand.

A comparison with very strong authoritarian governments reveals one element in common among the authoritarian group: They all attempt to restrict and control the expression of ideas. Governments run the media, whether they are newspapers, radio, or television. For that reason, one of the first activities of a revolution is to take over the media centers. Totalitarian governments forbid the free flow of information and spend enormous resources searching luggage for forbidden books or newspapers and jamming radio and television signals that are not under their control.

Power of Speech, Progress of People

In many ways, U.S. history can be seen as a continuous journey toward an increasing tolerance of the free expression of ideas, no matter how distasteful, idiotic, bizarre, or offensive they may be. Every year, there is an increasing number of court cases that test the limits of free expression and government's ability to regulate that expression.

Free Expression

One after another, challenges to restrictions have been upheld by the courts, and the protection of speech now includes almost all forms of verbal and nonverbal expression—from the traditional oration and newspaper editorial to art, film, and even flag burning. Many people feel that it is precisely because of a tolerance for a broad range of ideas, opinions, and expressions that the violence of the revolutionary tradition has been avoided (Arnett, 1990). As scholars in speech communication put it:

> The success of a democratic system depends upon an open and continuing dialogue between the citizenry. . . . You as an individual not only have the constitutional right to speak freely and to assemble peaceably, but it is often your social responsibility (Gruner et al., 1972).

Our Voices

Speakers of every sort have used their talents as public speakers to create and further a cause or a campaign. These speakers included well-known, early leaders of Congress, as well as seekers and holders of the presidency such as Webster, Clay, Calhoun, Randolph, Douglas, and Lincoln. Others created or supported social reform outside of government; they included Lucy Stone, Susan B. Anthony, Sojourner Truth, and John Brown. The reform speakers from the late 1800s into this century helped to improve social conditions, sparked the labor movement, established political parties, and created the civil rights movement (Duffy and Ryan, 1987a).

Speakers such as Eugene Debs, William Jennings Bryan, Clarence Darrow, the Roosevelts—Teddy, Franklin, and Eleanor—Marcus Garvey, and Martin Luther King, Jr. are all remembered for the power of their spoken words. The field of speech communication has always been concerned with this power, which has played a continuous and dramatic role in U.S. life (Duffy and Ryan, 1987b).

DIVERSITY IN COMMUNICATION

Sojourner Truth

One of the most interesting speakers to arise out of the early 1800s was a woman named Sojourner Truth. As a slave, she knew firsthand the oppression of that system. She had intelligence and ambition, and she escaped, fleeing to the North, where abolitionists helped her to gain wide audiences for her antislavery appeals. A large, imposing woman, she used biblical references, common sense, and powerful personal stories to win over her audience. She faced double barriers to speaking in public: being a woman and being black. Neither group was permitted to speak in public in many places, even in the North. She was so powerful, and had such a deep, resounding voice, that some accused her of being a man dressed as a woman. One story about her is that on being shouted down at one meeting as an impostor, she threw open her blouse and told how the children she had nursed at her breast had been taken from her and sold.

SPEECH COMMUNICATION

When the early settlers from England arrived in America with their British traditions, they found that Native Americans also included public speaking in their culture. The Iroquois and Algonquin nations had thriving systems of self-government that depended on skill in public speaking. Speakers often addressed a community council and were expected to follow a standard outline. One famous speaker, known to us today as Red Jacket, is still studied in speech classes as an example of an orator from this tradition. However, the English brought their own traditions and set up their own schools. When John Harvard endowed a college in Cambridge, Massachusetts, in 1636, one of the principal subjects in the curriculum was rhetoric, and a professorship was created especially for brilliant scholars to teach it.

Traditions in American Life

As the number of colleges and universities grew in the following years, speech continued to be an important subject. The link between good oral expression and good written expression was maintained, in that the same teachers taught both subjects. They emphasized the standard, Roman canons that had been passed along through the centuries. Free speech and public debate were important to aspiring leaders of political, social, or legal enterprises. They needed the training in rhetoric, the insights, and the skills it provided. The study of rhetoric ensured skills in research, good organization, and polished presentation. The writing of Thomas Jefferson is a good example of these elements; students study the Declaration of Independence not just for its political ideas, but also for the grace and eloquence of its expression.

The Elocutionists

A revived interest in classical Greece began to compete for attention with the Roman tradition in the late 1700s and early 1800s. This revival affected art, literature, architecture, and even public speaking. The shift of attention to the Greeks involved special interest in their ideas about beauty. Keats's "Ode on a Grecian Urn" is but one of many examples proclaiming that truth is beauty.

Unfortunately, this single-minded attention to beauty meant that in public speaking, the grand gesture, an elegant vocabulary, and flowing vocal tones received so much attention that matters of substance, thought, research, and precision were nearly forgotten in many schools. Teachers of this florid style were called **elocutionists,** and their schools dominated speech education for most of the 1800s. Movies set in this period often show a stereotyped politician or preacher, puffed up with grand oratory, who are reminders of this style.

Traveling groups of performers crisscrossed the country during this period. Their programs were called *chautauquas* after a series of summer seminars originating in the town of Chautauqua, New York, at an Episcopal summer camp in 1874. These performances often included music, dramatic presentations, poetry recitations, and recreations of the famous speeches of historical figures.

Academic Discipline

It was during this time that U.S. higher education also began to take the shape that it has today. As knowledge began to expand, academic departments began to form around history, philosophy, and the sciences. Eventually, English split from departments of rhetoric to become the study of literature and, to a lesser extent, grammar. These new English departments left the often silly extravagances of the elocutionists behind, thereby aiding the decline of rhetoric's reputation.

Many scholars were occupied with the emerging disciplines of psychology and sociology. These scholars were doing important research around the turn of the century and carried with them vivid memories of elocution training. They used their knowledge of the study of rhetoric. However, since these emerging disciplines were concerned with their own particular academic approach to communication, they produced their own research and publications about how people interact with each other.

At the same time, the excesses and shallowness of the elocution movement in public speaking began to be even more apparent, and a new association formed in 1915 called the Academic Teachers of Public Speaking. This organization has grown and changed names several times to become the current Speech Communication Association. Unfortunately, and in spite of changes in the field, many people still associate speech communication with the old, superficial style of presentation without substance.

The Modern Emergence of the Discipline

With the explosion of knowledge in this century, speech communication has taken on an enormous burden. Studying communication in all its richness is a difficult and enormous task. Since communication affects almost everything we do and weaves through every part of life, communication scholars must look everywhere to learn about its processes and effects. A definition of the field formulated by the Association for Communication Administrators (1981) gives the following broad outline:

> Speech communication is a humanistic and scientific field of study, research, and application. Its focus is upon how, why, and with what effects people communicate through spoken language and associated nonverbal messages. Just as political scientists are concerned with political behavior, and economists with economic behavior, the student of speech communication is concerned with communicative behavior (p. 1).

As we move to the twenty-first century, we find departments of speech communication with a variety of names and concerns. Some departments emphasize the classical study of rhetoric and still call themselves by that name, as at the University of California, Berkeley, while others are heavily involved in mass-media concerns and public policies, such as the Annenberg Schools at Pennsylvania and Southern California. Some departments still include a relationship with theater, while others are connected with journalism or speech therapy and hearing. These departments hold in common an intense interest in humans communicating with each other. The various areas of speech communi-

---

IMPROVING COMPETENCY

Communication in Careers

One of the valuable competencies is an understanding of the role of communication in everyday life. Conduct an informal survey of four or five people—parents, friends, or workers you meet during one day. Ask them to describe briefly the role of communication in their careers. What would happen if they were unable to communicate well? Do they feel a need for, or would they benefit from, improving their communication skills? National surveys confirm that communication skills are of primary importance in virtually every career. (*Pathways,* 1995).

---

cation are defined in the next chapter, along with a model that describes the communication process.

Current and Future Trends in Communication Studies

Although it is difficult to predict the future, the interests of today's investigators in the field provides some clues to where the study of communication behavior is going.

Currently, in addition to the established areas of rhetoric, public address, oral interpretation of literature, speech correction/audiology, linguistics, interpersonal communication, group communication, mass media, nonverbal communication, and organizational communication, many speech communication people are working with communication and gender, multicultural communication, health communication, and communication and aging. New perspectives are enriching our Eurocentric tradition. Afrocentric and feminist research paradigms in communication are now the focus of many researchers (Asante, 1987). These investigators use a variety of methods to help them study, including historical research, descriptive approaches, critical analysis, empirical observation and fieldwork, experimental and statistical data gathering, and analysis. The impact of technology on our communication behavior and the use of technological tools to study communication are both changing our knowledge of this ancient subject (Wood and Gregg, 1995). It is as complex a field as it is a subject. If you have the time or interest, your school probably offers many opportunities to study in a variety of these areas and approaches.

SUMMARY

From the beginnings of human history to the latest in electronic message processing, speech communication has been at the center of interaction. In a few pages, you have seen some 50,000 years of communication activity bring us to where are today. How did we get here? Through our ability to communicate. Sometimes our messages are helpful, passing on important knowledge about our environment and ourselves. Sometimes it is hurtful, inciting one group to hate, fear, or destroy another. Often it is hopeful, inspiring us with a vision of future well-being and extending the human spirit.

The tools of communication are indifferent about what use we make of them, as Aristotle pointed out. Just as a fine new hammer can build a shelter, so it can crush a skull. The hammer does not care. It is amoral; only the user determines its purpose. So it is with your knowledge and skill in communication. Your applications and choices will determine the outcome of your communication behavior.

KEY TERMS

Indo-European, *p. 2*
Rosetta Stone, *p. 3*
Socratic method, *p. 3*
Aristotle, *p. 4*
sophists, *p. 5*
rhetoric, *p. 5*
canons, *p. 5*
invention, *p. 5*
organization, *p. 6*

style, *p. 6*
memory, *p. 6*
delivery, *p. 6*
Eurocentric perspective, *p. 6*
storyteller, *p. 7*
Magna Carta, *p. 11*
Parliament, *p. 11*
elocutionists, *p. 16*

EXERCISES

1. Go to a large, comprehensive dictionary and find five different words with different root languages. For example, most of the words you find will list a Greek or Latin origin, but try to find some with Sanskrit, Indo-European, Japanese, Celtic, or African roots. Share your findings in class and see how many different root languages you and your classmates can find that have contributed to the development of modern English.

2. Which is more valuable to civilization: written or spoken communication? Write a two-page essay defending your choice, then be prepared to read your essay and defend your position to your class.

3. Interview ten people from ten different occupations, such as student, professor, librarian, bank teller, and service station attendant, asking each one to define *rhetoric*. How many included the classical origin of developing, supporting, and expressing messages? How many talked only about the modern media usage? Compare the definitions you gathered with those of a classmate and see whether you can pick out the common themes.

4. If you were going to make a career of studying communication, what area would you like to work in: business, health, or politics? What particular skills do you think would be important for your chosen career? Why?

REFERENCES

Arnett, Robert. "The Practical Philosophy of Communication Ethics and Free Speech as the Foundation for Speech Communication." *Communication Quarterly* 38 (Summer 1990), 208–217.

Asante, Molefi K. *The Afrocentric Idea.* Philadelphia: Temple University Press, 1987.

Ascher, M., and R. Ascher, *The Code of the Quipu.* Ann Arbor: The University of Michigan Press, 1981.

Association for Communication Administration. "Communication Careers." Annandale, VA: Association for Communication Administration, 1981. 1.

Brehart, Ernest, *An Encyclopedist of the Dark Ages—Isidore of Seville.* New York: Burt Franklin, 1912.

Campbell, Joseph (with Bill Moyers). *The Power of Myth.* New York: Doubleday, 1988.

Carter, T. F., "Paper and Block Printing—From China to Europe." *The Invention of Printing in China and Its Spread Westward.* Rpt. in *Communication in History—*

Technology, Culture, Society. Ed. David Crowley and Paul Heyer. White Plains: Longman, 1991.

Cooper, Lane (trans.). *The Rhetoric of Aristotle.* New York: Appleton-Century-Crofts, 1932.

deBarry, William T. *Sources of Japanese Tradition.* New York: Columbia University Press, 1958.

deBarry, William T. *Sources of Chinese Tradition.* New York: Columbia University Press, 1960.

Duffy, Bernard K., and Halford Ryan, eds. *American Orators before 1900.* New York: Greenwood Press, 1987.

Duffy, Bernard K., and Halford Ryan, eds. *American Orators of the Twentieth Century.* New York: Greenwood Press, 1987.

Gruner, C., C. M. Logue, D. L. Freshley, and R. C. Huseman. *Speech Communication in Society.* Boston: Allyn and Bacon, 1972.

Isocrates. *Antidosis.* Trans. George Norlin. Cambridge: Harvard University Press, 1929. 2.

Pathways to Careers in Communication. Annandale: Speech Communication Association, 1995.

Ryan, Halford. *Classical Communication for the Contemporary Communicator.* Mountain View: Mayfield, 1992.

Sawyer, Ruth. *The Way of the Storyteller.* New York: Viking, 1962.

Smith, Goldwin. *A History of England.* New York: Charles Scribner's Sons, 1957.

Solmsen, Fredrich, ed. *The Rhetoric and Poetics of Aristotle.* Trans. W. Rhys Roberts and Ingram Bywater. New York: Random House/Modern Library, 1954.

Wood, Julin T. and Richard B. Gregg. *Toward the Twenty-First Century: The Future of Speech Communication.* Cresskill: Hampton Press, 1995.

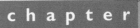
What We Have Learned: Communication Principles

After reading this chapter, you should be able to:

- Provide a formal definition of *communication*.
- Describe three major principles of communication.
- Discuss communication competency and the communication model.
- Understand sources of, and responses to, communication anxiety.
- Apply the formal study of communication to your daily life.

*F*rom the brief review of the history of communication in Chapter 1, it is evident that communication study has come a long way and that many great minds have contributed to its development. Because human communication is such a broad field, with application in so many areas, a simple definition is difficult to formulate. Therefore a few approaches may help to clarify what is meant by communication not only in this book, but in most formal works dealing with communication and people. We will begin with a definition of communication in general, follow with an examination of the areas of study, and then look at each part of the communication process.

A FORMAL DEFINITION

Because this book is focusing on human communication, several other popular uses of the term *communication* will not be considered here (for example, communication between animals or computer interfacing). The definition used in this text emphasizes "the process of people interacting through the use of messages" (Zeuschner, 1994). This interaction takes place in each of the intrapersonal, interpersonal, small-group, public communication, mass communication, organizational communication, and intercultural communication settings described in this chapter.

PRINCIPLES

A formal definition of communication is based on certain principles of communication.

Communication Is a Whole Process

Two contemporary writers about speech communication, Malcolm Sillars and Charles Mudd, suggest that communication is a human activity; it is interpersonal, it is purposeful, and it is a process (Mudd and Sillars, 1991). The communication process is dynamic, continuous, irreversible, and contextual (Berlo, 1971). It is not possible to participate in any part of the process without implying the existence and functioning of its other parts.

Communication Is Inevitable and Irreversible

The desire and capacity for communication is inherent in us. People are equipped with both the brain functions and physical attributes that make communication possible. Even people without the ability to use their voices or their hearing have both the capacity and the ability to communicate. Helen Keller, who was both blind and deaf, set a dramatic example, proving that the communication impulse is strong in everyone.

Communication is inevitable. It is also irreversible, which means that once a message goes out, it cannot be called back. You can try to modify, rescind, neglect, distort, amplify, or apologize for a message already sent, but you cannot delete it. A Greek sage once said that you cannot step into the same stream twice because you are not the same person from one moment to the next, and the stream changes as well. So it is with communication; it takes place in a constantly moving stream of time, and time is not reversible.

Communication Involves Content and Relationship

The twin elements of content and relationship mean that a message tells us at least two things in the communication process. The first, content, is the substance of the message—the meanings and definitions of the message parts. The second, relationship, tells us about the sender and the receiver and how they perceive their interaction. For example, consider the difference between the following sentences:

"Excuse me, but I was hoping that the materials belonging to you in this room could be put away, if it wouldn't be too much trouble."

"Clean up your room!"

The content of the statements is similar, but the relationship in each one is clearly different.

The fact that a person communicates at all indicates some perception of relationship. For example, in an elevator in a large city, you are unlikely to start a conversation with the strangers around you. However, in the university library elevator, you may feel less inhibited about making small talk or a casual remark because you already feel a relationship in general with your fellow students.

A relationship potential refers to the possible basis for connection you sense in the specific context (Caputo et al, 1994).

Communication Happens in a Context.   Communication cannot happen in a vacuum; there is always a setting or context in which the communication takes place and derives much of its meaning. The context may be a culture, a location, or a relationship. Waving at someone in Japan may be a way to call them back to you. Waving at someone driving toward an accident may be a way

Anne Sullivan Macy and her most famous student, Helen Keller.

DIVERSITY IN COMMUNICATION

The Miracle Worker

Helen Keller is known here and in other countries as the blind and deaf girl in the famous book *The Miracle Worker*. The worker was Helen's teacher, Anne Sullivan Macy, herself nearly blind. Sullivan taught Helen the means to communicate, and that was the miracle. She opened Helen to the world through the communication link of finger spelling. Helen went on to become a voracious communicator—reading, writing, and graduating from Radcliffe College in 1904. For all her impairments, she viewed the ability to communicate as the most wonderful way to participate in the world. She believed that life is nothing unless it's a daring adventure.

to warn them to slow down. Waving to your best friend across a crowded classroom before an examination may be a way to say, "Good luck!"

These universal principles of communication are constant, and they work in a process that can be delineated for the purpose of definition and study. Note, however, that these parts are not distinct and easily seen in isolation. They are always interacting with each other.

Communication Takes Place in a Variety of Settings

People who study communication usually focus on one of seven major settings: intrapersonal, interpersonal, small-group, public communication, mass communication, intercultural communication, and organizational communication. While there may be some overlapping of areas, each can be easily defined.

Intrapersonal Communication.   You can probably guess that this means communicating within yourself. When you think, daydream, solve problems, and imagine, you are in the realm of **intrapersonal communication.** Some investigators also include in this area all physical feedback mechanisms, such as the sensations of hunger, pain, and pleasure.

Interpersonal Communication.   This form of communication describes the interactions of two or more people. The most significant setting for **interpersonal communication** is the one-on-one, or dyad setting. An interview, a conversation, and intimate communications come under this heading. In the broadest sense, all communication involving other people and oneself is interpersonal, but it is usually associated with oneself in direct contact with one other person or a few other people. A different set of communication dynamics comes into play when three or more people get together in a discussion. That is the area of small-group communication.

Small-Group Communication.   **Small-group communication** requires the following conditions: leadership, equal sharing of ideas, peer pressure, roles and norms, and focus on a common goal. Although the number of members of a small group is not absolute, most studies show that four to six people make the best use of small-group potential. Fewer members reduce the opportunity to express a broad range of ideas. A group of more than seven members begins to crowd the channels of communication, so people get left out of the discussion, and may form subgroups or pairs. The small group is one of the most important communication settings. It exists everywhere, from the family to interview teams, roommates, work groups, legislative subcommittees, and military and business groups.

Public Communication.   When one person talks to several others and is the dominant focus of the communication, the setting is said to be public. A good example of this is a speaker and an audience. Again, numbers are not that important. A single person could be talking to three or four others or to three or four thousand others. The defining characteristics of **public communication** are that one person is identified as the primary sender of messages, while others function primarily as receivers of those messages.

Mass Communication.   When a message needs help to get from its source to its destination, **mass communication** begins to function. Usually, some form of medium—one meaning of which is "between"—is needed to connect the sender to the receivers. These media may be print (newspapers or magazines), electrical (radio, television, or video), or even electronic (computer modems). The common characteristics are that something comes between the direct communication of the sender and the receivers, there is usually some delay in sending and receiving, and there is often considerable delay in the feedback, if any, that the sender gets from the receivers.

Organizational Communication.   This specialized area focuses on interpersonal, small-group, public, and mass communication as they interact in a complex, multigroup setting. Especially important to business, government, and educational institutions, **organizational communication** analyzes what

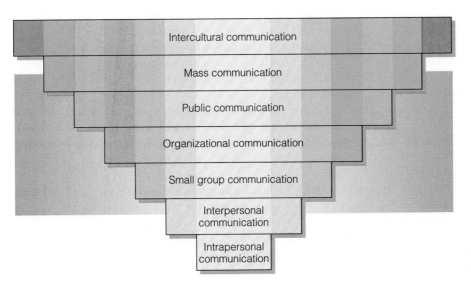

The contexts of communication build off of each other and are interrelated.

IMPROVING COMPETENCY

Review Your Communication

K eep track of the various communication settings you are in today. Which small groups are you active in? How many people from different cultures do you interact with? Are you part of an organization?

The basis for building communication competency is knowledge, so study the definitions on pages 24–26 and see how many apply to your everyday life.

happens to messages as they travel up, down, and around a large collection of individuals and groups bound together in some formal way.

Intercultural Communication.   Sometimes called *cross-cultural communication,* this setting describes what happens when the sender of a message is from a different cultural background than the intended receiver. In reality, **intercultural communication** can be present in any of the previously described settings. Rarely does one culture communicate with another culture. Rather, one *person* communicates with other *people* who do not share the same culture. Nevertheless, it is an area of much interest, importance, and study. It is easy to think of the primary settings in which one national or ethnic group meets another. Some studies are also investigating between-gender communication and the more subtle interactions such as various regional or even occupational differences as intercultural communication.

Each of these settings is the subject of its own chapter later in this book, but right now you should be aware of how complex and enormous the study of communication can be. Even though they seem to differ greatly in size and attributes, these settings are all subject to the universal principles outlined above, and they all involve very similar qualities.

A Communication Model

There are six primary elements in the **communication model.** They include context, messages, channels, senders/sources, receivers/decoders, interaction, and feedback/interference/noise. Each of these elements is explained to clarify the definition of communication.

Context indicates that communication takes place in a setting, sometimes called an environment. That means that there is no communication in a void. The place, time, surrounding events, physical and psychological climates, what has come before, and what is likely to follow—all of these factors are included in context.

People are an obvious element of communication, given the reference to *senders/sources,* but in a technological society, the word *communication* is often used to describe computer interfacing or machine transmissions to other machines. For the purposes of this book, electronic messages are not, strictly speaking, part of the human communication process—a human is always the originator and the ultimate destination of a message. In other words, people use

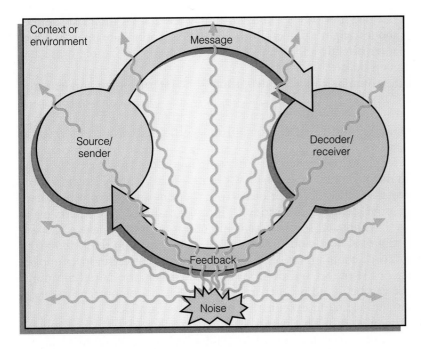

The model of communication.

machines to help in the transmission of their messages, but as yet the machines do not originate the messages, nor do they define the purpose of the messages they carry.

Messages are the content of the communication process. They may be verbal (written or spoken) or nonverbal (everything else, from gestures and movements to smells and objects). Messages can be transmitted through the use of *channels,* such as sound waves, light waves, or other sense-stimulating means.

Receivers and decoders are also part of the people orientation, in that they are the ultimate goal of any message and they are needed to translate the message finally into a form that people can comprehend. This link between senders and receivers is where communication interaction happens.

Interaction should call your attention to the back-and-forth nature of communication, sometimes called a *transaction.* Even within yourself, you consider and weigh alternatives, so a response is built in. That response may not always be the one you intended, but it is a necessary part of the process. The term *transaction* calls attention to fact that all parties in the communication event influence and are influence by the event.

In formal terms, responses, interruptions, or blockages to that interaction come under the heading of *feedback/interference/noise.* These terms are just what you imagine them to be: the response you have to the message or the factors that inhibit a clear response. For example, you may give an answer when questioned, you may just think about it, or you may try to respond even though you didn't fully hear or understand the question. The interference or noise can be external or internal. You may have tried to hear a message, but a lawnmower going by the window got in the way. Or you may have been trying to read an article, but someone spilled coffee on the page. In these cases, the machine and the beverage are forms of external noise. On the other hand, you may be able to see and hear just fine, but you get to daydreaming about a vacation last summer or worrying about tonight's dinner. Both of these disruptions are internal noise. The next chapter directly addresses the problem of how to handle noise and improve listening skills.

Part of the communication model includes the internal noise you generate when you are anxious about communicating. Because the internal anxiety associated with many types of communication can be an important factor in everyone's communication, the next section introduces this topic. More information and methods to respond effectively to this anxiety come in subsequent chapters.

You can see that this simple model of communication has a variety of components, and these components interact with each other. As a convenient way to study the process, we can break it down into sections and attempt to isolate each section as we define and describe it. But just as a molecule's parts make sense only as they interact, so does the communication model make sense as a whole—not as pieces. The model is a useful guide to help you think about the different aspects of communication, but keep in mind that each aspect implies the existence of the others and depends on those others for its full meaning. Because noise can be found in any part of the model, it is important to take a moment now and begin our examination of this important idea.

One of the most difficult times to listen effectively is right before you are called on to present your message. Especially if you are just about to give a speech, the internal factors of worry may be so great that your physical and psychological makeup is going out of control. The anxiety associated with public communication is well known to everyone who has ever given a speech in public and was well known to the ancient Greeks as well. We have stories of the great orator Demosthenes, who worked painfully hard to overcome his inhibitions and perceived limitations as a speaker, shouting out his speeches to the

It took Demosthenes years of practice to become the great orator of his time.

ocean waves, putting pebbles in his mouth to speak more clearly, and continually practicing so that he could finally summon the courage to address the Athenian crowd. Some 2,500 years after his death, his speeches are still reprinted and studied as models of excellent oratory.

Communication apprehension seems to be a core part of communication, cutting across contexts, situations, cultures, languages, and individuals. It can be seen as a fundamental factor in the study of communication. So let's take a first look at this problem—speech anxiety—and see what it is and what can be done about it.

 ## COMMUNICATION APPREHENSION

What is commonly called *nervousness, stage fright,* or even *shyness* is called *communication apprehension* by people who study this reaction. Some link it to a broader concept—performance anxiety—to cover the following situations: athletic performances, music recitals, stage productions, business deadlines, test taking, or even interpersonal situations, such as asking someone for a date.

Sources of Anxiety

The one thing that all of these events have in common is that by taking part in them, a person's actions will be judged or evaluated. Researchers have demonstrated that a person is likely to suffer an attack of this anxiety in any number of different situations (Richmond and McCroskey, 1995). The more the person cares about the outcome, the greater the anxiety (McCroskey, 1977). Whenever a person begins to dread the possible failure of his or her actions, anxiety begins to take hold. It is a universal reaction, and its immediate effects are predictable.

Anxiety Reactions

The human body is well equipped to deal with fear. People are genetically programmed to shift into a heightened state when they are, or believe they are, confronted with a threat.

The fear can be of mountain lions or of making a mistake. This reaction is often called the flight/fight response, and it begins with a message from the brain's danger perception center to the adrenal glands, telling them to start pumping. With adrenaline flowing almost instantly into a person's system, the person is ready to run or to fight. Unfortunately, the brain's danger center does not differentiate between reactions appropriate to facing an angry lion as opposed to giving a speech, and it prepares us for both in the same way. Breathing becomes tense and shallow, hands and feet get cold and sweaty, the heart rate increases, the stomach and digestive system go into spasms, large muscles become tense and may twitch from all the energy flowing into them, the voice tightens, and the mind seems to go blank.

Each of these reactions may have roots in a survival mechanism used in a more primitive time. For example, hands and feet get cold because blood leaves the surface capillaries and flows to the large muscles, allowing for more energy to be available to the arms and legs to do battle or run away. Moreover, with less blood near the surface of the skin, an injured person is less likely to bleed. This mechanism may offer some protection from an angry lion, but it is hardly useful for a business presentation!

Sweaty hands and feet also can help when facing an angry lion because a small amount of moisture increases traction. When turning a page in a book or newspaper, what do most people do automatically? Lick their finger. In the past, better traction helped people hold onto a weapon, grab a vine and swing, or scale a tree or a cliff, but traction does not get someone a date for Saturday night or a better grade on a class speech.

Blood also leaves the viscera and travels to the large muscles. Tension in the midsection and shallow breathing also give a person more strength. Think of karate demonstrations. Just before an expert smashes a brick apart, she shouts, "HA!" Why? Is she trying to scare the brick into breaking? No; she is tightening up her midsection to focus her energy. During a speech, a person's body automatically tries to do the same thing. Tension in the muscles affects the throat, extra energy is bottled up in the large muscles, and some blood flows from the frontal cortex, where the mind operates, and goes to the medulla to help coordinate the right and left sides of the brain. The net result is a person who feels out of control. What can be done?

Responses to Anxiety

After the body has reacted, it is time for the person as a whole to respond. There is no way to prevent communication anxiety, so the best response is to prepare for it. Many students set the unrealistic goal of trying to get rid of their physical reactions or conquer them somehow. A better goal is to respond so that *you* direct the anxiety reaction and eliminate the effects that detract from your performance. Then you can use the rest of your energy to make the communication more interesting, dynamic, and appealing to the listeners.

Unfortunately, many people block their own success by falling into traps of irrational thinking (Adler and Rodman, 1994; Ellis, 1977). For people in communication situations, these traps can be classified as fallacies.

The Fallacy of Catastrophic Failure.   This fallacy refers to focusing on a disaster that people imagine will happen, often making it happen by their own certainty. They imagine forgetting everything, and they think their messages will be rejected so totally that it is not worth the effort to even try giving them. Yet in reality, most listeners are sympathetic to a speaker. They want to hear, they try to understand, and they overlook the minor errors that almost everyone makes in any message presentation.

The Fallacy of Perfection.   This problem is the counterpart, and often the companion, to the first. People who believe this fallacy tell themselves that they should be perfect. Not a single "um" is allowed in their presentation. Every word must be precisely in the proper place, delivered in the best tone and at the best rate of speed. Only a perfect score on an exam will do, and all experiments must be flawless.

Yet successful communicators are rarely even close to such a level of perfection. Often these people focus on presentation details to a point at which they

THE STORY OF COMMUNICATION

Performance Anxiety

Universally recognized performers are not immune to attacks of anxiety. One of the finest actors of our century, Sir Laurence Olivier, used to tell of being so frightened right before he went on stage that he would run to the bathroom and vomit before every performance. The great opera tenor Enrico Caruso told how he would pace nervously in the stage wings, waiting for his entrance. A young tenor came up to him and asked, "Why are *you* nervous? You're the great Caruso!" Caruso replied, "Young man, you can just go out there and sing and all will be fine. But night after night, *I* have to go out there and sound like Caruso!"

forget that listeners are interested in content. Listeners want to know the value of the message and are only superficially concerned with extraneous slips. Perfection is an unrealistic goal in virtually every human activity, and communication is one of the activities that is farthest away from perfect of all of our undertakings. Setting perfection as a goal can become a psychological compulsion that actually inhibits our ability to do an excellent job.

√ **The Fallacy of Approval.**   A person who thinks he or she must have 100 percent agreement or support from everyone is a victim of the fallacy of approval. Everyone needs approval (Schutz, 1958), and seeking it helps people integrate into society. However, it is unrealistic to think that it's possible to please everyone. People who are always trying too hard to be friendly, actually drive people away. These people create the opposite effect from the one they seek because they are trapped into thinking that they must always please everyone, which is yet another irrational goal.

√ **The Fallacy of Overgeneralization.**   In this circumstance, a person holds onto a previous experience or exaggerates it until he or she thinks it is the norm for behavior. Because a previous situation was not as successful as the person had wanted it to be, it's easy to believe that future situations will be just as unpleasant.

To counteract this fallacy, it helps to recognize that each of us is always changing and growing in experience and ability. No one steps into the same river twice; you are not the same, and the river has moved on. Moreover, it's possible to take several positive, proactive steps to counter the undesirable effects of communication apprehension.

Coping Strategies

There are ways to counteract these fallacies by focusing on reality, your own potential, and the actual situation. These fallacies can be avoided by taking a rational approach and thereby become less bothered by the physiological reactions to the stress. This approach includes both physical preparation and psychological preparation (Zeuschner, 1994).

Proper preparation and practice can help to overcome communication apprehension.

Physical preparation includes deep, relaxed breathing; selective tensing and relaxing of muscles; and movement to burn off excess energy. Psychological preparation involves developing a positive self-image, becoming aware of and mastering the areas of communication competence covered in the next section, and creating confidence through thorough preparation and practice (McCroskey and Richmond, 1982).

Research about Communication Apprehension

After years of studying people who experience communication apprehension, researchers have come to several conclusions about its nature and ways in which to lessen its effects. Communication apprehension is tied closely to self-concept, and for that reason, the subject is discussed again in Chapters 7 and 12. For now, suffice it to say that communication apprehension is widely felt, although most people can and do carry on their communications in spite of it.

A critical evaluation of what is probable, likely, and logical can be a way to counteract unproductive anxiety. Four levels of communication apprehension (CA) are identified in the extensive research of McCroskey and Richmond. They found that some persons have CA as a general trait. That is, they always experience high levels of anxiety in all communication situations. Their condition is extremely limiting, for they may be unable to talk on the telephone, answer a question in class, or even make a request of a store clerk. A second type experiences extensive apprehension in situations requiring some sort of solo presentation or participation in a group discussion, presentation, or speech. Their level of anxiety may change from one situation to another, but it is usually present. The third type of person experiences apprehension in the presence of a given individual or group. For example, a certain teacher will always cause that

CRITICAL THINKING IN COMMUNICATION

Anxiety and Imagination

One of the ways to use critical thinking skills is to examine what creates fear and tension in communication situations. For example, confront negative thought patterns by making them overt—that is, by bringing them to the surface. Specifically, create a list entitled "What's the worst that can happen?" If, let us say, you stumble over a word while giving a book report, will you fail the course? No. Will your parents stop loving you? No. Will someone in the class giggle at you? Unlikely, but perhaps someone will. Pretend that the class roars with laughter at your lapse. What will happen then? Go through the experience mentally, and follow up by asking what is likely to happen next. Next, stop and recover, and then go on. What next? Finish the report. They will forget the error, and the sun will still come up tomorrow.

Dealing with the logical consequences of a worst-case scenario accomplishes two things. First, it becomes clear how unlikely and inconsequential the worst case would be; second, you will have mentally prepared a strategy for getting out of the situation if it does happen. By creating a mental image of following through, you will have rehearsed a method for getting past the feared moment.

particular person anxiety, but not teachers in general. Along the same lines, a special or significant person—parent, police officer, boss—will always get adrenaline flowing no matter what the circumstances. Some say that falling in love produces a similar reaction. Finally, most people experience CA in a particular situation—for example, when a teacher calls a student in for a conference, when a boss demands an unexpected meeting, or when a person is put on the spot for whatever reason (McCroskey and Richmond, 1988). In all these situations, CA is evident, but it is possible to respond to it in a way that limits its negative effects on the ability to send and receive messages effectively.

COMMUNICATION COMPETENCE REVIEWED

Repertoire, Selection, Implementation, Evaluation

The four elements required to be a competent communicator are developing a broad range, or *repertoire*, of skills and perspectives; learning how to *select* from that background, using appropriate criteria; putting into practice, or *implementing*, certain skills in the presentation and delivery of the message; and finally, learning to *evaluate* the communication so that you can adjust your future efforts based on an analysis of your past efforts. In a way, this entire text is aimed at helping you to develop one or more of these competencies. They are somewhat general at this point, so let us consider what experts in the field of speech communication have defined as **communication competencies.**

Knowledge, Feelings, and Skills

A widely read educator, Benjamin Bloom, created a system of organizing educational goals and outcomes that he called the cognitive, affective, and psychomotor dimensions of education (Bloom, 1956). Another way to label these ideas is to call them knowledge, feelings, and skills. These words describe many of the communication abilities covered in this text.

Knowledge, as a competency in the field of speech communication, means gaining information about the subject. It refers to an understanding of the history of the field, its concern with ethics, its universal principles and applications, and its place in the development of culture, especially Western civilization. It includes knowledge about the contexts of speech communication, from intrapersonal to intercultural, and about the elements of the communication process.

In terms of *feelings,* the field offers an opportunity to experience a growing level of ability and the associated sense of pride that comes from working competently. People need to feel both responsible for their messages and for being effective receivers of other people's messages. Responsible communicators play a valuable part in society by developing a sense of self-worth, the worth of other people, and the value of ideas, even if they are different from one's own (McBath, 1975).

Skills are the obvious focus of several aspects of this text and often the reason why schools offer or require courses in communication. "What can I *do* with this class?" is a frequent question from students, their parents, and others in the academic community. Although skills are certainly the most easily measured and observed of the three competencies, they are best used in conjunction with the other two. Someone who is skilled in organizing and presenting messages has surly gained something important; but without a clear understanding of background and principles, coupled with a sense of responsibility and value, these skills are somewhat superficial.

At the end of each of the following chapters, a reference is made to how that chapter contributes to your knowledge, your feeling, and your skills. From those areas, you build your communication competence. Your expanding knowledge and skills increases the choices you have available—your *repertoire.* Some of the chapters discuss different circumstances and applications that are appropriate, helping you to learn about how to *select* a choice. The concern for an appropriate choice means that communicators are following the accepted behavior for their relationship and the context (Spitzberg and Cupach, 1984).

Other chapters are aimed at building skills—your *implementation.* Finally, *evaluation* is present in the various exercises at the ends of the chapters as well as in the various assignments you will complete for the class and the daily interactions you have that involve communication.

SUMMARY

This course is a beginning, designed to launch you in the study of a rich discipline. It is a discipline abundant in history, revealing about ourselves, and useful in every aspect of a successful life. The effects of good communication are far-reaching.

You have seen how the principles of communication work in a variety of settings. Communication is a whole process, inevitable and irreversible, that involves both content and relationships. The principles of communication operate within everyone;

when a person talks to another person; when a person participates in small groups, in meetings, in careers; or when a person is involved with the mass media and people of different cultures. Each message takes place in a context, has a source and a destination, travels over a channel, and is subject to internal and external interferences. Feedback is the single most important element in making messages accurate.

Communication anxiety is a normal part of the communication process, and extreme anxiety can be dealt with so that communication flows more smoothly.

Finally, being a competent communicator involves enlarging your pool of resources, selecting carefully from that pool, putting choices into practice, and evaluating performance. By enlarging your repertoire, you will gain knowledge about communication and your feelings of self-worth, and you will enhance your skills.

Becoming a competent communicator probably does not happen at any particular point in time, but can be a lifelong endeavor. Specific goals, however, are discernible and achievable, even in a single course of study. This book is an effort to lead you farther along the path of your own development.

KEY TERMS

intrapersonal communication, *p. 24*
interpersonal communication, *p. 24*
small-group communication, *p. 24*
public communication, *p. 25*
mass communication, *p. 25*

organizational communication, *p. 25*
intercultural communication, *p. 26*
communication model, *p. 26*
communication apprehension, *p. 29*
communication competencies, *p. 33*

EXERCISES

1. There are many different ways to study communication, and each one defines *communication* differently. Find five different dictionaries (law dictionary, medical dictionary, dictionary of psychological terms, business dictionary, general-use dictionary) and record the various definitions you find. Bring them to class for a discussion of the meaning of the word *communication*.

2. Describe how the elements of the communication model work in at least three different communication contexts. In your description, identify each element and indicate how it relates to the other elements in each of the three contexts.

3. What was your most recent experience with communication anxiety? Answering a question in class? Giving a report for an organization you belong to? Asking someone for a date? Being interviewed for a job? What was your reaction to the anxiety? What did you do about it?

4. Make a list of three or four activities in which you think improved communication skills might help you. Be specific about the type of skills that would be most beneficial to you. Keep the list in the back of your notebook for later use.

REFERENCES

Adler, Ronald, and George Rodman. *Understanding Human Communication.* New York: Harcourt Brace, 1994.

Berlo, David K. *The Process of Communication,* New York: Holt, Rinehart and Winston, 1971.

Bloom, B. S. *Taxonomy of Educational Objectives.* New York: McKay, 1956.

Caputo, J. S., H. C. Hazel, and C. McMahon. *Interpersonal Communication.* Boston: Allyn and Bacon, 1994.

Ellis, Albert. *A New Guide to Rational Living.* North Hollywood: Wilshire Books, 1977.

McBath, James H. *Forensics as Communication,* Skokie: National Textbook Company, 1975. 14.

McCroskey, James. "Oral Communication Apprehension: A Summary of Recent Theory and Research," *Human Communication Research* 4 (1977): 78–96.

McCroskey, J. C., and V. P. Richmond. *The Quiet Ones: Communication Apprehension and Shyness.* Scottsdale: Gorsuch Scarisbrick, 1982.

McCroskey, James C., and Virginia P. Richmond. "Communication Apprehension and Small Group Communication." *Small Group Communication.* Ed. R. Cathcart and L. Samovar, 5th ed. Dubuque: Wm. C. Brown, 1988.

Mudd, Charles S., and Malcom O. Sillars. *Speech: Content and Communication.* Prospect Heights: Waveland Press, 1991.

Richmond, V., and J. McCroskey. *Communication: Apprehension, Avoidance and Effectiveness.* 4th ed. Scottsdale: Gorsuch Scarisbrick, 1995.

Schutz, William. *FIRO: A Three Dimensional Theory of Interpersonal Behavior.* New York: Rinehart, 1958.

Spitzberg, B., and W. Cupach, *Interpersonal Communication Competence.* Beverly Hills: Sage, 1984.

Zeuschner, Raymond B. *Effective Public Speaking.* Dubuque: Kendall-Hunt, 1994.

What We Know about Listening

After reading this chapter, you should be able to:

- Define the difference between listening and hearing.

- Describe the four steps of active listening.

- Understand the similarities in and difference between listening critically, listening for appreciation, listening for comprehension, and listening to empathize.

- Apply the steps of active listening to your own behavior.

*L*istening is a communication skill that is one of the primary communication interactions. It is vital to the transmission and reception of oral communication. To provide feedback, you need to *listen* to the messages. There are at least two ways to listen: passively and actively. There are a variety of reasons for listening: to make sense of potentially important information, for fun and entertainment, to learn in class, and to understand the messages of people who want you to act in a variety of ways. Each of these elements of listening is discussed as a primary tool of communication (Wolvin and Coakley, 1991).

LISTENING: THE FIRST COMMUNICATION EVENT

Listening is a "first" in several respects. It is the communication interaction that everyone encounters first. Some research indicates that fetuses react to sounds that reach them in the womb. They can begin to recognize voices and react to them. After birth, listening is the primary means by which babies learn to speak. They hear sounds, they pay attention to them, they remember and recognize them, and finally they try to imitate them.

But listening is also a first communication event in another sense. It occupies more of a person's time than any other type of communication; in fact, listening takes up more of the day than *all* other kinds of communication combined (Pauk, 1989), ranging from 60 percent of college students' time as reported in one study to 53 percent as reported in another (Baker et al., 1981).

The time spent listening represents a significant portion of a person's life. Yet, like speaking, it is so common that it is easy to forget to pay any attention to it. Like speaking, everyone listens, but few are trained to do it well. A distinction can be made between *adequate* listening and *effective* listening. A person can listen adequately, get through the day, follow directions fairly well, take sufficient notes in class to perform decently on tests, and get along with associates, but could improve in nearly every area. That is *your* goal: improving listening so

---

IMPROVING COMPETENCY

Your Listening Profile

*D*o you think the estimates about your communication time are accurate? Try to review the way you spent yesterday. First, block out time segments on a piece of paper, from when you awoke to when you retired. Now estimate whether you were listening, speaking, writing, or reading. TV time, music time, and conversation time all count as listening. Since the numbers mentioned in the text are averages gathered from many college students, yours may be slightly different, just as mine are different as I spend an intense day writing. Nevertheless, over the course of several typical days, patterns emerge. Listening takes up more than half my communication time.

that you are effective with your time and energy. Let us take a closer look at this, your first communication skill.

Listening Contexts

There are at least four different reasons we listen—appreciation, empathy, comprehension and criticism. Each of these contexts applies to activities we do everyday (Wolvin & Coakley, 1992). For example, listening for **appreciation** means that your enjoyment of the event is your primary purpose. As you listen for recreation to music, you are engaging in appreciative listening. *Empathic* listening is involved when a friend shares his troubles with you, and you respond by giving him your time and attention. You demonstrate care and concern by listening; you communicate empathy. Your classroom listening is probably a clear example of listening for *comprehension*. You take notes, pay attention to the lecture, film or discussion in an effort to understand the material. Finally, you engage in *critical* listening when you gather information about a new car you might purchase, or when two candidates for office debate in an attempt to win your vote. You apply the principles of critical thinking as you listen to help you make effective decisions. Each of these areas will be discussed further in the section about improving your listening competency.

Effective Listening

Listening is not studied simply because it is so obvious. Unlike trigonometry, which everybody knows that you cannot just do, but need to learn, effective listening is taken for granted. Even with daily reminders of how wrong that assumption is, most people still neglect to train themselves for the single activity that they spend most of their time doing (Sypher, et al, 1989). There are several

We spend most of our communication time as listeners.

reasons why people gloss over the importance of listening. Most of the reasons are related to several misconceptions about the activity.

First Misconception.   Many people assume that listening is the same activity as **hearing.** Actually, hearing involves only the physical reception of sound waves by auditory mechanisms. Most people are quite capable of receiving many sounds that they do not listen to at all. For example, as you are reading this paragraph, there are may sounds around you that your hearing mechanism is picking up, but you are not paying attention to them. There may be cars driving by, people talking at a distance, or a television or radio on in another room, or the fluorescent light in the room may be making a sound. Sometimes, people hear sounds and *appear* to be listening, but they may be attending to internal dialogue or noise. This appearance is called *pseudo-listening* (Caputo, et al., 1994).

Of course, the first step in listening *is* hearing—the reception of sound waves by the hearing reception mechanism in the ear. The next step is to pay attention to those sounds and organize them into a meaningful pattern, which begins the process of understanding.

We do not always understand the sounds to which we pay attention. For example, the sounds of an unfamiliar language are sounds that a person hears but is unable to organize so that they make sense. Bird calls may mean something to a bird, but most people cannot translate them. However, it's common to think that because someone hears a sound, that person therefore understands it. That notion is the next misconception.

Second Misconception.   Some people think that understanding comes automatically from paying attention. However, think about listening very hard to movie dialogue in another language. You can concentrate carefully on every

We filter out sounds that are not relevant to us at the moment.

sound and still not understand much. **Comprehension** means organizing sounds into meaningful patterns and associations. Unfortunately, everyone may speak a language that is "foreign" at one time or another—even to friends and family. In one study of listening comprehension, the findings concluded that people grasp only about 50 percent of what they hear (Steil et al., 1983) As you will explore more thoroughly in Chapter 6, on verbal communication, we all have different vocabularies and different associations with words in our common vocabulary, so our everyday interactions are filled with errors in understanding, from slight and unimportant to large and consequential.

> ## TECHNOLOGY IN COMMUNICATION
>
> ### Edison's Deafness Gave Us Sound
>
> Hearing sounds is a first step in listening, and people who have limited hearing ability have many systems available to increase their reception of sound. Most of these systems owe their existence to America's great inventor, Thomas Edison. Edison was deaf for most of his later life, and the invention of the phonograph came as a result of his efforts to produce a hearing aid. In fact, the horns that you see on old Edison phonographs are based on the ear trumpets that deaf people used to amplify sound in those days. Edison's expert technological skills and creative insight brought about improvements in the way we understand hearing as well as the development of one the world's great forms of entertainment and education: recorded sound.

There are ways to counteract these misconceptions and increase your ability to understand the sounds you receive. Such systems are often called *active listening*.

Active Listening

Active listening involves four major steps. By going through each step, you can dramatically increase your understanding, appreciation, and retention of information that you hear. This process includes: (1) getting prepared to listen, (2) staying involved with the communication, (3) keeping an open mind while listening, and (4) reviewing and evaluating after the event. These steps can be applied to each of the four types of listening contexts. Let's take a brief look now

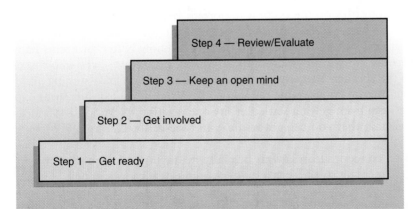

Step 4 — Review/Evaluate

Step 3 — Keep an open mind

Step 2 — Get involved

Step 1 — Get ready

The steps of active listening.

at the steps of active listening before applying them to the types of listening behaviors you might engage in every day.

Getting Prepared.   To be fully prepared to listen, get ready both physically and mentally. In terms of physical preparation, it's important to be able to hear the sounds. You might need to move closer to the source; eliminate interfering noises, such as sounds from a radio or television set; or adjust your seat in order to see better. If you want to remember specific ideas or materials for later use, such as for a test, then bring to class note paper, pens, and pencils, and sit in a place where you can write comfortably. If you do not see well at a distance, sit near the front of the room. If your hearing is a little impaired, move closer. If you are easily distracted, do not sit next to an open door or near a window. Give yourself as many advantages as possible in your physical placement so that you get the most out of the listening experience.

Mental preparation includes reading about a topic ahead of the event if you need background information and clearing your thoughts of extraneous ideas before the event. Suppose you are going to listen to a world-famous expert on the Galápagos Islands. You could strengthen your listening ability by first investigating material about the islands. Even a few minutes of reading in a general encyclopedia would help create a context for the event and would greatly increase both the amount of material you can comprehend and the speed at which you can absorb it. In a classroom situation, reading material that was assigned before the class makes any lecture or discussion much more meaningful. Some students read the entire texts for their classes before the term even begins. At a minimum, mental preparation means that you are making a commitment to listen actively to the source of the message.

Staying Involved.   The next step in active listening is to stay involved. Keeping your attention focused on the speaker may be one of the most difficult parts of the listening process because distractions are everywhere—inside your mind and outside. Staying involved requires both physical and mental actions.

Physically, you should keep eye contact with the speaker, watching for important nonverbal cues in his or her facial expressions and gestures. Some speakers use visual aids, such as charts, objects, or slide projections, which require your attention.

Keeping your eyes on the event is important because there may be distractions all around you—someone walking by the door, an attractive person three rows to your right whom you would like to get to know better, or events happening outside the windows. In spite of these distractions, you must stay focused on the speaker. You also need to keep yourself alert by assuming good posture. Getting too comfortable can make a person drift off, so shift around in your seat to keep from getting settled in any one position. Next, jot down ideas and make certain that you can always hear and see easily. Get up and move if necessary.

Mentally, concentration is your best ally in staying involved. Summarize each message mentally as the speaker moves from one idea to another. Memory devices can help you to associate an idea you are hearing for the first time with something familiar. For example, if the speaker is discussing dressage, you might associate the *dress* part of the term with dressy clothes and then remember that dressage is a formal type of competitive horseback riding. Make up any associations that work for you as ways to stay mentally involved, especially when the subject matter is not familiar. If there is going to be a question-and-answer period after the presentation, make notes about questions you might like to have answered. It is important to concentrate on the speaker, however, so do not get distracted by making up complex associations or questions. If you do, you may come back to the speaker after several minutes and feel lost, because there has been a change in the direction of the presentation.

Keeping an Open Mind.   One of the major barriers to staying involved with a speaker is the tendency to react to something that is said and to dwell on it to such an extent that the speaker leaves you behind. This reaction, called quick judgment, is most likely to occur when the speaker touches on a subject about which you feel strongly. Your mind may jump to make a judgment, and you stop listening. For example, if a speaker uses a term that you find offensive, you may pay so much attention to the term itself that you miss the fact that the speaker is also offended. Or you find that a speaker shares a favorite interest of yours. The speaker makes a comparison to your favorite baseball team, and you may react by thinking how wonderful the speaker is to admire the same team as you do. You may miss the point that the comparison is faulty and irrelevant.

This third step in active listening—keeping an open mind—is a very difficult aspect of good listening, and it must be conscientiously exercised to be effective. Otherwise, a person simply stops listening when a speaker uses terms or references or analogies to which this person has a very strong reaction. Keep listening for the idea, and then wait to make your judgment.

Keeping an open mind does not mean accepting as true everything you hear. It does mean listening as completely and carefully as you can but not uncritically. An open mind allows you to assimilate the *complete* message before

DIVERSITY IN COMMUNICATION

Are You Invisible?

What words make you cry or make you angry? Do you find all pejorative references to ethnic groups infuriating or just those to *your* ethnic group? Sometimes, members of an ethnic group use slang terms among themselves that would be very offensive if others used them. How do these words help or hinder listening? If you have emotional reactions based on the appearance, race, gender, or age of a speaker, how do these reactions help or hinder your listening? Ralph Ellison, in his book *The Invisible Man,* talked about the frustration he felt when people treated him almost as if he did not exist.

Some speakers feel the same when they sense that their intended listeners are not paying attention to them. A frequent research finding in studies of gender and communication shows that boys' answers in class are responded to by both male and female teachers more often than girls' answers (Rowe, 1986). How would this experience affect you? Would it make you feel invisible?

CRITICAL THINKING IN COMMUNICATION

Reactions Inhibit Clear Thinking

You can probably recall the effect of a powerful speaker on your emotions and feelings. Often, political speakers will tell an especially moving story—one that makes you angry or sympathetic. While stories are useful for getting attention, they do not substitute for content. A critical listener will think about the ideas in a presentation, as well as experience the feelings it evokes. Unfortunately, just when we need our thinking skills most, emotional reactions may prevent a careful evaluation. Pausing, questioning, and testing ideas can help you to engage your critical thinking skills while you listen.

---

passing judgment. Judgment, however, is an important part of the active listening process. It is *quick* judgment that is the problem, not judgment itself.

Reviewing and Evaluating.   After an event is over, it is time to review and highlight its main ideas and themes. You may wish to look over your notes and fill in any sketchy areas. It is a good idea to try to remember immediately any of the supporting materials the speaker used. Were there any statistics? Stories? Quotations? Examples?

Some students do this type of reviewing daily. When they have a break between classes, or when they arrive home for the day—and before they leave again for other activities—they quickly go through their class notes for that day and fill in any unfinished phrases or partial notes. In twenty or thirty minutes, they can fill in the incomplete notes for several classes. They do not study at this point; they review to eliminate blanks that they left as they were listening. Then, when it *is* time to study, they have a complete set of notes.

Others may neglect to review immediately, wait days or possibly weeks, and then try to recall what was once clear but is now lost. You may have a piece of paper next to your telephone right now with a telephone number on it in your handwriting. But you forgot to write down the name next to it. Now the number is a mystery, but it was perfectly clear at the time you wrote it. Reviewing notes immediately just to fill in content is one of the most powerful study aids for people trying to stay on, or get on, the dean's list.

Once you have the information clearly and completely in hand, it is time to evaluate it. There are many ways to evaluate information. You can look at its form, delivery, subject, presentation, use of supporting materials, and fairness or relevance. You can evaluate whether or not the presenter adapted to the relevant needs and concerns of the listeners. You can look at the recentness of the evidence; determine whether there was any evidence at all, or note which, if any, experts were cited.

While presentation and delivery skills are often the most immediate items to be evaluated, an evaluation does not begin and end with the presentation skills of voice, eye contact, and movement or gesture. Some critics think they have done a good job if they count the "ums" and "uhs" in a speech. To have done that and missed its content and substance, is a waste of listening time. It is prob-

> ## THE STORY OF COMMUNICATION
>
> ### The Gettysburg Address
>
> **N**ovember 19, 1863: Fourscore and seven years ago our fathers brought forth on this continent a new nation, conceived in Liberty, and dedicated to the proposition that all men are created equal.
>
> Now we are engaged in a great civil war, testing whether that nation or any nation so conceived and so dedicated, can long endure. We are met on a great battle-field of that war. We have come to dedicate a portion of that field as a final resting place for those who here gave their lives that that nation might live. It is altogether fitting and proper that we should do this.
>
> But, in a larger sense, we cannot dedicate—we cannot consecrate—we cannot hallow—this ground. The brave men, living and dead, who struggled here, have consecrated it, far above our poor power to add or detract. The world will little note, nor long remember what we say here, but it can never forget what they did here. It is for us the living, rather, to be dedicated here to the unfinished work which they who fought here have thus far so nobly advanced. It is rather for us to be here dedicated to the great task remaining before us—that from these honored dead we take increased devotion to that cause for which they gave the last full measure of devotion—that we here highly resolve that these dead shall not have died in vain—that this nation, under God, shall have a new birth of freedom—and that government of the people, by the people, for the people, shall not perish from the earth.

ably true that great speakers avoid verbal irrelevancies ("ums" and "uhs"), but there is much more to a worthwhile message than a smooth presentation. Some very smooth presenters in history have carried the most profoundly evil messages. Adolf Hitler is a case in point. On the other hand, some profound ideas have been presented in a plain, flat style, as is evident in the newspaper accounts of Lincoln's speech at Gettysburg.

To summarize, evaluation should help you to obtain a complete picture of the message from the dual perspective of both its content and its delivery. Some of the most memorable speakers of all time did full justice to both.

The steps of active listening, getting prepared, staying involved, keeping an open mind, and reviewing and evaluating are important to apply as much as you can. These steps are ready for you to start, now! It is your first communication assignment for an activity that you can begin to do immediately. You will have 40 to 60 percent or more of your day, every day, to try to put these principles into practice. To get you started, let's look at the purposes and places to work on your listening skills.

Listening Skills in Context

The four contexts for listening—appreciative, empathic, comprehensive, and critical—were identified at the beginning of this chapter. Let's examine how the techniques of active listening can be applied in each area.

Listening for Appreciation.   Probably the event that is easiest to look forward to is listening for recreation. Your favorite radio station, your cassette or CD player, and live concerts are quick examples. In the listening for recreation category, you can still apply the principles of active listening. Get yourself ready to relax. You might increase your enjoyment if you know something about the music or the artist. In fact, many newspaper and magazine articles about recording artists help to fulfill this part of listening preparation. Reviews of concerts or new releases also provide background information that may help you to prepare for better recreational listening. Getting involved and staying involved are accomplished by using headphones or volume controls or just closing your eyes and shutting out distractions. You may also increase your enjoyment by listening to new or unfamiliar material with an open mind. It might take several attempts before you appreciate a new approach, sound, artist, or style. Finally, you can review the material and decide whether you want to hear more or move on to another listening experience. Some people constantly flip through radio stations until they finally hear a familiar, favorite song. They give no time to a station unless they recognize the material immediately. A good recreational listener will be more tolerant and withhold quick evaluation in favor of thoughtful review and judgment.

Listening for Empathy.   Part of being in social interactions requires that you function as a sender *and* a receiver of information—that you remember that communication is a transaction in which meanings and understanding result from the interaction of the communicators. When your primary role in an interaction is to support your relationship with another person, you are probably engaged in a lot of empathic listening. **Empathy** means to "feel within" someone else's emotional state. Empathic listening means trying to both understand the content of the message and relate to the feelings of that message. You might be discussing with a friend or close co-worker some problem or situation in which feelings are important. Suppose your roommate has just received a low grade on an assignment and tells you about it. You could say, "Hey, no big deal, you'll do better next time." Although you might be trying to help, you have not engaged in empathic listening. Instead, if you say, "Sounds like a real letdown," you are letting your friend know that you understand about both the low grade and how your friend feels about the situation. Much counseling— both professional and informal—involves the ability to provide empathic listening. When you really like a friend, often it is because that person listens, *really listens,* to you and provides feedback indicating that he or she identifies, understands, and supports your feelings.

Applications of active listening in the empathic setting may mean putting aside your communication agenda for the moment to get ready to listen to your partner's message. Certainly, being nonjudgmental in this situation helps your partner to avoid feeling defensive and may invite your partner to explore further his or her ideas and reactions. Keep involved by providing appropriate feedback, making brief references to similar situations or feelings you have experienced, and yet restraining your own talking so that your partner can fully express himself or herself. An important part of empathic listening may be to help your partner by providing a summary of what he or she has told you. Hearing it back may help your partner to reevaluate the situation. Certainly, you can do your own personal evaluation by thinking how your partner's experiences can be applied to your own situation.

Listening for Comprehension.   This listening environment becomes a major part of your activity as a student. Research indicates that effective listening correlates directly with academic success. Students who tested best on listening skills also had the highest grades (Coakley and Wolvin, 1991). Listening in the classroom is probably going to focus primarily on remembering ideas and content presented by your instructors and others. In a learning environment, much of your comprehension depends on your ability to recall major ideas and their supporting details. You may have to learn complex mathematics or engineering formulae or dates, names, and locations in history. You may be asked to do both remembering and criticizing. You could be asked not just when the French Revolution started, but why, and what you think might have been done differently. In communication classes, you may be asked to be a critic of other students' speeches or presentations, and your teachers will be seeking both summary and evaluation from you.

Classroom listening is difficult because of the many barriers that are potentially at work, interfering with your ability to listen effectively. For example, most classrooms are not furnished with comfortable chairs, the lighting may be poor, or the temperature may be uncomfortable. Other barriers to good listening may come from your teachers, most of whom have not have courses in how to lecture effectively. Your mathematics professor may have no idea of how to organize a lecture, how to do effective previews and transitions, or how to enhance content with clear visual aids. Your chemistry teacher might be so involved in working out a formula construction problem that no effort is made to tie in fast-appearing work on the board with your note-taking speed. Finally, you may provide barriers by having a poor attitude, since the class is required for general education and not in your major area of interest. Or you might be preoccupied by an exam that is coming up in the next hour in another class. You might be distracted by home or personal concerns that pull your attention away from the subject at hand. Each of these problems is a form of noise, which we discussed in Chapter 2 as part of the communication model. Good listening in the classroom is a challenge, and you will need all the skills of active listening to help you meet that challenge.

Increased attention to classroom listening can improve your classroom experience. Get prepared by reading the assigned material, having pencil and paper handy for notes, sitting where you can see and hear, and avoiding hunger and fatigue. Stay involved by taking notes, rephrasing the ideas, connecting material to other things you know, asking questions, and paying attention to other classroom comments. Withhold quick evaluation, as it becomes internal noise to distract you. Avoid mentally wishing you did not have to take this class or critiquing the instructor's appearance or presentation. Finally, the best students always review shortly after class to refine and complete their notes, connect ideas to the reading materials, and prepare questions for the next session to get explanations for ideas that they still find unclear or incomplete.

Listening Critically.   A major function of training in listening is to enable you to become a wise consumer of the information that flows at you daily. If you watch about twenty hours of television weekly, a fairly low average for people in the 16 to 25 age range, you will be exposed to about 280 commercial messages a week urging you to buy some product or service. Some estimates go as high as a million commercials by the time you are 20 (Postman, 1981). By the early 1970s, it was estimated that the average college freshman had been exposed to 22,000 hours of television programming (Burmeister, 1974). Add to that number any hours of radio listening and think about how many commercials you see or hear in an hour of broadcasting, and you have a sizable number of messages designed by professionals who are trained in persuading you to act in a manner of their design. Not all of these actions are for your benefit; in fact, they are likely to be for the benefit of the advertiser's sales figures. **Critical listening** means taking information and looking at it carefully. It means being able to analyze the content and form of the message so that you make informed decisions about the value of the information for you. As you follow the steps for active listening, add these items to your mental checklist:

- How was the quality of supporting material?
- How adequate were the reasons expressed?
- Were there reasons that were not expressed? Why?
- Were the appeals logical, emotional, or personal?
- What will I gain from the proposed action?
- What will the presenter gain from my action?

As you are involved in listening, these questions can be present; and certainly at the end of the event, they should form a major part of your evaluation. Does

Watching television is an opportunity to listen critically.

the speaker want you to act immediately, before you have a chance to evaluate the message? What does that say about the speaker's purposes? One way to apply your critical thinking ability is to take advantage of the thought/speech gap to evaluate messages. People usually speak about 120–150 words per minute, but you can *think* at about 400–800 words per minute (Wolff and Marsnik, 1992). This gap between how fast someone is talking to you and how fast you are thinking is the space in which you can apply your critical thinking skills.

Listening happens in almost every waking moment of our lives. It is an event that has great importance for us every day, yet one that is generally little studied and seldom taught. In this short introduction to listening, you saw how the four steps of active listening can help you to improve your listening abilities. This can lead you to become a better critic of the persuasive messages from advertisers, a more informed classroom receiver of ideas, an enhanced recreational listener, and an empathic friend.

IMPROVING LISTENING COMPETENCY

Let us first take a brief look at each part of the communication model to see how a barrier is formed and how it can be overcome.

Eliminating the Barriers

The first step in improved listening competency is to remove the **barriers** that prevent active listening. These barriers are found in any part of the communication transaction, as described in the communication model in Chapter 2.

Context. The first part of the model, context, can help or hinder listening ability. If you know that you are in a classroom, listening to a lecture, a certain context has been set. You know something about the subject matter and may be familiar with the person who is speaking and with the content of the message. On the other hand, being in church and listening to a sermon probably do not call for a note pad and a pencil, nor does sitting in a friend's apartment.

Your expectations can set your frame of mind so that you are ready for certain kinds of information and certain kinds of listening behavior. Feedback in the form of questions may be appropriate, but it is controlled by raising a hand in the classroom. However, raising a hand in church is not appropriate; and in your friend's room, feedback is likely to be spontaneous rather than regulated.

Context, then, helps to determine how you prepare for listening and how you behave. Barriers to good listening arise when a context is unclear or is counter to normal expectations. Awards shows on television have run into the problem of an award-winner taking the opportunity to lecture the audience about a favorite cause or issue. The context would normally call for a simple statement of thanks and appreciation, so those who violate the expectations of the audience often find that their message is received with hostility. In a different setting and time, the same message might be well received and perhaps even supported.

Source.   The next part of the communication model is the source/sender—where the message originates. Usually, the source is a person who creates, or encodes, a message. Because we all have different associations and vocabularies, a problem can arise at this point. If the sender of a message uses a term or sentence construction that is unusual or unknown to the listeners, a barrier has been created. The source needs to pay attention to both the message and the target audience so that the message is sent and received with clarity. Being organized, following a clear pattern of development, using transitions and internal summaries, and restating main ideas are ways in which the source can help listeners to remove, or at least lower, the barriers to good reception. One way in which you can help a source respond to your needs as a listener is to provide feedback. You can nod in agreement if you understand the source's message or perhaps ask the sender to stop and rephrase or repeat an idea that you do not understand.

Message.   Because the message is an output, or product, of the source, any barriers in the message probably stem from the source. The best way to keep a message clear is for the source to check it as part of his or her self-monitoring.

This self-checking occurs when you have a clear message in mind but when you express it, it just "doesn't come out right." You say something like, "That didn't sound right; let me try it again." Then you rephrase the message. You may rearrange the word order or substitute one unclear term for a different term that better conveys your idea. This process is a way of editing your message, similar to the process you use to edit a written paper. In other words, problems occurring in the message are usually extensions of barriers originating in the sender.

Channels.   One common place for barriers to arise is in the various channels that carry communication. For example, if you cannot see a speaker, you are unable to pay attention to the nonverbal aspects of the message carried by the visual channel. If you cannot hear the message adequately, the audio channel has a problem, so it is impossible for you to listen carefully.

Often, you can make simple changes to eliminate these barriers. You can move to a place where you can see better, or you can turn up the volume on the radio or television. In an audience, you can ask the speaker to speak louder. A good speaker depends on this immediate feedback to enhance his or her presentation. You can also move your chair, turn down the sound of competing or interfering sources, ask others to be quiet or to speak louder, or make any other quick, physical changes to clear the main channel of interfering noise.

Receivers and Decoders.   The destination of a message is usually another person or group of people who are the focus of your communication. Within each person are potential barriers to clear reception of a message. As a receiver, you may not be adequately or properly prepared for a message, you can let internal thoughts distract you, or you can make a premature evaluation of the message or give your attention to ideas other than the one being presented at the moment.

When you function in the receiver role, the steps of the active listening process will help you to remove or reduce the barriers to effective listening, and in this sense, you have a great deal of control over this part of the process. It is one of the more difficult areas to control completely, as our minds are constantly active, often moving to areas that are unrelated to the event at hand.

Feedback/Interference/Noise.   Good listening depends on good **feedback,** both internal and external. Internally, you use feedback when you summarize or when you link ideas from the source to those that are important or relevant to you. Externally, you provide important feedback through nonverbal responses to a speaker or through verbal reactions when you make comments or ask questions.

Interference with the feedback process becomes a barrier to good listening when you cannot see the source or when the source cannot react to you. Noise is any disruption that occurs at any place or time in the process. Noise may be an internal distraction experienced by the sender, a clattering fan in the room, or a lawnmower going by outside. It may be a faulty picture tube in a television set or stray ideas and thoughts in the minds of listeners as their attention wanders from the source to personal concerns.

Removing these barriers depends on the location of the barrier and your ability to react to it. You probably cannot change the schedule of a person mowing the lawn, but you can get up and close the window.

Of all the ways to improve listening, providing feedback is perhaps the most useful. In each barrier situation, you can see that direct feedback, when possible, is an immediate way of reducing the barrier and promoting clarity and under-

Feedback and response complete the communication cycle.

IMPROVING COMPETENCY

Barriers to Listening

As you pay attention to your listening today, try to take one active step to help eliminate a barrier. Get up and close a window deliberately, and think, "I have just helped to eliminate a listening barrier." Or conscientiously move closer to a speaker if you are having difficulty hearing, and tell yourself what a good job you've done to improve your listening. By becoming aware of your active control over the listening situation, especially its barriers, you will become more sensitive to the listening experience, and you will acquire greater competency in being an effective listener.

standing. By recognizing that there are many ways and places for barriers to arise, you have already taken an important first step toward eliminating them. The principles of active listening, combined with your knowledge of the communication process, can help you to become a more effective listener.

Responsible Listening

The improvements that you can make in your listening skills are likely to fall into two phases: your responsibilities as a listener and your responsibilities as a sender.

Listener Responsibilities.   Try thinking about your efforts at listening as focusing on the information, focusing on learning, and focusing on wise consumer attitudes.

The focus on information means that you pay attention to the key ideas and ignore distractions or irrelevancies. You practice active listening to connect ideas in a message, even if the speaker does not. You try to apply ideas to your own experiences and needs. At the end of a lecture, you should be able to review the main ideas and a few of the subpoints and supporting materials such as examples, personal experiences, stories, or statistics. As a responsible listener, you should try to review at the end of each listening event. You will gain in the amount of information at your disposal and not waste time or energy on irrelevant efforts at noticing the speaker's haircut or clothing choice. Focus on the information. Take the job of listening seriously.

Next, try to keep learning about communication as a goal, even though the content of the message may be about something else. For example, if the speaker is talking about physics and uses an exceptionally clear diagram, make a quick mental note about the qualities of the diagram so that you can emulate them in your next visual aid. You are surrounded by good and not-so-good examples of communication; and if you can use the situation to help you discover what works and what doesn't, you can incorporate or avoid those behaviors as appropriate. While you are listening to speeches, you can learn something about how to be a better speaker. As you listen, you may discover that one person gets a strong positive reaction because of the enthusiasm of the delivery, whereas another bores the audience with dull, listless presentation skills. Take those experiences as messages not just about *those* speakers, but about yourself as well. Remember the best experiences to inspire your own presentations. These experiences also help to build your skills as an evaluator of messages.

In addition to ideas about strong or weak alternatives in presentation, you may gain ideas that you can use later in your presentations. For example, if Angela uses a quotation that you enjoyed or thought was powerful, remember the source and investigate it on your own. You may discover a new source of supporting material for your own presentations. If Thran has an interesting topic that catches your imagination, you may want to remember it so that in another setting, you can refer to those ideas to help make your own clear. Being inspired by other people is a constant source of information and a compliment to them. You can use your listening time to be on a constant search for ideas to develop and take in your own original directions.

Finally, listening responsibly can make you a more informed consumer. As you get bombarded with a constant flow in ideas and messages, the ability to listen critically becomes an important job of every receiver. One of the challenges of your lifetime is to take all the information that comes to you daily and make sense of it. Many people get overwhelmed and simply stop paying attention. They get into a habit of *not* listening; they avoid the news, they stop reading anything but material assigned, and they bypass magazines or newspapers with substantial or challenging content and style. Several commentators have identified this trend as part of the "dumbing down" of America (Hirsch, 1988). Fewer and fewer people get involved in running their lives, they fail to attend political forums, they avoid public lectures, they skip school board and city council meetings, and they decline to take part in voting or other expressions of opinion that count. These people can be called *listening dropouts,* for they failed to listen responsibly. At the other extreme, people who try to pay attention to everything do not act as critical consumers. A careful consumer selects information from among the huge variety available on the basis of the quality it offers. Listening consumption is much like other forms of consumption: You want to get value for the time and effort invested. One way to get value for your effort is to put into practice the simple training from this chapter, sifting out the valuable and relevant and deciding whether the information, the message, or the recreation gained from your time is worth it. Good consumers become *selective* consumers and put their time and effort into high-payoff activities. Are three hours a day of soap operas worth that much of your recreational time? Perhaps a listening budget would be an appropriate step, in which you devote a certain number of hours each week to informational listening, persuasive or motivational sources, or recreational uses. You might even want to keep track of how much of each type you engage in for a week to see whether your personal budget is getting you the most value.

Skill in Note Taking.   As part of your listening responsibilities, you can improve your competency by becoming a skilled note taker. Focus on key ideas, and jot down information in a form that keeps ideas and relationships connected and in order. The most effective tool for creating good notes is to follow an outline pattern in you note taking. The relationship of main ideas to subordinate ones needs to be clear when you scan your notes. Keep main ideas to the left of your sheet of paper, and cluster related ideas under those by indenting to the right. When the speaker moves to a new main idea, put that key term to the left and create a pattern for your notes. Remember, you're not taking dictation; don't try for every word or attempt to write full sentences. Just include main ideas expressed as key words. When you apply what you learn about outlining as well as skills in critical thinking, you will find yourself becoming an effective note taker as well. It takes practice; but each time you put your ideas into a brief form, you will find it becoming progressively easier.

All of these suggestions are for you when you are acting primarily as a receiver of information. However, there are also actions that you can take as a sender of messages to help improve the listening process.

As a Speaker. When you are a listener's primary source of information, you can help that person enormously in several ways. In general, start by being clear in you own mind about the purpose and focus of your message. Think back to the barriers that were mentioned concerning source/sender, and think how to make yourself clear to others. Then build your message for clarity with a clear outline that develops a central identified thesis or main idea. Use transitions and restatement to assist listeners in moving through your presentation with you. To help them maintain attention, add interest by telling stories or providing examples that are relevant to your listeners and captivating as well as relevant to your purpose. Use a vocabulary that suits their level of experience and background. If you need to include unusual or new terms, maker certain that you provide plenty of definitional information in the form of examples or similarities. Keep your voice loud and clear, and make eye contact around the room so that everyone will feel included and so that you can determine whether your listeners are interested, puzzled, or in agreement with you. If you decide to use visual aids, make them large, simple, and clearly directed to a main idea and make sure that they provide visual information better than you could communicate with words alone. Public speaking training deals extensively with details about preparation and presentation of speeches for impact and clarity. You should think back to this section and remember that good listening is a shared responsibility of the receivers and senders of messages.

Listening beyond the Classroom

When you leave your school setting, think about the importance that listening has in your everyday life. On the job, in family interactions, and during the reception of constant media messages, your skills at effective listening are a valuable asset.

As a listener in society at large, you receive many messages about products, ideas, people, and policies that ask you to make a decision or a choice. Use the skills of good listening to make informed decisions about the politics, services, and products that are competing for your attention. As a critical consumer of information, you can quickly identify slogans or catch phrases lacking substantial support. As a competent listener, you do not permit superficial, incomplete, emotional, or distorted messages to influence your behaviors or beliefs. By practicing active listening, you are on the lookout for a clear and detailed development of ideas, and you demand convincing, comprehensive supports for those

> ### *IMPROVING COMPETENCY*
>
> **Listening Applications**
>
> Training in listening is designed to increase your options—to build your repertoire of knowledge and skills. From that increased repertoire, you can select the appropriate listening technique, probably that called active listening. With the many examples given, you can then apply the skill or technique with confidence that you have a good chance of improving your listening behavior. Finally, review and evaluate your experience, and determine whether the desired improvement in your communication competency has been achieved.

ideas. Active listening is training you to become a discriminating, intelligent consumer of any and all information that comes your way.

SUMMARY

Both the reasons to be a good listener and the skills to allow you to become one were discussed in this chapter. Now you should be able to distinguish between the process of hearing and the activities that are involved in comprehensive listening. The four main principles of getting prepared, staying involved, keeping an open mind, and reviewing and evaluating afterward were outlined. The common barriers to effective listening were related to the parts of the communication model from Chapter 2. We looked ahead to information about how preparing and presenting speeches will help you to develop further competencies in listening. Overall, you should remember that listening most likely occupies more of your time than do all other communication activities combined, and an investment of your time and energy into applying these principles will pay handsome dividends for you every day.

KEY TERMS

listening, *p. 38*
empathy comprehension, *p. 39*
appreciation, *p. 39*
hearing, *p. 40*

active listening, *p. 41*
critical listening, *p. 48*
barriers, *p. 49*
feedback, *p. 51*

EXERCISES

1. Compare listening to an event on the radio and watching the same event on television. For example, listen to a sports event, a major news event, or some other presentation that is simultaneously televised and broadcast on the radio. Turn off the sound on the television and turn on the radio. What does the radio announcer do differently from the television announcer? What are your reactions when you close your eyes and listen only to the radio?

2. Keep a listening log of the amount of time you spend on a typical day listening to the radio, in class, on the job, and with friends. Do your percentages match the research discussed in this chapter? If they are different, can you explain why?

3. Sit in your room in silence for ten minutes, keeping your eyes closed and the lights out. Listen to the sounds around you. How many different sounds can you identify in that period of time? Include such things as other people's voices, vehicles, animals, television or radio broadcasts, creaks, and wind noises.

4. Count the number of advertisements you hear on the radio for one hour. Include public service announcements, political advertisements, and commercials. Then do the same thing during one hour of television. What similarities and differences do you notice? How do you explain these?

REFERENCES

Baker, L., R. Edwards, C. Gaines, K. Gladney, and F. Holley. "An Investigation of Proportional Time Spent in Various Communication Activities by College Students." *Journal of Applied Communication Research,* 8 (1981), 101.

Burmeister, David. "The Language of Deceit." *Language and Public Policy.* Ed. Hugh Rank. Urbana: National Council of Teachers of English, 1974.

Caputo, J. S., H. C. Hazel and C. McMahon, *Interpersonal Communication.* Boston: Allyn and Bacon, 1994.

Coakley, Carolyn, and Andrew Wolvin. "Listening in the Educational Environment." *Listening in Everyday Life.* Ed. Deborah Borisoff and Michael Purdy. Lanham: University Press of America, 1991.

Hirsch, E. D. *Cultural Literacy.* New York: Random House, 1988.

Pauk, Walter. *How to Study in College.* Boston: Houghton-Mifflin, 1989.

Postman, Neil. Interview. *U.S. News & World Report* 19 Jan. (1981), 43.

Rowe, Mary Budd. "Wait Time: Slowing Down May Be a Way of Speeding Up." *Journal of Teacher Education.* Jan./Feb. (1986), 43–50.

Steil, Lyman, Larry Barker, and Kittie Watson. *Effective Listening.* Reading: Addison-Wesley, 1983.

Sypher, Beverly D., Robert N. Bostrom, and Joy H. Seibert. "Listening, Communication Abilities, and Success at Work." *Journal of Business Communication* 26 (1989), 293–303.

Wolff, Florence I., and Nadine C. Marsnik. *Perceptive Listening.* 2nd ed. Ft. Worth: Harcourt Brace Jovanovich, 1992.

Wolvin, Andrew, and Carolyn Coakley. "A Survey of the Status of Listening Training in Some Fortune 500 Corporations." *Communication Education* 40 (1991), 153.

Wolvin, Andrew, and Carolyn Coakley. *Listening.* 4th ed. Dubuque: Wm. C. Brown, 1992.

What We Know about Critical Thinking

- Define the elements *critical* and *thinking* in combination.
- Describe the processes of deductive and inductive reasoning.
- Understand how the Toulmin model represents everyday thinking.
- Use appropriate tests to evaluate information, sources, and supporting materials.
- Apply critical thinking to your own decision-making processes.
- Communicate the results of your critical analyses to improve communication and thinking skills.

f listening is the first communication event, then trying to make sense of the sounds we hear follows naturally as the second event. When we focus effort, interpretation, feelings, and imagination on those sounds and start to associate them with things, events, people, and, later, ideas, we begin the process of thinking. Thinking is the use of the mind to process information. One thesaurus lists the following synonyms for the word *thinking*:

consider	recollect	suppose
contemplate	remember	create
meditate	conclude	envision
ponder	judge	imagine
reflect	presume	invent
recall	reason	conceive

Each of these terms also has a list of synonyms, so you can see that the word *thinking* involves a variety of meanings and associations.

Like emotion and intuition, thinking is part of our human makeup, and we do it all the time, with greater or lesser efficiency and precision. Improving the quality of our information processing, or thinking, is not a matter of luck or chance but a learnable skill. The term that is used in most academic settings to describe this enhanced ability is *critical thinking*. Let us take a moment to define this skill and then look at its components and how they affect our ability to make quality decisions. Finally, let us see how reasoning can be used as a mental habit to increase communication competency.

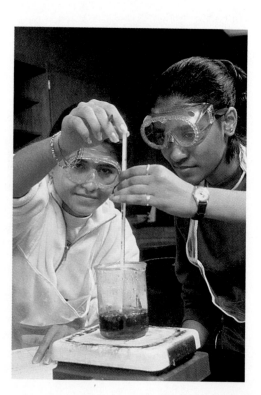

The scientific method is one formal system of critical thinking.

CRITICAL THINKING DEFINED

You get a good idea about the *thinking* part of the term from the list of synonyms, but you also need to focus on the use of the term *critical*. The word *critical* can have a variety of meanings, many of them with unpleasant connotations, such as: *acute, dangerous, grave, grievous, serious, crucial, decisive, important, momentous, pivotal, derogatory, disparaging, faultfinding, finicky, picky, analytical, discriminating, judging.*

It is important to consider your own associations with the term *critical*. Teachers in many colleges and universities have found resistance to courses or lessons in critical thinking because many people confuse negative meanings such as *faultfinding* or *derogatory* with the skills of critical thinking. Yes, you may become expert at finding weaknesses in much of the communication you encounter, but that is not a goal of critical thinking so much as it is a reflection on the sad state of much communication.

A critical thinker is skilled in serious, crucial, decisive, important, pivotal, analytical, and discriminating thinking. Some of that thinking may produce positive evaluations, and some may produce negative evaluations. Critical thinking will help you to judge the accuracy of statements and the soundness of the reasons that lead you and others to certain conclusions and actions. It will help you interpret complex ideas, appraise the **evidence** offered in support of arguments or claims, and make a distinction between reasonable and unreasonable communication (Ruggerio, 1990).

Thus critical thinking forms a complement to other ways of gathering and using information, such as your experience, intuition, and feelings.

These abilities are important in many ways, not the least of which is in your school work. Drawing conclusions from information involves much more than summarizing or rephrasing the information. Your training in critical thinking should equip you to evaluate the information that comes to you through careful

IMPROVING COMPETENCY

Creativity, the Workforce, and the Classroom

Observe your classes. What is the climate in the room regarding the asking of questions? Are questions and challenges encouraged, discouraged, or ignored? Can you find a relationship between the size of the class and the tolerance for questions?

One of the criticisms of business and industry in this country is that they lack the imagination to solve problems or to create new products. Do you think those criticisms are justified? If so, could there be a link between the way students are taught in school and the quality of the workforce? How many questions are asked on average in your classes? The imaginative use of questions can begin in the home and school. Building your questioning skills so that they reflect critical and creative processes can be an important part of improving your communication competency.

analysis of that information—its content, sources, biases, **assumptions,** methods, implications, applications, and limitations.

Thinking critically does not come automatically; in fact, the influential people around you may have discouraged you from developing critical thinking skills. For example, students who constantly challenge assumptions can be annoying and take up a lot of time in the classroom. Children who constantly ask their parents, "Why?" can become tiresome. So when people discourage habits of questioning and examining for the sake of expediency, they run the risk of extinguishing skills that will be needed later on.

Critical thinking skills are also important beyond the classroom as you make important decisions affecting your life. In her book *Reasoning and Communication,* Josina Makau (1990) underscores both these skills and their value as follows:

> These skills include the abilities to ask relevant questions, find, evaluate and effectively use relevant information, draw reasonable inferences and evaluate inferences. Proficient critical thinkers share at least several basic characteristics. They are committed to careful decision making. They make effective use of freedom of choice in their personal and professional lives. And they understand that exercising our liberties requires the development and use of critical thinking skills.

Critical thinking becomes a lifelong skill, to be used in the way you look at the world and evaluate the information you get every day. It should become a habit—a habit of mind—that enhances your ability to live successfully.

Critical thinking is the process of finding, interpreting, integrating, and evaluating information. At its base is the concept that all evaluation depends on a series of judgments, reports, abstractions, perceptions, inferences, and predictions. For example, if you are asked, "Who is the best singer in the world?" the immediate temptation is to begin tossing out names based on feelings or associations you already have in your mind. A better approach is to ask for some systematic method by which you can judge. "It all depends on what is meant by 'best,'" would be a good way to start. Even the most subjective-sounding questions, like the one just stated, have some **assumptions** or criteria that are the basis for the answer. Whether the criteria are sound can be evaluated according to the standards of critical thinking, and thus their reasonableness can be established. Applying the skills of critical thinking can help you to make better use of information so that you can improve your reasoning and thereby improve the quality of the decisions you make daily. To apply these skills, let us first define the ways in which reasoning can be approached.

APPROACHES TO REASONING

The formal study of reasoning is several thousand years old and was one of the subjects included in many of the early Greek texts on rhetoric. As philosophy and rhetoric interacted in the past, one major connection between them was the use, or lack thereof, of logic in thinking and speaking. Formal approaches to thinking and speaking were guided by the principles of **deduction;** less formal

THE STORY OF COMMUNICATION

Tension with Logic and Reason

The concern for logic and reason is especially strong in Western European traditions and cultures. These cultures followed the Greek and Roman models, which emphasized the mental, knowable, factual base of learning—often called *Aristotlean thinking*. While this base of learning led to many material advances, other cultures emphasized feelings or intuition or insight.

Many societies struggle with the tension between too much emphasis on one or the other, while some try to blend elements of both. In very materialistic societies, counterculture movements, such as that of the hippies in the late 1960s and early 1970s, will appear from time to time. In societies with a more spiritual emphasis (e.g., Native American, religious communities, Afrocentric traditions), there are struggles over whether or how much to accept the material approach and how much rational thought should influence personal, social, and cultural development.

The Western model has tended to dominate in the United States and elsewhere, but it has not done so without causing stress and tension. Your own communication style and preferences reflect degrees of influence from this variety of models.

conclusions were obtained by another reasoning process: **induction.** Both forms of reasoning are examined here, and this section concludes with a modern method for examining the reasoning process proposed by contemporary philosopher and rhetorician Stephen Toulmin.

Deduction

The formal processes of reasoning were expressed in structures and rules early in the teachings of the ancient rhetoricians and philosophers. This is called *deduction.* They devised careful systems to lead speakers, thinkers, and listeners from **premises** to **conclusions.** The most popular and seemingly simple form was the **syllogism,** which consists of three parts: the major premise, the minor premise, and the conclusion.

The major premise usually expresses a main idea or universal law or principle. The minor premise connects some specific example to one part of that main idea. The conclusion makes a connection to the other part of the main idea through a logical link. You are probably familiar with the following classical example:

Major premise: All men are mortal.

Minor premise: Socrates is a man.

Conclusion: Therefore Socrates is mortal.

This is a good example because it is short, it is based on sound premises, and it exactly follows both the form and the rules for a syllogism.

Unfortunately, there are many ways in which people reason that look and sound like correct syllogisms but are not. These errors are called **fallacies,** and, using the above example, you can see them plainly:

All men are mortal.

Socrates is mortal.

Therefore Socrates is a man.

In this syllogism, Socrates could be my pet goldfish and still be mortal but not a man, so watch for incorrect assumptions.

What went wrong with our reasoning here? The major premise is the same in both cases, and the premise is true. The minor premise in both cases may also be true, yet the conclusion in the second example does not necessarily follow and may be false. The problem is in the format. Look at this example:

Socrates is a man.

Socrates is a mortal.

Therefore all men are mortal.

Each statement in the syllogism is true, but the syllogism itself is not logically valid. You cannot make the claim that all men are mortal on the basis of the one example of Socrates.

Let us take a closer look at the two components for analyzing deduction: the **truth,** or accuracy, of the premises, and the **validity,** or rule following, of the logic. It is important to get behind the appearance of logic and test ideas and arguments that are expressed in logical form, because many people may be persuaded by only a resemblance to logical. A rhetoric scholar, Jesse Delia (1970), has pointed out the following:

> Since form conveys reason directly to the mind of the receiver, an argument cogently laid down according to the rules of logical form inherently has the power to . . . persuade.

Knowing something about logical forms will enable you to examine the flood of information that you get every day—asking you to buy, believe, behave, or vote in a certain way—and put it into logical form.

Truth.   The truth of the premises is usually easy to test but often difficult to see. Three questions help to determine the truth of premises: Are they based on what is known? How was that knowledge derived? How is that knowledge expressed?

First, the premises must be founded on accurate observations and reports of information. These data can be tested by rules of information accuracy. For example, is the major premise the result of carefully observed and tested examples? Or is it rather the impression of an observer? Is it the result of untested tradition or uninformed bias? There are several other ways to examine the accuracy of the premises. Does the statement or claim made in the premise agree with general knowledge? That is, does it seem, on the face of it, to agree with generally accepted ideas, or does the statement or claim call for special expert knowledge? The premise "All men are mortal" fits very well with what we generally know, but if the major premise is "All recombinant dynacarbo nucleic modules are the result of metathermal hydrosis," you would probably want to ask an expert in biochemistry about it. (She or he would tell you that the statement, though it sounds impressive, is meaningless.)

Since major premises are usually the result of an analysis of many specific instances, you can evaluate the soundness of a statement by looking at how it was derived. Were the facts on which it is based both sufficient and representative to justify the statement? For example, the facts that everybody who has ever lived has also died and there are no recorded cases to the contrary give us enough justification for the premise "All men are mortal." But how about "Bodybuilders eat sushi" as a premise? (At first, you might reject it as being without support, but suppose you know four competitive muscle builders and each one of them eats rice topped with raw, Japanese-style fish? You might feel justified in making your statement, but it would not pass an objective test of sufficient and representative data.)

Many of our cultural premises and values can be subjected to the same test. "Honesty is the best policy," "Men are better drivers than women," and "Mexican food is spicy" are similar in that they have no known sample or data behind them. They are generalities without support, yet many people believe them for the simple reason that they are repeated often. Check the underlying support, if any, of a premise that passes as a rule. Many elegant, perfectly formed, and articulately expressed arguments begin with a false premise.

In addition to lacking a valid premise, an argument might not be expressed completely. Some part of it could be left out, with the assumption that the listener will supply it mentally. Aristotle called this partial syllogism an **enthymeme.** He pointed out that most arguments and public presentations simply omitted premises or conclusions that the speaker thought the audience would think of themselves. For example, take any of the syllogisms presented here and block out one of the three parts. You can probably guess the missing part and mentally supply it to complete the connections. These missing parts are possible danger points, however, because there is always a chance that the audience will fill in that part in a manner you had not intended. More examples of enthymemes follow in the discussion of the Toulmin model.

Truth, therefore, may have another dimension. The language that is used may be unclear, have shifting meanings, or be ambiguous. The recombinant dynacarbo nucleic example mentioned earlier is filled with such problems. But you do not need bizarre words to be led astray. Often, the simplest words can be used in a variety of ways, and such variety can create a problem in a premise. For example, consider the following syllogism:

> All men are created equal.
>
> Women are not men.
>
> Therefore women are not created equal.

or

> Good taste is hard to get.
>
> Ice cream is good to taste.
>
> Therefore ice cream is hard to get.

or

All dogs have fleas.

My used car is a real dog.

My used car has fleas.

These examples may or may not seem amusing to you, but they reflect a real difficulty in creating sound premises. When a word shifts meaning or has a meaning that is unclear, a conclusion may be drawn that is tempting to believe but is erroneous because of the use of ambiguous language. Is abortion murder? Is capital punishment murder? Is beef or pork packing murder? Is polluting our environment murder? "It all depends," says the careful, critical thinker, "on what you mean by. . . ."

The fallacy of *ambiguity* means that a word may reasonably have two or more distinct interpretations. A second fallacy is *equivocation*—starting with one sense of a term and then shifting to another sense. In the syllogism beginning "All men are created equal," it is very clear that the word *men* in the major premise is used in its generic form to mean "people." In the minor premise, the meaning clearly shifts to mean only the males of the species. The equivocation fallacy is also seen with *good taste* and *dog* in the second and third examples.

Vagueness is the third fallacy of premises gone wrong, and it is often seen in platitudes such as "I will do only what is good for the country." What does that mean? Does it mean "I will stand up to the crooks and swindlers who have invaded our sacred halls of freedom and justice and will resist their efforts to bring down all that has made us great." If that is what your statement means, just what will you do, how, and to whom? When words soar to high levels of abstraction, referring to concepts so broad that they have no concrete referents, you are probably witnessing the vagueness fallacy. The danger here to critical thinking is that the major premise is *supposed* to sound like a general or universal principle, so how can you tell whether it is sound? Go back to the principle of testing or verifying with facts or examples.

Finally, *obscuration* is the term that is used to describe the use of unusual words, highly technical words, technical-sounding words, jargon that is specific to a group of insiders, or a highly complex and convoluted sentence structure. The statement concerning metathermal hydrosis is an attempt to obscure the message by hiding behind complexity. You can detect and guard against this fallacy by breaking down a complex message into small, simple parts and carefully examining those parts.

Examining premises means that you test them for any truth they may contain. Truth is measured by what is known, how it was derived, and how it was expressed. If you are satisfied with the truth of the major and minor premises, you need to move to the next area involved in testing deductive syllogisms and examine the process that was used to link the ideas in the premises to the conclusion. That process determines the validity of the deductive logic that is used to reach the conclusion of the premise.

Validity.   In formal logic, *validity* means that the conclusion of an argument must not be false if the premises are true. If, on the other hand, the premises are true and the conclusion is false, the logical process that is used to reach the conclusion is invalid.

DIVERSITY IN COMMUNICATION

The Treaty in Walla Walla

Cultural premises in decision making can vary to the point at which people may talk past each other. In 1855, Native Americans and representatives of the U. S. government met to work out a treaty in Walla Walla, Washington. Consider these excerpts from that meeting:

General Palmer: "I have made treaties with all the Indian tribes in the Willamette Valley, with all in the Umqua Valley, and all in the Rogue River and Shasta country. They have agreed to remove to such tracts as shall be selected for them. They have agreed to be friendly with the whites and all the other Indians. They have sold us all their country except the reservations. We have agreed to build them mills, blacksmith shops, a wagon maker's shop, to erect a tin shop and gun shop, to build a school house and hospital, to employ millers, mechanics, school teachers, doctors and farmers. . . . Do you want these things? . . . The Buffalo are not as plenty as they were once. Where are they now? All gone. . . . If we make a treaty with you . . . you can rely on all its provisions being carried out strictly."

Chief Peo-Peo-Mox-Mox: "We have listened to all you have to say, and we desire you should listen when any Indian speaks. . . . [You] want an answer immediately, without giving them time to think. . . . In one day the Americans became as numerous as the grass. . . . I know that it is not right. Suppose you show me goods, shall I run up and take them? Goods and Earth are not equal. Goods are for using on the Earth. I do not know where they have given land for goods. . . . I do not wish you to reply today. Think over what I have said."

Young Chief: "We did not understand each other on both sides about this country. Your marking out the country is the reason it troubles me so and has made me sit here without saying anything. . . . The reason why we could not understand you was that you selected this country for us to live in without us having any voice in the matter. We will think slowly over the different streams that run through the country. . . . I cannot take the whole country and throw it to you. . . . I think the land where my forefathers are buried should be mine; that is the place that I am speaking for. . . . My brothers, that is what I have to show you. That is the place I love, where we get our roots to live upon. The Salmon comes up the stream. That is all."

The Nez Percé War began twenty-two years later, in 1877, as the result of an attempt to drive the Nez Percé tribe out of a large portion of the reservation that this treaty guaranteed to them (McGlone and Fausti, 1972).

Chief Joseph led his people in resisting the takeover of their lands. He is remembered for his eloquent speech.

For example, the conclusion "Socrates is a man" was quite possibly false, since Socrates could have been the name of my goldfish. Even though the premises were both true, they did not necessarily lead to a true conclusion, because something was wrong with the deductive reasoning process. We confused, reversed, or inverted the statements so that, while they were still true independently, they no longer connected correctly to lead us to a single, necessary, true conclusion.

Truth, then, is the evaluation of each statement, or premise, by itself, whereas validity is the evaluation of the connections that are made in combining the statements. There are many rules of deductive validity, for there are several kinds of deductive syllogisms. A simple test of validity is that the general subject or condition of the major premise must appear as the result in the minor premise. For example, look at this syllogism:

> All dogs have ears.
>
> John has ears.
>
> Therefore John is a dog.

This syllogism violates the test of validity that was just described. The subject of the major premise is dogs, but the predicate, or result, of the minor premise is not dogs, but ears. Only a conclusion about dogs is possible in this syllogism, as follows:

> All dogs have ears.
>
> John is a dog.
>
> Therefore John has ears.

The connection is now valid because the term *dog* has been properly placed. But are the premises true? Check John for canine characteristics! If indeed John is your pet collie, he does have ears. If John is your pet hamster, the conclusion

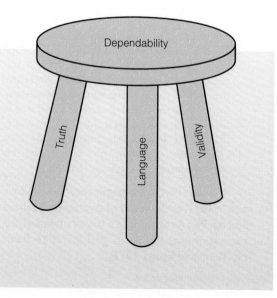

Would you stand on a two-legged stool?

may be valid, but the minor premise, "John is a dog," is not. Perhaps John is a fish, like his friend Socrates, and both are swimming in a goldfish bowl. Check truth, check the language, then check validity. You need all three to draw conclusions that are absolutely dependable (Reinard, 1991).

But what if you cannot investigate all the areas necessary for deductive reasoning to work, and you are interested not in absolute dependability, but just good, strong *probability*? The kind of reasoning that helps you decide the likelihood, or probability, of your conclusions being true is induction.

Induction

Induction shows how most of us think. It is the drawing of conclusions on the basis of a review of the evidence. Induction tells not what is true, but what is likely to be true on the basis of the weight of the evidence. Whereas deduction is concerned with what is true and valid, induction deals with what is *probable*.

Determining what is probable means to evaluate the evidence or support behind any conclusion. Are elephants gray? How do you know? Better yet, why do you believe that elephants are gray? This simple question of elephant coloring could be answered by saying that every elephant you have ever seen is gray, every photograph of elephants you have ever seen shows them to be gray, you have heard of no other color ever being associated with elephants, and therefore elephants are gray.

In this example, you can see the elements of induction. A number of examples or samples are examined; they are combined by something they have in common; and they lead to a conclusion that seems acceptable.

As is true for deductive reasoning, there are some accepted rules for good inductive reasoning. These rules are related to the quality of the evidence and the process that is used to link it to the conclusion. There are three basic rules to apply in evaluating supporting evidence.

Is the Sample Known?   This rule might seem simple, but many conclusions, especially ones that are held dearly and passionately, often lack any supporting sample. "She's the most wonderful girl in the world." "The Dodgers are the all-time greats!" "Republicans are rich." "Democrats are big spenders." The list could go on and on.

Most of these statements are based on assumed or implied evidence, and a person could probably make up samples that could lead to the conclusion expressed. You could, for example, offer comparisons of the favored female's qualities with those of others and conclude that she is indeed wonderful. Or you might list the accomplishments and statistics of the Brooklyn/Los Angeles baseball franchise and conclude that they are impressive. If you have met or heard of several people identified as Republicans, all of whom appear to be well off, you could draw the conclusion that Republicans are wealthy. Likewise, if the voting record of a number of Democratic politicians reveals that they support big government budgets, you might feel that you have support for your conclusion.

On the other hand, you may be guilty of believing unsupported conclusions when you simply repeat what you have heard before, trusting in some sort of logic of longevity, thinking that if a statement has been around a while and has been repeated, it must be true. The first step, then, is to look for a sample: Is one present, or is it implied? Asking people who make conclusions to reveal their evidence is often the best clue as to how sound their reasoning is. Once you establish the existence of a body of evidence, the evidence can be analyzed further.

Is the Sample Sufficient?   This step in the analysis of the evidence asks whether enough information has been gathered for the conclusion to be sound. How many people are included in the comparison? How many years of baseball need to be examined? How many Republicans or Democrats need to be in the sample? The answer is not always the same, but there must be enough evidence to give you a reliable picture of the event. In induction, conclusions will almost always be drawn on the basis of incomplete evidence. You cannot survey every Republican or have the Dodgers come out in first place in every possible measure of greatness. What you can do is guard against using a limited sample that is too small to be useful.

Is the Sample Representative?   This question asks that you examine the supporting evidence to see whether it is typical, based on a fair cross-section of the total group. For example, you might take a random sample of 100 students and ask for their grades to determine the projected average GPA of your school. If you took your sample from 10:00 to 11:00 A.M. on Tuesday, you would miss those students who are on campus only in the evening. If you got your sample from the room where the school's honor society holds its annual installation ceremony, your results would not be typical of all students.

The rule of representativeness is often stated to give every member of the base group an equal chance of being selected for the sample. Advances in the scientific identification of target respondents have enabled professional samplers, such as pollsters, to become very specific and accurate in their sampling methods. For example, the Gallup Poll, one of the most used and best known of our national survey organizations, contacts only about 1,400 people in each survey, yet it can be very accurate about what 250,000,000 people think. It makes absolutely certain that its sample is representative, and it can achieve reliably within three percentage points on a 100-point scale. Often, its results are more accurate than that.

Make certain that *your* evidence is based on a full cross-section of the entire possible base. You should also ask others how, where, or when their evidence was gathered. For example, people responding at one time may change their minds later. In presidential elections, polling is done weekly or even more frequently to detect trends. On important issues, people may change their opinions frequently. In just ten years, one university went from having an incoming freshman class in which 48 percent of students smoked cigarettes to having one in which fewer than 5 percent smoked. Any conclusions about college students and tobacco had better be based on the most current information.

Later in this chapter, you will read about *informed decision making* and will be given further guides for evaluating information, sources, and supporting materials. For now, remember that inductive reasoning asks you to evaluate the likelihood or strength of a claim or conclusion and that evaluation must begin by looking at the information that led to the conclusion.

Once you are satisfied with the evidence, you can construct a logical format for induction similar to the syllogism used in deduction. That format might look like the following illustration:

Person A lived and then died.

Person B lived and then died.

Person C lived and then died.

Person D lived and then died.

Persons E through 7 billion others lived and then died.

Therefore people are mortal; that is, they die.

Notice that with induction, a general conclusion comes from a series of observations. Clearly, the number and accuracy of the observations will determine the believability of the conclusion. Therefore induction takes specific examples or instances, connects them with a common factor, and draws a conclusion based on the connection. The example takes everyone who has ever lived, connects each person with the common factor of death, and then draws a conclusion. Following the rules described above, we had a known, sufficient, and representative sample. However, it wasn't necessary to research every person who was ever born, simply because the evidence is universal. But what about Republicans? Sushi eaters? Mexican food? Chemistry teachers? Can these rules still apply? The answer is that they do, and the guidelines for evaluating them will be discussed in the final section of this chapter.

At this point, it is evident that induction and deduction are related, even if they are different. Deduction begins with general principles, and induction ends with them. In fact, induction is the process that supplies deduction with its major premise. The two processes are connected at the point of generalization. Compare the following example of deduction to the previous example.

All people are mortal.

Socrates is a person.

Therefore Socrates is mortal.

Induction and deduction intersect at the generalization "All people are mortal." The truth of that major premise is discovered through the processes of induc-

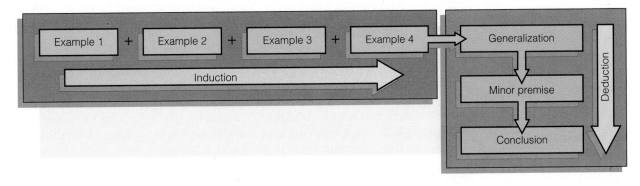

Induction and deduction connect with generalizations.

tion, and now it can be applied with great certainty to any particular person we meet. We must, of course, follow the rules. One way to look at the rules of logic was introduced in 1958 by Stephen Toulmin. It is yet a third way to engage in formal critical thinking.

The Toulmin Model

Because so much attention was paid to developing complicated systems of logic and mathematics, there were no simpler systems to use in ordinary thinking situations. Stephen Toulmin devised such a system when he began to examine the way most people think (Toulmin, 1958). This system is often called the **Toulmin model,** and it consists of three main elements: the grounds, or data (Toulmin et al., 1978), the warrant, and the claim. The **grounds** are the pieces of information you think about or collect that relate to a topic, the **claim** is the conclusion you draw when you look at the information, and the **warrant** is the connecting principle that allows you to link the information to the conclusion. This model can be illustrated as follows:

These three elements are the basis for drawing conclusions about the world. In some ways the warrants exist before the other two elements in the habits and manners you use to organize and connect information. Warrants are the general approaches or rules that you use to guide your thinking processes. They are often derived from values and beliefs about the way the world works, and you probably put them into practice automatically and without thinking.

When you draw a conclusion in a statement such as "I can't go to the movies tonight; I have a midterm exam tomorrow in my critical thinking class," your listeners will take the grounds (midterm exam) and connect them logically to your claim (can't go to movies) by filling in the implied "because" between the two automatically. They will supply the warrant for this situation (One should stay home and study the night before a test) without anyone ever actually mentioning it. It is an assumed, trustworthy "rule" that is understood by anyone going to school. The warrant is the reason to believe that the grounds justify the claim.

Sometimes, however, people supply a warrant that different from your own, and you may be puzzled by the conclusion they draw from the same grounds. For example, they may have a warrant that says, "You should relax before a big test." In that case, they would insist that you join them for an evening out, while you would insist on staying home. Both of you would wind up thinking that the other person's behavior is strange. An important part of critical thinking is to recognize the assumptions—the unstated warrants—that operate in all of us.

Notice that a warrant is much like the generalization that is used to begin a deductive syllogism or to conclude an inductive chain. Thus you could easily show the following:

People having examinations the next day should not go out the night before.

Sue has an examination tomorrow.

Therefore Sue should not go out tonight.

The usefulness of the Toulmin model is that people seldom talk in syllogisms. They make statements, sometimes offer grounds for those statements, and that is all. They are often unaware of their reasoning and rarely express their underlying logic. The Toulmin model, even in its basic form, guides our attention to the elements that operate each time we communicate our reasons for taking on action, reaching a decision, and so on. Even in the following brief interchange, you can fill in the missing elements once you know how to look for them:

Hi, Sue. We're going to the movies. Want to join us?

Sorry, midterm tomorrow.

The rest of the group nods with understanding in response to this enthymeme. Reasoning clearly exists here without the need to use formal syllogisms.

On the other hand, you must exercise caution in assuming warrants. If you were to say, "Let's study for the critical thinking midterm and invite Brad to join us," and your friend replied, "Not Brad, he's a Gamma Alpha Gamma!" some kind of warrant is operating here. It may be that members of that fraternity have a reputation for being poor study partners or that they have scheduled a dance for the same time period. One way to discover the unstated warrant here is to ask, "What does being in Gamma have to do with studying for the test?" When you discover the missing warrant, you need to evaluate the warrant's trustworthiness to be applied universally.

You do this evaluation in much the same way in which you evaluate any generalization. (This evaluation process can also be applied to the other two sections of the basic model to provide a more complete picture of the reasoning process.)

The first step of the evaluation is to look for **support** or backing. The warrant is the place to begin, but you can also look for backing for the grounds. If you were examining the warrant in the case of Sue, you might look for backing by asking, "Do you really need to study more than the seventeen hours you've already put in during the past three days?" You could seek support for the grounds by asking, "Wasn't that midterm rescheduled for next week?" In the case of Brad, you could look for support in the warrant (Gammas are poor study partners) by finding out what the sample was, how recently it was surveyed, whether it was representative, whether it was sufficient, and so on. Stereotyping is one especially limiting and usually unfair form of unexpressed or unsupported warrant. One of the dangers of using enthymemes in communication is that listeners can fill in a missing logical link with stereotypical and other kinds of illogical thinking.

A second way to test the logic of statements is to look for **rebuttal** materials. A rebuttal allows us to consider exceptions or unusual circumstances that might apply in a particular instance. For example, perhaps the movie is short or offers a once-in-a-lifetime chance to meet the star, or Sue is already assured of an A in the course, or Brad might be the top student in the class. Any number of individual circumstances can and often do call grounds or warrants into question. The Toulmin model does ask us to examine possible rebuttal information.

Finally, **qualifiers** are applied to the claim to test how strong or confident we are in our conclusions. When you say that you are *probably* going to pass the test or that you are *possibly* going to pass it, you are expressing two very different degrees of confidence in your claim of being able to score sufficiently on the exam to pass it. We hear these types of qualifiers all the time, especially in such daily occurrences as the weather report. If a television weather forecaster says that there is a 20 percent chance of rain, do you pack an umbrella? How about a 50 percent chance? A 90 percent chance? Those percentages constitute qualifiers to the claim that it will rain. We react differently to the claim, depending on its strength and the reliability of previous forecasts.

Given the importance of evaluating all statements for their logic, we can add the elements used in our evaluations to the basic Toulmin model. An expanded Toulmin model looks like the following diagram (Toulmin, 1978):

Once all the elements are in place, they may appear complicated, but nearly every conversational claim and every formal conclusion can be analyzed by using these elements. It is important to remember that these elements remind us where to look for missing parts of our reasoning or what else needs to be expressed in someone else's statement so that we can trust the conclusion. Get into the habit of asking for backing in the grounds, expressing warrants in your own statements, examining qualifiers, and presenting potential rebuttals. These are good mental traits, and the mind that does not accept a simple grounds-to-claim statement is one that is well on its way to being a critical-thinking mind.

People who understand the basic logical relationships that are involved in reasoning truthfully and with validity from **generalities** (deduction), in creating reliable generalities from evidence (induction), and in testing reasoning in everyday communication (Toulmin) will likely make better decisions.

INFORMED DECISION MAKING

We all make decisions, virtually minute by minute. Some are so common and made so often that we no longer even think about them as decisions. The question "Shall I have a cup of coffee with breakfast?" is a good example of such a decision. Others are so weighty and consequential that we may agonize for days or months over them. "Shall I apply to a college far away, even though the person I love most in the world is staying behind?" is a question involving a very serious decision. Making quality decisions is a goal of critical thinking, even if the decision is not one of action but only of judgment such as "Who is the best singer in the world?"

To make decision making a manageable process, look at the bases for decisions and the likely consequences they may have.

Evaluating information, sources, supporting materials, and probable outcomes requires a usable evaluation system. This system is based on specific **criteria,** and can be divided into the four areas of **decision making** that we discuss next.

When you ask, "What do you mean by the 'best' singer?" you are asking for a criterion—a measure by which to define the term *best*. Without criteria, no informed decision is possible. The criteria that we use, however, are often unexpressed, assumed, unknown, or hidden. Here is where critical thinking comes into play. By demanding that criteria be expressed, we as decision makers can become aware of the forces that drive our decisions. We can examine them, evaluate them, and clarify or modify them as appropriate. Let us look at each of the four criteria of informed decision making.

Evaluating Information

Information is the data we get through our senses or manufacture in our minds. As the previous chapter pointed out, much of our knowledge about the world comes to us through listening. Good, critical listening helps us to retain and evaluate information. We can listen for information, for recreation, and for evaluation. These types of listening are not necessarily mutually exclusive; we can do all three at once. When evaluating information from a critical-thinking perspective, examine four areas: premises, consistency, completeness and coherence.

Each of these elements is important, but a premise is perhaps the most difficult element to find and the most significant in terms of evaluation. A well-expressed idea based on a faulty premise is still faulty at its core. On the other hand, a soundly based claim may have shortcomings in the way it is expressed but still be sound. *Premises,* then, are the general statements that precede conclusions. A critical thinker will attempt to discover the premises in any communication event. Once discovered, the criterion for judging whether the premises are correct is fairly simple to express: They must be based on known, sufficient, and representative facts.

Consistency means that the information in the premise must agree with the known world and within itself. For example, studying for midterm exams is a consistently reliable way to pass them. However, if Sue has never before studied when she said she was staying in for that purpose, we may suspect that her premises are not consistent with her behavior. External consistency means that warrants, grounds, conclusions, and premises are based on reliable information. Internal consistency means applying information in a similar manner in similar circumstances. The language must be consistent—not shift in meaning midstream. Definitions must remain the same throughout the reasoning process.

Sufficiency, or **completeness,** requires that you account for the information that you have. Are your samples or data missing key elements? Have you met the test of representativeness? Have key parts of the reasoning process been omitted? Check especially for the warrants, or underlying premises, to make certain that they are clear and explicit, not implied or left to inference. Can you account for any contradictory evidence? How do you explain data that go against your conclusion? The requirement of completeness is often overlooked by people who, when they find just what they were hoping to find, stop investigating.

Coherence is the last guidepost to good decision making. It means that you evaluate messages partially on the care and precision that are used to express them. Do the premises, the data, and the conclusion all relate to the same underlying concept? Can you follow the development of the ideas? Is there a pattern or sequence that builds logically from one step to the next? Or is a scattering of thoughts, irrelevant information, and asides mixed in with the data? Coherence of expression communicates a clear goal and is perceived by listeners and readers as a sign of both the intelligence and the logical force of the ideas. Therefore it is important to keep ideas focused on the topic and clearly linked.

Evaluating Sources

Your reputation is important so that others around you know how to relate to you. In the same way, the reputation of the sources of information you use to draw your conclusions about the world is very important. Did you get your information from *Time* magazine or from a clerk in a store? From the *California Law Review* or from your instructor? Each source of information can be evaluated by some standard tests, which generally involve reputation.

For example, *Time* magazine is known and respected for being honest in its research and truthful in its reporting. The magazine certainly has an editorial bias; but when citing a statistic found in *Time,* you can be certain that it was thoroughly checked before it was printed.

However, any conclusions that the magazine's editorial writers drew from that statistic would have to be evaluated as opinions—informed, educated opinions, yes, but not at the same level of reliability as the statistic itself. In the same way, when a friend recommends a movie, a restaurant, a teacher, or a book, you need to evaluate the reliability of that friend's previous recommendations and respond accordingly. Does your friend have the same tastes in film, food, faculty, and fiction as you do? If your friend's recommendations have been reliable in the past, you can trust them again. Generally, the longer you have known the source, the more reliable the information is likely to be. Encyclopedias tend to have been around for a long time, so they make good references (in an uncensored society). Tabloid newspapers are out to make sales based on sensational stories and may need to be examined very carefully before you accept any of their unusual, eye-catching claims.

Look for qualifications and expertise in your evaluation of sources. Does a Ph.D. degree in chemistry qualify someone to give medical advice? Tax advice? Baseball advice? Make certain that an expert is in the right field. Tests for evaluating information could also be adapted for use here. Are the premises clearly stated and in agreement with what you know about the world? Are they consistent with the knowledge of other experts? With the same expert's body of work? Is the information complete—that is, is the expert telling you the whole story? Finally, is the information coherent? Does it make sense when you read or hear it?

Evaluating Supporting Materials

The test of recency of information is especially important when you evaluate supporting materials. Time changes data. What was true about a certain place, person, or event a few years ago may no longer be true today. You may have an excellent textbook, written by an outstanding professor in the proper field, but if it is about Middle East politics or the former Soviet Union, you had better check its date of publication. Even maps may become incorrect in a very short span of time. To the four elements previously discussed—premises, consistency, completeness, and coherence—we now add a fifth. When you evaluate information, be sure that it is *current*. A simple thought such as drawing a conclusion about a restaurant may be incorrect if the chef left between the time your friend went there and the time you received the recommendation.

Critical and Creative Thinking

Although you may be tempted to see these two kinds of thinking as separate, they can actually enhance each other. Some intuition and imagination can help you to discover premises and warrants, whereas wild **creativity** can lead you down many unproductive routes if there is no evaluation of the ideas at some point.

Brainstorming is a good exercise for demonstrating the reciprocal activities of creativity and criticism. Brainstorming has two parts. In the first, a group of people come up with an idea. They do so without restrictions or evaluations. In about ten minutes, or once they have generated several ideas, they stop and move on to phase two. In this phase, ideas are examined for their ability to solve a problem or for their practical use.

Creativity and critical thinking can also work hand in hand to improve your thinking skills. Albert Einstein, one of the most gifted people we know of, believed that imagination is more im-

TECHNOLOGY IN COMMUNICATION

Where Do Our Inventions Come From?

Albert Einstein, one of the smartest people we know of, once said, "Imagination is more important than knowledge." In helping to provide modern society with some of its greatest advances, Einstein knew the value of applying the creative eye to questions of science and technology. Critical thinking coupled with imaginative applications has helped us to apply Einstein's ideas and priniciples to develop incredible technological creativity.

Often thought of as the great thinker of our century, Einstein knew the power of creative and critical thinking.

portant than knowledge. Consider this passage from *The Wizard of Oz:* (Baum, 1956)

> "I don't know enough," replied the Scarecrow cheerfully. "My head is stuffed with straw, you know, and that is why I am going to Oz to ask him for some brains."
>
> "Oh, I see," said the Tin Woodman. "But, after all, brains are not the best things in the world."
>
> "Have you any?" inquired the Scarecrow.
>
> "No, my head is quite empty," answered the Woodman; "but once I had brains, and a heart also; so, having tried them both, I should much rather have a heart."

By using both critical and creative thinking, you can use the dimensions of both knowledge and feeling. Remember, knowledge and feeling are two of the three competencies that were mentioned in the introduction to this field.

Selecting among Alternatives

The whole purpose of critical thinking is to equip you to make intelligent choices. When you consider the multiple choices you face every day, you can materially increase the quality of your life by making those choices with a critical and creative mind. Examining the grounds for your decisions, their underlying assumptions, their consequences, any qualifiers or reservations you may find, and the quality of any supporting materials is the essence of critical thinking, and can become an excellent habit of mind.

This brief introduction is only that—a place for you to learn about the main elements that you can use when you attempt to make sense out of all the information you encounter daily. To sift through the enormous flow of data to which you are subjected every day requires rigorous effort. This effort is made easier with tools that help to divide the information into manageable units. The deductive and inductive patterns show how generalities are used to produce premises and conclusions about the world. The Toulmin system is an especially clear and useful way to categorize parts of the reasoning process to help you sort out and test the rules of logic as they operate in your life.

SUMMARY

The process known as critical thinking is defined as a way of processing information so that reasoning guides our mind. To think critically, we must find, analyze, interpret, and apply information in such a way that we can rely on our conclusions. Although the rules for deduction and induction could fill entire textbooks, they are based primarily on the idea that they either create a generalization (induction) or take a generalization and apply it to a specific case (deduction). If you remember to check for the truth of statements, find out how the information was derived, and examine the process by which each step was taken, then you have a start at applying the rules of logic to your information processing.

In short, the use of critical thinking in formulating informed decision making involves the following: the evaluation of information, sources, and supporting materials so that you can make decisions that have a strong base and in which you can feel confidence. Critical thinking is an old study, founded in logic, with applications to every decision we make every day. When critical thinking is combined with creativity and feeling, we can make good use of both our brains and our hearts.

KEY TERMS

evidence, *p. 59*
assumptions, *p. 60*
reasoning, *p. 60*
deduction, *p. 61*
induction, *p. 67*
premises, *p. 61*
syllogism, *p. 61*
fallacies, *p. 62*
truth, *p. 62*
validity, *p. 62*
enthymeme, *p. 63*
Toulmin model, *p. 70*
grounds, *p. 70*

claim, *p. 70*
warrant, *p. 70*
support, *p. 71*
rebuttal, *p. 71*
qualifiers, *p. 72*
generalities, *p. 72*
criteria, *p. 73*
decision making, *p. 73*
consistency, *p. 74*
completeness, *p. 74*
coherence, *p. 74*
creativity, *p. 75*

EXERCISES

1. Clip an advertisement for any product from your favorite magazine. Try to identify the elements that serve as the major premise, the minor premise, and the conclusion. Some of these elements may not be expressed, so you may need to provide them in your own words. Bring your advertisement to class and share your analysis.

2. Search the newspapers for a report from one of the major polling firms—Gallup, Roper, Field, and so on. What information does the article give you about the poll? Do you find polls credible? Why or why not?

3. Examine a letter to the editor or an editorial in a local newspaper or your campus paper. Apply the Toulmin model to the information presented to see

whether you can identify the data, the claims, the warrants, the backing, the reservations, and any qualifiers. Does your analysis help you to decide whether to support the point of the letter or editorial?

4. Review a recent disagreement you had with a friend. Can you identify any warrants that may have been involved?

REFERENCES

Baum, L. Frank. *The Wizard of Oz*. New York: Grosset and Dunlap, 1956. 41.

Delia, Jesse G. "The Logic Fallacy, Cognitive Theory, and the Enthymeme." *Quarterly Journal of Speech* LVI (April 1970), 141.

Kellogg, Mary Alice. *Hard Choices, Easy Decisions*. New York: Simon & Schuster, 1991.

Makau, Josina M. *Reasoning and Communication Thinking Critically About Arguments*. Belmont: Wadsworth, 1990. 4.

McGlone, Edward L., and Remo P. Fausti. *Introductory Readings in Oral Communication*. Menlo Park: Cummings, 1972. 312–319.

Reinard, John C. "Structural Tools for Testing Arguments." Chapter 9 in *Foundations of Argument*. Dubuque: Wm. C. Brown, 1991.

Ruggerio, Vincent Ryan. *Beyond Feelings: A Guide to Critical Thinking* 3rd ed. Mountain View: Mayfield, 1990. 14.

Toulmin, Stephen E. *The Uses of Argument*. Cambridge, England: Cambridge University Press, 1958.

Toulmin, Stephen E. Richard D. Rieke, and Allan Janik. *Introduction to Reasoning*. New York: Macmillan, 1978.

What We Know about Nonverbal Communication

After reading this chapter, you should be able to:

- Understand the important role of nonverbal communication in your daily experience.

- Describe some of the contexts and rules that govern nonverbal communication behavior and our understanding of that behavior.

- Define the concepts of paralanguage, movement, objects, space and time, and the senses as they function in nonverbal communication.

- Feel competent to improve your nonverbal decoding and encoding skills.

ou may already know that **nonverbal communication** generally means communication without words. It can involve words, such as when you use voice inflection to color the meaning of your message. Nonverbal communication can also include your use of gestures and movements or the way you use objects and your personal appearance to show the meaning of your information to another person. Your nonverbal communication can be filled with purpose and the desire to send a message, or it may be accidental and unintentional. Whatever the mode or the meaning of the nonverbal communication that you select, it is a powerful aspect of your communication ability. Let us look at the definition of nonverbal communication and then examine the impact that it has on your overall communication. We also consider some contexts and rules for nonverbal communication, types of nonverbal behaviors, and how you can improve your ability to communicate nonverbally.

A DEFINITION OF NONVERBAL COMMUNICATION

Nonverbal communication refers to the information that is transmitted from senders to receivers when the dominant meaning is not conveyed by the use of words. Another way to put it is that nonverbal communication is your use of interacting sets of visual, vocal, and invisible communication systems to convey and interpret meaning (Leathers, 1992). It includes several major categories: paralanguage, or vocalics; posture, movement; objects, or artifacts; space, or proxemics; time; and the five senses. **Vocalics** is the use of the volume, tone, rate, pitch, and quality of your voice to give dimension and meaning to your words. For example, you raise your pitch at the end of a sentence to indicate a question. Since you use your voice to surround the words you speak, this aspect of nonverbal communication is also called **paralanguage.**

Proxemics means using space to communicate. For example, you may feel uncomfortable if someone sits right next to you in the library when the whole table is empty.

Artifacts are those objects—clothing, jewelry, even an automobile—that relay a message about you. Do you wear three earrings in your pierced ears? Do you wear one in your nostril? People will sense a message about you if you do.

Movement includes your posture, gestures, eye contact, and facial expressions. When you wave, smile, or slump at your desk, you are using movement, and those movements communicate something about *you.*

Time, or chronemics, can communicate attitudes or status. Are you showing respect by arriving early to an appointment for a job interview and a lack of respect by coming a half-hour late to your study group meeting?

Finally, the five **senses,** which include taste, touch, and smell, convey information to you from others.

All of these elements constitute the basic components of nonverbal communication; and when you use them to enhance your communication techniques, they can have significant impact on your messages.

THE IMPACT OF NONVERBAL COMMUNICATION

What you are about to read may cause you to smile, frown, shake your head in disbelief, or nod in agreement. In any case, you will probably acknowledge the message of the material immediately and indicate your reaction in a nonverbal manner. Someone watching you could probably tell by your actions just what your response to the message is. That is because nonverbal communication has a powerful impact on your total communication process. Some early estimates about the impact of nonverbal communication ranged from about 65 to 93 percent of the overall meaning of any message (Mehrabian, 1968). Subsequent research suggested that closer to one third is derived from nonverbal information (Birdwhistell, 1970). In a project that examined twenty-three studies of nonverbal communication, more recent research suggests that about two thirds of the meaning of messages is communicated nonverbally (Philpott, 1992). If those estimates are even close, they strongly emphasize the importance of our nonverbal communicative behaviors.

Whereas you may have spent ten to fourteen years studying writing and reading skills and perhaps have had a few short lessons on listening and public speaking, you probably have not had any formal instruction in the skills of nonverbal communication. Yet you do it, usually pretty well, and almost constantly. How is this so? Is it a natural, inborn ability? Is it something you just picked up along the way? Researchers have put their efforts into answering those questions and have concluded that the *instinct* to want to communicate—both verbally and nonverbally—is innate in humans. The distinctive *symbol codes* that we use in our culture are learned. Generally, we learn at first by imitation and reinforcement and later by formal practice and instruction. Nonverbal communication is similar to our use of words in that there are specific forms, functions, and rules that govern our ability to create clear meanings, and these rules vary by group and culture as do our verbal practices. Let us now consider some of the principles that are involved in using nonverbal communication.

NONVERBAL COMMUNICATION FUNCTIONS AND RULES

Functions

You use nonverbal behaviors to communicate in a variety of situations. Sometimes, you wave your hand instead of saying hello. At other times, you point to show a direction, raise your hand in class to be called on, or smile when you see someone do a good job. Each of these actions illustrates one of the following six **functions of nonverbal communication** behaviors: (1) substituting, (2) reinforcing, (3) regulating, (4) contradicting, (5) managing impressions, and (6) establishing relationships.

For example, waving or nodding instead of talking illustrates the *substituting function*. Here, an action has replaced, or substituted for, a word. Replacement

IMPROVING COMPETENCY

An Hour of Silence

Can you keep totally silent for one hour? Try it, and keep track of how you managed to respond to other people. Keep track of your observations as well and of how much information was being exchanged around you without the use of words. Do you think you could go through an entire day of your regular schedule without speaking?

can range from the easy examples above to more complex ideas, such as the hand and other signals that ground personnel use at airports in directing pilots as they guide an airplane to the proper place at the gate. There are complete languages that use only movements for communication, such as the sign language developed by Native Americans in the Great Plains and American Sign Language (ASL), which is taught on many campuses and used by millions of hearing-impaired people every day. The simple movements and gestures of everyday life, such as waving, were the foundation of more complex movements used to build whole sentences and communicate sophisticated concepts.

In addition to using nonverbal communication substitutes for words, we communicate nonverbally to *reinforce* or complement our verbal sounds. When you point to clarify your meaning, nod your head while you say, "Yes, of course,

Gestures have meaning within a cultural context.

Sign language is one form of nonverbal communication.

I see what you mean," or pound the table with a fist in anger, you are reinforcing your message and complementing your words.

If you want to join a conversation, you use nonverbal signals to indicate your interest. Such movements *regulate* the flow of interaction. In class, you use a formal motion to get the instructor's attention—the raising of a hand. In

CRITICAL THINKING IN COMMUNICATION

American Sign Language

In the late 1800s, a French priest, Abbé Sicard, developed what we now know as American Sign Language. Many of the signs he created were based on wild-West views of the United States that seem funny to us today. For example, the sign for the United States is made by putting the fingers of both hands together so they alternate. This action was designed to simulate the wall of a log cabin.

The system was not always based on logic. Another example that did not use critical thinking is the development of the sign for the thick, red tomato sauce we put on hamburgers, hot dogs, and french fries.

The sign originally had two parts. The first part used both little fingers to make a "mustache" motion and was the sign for the four-legged, feline animal, or cat. The second part of the sign consisted of pointing upward with the index finger. The relationship of these signs to the tomato sauce—ketchup or catsup—was that it *sounds* like those two signs when spoken! Now, however, the sign has changed and consists of making a fist with one hand, then pounding the fist with flat of the other hand twice. As you can see, the new sign is much more logical.

ordinary small-group conversations, people who want to join in usually nod, raise their eyebrows a little, and open their mouths slightly as they sense that the speaker is coming to a pause. Sometimes people use a pencil or pen, raising it and tapping it lightly when they want to begin speaking. Or, if you are speaking, you may raise your hand slightly, palm facing the listener, and thereby "ask" the listener to hold for a moment while you conclude an idea.

If you want to *contradict* your verbal message, you can easily do so by displaying an opposite nonverbal behavior. For example, if you want to relay the message that you do not like a certain food, you might choose vocalic sarcasm as a strategy. Thus you could say, "This turnip is really wonderful," using your voice to stress the words *really* and *wonderful* and placing an elongated and exaggerated stress on the syllable *won*. At the same time, you might crinkle up your nose and perhaps use your thumb and index finger to pinch your nostrils together. Your message is accurate only if the receiver gets the nonverbal information from your paralanguage and facial gestures as well, because the words alone give information that is opposite to the message you intended.

Deceiving another person with your nonverbal messages is another form of contradiction. For example, you may be bored on a date or in a class but you do not want to communicate this feeling. So you pretend—you simulate interest by keeping eye contact, nodding, sometimes smiling, all of which are not truthful messages about your feelings. Much research has been done on **deception** in nonverbal communication, from the cues we all use in social situations to the efforts criminals employ to deceive their victims or police investigators (Hocking and Leathers, 1980; Leathers, 1992). In their studies, Hocking and Leathers have looked at eye contact and hand-to-face gestures as clues to deception. The size of the pupil of the eye also reveals heightened anxiety or interest or arousal. Measurements of the electroconductivity of the skin, as measured by the galvanic skin response "lie detectors," also provide clues to deception.

TECHNOLOGY IN COMMUNICATION

From GSRs to Videotape

The use of scientific instruments to record and measure nonverbal communication took a leap forward when psychologists discovered that the skin's ability to conduct electricity changes with emotional states, as do the heart rate and breathing rate for most people. Researchers devised a machine to record all of the changes and then attached the machine to people who were undergoing questions. For many people, the galvanic skin response (or GSR) machine was capable of indicating when they were truthful and when they were not. More recently, similar claims have been made by inventors of machines that can measure tiny changes in vocal stress pattern and video cameras that can record the pupil dilation of the eyes. Both are thought to be uncontrollable consciously, and both are thought to reveal truthfulness.

A fifth dimension of nonverbal communication is *impression management*, that is, creating and controlling the way other people perceive you. You arrange your hair in a certain way, you speak with a chosen pitch or tone of voice, you want a particular car, dog, bicycle, wristwatch, ring, shoe, or eyeglasses that will represent *you* to the rest of the world. You spend a great deal of time selecting the right outfit for a job interview or for a lunch with the parents of someone whom you are dating.

How you choose to look conveys a message to others.

In each of these situations, you are attempting to create a message about yourself based on the impression that these items and behaviors may form in the mind of the intended audience. When you listen to others, respond to them, wait for them to finish talking, or cut them off in midsentence, you are creating an impression. Sensitive nonverbal communicators try to make sure that the impression their listeners receive is the same as the one they intended to send. On the other hand, you probably have met people who seem to you too loud or too pushy, stand too close, or lean into a group and interrupt whomever is speaking. If these people are violating social norms for acceptable nonverbal behavior, they are not managing their impressions well. This chapter offers some suggestions for improving nonverbal communication later on.

Finally, we can use nonverbal messages to establish or reveal a *relationship*. The simple gold band on the third finger of the left hand is one way to communicate the existence of a relationship by using an object. Standing at the head of a table around which others are seated communicates the existence and type of relationship by using posture and proxemics. A police officer in uniform has a clear relationship to a traffic accident. In a clinic, people wearing white jackets and stethoscopes communicate to us that they have a relationship to medicine. Whether you touch someone else, how you touch that person and when and where you touch communicate information about the relationship.

Rules

These six functions of nonverbal communication can be conveyed in a variety of ways and with a variety of outcomes, but there are some rules or principles that apply to all areas.

First, because everything about you—looks, dress, action, inaction—can be interpreted, you are continuously communicating. Even if you close the door and turn off the light to avoid your friends, you are giving your friends a message that they are quite capable of understanding. You can be asleep in the library, and everyone who walks by you will get some impression of who and what you are. If you have an early-morning or late-afternoon class and you doze off during the lecture, you will be communicating something to the teacher. This rule is often stated by communication teachers as "You cannot not communicate." Even without other people present, you communicate with yourself in dreams and thoughts. So, through nonverbal communication, you are always communicating. You can't *not* communicate.

Next, nonverbal communication is often ambiguous. By themselves, gestures, movements, objects, and so on may tell you only part of the story. You need to see the context, the relationship, the accompanying verbal behavior, if any, and the responses. Students yawn in class sometimes because they are bored, sometimes because they ate a big lunch and are sleepy, and sometimes because they stayed up all night studying for an exam. All of these situations are perfectly plausible, but each represents a very different response.

Or you may see someone gazing out a window. That person could be day-dreaming, avoiding someone, bird watching, or evaluating the possibility of snow over the weekend. Because so many contexts are possible, you might attach implied meanings to them that turn out to be erroneous. Although you can make a tentative conclusion about the nonverbal meaning, you must keep it tentative unless you get more information from the situation or other clues about the message. Someone standing by a curb in front of a college campus, backpack filled with books, facing oncoming traffic with a thumb extended provides a clearly implied context, but not just from the thumb. All the factors together help to dissipate ambiguity.

My son was involved in track in eighth grade, and I watched from the stands as he ran in the 100-yard finals in a large meet. The finish was very close, but it looked as though he might have won. A teacher who was helping to record the official times knew where I was sitting; and after several moments of huddling by the officials, she made eye contact with me, smiled, and held up two fingers. "Well," I said to my wife, "second place at the county finals is pretty good!" A few moments later, they announced my son as the first-place winner, and the same teacher smiled again and again flashed her two fingers in the air—in a victory sign! The moral of this story is to be careful of the potential for ambiguity in nonverbal communication.

Third, remember that all communication exists in a culture, including nonverbal communication. We learn a set of gestures, movements, habits, styles of dress, and so on within one cultural setting and that may not even be close to the set someone else has learned in another culture. Especially bothersome for international travelers are the gestures that are used to substitute for or accompany verbal expression. You might point to clarify what you mean, but people in

DIVERSITY IN COMMUNICATION

Signs in Europe

I traveled with a group of U.S. college students in Europe for several months, and we attended a soccer game in London, sitting with the home team fans. We thought we would be amiable and root for them as well. When they finally scored, one of my more enthusiastic students jumped up, put his fingers in his mouth, and whistled loudly and continuously. The local fans looked at him with ugly, menacing expressions while I tried immediately to quiet him. Whistling in Europe is the equivalent of booing in the United States.

This same student went, with a few companions, to a small tavern in Greece, where he ordered and ate a fine meal. When the waiter asked in very limited English if they liked the food, my student gave the supposedly universal sign for okay: index finger touching the thumb to make a circle with the rest of the fingers flared out and making a slight back-and-forth motion. This sign, unfortunately, is not universally positive. In fact, it is often interpreted in Mediterranean areas as meaning something vulgar. My student was promptly punched by the offended waiter and tossed out of the café. Thanks to these encounters, he slowly began to learn about cultural context, ambiguity, and the nonuniversality of nonverbal communication.

other cultures are offended by the movement. Anyone who has traveled can tell stories of mix-ups and even altercations following a culturally improper use of nonverbal indicators. In the United States, we whistle to cheer our teams on at sporting events, whereas in most parts of Europe, whistling is derisive.

Finally, nonverbal communication is probably best used to express attitudes, feelings, and relationships. A couple walking down the hall hand in hand are clearly expressing a relationship. Whether you talk to someone face to face or facing away, standing up or sitting down, or even whether you address that person at all, indicates something about the feelings and relationship that are involved. A surprised look on your face, a deep frown, and a warm embrace are good examples of this use of nonverbal communication.

Now that we have examined some of the rules and contexts for nonverbal communication, we are ready to consider the actual types of nonverbal communication with which these patterns are used.

TYPES OF NONVERBAL COMMUNICATION

There are many ways to classify all possible nonverbal behaviors and objects, but the following elements, defined at the beginning of the chapter, seem to cover most situations: paralanguage, posture, movement, objects, space and time, and the senses—especially touch, smell, and taste.

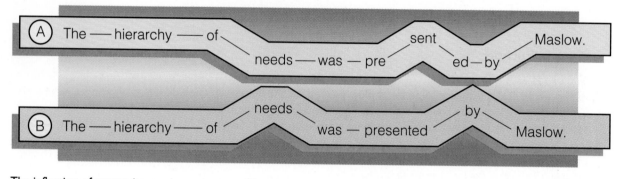

The inflection of your voice carries a message of its own.

Paralanguage

When you use your vocal apparatus to surround your words with color, tone, and inflection—or even pauses, mumbles, or noises—you are using paralanguage. Sometimes called *vocalics,* this kind of use of your voice is one of the most common aspects of nonverbal communication. Every time you ask a question, raising your inflection at the end of the sentence, you are employing vocalics to make your meaning clear. Every time you use the same inflection at the end of a declarative sentence, you are letting your listeners know that you may not be sure or confident of your information.

Sometimes you say "hmmm" when thinking about an answer to a tough question. The "ums" and "ers" that many people put between words to give them time to think are examples of paralanguage. Even the words *okay* and *you know,* when used as fillers, have ceased being actual words and have become just part of the noise stream.

The volume, rate, pitch, and tone of your voice can all be varied to create meanings. You can also substitute for words, as when you make the sound "huh?" with a rising inflection instead of saying "What?" or you can intensify your meaning by shouting or whispering. You can communicate a friendly or intimate relationship by adopting a warm tone, or you can shift into a shrill or clipped vocal pattern to suggest a hostile relationship. Sarcasm is an obvious way to use this type of nonverbal behavior to contradict your verbal message. Saying "I had a really wonderful time on our date tonight," while giving a prolonged stress on the word *really,* gives a contradictory message, but one that is clear nevertheless.

Posture

Sitting up straight is not just for your health, but you may also do it because a speaker once told you that your slouching posture communicated a lack of interest or respect. Lounging back in a chair during a job interview, with your body leaning away from your interviewer, will probably not help your prospects of getting the job. In public speaking situations, some speakers lean on the lectern in a posture that may communicate sloppiness to the audience or a lack of dynamism or interest. Thus you can use posture in the various ways to reinforce or contradict your verbal message, to communicate its own message in place of words, and to control an impression or indicate a relationship. You sit closer to those you like, as you have probably noticed, and you stand at the head of the table when you are in charge of a meeting. Posture can be used in all of these ways. But remember that the message conveyed by posture may also be ambiguous. A person who is slumped in a chair after a date with you may really have had a great time and like you very much but may be exhausted from studying all night. As in other areas of communication, be sure to consider all the information about posture before drawing absolute conclusions.

Movement

Included in the category of movement are general motions such as walking, as well as the specific gestures associated with animated communication. Sometimes called *kinesics,* the study of bodily and muscular movement is a rich area of investigation by communication scholars because of the great variety of possible kinesic combinations. When you stride confidently along, you communicate to onlookers a sense of strength and deliberateness. On the other hand, slouching while walking—with head down and taking small steps—may communicate weakness, passivity, or fear. People who work in the field of assertiveness training and those who teach others how to avoid assault say that attackers are often drawn to potential victims by their seemingly weak posture and movement behaviors.

Gestures comprise an entire subset of behaviors involving movement. Some are cultural indicators and are specific to a particular group, as in the two examples regarding a student traveler (refer to the Diversity in Communication box on page 87). Others may be connected to a job or an occupation, as in the signals used at airports or the hand signals used on a noisy construction site. Every day, you may be using gestures constantly and without much thought—wrinkling your nose when discussing something unpleasant or shrugging your shoulders when a friend asks for your opinion and you are not sure you have one. Platform speakers often use gestures to punctuate their words. In a review of research on gestures that was compiled several years ago, thousands of gestures and combinations of gestures from a variety of studies were identified and cataloged (Burgoon and Saine, 1978).

Facial expressions constitute yet other movements that have rich meaning, and the face is usually the first place that listeners look to discover the overall meaning of a message (Keman et al., 1972; Berry, 1990). Think of your facial expressions as gestures with which you can produce thousands of combinations. Most of the research on the communicative power of the face has been done with the communication of emotion. In fact, one of the earliest published works dealing with facial expressions was written in 1872 by Charles Darwin (Darwin, 1872).

More recently, the Facial Meaning Sensitivity Test was developed by Dale Leathers to determine the accuracy with which people can guess the emotions of someone else through facial expression alone (Leathers and Emigh, 1980). Leathers found five areas of meaning associated with facial expressions: (1) evaluation—we communicate pleasant and unpleasant, good and bad reactions; (2) interest—we tell others whether we are bored or attentive; (3) intensity—we show the amount or degree of interest of boredom or disgust or liking with facial expressions; (4) control—whether we are in control of ourselves, our emotions, and our feelings is communicated by our face; and (5) understanding—we let others know whether we are clear or confused about their messages. Several expressions were almost always agreed on, while others were judged to be ambiguous (Motley and Camden, 1988). Again, the clearest communication occurs when you know the speaker's context, can see his or her face, and hear the accompanying words. Given that much information, a frown might correctly be interpreted as an indication of anger, disappointment, or thoughtfulness. It all depends on the information.

Objects

Objects are the things that you have around you, that you wear, or even that you drive or ride on. Jewelry, clothing, eyeglasses, even a pen or pencil can have communicative significance.

These objects exist in a cultural setting, so a certain type of hat may mean nothing to you, but in another place it may indicate marital status or occupation. A uniform is an obvious example of an object that helps us to distinguish between a police officer and a firefighter, a marine, and a tennis player. There are places a person cannot go without the right uniform, such as restaurants that insist on coat and tie for men and skirts or dresses for women. Attention to clothes changes with the fashions and cultures of the times, but the nearly worldwide influence of U.S. culture has made blue jeans an international costume.

Objects symbolize certain jobs or characteristics. In filmmaking, for example, the director or writer may use an object to tell the audience about a character's interests, values, background, or job. What does it tell us if the heroine drives around in a jeep or a Porsche? Or takes a bus? Or is in a wheelchair? Or rides a ten-speed bike or an old contraption with a wicker basket on the handlebars? All these variations are choices to be made so that the audience will have some information about the person who is being portrayed. Nonverbal communication discloses information about self-concept, expectations, and experiences.

THE STORY OF COMMUNICATION

Woody Guthrie's Lyrics

Woody Guthrie wrote "This Land is Your Land" and hundreds of other songs about people's experiences during the Great Depression of the 1930s. In one song, "Pretty Boy Floyd," he describes a bank robber in Oklahoma who was reputed to have given the money he stole to poor farmers. In the last line of the song, Guthrie says that some men use guns to rob people and others use fountain pens. How can someone rob you with a fountain pen? Who used fountain pens in the 1930s? Guthrie uses a simple object to communicate a whole picture of the banking business.

The use of proxemics varies by culture and context.

When you go to a job interview, wouldn't it be wise to consider the nonverbal power of objects and find out what the dress code and other standards are for the prospective place of employment? The owner of a corner hot-dog stand will not require you to wear a business outfit on the job but will probably be impressed if you wear neat, clean, casual clothes—not shorts and a tee shirt and not a suit.

Space and Time

In all cultures, definitions of space and time communicate a great deal about relationships and status. If you have the largest office in a building all to yourself, and other people find themselves crowded four or five in a same-size or smaller room, you can be sure that the status and power implications of your space are clear to everyone. Often called *proxemics,* the study of how space communicates nonverbally has been the subject of much research. You already know that you move closer to those whom you like and that you feel uncomfortable if you are sitting in the library at a large, empty table and someone sits directly next to you. On the other hand, if that seat is the only vacant one at a very crowded table, you do not feel nearly the same discomfort.

Again, context and culture determine our use of space. North Americans have a personal "space bubble" that extends about twenty-four to thirty inches out and around them in normal conversations. Latin Americans, Mediterraneans, and Arab peoples have a much smaller "bubble" and feel uncomfortable if you keep a large distance from them while talking one to one. You may feel invaded by their bubble, while they may feel rejected by yours.

Time is another nonverbal area in which we communicate relationships and controls. Suppose you are trying to petition the dean of your school to exempt you from a certain required class because you already know a great deal about the area. You set up an appointment for 3:00 P.M. What time should you arrive at the dean's office? Since the dean has a higher status than you, has power over your request, and is probably older and better educated than you are and because you are the one seeking the appointment, you should arrive a few minutes before 3:00 P.M. Getting there at 2:50 P.M. or 2:55 P.M. is fine. Arriving at 2:40 P.M. is too soon and may seem presumptuous. However, arriving at 3:02 P.M. may be seen as rude or insincere. How about the dean's arrival time for the same appointment? Is 3:05 P.M. acceptable? Even 3:10 P.M. is probably fine. If the dean arrives after 3:15 P.M., some quick apology may be offered, such as "Sorry I kept you waiting; come on in." If the dean arrives after 3:20 P.M., you may get a brief explanation to accompany the apology: "Sorry I kept you waiting. I was on the phone." How long would you wait? This scenario demonstrates one possible function of time in our communication activities. Again, culture plays a big part in how time is used in nonverbal communication. Some places—generally in southern climates—seem to have broader and more flexible boundaries to being on time, while those having Northern European cultures have a much more exact standard. While traveling in the former Soviet Union several years ago, our group needed to be reminded that when the tour bus guide said the bus was leaving at 10:00 A.M., the guide really meant that at 9:57 A.M. the bus engine was started, people buckled up, the door closed two minutes later, and the bus left the curb just as the second hand swept past the 12 o'clock position. Several members of our group would leave their hotel rooms at 9:57 A.M. and arrive at the bus stop four minutes later to find only exhaust fumes. What *just on time* means in Madrid is *late* in New York and *early* in Bangkok.

Time and space are two fascinating areas of research and study, and the variations of these elements among cultures are important to understand if you are to become an expert in nonverbal communication.

The Senses

Your five senses—taste, touch, smell, sound, and sight—are the avenues along which messages come to you. Most nonverbal messages arrive at your brain's message center through your eyes or ears. Others come to you through the sense of taste, as when you discover food that is going bad, or through the sense of smell, as when you discover fire by smelling smoke.

Advertisers know the power of these senses, and they appeal to taste in food and drink commercials. Perfumers are selling not just a smell, but the feelings and emotions that they can conjure up with their product. Has anyone ever shaken hands with you so that you actually feel pain? You probably have had a gentle pat on the back or a warm hug. Those gestures are the ways in which touch gives and receives messages.

There has been a good deal of investigation into extrasensory perception (ESP), but the results are more intriguing than certain. Some people claim to be able to read cards face down or get impressions from other people or objects over long distances. Certainly, you have heard of police investigators who occasionally consult psychics to help find missing persons. This area is the subject of ongoing studies all over the world, but trying to observe ESP is very complex.

Control of experiments and agreement on definitions are difficult to develop, given the unseen nature of the phenomena. However, it is an area we may read more about in the future.

IMPROVING NONVERBAL COMMUNICATION COMPETENCY

Becoming aware of the ways in which you communicate nonverbally, and knowing that different people may have very different ways of using their nonverbal communication, is the best first step to improving your abilities. Self-awareness can be developed simply by getting into the habit of monitoring your behavior and taking note of your posture, movements, and objects. You may want to get some outside assistance by asking friends for feedback or even arranging for someone to videotape you in action during a conversation or a speech or as you participate in a group. All these activities will provide you with increased sensitivity to your own and others' repertoire of nonverbal interactions.

Once you develop awareness, you might try to expand your repertoire of nonverbal activities. You can expand your ability to decode the messages of others more accurately if you expand your own vocabulary for sending messages. There are ranges of behavior to be explored that can add depth to your abilities as a receiver if you learn them and practice them in your own communication.

Finally, remember that good communication focuses on the receiver of the message. If you become self-aware, then aware of others, and try to stretch your own abilities, you will have many choices from which to select to create a clear message for your listeners. You can send appropriate signals to amplify or intensify your verbal messages. You can also look to your listeners and read their nonverbal messages to evaluate your performance and then adjust or adapt your messages. A powerful tool, nonverbal communication is an essential part of overall communication. You may even be able to take an entire course in it at your school.

SUMMARY

The impact of nonverbal communication is at least as significant as verbal communication and accounts for much of the research in the field of communication. Like its counterpart, nonverbal communication is subject to some principles. It is always present, is usually ambiguous when used by itself, exists briefly in time and space, and is probably best used in conjunction with verbal symbols.

You can study your own use of posture, gestures, facial expressions, voice inflection, objects, space, and time to send messages, and you can study the information that you take in through your five senses. You may even be capable of receiving or sending information through means as yet unknown. Improve your communication skills by remembering the four areas of communication competency: repertoire, selection, implementation, and evaluation. Being aware of yourself, others, culture, and context builds your repertoire. Analyzing your behavior helps you to select appropriate nonverbal messages. Receiving feedback helps you to evaluate your style and effectiveness and to change if necessary. So apply your knowledge and expand it to become an effective communicator.

KEY TERMS

nonverbal communication, *p. 80*
vocalics, *p. 80*
paralanguage, *p. 80*
proxemics, *p. 80*
artifacts, *p. 80*

movement, *p. 80*
time, *p. 80*
senses, *p. 80*
functions of nonverbal communication, *p. 82*
deception, *p. 84*

EXERCISES

1. An interesting way to study nonverbal communication is to watch a television comedy show without the sound. Can you follow the plot and anticipate the next action? One of the great geniuses of comedic movement was Lucille Ball. If you can spend some time watching "I Love Lucy" reruns, you will have the chance to see a real master at work.

2. Spend one hour or one day without speaking. Keep a log of how you were or were not able to communicate clearly to others. What strategies and inventions did you use to keep your messages flowing clearly?

3. Sometimes, you may see students wearing blindfolds and being guided by others around campus. These students are participating in a blindwalk, sometimes known as a trustwalk, because the blindfolded person really needs to trust his or her partner to make it work. If you feel comfortable about trying this experiment, do it with special emphasis on both partners being quiet the entire time—except for minimal directions such as "We're coming to a stair step now." If you do not have a way to do this at school, blindfold yourself at home and try getting around in a very familiar space without your vision. Listen for sounds, be aware of smells, touch surfaces, and so on, all of which can help you understand where you are.

4. Pair off with a partner in class or a friend outside of class and do a nonverbal audit of each other. Start with objects, such as jewelry and clothing, and list what your partner is wearing and what messages you infer from those objects.

5. Learn the letters of the finger spelling alphabet used by deaf people. Pair off with a partner and conduct a brief conversation using only finger spelling. Pay attention to other nonverbal communication systems as well, especially the facial expressions that accompany the finger spelling.

REFERENCES

Berry, D. S. "What Can a Moving Face Tell Us?" *Journal of Personality and Social Psychology* 58 (1990).

Birdwhistell, R. L. *Kinesics and Context*. Philadelphia: University of Pennsylvania Press, 1970.

Burgoon, Judee K., and Thomas Saine. *The Unspoken Dialogue*. Boston: Houghton Mifflin, 1978. 54.

Darwin, Charles. *The Expression of Emotions in Man and Animals*. London: Murray, 1872.

Hocking, J. E., and Dale G. Leathers. "Nonverbal Indicators of Deception: A New Theoretical Perspective." *Communication Monographs* 47 (1980), 119–131.

Keman, P. W., V. Friesen, and P. Ellsworth. *Emotion In the Human Face: Guidelines for Research and an Integration of Findings*. New York: Pergamon Press, 1972.

Leathers, D. G. *Successful Nonverbal Communication*. 2nd ed. New York: Macmillan, 1992.

Leathers, D. G. and T. H. Emigh. "Decoding Facial Expressions: A New Test with Decoding Norms." *Quarterly Journal of Speech* 66 (1980), 418–436.

Mehrabian, Albert. "Communication Without Words." *Psychology Today* 2 (1968), 51–52.

Motley, Michael, and C. T. Camden, "Facial Expression of Emotion: A Comparison of Posed Expressions Versus Spontaneous Expressions in an Interpersonal Communication Setting." *Western Journal of Speech Communication* 52 (Winter 1988), 552.

Philpott, J. S. *The Relative Contribution to Meaning of Verbal and Nonverbal Channels of Communication: A Metaanalysis*. Master's thesis. Univ. of Nebraska, 1983. Cited in Leathers, D. G. *Successful Nonverbal Communication*. 2nd ed. New York: Macmillan, 1992.

What We Know about Verbal Communication

- Understand how the use of symbols creates a communication environment.
- Describe the process we go through from childhood onward to acquire and enhance language skills.
- Define the similarities and differences between written and spoken communication.
- Sense the appropriateness of a variety of types of English, and be aware of how language can be misused to attack others.
- Feel confident in using your forms of English in a variety of situations.
- Improve your skills in understanding and using language.

We have finally arrived at the subject of language, which is often the first thing people think about when discussing communication. From all that you read in the previous chapters, you understand that language is only a part of a much larger communication process. A great deal has to happen before you are ready to acquire and use language effectively. You need to be able to hear and think and to receive and process information. Once you have made sense out of the sounds around you, you begin to imitate those sounds to get reactions, solve problems, or simply enjoy life. Let us begin with a look at symbols, the basic building blocks of language.

SYMBOLS, UTTERANCES, AND MEANINGS

Your communicating self—listener, thinker, and person aware of nonverbal communication—has many of the tools that you need to be effective in a variety of situations. Even though you spend most of your communication time listening and thinking, your most frequent interaction with others will probably focus on verbal messages. To be complete, those interactions and messages will be carried on both nonverbal and verbal channels. In the previous chapter, you learned about nonverbal communication. Now it is time to look closely at another component: verbal communication.

The way we use words—that is, verbal communication—is one of the distinguishing characteristics of our species. We are able to turn our reactions to the world around us into symbols, that is, not the things themselves, but symbols that stand for the physical aspects of the world and our responses to them.

Like nonverbal systems, verbal communication is fraught with confusion and misunderstanding caused by a mismatch between the messages people think they have sent and the messages others think they have received. Language is complex, and the processes that we use to guide and build our use of language depend on understanding its nature. Let us first turn to learning about the symbolic nature of language and how the sounds we utter take on meaning for us and for others.

Language as Symbol

A **symbol** is something that stands for something else; in our minds, it replaces what it stands for with a form of shorthand. For example, in our culture, a square red cross on a white background is a symbol for medical services in general and for an organization—the Red Cross—in particular. It is seen on emergency vehicles, hospital ships, and the uniforms of disaster relief workers. A red octagon, on the other hand, is the color and shape of our stop signs. The letters that spell *dog* have nothing in common with the shaggy canine that scratches its fleas on the doorstep. The word is merely a symbol for that animal and a multitude of similar animals.

The very letters that we use to write in English are arbitrary. Anyone who has studied Russian, Japanese, Hebrew, or Greek realizes that the sounds we make when we see our symbols, other people make when they see other symbols. Even though there may be some common agreement among speakers of the same language regarding the meanings attached to symbols, we all may make different connections in responding to a certain symbol. For example, a dictionary is good for recording the general meanings that speakers of a language have for certain symbol combinations. However, it cannot tell us exactly what *your* meaning is. If you look up the symbol combination *c-a-t* in a dictionary, you will find several general meanings, but there will not be a picture of Fluffy, the pet you have had for ten years. In a dictionary, the difference between a literal definition—**denotation**—and the specific associations and reactions you may have with a word—**connotation**—is one source of confusion in verbal communication. That difference can also be a source of enrichment for symbolizing ideas. For example, if you wanted to create a romantic setting for a novel, would you be more likely to place the story in New Orleans or in Cleveland? People in Cleveland certainly fall in love and have romantic relationships, but the sound of a bayou, the charm of Creole-accented conversation, and the smell of Cajun cooking all combine to suggest a New Orleans setting. Of course, you may well try to place a warmly romantic story in Cleveland, but most people's connotations of Cleveland do not include romance, a fact that must be considered when you decide on the setting of the story. These examples are broadly drawn, although we probably do have connotations for most words. *Home, car, Mom, job,* and *bread* probably have a wide variety of connotations among your classmates.

Differences in background and experience create differences in the reactions people have to words. If you have eaten only the mild, Cantonese version of Chinese food, you will tend to think of Chinese food as mild and slightly exotic. If the only Chinese food you have ever had is the extremely spicy, mouth-searing Hunan variety, your impression of what Chinese food is will be quite different. The denotation of the word *Chinese* is the commonly used, dictionary meaning. The connotation of *Chinese* is the feeling or personal reactions you have to the word.

People have always been interested in their own use of symbols and in the development of written and spoken symbols to represent and communicate about their world and experiences. In our time, two notable writers—Alfred Korzybski and S. I. Hayakawa—have been strongly identified with study in this area (Korzybski, 1933; Hayakawa, 1990). Their writings concern the way people use and misuse language.

Korzybski and Hayakawa felt that our misuse of symbols is partly responsible for many social ills. They stressed that "the symbol is not the thing." By this statement, they meant that symbols are representational and artificial and not worth fighting over. Our words, as Hayakawa pointed out, are like maps to a territory, but they are not the territory itself. For example, rather than block a bill in the legislature because it contains a socially impolite term—*venereal disease*—it was, they argued, much sounder to attack the disease. They urged that we look at the reality, not at the symbol. They believed that if we could change the way we react to symbols, especially those of language, we could improve our orientation to reality and get to work solving real problems instead of arguing about what to call the problem. Their philosophy is called **general semantics** and is related to the study of how meanings and symbols interact.

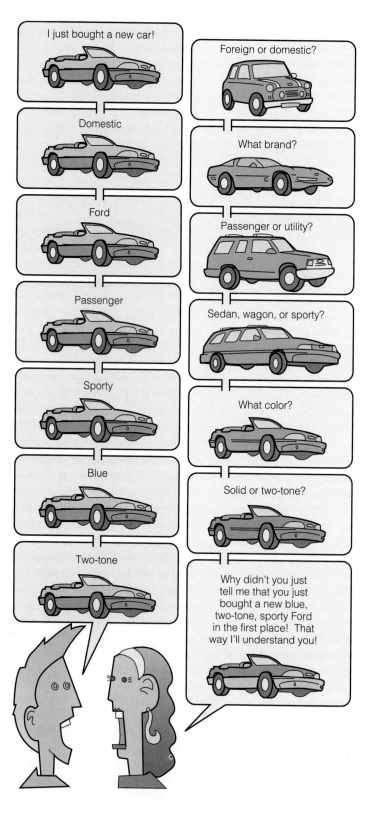

The message that is sent may not be the message that is received.

THE STORY OF COMMUNICATION

S. I. Hayakawa

One of the most interesting people of our time, S. I. Hayakawa, was born in Canada in 1906. Later, he moved to Chicago, worked with Alfred Korzybski, and published *Language in Action* in 1939, just as World War II was beginning. Although a Canadian by birth and citizenship, he was classified as an enemy alien on his U.S. passport during the war. He was a faculty member at Illinois Technical University for a time, then transferred to San Francisco State University and was its president during the troubled times of student and faculty unrest over the Vietnam War and campus issues. His confrontational style made headlines, and he eventually won a seat in the U. S. Senate representing California. After his term as Senator, he continued to write and lecture on communication, culture, and politics. He died in February 1992.

In addition to semantics, or the study of meaning and words, we can also look at the study of **phonologics,** the study of meaning and sound, and syntactics, the study of meaning and forms. These methods of looking at how we use symbols and signs are known as **semiotics.** We examine semiotics by focusing on each of the three parts identified here.

Semiotics

Semantics.   The way we attach meanings to words is known as **semantics,** and there are rules of semantics that we follow in putting meaning into those words. The meanings of words are given to those words by the users of those words. For example, you and your friends might have a special word for taking a break or eating a certain food. The dictionary is not likely to have it listed, yet the meaning of the word is perfectly clear to you, the users. Often, children make up a language or a code, perhaps to fool parents or other children. Special codes like these underline the principle that *use creates meaning.*

When you are told to look up a particular word in a dictionary if you do not understand it, you are getting good advice only if the user of the word was using its general application as found in a dictionary.

A few words about word books may be in order here. An old dictionary functions like a history book. It records how educated speakers used words in the past. However, a dictionary cannot tell what a particular speaker may have meant when that speaker departed from past usage. The job of current dictionary writers is to review a wide variety of sources to see how people are using words and then record and tabulate the results. If a word is no longer in use by anybody, the writers drop it from the current list or keep it but perhaps mark it *archaic.* On the other hand, if the writers discover a word in wide usage that has not previously appeared, they add it.

Every time a new edition of a dictionary comes out, there are newspaper articles about the number of new words in it. Most of these new words are already well known to readers of the newspapers because the words have been in use for

TECHNOLOGY IN COMMUNICATION

Webster's Contributions

The widespread use of books did not develop until relatively recently in our history. The combination of printing technology and wide distribution made it necessary for some standards of communication to be established, such as standard spelling and grammar. You know of *Webster's Dictionary*, named after Noah Webster (1758–1843).

Webster was concerned about the lack of standardization of American English in both grammar and spelling. Of his several books, the *American Dictionary of the English Language* was first issued in 1828. It has been reissued and updated for nearly 170 years now. A new edition is due out shortly, and it will be available in hard copy as well as CD-ROM format for your computer, and an on-line format is not far behind.

Webster thought that his work would do much more than just get people to be good spellers. He also thought that he would increase patriotism and improve morals through better communication, made possible then by improved printing technology and now via the electronic media.

several years before being entered in the new edition of the dictionary. Some words are transitory and faddish and never last long enough to be included in a dictionary. Others catch on and become permanent fixtures. For example, before 1960, no dictionary listed *countdown* as a word, yet it was widely used. Now it appears in every edition. *Compact disc, microprocessor,* and *byte* will appear in new editions, but they are not in many dictionaries published before 1985. However, their absence from dictionaries does not mean that they are not perfectly good, communicative words. It means only that dictionaries are slow to record word history. The best source for clearing up doubts or confusion about the meaning of a word is to ask the word's users. Do you remember the following scene from *Through the Looking Glass* by Lewis Carroll (1949)?

> "I don't know what you mean by 'glory.'" Alice said.
>
> Humpty Dumpty smiled contemptuously. "Of course you don't—till I tell you. I meant, 'there's a nice knock-down argument for you!'"
>
> "But 'glory' doesn't mean 'a nice knock-down argument,'" Alice objected.
>
> "When *I* use a word," Humpty Dumpty said, in rather a scornful tone, "it means just what I choose it to mean—neither more nor less."
>
> "The question is," said Alice, "whether you *can* make words mean so many different things."
>
> "The question is," said Humpty Dumpty, "which is to be master—that's all."

Which is to be master—you or the word? The study of semantics would say that you control both the meanings of and the reactions to the words around you. But mastering the meaning of our language systems also means being familiar with the other ways in which our symbols create meanings—that is, sounds and structures.

Phonologics.   The way a word sounds gives it meaning when we hear it. There are combinations and rules of language that clarify meaning and others that create only nonsense. You recognize *train* from its sounds as being different from *drain*, even though the sounds /t/ and /d/ are nearly identical. The phonemes, or sounds, change slightly, and the meaning changes completely.

A word means just what I want it to mean.

The meanings of words are determined by the users of words.

Through sound, we provide not only differences in meanings, but also information about ourselves. Are you from Brooklyn? Atlanta? Fort Worth? Calcutta? Edinburgh? We all can say the same words, but slight variations in pronunciation give listeners quite a bit of information about us. It is really sounds that govern meanings, since written language represents the results of our ancestors having recorded the sounds they made. Sometimes the original spellings remain, but over the years, the actual sounds have changed, as in the word *subtle*. Say it, and you will not hear the *b* pronounced. The rules for meanings that come from the way we sound our words are one more part of the whole symbolic process.

Syntax.   Finally, meaning comes from **syntax,** which is the rules of order of a language. You can probably guess the meaning of this sentence: "Dog, a large one there down the road coming is." You also know exactly how to change it to make it fit the rules for English sentence structure. Yet speakers of Japanese or Hungarian would prefer a word order close to the one illustrated. Sometimes, a writer or speaker will deliberately invert word order or sentence structure to make his or her particular use of syntax stand apart from normal structures. Dylan Thomas, a master of the English language, begins an essay as follows (1954):

Across the United States of America, from New York to California and back, glazed, again, for many months of the year there streams and sings for its heady supper a dazed and prejudiced procession of European lecturers, scholars, sociologists, economists, writers, authorities on this and that and even, in theory, on the United States of America.

This sentence stretches our ability to follow its syntax and is typical of Thomas's writing in both his prose and poetry. We recognize that the syntax is unusual, and perhaps we look more deeply into the meaning of his words than we might have if he had used simpler patterns. There is always a chance, however, that the reader will give up on complicated syntax, in which case there is no communication at all. That is why it is wise to follow the rules of syntax for general audiences until they are committed to following you. Audiences expect you to follow these rules, and a barrier may arise if you do not meet their expectations. The language you use, and that of everyone else, should follow the understood rules of definition, sound, and structure.

Robert Zimmerman, born in 1941 in Hibbing, Minnesota, was a great admirer of Dylan Thomas. He began to write poetry for dozens of powerful song lyrics. He was a composer as well and played both guitar and harmonica, his favorite instruments. Though he lacked a musically trained voice, he sang and recorded hundreds of his own songs and influenced many other singers who responded to the incisive and creative communication of his material. He was nearly killed in a motorcycle accident, and it took more than a year for him to recover to the point at which he could once again lift a guitar. He has recorded more than twenty gold albums under the name Bob Dylan.

The language that you use, and the languages of everyone else, follow the understood rules of definitions, sounds, and structures. One of the universal connections of all people is that we have the capacity of language and acquire and use language—all languages—in the same manner.

ACQUIRING LANGUAGE SKILLS

When you first listened to the sounds of others around you, your brain had the capacity and the impulse to sort through these noises, recognize patterns, and begin to attach meanings to those patterns. You had the phonological ability to make every sound of every spoken language on earth. If by some chance you had been whisked away as an infant and reared in a Nepalese family, you would speak Nepali without any hesitation or trace of an accent. As we grow and acquire language, we drop the sounds that are not used or needed and concentrate on the ones we do need. Sometimes the early ability is very difficult to regain as when, in high school, you try to learn to roll your *r*'s in French class. The French *r* comes from the back of the tongue. English-speaking people are not accustomed to using this area when they speak. At the southern tip of Africa, the Xhosa people make a sound by closing the top of the throat and quickly releasing it on a breath to create a pop, or click, represented by, but not sounding like, the English letter *x*. Therefore to say the name of the language, Xhosa, you need to be able to make this sound.

More important than the ability to make the right noises involved in language, is the aptitude to make sense out of those noises. The primary language

DIVERSITY IN COMMUNICATION

One Hundred Sounds

The International Phonetic Alphabet is a widely used system of recording the sounds of spoken languages. First codified about 1889, it includes symbols representing the sounds that are used in every language. Nearly one hundred such symbols are in common use. American English speakers use only about fifty of those symbols. Around the world, some of our sounds are used, others that we do not use are added, and others are dropped altogether. Diverse languages either use or do not use certain positions of the teeth, tongue, lips, palate, and throat. The rich diversity of thousands of languages around the world tells us that while we may be diverse, we are also unified in the human family by our linguistic capabilities.

center, located in the left hemisphere of the brain just above the ear, is capable of organizing sounds into meanings. The brain is a complex organism, and we have discovered that other areas of the brain also can interact to make sense out of language. If damaged, parts of the brain will cease to function, but other parts can sometimes be trained to take over the functions of the damaged part. Research is being done on this phenomenon, and each year researchers learn more about how these areas interact. Later, you will read about how children develop these skills, but for now you can see that you have acquired them through living and responding to the world around you.

Your culture is also an important factor in determining your language skills. Research has been done on the way English speakers think compared to the way speakers of other languages think. There is a theory called the **Sapir-Whorf hypothesis** that explains differences among cultures by looking at the linguistic patterns of their languages. Simply stated, this theory says that you think within the linguistic patterns and boundaries of your language. Your vocabulary and your language structure determine what you think about and how you think about it. For example, some Native American languages (especially Hopi and Navajo, which Edward Sapir studied extensively) talk about *processes* in the world rather than events. Thus you would discuss *dining* rather than *dinner,* or *singing* rather than *a song,* and so on. This dynamic flow of language is related to these cultures' patterns of thinking about the processes of world. By contrast, English places much emphasis on names and nouns for events and may be said to be more static in orientation.

Language is a miracle in the sense that it helps us—through our thoughts, ideas, and feelings—to travel across time, space, and culture. Why do people carve their initials on a tree, spray *Phil loves Elisa* on a rock, or mark up the walls along highways? They know that others who follow will read these symbols. Thus the originator is, in a sense, still there—captured and frozen in time. Long after Phil and Elisa have gone their separate ways, people will still be finding out about them and their relationship. You have the opportunity to learn from Socrates, long after he died, because Plato and Aristotle took the time to write about Socrates. Then someone else took the works of Plato and Aristotle and

---

THE STORY OF COMMUNICATION

Shakespeare's Sonnet 18

Shall I compare thee to a summer's day?
Thou art more lovely and more temperate.
Rough winds do shake the darling buds of May,
And summer's lease hath all too short a date.
Sometime too hot the eye of heaven shines,
And often is his gold complexion dimmed.
And every fair from fair sometime declines,
By chance or nature's changing course untrimmed.
But thy eternal summer shall not fade,
Nor lose possession of that fair thou owest,
Nor shall Death brag thou wanderest in his shade
When in eternal lines to time thou grow'st.
　So long as men can breathe, or eyes can see,
　So long lives this, and this gives life to thee.

---

put them into a form we can read. Because you have language, you can share the sagas and stories of Native Americans or Vikings who lived a thousand years ago.

At the end of one of his sonnets, Shakespeare wrote, "So long lives this, and this gives life to thee," meaning that while there is someone to read about his loved one, she remains alive—at least in our minds. You can send your thoughts and ideas around the world for less than the cost of a gallon of gas because you have language; you can write, and someone on the receiving end can read. One of Western civilization's greatest moments occurred in 1799 when soldiers of Napoleon's army discovered a large stone tablet that is now called the Rosetta Stone. On this tablet, ancient priests had inscribed the same message in three languages, including Greek and Egyptian hieroglyphics. Until then, the writings of Egypt were not understood, and this great African civilization was known only through its objects, paintings, and what other people wrote about it. When we finally unlocked the key to the Egyptian language, thousands of messages became available to us and filled in several thousand years of blank pages of history.

Your ability to use language is special and important. That is why there are classes like this one—so that you can understand, appreciate, and enhance your abilities. Your ability to build language skills did not stop in childhood; and if you wish, it may keep growing as long as you live.

SPEAKING AND WRITING

As was mentioned earlier, there is a direct relationship between speaking and writing. You first listened, then thought, then spoke, and then wrote. The symbols that you use to write were created in an attempt to capture the sounds of spoken language. A quick example of this phenomenon is easily seen in our use of the indefinite article *a* before any word except those starting with a vowel. *A book* is fine, but *a umbrella* is not. Why not? Because *a umbrella* is harder to say than *an umbrella*. Notice that *a umbrella* is not harder to write; in fact it is a bit easier to write. Furthermore, it would be more economical to use *a* all the time in our writing. But our speech pattern came first, and we retain in the rules for writing the rules that we developed in speaking.

There are some differences, however, in *style*. Written communication can be more complex than oral communication for several reasons. In writing, the reader has an opportunity to go back over what was written. You can put a book down, get a drink of water, check your mail, get a snack, and then pick up right where you left off or at any other place you like. When listening to a conversation, you have no such opportunity. Even if there are many participants, if you get up and leave for a few moments, you cannot rewind the conversation back to where you left it. Therefore written communication can be more complex, having longer sentences and fewer summaries than oral communication. The aware public speaker knows that he or she cannot simply read an essay and expect an audience to follow it as if they had a copy in hand. A speech is not an "essay on legs." A speech is different because it *needs* to be different. A good way to think about the relationship between speaking and writing is to see them as complementary functions. Being skilled at one can help you to be skilled at the other, but one cannot replace the other.

 ## USE AND MISUSE OF LANGUAGE

Because language is a powerful tool, it can help to guide us to new achievements or it can damage and degrade ourselves and others. As poet Robert Frost once said, "The first tool I stepped on turned into a weapon." The tool doesn't

Communication, like any tool, can be used in positive or negative ways.

care how you use it. You can cut wheat or kill a person with the same scythe. Anyone who has seen any of the "chainsaw" genre of films is familiar with this tool/weapon dichotomy.

On the positive side, you live in an English-speaking culture, and at the moment, you are involved in higher education—a subculture within the mainstream culture. In a college environment, certain kinds of language use are dominant and expected. In other times and settings, other forms of English may be expected.

Mainstream American English

Mainstream American English is really the language we hear on the network news and national television programs. It is the common language of commerce, government, entertainment, and business. When new arrivals come to this country, one of the first steps they must take to integrate into the culture is to learn at least the basics of Mainstream American English. Some may live in an ethnic community where the native language is spoken in every store and home; but historically, European-based neighborhoods seldom last more than one or two generations beyond the original families (Gans, 1979). The native speakers die or move on, and their children and grandchildren pick up the forms of the major language.

Where there is an enforced isolation of neighborhoods—usually consisting of people from non-European backgrounds—group patterns may persist longer

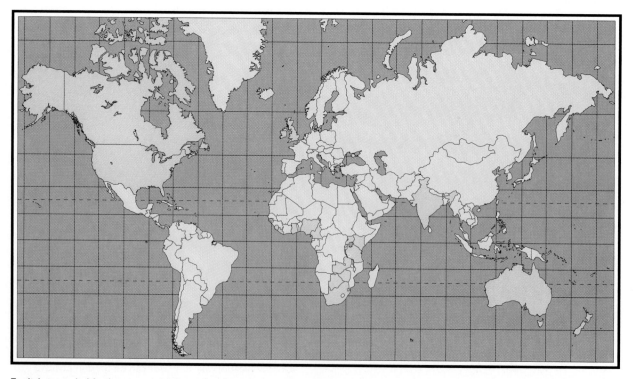

English is probably the most widely spoken language in the world.

and be carried from one ethnically similar neighborhood to another. For many years, racial segregation was legal and enforced in many states. In others, it was tolerated by government at all levels. Although the legal barriers are gone, families from racial minorities may still find reluctance or noncooperation if they attempt to live as the only minority residents in a neighborhood. Communities that are composed almost entirely of African Americans, Puerto Ricans, Chinese, or Latinos are still the norm in most large cities, and are exceptions to the pattern of moving that was noted earlier. Most people in these communities have bilingual capabilities. They understand and can use Mainstream American English but often communicate in other forms of English with friends, family, and local businesses. The language patterns of these groups are reinforced by the people around them, so they persist. Yet it is likely that with the influence of schools geared toward Mainstream American English and of television, these other forms will decrease over the coming years.

Mainstream American English is the form that this book uses, and it is different from other forms of English, such as those used in England, Ireland, South Africa, India, and Scotland. A wonderful television series, "The Story of English," took viewers around the world to show how English, in its many varieties, has become the world language. It was interesting that many of the people who were interviewed had to have their words displayed as subtitles on the screen for Americans to comprehend them. Our English may differ from theirs in spelling, pronunciation, vocabulary, and syntax. But you do not need to travel overseas to experience variety in English, for many forms are used in the United States.

Variety in American English

Probably most noticed and widespread, **Black English** is a variation of Mainstream American English that most Americans have heard or used. With popular African American musicians leading the way, people outside that culture often get a glimpse of this form of the language. Black English involves much more than a shift in vocabulary, or the rhymed, accented lyrics of a rap artist. The grammar rules differ in many ways and form a logical system that is independent of Mainstream English. Black English has at least two major forms (Jenkins, 1982). It developed over several centuries in African American communities and persists today because those communities have stayed intact.

One scholar described Black English as "an Africanized form of English reflecting Black America's linguistic-cultural African heritage and the conditions of servitude, oppression, and life in America." (Smitherman, 1972). That description emphasizes the growth of Black English in the context of African American history. For example, linguists can trace patterns and styles of the language to similar patterns and styles in West African languages spoken by the ancestors of modern African Americans (Hecht et al., 1993). Black English will likely continue to be used for three reasons, contends Dr. Shirley Weber, African American studies scholar. First, African Americans experience the world differently from other groups (Covin, 1990), so their language reflects and communicates that experience. Second, Black English is a common element that binds African American people together, even though they live in different areas or find themselves in different social or economic situations. Finally, the language can be seen as a political statement that reflects connections with, and pride about, a common African heritage (Weber, 1991).

Another variety of English includes forms that are associated with Hispanic cultures. This blend of languages is sometimes called *Spanglish* (Castro, 1988). This form uses both syntax and vocabulary that are related to English and Spanish, and it serves the functions of community identity and solidarity as well as group communication. Whether Spanglish will persist as long as Black English and develop an enduring linguistic identity remains to be seen. If the social forces change so that these groups no longer experience a markedly different experience from the mainstream culture, the reasons to maintain a separate linguistic identity will also begin to disappear (De Vos and Romanucci-Ross, 1982).

Professional, Personal, and Popular Codes

Certain forms of English, commonly called *jargon,* are associated with individuals by virtue of their occupation, interests, or relationship to current events in popular culture. For example, there is medi-speak which uses medical terms and shorthand, and computer-speak which everyone inside the computer community understands. Ten or fifteen years ago, only a few people knew the terms *CPU, motherboard, byte,* and *mouse.* The widespread use of computers has made these words more common, yet some terms are still the province of computer experts or hackers.

As for personal forms of English, you may share a personal code with a few members of your family based on common experiences or traditions. For example, my cousin Candace and I were about eleven years old when we went to another cousin's wedding celebration. Being mischievous, we tried to sneak sips

Advances in electronic communication have lead to new professional and popular codes.

of champagne from other guests' glasses without being caught and set a record of four consecutive sips. Ever since that day, whenever we think someone is drinking too much, one of us says "Four!" to the other, and the meaning is perfectly clear to us.

Popular codes stem from music, television shows, personalities, and movies. Terms from the 1960s surf culture, such as *fuzz* to mean "police" have largely disappeared, and only a few people left over from the hippie era still say "Groovy!" with any regularity. Current listeners to the music of Simon and Garfunkel are sometimes amused to hear the words to the "59th Street Bridge Song"—*Feelin' groovy!* The Valley Girl talk of the 1980s was replaced by the modern surf terms *tubular* and *barney,* which, in turn, are not heard much anymore. Some terms have staying power and enter the mainstream language; others, called *neologisms,* are current and reveal their users to be part of some popular movement of the moment. These terms can be both fun and useful, and they keep the language vibrant and colorful.

Linguistic Oppression

One of the more controversial aspects of language is its association with stereotypes and insults, or **linguistic oppression.** Racism, sexism, ageism, handicapism, and probably other areas of offensive discrimination are associated with actions, attitudes, and especially language. The user's intention is an important aspect of determining meaning. Men who call women *girls* and whites who use

CRITICAL THINKING IN COMMUNICATION

Computer History

In 1965, oversized computers worked with vacuum tubes. The simple machines needed to be housed in large rooms or sometimes entire floors. They processed information much faster than a human could, and a time frame of several hours to process a batch of data was considered good. Data were recorded on cards, about three inches by seven inches, that had hundreds of places for small, rectangular holes to be punched out by machine. These holes were then read by the computer to process the data.

At that time, Charles Thacker, a senior at the University of California, Berkeley, envisioned a computer "the size of a college notebook binder." It was impossible to believe the hyperbole of such a bizarre vision. Later, Thacker went to work for the Xerox Corporation and then became an independent professional.

The introduction of the personal computer (PC) in the late 1970s and the now widespread use of laptop and notebook computers, have made Thacker's vision part of our everyday reality. Incidentally, the tabletop PC that you use at home or at school can perform hundreds more operations than the roomsized computers of 1965 at a fraction of the time and cost. The analytical and logical processes of critical thinking, combined with a creative vision, have changed forever the way we communicate (Chesebro and Bonsall, 1989).

boy in referring to a black man are both considered offensive. Members of the reference group who use these terms may be able to do so within the community with less offense. The terms may even communicate affection, as is commonly done when African American women refer to each other as *girl* or a gay man refers to another as *queer.* Used by outsiders to attack, these terms are offensive; used by insiders, the intended meaning may be just the opposite.

These labels have, of course, changed over the years, most notably in relation to African Americans. Already popular, the term *African American* is rapidly overtaking *black* as the preferred expression. In less than fifty years we have come from terms such as *colored, Negro,* and *black* to *African American,* so the process seems well established (Hecht et al., 1993). The insulting word *nigger* is still around and communicates as much affront and attack now as it did in the past, as do *kike* for Jews, *honky* for Anglos, *spick* for Hispanics, *fag* for homosexuals, and so on. We seem to be capable of producing long lists of insults for people we find different from ourselves.

Often, older people are not referred to as *elderly* these days, but as *seniors* or *senior citizens.* A senior center is a place for people over the age of sixty to participate in a variety of activities. The context tells us that a senior there is a different kind of senior than someone in the last year of high school or college. Our study of semantics shows how words develop meanings as people use them. Both the user's intention and how the listener reacts to words are involved in this active process. If you can remember to supply a context to your communication, you will help listeners to understand your dynamic use of language.

Linguistic oppression is a topic that arouses deep feelings in many who are on the receiving end of deliberate acts of attack through language. The whole issue of hate speech concerns language on the attack, and issues of the right to free speech are sometimes in conflict with the right to be protected from attack. Speech codes on many campuses are an attempt to guide behavior and protect people from language that is used to attack or belittle. Some communication texts, such as this one, attempt to address the issue in a way to help people learn about the negative effects of such hate speech. Some communication classrooms use discussions, exercises, or simulations to accomplish the same goals (Jensen, 1993).

Labels can both communicate contempt for the target and reveal the speaker's attitudes. Another difficulty is that people will sense a put-down and may, if they hear it often enough, begin to incorporate the connotations of the term into their own self-concept. Thus women who are referred to as *girls* may develop an immature attitude toward themselves, believing that they are dependent and incompetent.

Although it is true that words are only symbols and are not reality—I can address you as "Your Majesty," but that will not make you ruler—they nevertheless have the powerful ability to help us construct our reality. The Sapir-Whorf hypothesis supports the possibility that linguistic oppression, especially in the labeling of distinct groups within a culture, can be harmful. Many Native Americans remember being forbidden to speak any language other than English at reservation schools. French-speaking Cajuns in Louisiana had a similar experience. The implication was that their native tongues were not valuable or important. American tourists are criticized for expecting people in other coun-

---

IMPROVING COMPETENCY

Attacks on Self-Concept

An activity that was suggested by law professor Geoff Cowan is to write about an incident during which you felt humiliated or abused by the use of hate speech. Search your memory for a time that may still be painful to recall. As you reflect, keep in mind that almost everyone can be a target and victim of language on the attack. Probably, you will recall an incident when the words were aimed at you on a personal level, perhaps by someone you know. Cowan uses the example of his brother, who suffered from severe acne as a teenager while attending an exclusive prep school. Because he was Jewish and in a decided minority at the school, he was sometimes attacked with the words *kike* or *Jew*. While certainly hurtful in both intent and effect, these insults did not remain as memorable to him as when he was taunted with the word *pimpleface*.

---

tries to speak English. When this message comes from a powerful source, it can affect the development of positive self-worth.

Be careful of your choices of words, for they can have tremendous impact on those who react to words in forming a self-concept. In reality, that probably means almost all of us. Whether we like it or not, most of us are not at a point of sophistication at which we realize that words are just the noises of other people. We both hurt others and get hurt by rude remarks. One way to break out of this cycle is to understand that certain labels can have an oppressive effect on those being labeled.

Magic, Taboo, and Ritual

Other important functions of our verbal code are expressive—that is, they serve to provide us with some psychological release.

Magic.   In earliest times, our ancestors thought that language was a gift from the gods or was otherwise divinely inspired. The Book of John in the Christian bible begins "In the beginning was the Word," equating God with the Word. Humans have used special prayers and ritualistic chants longer than recorded time. The ability to cast a spell means to make something happen by saying it. **Magic** may also involve a simple wish: "I *will* get taller! I *will* get taller!" It may involve a complex voodoo curse that makes its believers sick. When certain words are said, a special process is invoked—magic!

Our relationship to the magic power of words is why you may not say a wish aloud and thus break the spell. Or you may express a hope about a potential loss or danger. A statement like, "I'll pick you up tomorrow if the car doesn't break down—knock on wood!" is accompanied by a knock on a handy wooden object. Here, expressing a magic idea is complemented by a magic act. But when standing in line to board an airplane, you do not say aloud, "Gee, I hope the plane doesn't crash!" (Even the word *Gee* is a magic shorthand for the name *Jesus*, so that you do not violate the injunction against using the Lord's name.)

Taboo.   The ancient commandment "Thou shalt not take the name of the Lord in vain" is one of our earliest records of **taboo**—words that are forbidden. The ancient Hebrews would not write or pronounce the word *Yahweh*—later, *Jehovah*—which is said to be God's personal name, and instead used substitute words, or euphemisms, to discuss their deity. In fact, many strictly observant Jews to this day will not write the word *God* but will leave out a letter in order not to violate this taboo. The development of *gosh darn* and *gee whiz* was a response to the prohibition against religious names in Christian culture. And the power of words to live beyond their utterance is recorded in the New Testament: "For I say unto you that every idle word which you shall speak you will account of on the day of Judgement. For by thy words shalt thou be justified, and by thy words shalt thou be condemned," (Matthew 12:36–37).

We also include forbidden subjects, such as sex, death, and bodily functions in our taboo list. Certain words are considered crude and vulgar, others as acceptable or polite, even when the reality to which they refer is identical. Anatomy is a favorite target for taboo, especially when the body part may have sexual connotations. The Victorians were famous for **euphemisms** and required that polite people avoid the words *leg* and *breast.* Chicken and turkey parts were termed *light meat* and *dark meat,* and table legs (limbs) were covered with long cloths. The term *sleep with* someone is a euphemism to describe not really sleeping at all. You can probably list a dozen words to discuss death without mentioning the word itself. *Passed away* and *gone to heaven* have a gentle touch, while *kicked off* is rather crass. Nevertheless, we avoid the word *death* in many social situations, especially when talking to someone who has recently experienced the death of a close friend or relative.

Taboo is valuable as an index of the comfort or importance of a topic to a person or a culture. Taboo words themselves change over time, and what is not permissible now in some places will be common in a few years. New euphemisms are constantly taking the place of older ones, which may become so closely identified with the vulgar term itself that they, too, slide into the taboo area. Each culture has its own terms, but it is interesting to note that the taboos are often about the same subjects—religion, sex, death, and bodily functions. In Wichita, Kansas, you may need to *use the bathroom,* but in London, it's a *visit to the loo.* In Ohio, to avoid the subject of death, you may say that your grandparent has *departed;* in Tokyo, to observe the same taboo, you may avoid saying the number *four,* pronounced *shi,* as it is also the sound for the word *death.*

We react to these words because we have been trained to react to them. If someone swears in another language, we have virtually no response, even if we can translate the term. Only when we are inside our own culture with its associations do we readily blush or get angry.

Ritual.   **Ritual** is another formal, cultural way of using language to convey a sense of power or mystical union. The Roman Catholic Church used to hold its religious services in Latin as a way of demonstrating a link to previous ages. For

*Rituals help us to feel part of
a larger group or culture.*

Muslims gathered in prayer, the service is repeated in a formal way and creates a sense or unity among the participants.

Your physiology changes in response to the ritual use of language that is meaningful or important to you. Do you feel a swell of pride as "The Star Spangled Banner" is sung at a Veteran's Day service? When you join in the recitation of the "Pledge of Allegiance," do you feel a union with others reciting the pledge? Does the "Battle Hymn of the Republic" or "We Shall Overcome" bring a lump to your throat or a tingle to the back of your neck? If so, you are participating in a ritual response to words, linking you to the rest of the people who are also participating.

One of the interesting developments in popular culture during the past two decades is the addition of Canadian baseball teams to the major leagues. Now, whenever Toronto or Montreal plays a game with a U.S. team, two national anthems are sung or played. Future generations of U.S. baseball fans may come to know "O, Canada!" as well as their own anthem. Repeating familiar words, especially words that may also carry mystical connotations, helps to provide comfort and security to those participating.

 ## IMPROVING LINGUISTIC COMPETENCY

As with each part of the communication process, you must be aware of the component, understand its relationship to the rest of the process, and see how you use it before you can begin to develop improvements. Also, as with any other element, virtually no one is perfect, and virtually everyone could use some refinement.

So step 1 is to understand that words are symbols; they are arbitrary and abstract. They represent things, ideas, and responses, but they are not realities in themselves beyond their existence as sound waves or markings in ink on paper. We need to understand that they are wonderful aspects of our humanity, but they are given meaning only by those who use them and react to them. The development of meaning is always dynamic; it may change with each speaker, each writer, each situation or context, or each time frame. An understanding of language can start you on your way to mastery of it.

Second, an expanded awareness and understanding of word usage should lead you to expand your practice. Gather a larger vocabulary by reading widely, looking up words you encounter, or asking people to explain their use of terms. A better question than "What does that mean?" would be "What do *you* mean when you use that word?" An expanded vocabulary can be obtained by keeping your awareness level high as you read books, newspapers, or magazines. You can listen closely to dialogue in films and television shows for new terms or expressions. You may even want to buy a word-a-day calendar to enlarge your repertoire of words. With a greater vocabulary comes the possibility of greater precision in your communication.

The result of increasing your vocabulary is an increase in your options—an expanded repertoire. Instead of making a general term convey all your ideas, you can select from several related terms to find the one that best relates your meaning. You can help your listeners to come closer to understanding you if you can select words that they can interpret more precisely than generic terms. The sentence "I got a lot of stuff at the store" probably leaves your listeners only a little more informed on your return from shopping. "I bought a dozen kiwis at the Import Grocery" is more precise and informative. Some people take vocabulary-building courses, which can be an excellent start. Others work on self-oriented games or processes such as writing down unfamiliar words or solving word quizzes in magazines and newspapers.

Language can inspire us or depress us. Our ability to use and control our communication rests heavily on our verbal skills.

SUMMARY

Since words occupy so much of your education and will continue to be a part of your future interactions in career, family, social, and recreational settings, it is important to know how words function as symbols of our world. Language is a means of providing control over our environment. It develops in the same way in all humans regardless of place of birth, and the language that you learned is merely an accident of where and to whom you were born. Your language helps to shape your thought processes, and skillful users of language can expand their options for describing their world and for interacting with others.

We know that English comes in many forms, all useful at times to their speakers. Accents, region-alisms, and cultural variations of English help to identify one's background, provide a sense of connectedness to a group, or simply create variety in the communication setting. We know, too, that some reactions to language can be psychologically oppressing and can, in turn, create physiological reactions in us.

With attention and effort, you can improve your use of language and continually acquire a broader verbal repertoire to expand your potential interactions. You can be a better listener as well as a better speaker, writer, and thinker if you improve your language skills.

KEY TERMS

symbol, *p. 96*
denotation, *p. 97*
connotation, *p. 97*
general semantics, *p. 97*
phonologics, *p. 99*
semiotics, *p. 99*
semantics, *p. 99*
syntax, *p. 101*

Sapir-Whorf hypothesis, *p. 103*
Mainstream American English, *p. 106*
Black English, *p. 107*
linguistic oppression, *p. 109*
magic, *p. 111*
taboo, *p. 112*
euphemisms, *p. 112*
ritual, *p. 112*

EXERCISES

1. At the front of most major dictionaries is an introduction that may discuss the history of English, language in general, and the processes used to compile that particular edition. Select two dictionaries, and read the introductions. Take notes, and be prepared to present a short report or to participate in a group discussion about the material.

2. Make up a nonsense word to replace a common word such as *pencil*. Now create four sentences using the nonsense word, and give the sentences to a partner from class. Have your partner figure out the definition of your word while you figure out the definition of his or her word.

3. A popular game called *dictionary* has one person find an obscure word in the dictionary and then ask each of the other players to invent and write out a short definition for that word. The leader then reads all the definitions aloud, including the actual one from the dictionary, and the players try to guess which is correct. This game is now sold under the name "Balderdash" and can give you insights into how definitions are created. Try playing either version of this game with friends or classmates.

4. Buy a word-a-day calendar, and remember to use it!

5. Buy a popular newspaper or magazine written by and aimed at an ethnic group that is different from your own. Pick out vocabulary or syntax that is unfamiliar to you, and bring these examples to class to share with other students. How can you determine the meaning of the unfamiliar material?

6. Make a list of your taboo terms. You may do this task mentally if writing the words violates your behavior code. What are the first five about? Where did the list come from?

REFERENCES

Carroll, Lewis. *Alice's Adventures in Wonderland and Through the Looking Glass.* New York: Harper and Brothers, 1949.

Castro, Janice. "Spanglish Spoken Here." Time, 11 July 1988.

Chesebro, J., and D. G. Bonsall. *Computer-Mediated Communication.* Tuscaloosa: University of Alabama Press, 1989.

Covin, D. "Afrocentricity in O Movimento Negro Unificado." *Journal of Black Studies* 21 (1990), 126–146.

De Vos, G. A., and L. Romanucci-Ross, eds., *Ethnic Identity: Cultural Continuities and Change.* Chicago: University of Chicago Press, 1982.

Gans, H. J. "Symbolic Ethnicity: The Future of Ethnic Groups and Cultures in America." *Ethnic and Racial Studies* 2 (1979).

Hayakawa, S. I. *Language and Thought in Action.* New York: Harcourt, Brace, 1990.

Hecht, Michael, Mary Jane Collier, and Sidney Ribeau. *African American Communication.* Newbury Park: Sage, 1993.

Jenkins, A. H. *The Psychology of the Afro-American: A Humanistic Approach.* Elmsford: Pergamon, 1982.

Jensen, M. D. "Developing Ways to Confront Hateful Speech." The Speech Communication Teacher 8 (Fall 1993), 1.

Korzybski, A. *Science and Sanity: An Introduction to Non-Aristotelian Systems and General Semantics.* Lancaster: Science Press, 1933.

Smitherman, G. *Talkin' and Testifyin'.* Boston: Houghton Mifflin, 1972. 2.

Thomas, Dylan. "A Visit to America." *Quite Early One Morning.* New York: New Directions, 1954.

Weber, S. "The Need to Be: The Socio-Cultural Significance of Black Language." *Intercultural Communication: A Reader.* Ed. L. Samovar and R. Porter. 6th ed. Belmont: Wadsworth, 1991. 282.

Intrapersonal Communication

After reading this chapter, you should be able to:

- Understand how communication within yourself affects self-concept and the way you communicate with others.

- Describe the role of experience in the development of the self.

- Define values, attitudes, and beliefs.

- Explain the differences between functional and dysfunctional communication systems.

- Take steps toward improving self-communication competency.

C ommunication is part of your social self. Because we are using a person-centered definition of communication, not one related to machine or animal communication, it is important to see how a person's self is at the heart of all communication interactions. You think, you listen, you respond, and you speak, and you do all of these things from your self-perspective. You need to look to the self—*your* self—to understand the key to any communication event.

A DEFINITION

Intrapersonal communication is communicating within yourself. You engage in intrapersonal communication when you are thinking, daydreaming, studying, creating, contemplating, or dreaming.

You are both the source and the destination of this type of communication. You use your brain waves as a channel; and the outcomes are thoughts or ideas, sometimes decisions, and sometimes actions or behaviors. You still communicate within a context, or environment. That environment is shaped by your language and other social considerations.

If the Sapir-Whorf hypothesis, discussed in the preceding chapter, is true, then your thoughts are formed, shaped, organized, and expressed only in the language(s) that you speak. You sequence your ideas and decisions in certain ways that are parallel to the way your primary language is structured. For example, in Japan, students who engage in high school and college debates do so in English because Japanese does not lend itself to direct clash and counterargument as English does. In other words, you think of ideas and relationships in a linguistic

---

DIVERSITY IN COMMUNICATION

Culture and Self

H ow you think about yourself is influenced greatly by your culture and its linguistic patterns. For example, the practice of name usage is different in different places around the world. In the United States, people usually give their names by stating the personal name first, then the family name: "Hi, I'm Ray Zeuschner." This pattern is opposite that found elsewhere. In Japan, China, and Hungary, for example, the family name is usually given first, followed by the personal name: "Hi, I'm Zeuschner Ray." Some scholars attribute this pattern to the importance that is placed on the individual or on the family. In some places, it is important to establish your family affiliation first, because your identity and meaning as an individual are secondary and follow from your connection and identification with your family. These patterns may be reflected in your intrapersonal communication as well as how you place yourself in a cultural context.

Similarly, when asked to introduce yourself in a two-minute speech to your classmates, would you begin with your physical attributes or your major? Your hometown or your religion? Family details, parents' occupations, class level? Hobbies? Awards? These choices may reveal how your culture influences you to think about yourself.

context. If you are bilingual or multilingual, you may be able to shift from one pattern to another. You have a real intrapersonal advantage if you can think in a variety of languages, because then you will have a variety of perspectives to use in your approach to many ideas, problems, or creative thoughts.

DEVELOPMENT OF INTRAPERSONAL COMMUNICATION

At the center of yourself are your experiences, self-concept, values, and perceptions. These elements have developed in you from your being alive, from messages you have received from others, and from those you have sent to yourself. Together, they form the well of experience on which you draw for your thoughts and messages. Each of these sources of your intrapersonal communication can be examined to understand better how you have become the type of communicator you are.

Experiences

You selected some experiences; others were given to you. As a small child, you may have chosen some toys to play with and ignored others. At the same time, someone else put that array of toys within your reach, chose to talk to you or read to you, put you in front of the television set, or left you alone. As you grew, the number of choices you had to make increased, and the opportunity for self-directed experience expanded greatly. You may have tried playing a musical instrument, gone skin diving, or tried to ski or bungee-jump or surf or play chess.

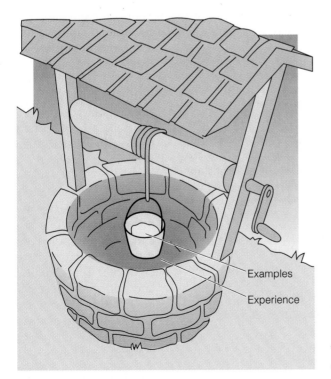

Examples

Experience

We select examples from our well of experiences.

Each of these choices gave you experience, and now you are ready for more. One of the joys and challenges of attending college is selecting new experiences. For instance, have you become involved in a club or activity as a means of enhancing your life experience? Perhaps you do some sort of volunteer work set up through your college. You might take a particular course as a means of trying a new or potentially difficult experience. Travel may be a method for you to expand your perspectives. Many schools offer foreign-study and travel opportunities.

Of course, not all experiences turn out perfectly. Nevertheless, you can learn from those as well, for they also broaden your range of options and increase your repertoire of communication experiences and choices.

An increase in your repertoire is the first dimension of communication competence. The accumulation of a variety of experiences builds your intrapersonal communication repertoire by adding depth and variety to your storehouse of ideas.

Self-Concept

Self-concept is what you believe about yourself. It is your own impression, opinion, attitude and description regarding yourself. Your self-concept includes your physical, mental, and emotional makeup. Self-concept is the way you identify yourself. All of these factors affect your overall self-concept, and, in turn, your self-concept contributes to the formation of your personality.

Your personality probably has the most direct bearing on your communication interactions. Although a complete discussion of personality is better left to the psychologists, there are some inescapable connections between your personality and your communication. Let's start with the social self, the way to see yourself in *relation* to others. This part of your personality is your communication self because communication is the means you use to create a relationship to others (Fine and Kleinman, 1983). As you look at communication within yourself, it is important to examine that process and what it produces.

Your self-concept may flow from many sources. You have a sense of your body, your talents, your roles, and your expectations. You have emotions, self-appraisal and reflection, predictions, and apprehensions. Each of these parts form a portion of your view of yourself.

TECHNOLOGY IN COMMUNICATION

Feedback Affects Self-Concept

Two tools to help you improve the accuracy of your self-perception have been audiotape and videotape. Remember the first time you heard your voice recorded—or, worse, *saw* yourself on videotape? These experiences can be unsettling because the feedback we get from these machines might not match the self-perception we had. Usually, the machines are more accurate. With repeated exposure to this feedback, you can begin to develop a realistic self-perception. I know one person who had thought she was tall because in the early elementary grades, she was much taller than the other children in her class. Her growth also stopped early, and she remained 5'3" from the time she was about ten years old. Only when, as an adult, she saw herself in a videotape, lined up with a crowd of her friends, did she exclaim, "I'm the shortest one in our group!"—a fact that everyone else in the group already knew.

The feedback that widespread access to technology makes possible may or may not be pleasant, but it will likely be accurate.

Body Image

You may be familiar with the way some psychologists have divided people into three general categories based on body type. The *ectomorph* is thin and lean, the *mesomorph* is athletic and muscular, and the *endomorph* is soft and round.

These categories may also form our image of our own bodies, even if the image is not accurate. We may wish to be thin and perceive ourselves to be overweight. The U.S. ideal of a slender, healthy, slightly tan, blond young athlete is an image that is projected relentlessly in advertising and films, but it is only a subjective view created by social norms. The paintings of Michelangelo, Leonardo Da Vinci, and Peter Paul Rubens show plump, dark-haired, pale-skinned nudes. Those artists did not paint any unusual image of beauty; they were idealizing, through their painting, the social image of women of their time. They probably would find our current image scrawny and unappealing. Social norms, therefore, define body image, and those norms are either reinforced or rejected by family and friends.

A major problem of young American women, especially those of college age, is their feeling of having an inadequate body image. This feeling may lead to pressure to change and can cause anorexia or bulimia, two eating disorders that are associated with negative body image. Young men are faced with stereotypes about strength, height, and other physical attributes.

Body image therefore, is the way we perceive ourselves in relation to the social standards of our culture. This image, in turn, influences our communication patterns. If you think you are far from the ideal image, you may become reluctant to participate in class or to stick out in a crowd by expressing your opinion. You may become withdrawn or defensive, conditions that modify your attempts to send messages to others and that also affect your interpretation of the messages you get from others.

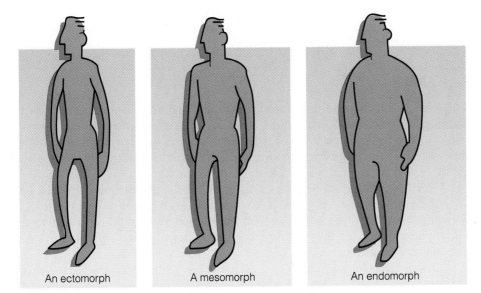

An ectomorph   A mesomorph   An endomorph

Somatyping categorizes people on the basis of three body types.

Cultural norms of beauty change with time and place.

Personal Attributes

Your talents are an important part of both your objective and subjective selves. You may have hidden talents, but you may be unaware of them because your self-concept does not yet acknowledge them. For example, I had a difficult time with arithmetic, so I assumed that I was not talented in mathematics in general. In graduate school, I needed to take a statistics course and found to my surprise that not only did it make sense to me, but I actually liked it. My self-concept changed as a result of that experience.

Often, self-concept formation comes early in our experience, so we may prematurely and incorrectly label ourselves as being shy or dull. When we are young, we are simply not as talented, intelligent, or competent as we are when we get older. A self-concept can and should change to meet the realistic changes in our lives. As we find and explore previously unknown talents and abilities, we can enlarge our sense of competency in a variety of areas—from public speaking to statistics.

Social Roles

The roles in which you find yourself may vary. You are a student, a son or a daughter, a friend, a volleyball player, a pianist, a poker player, a cousin, a hospital volunteer, a sales clerk. Each of these roles is a real part of you, even though the word *role* sometimes means "something artificial." Here, the roles you play are those that are normally associated with different aspects of your life.

The roles we have are sometimes assigned *to* us and sometimes adopted *by* us. For example, when you go for a job interview, your role is to be a polite listener, interested responder, and discreet questioner. You would be out of your role if you appeared at the interview dressed in casual beach clothes or made demands on the interviewer.

Most of the roles we follow are those we see in the models around us—that is, those which social values and customs tell us are appropriate. Your parental role might be a repetition of the role as you observed it in your parents. Or you might form it by watching the mother and father characters in a popular television program such as *The Bill Cosby Show*. You might want to be like the father in the novel *To Kill a Mockingbird* or like the mother in the book *Sounder*.

We play our roles through our communication behaviors. We are thoughtful listeners with ready answers in the parent role if we follow the Cosby model. We can be aggressive poker players who try to deceive others with our nonverbal communication, especially our facial expressions. We may be knowledgeable and deferential sales clerks, attentive and responsive students, and modest concert recitalists, depending how influential our models have been and how much self-appraisal of these behaviors we have done. Our communication in these contexts tells others what we perceive our role to be.

Of course, roles can and do change. For example, you went through a series of roles as a child. At an early stage, you were compliant with your parents' requests. You may then have gone through a rebellious stage during your early teen years, and now you are likely to be functioning on an adult-to-adult basis with your parents. Or you may have started out in a store as a temporary sales clerk, but now you are moving up to a shift supervisor role. With your change in role comes a change in role communication. Researchers on personal identity have concluded, "Thus, identity is formed and shaped through social interaction. Once formed, identity influences the flow of social behaviors and continues to be influenced by social interaction" (Hecht et al., 1993, p. 47).

Your perception of yourself and the social expectations of the various roles you play throughout the day determine your communication patterns and behaviors. You communicate from your self-perception, and, at the same time, you create an impression—that is, someone else's perception of you. How well you meet the social expectations of your roles determines other people's evaluation of you as a student, parent, sales clerk, child. The evaluation of good or bad in this case is determined by how closely your behaviors match the idealized expectations of those who observe your behaviors. You could, of course, become adept at playing the role of a bad student, but for now, what we mean is, How close do you come to the positive ideal of a particular role? Both the communication you send and the way that communication is perceived by others are based on a broad *social* sense of what is proper for a given role. These expectations are part of our social value system, and they create powerful pressures on role formation and therefore on your communication.

Values, Attitudes, and Beliefs

You might use those three terms interchangeably in conversation, but in communication and human psychology, they usually have three distinct meanings. *Values* are very broad, life-orienting, social principles that are shared by enormous groups of people, such as nations or civilizations; *attitudes* are more focused interpretations of values, applied to your own circumstances; and *beliefs* are specific applications of your values and attitudes. Let us examine each of these concepts in relation to intrapersonal communication.

These three aspects of yourself are especially important because they influence the way you see not only yourself, but everything around you.

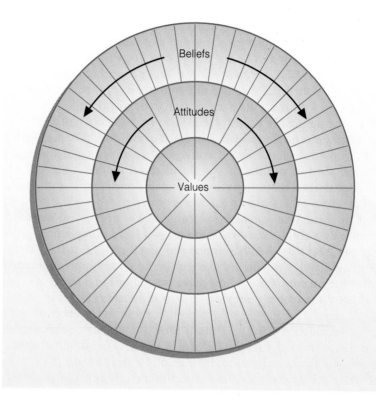

Your core values lead to many attitudes that are the basis for a multitude of beliefs.

Values.   Your **values** provide you with a general orientation about the *right* and *wrong* aspects of your ideas, thoughts, and actions. Values are broad, life-orienting concepts that are usually formed early in life and are heavily influenced by the family. For example, you think that education is an important part of life. Your family and closest friends are also likely to value education. In fact, you will probably find it difficult to remain in a relationship for long with anyone whose core values are very different from yours. Although your values can and do change over time, they are likely to change slowly, for values tend to be enduring.

Attitudes.   **Attitudes** are the ideals that stem from your values and that you apply to specific situations. They also affect the way you take in information from the outside world and apply its meaning to your experience. Moreover, you constantly explore and alter your attitudes but always as expressions of your basic value system. For example, continuing with the idea that education is good, you decide to enroll in college. You also think that paying taxes for good schools is the right thing to do. Your basic value—the goodness of education— orients your thinking to evaluate college education in a positive way and to be in favor of financial support for educational purposes. However, each case involving education might cause you to examine specific instances differently. Should private money support higher education? Should public money be used? Those specific areas come under the heading of beliefs.

Beliefs.   **Beliefs** are, in a way, the most subordinate of these three principles, and you have many more of them than you have of either values or attitudes.

Continuing with our example, you may value education and have a favorable attitude toward college education but believe that school X is better than school Y. Or you might believe that majoring in sociology is better than majoring in mathematics. You might be in favor of spending public money on education but believe that a particular bond issue in your town is not needed at this time. When you apply your values and attitudes to single cases, you are dealing with beliefs. The beliefs that you express are instances of the specific, case-by-case operation of your core values and long-term attitudes.

Perception and Self-Concept

Your values, attitudes, and beliefs affect the way you perceive the world. These aspects of your thinking constitute a sort of camera lens through which you view others as well as the events around you. These views of the outside world are called your **perceptions.** The way you view yourself is called your *self-concept.* Perception and self-concept are so closely intertwined that you can think of them as constantly interacting. What you think about yourself colors, shapes, and in some ways determines what you see around you. Conversely, the information that you get from outside of yourself provides valuable feedback and helps you to create an image of who you are. For example, your self-concept might include the notion that you are a wonderful cook, so you take every positive comment anyone may make about your skill in the kitchen as support for that notion. Any disparaging remarks, on the other hand, you dismiss; if you think about them at all, you interpret them as signs of jealousy or humor or as being just plain wrong.

Your perception of yourself may be accurate or distorted. The "real" you may be different from your perceived you. For example, you may have had a terrible experience in a public-speaking situation early in your life and have therefore insinuated the idea "poor speaker" into your self-concept. The reality may be that you are quite competent as a public speaker, but your memory of that one experience prevents you from viewing yourself objectively. This memory may become a self-fulfilling prophecy, causing you to do poorly in situations in which you might have succeeded. You may find examples in which people fail to give themselves credit where and when it is due and others in which people overrate their talents. You may know people who insist on singing because they believe they have a beautiful voice, when in reality they constantly sing off-key, in a grating tone of voice, or both.

Expectations

Your self-concept and your perceptions also affect the expectations that you have of yourself. Expectations are future-oriented messages that you send to yourself about what you ought to do. Some writers refer to these expectations as *life scripts*—that is, well-developed, long-term roles for you to follow. Your script predicts what you will do in the future and may be given to you early in life, or you may develop it yourself.

For example, you may come from a family in which traditional sex roles are important and are reinforced by your parents. They may often have said, "When you grow up and become a mommy, you can take your children to the park while daddy is at work." Though not ordering you to follow a traditional sex-

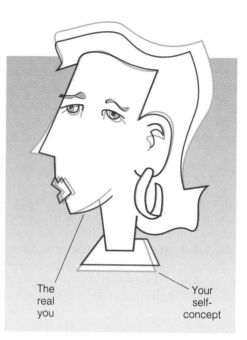

Your self and your self-concept should be close but may not be exactly the same.

The real you

Your self-concept

role pattern, the messages nevertheless were incorporated into your scripting process and told you what your long-term expectations were. On the other hand, your family may have sent you messages such as, "When you grow up to be a woman, you might like to be an attorney or a physician. How would you like to be a firefighter and ride in a shiny, red fire engine?"

Expectations can exert a very powerful force on your self-concept. Even now, as you go through college, you may be evaluating some of your expectations. Are they ones that you accept, or have they just been in your mind forever, without examination? Are there roles that you would like to create for yourself? If so, you are thinking about what we call *self-fulfilling prophecies.*

Self-Fulfilling Prophecy

Prophecies are messages about what you expect. Moreover, you can strongly affect whether or not they come true. For example, you may convince yourself

---

IMPROVING COMPETENCY

Self-Fulfilling Prophecy

Try composing a list of the prophecies you think you have heard in your family regarding your career. Can you list the ones from each parent or from other figures in your past—perhaps a teacher or a friend? Once you have your list, see how many of the prophecies you have examined consciously and which ones you have simply accepted. Share your list with a classmate.

THE STORY OF COMMUNICATION

The Power of Imagination

The world's greatest diver, Greg Louganis, was featured on the cover of *Sports Illustrated* after he won the 1988 Olympics. When asked about his dive practice, he said that the most important part of it was going home, sitting quietly in his room with his eyes closed, and mentally rehearsing every dive until he could do it perfectly—in his head. This practice session would last 20 or 30 minutes a day, and it was one he never skipped.

that you will do poorly on an exam, and when the results come back, you have indeed done poorly. Attitude can affect outcome, which also means that you can create a positive outcome.

The field of sports psychology is filled with positive-expectation training for athletes. For instance, athletes use visualization to create a positive image of themselves in performance—a mental image that helps them to practice and reach the prophesied level of performance. You can find positive visualization in many areas of performance—speaking, singing, business management, and sports.

If a teacher tells you, "I'm sure you'll never understand this material," that teacher is suggesting a negative expectation to you. Some people have a self-concept that is highly susceptible to such suggestions, and they may wither under such a comment. A person with a strong self-concept will react differently and may suggest a counterprophecy by saying, "Oh, yeah? I can pass any test you can make up!" While the strong response is a sign of positive imagery, the student who says it still needs to counter the teacher's perception by actually passing a test or in some way showing that he or she does indeed understand the material.

THOUGHTS, FEELINGS, AND DREAMS

Thinking, feeling, and dreaming are important parts of your self-concept—your communication with yourself. You respond to an array of factors within your mind. You have values, attitudes, and beliefs, images, roles, and expectations. You have a reservoir of talents and abilities but an awareness of only some of them. You process information only partially, because your perceptions are limited by your thinking style and your physical ability to handle information. You are also limited by the psychological filters and screens about which you learned in Chapter 3—the barriers that come between incoming information and your reception of it. Each of these factors varies in different people, but each barrier is at work in all of us.

Thinking Style

Much work in educational research has been done recently on cognitive style—the way in which you typically receive and process information. You may be pri-

Your style of thinking helps to create your self-image.

marily a visual learner—that is, you attend to and best comprehend the information you can see. People who prefer this style of learning like to diagram, outline, sketch, or read. Or you might be a verbal learner, most responsive to auditory information, in which case you prefer to listen—to descriptions, sounds, or impressions. Some people learn by physically doing something; this is the kinesthetic style. When you communicate intrapersonally, do you doodle or sketch? You might have a visual or a kinesthetic learning style. Do you mumble aloud or even shout at yourself? If you are alone and you hit your finger while hammering, do you comment out loud, exclaiming, "Ow! That was really dumb!"? If so, you might have a verbal cognitive style.

The manner in which you communicate to yourself may provide clues to the cognitive style you prefer. In trying to improve instruction, many teachers are now looking at cognitive styles—their own and those of their students. If a teacher is providing information in only one style, that message may be lost on students who are working primarily in other styles. Good teaching, like good communication, probably means being able to recognize and function in a variety of styles. An aware teacher may try to communicate at least the important points in the information in a variety of ways. An aware student who is not easily following or comprehending a particular teacher should try to get help from someone who communicates in a more compatible cognitive style than the teacher does. Perhaps a mismatch in cognitive styles is at the heart of the miscommunication between teacher and student.

In addition to taking the critical-thinking approach to communication described in Chapter 4, you can also approach the subject of thinking from an intrapersonal communication perspective. Three functions of thinking have been identified as follows: (1) to interpret, (2) to solve problems, and (3) to create (Jabusch and Littlejohn, 1981).

Interpretation.   When you think to interpret, you are communicating with yourself to classify, group, or cluster information coming in through your perceptions so that they make sense. You may make broad connections, as when people connect Chinese food and Japanese food by saying, "They're really about the same, right?" Wrong, actually, but they are both Asian, and both use rice, so for many people with limited experiences, these two bits of information are sufficient to form a single concept—Asian food—and then cluster or classify many items under this concept. Another way in which we use interpretation is to reason from one idea or bit of information to draw conclusions about that information. The syllogism and the Toulmin model described in Chapter 4 are examples of this aspect of your thinking processes.

Problem Solving.   If you are communicating within yourself to solve a problem, you probably begin with a few ideas and then compare potential outcomes with desired benefits. Or you are engaging in reflective thinking to solve a problem when you decide which class to take next term or whether to change your major. When you finish reflecting, you may take the next step: planning. With this type of self-communication, you plot out a strategy, make a list or create a sequence of ideas, think about them, and evaluate their likelihood of getting you to a desired goal.

Creativity.   The final area of thinking—creativity—may be the most fun to do and the most difficult to describe. When you brainstorm by letting your mind wander around a certain point, idea, or problem, you are tapping the creative dimension of your intrapersonal communication processes. Sometimes, you will have an instant insight into the problem or idea. Called by many investigators the *"Aha!" phenomenon,* it refers to the experience of getting an idea "out of the blue." Actually, the idea or solution to the problem is a product of the creative connections that your thought processes make when you switch from the focused, step-by-step orientation of interpretation and problem solving into a free-flowing, associational mode of thinking.

Much of the time, unfortunately, you are not called on to be creative in the school setting. The emphasis there is on the more routine methods of learning terms, concepts, and facts. Traditional, American public education could pay more attention to developing the creative ability in students, and some changes are taking place. For example, many high schools now require some form of creative arts class before a student can graduate. Being able to shift gears appropriately among your intrapersonal communication styles—to interpret, solve problems, or be creative—is a valuable communication skill. Some courses can actually help you to develop that ability and to realize your potential for rich, intrapersonal communication.

Physical Limitations

Given the obvious limitations that blockages such as deafness or blindness cause, each channel of communication has only a finite capacity to carry information. The notion of **channel capacity** means that you can process only a certain amount of information before you reach overload. You have probably been to a party in a crowded room with many people talking, loud music, and the visual distraction of people moving in and out of your line of sight, dancing in one area, eating in another. In that setting, it is difficult to remain focused on a person who is talking to you. Your channel for active listening is receiving its maximum input.

After the party, you might be at home, sitting alone quietly. But you might be worried about a test coming up the next day, a problem with your roommate that needs settling, bills that are due in the next few days, an important date coming up with someone you hope turns out to be special, and a phone call that you have not yet returned. Now you are reading this chapter and trying to remember everything about intrapersonal communication. But are you really reading this chapter? When your *internal* channel is overloaded, it is virtually impossible for you to take anything in from the outside. Go pay a few bills, get the problem with your roommate straightened out, return the phone call, and then come back and finish reading. You did not clear out all of the competing information, but you cleared out enough of it that you now have the capacity to read these words and worry about just one other thing. Recognizing overload is a skill in that it lets you know when you are getting close to breaking down. Breakdowns lead to extreme fatigue, lack of concentration, depression, or mental illness.

Finally, we all use psychological filters and screens to let some information in and keep the rest out. These filters may come from our values, as when we pay more attention to the advertisements for products, candidates, or speakers we like. Filters may also come from previous experiences, fears, or expectations. Our self-concept may prevent us from hearing negative feedback from a friend or may allow us to hear only negative feedback. When our ego, emotions, or fears are involved in a communication experience, our filters and screens work overtime. In a way, then, filters are part of our ego defense system. They help us to protect our self-concept and, as such, perform a kind of survival function for us. On the other hand, they also serve to inhibit the honest feedback we need to help us change in a positive direction. For example, the French Queen Marie Antoinette said, "Let them eat cake!" when she was told that the people of Paris had no bread to eat. Because of the way she filtered information, she had no idea that people could be living in such poverty that running out of one kind of food did not mean simply switching to another, as she would have done. The extreme form of using filters as a defense mechanism can be called *denial*. This term describes behaviors in which people refuse to recognize, deal with or even see an event that is too painful, horrible or threatening. Victims of various types of abuse often protect themselves by shutting out any aspect of the abusive behavior.

FUNCTIONAL AND DYSFUNCTIONAL COMMUNICATION SYSTEMS

One of the first signs you may have about how someone is feeling is that his communication behavior undergoes changes that reflect those feelings. Obvious examples are a constantly downcast facial expression and a voice that is consistently low in tone and cadence. Someone with a habitually self-effacing style

CRITICAL THINKING IN COMMUNICATION

Filters and Screens

One of the basic elements of critical thinking is to gather complete, relevant information, or data. As your data pool grows, you have more ways in which to look at and process information.

Unfortunately, Marie Antoinette was not alone in her ability to filter out data. At a convention of educators in Los Angeles, I heard one highly placed, well-educated official of the U. S. Department of Education suggest that the way to solve discipline and drug abuse problems in the public schools was to have "Dad lay down the law" more, while "Mom could visit the school, volunteer her time, and read to the children more at night." However, many of the homes to which children return every day have only one parent, who often works several jobs. Visiting school and reading more at night are simply not options for these single parents. Yet the government official spoke as if the ideal of the traditional nuclear family, with a strong father to enforce rules and a housewife-mother with plenty of time to volunteer in the schools, is the norm in Los Angeles—or in any major city, for that matter.

Perceptual screens and filters are at work in everyone. The critical thinker is aware of that fact and attempts to gather as much information as possible, even if some of it is unpleasant and contradictory to what he or she would like to believe.

who also avoids contact with people may be experiencing stress in terms of his or her mental health.

Communication and Mental Health

The internal communication system is your own private monitor of your mental health. When your internal messages get scrambled, when you cannot make sense of the data you get from the outside world, when your conclusions are consistently refuted, you may be experiencing signs that your mental health is at risk. An extreme example of this phenomenon is schizophrenia. Someone may say, "Hello, Jeanie!" and the person listening may *hear* "Hello, Marie Antoinette!" because she believes that she is the former queen of France. People suffering from schizophrenia do not function as realistic communicators. One way to approach the treatment of mental illness is to look at its communication-related attributes. Autism is a mental illness that precludes any interaction or communication with stimuli outside of the self. The image of a child rocking alone in a corner is a good representation of autism—a condition of total, exclusive self-communication. Autism is intrapersonal communication carried to the extreme of excluding any other source but the self.

Is mental health the same as *not* being mentally ill? In other words, if you are open to messages from outside yourself and are in touch with reality enough to know that you are a college student and not the monarch of France, are you mentally healthy? Positive intrapersonal communication goes beyond the mere

THE STORY OF COMMUNICATION

Autistic Savants

You may have seen the film *Rain Man,* in which Dustin Hoffman plays an autistic savant—that is, someone who has very low interpersonal communication abilities but fantastic mental abilities in other areas. Not all people with autism have these abilities, but some do, and their stories fascinate professional communication researchers as well as the general public. In this film, the character Raymond actually functioned beyond the level of most autistic people; but through Hoffman's powerful performance, viewers did get a glimpse of the kind of intrapersonal communication that such people experience.

absence of problems; it means to improve your internal message sending and responding constantly so that you reach *optimal* levels of functioning. You can be adequate but still have room for improvement. A positive ability to communicate well within yourself leads to a positive mental outlook. Self-fulfilling prophecies become important in this context. If you send yourself positive messages about yourself, you can guide your behaviors toward matching the messages.

Communication and Achievement

As was previously noted, athletes the world over practice positive imaging to become better at their sport. If you repeat a message over and over, it becomes part of your subconscious—an almost automatic source of internal messages. You can use this intrapersonal communication strategy to enhance your mental well-being and your levels of accomplishment. For example, some Olympic weight lifters were told that the weight on some barbells was the same as barbells they had already lifted successfully. In actuality, the weight was greater than what they had ever lifted before. Because they thought they could, they did in fact lift the heavier weight. Later, they were given the same barbells to lift but were told the real weight. They failed to lift the weight, and they failed because they thought they would fail.

Clearly, optimal intrapersonal communication functioning needs to be a product of both your skills and your attitudes. When you examine your attitudes, adjust them to reflect a positive mental outlook. Recall that in Chapter 2 you learned about communication apprehension (CA). One of the strategies for dealing with apprehension was to change your vision of yourself. You learned that you can reduce your levels of anxiety and thereby increase your level of performance—a good example of how you can actually make important mental adjustments.

People with CA are often painfully aware of it, and their awareness may lead them to have low self-esteem. They may feel inadequate, and their internal messages are those of incompetence and lack of personal worth. Again, both mental health and achievement are negatively affected in people with high levels of CA. You probably experience some anxiety or tension before giving a speech or going to an important interview. While those sensations are perfectly normal and universal, even those levels of apprehension may affect you slightly in the form of negative communicative outcomes. You may increase dysfluencies—your "ums," and "uhs," during a job interview—or you may lose your train of thought during a speech. These minor dysfunctions may create a negative impression in your listeners; they can also reinforce a negative self-image. For those reasons, it is important to work on improving intrapersonal communication.

IMPROVING SELF-COMMUNICATION COMPETENCY

You have already taken an important first step toward developing optimal intrapersonal communication abilities by learning about yourself, the factors that make up your values, your perceptions, and your internal message systems. Remember the four areas of communication competency: repertoire, selection, implementation, and evaluation. Each of these can be developed at the same time that you enhance your intrapersonal communication abilities.

You can expand your repertoire by understanding the variety of ways to process information. You can try to see new perspectives, take another point of view, and question your repeated use of strategies that do not seem to get the results you want. As you expand the number of ways in which you receive information and process it, you can experiment with selecting different ones as appropriate. After analyzing a situation and remembering past responses to it, you may elect to withhold a quick judgment of information, or you may try to evaluate a comment from several viewpoints before you react. You may experiment by shifting from one thinking pattern such as problem solving, to another one, such as creativity.

Putting these insights into practice will allow you to implement different skills. Try a new way of reacting. For example, respond from your rational self rather than your emotional self the next time you think you are being slighted. Conversely, try reacting with your feelings when you are faced with a tough problem that defies logical solution. Finally, take careful note of how these new strategies are working or failing in a given situation. Evaluate your success and make any adjustments that are needed. The important thing is to keep trying, to keep evaluating until you sense improvement in your intrapersonal communication skills.

SUMMARY

You are a social being, and the basis for your interactions in the social world is your self. You have inside you a flexible core of values, attitudes, and beliefs that shape the way you think, the way you process information internally, and the way you send messages out to the rest of the world. Your perceptions are both the product of your internal communication patterns and a screen through which information must pass to become meaning-ful to you. Both your thoughts and feelings are important to your becoming an integrated communicator. The messages you send yourself about yourself create your self-concept. Your message sending and receiving can result in positive feelings and enhanced abilities, or they may become negative and damage your self-worth. Your ability to communicate well internally affects your ability to communicate well with the world around you. You can unlock much potential for success if you can first develop and expand your intrapersonal communication skills. Overcoming the negative effects of severe communication apprehension is one positive, proactive step you can take to launch yourself on the road to optimal communication experiences.

KEY TERMS

intrapersonal communication, *p. 118*
self-concept, *p. 120*
body image, *p. 121*
values, *p. 124*

attitudes, *p. 124*
beliefs, *p. 124*
perceptions, *p. 125*
channel capacity, *p. 129*

EXERCISES

1. List the five or ten most important values you hold. Test them against your actions. Do you behave in ways that are consistent with your values? What circumstances cause you to modify, or add qualifiers or reservations to, your values?

2. Take five minutes to create an idealized vision of yourself. What do you look like? What talents do you possess? What are your living circumstances? Now select one aspect of your vision that you think can come true, even partially, in the next few weeks or months. What steps would you have to take to bring it about?

3. Ask a friend to describe three things about you in writing, such as height, personality traits, and likes or dislikes. At the same time, write your own description of the same three items. Now reverse roles, and do the same for your friend. Compare notes, and see how closely your description of yourself matches your friend's description of you.

4. Describe to a classmate one special activity or interaction you had with your parents that you think was worthwhile and that you would like to do if you were a parent. Is there one thing you would do differently? Compare notes with your classmate to discover whether there are similarities.

REFERENCES

Fine, G. A., and Kleinman, S. "Network and Meaning: An Interactionist Approach to Structure." *Symbolic Interaction*, 6 (1983).

Hecht, M. L., M. J. Collier, and S. A. Ribeau. *African American Communication*. Newbury Park: Sage, 1993.

Jabusch, D. M., and S. W. Littlejohn. *Elements of Speech Communication*. Boston: Houghton Mifflin, 1981.

Interpersonal Communication

After reading this chapter, you should be able to:

- Define interpersonal communication and its relationship to affection, inclusion, and control needs.
- Describe communication and relationship development.
- Feel confident with your everyday interpersonal interactions.
- Understand communication climates and conflict.
- Develop conflict management strategies.
- Improve your interpersonal skills.

he social self meets another's self as you take your internal messages and send them out. When you turn from thinking, dreaming, and other internal forms of communication, it's time to step out and face the world and connect with other people. Just as you move from dreams and get up each morning to begin interacting with others during the day, this chapter moves from the intrapersonal world of thoughts to the interpersonal world of interaction. Of course, you never leave the self behind, just as you can often recall your dreams during the day. For purposes of breaking the study of communication into manageable units, we divide the chapters, but all the elements of communication are constantly present and constantly interacting—listening and thinking, verbal and nonverbal communication, and intrapersonal and interpersonal communication. We look in this chapter at what happens when you take your self out for a walk and it meets another self.

DEFINITION OF INTERPERSONAL COMMUNICATION

Simply put, **interpersonal communication** is a communication transaction involving two or more people, but this chapter emphasizes the one-to-one setting. Even this general definition implies so much and includes all the rich interaction that takes place in a socially meaningful pair. For example, when you buy gas and give the station attendant your money, you are engaging in an interpersonal exchange, but it is not the meaningful relationship you have with close friends or even with other members of this class. A useful distinction can be made between the brief, transaction communication of the sales exchange and the personal relationship that builds over time and involves your thoughts and feelings beyond a superficial level. Therefore a full definition of interpersonal communication is communication transactions between individuals in a personal relationship.

Personal relationships are part of our daily lives. They affect us constantly and in meaningful ways. As interpersonal communication researcher Stephen Duck (1985) put it, "People's lives are fabricated in and by their relationships with other people. Out greatest moments of joy and sorrow are founded in relationships." The values and attitudes that were discussed in the previous chapter were developed in our relationships with others. Self-concept is derived largely from the messages we received in interpersonal settings.

These messages are part of the interaction—the give-and-take—of a personal setting. The messages can be intense largely because they are so direct and focused. Just you and one person, or perhaps two others, are involved in the interaction. The message cannot get lost in a noisy crowd, and the feedback is immediate and clearly directed.

There are, however, some risks in this type of communication because of the private setting. What we talk about in these situations is often ourselves and our immediate relationships. We discuss things we think about, feel, worry about, and things that are important to us. Good interpersonal communication also includes discussing matters that are important to the relationship. All of these topics come under the heading of self-disclosure. When you talk about things that others are not likely to know about you without directly asking you, you are engaging in self-disclosure.

The Johari Window

One useful way to think about self-disclosure is the **Johari Window** (Luft, 1969). The Johari Window is a diagram that represents your self, how much you know about yourself, and how much others know about you. Four possible combinations of knowledge about yourself are illustrated in the diagram: (1) things you and others know about you, (2) things you know but nobody else knows, (3) things others know about you that you do not know, and (4) things about you that are known neither to yourself nor to others. These four possible types of public and private knowledge are represented by the four quadrants of the diagram, which looks somewhat like a window with four panes of glass. Moreover, the term *window*—that is, a place for looking out and looking in—is especially appropriate in the interpersonal communication context. Let us look at each quadrant of the window and see how these possibilities operate in communication involving self-disclosure.

Things everybody knows fall into the quadrant called the *open* pane. Your physical appearance, gender, hair color, occupation, and general economic situation can all be inferred by anyone who observes you or listens to your spontaneous conversations in your public moments.

The *hidden* pane covers those things that you know about yourself but conceal from others. You may have secret fantasies or aspects of your past or your personality that you wish to keep private. You may have habits you conceal, tastes in food, or a secret ambition that no one else knows about. Even in the context of very close, long-term, personal relationships, you may still keep some information hidden.

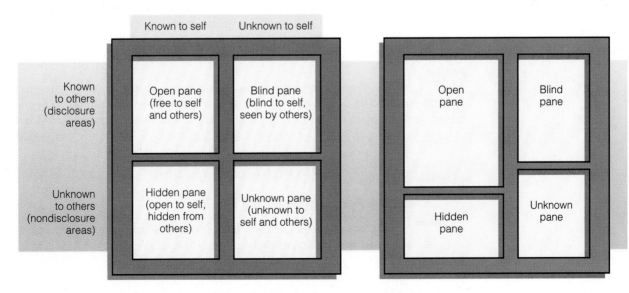

The Johari window is a way of looking at your self-disclosure and self-knowledge.

THE STORY OF COMMUNICATION

The Origin of Johari

When you first saw the words *Johari Window*, what did you think about the term *Johari*? Is it a town in Pakistan where this idea was born? Is it the name of the Japanese communication scholar who developed it? Is it the name of an exotic animal from Bali or a rare wood from India? Many students have suggested these and other ideas. The second idea comes closest to the truth. The window is associated with Professors Luft and Ingram, who devised the concept. *Luft-Ingram Window* did not seem very interesting to them, so they combined their first names—Joseph and Harry—to form *Johari*.

The area that represents things that others know about you but that are unknown to you is called the *blind* pane. You may have heard it said that someone has a "blind spot" about a certain issue or person. This expression means that a person simply does not recognize in himself something that is all too obvious to others. Your self-concept may be such that you think you are taller than you really are; or you might not believe that you have a good voice, though others like your voice very much. You may have a talent for doing a particular job, building relationships, or solving problems—talents that others recognize in you—yet you may be unaware of these qualities. Having a blind spot can often mean quite the opposite. You might give yourself credit for having a great sense of humor and not notice that others never laugh at your jokes.

Finally, there are probably things about you that are as yet undiscovered by anyone. You may have a talent for harmonica playing but have never tried it. You may have likes or dislikes that have never been called on or tested and thus are part of the *unknown* pane. If you have not thought about, read about, heard about, or tried something, you simply have no exposure to it or information to guide you in self-knowledge about that thing. Since we cannot know or try everything, we are bound to always have some unexplored territory in ourselves.

The processes of interpersonal communication often deal with the areas (panes) just described. You can try opinions or ideas about yourself out on your friends to develop them or modify them. If these ideas were previously hidden

IMPROVING COMPETENCY

Check Your Perceptions with a Friend

Try filling out your own personal Johari Window. How much area do you think you should allot to each quadrant? Next, ask a trusted friend or two to make up a Johari Window diagram showing how they perceive you. Do the diagrams resemble each other? If not, what significant differences do you find? How can you explain these differences?

from others, then the hidden pane of your self gets a little smaller, and the open pane gets a little larger. The Johari Window is a kind of shorthand that describes how we act in interpersonal settings. Some of us have large open panes; others have larger hidden or blind panes. The process of interpersonal communication, if it is authentic, inevitably involves enlarging the open area and making some combination of the others smaller.

What motivates us to engage in this type of communication? One explanation is provided by looking at our interpersonal *needs*—that is, those needs that can be met only through interaction with others. These interpersonal requirements have been classified as *affection-inclusion-control* needs and have been the subject of study of researcher William Schutz (Schutz, 1958).

Inclusion, Affection, and Control Needs

One of the ways we use communication is to express and receive **affection.** Schutz contends that a basic component of human makeup is the need for affection, and we fulfill that need with our interpersonal relationships. The range of our emotions goes beyond affection, of course, but the positive regard, or affection, that we get from others is a central and motivating force behind our interpersonal interactions.

You will find affection in many situations and dimensions. You can have an affectionate regard for family members and loved ones. Another dimension of affection is close friends, such as roommates or team members. You may feel affection for some associates at work or fellow members of your organizations or clubs. Of most importance in your life will most likely be a long-term interaction in a relationship with a significant other person.

The messages you send and receive that exhibit warmth, support, respect, genuine interest, and empathy are all mechanisms to communicate affection to others and to help you meet this need in yourself. The reciprocal nature of interpersonal communication is most evident in the area of affection. If you have ever been in a one-way relationship involving affection, you know how frustrating and ultimately unsatisfying such a relationship can be. The need to give and receive affection seems to be a central, motivating force in our lives, and affection is most likely to be found in our interpersonal communications.

Schutz describes **inclusion** needs as the desire to be part of the events and interactions around us. A person who wants to be asked along on every outing or short trip to the store is exhibiting this need, albeit excessively. We may want to join groups or clubs and have seen the tremendous pressures that the need to belong can exert on people. The need to be included is one of the strongest motivating factors for membership in gangs. In fact, it is doubtful that gangs would exist without this powerful need. In the interpersonal realm, wanting to be noticed by others and included in their relationships is an expression of the need for inclusion.

Finally, **control** needs relate to the desire to feel secure and safe in our surroundings. We want to have power over our environment, ourselves, and other people, or we want to feel that structures, systems, and rules are in place so that we can have a sense of security. On one level, this need for control may express itself as the ability to influence another person—to have someone listen to our opinion and react to it in a significant way. On another level, the need for control

We relate most easily to those whom we perceive to be similar to ourselves.

may involve dominating another person through manipulation or bullying tactics. Emotional blackmail, another example of control needs, begins for many children at a very early age with the playground message "Let me have that or I won't be your friend!" This type of message is a control strategy, and it uses our need for affection and inclusion as the tools of its control.

Each of these three needs is part of the dynamics of interpersonal interaction in that the needs drive us to engage in relationships in order to be fulfilled. Next, we will see that our communication develops in a regular pattern during the course of a relationship. That pattern has come under increasing scrutiny by experts in the field of relational communication.

COMMUNICATION AND RELATIONSHIP DEVELOPMENT

You are a social being, which means that you exist partly in terms of your relationships with other social beings. As you live your life, there are various stages that you must experience. We are first infants, then children, adolescents, young adults, middle-aged adults, and senior citizens. In much the same way that life stages follow a predictable course, the **relationship development** has typical patterns which can be described and understood.

Although each relationship has its own unique aspects, there are general patterns that seem to be consistent, no matter what the setting happens to be. Communication scholar Mark Knapp has studied these patterns and has identified ten stages in the relationship process from beginning to end (Knapp, 1984). The coming-together stages include the following: initiating, experimenting, intensifying, integrating, and bonding. When a relationship begins to come apart, it goes through the following five stages: differentiating, circum-scribing, stagnating, avoiding, and terminating. While other scholars' research brings up questions about Knapp's descriptions (Baxter and Wilmot, 1983), his terminology can provide a useful reference point for identifying and examining different aspects of an interpersonal relationship. Each of these stages is discussed here as a way of viewing the communication changes people go through as relationships grow and then decline. Your interactions may or may not follow this pattern, but having this information may help you to understand what is happening in your relationships.

Coming Together

The first stage, *initiating*, is filled with communication data. You may have heard that you "never get a second chance to make a first impression." That observation stresses the importance of the interaction that takes place during an initial meeting. Your first contact allows you to form an immediate, complex, and lasting impression. You make an evaluation of a person's potential for future relationship development, and you may also draw a host of other conclusions about his or her intelligence, interests, economic status, and so on. The other person is doing exactly the same thing while meeting and observing *you*.

The other person's physical aspects are easiest to observe, and the attention and effort we put into our appearance reflects our understanding of this fact. During this stage, you make contact, say hello, and engage in conversation about impersonal matters that you may have in common—the course you take together; the concert you are both attending; the restaurant, day, or event you are currently experiencing; and, if all else fails, the weather. This stage may take a few minutes or a few weeks.

When you have sufficient information and responses from the other person to establish an open channel for communication, you are ready to move to the next step: *experimenting*. In this stage, you make an effort to continue the inter-action and to include other topics of a more specific and perhaps more personal nature. You might engage in an evaluation of the shared event or class. You venture opinions on different types of food or restaurants or movies.

This experimenting can involve an exchange of information about a wide variety of topics. Much of the information that you would include in the open segment of your personal Johari Window would come from the communication that takes place at this stage of a relationship.

Notice that a relationship moves from one stage to the next only if both parties continue the pattern. If the other person ignores you or keeps the subjects of conversation focused on weather and other impersonal topics, then you are getting a signal that the relationship is still in the initiating stage. It is likely that you have been in a situation in which someone initiates contact with you but you have no interest in further development, so you try to find a way to discourage the sharing of personal information. You can do this by not responding; by responding in short, neutral, and noncommittal tones; by not volunteering information about yourself; and, when pressed, by declining to respond or responding on only the most general level. Suppose that someone at a party wants to initiate a relationship faster than you do. She asks, "So, where do you live?" You might respond, "Around campus." The person might persist, saying,

"Really? So do I! What street?" You could avoid continuing the interaction and furthering the relationship by keeping your communication at the same level as the previous answer. You could say, "Well, let's just say it's close enough to walk." You have given a clear signal of disinterest, and you hope that the other person is sensitive enough to understand the full meaning of your response. If she is not and continues, "So, tell me your address," you might need to reply, "Excuse me, I'm going to try some of the snacks," and literally walk away from the person.

Stage three, *intensifying*, assumes that both parties are mutually interested in developing the relationship further on the basis of the information and responses that occurred during the experimenting stage. One of the main indications that this stage has begun is the amount of time you spend in each others' company. In potentially romantic relationships, you begin dating. Going to places that you discovered were of mutual interest in your experimenting conversations is one dating idea. Virtually all of the open information in each one's Johari Window is known to the other, and you begin to disclose to each other some of the topics reserved in the hidden pane. You may even offer each other some feedback about information observed in your blind panes. At this point, the feedback regarding your blind panes is likely to focus on the positive attributes you see in each other and less likely to involve any criticism.

This pattern is more likely to occur in a developing romantic relationship. Physical contact is likely and becomes more frequent. In friendship relationships, there may be some borrowing and using of personal items, such as an article of clothing, music items, and money. As the relationship develops, a series of mutual experiences begin to accumulate. A mutual code, such as a set of shorthand references to events that only the pair understand, begins to emerge. Perhaps they were eating out together and the cashier dropped their check and exclaimed in an unusual voice, "Excuse me. I'm *so* clumsy!" From then on, whenever anyone drops something, one will start the code sentence by saying "Excuse me . . . ," and the other will finish, often mimicking the unusual voice of the cashier, ". . . I'm *so* clumsy!" after which both parties laugh intensely, leaving others in the room wondering what the reference is. Signs of such communication interactions strongly indicate that a relationship has moved into the intensifying phase.

If both parties find that their interpersonal needs are being met in a particular relationship, and if they feel comfortable enough, they may move on to the next step: *integrating*. At this stage, they are together often enough that their friends and associates begin expecting to see both of them when they see one of them. Mutual friends now feel that they can inquire about the absent one with the expectation that the one who is present will know the answer. Meanwhile, the partners themselves may divulge more and more private information to each other and develop a feeling of strong, mutual trust. They may freely use each other's personal items without first asking permission. They may make social and other commitments for each other on the assumption that they know each other's schedule and likely response. People will ask one of them about the other's tastes, preferences, and opinions. For example, if Pat and Chris are very good friends, you could ask Pat, "Do you think Chris would be interested in going out with my roommate?" People both perceive and treat the relationship as a single unit. Inviting one of them to a party means inviting both. If they are

Could improved interpersonal skills be useful to you?

in a romantic relationship, they will be treated as a couple; in a strong friendship, they will be treated as best friends.

In your lifetime, you will probably have only a few such relationships—perhaps with a family or school friend and with a marriage partner. Your personal Johari Window has a very large open pane because of the nature of your communication with these important people in your life. Any negative information from your blind pane can now be shared in the form of feedback from them. Their personalities may be different from yours, but they most likely hold and respect essentially the same values and enduring outlook oil the world that you do.

The final stage in developing a close relationship is called *bonding*. This type of formal coming together may, at one level, be exemplified by an agreement to rent an apartment or lease a house together. Initiation ceremonies in sororities and fraternities also contain elements of formal bonding. At another level of bonding, as in romantic relationships, there may be an engagement announcement or a joining together of household or financial matters in a public, formal way.

Marriage, of course, constitutes the most formal bonding activity in the area of interpersonal relationships. At this stage, communication patterns between the two members of the relationship are fully integrated and intense. The marriage partners constitute a formal unit, and even people who barely know them will be able to ascertain the status of the relationship and treat the pair as a unit. Their Johari Windows will continue to change in the same direction as before, with the open pane growing and the other three diminishing correspondingly. You are a unique and complex individual; and although it could take a lifetime for a partner to get to know everything about you, the impetus of a continuing, bonded relationship is always to create larger and larger open areas. One of the factors that may, in fact, contribute to a stable, long-term, bonded relationship is a sense of continual growth in knowledge— of both the self and the other.

Not all relationships go through all five of the coming-together stages. In fact, very few get past the first stage, and most people have just a few relationships that make it to the bonding level. Knapp indicates that each step follows and builds on the previous ones. In fact, a relationship may even reverse direction or terminate. Depending on several factors, including the type of relationship (romantic or friendship) as well as the uniqueness and flexibility of the communication, the reversal or termination may take several forms (Baxter, 1983). Knapp believes that when a relationship begins to deteriorate, there are five levels that they can go through. This view can provide a useful way to talk about your relationships.

Coming Apart

Knapp calls the first stage of coming apart *differentiating*. This phase of the relationship mirrors the initiating stage; but instead of focusing on what the two people involved have in common, it is characterized by the communication of differences. Conversations begin to be dominated by what one person does, likes, thinks about, admires, or tolerates that is different from what the other does, likes, and so on. "Chinese food again! I never did care for it," or "Do we always have to listen to your CDs? I'd much prefer something else." If communication goes beyond simply acknowledging or pointing out differences, conflict is the likely result. You may have visited friends who are at this stage in their relationship and found yourself in the middle of such conflict. They may even ask you to side with one or the other or to arbitrate the conflict. In romantic relationships, stress is placed on communication when the initial positive regard the couple used to feel for each other is replaced by the constant, mutual identification of areas of difference. They may begin encoding messages—discussing each other in the third person even when they are both still in the room. "Did you see what he does? Leaves his dirty dishes right there all day, as if I were his mother." These types of messages lead to hostile and defensive behavior, and the Johari Window begins to revert back to the earlier configuration of a smaller open pane and a larger hidden pane.

The next stage is called *circumscribing* and can, once again, be identified by the message patterns that are evident in the relationship. Instead of taking telephone messages for each other, they simply tell a caller to call back and speak directly to the absent partner. They begin to deal together only in matters of little substance and to avoid issues of personal importance. Requests for information or assistance become routine and brief. If there is a strong desire to continue the relationship, conversation may turn to the state of the relationship itself.

If friends or roommates are having the conflict, an honest and frank discussion may clear up the problem and return the relationship to a positive mode. A third party may have to assist, or the two people involved may be able to work on the relationship together. Obviously, if one party does not wish to continue the relationship, any attempts to focus on its improvement will be met by an attitude of neutrality and a minimal response. It is also possible that focusing on the relationship will bring out further dissatisfaction. Additional areas of discontent may be revealed and old problems revived, so that renewed conflict flares up. In couple communication, focusing on the relationship often increases the difficulty rather than resolving it. If there is a mutual desire to maintain the association, a professional third party, such as a qualified counselor or therapist, may be consulted. Such a person can teach the couple alternative ways of managing conflict so that it is resolved and not simply deferred, only to return repeatedly in new rounds of circumscribed communication.

While they are in this stage, even if they are actively involved in counseling, the partners in the relationship will probably still be perceived as a viable pair by others and will continue doing together the things they are used to doing together.

By the time a relationship reaches the third stage, *stagnating*, it is well on its way to coming apart. Silence is the hallmark of this communication pattern. Brief exchanges of a necessary nature, such as "Please hand me the bread" or "It's time to pay the rent; I'd like your half today or tomorrow," are typical. A neutral, flat feeling accompanies interactions at this stage. You might think that this is a short stage, but some couples fall into this pattern and remain in it for years. Sometimes, religious belief concerning marriage, restrictions on finances, housing needs, children, social pressure, or other factors may keep the relationship together so that it has the appearance of the relationship as it existed in earlier stages. But for the two people involved, stagnation is all too obvious.

Overt unpleasantness in virtually every interaction is indicative of stage four, *avoidance*. At this stage, it is annoying to be around each other, hostility is usually in their tones of voice, and direct antagonism permeates their interpersonal communication. In a friendship situation, they avoid seeing each other, and one perhaps makes a direct request of the other to discontinue the interaction. Couples will come and go without acknowledging their actions to each other, eat and sleep at different times and in different places, watch television in different rooms, and so on. Roommates may alter their patterns so that one of them is not around when the other is home, choosing to stay late at the library to study or spending more time in friends' apartments. If there is a time dimension to the relationship, as with school roommates who are nearing the end of a term, preparations begin for the termination of the relationship. New roommates are sought, and new places to live are explored without the other being involved. In other circumstances in which no obvious or natural break occurs, the final stage, *termination*, begins.

In termination, Knapp has identified three distinct types of message that can be expected as the relationship comes to a formal end (Knapp et al., 1973). Partners signal this stage by first summarizing the relationship. "Well, we sure had some good times at first, didn't we?" or "Well, this semester together has had its ups and downs." Much like the conclusion of a speech, the summary tells the receiver that the interaction is coming to closure. Next come statements telling the other that interaction will be limited or stopped. Someone might say, "We just can't see each other again" or "We'd better limit ourselves to just finishing English class and not get together anymore outside of class." One could, of course, be more restrictive with a message such as "Don't ever call me again!" In the final-message form of terminating a relationship, you point out what you would like the future relationship to be like. It could range from "I still like working with you, so I hope we can get together on some projects in the future" to "I hope I never see your face again!" In a school setting, you may run into the other person again inadvertently, so such a total termination may be impossible to maintain. In a marriage with children, unless one partner will never again be involved in the lives of the children, future interaction is almost impossible to avoid. There are graduations, weddings, birthdays, and other events in the children's lives at which both parents are likely to be present. So even if the termination occurs under painful and angry circumstances, the partners may agree to try to avoid further stress on the children through some sort of contract. For example, one of them might say, "Since we'll probably see each other at events for our children, I hope we can be cordial to each other." Ending a relationship is never easy, but communication scholars have found that we can learn and use certain patterns or strategies (Baxter, 1982) that should help us to understand the termination process and assist us as we go through its stages.

This approach to understanding relationships is useful in helping us to understand our interactions, but you should realize that not all relationships follow such a steady or predictable path. Your particular relationship may follow many paths and directions, depending on the choices and events that are unique to your life. What researchers select to observe in any relationship may vary, and so their results may show a variety of trajectories for any specific interaction (Duck and Miell, 1984). Use these patterns simply as a guide to what often happens and what is likely to happen in relationships, taking care to allow for your own individual applications.

Everyday Interpersonal Interactions

Needless to say, most interpersonal communications will not travel the road of full relationship development and decline. In everyday situations, you may have a brief initiating interaction and then move on with hardly a thought about the event. However, important relationships do go through at least some stages of coming together and coming apart and take up some amount of time. When that happens, you are likely to take your attitudes, values, and beliefs further into the relationship. Because we all have slightly different values, attitudes, and beliefs, there is a potential for conflict. The longer and more intense the relationship, the more you reveal of your hidden self. With an increase in interaction involving personal and private matters, there is a greater chance of running into conflict with the other person's self. Moreover, when the social self meets another social self, the potential for conflict is present. This conflict may have both positive and negative effects. Because they are such a constant factor in everyone's life, the elements of this conflict deserve greater attention.

COMMUNICATION CLIMATE AND CONFLICT

What factors contribute to a positive, sustained communication interaction? What helps a relationship stay on track or go sour? Communication scholars have looked at this important question, and the answers to it can help make our relationships work better.

Think about the relationships you have. Some are pleasant, some are uncomfortable. You may be offended if someone signs you up for an activity without asking you first. Or it may bother you when someone expresses his or her ideas so forcefully that they leave you no opportunity to express your opinions. You may be irked by people who always seem to be talking about their exploits—adventures in which they always perform better than anyone else. You may go to a party where you don't know anyone and the other guests ignore you as if you didn't exist. Each of these situations helps to create a *climate*—a feeling or tone to which you respond with dislike. Maybe you become a bit rude or touchy and snap back at others or put a sarcastic tone into your voice. Perhaps *you* are one of the people practicing one-upmanship, ignoring a newcomer, or expressing opinions with absolute certainty. Either way, communication researchers have given much time and attention to the study of communication climate and have achieved some good insights.

The most prevalent description of the environmental factors that help or hurt relationships was developed by Jack Gibb. In the process of observing and studying small-group dynamics, he created six categories of behaviors and identified a *defensive* and a *supportive* style of communicating for these categories (Gibb, 1961). Like Knapp, Gibb may be simplifying and idealizing the situation (Eadie, 1982), but the categories are also a useful way to open up the concepts of communication climate and how conflict arises and may give us some sense of how to avoid or solve conflicts.

The Gibb's Climate Factors are as follows:

Supportive Behaviors	*Defensive Behaviors*
Description	Evaluation
Equality	Superiority
Problem orientation	Control
Spontaneity	Strategy
Empathy	Neutrality
Provisionalism	Certainty

Each style of communicating helps to establish and maintain a particular **communication climate**—that is, a general sense of the tone of the interaction. Some people call this sense or tone the *communication environment,* but it refers to the same feeling or sense or tone of a communication. Each of these styles—supportiveness and defensiveness—is examined in detail to give you a better understanding of how we create and continue a certain tone in our interaction.

Supportiveness

The six styles of a **supportive communication** climate help to maintain an open, inviting, encouraging, positive, accepting, and continuing communication atmosphere. Each of these styles is easily recognizable.

Description is the way you talk about the observed world rather than the inferred world. You talk about what you see, not about what you think might be behind what you see. For example, your roommate comes in and slams down her book. A descriptive comment might be "That was pretty intense. I do that, too, when I'm upset or angry." The statement does not include a reason or guess as to the cause or motive of the behavior, it just describes the observed behavior and invites further clarification.

Equality means that you view the other person in the relationship as being on the same level as you, neither superior nor inferior, and that you communicate such feeling authentically. You would ask this person, "Can I help?" as an expression of cooperation. You would not say, "Here, let me do it for you" as an offer to take on a task that is beyond the other's level. Equality cannot reflect an absolute sameness in talent or ability, but it does imply a regard for the other person as being worthy and deserving of respect.

Problem orientation requires us to look at a situation as an event to be dealt with in a mutually satisfactory way. Otherwise, it may become a contest over who is in control or whose solution is adopted, regardless of the relevance of the outcome to the original problem. Thus people fight over solutions to problems not to find the best one, but to get recognition for having had the winning idea. When one partner in a relationship drops a bowl of spaghetti sauce on the kitchen floor, a problem orientation response is to look for a mop, not to spend time berating the person for being clumsy. A problem orientation looks to the value of an idea per se, regardless of the source. The best solution to a problem may come from an insufferable braggart. That does not matter. Try to get past the person and focus on the worth of the idea. A positive communication climate will be one of the results.

Spontaneity means that you are uncalculating and nonmanipulative in your communications and that you react authentically to people and situations. You do not hold back to calculate a response but are honest in your reactions. Someone who is spontaneous communicates that he or she is open, trusting, and self-confident. You may be thinking about all the times when you need to be less than authentic to be socially correct. For example, when your aunt wears a new perfume that she loves but that reminds you of decayed lilies, you probably say, "It reminds me of garden flowers!" In other words, a certain measure of tact and sensitivity is an important part of our social being and helps us to avoid causing defensiveness in other people. So a balance between always saying just what you think without hesitation and never venturing an honest opinion is the goal of spontaneity in communication.

Empathy as a style of communication means that you share a common core of feelings with the other person. You give the person positive regard, and you identify with his or her emotional state. Having empathy means that you understand a situation from the other person's point of view. Even if the other person's point of view is not exactly the same as your own, you are nevertheless capable of looking at a situation from his or her perspective. It means getting into the other person's shoes and seeing his or her reactions from that person's perspective. Sympathy may simply consist of offering a pat on the back or saying, "That's too bad." Empathy takes more effort, and the effort itself can be felt by the other person as genuine support and caring, rather than impartial concern offered out of courtesy or social obligation. When you make an effort to create empathy, you show that the other person is valued, that his or her feelings are respected, and that the person has worth that you acknowledge.

Finally, by indicating your willingness to wait, *provisionalism* helps to create a supportive communication climate. You wait to consider your responses in order to make them appropriate. You wait before insisting that your solution to a problem is the best so that you can hear all sides of an argument or so that you can listen to your partner explain a different idea or approach. You wait before

CRITICAL THINKING IN COMMUNICATION

Think before You React: Provisionalism

The critical thinker is trained to seek out supporting data—information to support his or her ideas—before accepting them. If critical thinking becomes a habit of mind, then you will apply this skill to interpersonal conversations and interactions as well as to more formal communications. The practice of waiting before reacting buys you the time to engage in some critical thinking. Is a particular statement consistent with what is known? Is it consistent with previous information from this source? Making assessments of information is easier and more accurate if you can give yourself a little time to think about that information—to check it and make logical connections between what is known and what can be assumed. What inferences can you draw that are warranted, and which are not? The critical-thinking mind is always on the alert to such questions, even in conversations.

you make a judgment so that you can check details and make certain you have the necessary information. An open mind helps you to try different ways of looking at a situation or problem, to respect other peoples' approaches, and to let go of your own idea or method if a better one comes along. If you are always sure that you are right, you spend your time and energy defending your ideas, perhaps without listening very well to others. When you start defending, they start defending, and the climate shifts from one of support to one of argumentative, nonproductive bickering.

These six styles of communication—description, equality, problem orientation, spontaneity, empathy, and provisionalism—create a supportive communication climate so that authentic interpersonal communication can take place. You have a direct influence on the creation of a communication climate; and although these styles stress positive, supportive actions, you probably are already aware of the numerous times, perhaps daily, that your relationships are not characterized by supportive communication. You may experience what Gibb describes as a defensive climate.

Defensiveness

Defensive communication climates are characterized by six counterparts to the six supportive communication styles previously discussed. They are all too common in most people's interpersonal communication situations. If that is true for you, too, you will want to know what they are so that you can recognize when and why they come into play. After you have read the brief discussion of the six styles, you will see how to take steps to manage conflict and improve your interpersonal skills.

Evaluation, the first characteristic of defensive climates, is ubiquitous. Your teachers grade you, your friends evaluate your housekeeping skills, and your peers ask you how you did on a test. Your parents want you to stand up straight and eat right, your boss gives you a performance appraisal, and the coach of your softball team yells at you for striking out or flubbing a play. Any judgment, direct or implied, negative or positive, comes under the heading of evaluation and can lead to a defensive climate. The supportive behavior, description, balances evaluation by focusing on objective, observed actions without attaching a value judgment to the communication.

The counterpart to equality is *superiority,* and you will run into this type of communication style all the time. When someone says, "Here, let me show you how that's supposed to be done!" that person is communicating a tone of superiority. The defensive response is often silence or a withdrawal from the communication interaction, resentment, and possibly counterattack. When you perceive that your self-esteem is threatened, you normally make an effort to defend yourself, and a defensive climate is the result of feeling threatened.

Messages of superiority can be verbal or nonverbal, as when someone makes a grimace when you tell her that you are going to cook your famous lasagna for dinner or when your peers roll their eyes in response to your offer to work on a project. You may often have perfectly valid grounds for feeling superior to someone—you are a better basketball player, you do better in mathematics, you play the piano very well, or you are very good at repairing cars. People do vary in their skills, development, and ability. But when the fact of that superiority is communicated and allowed to dominate the message, a defensive communication climate is created.

Equality, on the other hand, is the willingness to take other people on their own terms, at whatever level they may be. Equality also recognizes that people change, grow, and develop and that the other person may need some space and time to expand his or her talents. Superiority in a message cuts short the other person's potential by diverting energy away from positive growth to negative defensiveness. You may remember having to remind your parents that you are no longer at a former, now inappropriate stage of development but have moved on. They may nevertheless insist on acting in a superior way, giving unasked for advice about choices you are going to make. This parental superiority may last long past adolescence—perhaps even as long as both parents are alive. But no matter when or under what circumstances a superior communication style occurs, the result is sure to be a defensive communication climate.

Control creates defensiveness by communicating to another individual that you know how they ought to behave, think, or feel. Even a remark as innocent-sounding as "I know you're going to love this movie!" can communicate a control message. Control is seen most clearly in messages that begin with phrases such as "You should . . . ," "What you need is . . . ," or perhaps "You'd better . . . (not) . . . ." Warnings, threats, orders, directions, commands, guidance, suggestions, and recommendations are all likely to be perceived as control messages by the other party, and they may invite a defensive reaction. What can you do, then, if you are the teacher or boss, to avoid defensive reactions? It is a difficult situation, since your role requires that you exert control in many situations, while at the same time, you may wish to encourage a supportive atmosphere. There are ways to combine authority and supportiveness.

Adopting a mutual problem-solving approach to issues such as classroom behavior or job performance is one way to counter potential defensiveness. For example, in a noisy classroom, a teacher may say, "There is too much noise for people to work. Can we work quietly for fifteen minutes and then have discussion? What can we do together to get the noise down?" The tools of active listening that were explained in Chapter 3 can be helpful approaches to creating a climate of mutual problem solving.

If you engage in *strategy,* you give to your messages a sense that there is an unstated or ulterior motive to them. People begin to see you as not being forthright, and they will lose trust in you. They will begin getting their defenses in place to protect themselves from any possible threat of being manipulated by you.

One of the temptations of engaging in strategic behavior is that it often works. You can often achieve a short-term goal or a quick gain by less than honest, or devious, behavior. The reason that the goal is usually short term is that people discover the manipulation. Trust is destroyed and usually the relationship with it. Manipulation can take the form of giving out dishonest messages, withholding information, making up stories, sending incomplete or distorted messages, and just plain lying. If you have ever trusted someone and then been lied to, you know how hard it is to regain that trust. Using strategy as a communication style is a sure-fire way to create a defensive climate in any relationship; and the closer the relationship, the more severe the effect. To counteract a tendency for strategy to be a part of your communications, be aware of the positive effects of spontaneity, and keep your communications authentic.

Neutrality is just what is sounds like. An example of neutrality is the statement "I really don't care, one way or the other." Saying something like this distances one person from another with an impersonal aura of detachment and noninvolvement. If you receive neutral responses to your messages, you are likely to feel that the other person is cold and uncaring, lacking any feeling or appreciation for you. Some people believe that even anger is a better response than neutrality in a relationship because at least it reveals involvement and interaction. The worst communication response in a relationship may be indifference, because it indicates that there is no sharing or commonality in feelings or perspectives.

Finally, Gibb observed that *certainty* in communications often creates a defensive interpersonal climate. In contrast to provisionalism, certainty allows little or no room for open exchange or a consideration of alternatives. If you are in a relationship with someone who is always certain about his or her opinions, ideas, tastes, suggestions, and demands, you may begin to think of that person as being close-minded, bigoted, egotistical, or some other similar term that describes the same quality. You can see how certainty is associated with superiority and probably evaluation as well. People who express certainty in many of their communications often refuse to recognize their own mistakes and instead rationalize them, blame others for them, or ignore them altogether.

The problems for others in these relationships are that they may feel worthless, they may fail to trust their own values or opinions, and they may be reluctant to express their own ideas until they have heard the person with certainty speak. Then they can agree with the partner and avoid upsetting him or her. You can see what a waste of human potential this situation creates, since only one perspective is used in examining ideas or problems; and as a result, the pool of ideas in the relationship gets smaller. If a relationship is in the early stages of development and one person is especially eager to please the other, a situation is created in which certainty becomes a frequent communication style, and a pattern may be set that inevitably leads to a defensive communication climate.

The six pairs of behaviors—supportive and defensive—can and do affect your life in every interpersonal communication situation. Sometimes, a relationship may be short-lived, and there will not be many consequences of establishing one climate or another; but even in a brief sales interaction, climate could be an important factor. Suppose you were shopping for shoes and a salesperson brought you several pairs of shoes that you didn't like or that were too expensive for your budget. Yet the salesperson kept insisting, "You really should get these." You might buy a pair of shoes from this person, but it is more likely that you will not and that you will not return to that store again. When it comes to your long-term friendships, your family, and your professional and affectional relationships, you can see the importance of establishing an enduring, supportive climate.

Having a supportive climate does not mean never having a conflict, however. Conflict is inevitable in every relationship in which you communicate honestly. Since we are all different and have a variety of likes and dislikes, we will probably experience a great many conflicts throughout our relationships. How we handle them can make the difference between a relationship that continues and grows and one that declines and terminates. Therefore, knowing how to manage conflict can be an important skill.

CONFLICT MANAGEMENT

Ask yourself, "What is conflict?" You might answer that conflict is a disagreement or an argument, perhaps a fight, a battle, or even a war. These situations all have certain elements in common. Communication writers Joyce Frost and William Wilmot have defined conflict based on four elements. These elements appear in the smallest disagreement—over a mixup in your food order in the school cafeteria—and in major, international confrontations. The four elements are included in the following definition: Conflict is an expressed struggle between at least two interdependent parties who perceive incompatible goals, scarce resources, and interference from the other party in achieving their goals (Hocker and Wilmot, 1985). You can see that *expression* is the first element and that it involves communication. Maybe you asked for a cheeseburger, and the server brought you cheesecake. Or maybe Israel and the Palestinians both claim the same territory. In both cases, an expression of the conflict is communicated so that both sides know about it.

The next element in the definition of conflict is that the parties involved must be *interdependent*. This means that they are somehow linked together in a particular situation. In the first case, you rely on the server for food and the server relies on you for income. In the second case, both Israel and the Palestinians occupy the same geographical space and have vital interests in its control and use.

The third element in this definition is that the goals of each party in the conflict need to been seen as being *incompatible*. If the server now has to pay for the mistakenly ordered cheesecake, there will be a conflict. Both Israel and the Palestinians express the position that the other must be excluded from certain places or roles.

Finally, the element of *interference* comes into play when your goal of eating a quick lunch is delayed or even defeated by having had the wrong order

Conflict management is an important interpersonal skill.

delivered. The current Middle East conflict has been raging for fifty years over troops, occupation, and aggression, so neither side has achieved any lasting goals.

Conflict Is Inevitable

As you experience more interpersonal relationships, you are going to experience some form or level of conflict. Conflicts can arise over something as simple as which television program to watch when two that you want to watch are on at the same time. Conflicts also can arise over decisions that have long-term implications, such as whether to marry a particular person, where to live, whether to have children, when and how many, or how to rear them. Since conflict seems built into any meaningful interpersonal relationship, learning how to manage the conflict constructively can have lifelong, beneficial effects. There are limits to time, money, patience, resources, energy, abilities, interests, enthusiasms, and desires. These limits affect the variety of personalities as discussed in Chapter 7; and when these limits and differences in personality come together—as they do whenever one person has a relationship with another—conflicts are bound to arise. Sometimes a problem may be internal, and you keep it to yourself, stewing over it in your own mind without involving the other person. That does not mean that there is no conflict. It means only that the problem has very little chance of being solved. If, on the other hand, it takes two people to create the conflict, then it is probable that two people are needed to manage it effectively. Keeping your conflicts internalized may put so much stress on your mind and body that illness results. Thus conflict is still expressed, but without much opportunity for resolution. Learning to manage your conflicts means learning to involve others. When it is done well, you may even find that conflict resolution has positive benefits for your personal development.

DIVERSITY IN COMMUNICATION

Conversation Styles

Communication patterns of African Americans differ from those of Anglo Americans, and one place to see these difference is in a conversation between people from these two groups. In one extensive study, African Americans were asked about their conversations with Anglo Americans. The research found several elements that contributed to both satisfying and unsatisfying interactions. Primarily, African Americans felt that these conversations could be improved if *they* were more active in managing the interaction and in asserting their point of view. They suggested that their Anglo American partners could improve the quality of the conversations by being more open-minded. The study quotes one African American male as saying,

> Blacks and whites may come away with different meanings from a conversation because concepts aren't defined in the same way. The members of the ethnic groups tend to think in a different manner. Most times blacks don't get a lot from conversations with whites, so when it occurs, it is highly valued—like the gates opening.

Open and honest conversations were seen as rare (Hecht et al., 1989). Perhaps one way to manage diversity is to follow the advice given here, that is, to be more open, more effective at conversation management, and honestly assertive about your ideas.

Conflict Can Be Constructive

We often feel negatively about engaging in conflicts. Cultural norms may lead us to resist conflict, or we may believe that a relationship is threatened if there is any expression of negative feelings. Actually, positive uses of conflict can unburden a relationship of factors that may be preventing the people in it from growing closer. At worst, conflict can reveal areas that need to be resolved or, if they are unresolvable, can allow us to choose to terminate the relationship or change our attitudes or values. Conflict, therefore, is actually useful in interpersonal growth and in personal development. The creative energy that can come from exploring, expressing, and resolving conflicts can be channeled toward improving self-esteem, developing greater social skills, and creating a wider repertoire of communication abilities, as well as improving relationships. For these constructive outcomes to occur, effective conflict management must become a regular practice.

Process of Conflict Management

There are several ways to keep conflict constructive. Unfortunately, when you are in the middle of a conflict, these methods may be forgotten, lost, and unused. Keeping them in mind may be the hardest part of the process. In many ways, a good conflict is similar to good listening, and the four areas of active listening presented in Chapter 3 are paralleled in the four aspects of constructive conflict.

Be Prepared.   This is the first aspect of constructive conflict. Think about what the conflict is *really* about, and then focus on that item. If it is only about your partner's constant reluctance to wash the dirty dishes, go into the conflict with that as your theme. Be careful not to expand the conflict by introducing other topics until you find yourself at the point of saying, "So everything you do shows that you don't care!" Such a conflict is a conflict out of control. On the other hand the *real* conflict may not be about dirty dishes at all, but about a deep resentment over feeling ignored or unappreciated. If that is the case, then make *that* your focus. Good preparation also means looking at your available strategies and selecting the ones that are most appropriate for your purposes. If you are relying on the conflict to strengthen your interpersonal relationship, be careful to avoid attacking and wounding the other person so that the relationship begins to reverse itself in the direction of termination. Review the supportive climates, focusing especially on description.

Be Involved.   Be an active participant in the conflict. Withdrawal and avoidance are two strategies that prevent conflicts from being resolved. Be clear about your own thoughts and feelings. They are not forced on you by others; you are responsible for them. If you use the word *I* more frequently than the word *you*, you will be communicating that you are involved as one of the parties. Keeping your messages direct and staying on the issue by identifying specific items will help the conflict to move toward resolution.

Withhold Quick Retorts.   As tempting as it may be to respond with a quick retort in a conflict, try to restrain yourself. When the other party hits you with an unfair statement and you think of a quick comeback—perhaps a sarcastic play on words—try to hold off for a moment. Remember, you are partially responsible for creating the communication climate. Withholding the quick retort can save you from introducing a communication into the conflict that will cause further conflict.

Review or Summarize.   When you believe that a situation has been thoroughly discussed and you are reaching closure, it is a good idea to summarize the discussion in descriptive terms: "So, I think the dishes shouldn't be a problem for me anymore now that I understand you will get to them a bit sooner. Thanks for listening to me." A good summary identifies the problem and restates the resolution. It may be that the conflict cannot be resolved in one session. A good summary might be stated as follows: "It's time for me to go, and we still haven't resolved the dishes problem. Could we get together between three and five o'clock this afternoon and pick up with your point about time being too short after breakfast?" This message brings the session to a close, if not the conflict. Moreover, it avoids simply letting the conflict drop without resolution. In international affairs, negotiators often take breaks in their sessions, sometimes staying away for weeks or months, to consider their goals and determine how to proceed next.

The best-selling book *Getting to Yes* offers four strategies for managing conflict constructively. The researchers were part of a group called the Harvard Negotiation Project, which looked at all sorts of negotiation and bargaining situations, from deciding which movie for a couple to see to international conflicts such as the Arab/Israeli situation. Former President Jimmy Carter has maintained his international profile as a skilled negotiator by using this approach. The four steps are as follows (Fisher and Ury, 1986):

1. Separate the people from the problem.
2. Focus on interests, not positions.
3. Generate a variety of options before coming to a decision.
4. Develop an objective standard to judge the result.

The first step means keeping your focus on the event or problem and avoiding attacking or diminishing the other person's interests, motives, or personal attributes. Rather than worrying about who wins, be concerned with what is gained. The second step advises that you focus on interests and avoid announcing a bottom line. Instead, think about what you are trying to gain. If a fair settlement is your goal, then be careful to have in mind a full idea of what *fair* means, not just a single position. The third step involves developing or enlarging the number of alternatives. Sometimes, this means simply taking a huge problem or desire and breaking it into multiple parts. Some parts may be more important to you than others. By creating a large number of choices, you increase the chances of giving alternative perspectives to your conflict resolution. Finally, insist on an objective criterion. This advice is also found in Chapter 4, on critical thinking. Asking the parties in a conflict to define in objective or measurable terms what the result should be will help both parties to recognize a settlement. You might use the *Blue Book* price in negotiating the cost of a used car, or you could settle on equal amounts of time spent on household chores. Try to develop objective criteria to measure your settlement before you try to identify that settlement.

If either of these approaches is used carefully, with practice, you can become better at managing the conflicts that are inevitable in your relationships. In turn, better conflict management will help you to improve your interpersonal relationships.

TECHNOLOGY IN COMMUNICATION

Light Up a Liar

You can purchase many devices to attach to your telephone that are supposed to tell you whether the person at the other end is telling the truth or lying. I frequently see these advertised in airline magazines. They are electronic measurement systems to detect slight changes in the tension level of the voice. The human ear cannot detect such changes, but they can be monitored by these instruments. The devices often use red, yellow, and green lights to indicate the other person's truth telling.

Negotiations in business take on new dimensions if the other side hears you say, "That's the highest offer I can make!" and the red light comes on, so they know it is not. These devices are extensions of the old "lie detectors" (polygraphs), which measured electroconductivity of the skin, heart rate, breathing, and muscle tension in an attempt to discover whether someone was telling the truth. Our advancing technology is often applied to areas of interpersonal importance, and truth telling is one such area.

IMPROVING INTERPERSONAL SKILLS

All the ideas in this chapter taken together would give you only a start in improving your interpersonal relationships. You can take entire courses, probably at your own college, that focus exclusively on interpersonal communication. There are several guidelines, however, that you can begin to use right now to improve the quality of your interpersonal communication.

Be Assertive

Being assertive means that you are willing to communicate. The passive, withdrawn, inactive person will not elicit much response from others, so to get interaction from others, *you* must first interact! Notice that the word *assertive* does not mean the same as *aggressive*—that is, pushing yourself onto other people, interrupting others, and telling strangers intimate details of your life story at great length. These behaviors are all associated with the overly personal behaviors that Shutz described earlier in his work on *inclusion, affection*, and *control*. Being assertive also means being responsible. This means that you acknowledge that you are an independent person—that is, you take responsibility for your own ideas, thoughts, and feelings. You also have a responsibility to communicate according to the social and cultural norms and expectations within which people feel comfortable and in control.

Be Considerate

You need to be aware of the other person as being another complete person. Other people have their own backgrounds, personalities, and experiences, which they bring to the relationship. If you try to practice empathy, you will find yourself becoming more aware of another individual's qualities. Then you will find more ways of communicating with that person.

Listen

This act sounds so easy to perform, but the skills of active listening that are described in Chapter 3 can be used immediately to help improve your interpersonal relationships. If you have already started putting them into practice, you have probably noticed an increase in both your understanding of others and your ability to send and receive messages with accuracy and clarity. You can actively listen to both words and nonverbal messages so that your feedback becomes more accurate and appropriate.

Develop Language Skills

Keeping in mind the information from Chapter 6 about the variety, richness, and problems associated with our use of language, you can be on the lookout for your own use of abstractions, snarled words, jargon, or cliches or for the many other habits of language that can interfere with clear communication.

Be Supportive

Putting all the qualities of supportive communication into an ongoing communication style can be challenging, but it is within your reach with self-reminders and practice. Large doses of good-natured humor can go a long way toward energizing your efforts. With a habit of approaching others with warm, positive regard, you can check the communication climate in which you find yourself, and change it, if necessary, by your actions.

At the heart of all good interpersonal communication is the positive regard you give to others. It is based on your authentic commitment to communicate well because you believe that the other person is genuinely worthwhile. That attitude may not be easy to maintain with everyone, but people who have it are excellent interpersonal communicators, and they, in turn, are warmly regarded by others.

Finally, try to apply either of the conflict management approaches outlined above. The first set may be easier at first because it parallels active listening. In formal situations, the Harvard Negotiation Project method may be more sophisticated, and you might want to get the book *Getting to Yes* and become fully informed about this system.

SUMMARY

Interpersonal communication is a topic so vast that many of the following chapters will continue to explore its various areas and settings. The general principles outlined here can serve as guidelines for your continuing interactions with others. Your need for affection, inclusion and control is evident in our one-to-one relationships, small groups, interviews, families, and even public life. Your life will probably follow, at least to some degree, patterns of relationship development and deterioration. You probably recognized yourself in some of the examples showing how people get to know each other and how they break off relationships.

If you can carry the practice of supportive communication into your personal life, you will find your interpersonal communication climate improving and providing you with greater satisfaction. Supportiveness helps to open clear channels of communication; defensiveness closes them down. Even though conflict is probably woven into our very nature, there are ways to manage it so that problems are resolved with minimal damage to the relationship and to the self-concepts of the people involved. Constructive conflict is helpful in friendships, on the job, and in romantic relationships. The ideas regarding conflict and conflict resolution are many, the behaviors complex, and the rewards rich and plentiful. Begin today to apply these skills and to reap the benefits they offer.

KEY TERMS

interpersonal communication, *p. 136*
Johari Window, *p. 137*
affection, *p. 139*
inclusion, *p. 139*
control, *p. 139*

relationship development, *p. 140*
communication climate, *p. 147*
supportive communication, *p. 147*
defensive communication, *p. 149*

EXERCISES

1. Keep a journal of your interpersonal interactions for one full day. Record whether you felt that your values, attitudes, or beliefs were similar to or different from those of the people with whom you interacted. Note one or two examples of contrasts or similarities in the values, attitudes, or beliefs of the people with whom you interacted.

2. List some interpersonal activities that fulfill your inclusion needs, affection needs, and control needs. Which activities fulfill more than one need at a time? Which activities are unsatisfying because they fail to meet any of these needs? Which activities meet one or more of these needs to a greater extent than you really like? Which activities are you likely to continue for a long time?

3. Pick three relationships in which you are an active participant, and indicate which stage of development you are in for each one. What do you predict will happen next in each relationship? What behaviors can you specifically identify that place one or more of your relationships in a particular stage of development?

4. Keep track of the defensive messages you received for one day. Record how you were able to respond—either defensively or supportively. Share these reactions in class and find out whether your classmates have any suggestions for altering the communication climate for any of these interactions.

5. Describe a recent interpersonal conflict. Write the details of the interaction just as it occurred. Now write a script showing how you could have applied some of the principles of conflict management to create a better interaction. Do you feel comfortable enough now to share both scripts with the other person who was involved in the conflict?

REFERENCES

Baxter, L. "Strategies for Ending Relationships: Two Studies." *Western Journal of Speech Communication* 46 (1982), 3.

Baxter, L. "Relationship Disengagement: An Examination of the Reversal Hypothesis." *Western Journal of Speech Communication* 47 (1983), 2.

Baxter, L., and W. Wilmot. "Communication Characteristics of Relationships with Differential Growth Rates." *Communication Monographs* 50 (1983), 264.

Duck, Stephen. "Social and Personal Relationships." *Handbook of Interpersonal Communication*. Ed. M. L. Knapp and G. R. Miller. Beverly Hills: 1985.

Duck, Stephen, and Miell, D. E. "Towards a Comprehension of Friendship Development and Breakdown." *The Social Dimension: European Perspectives on Social Psychology*. Ed. H. Tajfel, C. Fraser, and J. Jaspars. Cambridge: Cambridge University Press, 1984.

Eadie, W. "Defensive Communication Revisited: A Critical Examination of Gibb's Theory." *Southern Speech Communication Journal* 47 (1982), 163.

Fisher, R., and W. Ury. *Getting to Yes*. Boston: Houghton Mifflin, 1986.

Gibb, J. "Defensive Communication." *Journal of Communication* 11 (1961), 141–148.

Hecht, M., S. Ribeau, and J. K. Alberts. "An Afro-American Perspective on Interethnic Communication." *Communication Monographs* 56 (December 1989), 385.

Hocker, J. L., and W. Wilmot. *Interpersonal Conflict*. Dubuque: Wm. C. Brown, 1985. 22–29.

Knapp, M. L. *Interpersonal Communication and Human Relationships*. Boston: Allyn and Bacon, 1984.

Knapp, M. L., R. P. Hart, G. W. Friedrich, and G. M. Schulman. "The Rhetoric of Goodbye: Verbal and Nonverbal Correlates of Human Leave-Taking." *Speech Monographs*. 40 (August 1973), 182–198.

Knapp, M. L., and Gerald Miller. *Handbook of Interpersonal Communication*, Beverly Hills, CA: Sage Publications, 1985.

Luft, Joe. *Of Human Interaction*. Palo Alto: National Press, 1969.

Schutz, W. *FIRO: A Three Dimensional Theory of Interpersonal Behavior*. New York: Holt, Rinehart and Winston, 1958.

Interviewing

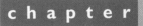

After reading this chapter, you should be able to:

- Understand the three common types of interviews.
- Follow the steps for preparing and participating in interviews.
- Explain where and why interviews are an important part of interpersonal communication.
- Feel more confident in being interviewed and in conducting interviews.
- Be at ease and assertive during a sales presentation.
- Evaluate your interview experiences to improve them in the future.

A graduating senior is seated in the office of the personnel director of a large and impressive company.

"First, tell me a little about yourself," begins the director.
"Well, I like sports," replies the senior.
"Oh? Any in particular?"
"Most of them."
"I see. How about some of your school activities. I see on your resumé that you were in the Wilderness Club. What was that like?"
"Fun."
"Just what was fun about that group?"
"Everything."
"OK. Let's see, I notice that you wrote that you'd like a job in management. That's pretty broad. Any aspect of management that you'd like to focus on or took courses in?"
"Not really."

A specialized form of interpersonal communication is the focused and purposive exchange of questions and answers—the interview. There are many types of interviews; the job interview is one that everyone will experience. As you can see from the responses of the senior in the example above, there is a skill to conducting a good interview, and he has yet to acquire it. Because interviewing will be required of you in a variety of situations—many of them having lifelong consequences—both knowing about interviewing and practicing the skills that will help you do it well are worth your time and energy.

We start with a definition of interviewing, then examine some different types of interviews, focusing on three of the most common ones. Next we present a variety of strategies that you can use to be skillful at both being interviewed and conducting interviews yourself. Let us begin by defining the interview and looking at a variety of interview situations that communication scholars have identified.

DEFINING THE INTERVIEW

Several elements are involved in a definition of interviewing. First, there are usually just two parties involved in an **interview:** you and one other person. At times, there may be several people on an interview team and one person being interviewed, but the idea of two parties being involved remains the same—one party primarily asking the questions and the other primarily giving the answers. The second element that defines the interview has already been mentioned, and that is questions. There are a great many questions in interviews, and most of them come from one of the parties and are directed at the other. As in most other communication situations, there is a purpose to an interview that both parties usually know and understand. So the interview can be defined as *a specialized, two-party communication primarily involving questions and answers directed at a preplanned objective.* The objective determines the type of interview, so let us now examine some interview objectives.

TYPES OF INTERVIEWS

In their extensive work on interviewing, Charles J. Stewart and William B. Cash, Jr. defined several important types of interviews (Steward and Cash, 1985). Some of these types can easily be considered together; for example, information giving and information gathering can be combined into information interviews. Five such distinct areas emerge for each of the primary interview situations (Skopec, 1986). Each of these types is examined briefly, and then three common techniques are identified that you will find useful when you interview another person. Finally, we look at ways to create a resumé and to increase your interviewing competency.

Information Interviews

This exchange involves one person as the source of information for another, as when you see your academic advisor or begin orientation for a new job.

In the information-*giving* format, one person may be new to the situation, and the other person is an expert who has information that will assist the first person in becoming acquainted. In this case, the expert has probably structured the communication situation, but the new person might do most of the questioning. The expert might be training you to operate a machine, follow a procedure, fill out a class schedule, or find your way around a building or the campus. A situation in which instructions involve you and another person and in which you can ask questions is an information-giving interview.

The information-*gathering* format is a common type of interview in which you might wish to gain information from an expert but the expert is not there with prepared orientation materials. You are the one who structures the communication. Journalists who interview people for news stories are gathering information (Biagi, 1986). Doing research for a speech and interviewing a faculty member for information is another example. Another common example is a survey or a poll, whether it is conducted in person or on the telephone. You might be asked to sample a new product and then answer questions about your reactions. A police detective who questions a witness to an accident or the associates of a suspect is also engaging in information gathering.

Selection Interviews

This situation includes any interview that has as its purpose the screening of individuals for hire, awards, admission, or placement or for any reason involves the individual's being chosen for something. The selection interview takes place in many settings besides a job setting. You might be interviewed to join a club, to get a scholarship, or to be chosen by potential roommates. However, it is the job interview that students seem to think of when they think about interviewing. Many campuses make interview-training services available to students who can practice their interviewing skills, often with videotape, so that their effectiveness during a screening or selection interview is enhanced. Specific advice that addresses the job interview situation is presented in the second half of this chapter.

Most of us hold between three and eight different jobs during a working career—a figure that does not include the part-time jobs held during the summer or while in school. If you have already been employed, you realize that every new job entails a job interview. These interviews are generally divided into two stages: screening interviews, which reduce a large number of applicants down to a few, and final-selection interviews, in which the chosen few are again interviewed and a single person is picked. Stewart and Cash (1985) distinguish between the two types by referring to them as *screening* and *determination* interviews.

The structure of these interviews is provided by the person or group making the choice, and the questions are directed to the applicant or nominee. Whenever you got a job, when the president of your college was hired, or when an admiral is up for promotion, a selection interview process is involved.

Appraisal Interviews

These can involve problems of the interviewee's behavior. Sometimes, a teacher or an employer will say, "Please see me," and you know that person probably wants to see you about a problem with your work. This type of interview is sometimes called a *performance review, an evaluation,* or a *counseling interview.* You might be called in for something as simple as correcting a minor behavior or for something as serious as being fired or expelled. In a formal situation, rules or regulations are probably involved, such as employer regulations or company policies that you have not followed. At school, this interview might involve a deadline for a paper or project or the performance level for a class. It could also involve something more serious, such as a school regulation that you have violated. This type of interview is very difficult for both parties.

A somewhat tricky situation involves the two parties in a reverse of the previous situation. Typically, the party who is not in charge is there to complain about something. You may recognize this form if you have ever interviewed a teacher about a grade on a paper or an exam. You may have felt that there were problems with the class or an assignment or an evaluation—problems that came from the teacher. In such situations, you need to express your complaint to the teacher, and that may be a difficult thing to do. On the job, an employee may seek redress from a supervisor, or there may be a formal grievance procedure that begins with the employee first interviewing the supervisor about the problem. Schools have formal procedures that allow you to express a complaint about a teacher, but the first step is almost always to discuss the problem with the teacher involved.

Problem Solving and Counseling

The *problem-solving* interview is a situation in which both parties share in both the problem and the solution. The problem is not that you are going to be fired or that you are about to file a formal grievance against a teacher. The problem must be *mutual,* and both parties must have a stake in the solution. The interview in this case focuses on what each party can contribute to identifying the elements of the problem and what each can contribute to finding and implementing its solution. Some clear decision should emerge as a result of the interview. A successful problem-solving interview will most likely follow these steps:

identifying the problem, defining it, identifying potential solutions, selecting criteria for evaluating the solutions, choosing a solution, and acting on it. These steps are also used by small groups that meet to solve problems.

On the *counseling* side, you may be the one who initiates the process. Perhaps you are having personal problems or difficulties in a relationship, or you might need help in deciding on a career or some other personal choice. You, rather than the other person, would then seek the interview. The problem might still be difficult to discuss, but the choice remains with you as to the course of action to follow.

Sales and Persuasion Interviews

The final category of interview listed by Stewart and Cash is the frequently encountered persuasion interview. Often, it is a sales presentation, and you might get involved in one of these several times a week. If a friend tries to convince you to try a new class, change your major, or buy a used stereo, you are in a persuasive interview situation. The more obvious of these situations include someone coming to your door to sell you a product or service or solicit a donation and telephone calls you receive for the same purposes. When you visit a used-car lot or stop in a stereo store to look around, you can expect someone to begin a persuasive interview with you. "Can I help you folks today? The model you're looking at is on sale this week, and the reviews it gets are terrific. Would you like a demonstration?" These questions and statements are typical of a persuasive interview. Of course, you can always walk away, close the door, or hang up the phone, so you do retain some control over the interview. Skilled persuaders, however, always seek to keep the communication flowing and connected. They do so by asking you simple questions and eliciting easy responses to engage you in their communication process.

The sales interview is one type of interview that has persuasion as its goal.

> ## *IMPROVING COMPETENCY*
>
> ### Entertainment Interviews
>
> **W**atch an interview show on television tonight, such as those featuring Jay Leno, Conan O'Brien, or David Letterman. These are good examples of a format in which there is one guest and one interviewer. Which of the seven types of interviews is exemplified by the show? What key factors determine the best type of interview for television? Look at the kinds of questions the host asks, and make a note of the ones that seem preplanned and those that seem to be spontaneous reactions to the guest's responses. As you watch these programs, think about the standards for a good interview that we set in this culture.

You may expect to engage in all of these various types of interviews during your lifetime. You will find that each one of the same type is a little different because of the personalities and circumstances involved. Recall from Chapter 8 that the interpersonal communication situation builds on the interaction between the people involved. Both the close give-and-take of friends and the intimate conversations of couples can benefit from some guidelines for improvement. Interviews can be improved by preparing for them in advance. We now look at some common interview techniques that could be applicable to all types of interviews and show how they can be used to build interviewing competency.

INTERVIEWING ANOTHER PERSON

The methods for successfully interviewing another person are similar to those used in active listening. To review, recall these four steps:

The first step is to *be prepared*. You might need to do some general background reading first, or you may wish to find out something about the person you are about to interview. I am sometimes interviewed by students working on the college newspaper or majoring in our department. Usually, they are doing a profile of faculty members, and the student conducting the interview will often ask me questions that are easily answered by other sources. For example, they often ask, "Where did you get your degrees?" This information is both in the university catalog and in a handout available at the department office. By preparing ahead of time, the interviewer could skip these questions and ask more interesting or conversational ones. For example, they could ask me to compare and contrast my teaching experiences at one college with those at another. I would also be impressed with their preparation. Prepare a variety of questions in advance so that you have a plan and a direction for the interview. Various types of questions are described later in this chapter.

Stay involved by listening and reacting to the answers to your questions so that a genuine dialogue develops. You may mentally be getting ready for the next question and miss an important idea that the interviewee is expressing.

Staying involved also means keeping careful notes of both the questions and the answers. A good record will help you later when you write up the interview.

By *keeping an open mind,* you should be able to listen to answers that you might not have been expecting. Sometimes, a student hopes that I will say one thing in an interview, but instead I say something else. I then read about the interview in the next day's student newspaper and wonder why he or she didn't listen more carefully.

Review your notes immediately after the interview, filling in the blanks you may have left while talking with the other person. You may have written down key words that are intended to remind you later of a complete idea, so get back to those words while the ideas are still fresh. You may be like many others and write a partial note or comment that has a very clear meaning at the time, but a few days later, you cannot recall the meaning. For example, you may have a telephone number written in your handwriting on a pad in your house or dorm, but you have no idea now how to identify the number. When this happens to me, I am tempted to call the number and sound like that television commercial: "Hello, do you know me?" But I never do. Instead, I keep the number around for days or even weeks, hoping I can recall the association, and finally wind up throwing it away. To avoid this problem with your interview notes, go back over them as soon as you can, and fill in the details while your memory of the interview is still fresh in your mind.

STRUCTURE AND SEQUENCE

It is important to keep the information-gathering focus of your interview in mind and not invade a subject's privacy. It is within the correct format of an interview to have some getting-acquainted, personal exchanges; or you might already have gathered some personal information on the interviewee. However, there is a difference between *personal* and *private* information. You can create a barrier to effective communication if you appear to be seeking private information. Defensive reactions on the part of your subject can lead only to a decrease in the sharing of information. Your subject will be much more cooperative and will provide you with more information if you are nonthreatening and sensitive to obvious social and cultural limits on questions than if you ignore these limits. Be courteous and respectful, and you will create a favorable impression with your interviewee.

When you are planning an interview, it is a good idea to consider the types of questions you are going to ask, not just the questions themselves. Variety in your question types can keep the interview fresh and dynamic. There are two major types of questions: directive and nondirective. **Directive questions** are those that require a clear answer, such as "What were the dates of your stay in France?" Directive questions force the interviewee to give a specific answer and do not try to elicit reactions or elaborations. **Nondirective questions,** on the other hand, allow the respondent to structure the content and the tone of the answer. For example, the question "I see you spent nearly two years in France. What were the most vivid impressions you still have of that time?" gives the subject an opportunity to structure the answer. Notice that these types of questions are not different because one is specific and the other is general. Both examples

DIVERSITY IN COMMUNICATION

Skilled Communicators Can Reach a Diverse Audience

Two of the most popular interview hosts in recent television programming are Oprah Winfrey and Montel Williams. Some of their appeal comes from the fact that they have guests who are interesting to a wide variety of people. Some of it may be because they make an effort to include different perspectives and ideas in their questions. Both of these hosts often refer to the experience of being African Americans in the United States, and both are active in African American organizations and associations. They seem to be able to identify strongly with their root culture and to communicate clearly and positively with a broad spectrum of people as well. It might be worthwhile for you to observe and analyze their communication skills as being an explanation for this ability.

ask for specific information. The main difference is in the latitude you allow your respondent to structure the answer and fill in details. You could also say, "So, tell me about your time in France." Then you would be asking a question that is both general and nondirective.

A good interviewer usually tries to provide variety in the types of questions asked, leaving some questions very open and using others to focus the interview or to gain a specific answer to a particular question.

Remember to wait and listen for the respondent to reply completely. A full answer may contain further information that you might need to use in later questions. If your time is limited—and it usually is for both you and your interviewee—you may need to move the interview along. If you are spending too much time on friendly, introductory questions and are missing the point of the interview, you may need to encourage your subject politely to move on. A good transition would be to say, "Let's turn now to your work on French politics. That's the theme of my term paper, and I'm really interested in your research."

Finally, you may find yourself in the particular information-gathering situation of having to introduce your subject to a group. It is, of course, necessary to gather biographical information about the subject, but try to go beyond names, dates, and places where the subject lived or worked. Be attentive to the whole person, and include in your introduction some of the impressions you gathered about the individual. That kind of information will help to fill out and add life to what otherwise could be merely a recital of fairly dull statistics.

By following these suggestions, you can make the information-gathering interview a productive interaction. When you put these suggestions into practice, you are building on your knowledge of personal communication principles.

In addition to conducting interviews for the purpose of gathering information, you will most likely be interviewed as part of the job selection process, to give information that you have and that others want, or its a receiver of persuasive messages. There are several things for you to keep in mind, especially during a job or selection interview.

BEING INTERVIEWED

In terms of life experiences, the job interview may be one of the most important communication events you have to go through. Even if you are the subject of only an information-gathering interview, you will want to present yourself and your ideas in the clearest and best possible light. Here are some suggestions to follow that parallel those for being a good interviewer. These suggestions can be divided into three steps: (1) preparation for the interview, (2) responses during the interview, and (3) follow-up after the interview.

Preparation for the Interview

Getting yourself ready to be interviewed means putting your information in order. Most job or other selection interviewers will want to know about your background, education, interests, and activities. They will often ask about these things during the interview, but they will usually require some written information from you before the interview itself. You need to prepare a short summary of your background and put it into a form the interviewer can use. The most common form is called a **resumé,** or sometimes a *vita*. This summary should be brief—rarely more than one or two pages long. Some people, particularly as they accumulate years of experience and a variety of training and education, prepare a complete version and a brief version. An interviewer who wants more details later can request the complete version. Initially, however, the short resumé will be the most valuable. There are many slight variations in resumés (Bostwich, 1985) but a typical resumé might look like the sample resumé on page 171.

This sample lists a variety of items, and you can see that there is an order to them. First, list only a little of your personal data, but emphasize your educational and training background. Use clear headings, and put the information in block form, not in sentences or paragraphs. The block format is designed to give the reader a quick, clear, and complete picture of you, and it stresses relevant, job-related information.

It is important for you to realize that this is a formal piece of communication and that it is usually the first impression of you that the interviewer gets. People often seek professional advice in preparing a resumé. Your campus probably has a placement service or counseling center where other samples are available for your use and where someone can help to proofread your resumé.

Notice that only certain information is given under personal data. Federal law recognizes that your race, age, sex, marital status, religious affiliation, cultural background, and so on are almost always irrelevant to employment. Indeed, your performance on the job is not related to those things, so it is almost always illegal for an interviewer to inquire about them and unnecessary for you to volunteer information about them. However, after you are hired, an employer will sometimes need to know about your dependents for insurance purposes or your age to fulfill bonding or licensing requirements or to plan for your retirement. Hard-fought battles over civil rights during the past thirty years have made only job-related items required on a formal resumé and in an

> ### THE STORY OF COMMUNICATION
>
> ### Equal Employment Opportunity
>
> Until the 1960s, the content of questions asked in job interviews was up to the questioner. With the passing of certain notable legislation—namely, the Equal Employment Act of 1963, the Civil Rights Act of 1964, the Age Discrimination Employment Act of 1967, and the Equal Employment Opportunity Act of 1972—employers were prohibited from inquiring about personal items that were deemed irrelevant to the job but possibly related to the applicant's ethnic, religious, political, or other characteristics that are immaterial to performing a job. More recently, the Americans with Disabilities Act expanded on these laws to include disabled people. This aspect of our communication content, then, is subject to regulation by government. The purpose of the regulation is to protect people from prejudice and discrimination. Some factors, such as race, ethnicity, age, and gender, are often self-evident, so employers can still use that information if they desire to. However, they would be open to charges of unfair discrimination in hiring if any pattern of consistent behavior against certain individuals or groups became evident.

interview. Other details can be saved for informal conversation after you are hired and if you wish to expand your Johari Window once you are on the job.

Part of your preparation should involve a little research about the prospective interviewer's organization. If you are applying for the Martha M. Holgate Memorial Scholarship, you might find out who she was and why a scholarship was named for her *before* you go to the interview. If you are applying for a job at ACME Tools, Inc., you can read copies of the company's annual reports or find out about the company from the local Chamber of Commerce or other business association. Having a little background information can help you to answer common questions, such as "What is it about ACME that inspired you to apply here?" You could answer, "I really don't know anything about ACME," or you could say, "I like the way your production has been expanding by 16 to 20 percent over the past five years, and I'm especially intrigued by your new operations in Japan and Singapore." You can figure out which answer is more likely to get you the job.

Responses during the Interview

Speaking of good answers, your responses during the interview are the major determinant of the success of the interview.

Your communication, as you know, has both nonverbal and verbal aspects. Effective, nonverbal communication during an interview can increase your communicative ability and the overall impression that you make. Begin by dressing appropriately. For your interview with the loading-dock supervisor at a local bakery, you probably would not wear a business suit; your clean jeans and clean pullover are acceptable. However, if you interview for a job as a bank

Chris J. Masterson
7865 Park Lane
Watertown, TX 50554
616-885-2553

Employment Objective: An introductory position in management in a medium-size company, eventually moving into personnel administration.

Personal Data

Date of Birth: January 24, 1973
Place of Birth: Chicago, Illinois
Health: Excellent

Educational Background

Central Texas University Parkfield, Texas	1995–97	BA: Business Management Minor: Communication
Brazos Community College Llano, Texas	1993–95	AA: Psychology
U.S. Army Technical School Ft. Lewis, New Jersey	1991–93	Data Processing

Employment Background

Bank of Parkfield 234 Main Street Parkfield, Texas	1995–present (part-time)	Teller
Brazos College Bookstore Brazos Community College Llano, Texas	1993–95 (part-time)	Assistant Manager
U.S. Army Central Motor Pool Fort Rollins, New Jersey	1991–92	Dispatcher
Watertown Electric Repair 342 West Elm Street Watertown, Texas	1989 (summer) 1988 (summer)	Sales Clerk Stockroom/Janitor

Activities

Parkfield United Way	1995	Funding Coordinator
Watertown Community Action	1989	Youth Activities Director

Hobbies include waterskiing, backpacking, singing with a country-pop band, and volunteering as a reader for the blind.

References are available on request from each employer listed.

teller, you might visit the bank beforehand to see what the employees are wearing. In any case, make sure you are appropriately attired for the message you wish to convey. A prospective employer who sees that you are sensitive to every aspect of the nonverbal communication situation will get a good impression of your awareness in general. If you are not certain what to wear, a low-key approach is best. Try to avoid the latest in trendy fashions and flashy jewelry. Your interviewer will be distracted from your good qualities if your clothing is "shouting" while the two of you are talking.

While you are presenting your answers, try to maintain an energetic, friendly, and relaxed nonverbal presentation. Keep good eye contact so that you can discern any nonverbal cues from your questioner that tell you how your answers are being received. Project energy in your voice and facial expressions, and balance this impression with a body posture that is at ease. This particular combination will create an impression of confidence and interest. If you show nervousness and fidget with pencils, rings, and so on, your listener will be distracted from the content of your message. It may be difficult to control your nervous energy, but by being aware of unwanted nonverbal signals, you may be able to stop them.

The techniques for controlling the effects of communication anxiety will be useful in the interview situation; deep breathing for several minutes before the start of the interview may be just what you need. It may be difficult to control your nervous energy. But by being aware of your nonverbal signals, just as in good listening, you may be able to stop tapping your pencil or twisting your ring around on your finger.

TECHNOLOGY IN COMMUNICATION

Police Interviews

One specialized interview is that conducted by police investigators with suspects in a crime. Police are on the alert for deception in this situation, and many agencies have turned to technology to assist them in detecting deceptive answers (Hocking and Leathers, 1980; Hocking, et al., 1979). One device that they use is a camera that focuses on the suspect's eyes and records the amount of pupil dilation that occurs during questions. When people are trying to deceive, their eye pupils change size briefly and in tiny amounts. Advanced camera technology can record these changes and assist investigators in detecting deceitful communication.

As for your verbal messages, recall the advice that was given earlier about listening in an information-gathering interview in which you are the interviewer. Use the same skills when you are being interviewed.

Most interviewers will give you clues about what they are seeking in the way they phrase their questions, and you can infer a great deal of information from a question by listening to it very carefully. For example, the interviewer might say, "Your experience has been in banking, but our need is for someone who is more people-oriented than money-related. Do you think you have more than money skills?" Rather than answering with a simple *yes,* try to respond to the question's implicit message: Your primary experience is not relevant. You might elaborate by saying, "Yes, I do think I have people skills. My position at the bank involved handling large sums of money, but it also involved customer contact. As a teller, my first priority was to make clients feel welcome and comfortable before I concerned myself with their money. I felt really good when people would wait until my window was available because they enjoyed interacting with me." This answer is not too long, yet it addresses the underlying concern in the interviewer's question by connecting your experiences with the needs and concerns of the interviewer. A good listener will respond to both the question's content and its intent.

Another important factor in effective listening and responding is to make certain that you are answering the question that was asked, not the question you wish had been asked, were hoping would be asked, or were afraid would be asked. Do not overanswer a question by digressing into long stories or examples.

Try to balance being complete with being concise. As you formulate complete answers, make certain that you cover the item completely, then stop. The interviewer has probably planned to cover several areas in a set amount of time. If you take too long for any single answer, the interviewer will have less information by which to remember you and to use in your evaluation. You can apply your nonverbal sensitivity to gauging feedback from your questioner. If the interviewer begins to talk, saying "Okay," "Ah, I see," "Umm, that was interesting," he or she may be signaling that it is time to move on. You can always try to check directly if you are not sure. In the sample answer about your people skills in the bank, you could give your one example and then say, "There were other aspects of my work that helped me learn about and use people skills. Would you like another example?" If the interviewer is genuinely interested in more information, he or she can say so. If not, the interviewer can move along with a response such as "Well, yes, if we have time later. Right now, I wanted to ask you about your community activities." Finding the right balance between completeness and brevity is not always easy; but if you keep it in mind during the interview, you will probably achieve it to some degree.

Many applicants take brief notes during the interview so that they can ask questions about the job or the company that they could not find the answers to during their preparation. Keep your note taking to a minimum, and do not

CRITICAL THINKING IN COMMUNICATION

Interviewing Skills

You can use your skills at evaluating communication options to help you decide how much of an answer is enough and what the intent of the question is. I was once on an interviewing committee that had allotted about thirty minutes for each candidate. There were seven or eight questions that we wanted to cover for each of the eight finalists. One person, in response to a general warm-up question, proceeded to give us his life history, talking for nearly twenty-five minutes before we were able to make him stop. Needless to say, the other questions remained unanswered, and the candidate was not hired. Had he used his critical thinking skills, he would have analyzed the situation, gauged the first question to be an ice breaker, and given it just a few moments, allowing the team to set the direction of the interview. By dominating the time, he showed his inability to assess the goal of the interview and thus called into question his critical thinking skills in general.

write more than one or two items at a time; otherwise, you risk taking your attention from the interviewer. Asking a few questions that you could not have anticipated before the interview can show that you are responsive and attentive.

Most interviewers conclude by asking you if you have any questions. Time may be short, so have a few in mind. You may have formulated some questions before the interview. If you have them with you, you can show the interviewer that you know how to prepare ahead of time and that you can anticipate future concerns. Try to keep these questions brief, and restrict them to areas that you could not find out about in another, easier way. You could ask about any job-related expectations that were not completely clear from the job posting or advertisement. You might ask when a final decision will be made, or you could reverse roles and ask the interviewer whether there is any additional information or work samples he or she might want from you. Be careful of the time, though; there might be another interview scheduled right after yours.

Sometimes, interviewers will ask you if you would like to have something to drink. While the interviewer may be sincerely trying to make you feel comfortable, you would probably be wise to decline. A cup of hot coffee or a cold glass of water is just one more thing to juggle, spill, or cough on. Even the most graceful person can accidentally knock over a glass under the stress of an interview. Dribbling coffee on yourself is bad; spilling it on the interviewer's desk is a disaster. Get a drink before or after the interview, but not during it. Smoking is increasingly frowned on in the workplace, so even if you do smoke, do not smoke during the interview.

The interviewer will indicate that the interview is coming to an end by saying, "Well, that's all the questions I have for you. Can I answer any questions?" or "Well, our time is just about up. Is there anything we didn't cover?" Be certain to respond by honoring the signal and keeping your closing remarks or questions to a minimum. You might conclude by saying, "Thank you for taking the time to see me. I enjoyed coming here and look forward to hearing from you when you make your decision."

These steps can help create a solid impression of you during the interview and will allow your best qualities to be clearly communicated to the other person. You might then complete the interview process with a short follow-up.

After the Interview

Once you have left the interview, check for any follow-up requested by the interviewer. Did the interviewer ask for a letter of reference? If so, contact that person immediately. Did the interviewer ask for a sample of your artwork? Send it the next day. In any case, always send a brief note of thanks that can also serve as an appropriate close to the interview process. You might wish to send something like the following letter.

This letter reinforces your interest in the job and will help to create a favorable impression of you in the interviewer's mind. In the letter, you come across as both serious and enthusiastic and indicate that you have responded to the request for a reference made during the interview. On the other hand, if you are not interested in the job anymore, it is a good idea to write and tell that to the interviewer as well. While you do not need to indicate any particular reason for withdrawing your application, you should be polite and remember to thank the interviewer for his or her time. You might say, "I find that my plans have

7865 Park Lane
Watertown, Texas
June 5, 1997

Ms. Susan Hernandez
Personnel Director
Wrightwood Electronics
4455 Arrow Highway
Crawford, Arizona

Dear Ms. Hernandez:

My visit to Wrightwood Electronics yesterday was informative and pleasant, due to the time and effort you gave to our interview. Thank you for making me feel welcome. I am convinced that I would enjoy working with your company if it turns out that I am offered the position of management trainee in your personnel department.

I have contacted Dr. Ralph Yamato, my advisor at Central Texas University, regarding the letter of reference you requested. He assures me that you will receive it next week. If there is anything else I need to provide, please do not hesitate to call or write. You mentioned that you will be making your selection by July 1, so I look forward to hearing from you around that time.

Thank you again for your time and for considering my application.

Cordially,

Chris J. Masterson

changed and therefore request that you withdraw my name from consideration." If you have already taken another job, you could allude to it by saying, "I have just taken a position with another company in the area, but I wanted to tell you that I appreciated your time during our recent interview," but skip the details about the other job's higher wages, better benefits, and nicer work environment. You may someday be back to apply for another job with the first company, and the impression that you make at first should remain positive. It is also possible that the interviewer will get another job with a different company and that you will run into him or her in that circumstance. In any event, leave a friendly, positive impression that shows you to be a responsible person.

The three areas of preparation—what to do before the interview, how to conduct yourself during the event, and how to follow up—are easy to remember if you place yourself in the position of the person doing the interviewing. Who would impress you? What behaviors would they show? What manner of preparation would communicate thoroughness and reliability to you? By adopting a little of their perspective, you can help remind yourself of these areas of preparation.

INTERVIEW FORMATS

As was previously discussed, the most common **interview format** is one in which you will be involved one on one—one person asking most of the questions, and one other person providing most of the answers. At other times, you might be part of an interviewing team on which several people share the role of questioner and one other person is the **respondent.** In this case, you will need to be sensitive to sharing time with the other members of the panel. Perhaps you will meet ahead of time and agree on different areas for each person to cover. You might even develop questions for each other and work out a sequence of turns so that you know when it will be your time to ask questions.

As a respondent to a panel interview, your tasks and goals are the same as they are for a one-on-one interview. However, you need to include all the panel members in your answers, and you need to keep track of everyone's nonverbal responses to you. A simple rule of thumb might be to give the person who asks you a question about 50 percent of your eye contact and spread the other 50 percent among the remaining members of the panel. If there are only two questioners, give the one who asks the question about 75 percent of your direct response, and spend about 25 percent of the time talking to the other person. This division of your attention helps to create a sense of having a direct conversation with the main source of the immediate question, but at the same time it does not ignore the fact that one or more other people are conducting the interview, are listening very carefully to your responses, and forming opinions and making judgments about you.

Some interviews follow what is called the *funnel format,* which is a technique in which the interviewer starts with very broad questions and then focuses on progressively more specific questions. To start off on an easy and general note, the interviewer or team will say something like "Tell us why you

Skills of interpersonal communication are useful in working as part of an interviewing team.

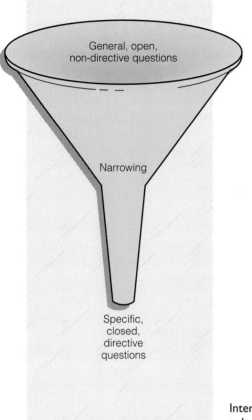

Interview questions generally follow a funnel pattern.

decided to apply to ACME." They will then become increasingly specific and narrow (hence the term *funnel*) and move to questions such as "Would you be comfortable working with a shifting job assignment?" and then to questions such as "How many out-of-town trips per month would you be willing to take?" The funnel format begins with nondirective type questions and moves to more directive ones.

Some interviews can also be described as directive or nondirective overall. A general interview with your professor about your ideas for a future career may be nondirective in total approach. Counseling interviews can have that dimension, allowing the respondent to structure the whole event. At other times, especially when there is limited time and a specific set of questions that are the point of the interview, a directive tone may characterize the whole interaction.

 ## IMPROVING INTERVIEW COMPETENCY

During your lifetime, you are likely to be both an interviewer and an interviewee. You can improve your competency in both areas by building on what you have learned about communication competency in general. First, increase your background and knowledge about interviewing. That knowledge will provide you with a greater *repertoire* of types of questions and potential answers. When you analyze a situation from the perspective of both the questioner and the respondent, you can increase the skill and accuracy with which you *select* the right kind of information to include on your resumé, in your answers, or in your questions. When you think about and practice framing questions or giving simulated answers, you are rehearsing the implementation of your choices. Then you can *implement* again in the actual situation. Perhaps going through a mock interview with friends or with professionals available to you on your campus will give you practice in implementation. Finally, after practices or after actual interviews, you can review and *evaluate* your choices. Sometimes you will also get feedback from your friends or others who have interviewed you. All of these steps contribute to your communication competency in interviewing—an important area in almost everyone's life.

In the interview at the opening of the chapter, the interviewer was trying to ask a variety of questions and to be open and encouraging. When you are the interviewee, interact with the tone, take the hints, and keep your messages clear and complete. Then the interview might look something like this:

> A graduating senior is seated in the office of the personnel director of a large and impressive company.
>
> "First, tell me a little about yourself," begins the director.
>
> "Well, I like sports, was involved in clubs in school, and have been working part time during all four years of college, so there's quite a bit to talk about. Where would you like me to start?"
>
> "How about sports? Any in particular?"
>
> "I was in a softball league and play some basketball on weekends, but my favorite sport is one that not many people consider a sport—orienteering. I got involved in it after I joined the Wilderness Club. In fact, this year I'm the coordinator."
>
> "What about orienteering makes it attractive to you?"
>
> "I like the challenge of being outdoors, working with a team, and facing the unknown—but with good preparation. I also get to know and work with a great group of people in an intense, focused, and personal contest. We divide up into teams, and it's always fun to have a few new people as well as some experienced people on your team. Each event, win or lose, teaches me something about myself and about other people."
>
> "That sounds like a great activity. Can we talk about your interest in management for a few minutes? Is there any aspect of management experience or involvement you'd like to focus on in particular?"
>
> "I took the standard business courses, but I want to get involved in a career in which I can use some of the approaches I'm learning from my orienteering experiences. I like teamwork, challenges, and a little risk. I'd be flexible about the specific assignment or division, but I'd like to keep some of these personal interests going in whatever position I'm in."
>
> "Okay. Let's talk a bit about your long-term goals."

Our senior is much better prepared to build from his experiences and ideas, and it is fairly certain that he has made a completely different impression this time.

SUMMARY

The three major interviewing activities to keep in mind are prior preparation, skillful conduct during the interview, and appropriate follow-up.

Preparation means doing some research about the subject. For example, if you are going to be the interviewer of applicants for a job, make certain you understand the job thoroughly. If your task is to interview people for an award, find out about the past history of the award and its requirements and intentions. If you have been sent materials beforehand, read them. Then you can focus your attention on the candidate at the time of the interview. You can adapt your questions to the specific person and avoid general, uninteresting questions. By treating candidates as individuals, you can help to put them at ease and elicit better answers from them.

Your conduct during an interview means more than just extending basic courtesy. As a trained communicator, you should also be able to apply the rules for active listening and give others the appropriate nonverbal communication they are seeking as feedback. Maintain eye contact with them, and keep your note taking to a minimum. Try to create an open and encouraging atmosphere so that your respondents can express themselves clearly and completely. An open, encouraging attitude on your part can assist the interviewee in providing the information you seek. Asking a variety of questions can help the interviewee to provide you with a variety of responses.

As the person conducting the interview, try to keep the interview moving along. You may need transitions and connections to guide and direct the conversation if it veers off into a long discussion of a hobby you have in common or a recent vacation one of you enjoyed. You are responsible for setting both the tone and the pace of the communication. If you are on a strict time schedule, you might want to tell that to your interviewee. Sometimes, job or selection interviews are deliberately structured to judge the candidate's capacity to handle stress and may include some tough questions. Otherwise, try to avoid making the interview difficult for the other person. Following up after an interview can be accomplished with a letter, phone call, or personal visit.

If you follow these steps, keeping in mind both the interactive and directive nature of interviews, you can improve your competency in being interviewed and conducting interviews. Your college may have workshops in interviewing, or you can take an entire course or read books dedicated to the interview situation. This introduction should be enough to get you started, but it is only a beginning. If you put these guidelines into practice to build on your communication skills, then interviews will become a successful and rewarding part of your communication competency.

KEY TERMS

interview, *p. 162*
directive questions, *p. 167*
nondirective questions, *p. 167*

resumé, *p. 169*
interview format, *p. 176*
respondent, *p. 176*

EXERCISES

1. Make an appointment to interview any of the following people on your campus: (1) a professor, but not one of your teachers, who is an expert on a topic you will be researching for a class presentation, (2) a professional in the counseling center at your college who advises students about job inter-

views, and (3) one of your own teachers, but the interview should *not* be about class matters. Instead, make it about some aspect of your teacher's professional work, research interests, or recent publications. Follow the suggestions for conducting an interview in each case, and make notes on how and why the interviews were similar or different.

2. Get some sample resumés from your career center. There are a variety of ways to organize a résumé: chronologically, categorically, topically, and so on. Which do you like the best? Why? Which are recommended, if any? Why?

3. Pair off with a classmate, and conduct an interview with him or her for twenty minutes. Then reverse roles. Did you learn anything from one role that helped you be more effective in the other role?

How does switching roles help you improve your interviewing skills?

4. Take some ads from the help-wanted section of the local newspaper and do the same exercise. This time you are the personnel director interviewing candidates for a real job you found in the newspaper. Switch roles again, and see whether you can create a realistic interview that might prepare you for the real event.

5. Prepare a resumé for the job interview in Exercise 4, and bring it to class on the day of the interview. Help your partner by evaluating the one you receive from him or her when you are in the role of the personnel director. Listen carefully to any suggestions your partner might have about your resumé.

REFERENCES

Biagi, Shirley. *Interviews That Work: A Practical Guide for Journalists.* Belmont: Wadsworth, 1986.

Bostwich, B. E. *Resume Writing.* 3rd ed. New York: Wiley, 1985.

Hocking, J. E., J. Bauchner, E. P. Kaminski, and G. R. Miller. "Detecting Deceptive Communication from Verbal, Visual, and Paralinguistic Cues." *Human Communication Research* 6 (1979), 33.

Hocking, J. E., and D. G. Leathers. "Nonverbal Indicator of Deception: A New Theoretical Perspective." *Communication Monographs* 47 (1980), 119–131.

Skopec, Eric W. *Situational Interviewing.* Waveland: Prospect Press, 1986.

Stewart, C. J., and W. B. Cash. *Interviewing: Principles and Practices.* 4th ed. Dubuque: Wm. C. Brown, 1985.

Small-Group Communication

After reading this chapter, you should be able to:

- Describe the factors that create small-group communication.
- Define the types of small groups in your life and their importance.
- Know how the elements of personal influence and leadership function in small groups.
- Understand how small groups, by working together, build organizations.
- Feel able and confident to participate in either member or leader roles in small groups.

M ost of the important decisions made about you have come from small groups. Most of the important influences that helped shape you came from small groups. Most of the important activities in which you are involved come through small groups.

Do you think that these statements are too bold? Think for a moment about the sheer number of rules and regulations that influence and govern your behavior. Speed limits, college admissions, and the amount of tax you pay on gasoline—all came about as a result of group decisions. Your family is a small group, and the way you functioned in that group, and the way your family members treated you, influenced the pattern of your development. In maintaining a relationship with your family of origin, with a small circle of very close friends, with a family of your own, with a work or career group, you will participate in most of the daily activities of your life as a member of a small group (Rothwell, 1995).

You may make a few important decisions on your own or with a significant other person, but most of your everyday interactions will probably be in relationship with others in a small-group environment. Simply because you conduct so many of your activities in groups, it is important to know something about them and to be good at working in them. If your experience is typical, you probably have been in some really good groups and others that were a real disaster.

This chapter introduces you to some important aspects of small-group communication. It gives you an opportunity to learn a little about groups and to expand your ability to make the groups in which you participate more effective. Let's begin with a definition of small groups.

SMALL-GROUP COMMUNICATION

Several characteristics need to be present in small groups for them to be more than just a collection of individuals. **Small-group communication** means that three or more individuals are involved in face-to-face interaction for a common purpose or goal. All of these factors need to be present for small-group interaction to take place.

Size

First, three or more people must be present, up to a limit of about ten or twelve. At least three people are needed because two people make a dyad, as for an interview. With three people, some sort of organization is necessary, social pressures exist, and interaction changes markedly from what it is with just two people. The upper limit of small-group membership should be about ten or twelve people so that everyone can communicate with relative equality, ease, and directness. As more people are added to the group, the potential lines of communication increase until there is a huge number of potential interactions within the group. The illustration on page 183 demonstrates the growth of a small group from the perspective of potential interactions.

Have you ever noticed how, in groups that are larger than ten members, people tend to start little conversations on the side? A person might turn to his or her neighbor and whisper a conversation, creating cross-talk, while the rest of the group focuses on someone else. This breakdown occurs because people want to be

Communication complexity increases dramatically with each additional person in a small group.

involved, and the more people there are in the group, the more difficult it is for everyone to have an opportunity to speak. The desire to communicate is still there, so people get that opportunity by forming small subunits out of the main group. Because the strain on the communication system in a small group increases with each additional person, ten or twelve people seem to be the limit. Many people feel that between four and six persons is the ideal number of people because it permits a smooth flow of ideas and should provide enough opportunities to speak.

Interaction

The stress on small-group communication patterns that is generated by an increase in the number of participants is related to **interaction,** the second part of our definition of small-group communication. As in any communication event, there are senders and receivers in a small group. Here, those senders and receivers **influence** each other in an immediate sense. They have a full view of each other, so nonverbal messages can be processed at once, and they can hear each other easily, so verbal messages come through quickly and clearly. Taking turns, developing roles, and building a group relationship are the desired outcomes of small-group discussion.

A Common Purpose

The group must interact about something, which is usually a common purpose or goal, the third major element in our definition of small-group communication. This purpose or goal is usually the reason that brings a group together in the first place and that holds it together in spite of tensions, conflicts, and strains.

Thus we can define a small group once again as a collection of three or more individuals, organized and interacting face to face for some common purpose. If you keep in mind the elements of interaction, organization, and a common goal and people have somewhat equal access to sharing the channels of communication, the exact number of members is not highly relevant. For example, a teacher lecturing to a room containing only four students does not constitute a small group because there is not much interaction during a lecture, nor is there equal sharing of the channels of communication. One person talks; the others listen and take notes. A common goal is missing as well. But when eight or ten people are focused on a common task, they are sensitive to each other so that everyone feels involved, and there are equality and sharing, they have the potential to become a successful small group with a **common goal.**

Organization

Most small groups are organized in some manner. **Organization** can be formed with either a set format such as a chairperson, a secretary, and so on, or it can evolve, informally, as when roles develop over time. For example, in one group,

---

DIVERSITY IN COMMUNICATION

Group Communication and Social Order

Among various cultures throughout world history, wisdom is to be seen in the use of small groups for various important purposes. For example, the Jewish culture requires a *minyan*—a group of ten—to conduct certain types of religious meetings. The council of elders or chiefs of many Native American cultures vested power in a small group of leaders. Japanese culture still places great value on the collective wisdom of work groups and social groups. Western European governmental institutions developed councils of ministers, and churches established synods. Successful use of groups can create successful institutions.

Anita might always start the discussion, Franco might bring the snacks, Art might keep good notes, and Willa will might remind the group to keep focused on the task and summarize the progress of the discussion.

These roles evolve from the group members' expectations and needs. At the same time, the mutual influences that they exert on each other eventually lead to the development of group **norms.** When people interact, they have certain expectations about how they should interact. For example, are we expected to be on time for the group? Discuss for an hour and then take a break? Interrupt the discussion with witty remarks? Look to the oldest person for expert help? Norms are like rules for acceptable behaviors in a particular group. In your classroom, one of the norms is that you raise your hand to get the teacher's attention and for permission to talk. In a small group of which you are a member, you may have norms about what you can and cannot do and still be perceived as a viable member of the group. Certain sororities may have a dress norm; a sports team may develop a celebration handshake or slap.

All these norms develop as a result of the interaction within the group. Of course, different groups have different purposes and different ways of interacting. At the same time, most small groups can be categorized into one of three main types: a social group, a work group, or a decision-making group. Although each of these groups has all the elements mentioned in our definition, they are nevertheless unique in their focus and purpose.

TYPES OF SMALL GROUPS

The division of small groups by specific type or focus is common, and there are several ways to cluster them. For example, the reason for a group's being together and staying together is an important characteristic and a good way to classify small groups. If being friends and interacting socially is your group's purpose, then you are interacting in a social group. If you have a task or job to do, then you would probably be classified as a member of a work group. If you are in a group whose goal is to come to some decision, then the development of that decision is your reason for being together, and you are in a decision-making group.

Each of these groups is described in some detail so that you can see which type you may be dealing with at any given time. Although the types have much in common, if the purpose of a group consisting of five people shifts, then the same five people will also shift from one type of group to another. Distinctions among groups come from the groups' purpose and behaviors, not from the members themselves. Moreover, the same five people may move back and forth between types of groups in the same meeting, so always observe group behaviors for clues as to the type of group you are in at any particular time.

Social Groups

Social groups include units such as families, roommates, or even a softball team. Throughout your life, you will find that there are structured times during which you engage in social interaction with others. Your family plans trips, vacations, meals, and conversation times. Your school has intramural sports, as well as clubs and outings. Your company sponsors annual picnics and a volleyball league. You may join a special type of social development group to learn about yourself, enhance your self-esteem, or confront and solve a personal problem. All these groups fulfill our need to interact with others. Do you recall the discussion of Schutz's inclusion, affection, and control needs in Chapter 8? Small groups provide us with the means to fulfill these needs. By creating social groups, we recognize the interactive dimension inherent in human behavior, and we sustain and support our psychological needs.

People form groups such as families, clubs, and teams to fulfill their social needs. We start out in life in a family, but we are so familiar with it that we might not think about it as one of the many forms of small groups. Recall in Chapter 7 the discussion of the many influences that helped to shape your self-concept. You can see how long-lasting the effects of the family group can be. In Chapter 17, you will read about the special communication environment in the family group, but for now, think about a family as a small group that sees itself as a family.

Usually, this vision of a family involves a long-term commitment to the relationships within the family, even if those relationships are not always within the traditional family group of two parents and their children. It is becoming more and more common to consider as families groups that are not always made up of a married couple and their children. Our definition of *family* might include a married couple, each of whom has brought children into the marriage, thus creating a blended family. It could also include a set of natural parents, their children, and adopted or foster children. Our definition also includes single parents with children and extended families having two or more generations of parents, children, uncles, aunts, cousins, and grandparents. Other family groups include people who are neither married nor related in any traditional sense, such as people living in communes and same-sex partners.

Each of these small groups acts as a **primary group**—one that is the major referent for its members, one in which its members share living and financial arrangements, and one that has certain characteristic and identifiable patterns of communication. These patterns flow out of the following characteristics: a long-term commitment, the ability to have and endure serious conflicts, a feeling of trust, and the development of roles and norms in the context of intimate and enduring relationships. Other social groups may be formed by a company or organization, such as a team or a social committee.

As was discussed earlier, people form and join groups to fulfill their social needs. We come from groups, live in groups, and organize our society around groups because we have social needs that only groups can provide. These needs include reference behavior, safety and solidarity, and esteem.

Reference Behavior.   **Reference behavior** begins quite early in our lives. As babies, we constantly try to copy the behavior of the significant adults around us. Babies see their parents walking and using knives and forks to eat, and they hear their parents talking. Babies respond by imitating those behaviors, and that is how they learn about the world and about their capacities and abilities.

This same primary group—the family—also tells you about yourself. Your self-concept and personality are strongly influenced by your family's reactions to your behaviors. We also look to other groups, such as friends, fellow club members, or even gangs to show us how to behave. Peer pressure from these groups is so strong because our reference need is strong. Many college students enjoy joining clubs as a way of fitting into a new environment. Groups such as an intramural volleyball team, a fraternity, a debating team, and a concert committee are examples of referent groups. Sometimes reference power is so strong that people dress or talk alike. You can find this phenomenon in businesses that have a certain corporate look for all of their executives or in groups of friends who always go together to the same restaurant. In general, these behavior modifications help distinguish one group from another, one culture from another, or one society from another. These differences are important because they provide us with some of the models and standards for our personal development and behaviors.

Safety and Solidarity Needs.   It feels better to walk from the library to the parking lot late at night if there are other people walking that way as well. Even if you are not walking with them, it is comforting to be in the presence of others. Have you ever watched a horror movie on television by yourself? Wouldn't you have felt more comfortable if someone else had been around? There is probably a very primitive instinct that reassures us of safety in numbers, and groups provide those numbers and answer that need. **Safety and solidarity needs** can be met simply from being around other people.

It also feels good to be part of the crowd at a concert or stadium event. You identify with others in the crowd by wearing certain colors, tee-shirts, or other emblems. In other words, you get a sense of solidarity from the group.

Unfortunately, this need for solidarity can go to an ugly extreme, as when groups get so large and out of control that people in the crowd take risks and engage in behaviors they would not even think of as individuals, There is a phenomenon known as the *risk-shift,* which means that people tend to shift their behavior from a conservative risk level to a higher risk level when they are in a group, whereas the same people would not make that shift when acting alone. We can lose our individual sense of responsibility in a group. The violent behavior of mobs is one example of that phenomenon.

Self-Esteem Needs.   Groups can also be a place for us to meet our **self-esteem needs,** as we seek and gain approval from members of our groups. The roommates and friends who tell us we have done a good job when we get a high grade on an exam and the award given to us by an organization for our outstanding performance are examples of how the need for esteem is satisfied in groups.

Groups also provide us with recognition and reaffirm our sense of self-worth. In addition to your membership in work and school groups, you may also hold memberships in several social groups, ranging from clubs, volunteer groups, or civic organizations. Personal development may come from therapy groups that form to help people overcome eating disorders, alcohol or other substance abuse, anxiety or depression, and low self-esteem. Facing such problems with other people in a small group can be a highly effective way of treating them.

To summarize briefly, social groups are groups that provide interpersonal satisfaction through rewarding interactions. These groups provide us with references for our behavior and attitudes, may give us emotional support in times of crisis, and often are the places where we find and build friendships. For most of us, the primary groups that are established in late adolescence consist of a few close friends from high school or college, a few work associates, and the members of our family. We may alter and modify these groups over time, as when we move to a new school, change jobs, or live in a different city. We can change location and still maintain contact with a few of our previous groups, but with only a limited number of them. New groups and new friends will come into our lives.

The amount of influence that a group can exert on you depends on how much you value the approval of its members. Both on and off the job, you will value some groups more than others. Thus groups can affect your attitude and behavior to a greater or lesser degree. Social groups help to modify or reinforce our behavior, and they play an important part in many of our communications and in our day-to-day satisfaction with life.

Work Groups

In virtually every occupation, employees are placed together in units to accomplish their tasks. **Work groups** like this can be found in your classroom. A project is due, and a team of students works together to complete it. Or you might be a member of a civic club or other campus organization that has undertaken a project, and a group of you joins forces to get the job done.

Task Orientation.   The notion of a task is what is important in all of these examples, and it binds the different settings described into the general category of work or task groups. These groups are different from social groups in that their goal is usually a visible, material product. In social groups, the *interaction* is the goal; in a work group, a *product* becomes the focus. The same elements of our original definition are still present, but the interaction will be centered on the accomplishment of a task, and the leadership will center on the skills and expertise of the members as they accomplish the task. While there may be personal dimensions to the interaction, and while the group may work better if everyone feels included and liked, the interaction is determined by and focused on the product.

In a career setting, the implementing of an idea or plan is often turned over to a task force, or group, to complete, even if that group had little to do with generating the idea or plan. Businesses, therefore, are constantly trying to find ways to handle the problems that arise when there is a conflict between the group that came up with the idea or plan and the work group that must carry out the plan or idea. The work group may resent not being included in the early phases of the project, and the group's work may suffer as a consequence.

A work group must, first of all, organize its task. It must define the task and divide the work into logical job units. If you have ever worked on a group project in class, you know that it is important that each person have some clearly stated responsibility for a specific segment of the task. Otherwise, everybody tries to do everything, or many tasks are left undone or partially done because nobody had direct responsibility for them. Some tasks can be done cooperatively, some independently. For example, only one person needs to go to the library to look up dates or resources on a specific topic, but everyone should cooperate in planning the overall organization or format of the project.

Resource and Feedback Utilization.   The wise work group will use the resources of the group members. If one person is an excellent typist but not a good proofreader, divide the job so that the appropriate person gets the part of the task that he or she can accomplish realistically. A common practice in Japanese business settings is to have workers rotate the jobs in a section of the company until, over a period of years, they have tried virtually every job in their related area. Often, a worker excels in one area but not others, and the company can either provide that person with training or keep him or her on rotation until there is a comfortable fit between the person and a job. Even people who are very good at one job get rotated. In this way, they expand their knowledge and skill base and perhaps demonstrate that they are good candidates for advanced positions in the firm (Hatvany and Pucik, 1981).

> ## TECHNOLOGY IN COMMUNICATION
>
> ### A Virtual Group?
>
> With the widespread use of computer networking, some people hold simultaneous computer conferences with others. By using speaker-phones, several people can talk in the same telephone conversation. The development of fiber optics for the transmission of sound and images has led to the visual telephone, and the use of hologram projection makes it possible to beam the image of someone in a three-dimensional likeness. Current virtual reality game simulation centers place players in the center of interactive, wholly realistic situations. Will our idea of face-to-face interaction for small-group communication change? Certainly, it is being expanded with the advances of technology.

Being open to change and feedback allows you to revise the task as necessary and to get a constant update on your progress. On the job, you might have a supervisor or manager who will help to establish a feedback loop for your group and who can help iron out any difficulties with the division of labor or establishing and meeting deadlines. A manager can be a resource for the group as well and will help you to understand that you are doing an important part of the task. Often, the success of one person depends on the success of the whole group and vice versa. The cooperative approach that most work projects demand makes it necessary for the group to understand how each member contributes to the completion of the goal.

As was mentioned earlier, in reality, groups are seldom completely task-oriented or socially oriented. Both group behaviors may be present. However, the social dimension of a work group can vary tremendously. A very concentrated project that has a high priority and little time to spare may have minimal social aspects to it. In a highly social group, the task almost becomes secondary.

Decision-Making Groups

A third type of group is characterized by a goal that asks for a decision at the completion of the group interaction. A city council or student senate may be such a group because it does not produce a tangible product, nor is its purpose to develop social interaction.

Decision-making groups are brought together for the purpose of planning something or deciding something about a task or about a question of policy. You have already been in many decision-making groups. When your family has a conference to decide where to vacation, you and your roommates meet to divide up household tasks, or your club tries to figure a way out of a financial crisis or how to raise money, you are participating in a decision-making group.

These groups may be informal, and they may or may not have a designated leader. They meet to work out satisfactory solutions to problems of mutual concern. They may explore many ideas and alternatives before coming to a decision. There are probably hundreds of decision-making groups on your campus that plan concerts, decide on admission requirements, advise the president, revise course offerings, and evaluate the faculty for promotion. In business and industry, decision-making groups discuss the allotment of resources, union contract provisions, ways to develop new products, how to move the company into the future, or how to represent the employees' concerns to management.

Problem Solving. A special type of decision-making group is the problem-solving group. This group focuses on finding the best solution to a particular problem and on developing a plan of action for putting that solution into practice. If your group reaches the decision to select a particular student to receive the Outstanding Senior Award, then no plan is necessary. But if you want to solve the parking problem on campus or end the business recession, you need a complete plan.

There are specific steps to follow to create an effective, formal, decision-making or problem-solving group. First, the group must *define the problem.* This step is like creating a topic for an essay or like the first step in the scientific method. Your group must also create and specify some *criteria* for judging the final outcome. "What are we looking for?" is a good question with which to start as you initiate your discussion about definitions and criteria. Thus a coher-

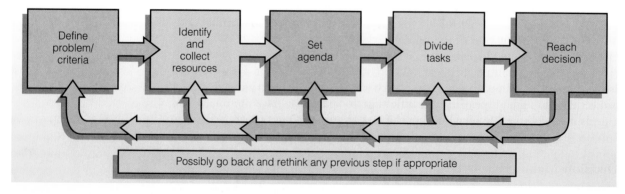

Group decision making is helped by following a clear pattern.

ent system for evaluating your results is one way to think about definitions and criteria.

At first, however, you may need to *brainstorm* for ideas, perspectives, and definitions. One problem with many decision-making groups is that the members stop brainstorming too soon. They take the first plausible definition of the problem and, in their eagerness to get on with the discussion, do not consider other possible definitions. Often, finding the best way to define the problem is part of the problem itself. For example, the county north of where I live was having problems with traffic congestion on a main highway. The decision makers used the most common perception to define the problem. They said, "The road is not big enough to handle these commuting cars every day." Therefore, as you can predict, the solution that they came up with was to widen the road. Suppose they had defined the problem by saying, "There are too many cars for this road." They might then have looked for solutions that decreased the number of cars, such as carpools, mass transit improvements, or a commuter rail system, rather than increasing the number of road construction projects. The definition of the problem may actually predict and control the solution at the very first stage.

We have seen a major change of definition regarding nationwide decisions about energy. For many decades, we looked at our energy needs and decided that they were constantly in danger of not being met. We defined the energy problem as being one of not enough energy. The solution, therefore, was simply to get more of it. For years, that definition both predicted and controlled our approach to a comprehensive energy policy. In the 1960s, and more extensively in the 1970s, policy makers and ordinary citizens began to rethink the problem, and some new definitions of the energy problem were generated. Inefficient use of the energy that we have could be said to be the real problem. This definition sparked a dramatic improvement in energy efficiency in everything—from refrigerators to automobiles. Another way to define the problem was to say that dependence on the wrong sources of energy is also part of the problem. This definition leads to the exploration of solar, wind, geothermal, and renewable sources of energy. The way we define a problem, and the way we *redefine* the same problem over time, can be the breakthrough to finding solutions. In the section on improving your small-group communication competency later in this chapter, some hints for good brainstorming are presented.

A good first step is to define the problem so that it is well thought out and well phrased. Taking the time to do this at the outset of your group's decision-making task can save you many difficulties later, in the discussion phase of the group's assignment. Work on getting a good definition of the problem and some clear criteria for later use in evaluating the solution.

Second, now that you have a clear definition of the problem, take stock of the *group resources*. Find out what expertise the members of your group have and what special abilities or backgrounds they have. You might find just the key people with talents or skills from which the entire group will benefit if they are used appropriately and effectively.

Third, *create an agenda*. An agenda can be a complete plan of action, or it can be the way you organize a meeting. By getting a plan in place, you can focus on the steps you need to take, and you can guard against skipping an important

CRITICAL THINKING IN COMMUNICATION

Brainstorming

One way to develop your critical-thinking skills is to engage in the process of brainstorming, in which *creativity* generates ideas and *judgment* evaluates them. The critical-thinking skills that are used to create and apply appropriate criteria to the solutions that result from group discussion will help your group make better decisions throughout the decision-making process. You might be tempted to skip the critical-thinking phase because of group pressures to conform. But it is important for any group to use critical-thinking skills, especially in specifying the evaluation criteria to be applied to the solution *before* specific solutions are actually offered. Sometimes, a brainstorming session on evaluation criteria at the very early stages of group interaction can help any decision-making group focus its energies and save its members from wandering off on tangents. A group may also decide to appoint a critical thinker, often called a devil's advocate or critical evaluator, whose job it is to hunt for and bring out any possible flaws or problems inherent in the group's ideas. Although the role of devil's advocate is not a particularly enjoyable one, it is not permanent, and it fulfills an important function; it brings the insights that can result from critical thinking into the decision-making process.

step. You might make an outline describing where and how the group is going to investigate the problem, the due dates and time frame for reporting information, or the dates and times of future meetings. You may also decide to break the problem down into small subunits so that your task will not appear to be so huge that it is overwhelming. After you have created the smaller topics, you can put them into a time frame to see how they fit and to decide which ones need to be addressed first, which come second, and so forth. Feel free to try different orders of priority until you have an agenda that satisfies both the group's definition of the problem and its resources. The group needs to be assured that the agenda fits the group's purpose, time frame, and goals.

Fourth, once you have divided the decision-making process into parts that make sense, you need to *delegate the work*. For example, if there are several questions requiring some research, these questions can be handed out to various members for information gathering before the next meeting. If there are assignments that people can work on independently, they need clear instructions and a deadline. Other jobs, such as brainstorming or final voting, will require that everyone work together.

Finally, *making a decision* combines the input that has been gathered from all sources—including appropriate results from the group's resources from the agenda itself. At this point in the process, you might need to adjust your definition of the problem or your evaluation criteria on the basis of the inputs, so the group interaction is very important.

The group can come to a decision by using many methods. Sometimes, a vote is taken, and the majority wins. At other times, it may be important for everyone to agree, so consensus will be reached by compromising or by merging ideas. Some groups allow just one person to make the decision. If that person has great expertise or power or is the one most affected by the decision, a group may want that individual to make the final decision. There are groups that cannot seem to come to a decision through discussion, so they average the suggestions offered. For example, you might need to decide how much to charge for admission to a concert. One way to decide is to add up all the suggestions for prices, get the average, and settle for that. Another way groups get out of a deadlock is to pick a decision at random. For example, drawing straws, flipping a coin, or pulling a name or number out of a hat are ways to let "fate" decide. The shortcoming of these methods is that they fail completely to take advantage of the intelligence, insight, and expertise of the group. They may not lead to hurt personal feelings, but they bypass the research the group has done, ignore the desires of the group, and eschew human communication as the way to find the best solution or come to the best decision.

COMMUNICATION PATTERNS IN GROUPS

Communication interaction in small groups follows predictable patterns, or networks. When you look at the way messages go from one person to another in a small group, you can observe some common lines or patterns of communication, also called **communication networks.**

An X pattern puts one person at the center of all messages, and everyone speaks to that person. This pattern is fairly formal and is used when a small group is holding its discussion in front of an audience, such as at a city council or board of supervisors meeting. The X pattern may also be used if there is a

The person at the center of an X network can be a gatekeeper or a facilitator.

There is feedback in the circle network, but it can be delayed because it might not be direct.

great deal of interpersonal tension in the group, so the chair serves as a neutral center.

A circle pattern is one in which each person talks only to one or two others. An office may have this pattern, or roommates who get along with two or three others may have it. In this pattern, not all members of the group communicate with each other. When they have one member in common to whom they all talk, they form a wheel pattern.

The chain, or line, pattern does not involve a group. It is simply a line of communication links in which one person talks to one or two others. No connection is made to provide a return, as in the circle pattern.

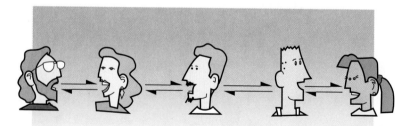

The line network suffers from status, control, and feedback problems.

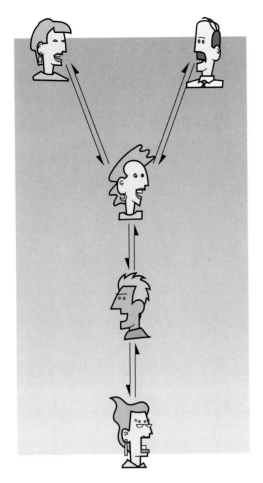

Many organizations have a Y network pattern.

A special type of chain is called the Y network. In this pattern, one person acts as a sort of center for three or four others. Everyone else gets farther away from the interaction as they chain out away from the center. Many business and other organizations have patterns like this, but it is very difficult for a small group to function adequately with a Y communication pattern.

The star network is the one that is used by most small groups that are communicating authentically. It is called the star because it is the best but also because it represents a pattern in which all members communicate with every other member. Some writers call it the *all-channel network,* which certainly describes it. However, calling it *star* will remind you of how important it is for everyone in an effective small group to communicate directly with everyone else.

Please note that these diagrams do *not* represent seating arrangements; they represent message flow. If you are seated next to someone but speak only to the chairperson, you are in an X pattern of communication. On the other hand, how you sit and where you sit are important considerations and are covered in the next section.

The star network allows all members to communicate with each other.

 **ENVIRONMENTS**

Much study has been done on the circumstances of small group meetings. Are the members seated in comfortable chairs? Can they see each other clearly? Is there a draft or noise? All these factors create an environment that can help or hurt group discussion. Think of the times you may have gotten together with others to study. Sometimes that worked well, but sometimes other people kept walking through the room, a television set was on in the next room, and the smell of pizza was coming down the hall. All of these intrusions from the environment can and do work against an effective group session. Perhaps you had to sit on the floor because there were not enough chairs, or there was no table to write on, or the light was poor. These examples illustrate how important a good environment is to good group functioning.

With a little thought, you can plan an effective workspace to get the maximum benefit from group interaction. Perhaps you need to reserve a room in your apartment or in the library or the conference center. You can make certain that someone is responsible for answering the telephone during the session and for keeping other sounds away. Are you going to set a meeting for 5:30 in the afternoon? Think again, or be prepared for eating habits to interfere with your plans. Some campus groups always schedule their meetings for 12:00 noon. People are typically fifteen or twenty minutes late for these meetings because they have had to stand in line to get a sandwich. Then they bring the sandwich, a drink, and some chips to the meeting, crunching, munching, and spilling during the entire meeting. The focus of the group gets off the topic and the task easily, and the groups that call these meetings continually finds low satisfaction and low productivity in their sessions.

If you pay attention to the environmental factors of time, space, setting, noise, and arrangements, you can enhance the value of the time you spend in small groups. One thing you cannot influence to any great extent is what your members bring with them to every meeting in the form of personal attributes. These attributes will be discussed shortly, but first let us look at the overall patterns that groups seem to follow as they progress through a typical session.

PHASES OF GROUP DEVELOPMENT

The communication patterns of group development change according to predictable **phases of group development**—usually divided into four distinct areas: orientation, conflict, consensus, and closure (Tubbs, 1995).

Orientation

The first phase of a group's interaction is called *orientation*. People get to know each other, get used to the setting, talk about the problem, look at the problem definitions, decide on appropriate evaluation criteria, and take stock of the resources and limitations of the group. Group members may assign, elect, or take on various roles, such as recording ideas, acting as moderator, or being in charge of social aspects of the group. Orientation, which can continue over several meetings, is a vital stage. If the group fails to take enough time to explore these areas, it runs the risk of skipping over a vital group resource or letting a job that is necessary for its work go unassigned. One of the most common reasons for a group's failure to create a positive outcome, and a common reason for members' dissatisfaction with the group process is a faulty orientation—an incomplete, rushed, first phase. Because members may be in a hurry, under some pressure to complete the project, or uninterested or distracted, your group may be tempted to run quickly through a superficial orientation. Take your time; good groundwork will help avoid problems later.

Conflict

Avoiding problems sometimes creates problems in phase two, which is called *conflict*. In U.S. culture, there is a tendency to avoid conflict. We are told, "Be polite! Don't argue!" Some personality types are very uncomfortable with any kind of conflict; and in groups, these people exert a pressure on the group to go along with whatever idea comes first, seems plausible, or is presented most forcefully. Be careful of group pressure to conform because it limits the use of group resources. Conflict is a necessary and valuable part of good group process. It helps with the evaluation of ideas so that the group comes to the best possible decision or outcome. To encourage healthy conflict in a group, think about the problems that are associated with a suggestion, and consider the positive and negative aspects involved in reaching a particular solution. Speak up about any concerns, reservations, or hesitations you may have, for example, about moving too fast. Others may have them too, and you can save your group problems in the decision stage if you voice your concerns *early* in the discussion.

Asch used this line diagram to test people's tendency to conform.

Engaging in conflict is not easy, for there are tremendous pressures to conform. You may have heard of the famous study of small-group pressures done by Solomon Asch (Asch, 1952). Asch hired a group of students to give wrong answers to a simple question. He then added a new person to the group, asked for the answer to his question, and tried to find out whether the new person would give the obviously correct answer or would conform to the clearly wrong one given by the paid students. He put three lines on a blackboard labeled A, B, and C and then another line nearby labeled X.

He asked each person to say out loud which line—A, B, or C—he or she thought was closest in length to line X. His paid students all said it was line A, one after another. When it was the new person's turn, he or she also said it was line A a significant number of times. Asch then brought in another new person, and this time all his hired students said that it was line C. The new person conformed and said that it was line C even though that was obviously the wrong answer. In fact, lines X and B were exactly the same length, but the pressure to

THE STORY OF COMMUNICATION

The Dangers of Groupthink

The pressure to conform is called *groupthink*, and there are numerous examples of this pressure resulting in bad decision making, even at the highest levels of government. The most famous example happened during the 1961 Bay of Pigs invasion of Cuba by a small force of troops trained by the U.S. government. President Kennedy had a small group of advisors who relied on poor information and an exaggerated sense of their own superiority to make a decision to overthrow Fidel Castro's communist government in Cuba. No one wanted to appear to lack confidence in the information or the training, so there were no comments that were critical of the plan, which turned out to be total disaster. The failed attempt nearly brought us to a nuclear confrontation with the former Soviet Union, Cuba's main ally. The high status of the planners and the pressures of time prevented the group from engaging in the conflict phase, so ideas were neither creatively formed nor critically examined. Peer pressure is not just a fact of life for junior high school gang recruits with low self-esteem. It happens among lawyers, teachers, government officials, physicians, and religious leaders. Just about everyone is subject to groupthink, and our history books are filled with examples of the resulting poor decisions.

The pressures of groupthink nearly brought us to war.

conform was so great that many people simply would not go against the rest of the group. But, when Asch repeated the experiment and had people *write* their answers, the unpaid subjects always wrote that it was line B. So the incorrect answers were not a problem of eyesight, of confusing directions, or of distance from the board. They were merely a matter of not going against the group.

Conflict is an important phase because it helps us avoid the pressures of conformity. Some groups even assign the role of critic, or devil's advocate, to a member to avoid quick unanimity in the group, which might short-circuit the critical-thinking skills of its members.

On the other hand, too much conflict can also bog down a group. If the conflict is repetitive, personal, or focused on issues outside of the group goal or task, then it is time to leave it. By returning to the orientation phase for a while—reexamining the group's goals, definitions, resources, criteria, or the personal attributes of the members—it is possible to let go of an unproductive conflict.

Consensus

The third phase of group development is called *consensus*. This period brings the conflict phase to an end by having members begin to compromise, merge ideas, or select from among the alternative ideas and solutions developed and debated about during the conflict phase. "I agree with Phyllis's idea and think we could start with it and add Franco's suggestion for the deadline" is a statement that shows that the group is moving into this phase. Decisions are actually reached at this time, and people add their input to the final product. If there is a holdout who will not join the group norm, then it may be necessary to return briefly to conflict or even orientation. If that does not work, you may have to move to an alternative decision-making strategy, such as a majority vote.

Closure

Finally, closure is a short phase during which the final decision or product is brought forth, a restatement of the group goal and the group consensus is made, and people reaffirm their support of the final decision. If any final, fol-low-through work needs to be done, it is assigned and accepted at this point.

A group may go through all of these phases each time it meets (Fisher, 1970) and, at the same time, have a long-term focus that carries through to each meeting. It is also possible to go through these phases for each item of business at a single, decision-making meeting. For example, your student senate or local city council may move through each of these four phases for every item on the agenda. Watch their communication behaviors, and you will be able to identify each phase easily. In your own small-group discussions, remember that effective groups go through all four phases, and skipping or unnecessarily short-ening any one, especially the first one, can lead to problems later.

PERSONAL INFLUENCES

Earlier chapters of this book discussed different aspects of communication and individual personalities. You may recall that some aspects of each person will always be evident in any group setting. Some of these attributes come about as a result of the small-group interaction, while some are independent of the com-munication within the group.

Group-Related Influences

Those personality characteristics that develop from small-group interaction include status and power. **Status** is the esteem or regard the members have for each other. It can come from previous success, reputation, or nonverbal com-munication signals that show wealth or experience. **Power** is related to status in that it is the ability to influence the group. For example, you can use your expertise to get the group to adopt your ideas. Or you may try using references to others by saying, for example, "I know the boss really well." Some people try to use rewards or punishments to influence the decisions and actions of others, and you commonly find these people in a work setting. Raises, bonuses, good grades and evaluations, and promotions are examples of rewards. Sometimes, you may be an elected leader and therefore have legitimate power over the flow of information in your group. These personal variables can affect group dynam-ics—who sits where, who gets listened to or ignored, or who will help shape the final outcome of the group effort.

Independent Influences

The personal influences that are generally independent of the group interaction are usually those that the members had before they joined the group. For exam-ple, a member's personality type is fairly constant. If you are an easygoing, open-minded individual, you will most likely be that way in a group. We all know someone who is bossy, pushy, demanding, close-minded, and authoritar-ian, and we dread working with such people in a group because we know they will bring those qualities to the small-group interaction.

Your age, gender, and health can affect the way you function in a small group, yet they are not consequences of the group interaction, and they will remain constant after the group has finished its task. However, they do affect the way the group as a whole operates. If you are significantly older or younger than the rest of the members of your group, you may be more or less likely to be selected leader or be more or less influential in the decision-making process. We tend to value experience, so if you are obviously younger than the rest of the group, you may find it difficult to have your ideas treated with the same intellectual weight as those of an older person. Even if your ideas have merit, they may be missed because of your young age. This problem is especially frustrating for young people recently out of college who enter a workplace filled with experienced employees. The existing group may be somewhat resistant to suggestions or ideas from new, younger personnel. For the same reason, a sorority on your campus will probably be headed by a senior, not a sophomore.

While much progress in equality for women has been made in recent decades, our culture still shows a bias for giving leadership, influence, and power in general to males rather than females and to people from majority cultures rather than minorities. Your gender alone may be enough for a group to ask you to be the secretary for the group, to bring the refreshments if you are female, or to chair the meeting if you are male. You may be utterly incompetent at a particular job and wonderful at another, but stereotypes persist and are difficult to identify and to overcome. That is why the step of *identifying the group resources* is so important, as was discussed earlier in this chapter. An objective assessment of the talents that are available among the members of the group will help you to use members' abilities realistically. In the same context, people with physical handicaps are often passed over because others are apparently reluctant to focus on their abilities rather than on their disabilities. People from minority races or cultures are also familiar with the reactions of others who ignore their potential out of prejudice.

You know intellectually that these factors influence our reactions, but so many of these reactions are subconsciously motivated. So you need to make certain you are conducting an objective analysis of peoples' talents. Monitoring your own communication behavior is the best way to develop sensitivity to the talents of people who are different from you.

LEADERSHIP INFLUENCES

When you think of small groups, you should automatically think about **leadership.** The two concepts seem to go so naturally together, and many people believe that one reason to teach about small-group communication is to help students develop their leadership abilities. To some extent, this perception is true. Unfortunately, many people also think of leadership in terms of a single person *directing* a group, when leadership is better defined as *any behavior that influences the group.* We like to think of leadership in its positive sense; therefore good leadership behaviors are those that help the group to attain its goal. Bad leadership prevents or deters the group form achieving goals.

Leadership may mean the ability to help meet task goals or the behaviors that help to meet social goals. You can find some people who are good at influencing part of the group discussion, but not others. For example, Todd reserved the room, sets up the tables and chairs, and adjusted the thermostat, but says very little during the discussion. Did Todd play a leadership role? How about Cora, who brought the encyclopedia and dictionaries that everyone used all evening? Then there was Maya, who called the meeting to order, and Greg, who brought chips and drinks and kept notes on what was said.

Each of these behaviors helped the group—influenced it for the better to accomplish its task. Some people would look just to the chairperson as having leadership, and they would miss all sorts of leadership activity going on in that particular small group. Influences can also be negative, as when Freida barges in late, asks the group to give her advice on purchasing a new car, then leaves without giving the group the piece of information they were counting on. In this example, Freida has exerted a negative influence on the group's task.

There are usually four types of group leadership climates, or styles, that can be identified for any particular group.

Authoritarian leadership is characterized by the dominance of one person and the acceptance of that dominance by others. A single member can have complete influence over a group, and the group goes along with it. If the group is in an emergency situation, it probably wants an authoritarian figure who is also an expert in the work of the group. Fighting a fire, running an army or a police force, or meeting a midnight deadline for a project will most likely produce leadership in the authoritarian mode. The problem is that most members do not rate having an authority figure as being personally satisfying, so the group will probably lose some of its resources.

Democratic leadership is one that we all seem to value in our culture because it rates high in both utilization of group resources and in member satisfaction. If time is not a big problem and members have an abundance of good input, then a sharing of power, decision by consensus, and consultation might be appropriate. You and other members of your clubs probably operate in a democratic mode, as do members of most voluntary associations.

Laissez-faire leadership is something you may remember from your political science or history classes. It is characterized by a let-it-happen or hands-off style of leadership. Minimal direction is offered, and the group just finds its way without much of an agenda or deadline. A party is a good example of laissez-faire leadership. Some planning is necessary; but once the party is launched, no goal or task need drive the group. You can see how well a laissez-faire approach might work for social interactions, but what a disaster it would be for building a house, producing a car, or fighting a fire.

The fourth type of leadership is barely visible, but it is seen in those brief periods when everyone in the group actively rejects any leadership at all. It is called *abdacratic* leadership, and it is almost a contradiction in terms. No one takes any steps to influence the group, and any attempts that are made are just as quickly rejected by the rest of the group. The group is in a state of rebellion, and group disintegration is often quick to follow. In large societies, anarchy and revolution are the expression of this behavior. Curiously, the style of leadership that is most likely to follow the abdacratic style is the authoritarian style, bringing our styles around to full circle. Imagine a study group in which the members start to wander off the topic, begin to play music, order out for pizza, drift to side conversations, and lose all focus. Someone may finally shout, "Let's get back to work!" and begin to turn off the music, put away the pizza, and try to

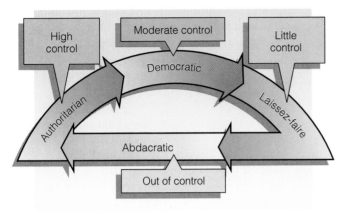

Leadership styles vary by amounts of control.

take charge. This person may become the authoritarian leader. This example is a good demonstration of how leadership styles can come around full circle.

OUTCOMES AND MEASUREMENT

Once you have settled on your group type, worked on creating an appropriate setting and leadership style, and taken into account all the personalities and resources in your group, you are ready to assess the **outcomes** of the interaction. How do you evaluate a group?

The easiest way to begin is to ask, "Did the group reach its goal?" If members set out to have a good party and did, then the group was successful. If members set out to get good grades on an exam the next day but instead had a good party, then the group did not reach its goal.

You can get a **measurement** of group outcomes in many ways. If the group is a task group, then you can look solely at the product. Sometimes, you may wish to measure member satisfaction. Often, a combination of the two is helpful, because people who are enjoying the group experience are likely to facilitate a good outcome. If a group is well organized, uses group resources, and establishes effective communicative interaction, then its final outcome will be better than that of a group that fails to create such a positive communication climate.

In an interesting series of experiments, communication scholar Dale Leathers measured the communication processes of a number of small groups and then had independent raters assess the quality of the products these groups produced (Leathers, 1969). A consistent finding was that if the discussion process was disrupted or faulty in any way, then the product was judged to be inferior. This latter judgment came from people who had no idea of how the group had behaved; they saw only the final product. So if you think that it does not matter how people are getting along and it matters only that the job gets done, you may wish to look at Leathers's research. It could change your mind.

Group process, as differentiated from group outcome, can be measured by looking at the good communication skills and attributes you have learned about throughout this text. Clear use of language, respect for others' opinions, good use of evidence and logical thinking, attention to criteria and definitions, and equal opportunity to expressing an opinion are among the important things to look for in evaluating the communication processes in small groups.

ORGANIZATIONS: GROUPS WORKING TOGETHER

When a collection of groups works together within a large system, they are most likely part of an organization. Many of the characteristics of small groups—networks and patterns, personal influences, leadership, and outcomes—are also seen in the larger, multiple group system of the organization. Sometimes, the effect on the group of one or more of these characteristics gets magnified and becomes very powerful. For example, status in an organization can become so strong that it is intimidating. Suppose you were a production line employee at a large company and the senior vice-president in charge of production came walking through your department one day, unannounced. If she were to ask you how things were going, you would probably say that things were just fine, even if you had a complaint. You are more likely to make a complaint to your immediate supervisor and to distort your messages in a positive direction as you give them to people of higher and higher status (Krivonos, 1976).

Communication in an organization takes time, and people who are at message intersections have control over the flow of messages and can become very powerful. For example, a secretary who gets all the messages and distributes all the memos can be an important person. By being at the crossroads where information meets, the secretary becomes very knowledgeable. People in this position are sometimes called *gatekeepers* because they can either let information pass through or hold it up. Message distortion is more likely to occur in an organization than in a small group for the obvious reason that in a small group, there is immediate feedback to check information. In an organization, not only do delays distort information, but all the people who get a message and then pass it along also filter and screen that message. If the message starts out from very high in the organization, it may become more and more negatively perceived as it travels downward. Rumor begins to color the message so that the message may be very different by the time it reaches the entire organization. Imagine a college president talking about impending budget cuts and saying, "We'll have to do more with less next year." If word spreads from one level down to the next, there will probably be rumors around campus of classes being canceled, salaries being cut, and people being laid off, all within days of the transmission of the original message.

Some organizations try to build in automatic correction mechanisms, such as bulletins, suggestion boxes, open meetings, and direct conversations to guard against and correct distorted messages. Yet distorted messages seem to be a fact of life for large organizations. A good communication tactic to counteract this phenomenon uses the small-group principles of feedback and response to help minimize the negative effects on messages due to the sheer size of the organization. For example, suppose a major corporation decides to expand its operations and build a new plant in another state. After hearing the news, someone might wonder aloud whether that means cutbacks or closing of existing plants. Pretty soon others are repeating that they heard from so-and-so that their jobs are being relocated. The rumor starts on the basis of some factual information, then, as the information was passed along, it is distorted. Finally, a worker asks the area supervisor about the "impending layoff plan," which motivates the supervisor to ask top management for clarification. The next day, a bulletin comes from top management explaining that a new plant opening will not affect the operations of the existing facility.

A final effect worth noting is that which is generated by the variables of competition and cooperation in large organizations. If resources and rewards are plentiful, it is fairly easy to get different small groups within an organization to cooperate. However, as is more often the case, if resources are limited, there will be a competitive atmosphere in the organization. If held to an optimal level, competition can increase both motivation and loyalty to the small group. At its worst, it can lead to the deliberate sending of misinformation, secrecy, suspicion, and even sabotage. A good management team is aware of the potential for communication conflicts in an organization and uses proven techniques of interpersonal and small-group communication to moderate them.

IMPROVING SMALL-GROUP COMMUNICATION COMPETENCY

One way to increase your effectiveness as a small-group participant is to understand the processes of small-group interactions and the influences that help those processes to become effective. For example, you know that a goal must be clearly defined for a group to reach it. If the goal for some people is social and the goal for others is to get some work done, you can help by initiating discussion about the purpose of the group so that the conflict has a chance to be resolved. Along the same lines, the most appropriate leadership style for situation A may be completely wrong for situation B. Can you move from a democratic to an authoritarian or laissez-faire style if that is what your group needs? By learning about the variety of group communication styles, you can increase your *repertoire* of communicative behaviors.

Selection of the most appropriate behavior from your repertoire is the second step to communication competency, and it is often a difficult one. For example, if you are involved in a strong disagreement, it may be hard to step back and analyze your own behavior to select a more appropriate behavior for that situation. If you have a personality clash, selecting a different style of group leadership may be a strenuous task. You may find it difficult to work with someone on decision-making criteria for the group if you have just gone through an extended conflict with that person. Selection can involve some experimentation as well. If you try one behavior and it does not work, analyze the situation again, go back to the alternatives you have learned about, and try another.

The process of analysis can involve the entire group. One useful method for generating possible solutions and then selecting from among them is called **brainstorming.** This method of small-group communication is one you probably have heard of, yet few people or groups use it when it is most needed or do it very well. The method is basic, and it has two phases. The first phase involves the generation of a large number of ideas as quickly as possible. During this period, any idea is acceptable, and no criticism, especially any that is negative, is allowed, either verbal or nonverbal. If someone tosses out an idea that you do not like, don't waste a moment thinking about it. Keep generating your own ideas or playing off their suggestions to come up with other ideas. Someone should be appointed to the job of recorder and should write down every idea mentioned—humorous, brilliant, bizarre, off-color, or nonsensical. The first phase must generate a large pool of ideas, and anything goes. Usually, between five and fifteen minutes are allotted for this phase. Do not be tempted to stop when there is a pause and give up by saying something like, "Well, I can't think of anything else; let's quit now." Give yourselves a set amount of time, and keep at it until that time is up. It is important that you avoid evaluating other people's ideas *and* that you avoid doing any *self*-criticism. For example, you might get a quick inspiration, then judge it yourself, decide that it sounds silly, and never mention it. Such internal censoring hurts the entire effort. You might be right, your idea might be silly itself, but it could very well inspire someone else in the group to come up with a spinoff idea that exactly solves your group's problem. If you hold back, you markedly diminish the total resources of your group. Does this advice mean that you never evaluate? Not at all. *Evaluation* is step 2.

Once your group has generated a number of ideas and has written down all of them, it is time for an *evaluation* of those ideas. Sometimes a short break helps to keep the two phases—brainstorming and evaluation—separate. Now go back over the list of ideas. People usually do not remember or do not care who said what. They want to pick through the ideas to select those that seem to fit the group's goal. If you are following the five-step decision-making model outlined earlier, you will have a definition of the problem or some evaluation criteria to help sort out the various ideas and suggestions into those that correspond to the group's goal and those that do not. Brainstorming and evaluation can be excellent tools for helping you generate and select the option which best fits your group's needs.

Once you have selected your plan, or strategy, it is time for *implementation*. Putting into practice or applying the selected approach to the problem will require the cooperation of the whole group. The interaction and mutual dependence of small groups are controlling factors that require that the group work together. If you have taken care that the brainstorming and the development of the evaluation criteria have been carried out in a fair manner, you will have an easier time putting the group's choice into practice. Implementation may require that jobs be identified and assigned appropriately, an aspect of communication competency that is also covered in a five-part decision-making plan.

The *evaluation* aspect of communication competency can take place in small steps throughout the duration of the group's work. When you gather feedback and incorporate that feedback into the evolution of the group's activities, you are making use of the strategy of evaluation. Of course, there is always the final evaluation. Your group had a successful party, built a great car, or turned in a highly rated project for your class. You can also evaluate member satisfaction, the quality of the group's communication interactions, and the quality of the project's final outcome.

Any increase in your communication competency is a result of your being able to use evaluation as feedback. You will be able to identify ways in which to

IMPROVING COMPETENCY

Overcoming Stereotypes

Many small group members carry around stereotypes about what kind of person is good at a particular job or role. Such attitudes block small groups from achieving full potential. These stereotypes may be based on age, gender, race, ethnicity, level of education, or other factors. They may be those you have about other members, or they can even be about yourself. Remember, one of the primary suggestions in this chapter is to utilize the resources of your group, and these resources must be recognized before they can be effectively included in the group interaction. This may mean that you need to volunteer for a variety of jobs or take on different role behaviors from those you typically assume in a small group. Give yourself some "job rotation" as mentioned in this chapter under the discussion about how Japanese often manage their organizations. In addition to exploring your own talents, remember to check with other members about their talents or preferences or experiences. Check your own assumptions about who knows the most about baseball or who can type fastest or who knows all the current television shows. Work for inclusion of resources as a way to make your group the most effective it can be.

do things differently in your next small group. Moreover, you will have increased your repertoire of potential behaviors, and the decision-making process in your next group can begin on a stronger footing.

SUMMARY

Small groups are a fact of life, and in this chapter, we have barely scratched the surface of the many factors that go into successful, small-group interaction. Many schools have entire courses devoted to small-group communication. Some courses focus on the skills that are needed to function well in small groups; others spend an entire term exploring the research that has been done on groups. You can begin immediately to improve your performance as a competent, small-group communicator, but you can also work at developing various aspects of your ability throughout your life. Because small groups are such a common and important aspect of our lives, the time and effort you spend enhancing your abilities as an effective communicator will be well worthwhile.

KEY TERMS

small-group communication, *p. 182*
interaction, *p. 183*
influence, *p. 184*
common goal, *p. 184*
organization, *p. 184*
norms, *p. 185*
social groups, *p. 185*

primary group, *p. 186*
reference behavior, *p. 186*
safety and solidarity needs, *p. 187*
self-esteem needs, *p. 187*
work groups, *p. 188*
decision-making groups, *p. 190*
communication networks, *p. 193*

EXERCISES

1. Make a list of the various groups in which you participate during a typical week. Identify those that are formal and those that are informal. Next, designate the ones that are primarily social, those that are task-oriented, and those that are focused on decision making. In how many groups do you participate in a week's time?

2. Consider the small groups that you identified in the first exercise. What roles do you play in each? Do you find yourself engaging in any leadership behaviors? What leadership styles—authoritarian, democratic, laissez-faire, or abdacratic—do you find in each of your groups? Do some styles seem more or less appropriate for a particular group than other styles? If so, why or why not?

3. Peer pressure is a force that often leads to conformity. What examples of peer pressure can you observe on a daily basis, either in yourself or in others?

4. The next time you are in a group, try to apply the five steps of problem solving. For example, it can be very stimulating to engage in brainstorming if, thanks to you, everyone is aware of the rules and follows them. Your continuing efforts with the remaining four steps can also help give your group focus and energy throughout their problem-solving discussions.

REFERENCES

Asch, Solomon. *Social Psychology*. New York: Prentice-Hall, 1952. 450–501.

Fisher, B. Aubrey. "Decision Emergence: Phases in Group Decision Making." *Speech Monographs* 37 (1970), 53–66.

Hatvany, Nina, and Vladimir Pucik. "Japanese Management Practices and Productivity." *Organizational Dynamics* (Spring 1981), 5–21.

Krivonos, Paul. "Distortion of Subordinate to Superior Communication." Meeting of International Communication Association. Portland, Oregon, 1976.

Leathers, D. G. "Process Disruption and Measurement in Small Group Communication." *Quarterly Journal of Speech* 55 (1969), 287.

Rothwell, J. Dan. *In Mixed Company*. 2nd ed. New York: Harcourt, 1995.

Tubbs, Stewart. *A Systems Approach to Small Group Interaction*. 5th ed. New York: McGraw-Hill, 1995.

Preparing Speeches

After reading this chapter, you should be able to:

- Understand and apply the principles of outlining and the organizational development of speeches.

- Describe and use techniques for analyzing an audience.

- Identify and locate a variety of supporting materials.

- Feel competent to create and present a speech in public.

- Have a commitment to communicating with your listeners.

- Create an acceptable, formal speech outline.

As you begin preparing a public presentation, you need to consider many factors—yourself, your listeners, your topic, the occasion, the setting, the amount of time you will have, the purpose, and perhaps many other things. Central to any message, however, is that it be clear. If you fail to have clarity, your message is likely to be misunderstood. The foundation of clarity is organization, and good organization will help you to accomplish all of your other goals. After learning about organization, you will learn how to analyze your listeners so that your message can be adapted to them. Different types of supporting materials and how to find them are also covered in this chapter. But as was mentioned above, organizing your message is the starting point. Two approaches to help you with organization will be discussed: outlining principles and organizational development in speeches.

OUTLINING PRINCIPLES

This section is intended as a review of the **outlining** principles and techniques that you have been studying for many years in language arts classes. You are probably familiar with the major symbols that are used to organize an outline: Roman numerals, capital letters, Arabic numbers, lowercase letters, numbers in parentheses, and letters in parentheses. This system is universally used in the composition of both written and oral discourse. These symbols have been developed over many years as a way to keep ideas in order, in terms of both sequence and relationship. Speaking well involves much more than just talking clearly. A coherent message is one that is carefully constructed and pays attention to techniques of organization from the very beginning. When you have selected a particular type of speech and the appropriate thesis to go with it, an outline will provide you with a complete structure to guide you in constructing a speech.

General Outlines

The outline format lends itself to a variety of purposes, and you can also select from among several patterns of development in speeches, all of which fit into

---

CRITICAL THINKING IN COMMUNICATION

The Logical Structure of Outlines

One of the things you will notice about an outline is that it is logical. If you can look at items and put them in a logical sequence of relationships to each other, you will be able to create an organized speech. The linking together of superior, coordinate, and subordinate ideas can help you to move from large subjects to specific, supporting materials. It helps to cluster ideas or examples because the items in these clusters will form the subdivisions for your speech outline. Look for main ideas (superior position in the outline) and for supporting details or explanations (subordinate position in the outline) that fit logically under the main ideas.

the same general outline structure. A simple outline that can be used in virtually any public-speaking situation has five main parts. Each of these parts is defined briefly, and then some rules and guidelines for creating an outline are presented.

Sample Outline.   A five-part speech outline looks like this:

I. **Introduction.** About 10 percent of your time can be spent on the introduction. A brief story, an interesting example or statistic, or a startling statement, quotation, or illustration can work well as an introduction.

II. **Thesis sentence.** This item represents the main idea of your entire speech. It also expresses the central purpose of your speech.

III. **Body of the speech.** About 85 percent of your time will be spent on the body of the speech. A preview of the main ideas in the body of the speech can be a good transition from the thesis sentence to the body itself. The body of the speech usually has between two and five main subsections. This example has four main subdivisions.
   A. First main subdivision
      1. Supporting material for A
      2. Supporting material for A
   B. Second main subdivision
      1. Supporting material for B
      2. Supporting material for B
      3. Supporting material for B
   C. Third main subdivision
      1. Supporting material for C
      2. Supporting material for C
   D. Fourth main subdivision
      1. Supporting material for D
      2. Supporting material for D
      3. Supporting material for D

IV. **Conclusion.** About 2 to 5 percent of your time will be used for the conclusion. A brief review of A, B, C, and D; the thesis sentence; and the introduction.

V. **Sources/bibliography/references.** You may list sources alphabetically by author or in footnote order—the order in which they appear in your speech. This section is not read aloud during your speech, but you may cite a specific source at the point in the speech when you are presenting information from that source.
   A. First source, listed in a standard format.
   B. Second source.
   C. Third source.

Introduction and Thesis.   The outline format presented here shows how you can link your ideas together. Each part has a function that relates to every other part. The *introduction* is where you capture the audience's attention so that your listeners will be ready to focus on your thesis sentence. You can take these moments—about 10 percent of your total time for a short speech—to become comfortable with the situation and to let your audience become accustomed to looking at you and hearing your voice. You can also set the mood you want for your presentation. Will it be humorous or serious? Let your listeners clearly understand your mood from the beginning.

The *thesis sentence* is the main idea of your entire speech, but should you start with it? Often, the audience is not quite focused on you; and if you begin by saying, "Today, my speech is on . . . ," they might miss your main idea. In addition, your listeners will be disappointed by such an unimaginative and uninteresting opening. Do not get to your thesis sentence until after the introduction. Then make it simple and to the point. Everything else in the presentation is controlled by your thesis sentence. The introduction must lead up to it, and the body explains and supports it. The thesis sentence is the most important—but smallest—part of your speech.

Body and Supporting Materials.

The *body* is where the speech takes shape and where 85 percent or so of your time will be spent. The body clarifies, explains, extends, defends, and supports your thesis sentence. Usually, the explanation of your thesis sentence can be broken down into two to five main subsections or subdivisions. Later in this chapter, you will see some examples of how to divide the body into logical patterns. For now, notice how each subsection has specific supporting materials under it.

Supporting materials are the specific items that you use to illustrate or prove your point. They may be examples, statistics, short stories, illustrations, quotations, visual aids, or statements. Supporting materials can include personal experiences; case histories; results of opinion polls, research studies, or experiments; and materials from songs, literature, or poetry. One way to enrich your presentation is to use a variety of supporting materials. Each of these is explained in more detail later in the chapter.

Conclusion.

The fourth subsection of the outline is the *conclusion,* which is a short review of the main subsections of the body (but not the specific supporting materials), the thesis sentence, and a reference to the opening material that you used in the introduction. The conclusion should be brief—about half as long as your introduction—and it should tell your listeners that you have come to a close.

Sources.

Finally, you need a list of your sources—Part V in the sample outline. Sources can be a standard bibliography, a list of references, or footnotes such as you add to the end of a term paper. You need to credit the sources of your material to avoid a charge of plagiarism. **Plagiarism** means using someone else's ideas or words without giving that person credit. It is dishonest—a form of academic and intellectual theft—and a serious crime in any field. Certainly, you need to use and probably depend on other people's work and ideas to create your own. By giving those sources credit, you acknowledge their contribution to your effort. In fact, you build your own credibility by making listeners aware of all the experts you have consulted. So for many reasons, make certain that you properly credit all work that is not your own.

There are several ways to acknowledge this credit. The Modern Language Association (MLA) format is the format that most colleges use. The MLA is a national group of English teachers, scholars, and others who are interested in the field of English. They publish the *MLA Handbook for Writers of Research Papers,* which presents standard ways to cite sources for everything, from books to interviews. Citations usually begin with the author's name, last name first, then the title of the article or book, then the name of the larger work if the material is only one section of it, then the publisher, city, date, and perhaps the page numbers. This is the format you have probably been using on every paper you have written since junior high school. For this book, the citation would look like this:

> Zeuschner, Raymond. *Communicating Today.* 2nd ed. Boston: Allyn and Bacon, 1997.

If you were using an article from a magazine or a journal, it would look like this:

> Rubin, Rebecca B. "Assessing Speaking and Listening Competence at the College Level: The Communication Competence Assessment Instrument." *Communication Education* 31 (January 1983): 19–33.

There are minor variations on these forms, but the important information is consistent throughout. You need to give listeners and readers enough information that they can easily locate the source. Although following the form makes your bibliography look correct, what is really important is that you credit all your sources in a clear and consistent way.

Subordination and Grouping

There are rules to keep in mind as you create any outline for any message. Outlines have a logical construction, and the simple rules of subordination and grouping can help you to create a logical structure to your own outline. Always remember that your ideas exist in *relationship* to each other, with the more abstract or general main ideas listed flush left and the smaller, detailed, supporting ideas indented to the right. The rule of subordination tells you whether something should be labeled with a Roman numeral or a capital letter—that is, whether the item is a main idea or a supporting detail.

The rule of grouping tells you that all related ideas need to be in the same group. If a supporting detail relates directly to subdivision X, it needs to be in X's group. If it's not related to X, then it belongs to Y's group or Z's group. If it is not related to any of these, it belongs in yet another group or in a different outline.

Sample Outlines.   The rule of grouping says that there must be a direct link among all the items in the group. At the beginning, it might look like this:

> I. Main idea X
>   A. First subordinate idea related to X
>   B. Second subordinate idea related to X
> II. Main idea Y
>   A. First subordinate idea related to Y
>   B. Second subordinate idea related to Y
>   C. Third subordinate idea related to Y
>   D. Fourth subordinate idea related to Y

   III. Main idea Z
     A. First subordinate idea related to Z
     B. Second subordinate idea related to Z

The rules of subordination could continue further under X—A and B; or under Y—A, B, C, and D; or under Z—A and B, as follows:

   I. Main idea X
     A. First subordinate idea related to X
     B. Second subordinate idea related to X
        1. Supporting material related to B
        2. Second supporting material related to B
  II. Main idea Y
     A. First subordinate idea related to Y
     B. Second subordinate idea related to Y
     C. Third subordinate idea related to Y
        1. First supporting material related to C
        2. Second supporting material related to C
     D. Fourth subordinate idea related to Y
 III. Main idea Z
     A. First subordinate idea related to Z
     B. Second subordinate idea related to Z

When an item is indented below another item, it must be related to the item directly above and must be of less importance, or subordinate to it. Thus you can see the main principle of outlining at work: *Keep the relationship in order.* The most important, comprehensive ideas are flush left. Less important ideas, examples, illustrations, or research results that *support* the important ideas are indented. All similar or coordinate ideas must be in the same group.

Let us put these principles into a real-word outline format. Look at the two examples below and determine which one follows these principles correctly and which does not.

Example A

   I. Television shows and entertainment
     A. TV and music
        1. MTV
        2. *Great Performances*
     B. TV and comedy
        1. *Seinfeld*
        2. *Murphy Brown*
        3. *Home Improvement*
     C. Sports programs on TV
        1. *Monday Night Football*
        2. Olympic games
  II. Television shows and information
     A. News programs
        1. *The News Hour with Jim Lehrer*
        2. *Nightline*
        3. CNN—all-news format

　　　B. Special series
　　　　1. *Nova*
　　　　2. Jacques Cousteau specials
　　　　3. *National Geographic* specials
　　　　　a. "Voyage of Columbus"
　　　　　b. "World of Antarctica"

Example B

　I. TV has comedy.
　　A. Television entertains us.
　　B. *Seinfeld*
　　C. *Murphy Brown*
　　D. *Home Improvement*
　II. Television news informs us.
　　A. Sports programs such as *Monday Night Football*
　　B. Olympics every four years
　　C. *The News Hour with Jim Lehrer*
　III. *Nova* and other PBS specials
　　A. *The News Hour with Jim Lehrer*
　　B. Jacques Cousteau specials
　　　a. Other specials are *National Geographic*
　　　b. The "Voyage of Columbus" and "Antarctica"
　　C. *Nightline* is another good show.
　　D. Specials and sports
　　　1. MTV has specials.

Even a quick glance will show that Example B is a hodgepodge of disorganization. Not only do the ideas not follow the principle of subordination, but the rule of grouping is also disobeyed, since many of the ideas do not belong

IMPROVING COMPETENCY

Practicing Subordination

Try looking at any system of organization and see how these relationships are present. For example, look at the college you are attending. If you think of the entire school as your main idea, then what would constitute A, B, and C? Perhaps you would put the words *Academic Affairs* as A, and then put *Student Activities* as B. *Facilities Operations* might be C, and perhaps D would be *Fiscal Affairs*. You could then take each one of those areas and begin listing Arabic numbers under them, so that academic departments become 1, 2, 3, 4, and so on under A. The various student clubs and activities would be listed with Arabic numbers under B. Try filling out such an outline for your job, church, club, family, team, or city government, and you will see how patterns of organization are present in every aspect of our lives. Learning and applying the principles of outlining can help you to see, understand, and use the patterns that operate in our daily affairs.

together. Items related to sports are listed under both II and III, and there does not appear to be any system at work. Which are the main ideas and which are subordinate? Go back to Example A and see that the more abstract concepts— the ones that are comprehensive or "bigger"—are to the left while the specific examples are indented to the right.

Note that Example A is a clear illustration of the principles of outlining: The main ideas are flush left, symbols are used consistently, there is one single idea per item, and all items in one group are related to each other and to the main idea above them. Although both examples follow the rules for indenting, in Example B one area has reversed the use of numbers and letters. Can you find the error? If you identified III, B as the problem and said that the a and b should really be 1 and 2, you understand how to use these principles. That example brings us to the next step in preparing a good outline: the consistent use of proper symbols.

Symbols

In preparing an outline for your speeches, use the *standard outline symbol system*. Remember to do the following: (1) Start with capital Roman numerals; (2) alternate between numbers and letters; (3) indent so that all capital letters are the same distance from the left-hand margin and all similar numbers are indented and aligned with each other. The following example illustrates these guidelines:

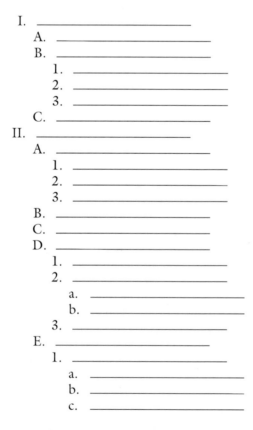

      2. _____

III. _____

     A. _____

     B. _____

Notice how each subsection is indented so that the relationship is clearly expressed. Superior ideas contain subordinate materials. Coordinate ideas are equally placed and are of equal importance. Thus E is superior to E.1 and E.2 but is subordinate to II. Which items are coordinate with E? If you said A, B, C, and D, you have the right idea. What do you know about the material to be listed under II. D. 2. b? You should be able to say that b is a specific supporting idea or fact that is similar to a in degree of importance and that they are both linked to 2, which is a subordinate idea under D, which in turn is a main category under the major concept II. If that little b does not relate back through its series of links, then it belongs somewhere else. If b is more than a very specific idea, then it probably needs to be upgraded to a number or perhaps to a capital letter. For most of your speeches, you will probably be able to express your ideas and their relationships by using just this level of detail and nothing more detailed. You may even stop at the Arabic numbers in a key idea outline.

TECHNOLOGY IN COMMUNICATION

Software Outlines

The importance of outlining can be measured by the development of software packages to help students and people in business develop outlines. Many of these packages have a template format that puts ideas into a format, automatically using the next correct symbol and providing the proper indentation. As you make internal changes and substitutions, the program then automatically renumbers the subsequent material. However, responsibility for what goes into the outline still lies with the writer.

Efficiency of Expression

Your main ideas should be expressed as simple, single ideas. You may use a full sentence or key words. Whichever you choose or your instructor assigns, be consistent throughout your preparation. Do not mix sentences and single words or phrases in the same outline. Keep each line focused on one single idea. This guideline will help you decide to which group or cluster a particular item belongs. Try to avoid the use of the word *and* in your sentences or key ideas. That word may indicate that you have two ideas in one item. For example:

Wrong

    I. It's hard to raise guide dogs because of the time and attention and the strain it puts on the owners when you have to give them up.

      A. They take a lot of time away from other activities, and you need training to give them proper attention.

      B. It is difficult to give them up after you've raised them, so be prepared.

Instead, try being concise and simple:

Right

I. Raising guide dogs can be a difficult task.
   A. You need lots of time.
   B. You need special training.
   C. You need to be prepared to give them away.

The second example correctly identifies three distinct areas of difficulty and keeps the sentences brief.

Outlining can be of real assistance to you in your speech preparation. If you remember the five major parts, you can put your thoughts in order and visualize the relationships among the parts. All parts connect to the thesis sentence.

In addition to the overall organization of an outline, there are a variety of ways to focus on the body of the speech and put it into a pattern.

ORGANIZATIONAL PATTERNS

As you can probably sense, a good speech does not just come out of someone's mouth on the spur of the moment. Many excellent speakers *appear* smooth and spontaneous as a result of spending many hours thinking about their speech, researching ideas and supporting materials, trying out a variety of ways to organize it, and practicing until they are confident and comfortable. If you are going to achieve your purpose with your presentation, you should think carefully about your ideas and how each is related to the others. Examine your thesis sentence, and decide whether there are ways to break it down into a few subordinate ideas. For example, some topics can be thought of in terms of a sequence of steps or stages, each following the previous one in a logical or systematic order. Another common-sense pattern is to arrange subordinate ideas according to particular topics or divisions among the ideas. Finally, in persuasive communication, you may wish to put the body of your speech into a motivational pattern to move your listeners to agreement or action. Let us take a look at each of these **organizational development patterns.**

Sequential Patterns

If your topic has an obvious, step-by-step order, or involves a series of ideas or events that move in a certain logical progression, you are dealing with sequence, or the *sequential pattern*. There are four major sequential patterns: time, space, size, and importance. The *time sequence pattern* is often called *chronological*, which means that you organize the A-B-C-D sections of the body of your presentation according to the relationship your ideas have, or have had, over time.

For example, it you are discussing an event in the past—an event leading up to World War I or the chronological events of your vacation trip—you start with the earliest events and finish with the most recent events. Many speakers find the past-present-future time pattern a convenient way to discuss items. If you use it, you'll find that the A-B-C parts of the outline are ready made for you. In the A section, you will cluster the information about the topic's history and about the events that led up to the current situation. The B section will describe

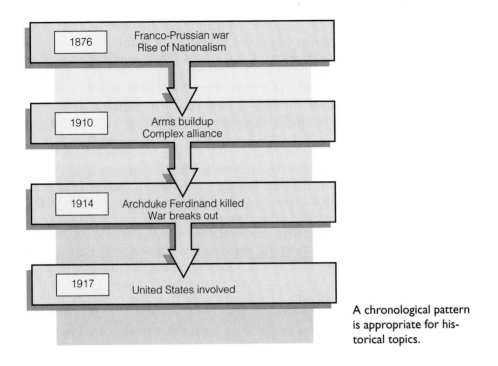

A chronological pattern is appropriate for historical topics.

what is happening now. In the C section, you can speculate on what will be coming in the future This pattern is popular because both the speaker and the audience can follow it and remember it with ease.

Another use of the time sequence pattern is found in the process, or how-to, speech. Follow the steps above until you have completed your description of

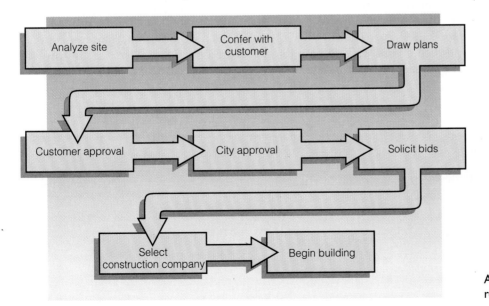

A sequence is a pattern of related steps.

the process. Are you building a house? Preparing lasagna? Producing a play? The time sequence pattern may be perfect for your presentation.

A related pattern that could work for some of the above topics involves *space*. For example, if your vacation started in Miami and you then went to Atlanta, then to New Orleans, and back to Miami, these events are connected geographically—that is, in space—as well as in time. The *spatial sequence pattern* is easy to see in an outline that explains things that exist in the material world. For example, you could give a speech about the Hawaiian Islands from the perspective of time—early volcanic activity, the settling by Polynesians, the kingdom era, European arrivals, annexation to the United States, and statehood. Or you could discuss the fact that the island start at Midway Island and end with the island of Hawaii. Your outline could also start with Midway Island and end with Hawaii. You could give a talk about your campus, starting at one end and moving in a spatial relationship from one building or section of campus to the next one that a person would come to if he or she were walking. Of course, you could also talk about the buildings according to the order in which they were built and then go back to chronological order. Do you want to discuss the solar system? Start with the sun and work your way out from there—chronologically *and* spatially.

The *size sequence pattern* is the third pattern, and it works well for certain topics. For example, your solar system speech may start with the sun, then move to Jupiter as the next largest, then Neptune, and so on until you got to Pluto, the smallest planet. Or you could reverse the order: Start with the smallest and move on to the largest. A speech on types of hawks, for example, might start with smallest species, continue to the middle-size birds, and end with a discussion about the largest member of the hawk family.

Finally, an *importance sequence pattern* could be used to discuss topics that make a judgment or use criteria to evaluate ideas. If you were running a political campaign, you might start your speech with a time pattern, or if you had only a few minutes to explain a complex idea, you could put the body of your speech into the order of importance of the items it contains. You could say, "The most important thing to do is . . ." and then, "The next most important thing is . . ." and then, "Finally, if you have the time or resources, consider. . . ." In this way, your listeners will grasp the relative importance of each item.

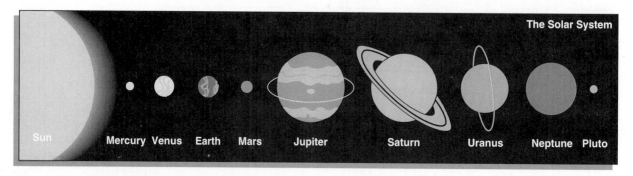

A visual aid can show objects related in size and space.

As you can tell from these examples, a speech can be logically arranged in a number of ways, all of which make some sequential sense. Your task is to select from among the sequential patterns and find the one that best suits you, your approach to the topic, your purpose, your research, your time frame, and your audience.

Topical Patterns

If your ideas do not fit the sequence format very well, you might try this group of patterns to provide a framework for the body of your speech. Topical patterns are based on the way we think about ideas or topics when we try to break them down or cluster them into logical divisions. This pattern is called the topical pattern because the subtopics of the thesis seem to flow naturally and logically from the subject of the thesis. The breakdown of the main ideas into subordinate ideas stems not from the relationship of those ideas in time or space, but from the logical way they can be put together.

One of the most popular topical patterns is one that shows the relationship of cause and effect. This pattern asserts that event X was the cause of event Y. For example, the Hawaiian Islands were formed by a series of volcanic eruptions, so you could give a speech about the series of events that caused the islands to form. The factors that caused the earthquakes could be the subject of a cause–effect topical pattern. This can be a tricky pattern. One of the most common logical fallacies occurs because many things are related only in time, but we make the faulty assumption that they also have a causal relationship. This fallacy is called *ergo propter hoc* (Latin meaning "After this, therefore because of this") or just the *post hoc* fallacy.

There is a similar pattern—a correlation—that sometimes looks like a cause–effect pattern but is not. For example, the failure to wear a seat belt is correlated with high death rates in motor vehicle accidents. The lack of a seat belt does not *cause* the accident, nor does it *cause* death. Smashing through a windshield or hitting the pavement with great force may cause death. However, the lack of a seat belt is connected, or *correlated,* with an increase in death rates in automobile accidents. Sometimes, correlation studies do show that one event *might* cause another. For example, all the studies of rates of cancer in smokers suggest that smokers have a much greater chance of getting lung cancer than nonsmokers. However, the fact that some people smoke and do not get lung cancer keeps this relationship from being, strictly speaking, a cause–effect relationship and places it in the category of a correlation. If you constantly miss class, will you get a low grade on the tests? Quite probably you will, but it is not certain that you will. However, it can be demonstrated that as a group, students who skip class frequently have lower grades than students who attend class regularly. You *might* be an exception; for example, if U.S. history is your hobby, you might be able to miss your U.S. history class and still do well on the tests. On the other hand, regular attendance correlates highly with high grades.

Parallel to the cause—effect pattern is the *problem–solution* pattern. In this pattern, the A section of the outline presents a particular problem, such as air pollution. The B section follows, with ideas and suggestions for solving the problem. You will find the problem–solution format useful in giving persuasive speeches. Many policy decisions are made through problem–solution approaches.

Watch television commercials, and you will see dozens of problem–solution presentations in an hour: "Do you have gray hair? Just use Young Forever Hair Cream." "How can you get rid of roaches in your kitchen? Easy, just buy Roach Bomb Spray!" "Are you tired of corruption in government? Vote for Zeuschner!" Examples of this format are everywhere.

Motivational Patterns

There are many explicitly persuasive patterns that speakers have used for centuries, and they belong in the motivational pattern group. Although each of the patterns previously discussed could probably be used to organize the body of a persuasive speech, motivational patterns have that application as their goal. One of the most widely used motivational patterns is called the **motivated sequence.** It was developed by speech teacher Alan H. Monroe over sixty years ago and has been popular ever since (Gronbeck, 1995). The five parts of this pattern are as follows:

1. *Attention:* Capture the attention of the audience and focus it on the topic.
2. *Need:* Present the problem so that the audience sees it as one that needs solving.
3. *Satisfaction*: Present the solution to the problem.
4. *Visualization:* Stimulate the audience's imagination by having them think about the consequences of either adopting or not adopting the solution.
5. *Action*: Get your listeners to take some specific step to put the solution into operation.

Although Monroe and his later collaborators used this five-part process to describe many types of speeches, its effectiveness is seen most clearly when the speaker asks the audience to take some action to solve the problem. In this format, your speech outline would have four parts to the body because step one,

---

THE STORY OF COMMUNICATION

Alan H. Monroe

Alan H. Monroe was one of the important figures in the development of the field of speech communication. His textbook *Principles and Types of Speech* was published in 1935. It included materials he had tested for nearly a decade in his own classes and in collaboration with scholars in psychology and business. He developed his organizational format largely on the basis of formats used in sales presentations. In 1940, while at Purdue University, he was president of the national Speech Communication Association. He continued to teach and influence an entire generation of teachers and scholars in the field with his use of social science approaches to a field then dominated by traditional rhetorical perspectives. Speech communication today continues to draw from a blend of the social sciences and the humanities, psychology and rhetoric. Professor Monroe died in 1975.

attention, would already be on your outline as *I. Introduction,* in the format presented earlier. Then, under *III. Body of the Speech,* you would list A as the need step, B as satisfaction, C for visualization, and D for action.

You can also motivate your listeners by using a *benefits* pattern, a pattern that describes all the good things they will gain if they adopt your thesis. Or you might take the opposite view and show them the costs they would incur if they took another course of action. Or you might combine the two into a cost–benefits pattern showing how much your suggestion costs and how much the alternatives would cost. Then you could compare the two on the basis of probable benefits.

From these organizational patterns—sequential, topical, and motivational—you can create the body of your speech so that it flows together in a logical order that makes sense to you and your listeners. Your presentations will be clear and will have the impact that you intended on your audience. When your main topic and its subordinate ideas are related in terms of size or time, you will probably use a sequential pattern. If the relationship is more like a grouping or cluster, you may want a topical pattern. Finally if you are trying to get your audience to do something, look to a motivational pattern to organize the body of your speech.

Each of these patterns is designed to help two parties in a communication transaction: you and your audience. To create a message that has both clarity and impact, you need to select a pattern that will enhance it. Communication in this setting takes place only if the audience gets the message that you intended, so make your message clear and strong by taking some time to think about the pattern that will best help you do that.

ANALYZING YOUR LISTENERS

A great deal was said in Chapter 3 about active listening from a receiver's point of view. In Chapter 7, you read about yourself as a processor of information. Now put those two ideas together, but see yourself as the *sender* of a message to a group of individuals who will try to listen to what you have to say. When you focus on the audience, you can begin the steps of **audience analysis.**

Aristotle's book *Rhetoric* devoted large sections to advice about how to approach a topic if older people or younger people were the audience. His reasoning was based on the values, attitudes, and beliefs that people bring with them when they are listening to a speaker. Values, attitudes, and beliefs as they relate to you personally are discussed in Chapter 7. Now it is time to think about how those aspects of your listeners might affect the way you create and deliver your presentation. The attitudes of your audience will affect their ability to listen. If they are in a good mood; if they like you, the speaker; and if they feel involved and connected to the topic, it will be easier for you to deliver your message (Lumsden and Lumsden, 1996).

Values are the social principles, goals, and standards that members of your audience have in common. Their values determine the overall guidelines for their life patterns, and they are generally few in number. If you are speaking to a college group, you can guess that they value education. A group of owners of small businesses probably value hard work and independence. These values provide the framework or foundation for their feelings and attitudes.

Audience analysis helps you to adapt your speech to the values and concerns of your listeners.

Several major **value systems** in our society have been identified that can help you to adapt your message to your listeners. For example, the Protestant–Puritan–Peasant system is known for its emphasis on hard work, family, religion, and education. Incidentally, these values are held by many more people than those who come from those three backgrounds. Jews, Catholics, Buddhists, and very wealthy people all may also hold these fundamental values. Another type of value system is the progressive value system, which stresses newness, invention, development, and exploration. On the other hand, some people hold primarily to the transcendental value system, which places an emphasis on spiritual feelings, intuition, and getting away from materialistic ties. Some researchers have identified Native American value systems, Mormon value systems, and specific corporate value structures (Reike and Sillars, 1983). The important thing to remember is that your listeners will apply whatever seems to them to be a relevant value, attitude, or belief to the message they hear—your message. Therefore when you function as the primary sender of a message, you need to consider how to connect your values to those of the audience. Consider the people listening to you and how *they* will react to your message.

To speak effectively to your audience, you need to gather information about it and the situation in which you will be speaking. Recall that in earlier chapters, you learned about communication as an interactive process—a transaction between senders and receivers.

Analyzing the Occasion

When you consider your listeners, think about why they want to hear your speech. What event or purpose brings them together? Think about the degree

DIVERSITY IN COMMUNICATION

Understanding Audience Diversity

Audiences come in all sizes and shapes, and that diversity challenges you to adapt appropriately to your listeners. Their age, gender, ethnic background, and other demographic factors can guide you to become a speaker who connects with the specific group of listeners you face. Be careful, however, of stereotyping. One student began her speech by saying, "Ladies, would you like to save money on your dresses, blouses, and skirts? I know I would, and I do by sewing many of my own clothes, so today I'll tell you about some simple sewing techniques you can use to make your own clothes or keep the ones you buy in good repair." Fourteen of the twenty-five people in the class were males. Does this mean that she picked the wrong topic? If you said yes, then you, too, are stereotyping. Are there good reasons why men should know some basic elements of clothing construction, maintenance, and repair? It seems to me that everyone could profit from this knowledge. In another class, a young man began his speech by telling "us guys" about automotive tune-ups and oil changes. Does this mean that women have nothing useful to learn about automobile maintenance and repair? Often, it is not the topic, but *what we choose to do with the topic* that adapts it to the diverse audiences who are likely to hear it. Even if you are one of only a few African Americans in a class, there are lots of reasons why your classmates should hear about the concerns and perspectives of your group. Likewise, age differences, gender, culture, and background can all be linked to members of a diverse audience as long as you take care to be inclusive, not exclusive. Find the common connections, concerns, interests or motivations, and build on those in the development decisions you make as you create your speech.

of formality of the **occasion**. If the speech is a classroom assignment, then one style of dress and presentation is appropriate. If it is a formal contest or the presentation of an award, a different mode of dress and style of presentation are called for. You may be giving a speech welcoming an important visitor to your business or school. Be aware that different occasions call for different norms of behavior. The joke that you have for the classroom may not be the right one to tell at a religious meeting in a temple or church. Formal approaches may work at a business presentation in the main conference room of a major corporate headquarters but not at an outdoor pep rally.

Many of you reading this advice probably think that it is unnecessary and that you would certainly adapt appropriately. You would be surprised at the number of people who forget to do so. Speakers who fail to consider the different demands of various occasions fail to reach their audience. If you violate listeners' expectations associated with the occasion, they will stop paying careful attention to your message. In addition, you also need to think about the setting—that is, where you will be presenting your message.

Analyzing the Environment

One of the most important environmental factors in your presentation is location. **Location factors** include the size of the setting. Will you be speaking in a small conference room or a large auditorium? Indoors or outdoors? Although this consideration usually relates to the probable size of the audience, it is not always the case. For example, you may be outside, but speaking to only twenty or thirty people. What if you are scheduled for a large convention hall or auditorium, and only thirty or forty people show up? You might consider stepping down from the platform, asking the audience to move to the first few rows, and increasing your interaction with them. You should also think about where to stand, where to put your chart or overhead projector, or even whether to use a chart if it is not visible to everyone in the audience. Other elements such as poor lighting, distracting views, windows, possible noise, drafts, and heating and air-conditioning vents must all be considered so that you can adjust your plans to the location or, if necessary, change the location.

Once you have become aware of your listeners' values, the occasion or context for your speech, and the setting in which you will give your presentation, you need to consider ways to support your message so that it is clear, relevant, and interesting. The way to do this is to add good supporting materials to a well-constructed outline.

USING SUPPORTING MATERIALS

Suppose that you have identified a topic that is suitable—for you, the occasion, the audience, and the setting. Suppose that you have put together a tentative outline, complete with major parts and two, three, or four major subdivisions. The next step is to find support for each of those subdivisions. You can provide interest and substance for your main ideas by including specific information about them. The following section presents the types of information to look for, and the next section helps you to find some specific materials. There are three classes of information that can support your ideas: verbal, numerical, and visual (Zeuschner, 1994).

Verbal Supporting Materials

Specific pieces of information that can be conveyed only in words are called *verbal supporting materials*. You already use these supports every day whenever you try to explain or describe something to someone else. When you tell your friends on Monday morning that you had a great weekend, then tell them about the football game and party on Saturday, and finally give them details about the picnic on Sunday, you are using verbal supporting materials to amplify or describe your thesis—that is, that the weekend was great. In your speeches, you will probably use short stories or anecdotes, definitions, descriptions, examples, and quotations as verbal supporting materials.

Short stories are sometimes called *anecdotes* and can be an excellent way to support your ideas. If you can tell a vivid, clever, funny, or moving story, your audience will have a chance to identify with the story and remember your point.

A good story for a speech should meet several criteria. It must clearly illustrate the point you wish to make, be complete so that your audience will understand the plot, and be appropriate to the situation. Do not tell a series of complex stories to an audience that is unfamiliar with your subject. Personal experiences are one type of story that, if used carefully, can both clarify ideas and show your connection with, or your interest or expertise in, the topic.

Keep off-color jokes out of a speech to a formal audience. Stories that are offensive because they mock gender, race, or age are sure to backfire. Your story must also be concise so that it does not take up too much time. If the story runs on, you risk having your audience forget the point. Remember that a story should not dominate the point, but support it. Look at the outline again, and notice that supporting materials are listed as 1 or 2, not A or B. This placement tells you that they are subordinate to the idea they support.

Definitions are sometimes very easy to find. Go to your dictionary and look up a term or concept. Sometimes you will find an encyclopedia or one of your textbooks to be helpful. If you cite your sources for your audience when you present a definition, you will give it greater impact. Definitions are good supports because they usually come from a professional source. They are also short and clearly written. Of course, you can always create your own definition and thereby possibly add an element of humor to a speech.

Descriptions are a combination of definitions and examples. When describing an object, an event, or even a feeling, you have to give your listeners only relevant, specific, information so that they can picture what you are describing. If you tell them that the Empire State Building is really very big, you are not being very descriptive. However, if you describe the number of floors it has, to what distance you can see from the top, and how many tons of steel and building materials it took to build it, you are approaching a good description.

By using the elements of *comparison and contrast,* you can describe something in terms of its relationship to something else. If your listeners are in Chicago, then comparing the Empire State Building to the Sears Tower will help them to understand their comparable sizes. A miniature pony can be described as being similar in size to a golden retriever. The texture of a mango can be compared to that of a peach. Descriptions like these will help to enrich your speech and make it interesting for your audience. If you go into a point-by-point comparison, you are probably drawing an analogy. These extended comparisons often have a poetic or figurative element. You may recall from your English classes the uses of metaphor and simile as forms of comparison that are rich in expression and vivid in content. Each of these forms—analogy, metaphor, and simile—can be usefully included in your supporting materials.

Examples are detailed, specific instances of an event, idea, activity, and so on. If you have a story that is not long enough to have a plot, it is probably an example. You should provide enough detail in your examples that the audience can appreciate and understand both your example and how it relates to the main idea it supports. If you are urging your classroom listeners to visit the campus counseling center, you can tell them the following:

> Many services are available at the center. For example, you can get free aptitude testing and other testing for career guidance. They offer career-planning small groups and interest workshops all year. If you need someone to talk to

about personal problems, they can help you immediately with someone on staff. Or they can refer you to a trained professional in many areas, including health. They can even help you select a graduate school. These are just a few examples of the free services that are available at the counseling center.

Quotations allow you to use someone else's direct words to support your ideas. You may think of quotations as being the lofty or clever words of famous people. Go beyond that framework, and think about quoting a newspaper article, a poem, a line from a song, even your grandmother or your next-door neighbor. Quote the words of great authors or well-known speakers, but you can also quote many others to support your ideas as long as the quotations are clearly relevant to the topic and capture your listeners' attention. Make certain to credit your quotation when you present it. Giving the source of your quotation *before* you present it helps the audience to focus its attention and realize that a shift in voice is coming up. Sometimes, and for a surprise effect, you may want to wait until after the quotation to give the source. A favorite example of this surprise strategy is a quotation about how young people these days are unruly, hard to teach, impolite, and academically ill prepared. Then tell your listeners that the author of the statement is Socrates, speaking nearly 2,400 years ago! Usually, however, you will increase audience attention if you present your source first.

As you have seen, verbal supporting materials are an excellent way to define, clarify, and add impact to your presentation. However, there are times when they do not fit the content or purpose of your main ideas. Another form of supporting materials may be just what you need—numbers.

Statistical Supporting Materials

When you collect several single examples into a unit of measure, you are using numbers. You would not talk about each baseball hit by a major-league player; you would give only his average. You cannot enumerate every donation to the local blood bank, so you say the following:

> Last year, our local blood bank collected over 1,200 pints of blood. That comes out to less than four pints a day. The need for blood transfusions was well over six per day. Clearly, we are failing to provide this blood bank with sufficient funds.

Since you cannot detail all the examples of needed transfusions, you collect them into a statistical support—"six per day." You might select one powerful story to bring the statistical support "six per day" to life for your class, but the sheer volume of many examples will force you to collect material into numerical units. Although not as colorful as stories, statistics can often have a significant impact on your audience if you use them wisely. Since numbers are not as easily remembered as stories and examples are, your impact will be stronger if you use only a few numbers during a speech.

Any time that you use numbers to show relationships, you are in the area of statistics. In the blood bank example, if you had mentioned only the 1,200 pints of blood collected by the local blood bank, your listeners would not have been able to relate to anything meaningful. However, when you applied that number to both a daily donation rate and a daily need rate, you were discussing the rela-

Comparing three objects is easy with a proportional visual aid.

tionship of those numbers to each other. In other words, you were using statistics, thereby increasing the impact of your message on your listeners.

You are probably familiar with such basic statistical concepts as rounding off, averages, trends, and percentages. These concepts will be familiar to your audience as well, so you should feel free to use them. If you are trained in more complex statistics and think that your audience would benefit from information about standard deviation, margin of error, or correlation coefficients, include that information as well. But do not assume, because you know what these concepts mean, that your listeners will as well. For most purposes, basic statistical relationships will tell your audience what it needs to know to understand your point. Remember to be accurate, clear, up to date, interesting, and relevant.

Visual Supporting Materials

Effective, total communication involves more than the sound channel; it includes the sense of sight as well. If you supplement the words you speak and the numbers you present with supporting materials that can be seen, you will increase the interest and clarity of your presentation for your audience. Using **visual aids** to support your ideas gives your listeners more ways in which to receive and understand your message, thus increasing your chances of success in transmitting your message. Using visual supporting materials also gives you an opportunity to add variety to your speech and to give your audience a break from listening to words.

As with any supporting material, make certain that your visual aids are linked to your ideas by placing them on the outline as a level 1 or 2 item. They should support, clarify, emphasize, define, or explain an idea better than words alone could possibly do. Sometimes, you might find an excellent photograph or

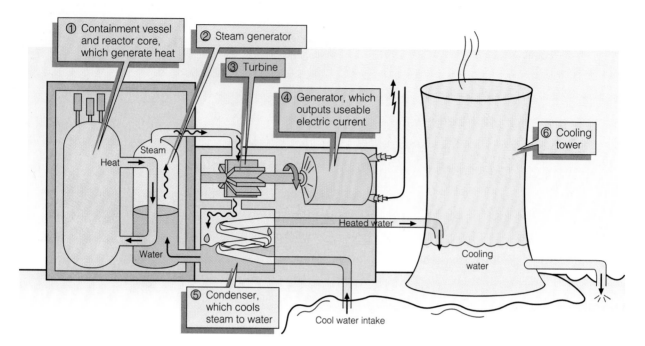

A schematic visual aid can help to explain how a complex process works.

object that has little to do with your main idea. Do not make the mistake of trying to use it. Make your visual supporting materials both relevant and uniquely valuable to your speech. For example, if you try to explain the beauty of the Grand Canyon without using a visual aid, you are probably making a mistake. If you want to explain the checks and balances of the federal government and show as your only visual aid a photograph of the White House, a drawing of George Washington, or a map of Washington, D.C., you are also making a poor choice.

There are several types of useful visual aids: pictures, maps, diagrams, objects, and models. You can also combine numbers and visual aids into graphs and charts.

Pictures and Maps.   Pictures and photographs are the most popular visual aids. You can use anything that will illustrate an item in your speech—a photo of your car, of the Eiffel Tower, of your pet calf, or of your apartment building. If professional photographs or pictures are not available, do not be afraid to make one yourself. You do not have to be an artist to create a reasonably clear line drawing or sketch. If it's the right size, is clearly drawn, and supports your idea well, do not worry about its aesthetic merit.

A picture can indeed be worth a thousand words. Try showing a photograph of the Yosemite Valley to an audience and then try matching it with a verbal description. Color, size, shape, scale, and setting are almost always easier to show than to tell about. How would you begin to describe the color purple when there are dozens of shades of purple? Bring in a sample of the shade you want to describe, and your description will be clear instantly. A description that is long, labored, and obscure in words can be quick, direct, and clear in a visual aid. Keep your visual supporting materials simple. Use them for one major item

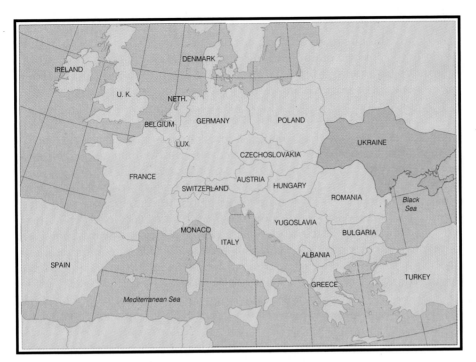

A map is an excellent way
to explain location.

or theme at a time. Make sure that people at the back of the room can see them. Make them interesting and colorful. Do all of these things, and you will have effective visual supports,

Maps, too, can be useful and effective. If you buy a professional map from a bookstore, it will be neat and clearly drawn. However, it might be too small or overly detailed for your presentation, so you could try drawing one yourself. Keep it neat and simple, and follow the suggestions for size, clarity, and color that were previously discussed.

The location of Ukraine may be too difficult to explain, but a map segment of Europe and the former Soviet Union, with Ukraine shown in a bright color, could be very helpful to your audience. If you want to give the audience directions to your favorite eating spot, you can draw the directions on a large poster board, using a city map as your guide. A good map shows details and relationships more clearly and precisely than you can with words alone.

Objects and Models.   Objects and models can also help you clarify your ideas if you can find any that are large enough to be seen by an audience. Do not ever bring a small object to class or to any other setting and say, "I hope everyone can see this." *Hope?* You should *know* whether it is large enough because you were supposed to have checked it beforehand. Even worse is the speaker who says, "I'm sorry most of you can't see this." This statement tells your listeners that you know they cannot see the object, but you had decided to use it anyway. Make certain that your object or model will be useful to your listeners so that they can experience it as support for your ideas. If it is not a good support, find something else to use. Show the types of rope used in sailing, or bring in three different kinds of bicycle helmets, or make a three-foot tall scale model of the Empire State Building or the Eiffel Tower. Do not let yourself be caught in the position of not knowing whether your object or model is providing the support for your listeners that it should. Go to the back of the room before your speech, turn around, look at your object, and see for yourself whether or not it can be seen from a distance.

Charts and Graphs.   Combining supports by using charts, graphs, or diagrams can also be an effective way to supplement your communication. You could create a chart showing the steps of a process, or the relationship of rising costs to declining profits. Graphs are an especially good way to show relationships among numbers. You might make some simple bar graphs to communicate the relative quantities of several numbers or amounts. Use different colors for different items, and your audience will be able to find them easily as you discuss them. A line graph can show trends over time, such as tuition levels over the past twenty years at your school, the price of automobiles, or population changes. If time is an important part of your idea, then a line graph would be a good supporting material to use for that idea. You might wish to show proportions of parts of a thing compared to the whole thing. In that case, use a pie graph. It can easily communicate that kind of relationship to your audience. A pie graph or chart illustrates the parts of a whole, and the relative sizes of all the parts equal the whole. Whether it is the distribution of your monthly expenses, the size of each department in a business, or the amount of calories in each part of a balanced meal, a good-size pie chart, with clear lines and a variety of colors, can do a great deal to support your idea.

In short, make sure that all of your visual aids are large enough to be seen; are easily made, handled, and presented; and are simple to operate. You probably should avoid electrical or mechanical devices that are subject to failure. Make certain that your visual aid is appropriate to both the audience and the

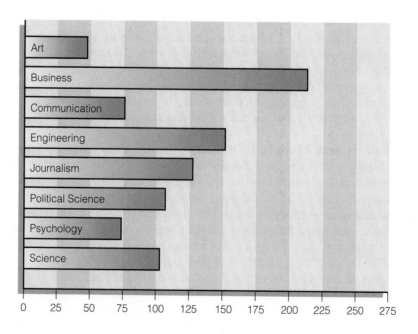

Bar graphs can help listeners to visualize comparative sizes or amounts.

setting. If you collect venomous snakes as a hobby and would like to bring them to your presentation on snakes, don't do it. Substitute a photograph for the real thing, and make your point that way. In the same vein, bringing in guns may be illegal, but diagrams of guns are not. If you are discussing drought and famine, you might be tempted to bring in pictures of dying or dead children to emphasize your thesis, but most people in your audience would be overwhelmed by such photographs and would probably stop paying attention to you. A student recently brought to class detailed photographs of an abortion in process to convince her listeners to oppose the procedure. The entire class avoided looking at her material, and two students left the room. So be careful about the appropriateness of your visual supports.

Time is also a factor. Does your visual aid take ten or fifteen minutes to set up and then dismantle? Be aware of the time limits you will have to cope with in any setting. Remember, your visual aid is just like any other type of supporting material. It is a support for a subordinate idea. It is a third-level event and should be allotted only that proportion of time in your presentation.

Finally, passing around small objects or handouts to the audience can be distracting. It is better to enlarge one object so that everyone can see it at the same time, you can control the time that it goes out of sight, and there will be no distractions in the audience while you are speaking. If the members of the audience really have to have something, hand it out to them at the end of the speech or presentation.

If you follow these guidelines, you can give a speech that has good supporting materials. The key to success here is to make sure the materials are appropriate and to lend them variety so that you can explain your ideas to your listeners in several different ways. Just how many of which type of support should you use? It all depends on you, your topic, your audience, and the situation. You can be sure, however, that a speech with a variety of supporting materials will go over better with an audience than a speech that is dominated by just one single type of material. Keep variety in mind as you look for supporting materials. Where do you look for these supports? The next section will answer that question.

RESEARCHING YOUR IDEAS

Finding interesting and stimulating supporting materials is one of the best reasons to do research for your speech. As you learn more about your subject through research, you add depth and interest to your presentation. Sometimes, you may be speaking about a personal experience—your trip from Miami to Atlanta to New Orleans. That does not exempt you from doing research. If you limit your speech to saying, "Well, then I went . . ." and "After that I went . . ." you will fail to provide both depth and variety for your listeners. Find out about the history of some of the places you visited. Quote from *Gone With the Wind*, get a map of the three areas from an auto club, use statistics about the populations of those cities. That type of supporting material will rescue your speech from being a self-centered, monotonous travelogue and turn it into a speech that is of keen interest to your listeners. Your presentation will be made more interesting by your personal touches, but they do not and cannot replace outside supporting materials culled from solid research.

So how and where do you find supporting materials? You can start with yourself, then talk to other people, and then research the print and nonprint resources available to you.

Finding and Recording Information

You will have to do some exploration to find all the supports that were discussed earlier—short stories, statistics, visual aids, definitions, descriptions, comparisons, and contrasts. Once you have found this information, you must record it so that you can both remember it and properly credit it in your speech. How much information should you gather? A good rule of thumb is that you should collect two or three times as much information as you have time for in your speech. For example, if you have a four- to six-minute speech, you should collect about fifteen minutes worth of supporting materials. That way you can go through your stack of stories, examples, statistics, and so on, and select the *best* ones for each subordinate idea. Evaluate each item for interest, clarity, and variety, and choose only the items that give your presentation the most value. Otherwise, if you have only four minutes' worth of material, you will have to use it. It may be good, bad, weak, strong, clear, or unclear. It doesn't matter; you are stuck with it. So give yourself an opportunity to choose.

Using Personal Resources

Think of yourself as an expert in experiences—your experiences. You have visited different places, taken classes in many subjects, had hobbies and jobs, and read a small mountain of books and magazines. All of these experiences make you a resource. Consider the cartoons you have clipped out, the books you have read, or your photographs of favorite stars, sports figures, or favorite vacations spots. Think about the variety of life experiences you have had, and use them as a starting point for gathering your supporting material.

Next, talk to some of the people you know. *Interviews* are an excellent way to gather quotations, and you have friends and associates who can lend their expertise to your speech if you ask them to do so. Your campus is filled with experts on hundreds of subjects, and most of your faculty members enjoy talking to students about their specialties. Most of the time, the main reason that students go to see teachers is to complain about a grade or ask about an assignment that the teacher thought had already been explained. What a pleasure it is for your teachers to have an intellectual discussion with someone who wants to know about their expertise. Remember to make an appointment and to prepare your questions in advance, as described in the section on interviews in Chapter 9.

Using Library Resources

Print resources are probably what you thought about immediately when you first read about doing research. Books, magazines, newspapers, and other printed material are some of the best sources of supporting materials. The best place to find these items is, of course, a library; and learning how to use a library can be a great advantage to your college career as well as to your speech preparation.

Interviewing people allows you to share their life experiences.

Books are an easy and plentiful source of information. Keep track of what you read so that you can list it properly in your bibliography. Small 3" × 5" or 4" × 6" index cards are useful for this purpose. You can write on them the important bibliographic information found on the copyright page of the book and still have plenty of room to note important information such as statistics, facts, or direct quotations. The library may have a card catalogue—a large set of file drawers containing cards—that lists the books that are available. These cards are filed in three separate ways: by subject, by title, and by the author's last name. Many libraries have electronic catalogues that organize their listings in the same way—by author, title, and subject. When you begin your research, it may be a good idea to browse through the listings of either types of catalogue to get an idea of the holdings. Remember, books are always somewhat out of date, since they take at least a year and sometimes two to get from the author to the library. If an author has spent a year or more doing research, the information in the book may be at least two, and sometimes four or more, years old. For many items, this time gap will not matter, but if you plan to talk about current world events, unemployment rates, the cost of automobiles, or stock prices, books are not adequate. You will need current sources.

Newspapers and magazines can give you that information. Libraries subscribe to dozens of newspapers and magazines from all over the world. Magazines such as *Time, Newsweek,* and *U.S. News and World Report* are all well established and provide weekly coverage of important events. Of course, each has a particular perspective; nevertheless, they are well known for their accuracy. Other magazines may have a special interest, a particular political point of view, or a perspective from a different culture or country, all of which can give your speech both comprehensiveness and depth. Consult the *Readers' Guide to Periodical Literature* to locate the specific magazines that have the information you seek.

The library is a treasure house of information for every speaker.

In addition, libraries collect booklets, documents, pamphlets, and flyers published on a variety of very specific topics. College libraries also collect professional journals in every subject taught on campus, and they can be a source of sophisticated and highly specialized information. Check the library's vertical file or the publication *Facts on File* for short articles about current research in a variety of fields. You might even call organizations that are related to your topic and request some of their publications. Most organizations are happy to share their information and they usually enjoy helping students. Community action groups, local government, and utility companies are more places where you can get interesting print materials.

Nonprint resources are increasingly important in a world of computers and electronic information processing. Traditional sources such as films, tapes, and records have been augmented by compact discs, videotapes, electronic data banks, CD-ROMs, and on-line services. If you are going to discuss the speeches of former Presidents, you will get much more information about the topic from films and videotapes than if you simply read transcripts of the speeches. A speech on Native American literature would be somewhat impoverished unless you took the time to listen to some recordings of tribal storytellers. If you want to give something unique and memorable to your listeners, you need to look beyond ordinary sources of information. Most libraries have extensive indexes of nonprint resources including catalogues, references, and microfilm readers.

Using electronic databases with a computer will help you to combine this electronic format with traditional print media. Since these resources are on-line, they may be updated frequently, even as often as daily, so they become a rich resource of current information. Your library or your own on-line service provider may give you access to *InfoTrac,* which includes several thousand separate periodicals. Its *Expanded Academic Index* would be an excellent place to start your search. You can also try *Magazine Index Plus* as well as the *New York Times* and the *Wall Street Journal*, which are probably available via your computer connection. Web browser programs and search engines make using the Internet a useful part of you research. One further labor-saving advantage to your computer search is to hook up to a printer; the printout will give you properly recorded information to include in your speech bibliography (Grice and Skinner, 1995).

You can also collect supporting materials from television and radio. Did you recently watch a good program, see an important news broadcast, or listen to a great song? Write them down so they will be available to you for your speeches in the future. The average American household watches seven hours of television a day, so you have an opportunity to do research while you are being entertained. News broadcasts, documentaries, weather reports, sports programs, comedy series, and special programs are all potential sources for an example, a great story, a funny description, a bold analogy, or a key fact. Intelligent and focused television viewing can produce excellent supporting materials.

Synthesizing Your Material

Once you have gathered your information, it is time to reconsider the basic speech outline discussed earlier in this chapter. To construct a speech that meets the goals of clarity and impact, you need to support your thesis, and the main divisions of that thesis, with materials that are lively, specific, colorful, memorable, relevant, and convincing. Your goal is to communicate a worthwhile message to your audience members so that they will both understand and remember what you said. The better the supporting materials you use, the more likely it is that your intended results can be achieved.

Consult your stack of index cards, and sort them into groups according to the divisions of the body of your speech (A, B, C, and so on). Some items may not be appropriate, in which case you can either adjust your ideas or put the items aside. A great story that does not fit in one place often can be used in another. The introduction of a speech, for example, is often a story, so that is a way to create an introduction from the materials you have already gathered. If you have twice as much material as you need, you can review your speech outline, checking all items for interest, variety, and impact, and keeping only the very best ones.

SUMMARY

Preparing speeches is like doing a term paper. You need to organize your speech by preparing an outline. You have to think about who your listeners will be and adapt your ideas to that audience. Then you must present your information clearly and in a way that will show your audience that it is relevant to them. If you do not address the needs, concerns, and values of your listeners, you will be speaking only to yourself. The best way to prepare a presentation that is both clear and relevant is to assess your audience accurately, then engage in the research of supporting materials to which you feel it will respond. Verbal supporting materials are the most commonly used, and they can be augmented with simple statistics and compelling visual aids.

The use of supporting material should follow some common-sense guidelines. The next chapter deals with this issue by showing you how to put your preparation into practice so that you meet your goals.

KEY TERMS

outlining, *p. 210*
introduction, *p. 211*
thesis sentence, *p. 211*
body of the speech, *p. 212*
conclusion, *p. 212*
sources/bibliography/references, *p. 212*
supporting materials, *p. 212*
plagiarism, *p. 212*
organizational development patterns, *p. 218*

motivated sequence, *p. 222*
audience analysis, *p. 223*
value systems, *p. 224*
occasion, *p. 225*
location factors, *p. 226*
visual aids, *p. 229*
print resources, *p. 234*
nonprint resources, *p. 236*

EXERCISES

1. Watch a frequently appearing commercial on television. Watch it several times so that you can verify your observations. Determine what pattern of organization is used in the commercial. You can probably identify a chronological or cause–effect pattern fairly easily. Are there any others? Bring a list of three or four differently organized commercials to class, and compare them with those observed by your classmates. Did anyone use the same commercial but classify it as having a different pattern from yours? Why might this happen?

2. Create a key word outline for an informative speech, making certain that all five areas of a speech are included. Now use the same topic and thesis sentence, but organize the body of the outline into a different format. Which one works better? Why?

3. Buy a packet of 4" × 6" note cards, and have them with you when you go to the library, watch television, and attend classes, lectures, or speeches.

On these cards, write specific items you might use in a speech or presentation as they occur or happen to you. For example, you might record an interesting anecdote, some compelling statistics, or a vivid example. Even if you are not planning to speak on the same subject as your example or statistic, you will find that items can often be transferred from one presentation to another. These cards will also help you to build a reserve of information in case you are asked to give an impromptu speech.

4. Substitute a visual support for a verbal one. Can you show something better than you can tell it? Now do the reverse. Take something you think would make a good visual aid, and put the content into words. Is this item easier to say than it is to show? These tests can be done any time that you use supporting materials. Do them mentally to see whether an item should be a verbal or a visual support.

REFERENCES

Grice, George L., and John F. Skinner. *Mastering Public Speaking*. Boston: Allyn and Bacon, 1995.

Gronbeck, Bruce E., R. E. McKerrow, A. H. Monroe, and D. Ehninger. *Principles and Types of Speech Communication*. 12th ed. New York: HarperCollins, 1995.

Lumsden, Gay, and Donald Lumsden. *Communicating with Credibility and Confidence*. Belmont: Wadsworth, 1996.

Reike, Richard, and Malcolm Sillars. *Argumentation and the Decision-Making Process*. Glenview: Scott, Foresman, 1983.

Zeuschner, R. B. *Effective Public Speaking*. Dubuque: Kendall-Hunt, 1994.

Presenting Speeches

12

After reading this chapter, you should be able to:

- Know the four types of speech presentation styles, the causes of speech apprehension, and the standards for presenting and evaluating speeches.
- Feel ready to give speeches to your classmates and other listeners.
- Have control over your nervous energy.
- Uphold ethical standards in communication.
- Present an effective speech, and evaluate it and other speeches you hear.

*W*hen you have done your research, gathered your supporting materials, put them in order, and developed your visual aids, you will be ready to start practicing your presentation. No matter how much effort you put into research, outline construction, revision of your thesis sentence, and organization of the body of your speech, without an effective presentation your speech is not likely to have its desired effect. It is true that you must begin with substantial information on a worthwhile topic. But once your preparation is in place, it is time to make sure that your presentation does justice to all your preparatory work.

As noted several times earlier in this book, your presentation should clarify your ideas and give them impact. Speech delivery involves coordinating your voice and your body in a way that makes your message come alive for your audience. This chapter presents you with several optional styles to use when delivering a speech, suggests ways to deal with the speech anxiety you probably will feel, and enhances your verbal and nonverbal presentation skills. Finally, you learn about standards for evaluating speeches—your own as well as those you hear in class, in the community, and in the media. Let us begin with the four styles of presenting speeches.

TYPES OF PRESENTATIONS

For as long as there have been speakers, essentially four different types of **presentation styles** have been available: memorized, with a manuscript, extemporaneous, and impromptu. Your speech will fall into one of these styles of delivery every time you speak. Depending on the time and place, one type will be more appropriate than the others. Yet each one will be the right one at some particular time. The appropriateness, strengths, and weaknesses of each type will help you decide when to use and when to avoid a particular style. Your instructor may assign you one style for your classroom presentations; but outside of the class, *you* will need to select the one you believe is most appropriate.

Memorized

A **memorized** presentation follows a word-for-word preparation. This process, although time-consuming and tiring, gives you the advantage of speaking without notes, of including every detail exactly as you had planned, and of knowing precisely how long your speech will last. In a formal setting, and when you need only a few minutes to express your thoughts, this style of presentation may be just right. However, this style has one major drawback: You might forget parts of your speech. The pressure that public communication can put on you may result in your forgetting a line or a word. If you memorize the way most people do, you depend on one line following another, like the links of a chain. Each sentence ties you to the next. If you blank out on one sentence or word, you might forget not only that line, but all the lines that follow. If this happens, then all the benefits of memorization evaporate, along with the lost lines. You are now unable to speak. Now you need your notes, your timing is off, and you may skip ideas or materials on which you worked very hard.

Unfortunately, many beginning speakers think that they *must* memorize to make a good impression. The more concerned and worried they are, the more they are tempted to control every second and every syllable of their presentation. Their very anxiety is their worst enemy. They forget their speech, and the disaster that they had nightmares about actually happens—caused by their own overpreparation. Memorized speeches are usually best left to very experienced speakers.

Another disadvantage of memorization is that all but the very best speakers tend to sound mechanical, stilted, and uninvolved when speaking from memory. Instead of establishing genuine rapport with their audiences, speakers who memorize often look and sound like robots, reciting lines with no direct connection to their listeners. If the audience does respond with some feedback, these speakers cannot adapt or respond to the audience, and communication interaction fails. The use of memory for most people is probably manageable if it is limited to very short speeches, such as a thank you or a brief introduction in a very formal setting. Memorization probably will not be appropriate for most of the classroom speeches you give or for most of the presentations you will give throughout your lifetime.

Manuscript

A speaker who delivers a speech from a **manuscript** usually writes out or types the speech word for word and then presents the speech by reading the manuscript. In the best manuscript delivery, speakers spend about 10 to 20 percent of their time looking down at the script and 80 to 90 percent of the time looking at the audience to establish eye contact and direct interaction. The speaker must always focus on the audience and not on the manuscript. The advantage of speaking from a manuscript is that you have no fear of forgetting. In addition, you have control over what you say, and your timing will be very accurate.

When you attend major events—graduations, dedications, presidential addresses, public ceremonies, or religious services—you will usually see a manuscript delivery. Often, the delivery is very good, but sometimes it is not. One reason that people use manuscripts is to lend an elevated tone to the event by using highly polished vocabulary and sentence structure. With this kind of preparation, they can be sure that they will make no mistakes. Generally, a manuscript speaker does not sound as mechanical as a memorized speaker, but a manuscript can still create a barrier to good eye contact, and it does not allow for much adjustment to audience feedback. Reading from a manuscript lacks both spontaneity and immediacy and runs the risk of making the speaker sound flat, recycled, stale, or not directly related to the listeners. Manuscript presentation is usually found in longer presentations—beyond eight or ten minutes—and when the ceremony itself or the accuracy of the information is the most important consideration.

Extemporaneous

An **extemporaneous** speech is the type you will give most often—both in the classroom and later in life. To deliver a good extemporaneous speech, you have to prepare and practice, but you must stop short of memorizing the words of your

The more formal the setting, the more likely you'll use a manuscript.

presentation or writing them out in sentences. Good extemporaneous speakers will carefully prepare a key idea or key word outline. The speakers then memorize the *outline* but allow the exact words of the body to emerge spontaneously. They practice out loud many times; and although the speech is very similar each time, it is never exactly the same. Moreover, they do not attempt to achieve exactness. If a phrase or a sentence reverses itself from one time to the next, that is permissible, as long as the point of the topic or idea is clearly made each time.

The advantages of an outline to you as a speaker are many. Using an outline gives you a comprehensive plan, helps you to be comfortable with the materials, and ensures that you will have the results of your research and organization readily at hand. An outline also allows you to practice sufficiently that you will know the length of your presentation. Finally, using an outline gives you the flexibility to be spontaneous and direct and to adapt to your audience immediately. You can remain conversational, thereby increasing audience attention and rapport, and you can create a directness in your approach that helps to give an impact to your ideas. In virtually every situation, audiences prefer extemporaneous speeches, and they rate the speakers who give such speeches very highly.

There are, of course, some potential disadvantages to this type of presentation. You do not have exactness in your wording or your timing. You need to smooth out your phrasing; and some speakers, especially if they are working in a second language, may not be as adept at spontaneity as others. However, because it is such an appropriate type of presentation for so many settings, it is important for you to develop skills in extemporaneous speaking.

Impromptu

When you deliver a speech on only a few moments' notice, you are engaging in **impromptu** speaking. You may find yourself at a meeting and decide to speak about the issue under consideration. In your career, you may suddenly be asked by a visiting team to explain your section of the company. In class, you may be called on to provide a lengthy explanation of a point or a defense of a position. At a business conference, someone may have heard of your creative work and may ask you to stand up and explain your latest project to a group or an assembly.

In each of these situations, you have not prepared an outline or rehearsed your presentation. However, it is a mistake to call impromptu speeches unprepared speeches. In a very real sense, you are prepared, and in many ways. First, notice that no one is ever asked to speak about something unless there is a reason or expectation that the person can do so. In class, you should know the material. In a meeting, you are there because of your interest. A career setting will find you explaining things that are directly related to that carrier. So you do have some research and some supporting materials that are with you always and everywhere: your experience, background, and knowledge. Moreover, this class and others have given you some preparation for organizing those experiences into a coherent speech. If you are asked five years from now to give an impromptu speech about something, you will already know that your speech should have an introduction, a clear thesis sentence, and a body organized into some pattern that has from two to five main divisions that relate to the thesis. You know right now that you need a quick review for the conclusion and supporting materials that are vivid, specific, and varied. You may not know it, but you are already writing your future impromptu speeches. When the time comes, you will need only a few moments to jot down some notes so that you can quickly create a basic outline, fill in spaces, and be ready to give your speech. All of your earlier speeches will have given you practice in modulating your voice, making eye contact, creating transitions, and using good body language, so those skills will also be with you everywhere you go.

The advantages of being able to deliver an impromptu speech will make your ideas more compelling than those of people who do not know how to make such speeches. Impromptu speeches are immediately adaptable to the situation and the audience, and they make it possible for the speaker to respond directly to any feedback from the audience. On the other hand, you may not remember to organize an outline, or your supporting materials might not be as strong or as varied as you would like. Your timing and phrasing might be off. Being a good impromptu speaker is a real challenge, but it is one that can be personally gratifying for the person who does it well.

IMPROVING COMPETENCY

Honing Your Presentation Skills

As you speak in your classes, on the job, or in your community, try applying the four different types of presentations. You might read notes in one setting and make an impromptu speech in another. You could memorize a short presentation or try the extemporaneous method. By being aware of the four different types of delivery, and by putting them into practice, you will expand your range of abilities. What is more, you can start today.

The four types of presentation can be selected and evaluated according to the circumstances of your speech. No matter which type you select, you will most likely have one experience each and every time you present a speech: some nervousness.

DEALING WITH APPREHENSION

As mentioned in Chapter 2, the mere thought of giving a speech is enough to produce apprehension in most people (Richmond and McCroskey, 1995). This reaction is common and normal. The symptoms—tension, "butterflies," sweaty palms, tight and shallow breathing, and a lump in the throat—are felt by everyone. These symptoms are the standard physiological reactions to fear and stress. Like many other fears, this one can be managed and reduced.

It is important to know that any nervousness you have is natural and that with preparation, you can respond to it so that it no longer hinders you when you are doing a presentation. You read about the source and effects of **speech apprehension** in Chapter 2, in which several approaches to the problem in general were recommended.

Apprehension may flow from one or more of three areas: excessive activation of your physical responses, inappropriate cognitive processing of the situation, or inadequate communication skills (Richmond and McCroskey, 1995). In this chapter, some very practical, specific suggestions are made that you can use when it is your turn to speak. Most people have a strong desire to appear competent in the eyes of others, and giving a speech puts a person in the spotlight. If you have never had any training in giving speeches, you might be afraid of making mistakes and appearing to lack competence. If you have never learned how to drive a car, you should keep out of the driver's seat. However, once you take a driver-training course and gain a little experience, you still

Give yourself the gift of practice.

won't be an expert driver, but driving should no longer be such a formidable experience that you avoid it altogether. In the same way, preparing and presenting a speech, when that task is approached with some knowledge and experience, can develop your competence and your confidence.

The bottom line is: To appear credible, you should *be* credible. Many of the ways to become credible have already been covered—select a substantial and worthwhile topic, give it the clear organization and preparation it deserves, provide yourself with significant supporting materials, and select a presentation type that is appropriate for both you and the situation. The last task of your preparation is to practice; and while you practice your speech aloud, you can also practice some physiological and psychological exercises that can assist you in your *total* preparation.

Physiological Preparation

If you have excess energy, you can learn to use your physiology to spend some of that energy. As you sit awaiting your turn to speak, you will probably experience your greatest anxiety. There are several physical exercises that you can practice ahead of time that will help train your muscles to relax. If you practice **physiological preparation** now, and again as you practice the spoken part of your speech, you will have some excellent tools to help overcome the negative effects of your natural tension.

Correct Breathing.   First of all, the best and proven method of helping you counter excess tension involves your breathing. In ancient cultures that taught us yoga and in modern Lamaze childbirth methods, correct breathing is at the heart of controlling and channeling energy. The importance of breath control is seen in sports, singing, exercise, acting, childbirth, and public speaking. These techniques can help you to gain control over your apprehension and ease the task of presenting your ideas to others. These breathing techniques are easy to learn and easy to apply.

The basic exercise is to breathe slowly and regularly from your diaphragm. The diaphragm is a large muscular tissue located beneath your lungs, just below the rib cage. As you push this muscle down, you create a vacuum in your lungs. Air rushes in from outside to equalize the pressure, and you inhale. Although this description sounds like a fairly involved way to describe something that you do without thinking, you do need to think about it when an anxiety reaction interferes with your presentation. To give you greater strength with which to face your "danger," the anxiety response tenses up your midsection, which in turn forces you to breathe in a shallow manner and with only the upper lungs. Singers and actors exercise to increase their lung power because they know they can support a stronger voice with full lungs. Like you, they need to overcome the effects of tension, so they practice deep breathing and continue with it when their physiology tries to make them breathe with only the top part of the lungs. Learning to feel your diaphragm and monitor its movement can help you to attack immediately one of the prime causes of continuing tension: incorrect breathing. Incidentally, your solar plexus, the place where you feel "butterflies,"

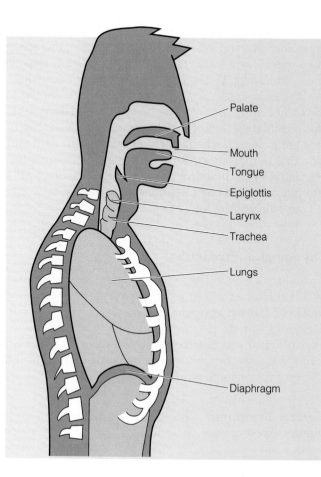

Palate

Mouth

Tongue

Epiglottis

Larynx

Trachea

Lungs

Diaphragm

The diaphragm is at the base of the lungs and supports the rest of sound production.

is at the base of the diaphragm; and by slowing down your breathing, you can chase the butterflies away as well.

Yoga teachers point out that when you relax the center of your body, a calming feeling spreads from there throughout the rest of your body. By breathing regularly and slowly, in and out, while you practice your speech, you will be creating an automatic reminder to do the same kind of breathing while you are waiting for your turn to speak. By so doing, you will supply your brain with oxygen, keep your butterflies under control, and begin to calm your entire body. You can practice slow, regular, and deep breathing while you are practicing your speech.

Muscle Relaxation. Another physical exercise that you can practice and then do while waiting for your turn to speak, is a tensing and relaxing of various muscles. Locate the calf muscle on your right leg. Now, keeping your thigh muscle relaxed, tense just the calf muscle. This exercise is not easy, but try to make the calf muscle tight. Hold it for a count of ten, then relax. During this exercise, you should be breathing slowly. Now switch legs, and repeat the exercise. Try the same exercise with the thigh muscles. Continue to breathe slowly. Now try tensing your forearm but leaving your biceps relaxed. Breathe slowly.

You can do these exercises very subtly so that even if you are doing them on stage in front of an audience, no one will be aware of what you are doing. In fact, what you will be doing is using up some energy—skimming off some of the tension so that your muscles will be more relaxed. You will still have plenty of energy to give a dynamic presentation, but you will not have the shaky knees or the quivering hands of speakers who tense up and then hold onto that tension. You might try the exercise at home with any combination of muscles. Try selective tensing, hold for five deep breaths, then relax. Airline passengers are often taught these and similar isometric exercises as a way of avoiding fatigue.

If you are not on stage but in a somewhat private setting, you can try shrugging your shoulders and rotating them forward and then backward. Another helpful exercise for reducing tension is to lower your head slowly until your chin rests on your chest. Then slowly rotate up one side, then down again, and slowly up the other side. A good, long yawn can help to relax the throat. You can even yawn on stage if you remember to keep your mouth closed. Try it now. Can you feel the stretch of your larynx? That stretch will relax your voice.

As you do the breathing exercises and the muscle tensing and relaxing exercises, remember that you are in control. If you practice these exercises often, doing them in a slow and regular pattern, you can build your confidence. You will, of course, feel the direct, physical benefits immediately. When you go to your presentation, remember to start your deep breathing as you approach your destination. Start your muscle tensing and relaxing as soon as you reach your seat. Getting in control of your physical reactions is a direct way to meet the challenge your physiology presents to you when you are under stress. Incidentally, many people use these techniques in many different kinds of situations: taking a

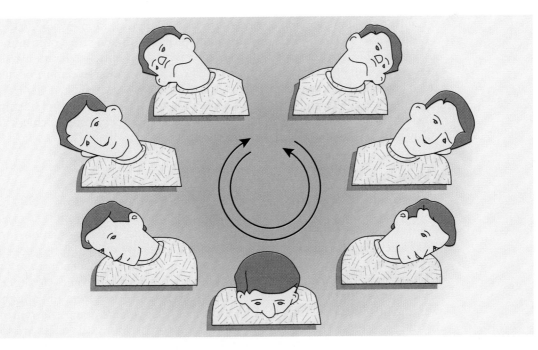

A gentle, slow head roll can relax tension.

THE STORY OF COMMUNICATION

Creative Visualization

A few years ago, the Public Broadcasting Service television stations ran a feature that described a basketball training camp experiment. The researchers divided students at the camp into three groups, and they were tested on their free-throw ability. The first group was thanked for its participation, sent home, and told to come back in a month. The second group was given four hours a day of instruction for four weeks and practice in free-throw technique. The third group was taken to a classroom, shown a film on perfect free-throw technique, and given instruction on positive visualization and self-imagery. For a month, these students sat in a quiet room for twenty minutes a day and *imagined* themselves shooting perfect free-throws. At the end of the month, the first group had a 10 percent decrease in average free-throw ability. The second group had a 23 percent increase in free-throws. The third group had a 21 percent increase in free-throw ability. Although visualization was not as good as the actual practice, the third group did improve significantly. This experiment indicates the power of visualization.

---

test, being interviewed, meeting a special person's parents, trying out for a team, or doing an audition for a show. When you are in a situation in which you begin to feel the flight-or-fight reaction, counteract it immediately with the physiological responses described.

In some cases, the extremes of physiological reaction can be reduced effectively by a six-step process known as systematic desensitization (Wolpe, 1958). This process takes extremely anxious individuals through a series of imagined anxiety-producing situations and, combined with deep muscle relaxation training, moves from low to high stress levels. The anxiety at each level must be mastered before moving to the next. This system has been widely applied (Hoffman and Sprague, 1982); and although the exact reason(s) why it works are not conclusively accepted, we know that it does produce significant improvement for many people (Richmond and McCroskey, 1995).

Psychological Preparation

The second part of the communication apprehension reaction is psychological. Your mind is the place where the danger signals begin, so your mind is where you can work on countermeasures. Remember, in most of these situations, you *should* feel that the occasion is important, and you have every right to be concerned about your presentation and its outcome. However, in an effort not just to control the reaction, but to eliminate it altogether, many people wind themselves up even tighter and create exactly the opposite effect from the one that was intended. Acknowledge the importance of what you are doing, but remember that control of the reaction, not its elimination, is your goal. There are several steps you can take in **psychological preparation** to enlist your mind to help you deal with communication apprehension.

Familiarity. Become familiar with the situation. This means that you need to follow up on your analysis of the setting. If you take that advice, you are already well on your way to having a good frame of mind rather than an anxious frame of mind.

People dislike what is unfamiliar, so getting to know your setting is a big step toward psychological control. Your efforts to become familiar with your listeners—their backgrounds, values, and listening goals—will also help you to know what the situation calls for and how to prepare for it. As you become more familiar with the speaking environment and your intended audience, you will have fewer uncertainties and greater confidence.

Involvement. Be involved in your topic. This step helps you to focus on your topic and its importance to your listeners and therefore to be less focused on *yourself*. Select a topic that you care about. After you have expended energy on research and preparation, you will develop a psychological investment in the topic. As the ideas in your presentation gain greater importance, your ego becomes less important. If you have a strong desire to communicate to your audience about something you find worthwhile and substantial, you will replace concern for your appearance or your nervousness with concern for your message. If you are genuinely involved in your ideas, your involvement and commitment to those ideas will show in your preparation, practice, and presentation. For that reason, you need to avoid a topic picked out of a magazine the night before the presentation or recycled from a friend. Create a sincere message, and your sincerity will be evident.

Concern. Show concern for your audience. After you have selected a good topic, take the time to demonstrate that you also care about your listeners. Do you have a sincere desire to communicate with them? Have you considered their reasons for being in the audience? Have you approached the topic from their point of view? By responding to these questions, you place the attention on your ideas and your audience, not on you. Center yourself on your listeners, and relate your speech to *them*. In that way, your psychological commitment is to the ideas in your presentation and to the receivers to whom you send those ideas, not to your own personal concerns. The message happens in collaboration with the audience or not at all. Review Chapter 11 to gain a deeper appreciation of your listeners. Remember that you are speaking not to a mirror but to real people. If you keep your listeners uppermost in your mind, you will have less time to become overly concerned with yourself. And don't forget to smile.

Imaging. Imagine yourself as a strong speaker. Do you recall the discussion about how powerful self-concept messages can be? Use that knowledge to help you create an ideal speaker in your mind—in other words, you. See yourself doing a good job. Imagine smiles on the faces of your listeners. Visualize your speech going smoothly and ending at just the right time and in just the right way. Many people dwell on negative thoughts when they are feeling apprehensive. They invest large amounts of psychological capital in all the awful things they fear might happen. As you learned in interpersonal communication, your internal messages are very powerful, but they are under your control. When you find your internal messages drifting toward negative thoughts, replace those thoughts

Positive visualization helps you
to reach your goals.

with positive visualizations. Imagine yourself as a calm, energetic, and dynamic person who thinks and speaks clearly. Imagine your audience's reactions as being positive—nods of agreement, smiles at your ideas, and applause at the end of your presentation. Keep this image in your mind when you practice, while you wait your turn to speak, and during your presentation. Positive visualization works for sports teams and is exactly what is meant by getting "psyched up" for an event. If you mentally predict success, it is more likely to come your way.

You know enough about public speaking by now to realize that the best way for physiological and psychological preparation to work is for them to work together. The mind and the body are a team, not independent entities. When you *concentrate* on your breathing, you will forget to get butterflies. In other words, the human mind concentrates best on only one thing at a time. When you create a positive mental image, your physical energy is channeled into that image, and both your mind and your body help you to realize it. Teamwork between physical exercises and psychological responses can give you the focus and confidence you need to make the image a reality. You will find that you are able to control your public-speaking energy. You can then direct that energy into making yourself a skilled public speaker.

EFFECTIVE PUBLIC SPEAKING SKILLS

Once your preparation is strong and solid, you can pay attention to the presentation itself. The success of your delivery will depend on how effectively you use your voice and body to deliver your message with clarity and impact. There are five elements of **vocal delivery,** and we begin with a discussion of those elements. Next, we look at how to use posture, movement, and gestures to enhance your message.

Verbal Skills

Volume is obviously the first element of good vocal delivery because your listeners must be able to hear you, at the very least. Speak loudly enough to be heard by every person in your audience. You may need to use a microphone if the room is especially large, so test the microphone for sound level and feedback—in advance if possible—and then practice using it. In a classroom or business conference room, a microphone is not only inappropriate, it is unnecessary. For the majority of your speeches, you will be in front of a small or medium-size group, and you will speak with a voice supported by good breathing from your deep-breathing routine.

You can find out whether the volume of your voice is adequate by practicing in the room in which you are going to speak and by having someone tell you how you sound. When you are actually giving your presentation, you can carefully observe your listeners as they relax and seem comfortable, or as they strain and lean forward to hear what you are saying. Keep in mind, however, that a room full of people absorbs sound, so do not practice in an empty room.

Another important thing to remember about volume is to have variety in the sound of your voice. You can emphasize ideas by varying your volume, but do not be misguided into thinking that *loud* means important. Although we often raise our volume to emphasize an important idea, we also drop the volume very low to show the same thing. At a wedding, for example, the bride and groom speak at a very low volume when they say some of the most important words they will ever utter. Variety means to speak louder and then softer; it is the *change* in volume that alerts listeners that a change is taking place in the message.

Articulation and pronunciation are also important to your vocal delivery in terms of being understood by your listeners and building your credibility. The way you make your sounds should be clear, and your pronunciation should be within acceptable ranges for your audience.

Articulation is the clear production of sounds so that they are crisp and distinct. It means involving your muscles and vocal structures so that these tools can be used to produce the sounds clearly and audibly. To develop clear articulation, you need to be able to hear yourself. Although that sounds like an easy task, it is actually somewhat difficult, at least at first. You are so used to the sound of your own voice that you might not be objective about the sounds you produce. Use a tape recorder. Then listen to your voice with a sensitive ear. You may want to use a dictionary pronunciation guide at first. It will give you the standard, correct pronunciation of any words about which you are uncertain. Be especially sensitive to the final consonants *t* and *d*. They are frequently ignored by many people. Sometimes middle syllables get altered, as when people say things like "fas'nating" instead of "fascinating." Some people add syllables to words, as when someone says "orientate," when the correct word is *orient,* or "orientated" instead of the word *oriented*. As you work on developing sensitive self-feedback, your articulation can become improved.

Sometimes people worry about pronunciation. Pronunciation is the use of clearly articulated sounds in any given word. You might try using a dictionary pronunciation guide at first; it will tell you how educated speakers of Mainstream English pronounce the word.

Your pronunciation can affect your credibility. Many listeners associate a level of competence with a certain pronunciation. Sometimes, if you have a strong regional accent, you might want to modify it when your audience is from a different region. In a well-known example, former President Kennedy was speaking to a group of ministers in Houston, far from his native Boston. In a recording of that speech, you can hear Kennedy modify at times his New England pronunciation of "Americur" to "America."

In many ways, once a word has been clearly articulated, most regional and ethnic differences in pronunciation can be perfectly acceptable, depending on the listeners. If you have a regional color to your speech, there is no need to be overly concerned as long as your audience can follow you easily and respond to you credibly. Follow the generally accepted standards of educated people in your audience. Sometimes an accent can add interest or uniqueness to your presentation, and it may be a genuine part of you that you wish to retain, even when you are not dealing with listeners from the same cultural or regional background. Can your present listeners understand you? Does your credibility remain high? If so, don't feel that you must eliminate every trace of your background accent.

However, some accents do create an unfavorable impression if they are associated with substandard speech. Saying "gist" for the word *just* is an example of pronunciation that is often associated with a lack of education. Again, your dictionary can help you with problems like this one, and it may even list several pronunciations for the same word. By following the standards of educated people in your community, you can be both faithful to your background and understood by your listeners.

Pitch is simply the musical note that your voice makes when it issues a sound. You may have a high soprano voice, or you may be a deep bass. In any case, your voice has a range that is comfortable, and you have a typical pitch at which you usually speak. When you are tense, there is a tendency to speak a note or two higher than your typical pitch. A closed-mouth yawn can help get you back to normal. If you feel that your pitch is too high in general, you can develop a lower voice by relaxing your throat and learning to speak in a lower, relaxed tone. In a private setting, you might try to tilt your head back slightly and slowly gargle air by letting your vocal bands relax and "flap" on the airstream. Lower tones also carry better than higher ones, so speaking in a low tone that is still within your normal range can help your voice to project farther out into the room.

Variety in pitch is also important. When you raise your pitch slightly at the end of an interrogative sentence, you are telling your listeners that your sentence is a question. You can also use the range of your voice to create interest and emphasis. A tape recorder can assist you in developing good variety in the pitch of your voice. Use it to learn how to enhance your message or to see what areas you need to work on if your voice seems to be stuck in a limited monotone.

Your *rate* of speech refers to how fast or slowly you speak. You have probably heard speakers who speed along so fast that you cannot follow them and others who seem to drag on for so long that it takes them forever to get to the point. As is true for the other elements of vocal presentation, variety can be a key ingredient to your success as a speaker. Going fast sometimes and then slowing down add interest in general to your speech, and you can also use this technique to emphasize key ideas for your audience.

A very important aspect of your rate of speech is silence. Pause at key places to emphasize an idea. For example, if you have an important word coming up, pause just before you say it to set up your listeners. During the pause, gaze around the room at your audience to heighten the expectation. "And the winner is . . . !" is a perfect example of the use of a pause before a key idea to create an impact. After you have presented an important idea, you may want to pause to give the audience a moment to absorb or think about what you have just said. Try going through your speech to discover the impact that a well-chosen pause might have on your message.

The final element, tone, is the most difficult to vary. This aspect of your voice is also called *quality*, or *timbre*. The tone of your voice refers to those qualities that are unique in your resonance and sound production. When Jim calls on the phone, you can distinguish his voice from Walt's voice. When a clarinet plays a note, you can tell that it is not a violin even if it is playing the exact same note. The instruments may be played at the same volume, rate, and pitch, but their tone is what distinguishes each instrument. Brothers or sisters may sound very much alike because they share many genes and have been raised in a similar environment. Therefore their vocal production and patterns may also be very similar.

It is difficult to provide variety in your tone of voice; and unless your voice is at one extreme or another of the tonal scale, it is probably not very important to do so. However, if your voice is excessively nasal or so breathy that people think you are trying to imitate a movie star, you may wish to work on altering your tone production.

When is a person's tone of voice excessive? When your audience pays more attention to the tone of your voice than to your ideas, you are probably a candidate for tone modification. You can alter a nasal voice by learning how to close off the nasal passages and open your mouth and throat more. You can reduce a breathy voice by using less air in your vocal production and by forcing that air through a slightly smaller opening. Of course, you can have fun playing around with your tone production, and that may be one way to discover some tonal variety that you can use to your advantage in your presentation. If your tone production gets severely in the way of clear communication with your listeners, you may need some sessions with a qualified speech therapist to develop some new habits of sound production.

All of these aspects of good vocal delivery are designed to bring clarity and emphasis to your message. The use of volume, diction, pitch, rate, and tone can be enhanced by appropriate variety. You can increase your ability to discover and use this variety by careful self-monitoring, especially through tape-recorded practice.

Nonverbal Skills

Studies of speech communication have found that the use of both voice and body are very important in giving a speech. In one experiment, a trained actor presented a speech to several different audiences. Although the speech was the same on each occasion, in one half of the sessions he stood perfectly still and simply gave his speech. In the other half, he took a few steps from time to time and used a few arm, hand, and head movements. The responses to the speech were markedly different. The second group of listeners thought that the speaker was more intelligent than the first group did. They also thought that he was better looking and taller than the first group did. What is most important, though, is that after a month, the second group *remembered the content* better than the first group did. Clearly, nonverbal communication, when it complements a verbal message appropriately, can make that message more effective. Physical communication delivery has four major aspects: appearance, posture, movements, and facial expressions.

Appearance is the first thing your audience will notice about you, even in a classroom setting. It is said, "You never get a second chance to make a first impression." That first impression is always made by your appearance, and it can affect the way listeners will receive your complete message. An easy way to be guided regarding your appearance is to ask yourself what is generally expected or worn in similar circumstances. Is your speech a classroom speech? Are you going to be interviewed for a job or a scholarship? Will you be doing a reading at a religious service, or are you going to be a commencement speaker? Each of these settings probably has a standard of dress and grooming that is appropriate to it. Why should you be concerned with such a seemingly superficial concept as appearance? For the same reason that you would be concerned about your voice or a visual aid. If receivers pay more attention to those factors than they do to your message, they will miss the point of your communication. All the choices you make should enhance and highlight the content of your message. The great fashion designer and perfume manufacturer Coco Chanel was reputed to have said, "If they remember the dress and not the woman, they have remembered the wrong thing." On the days that you present a speech in class, you need not wear a business suit. But you can dress at the better end of the spectrum of what people normally wear to class. Caring about your appearance is one way to demonstrate care and respect for your topic, your ideas, your listeners, and yourself.

Posture refers to your overall, general stance, or how you hold yourself when speaking. Usually, listeners expect speakers to stand up straight, not slouch, lean on the lectern, or drape themselves across a chair or table. Your posture need not be stiff and formal, but it should communicate alertness and energy. Posture also includes the way you position your body. You should turn from one side to another while speaking and eventually face all parts of the room. In this way, you can vary your posture in a comfortable, useful way.

Movements are the many shifts, turns, and gestures you make while you still maintain a consistent posture. Appropriate movement that assists in the clear transmission of your message is not only desirable, it is essential. Some speakers seem to be in constant movement, which can be distracting to the audience. But your standing perfectly still can be boring to the audience. Somewhere in between the two extremes is a level of movement that suits you and will enhance your communication effectiveness. Speakers who engage in a moderate number of movements and gestures are rated by audiences as being more credible than those who do not move very much or those who are in almost constant motion. If you are showing your listeners a picture or a chart, you may need to move so that they can all see it properly.

Smaller movements are called *gestures* and include everything from slight hand movements and head nods to the expansive and descriptive shaping of space with your arms or perhaps your entire body. Most people think of gestures as hand movements because they are the most common and most noticeable. You could, of course, lift your foot and point with your toe, but most people do not. Are you wondering what to do with your hands? Most people seem uncomfortable just letting them hang at their sides. Some people try clasping their hands behind their back, shoving them into their pockets, or folding them in front of the lower chest. These options severely restrict the opportunity to reinforce and complement your ideas with appropriate gestures. They may also have the effect of holding onto tension. Gestures are best used when they are natural and spontaneous—just the way you would use them if you were sitting in your living room or at a lunch table talking with friends. A relaxed, natural animation helps the audience connect with the speaker and creates a friendly rapport. Videotaping your practice sessions is one way to get some direct feedback on your use of gestures.

Facial expressions include a raised eyebrow, a smile, a wink, a frown, or wide-eyed surprise. Research suggests that the face is the most powerful, nonverbal communicator because of the hundreds of possible combinations of facial expressions you can make with your facial muscles. You are also capable of recognizing and giving meaning to these combinations. Make certain that the message your face sends is consistent with the message of your speech. Have a friend watch your presentation or, better yet, arrange to have it videotaped. Then check it for clear and communicative facial expressions.

TECHNOLOGY IN COMMUNICATION

Honest Feedback

Videotaping your practices may be one way to get some direct feedback on your use of gestures, postures, and vocal variety. The widespread availability of videocameras and players makes this tool one to which you probably have easy access. Each year, the cost of these cameras and players comes down, and the quality and capabilities of the equipment go up. Technological advances will allow you to see yourself in slow motion, freeze the action, or fast-forward to get an exaggerated picture of yourself. About ten years ago, I began the practice of videotaping my students' speeches and letting them view the tape later, one at a time. Since that time, their abilities to present oral communication have improved beyond the levels my students used to reach. Take advantage of this technology, and use it to provide accurate feedback.

Eye contact is an important element in communication. Having good eye contact means that you look at your listeners almost all of the time, establishing a direct link between yourself and individual members of the audience. Many students find this contact difficult to establish and maintain. Some are reluctant to use eye contact because they start thinking about the person they are looking at instead of the idea they are speaking about. Other speakers may come from a culture or tradition in which direct eye contact is considered rude. In traditional Asian and African families, it is often a sign of respect to look away from the person whom you are addressing. Some families maintain these cultural norms through many generations. However, the mainstream American social norm is to establish direct eye contact with the audience when you are in a public-speaking situation.

DIVERSITY IN COMMUNICATION

The Emperor and the Messenger

In Kyoto, Japan, the imperial palace has a reception hall where messengers used to bring news and information to the emperor. A lowly messenger could not speak directly to the emperor, so three floor levels were built into the room. The messenger would kneel at the first level and present the message to the shogun, or intermediary, who sat at the second level, about ten feet away. The intermediary would then turn to the emperor, who sat at the third level, also about ten feet away, and repeat the message. The emperor probably heard every word the messenger said, since he was barely twenty feet away. Nevertheless, cultural communication norms had to be observed. Consequently the emperor showed no reaction, not even to terrible news, until the intermediary repeated it to him. The same process was reversed if the emperor had a return message. First he told it to the intermediary, who then told it to the messenger. The messenger, of course, could give no indication that he had heard a single word spoken by the emperor.

It is difficult to think about your speech and simultaneously gaze around the room, looking at all the members of your audience. One common problem for classroom speakers is that they will find a friendly face and present most or all of the speech to that one person. Speakers are usually unaware that they are doing this. The best thing to do is to glance slowly around the room, looking directly at each person for only a brief moment, then move on to the next person. Although some members of the audience may not be looking back at you at that precise moment, most of them will be, and you will make them feel included. You can also be reading their expressions and postures for feedback as you look around. Do you see some puzzled looks? Maybe you should explain your idea from a different angle. Do some people seem bored? Tell a lively story, change the volume of your voice, or make a dynamic movement. Eye contact makes the audience feel connected to the speaker and the speech. This connection is called *rapport*, and it is a strong factor in getting your message across. One way to create and maintain rapport is through direct, but passing, eye contact while speaking.

Verbal and nonverbal presentation skills are important because together, they carry your complete message to your listeners. Good delivery enhances, but cannot replace, good content. The best speakers have both; they begin with a worthwhile message and then give it a good presentation. Each speaker will have some personal variations on the general suggestions presented here, so you can still demonstrate your individuality while working within this framework.

 ## EVALUATING PUBLIC SPEECHES

Every time you give a speech in class or a presentation in public, you will be evaluated. You won't always get a written grade for your outline or your speech, but you can be sure that people will be forming evaluations of you and your message. Because evaluation is integral to any communication event, it is appropriate to look at how people judge the communication they receive. One way to evaluate speeches is to judge them according to three **standards for evaluating speeches:** presentation, audience adaptation, and ethics.

Standards of Presentation

Included in this criterion are the preparation and speaking skills you exhibit in your speech. When you listen to others speak, and when they listen to you, the following aspects of your speech become important to the process of evaluation.

The *significance of the topic* means that the topic itself must be worth the time and effort that you invest in preparing it. It must also be important enough to warrant your audience's attention. The topic should inspire new insights and perspectives in the listeners. It should not be trivial or superficial. The ideas you express should address what you assume to be the best aspects of your audience.

Enhance, illustrate, and focus your topic with adequate and appropriate *supporting materials.* The research sources and factual basis for the speech should be solid and very clearly presented. The supporting materials should contain material of real substance. A quick look at one issue of *Time* magazine is not adequate to support a speech on changing our policies in the Middle East. Moreover, personal experience should not be considered more than a place to begin. Even a presentation on your trip to the Grand Canyon could include some statistics about the canyon, a quotation from John Wesley Powell (the first explorer to travel the entire canyon by boat), a reference to a Havasupai legend, and a published interview with a ranger stationed there. Finally, the material must be appropriate for the maturity level of the audience, as well as for the setting, the occasion, and the time limits.

For clarity of *organization,* your outline is the basic guideline. Do you have clear and distinct subordinate ideas? Is the thesis clearly stated? Are there clear transitions that link each major item together in a cohesive body? Remember,

CRITICAL THINKING IN COMMUNICATION

Critical Message Reception

One of the positive aspects of being a critical thinker is that you automatically become a critical consumer of information. This ability is called on when you evaluate advertising, marketing, and other information that you receive. For example, you can evaluate the speeches you hear in class or the advertising you see on television. As you read and gather information in support of *your* messages, keep in mind what you learned from evaluating the messages of others. You need to select from among many choices and options. Critical thinking helps you to compare your options and choose the best ones for the time, place, and circumstances of your communication. In short, applying critical-thinking skills will help you to listen more carefully to others and select more carefully for yourself.

the body must have its own internal logic. Use one of the patterns suggested in the previous chapter to create a complete and comprehensive outline.

Choice and *fluency* of language involve two aspect of your delivery that go hand in hand. One is the level and vividness of your chosen vocabulary. Do you select words that both communicate and create interest? Are you using too abstract a vocabulary? Do you talk down to, or talk at, your listeners? Fluency concerns the ease with which your words flow. Do they flow smoothly, and are they presented in a tone and at a rate to which your audience can respond?

The final standard—*delivery,* use of voice and body—is what many people think of when they discuss presentation. Many beginning speakers focus almost exclusively on these aspects of their presentation. But these criteria represent only one of the five areas of evaluation. On the other hand, you do need to speak loudly and clearly and use movement, gestures, facial expressions, and eye contact to enhance your message.

Evaluating speeches according to these five standards will probably be sufficient for most presentations. However, if presentations were judged only by these standards, the judges would be lacking in terms of two very important, additional criteria: the adaptation of the speech to the audience and the adherence of the speaker to ethical standards of communication.

Adaptation to the Audience

This standard means that any presentation should demonstrate the sender's clear attempts to make the content of the speech apply to the *particular* group that is listening to it. Such things as level of interest, complexity of ideas, clarity of sentence structure, and type of visual aids are included in this standard. References to the immediate listeners—to their values and to their reasons for being present—are also included in this standard. In short, the question to be answered in evaluating presentations according to this standard is: What is the value of the information to the audience?

Standards of Ethics

An **ethical communication** must meet several tests. It must be honest; that is, you cannot lie to your listeners. You must make certain that what you purport to be true is in fact true. Some speakers depend on the statements of others. Then, when the statements turn out to be erroneous or faulty, they blame their sources. The responsibility for the content of a speech rests clearly and solely with the speaker. If the speaker depends on others' faulty research, it is the speaker who bears the fault. That is why it is so important to do wide-ranging research. Any unusual or inconsistent information will become noticeable to you when no other source confirms it.

Sometimes a speaker will invent a story to illustrate an idea. This type of invention is fine, as long as the speaker makes it clear to the listeners that the story is only a hypothetical support. Speakers usually let the audience know that they are only telling a story when they say things like, "Let's imagine for a moment . . . ," or "Suppose that this happened to you . . . ," or "I once heard a story about a man who . . ." These phrases say very clearly that the information the audience is about to hear is fictional. Then you can be as creative as you wish. Otherwise, if you give your listeners the impression that what you are saying is true, it had better be true.

A second aspect of ethical communication follows from the first. That is, you must credit your sources. If you follow the five-part outline suggested in Chapter 11, you will include a bibliography in your own outline to document your research and give credit to the ideas that are not your own. But what about your audience? Since the spoken part of your presentation ends with the fourth section, the conclusion, you do not actually read your bibliography to your listeners. The way to include your citations is to work them into the flow of your speech. Instead of saying, "There were nearly 50,000 deaths on the highway last year due to drunk drivers," you might say, "According to the National Safety Council in their September report this year, there were nearly 50,000 deaths on the highway last year." This is a good citation, and it makes a strong impact. The audience will listen more carefully if you cite a respected authority. You do not need to include the complete citation, with page numbers, city of publication, and so on, but a reference to the source alone is sufficient to meet the ethical requirement so that your listeners know where you got the information.

A third area of ethical consideration relates to the way in which the audience is capable of using the information. The meaning of this statement can be shown in the following analogy: A high-power sales pitch for a set of expensive books is appropriate for a consumer who can afford them and who can benefit from them. A family that is struggling to pay the rent each month or has limited language skills would probably benefit from a gift of used books and information about free courses to improve their language skills. It would be unethical to try to pressure this family into a purchase. An ethical salesperson would give the first family a lively sales presentation and give the second family a list of resources where they might find free reading material, and language training.

Another way to evaluate the ethics of a message is according to its completeness. Not only must your message be true, supported, cited, and of value to the listeners, it must not deliberately leave out vital information. If a speaker tells you about a cure for cancer and fails to mention that it has been investigated and rejected by the American Medical Association, the speaker is being dishonest by giving you incomplete information.

To summarize, the hallmark of ethical speakers is that their speeches are truthful, complete, fair, and well documented. Anything less would be judged as not meeting the minimum standards of communication ethics.

IMPROVING PUBLIC COMMUNICATION COMPETENCY

There are four distinct ways to improve your competency as a public speaker. If you have ever admired speakers who exhibit excellent speaking abilities, you know that the first thing you notice about them is their **confidence.** The way to look confident is to *be* confident, and confidence can be achieved by following these steps (Zeuschner, 1994).

Know your subject well. If you have a comfortable feeling about your topic, you are well on your way to becoming a confident speaker. Of course, you need to select a topic that interests you or about which you already know something. Then you must spend time to develop your knowledge and interest in the subject. If you consult many sources, if you interview or find published interviews of experts, and if you have personal connections to the topic, you will enjoy the confidence that comes from knowing your subject well.

Know your speech materials. Once you have gathered and reviewed your material, you should feel that you have selected a comprehensive variety of the best information available to you. Go through the research you have collected, and check it for variety, interest, and impact and for how up-to-date the information is. Have you tested your ideas for their relevance to the audience, the situation, and the time limits? Have you chosen an interesting story or quotation for your introduction? Do your visual supporting materials meet the tests of clarity and impact? If so, you can feel secure with your materials.

Know your outline. This step requires that you fully understand and use the principles of outlining. Are all five parts of your outline distinctly labeled? Are the five parts clearly related to the thesis and to each other? Make certain that the body of the speech helps to explain, clarify, define, or defend the thesis and that it is broken into two, three, four, or five main subdivisions based on a logical pattern. Try using a few different patterns until you are sure that you have the most appropriate one for you, your topic, and your audience. If your outline stands up under careful analysis and alternative outlines do not work as well, you can have confidence that you have selected the correct outline for your material. As you know, good organization is the foundation of good communication.

Finally, *practice*—and practice again. The best method for developing competency is, and always will be, practice. But it works only if you are practicing correctly. Go over your presentation enough times so that *you know* that you know your speech. Say the words aloud six, eight, or ten times, until you can enunciate them clearly and naturally. Do not force yourself to repeat a sentence over and over or to work toward perfection in your recitation. Try to achieve a comfortable ease. It is the flow of your *ideas* that should be smooth. Your transitions should link one idea to the next. If you develop a direct, extemporaneous style, your speech will have slight variations each time you present it, yet the ideas will remain essentially the same. Knowing that you have the ability to present your speech comfortably will give you the confidence that is characteristic of a competent public speaker.

You can see how developing these areas increases your communication repertoire, giving you standards and criteria by which you can make appropriate selections from that repertoire. Practice in these activities and skills will allow you to enhance your implementation. Finally, the systems for evaluation presented above complete the competency cycle.

SUMMARY

You probably understand by now that you have control over your ability to become a competent speaker. In other words, this competency is not something you have, but is something that you *develop* through effort. First, you need to develop a repertoire of delivery styles and types, of organizational patterns, of research strategies, of supporting materials, and of presentational skills so that you can quickly and readily select the ones that are appropriate for you, your audience, your topic, and the occasion. Your selection of a subject that is both important and interesting to you and your audience is the next step. Then you can implement your choices with materials that support, clarify, and give impact to your topic. Furthermore, you will become more confident if you know that you have created an outline that follows specific guide-

lines for good organization and addresses the major sections of the outline format. Next, good speakers work at controlling excess energy, which is common to everyone. Not to be neglected in giving good speeches is the feedback from your teachers, friends, and even yourself with which you can evaluate both your own development as a speaker and that of others. Finally, you will gain a good deal of confidence if you give yourself sufficient time to practice your presentation until you know that you can deliver the ideas contained in your presentation with comfort and ease.

If you follow the steps suggested in this and other chapters, you will become like the vast majority of good speakers—a bit nervous on the inside, but also ready, willing, prepared, able, and confident when you appear before your audience.

KEY TERMS

presentation styles, *p. 240*
memorized, *p. 240*
manuscript, *p. 241*
extemporaneous, *p. 241*
impromptu, *p. 242*
speech apprehension, *p. 244*
physiological preparation, *p. 245*
psychological preparation, *p. 248*

vocal delivery, *p. 250*
appearance, *p. 254*
posture, *p. 254*
movements, *p. 254*
facial expressions, *p. 255*
standards for evaluating speeches, *p. 257*
ethical communication, *p. 258*
confidence, *p. 259*

EXERCISES

1. Describe specific examples of presentations that you have recently seen in which each of the four types of presentation was used appropriately by a speaker. For each example, describe the circumstances that made one type of presentation more appropriate than another. Can you think of a recent experience you had in which the speaker used an inappropriate style? What factors made the style seem wrong for the situation?

2. As you watch a sports program on television, identify some of the relaxation techniques used by the athletes that are similar to the ones you can use

before a speech. Jot down some examples to share with the class. Look for deep breathing, head and neck movements, tensing and relaxing muscles, and eyes closed in concentration or visualization.

3. The next time that you are about to take a test, try the breathing exercises and the exercises in tensing and relaxing the muscles described in this chapter. Evaluate the effectiveness of the exercises after the test. Try to teach the exercises to someone else. Ask that person to apply them in a tense situation. Find out later whether the exercises help to relieve the tension.

4. Listen to a speech on campus or in the community, and conduct an evaluation of the speech, just as your instructor does for your speeches in class. Rate the speaker according to the five criteria presented in this chapter. Some elements of a presentation are easier to rate than others. Why? Share your evaluation with the class in an evaluation session.

5. Pair off with a member of the class and become that person's speech buddy. Agree to listen to your classmate's practice sessions in exchange for your classmate's doing the same for you. Then practice—and practice again.

REFERENCES

Hoffman, J., and J. Sprague. "A Survey of Reticence and Communication Apprehension Treatment Programs at U.S. Colleges and Universities." *Communication Education* 31 (1982), 185.

Richmond, V., and J. C. McCroskey. *Communication: Apprehension, Avoidance and Effectiveness.* Scottsdale: Gorsuch Scarisbrick, 1995.

Wolpe, J. *Psychological Inhibition by Reciprocal Inhibition.* Stanford: Stanford University Press, 1958.

Zeuschner, R. B. *Effective Public Speaking.* Dubuque: Kendall-Hunt, 1994.

Informing Others

13

- Understand the purposes of informative speeches, and be able to use different types and patterns.

- Apply the standards that are used to evaluate informative speeches.

- Be confident and willing to create your own informative speeches.

- Present a short speech of definition, demonstration, or exposition.

- Follow the steps for improving your informative speaking competency.

O ne of the most common types of presentation or speech is one that informs the listeners. The speaker may be telling about a place or an event, describing a person or a process, or shedding light on an invention or a hobby. When your listeners' goal is to gain information, you are probably giving an informative presentation. The goal of an informative speech is to leave your audience with more information than it had before your speech. Your listeners should walk away saying, "That was really interesting. I never knew that before!"

The key to their understanding an informative speech, or any speech, is the thesis sentence. When the thesis sentence states, "The microchip was developed in four distinct steps," listeners can tell that they are about to hear an informative speech. The body will probably be divided into four subdivisions, and it will most likely follow a chronological pattern of development. If your thesis sentence states, "Yellowstone is a great place to visit," your audience will again probably hear an informative speech, but this time it may follow a topical pattern. On the other hand, if you say to your audience, "There are four reasons why you should vote for Smith," you are making a persuasive speech.

The difference between an informative and a persuasive thesis sentence is that the first talks about a thing or an event as the subject of the sentence, while the second makes the listener the subject. The word *should* indicates persuasion. When you say, "I'm going to inform you why you should give blood," you are about to give a persuasive speech. On the other hand, the goal of informative speeches is to convey information, and to do so clearly and accurately. The report on the speaking style of Sojourner Truth that appeared in an earlier chapter was an informative presentation, as would be for example, a demonstration of pottery making.

DIVERSITY IN COMMUNICATION

Informative Styles

I n some cultures, it is rude to be direct when asking for action or compliance. For example, an Asian speaker may present what appears to be neutral information to Europeans, yet it is really an indirect way of seeking compliance. Some writers believe that in the United States, some women's use of politeness in communication may seem to men to have informative functions. Some messages that women present in the form of questions may, in reality, be softened or polite forms of persuasion. For example, a woman who says, "Do you think it's time to go yet?" might not be looking for a "yes" or "no" response but instead be trying to influence the other party to hurry or to leave (Lakoff, 1979, 1990; Hoar, 1988).

By contrast, an American male might ask his female companion, "Do you want to make dinner tonight?" in an attempt to find out whether she has already planned a menu or whether he should go ahead with the one he planned. She might reply, "Okay, I will," treating the question as a request to make dinner even though she had not planned to and expressing compliance to the perceived request (Tannen, 1994).

When you are in a job setting, you may need to train a new group of employees, explain how a piece of equipment works, or clarify a new plan for organizing the work area. Your community life is also filled with informative presentations, such as the town meeting at which the new water plan is presented, or the city council meeting at which a person comes to explain the operations of a neighborhood crime watch.

The next section describes three ways of looking at informative presentations. Some applications of the patterns of organization covered in the previous chapter follow. The chapter concludes with a description of ways in which to evaluate your informative presentation and improve your competency as an informative speaker.

TYPES AND PURPOSES OF INFORMATIVE SPEAKING

There are different ways to categorize informative speeches, but the three following general categories are the most frequently used: speeches of definition, of demonstration, and of exposition. The differences among them are not great; in fact, you may notice a good deal of overlap.

Speeches of Definition

This type of informative presentation requires you to present an idea that is unfamiliar to your audience and tell them about it so that they understand something new. You need to divide the topic into logical units, describe the parts or aspects or history of the concept, and give your listeners enough detail that they fully comprehend the idea. Speeches of **definition** may be short and can be combined with others as a first step in a longer process. For example, you may be a member of a panel that is discussing an issue before an audience. The first speaker usually gives a speech of definition by defining the problem, describing the background, or clarifying the vocabulary or terms to be used in the rest of the discussion.

Defining ideas or concepts is not an easy task, and a good speech of definition is concrete, rather than abstract; is specific, not general; and uses multiple approaches to making the idea clear. There are several steps that you can follow to create a good definition of an idea or concept for your audience. These steps can become the body of your speech.

You might first turn to a dictionary for help and present your listeners with the definition(s) you find there. One way to work in some variety here is to use a variety of dictionaries. There are many specialized dictionaries, and even the popular, general ones may have slightly different, interesting ways to define the same term. You might begin with *Webster's New Collegiate Dictionary*, then turn to the *Oxford Dictionary of the English Language*. Suppose you were talking about issues concerning the freedom of speech, and you wanted to explain the concept of *libel*. A general description would be adequate for a start, but do not stop there. You could then turn to *Black's Law Dictionary* or *Ballentine's Law Dictionary*. You might find citations on the *Lexus* electronic search system

THE STORY OF COMMUNICATION

The Evolution of Modern English

If you lived in London in the year 1065, you would be speaking a form of Old German called Anglo-Saxon, and you might still be speaking a similar language today if William of Normandy had failed in his attack on England in 1066. William and his conquering armies spoke Old French, which was derived from Latin. As was true of most conquerors, the Normans took all the good jobs—king, duke, and baron—and left to the Saxons the occupations of servant and peasant.

The official language of England for about the next 400 years was French, and modern English grew out of a blending of Saxon syntax and French vocabulary. During those years, a great deal of tension and strife was associated with the two languages. The tales of Robin Hood, for example, pit the oppressed Saxons as represented by the Merry Men against Norman officials as symbolized by the Sheriff of Nottingham.

In England today, there are still strong associations with family names from the two cultures as well as the pronunciations used by different social classes and in different geographical locations. The United States, of course, also has linguistic stereotypes, as seen in a variety of regional accents or dialects. In other countries, especially those having a conquered minority, language differences, as a reflection of deep-seated nationalism, can cause persecution, punishment, and even war. The strife in many parts of the former Soviet Union and Yugoslavia is due to interethnic tensions and the desire of a national or ethnic group to have autonomy, including its own language. It took our English-language ancestors about 400 years to blend their languages, and the story of communication is still being written when it comes to languages.

to cases or rulings in the area of libel containing statements that you could include in your definition.

A next step might be to discuss the origin of the term *libel*. In that case, you would present the etymology of the word, which means that you would discuss its origins, roots, history, or development. Because much of the English language is derived from Latin and Greek—via the French of William the Conqueror—you may find yourself describing an ancient root for your audience, taking it apart, and delineating its meanings. If you are dealing with an idea or concept such as socialism, you could also research the origins, history, and evolution of the socialist movement.

One of the best ways to define any idea, word, or concept is by example. An example is a form of supporting material, so a speech of definition requires several clear, specific instances to help the members of the audience understand your point. If they are familiar with your examples, and if your examples are precise and clear, you will have made your subject understandable to them. For example, when telling your listeners about types of dogs—spaniels, retrievers, shepherds, and so on—make certain you provide an example or two of each so that your audience will see that a cocker and a springer are examples of spaniels, that a golden and a Labrador are types of retrievers, and that the Australian, German, and collie are examples of the shepherd group. Examples will make your presentation come alive.

If you tell your audience what something is not, you are defining by negation. For example, you might say to your listeners,

> "Let's talk about transportation for a minute. No, I'm not talking about fancy luxury cars. I'm not talking about all-terrain vehicles, nor am I interested in high-performance, two-passenger sporty models. I want to focus your attention on the economy transportation car."

By eliminating some factors from your definition, you focus the attention of your audience on the definition of your topic. The problem with using this pattern for an entire speech is that you spend too much time on the areas in which you are *not* interested. This pattern can be useful if, for the sake of variety, you work it into a larger, positive speech of definition.

Finally, you can define something by providing additional words about it. This type of definition is called *rhetorical* and uses synonyms, rephrasing, or context to add clarity to your definition. For example, if you use a word that is unfamiliar to your listeners, you might give them some synonyms to help them understand the word's meaning. "The family was distraught—anxious, distressed, upset, and frantic—when their child got lost." Not only has your rhetorical technique helped anyone who did not know the meaning of the word *distraught,* but you have also reinforced the feeling and meaning of the term. Context refers to the setting, situation, or circumstances that may affect the meaning of a word. For example, the word *spare* in the context of bowling is very different from the word *spare* in the context of auto repair. A *citation* may be very desirable when it is from the Red Cross, very undesirable when it is from a police officer, who has stopped your car, but desirable when it is from the Chief of Police for valor.

These approaches to speeches of definition can be used together; and by using several forms for your ideas, you can be reasonably assured that your audience will understand your definition. A combination of approaches will also help you to create interest through variety. As noted above, a speech of definition can function as the first part of a longer speech. The definition clarifies your idea, then the rest of the speech explains its details. For example, if your topic is nuclear energy, step one of your presentation might be to define the words *fission* and *fusion,* giving your listeners several approaches to definition to clarify these important terms.

Speeches of Demonstration

One popular informative speech, both in class and in your career, is the "how-to" presentation, or the speech of demonstration. Whenever you show your listeners a process or illustrate or teach them how to do something, you are giving a speech of **demonstration.** When you teach someone how to assemble a model, stand on a surfboard, play the guitar, perform CPR or *t'ai chi,* or even breathe deeply as a relaxation exercise, the demonstration speech is the form you will probably use. We learn most of our skills from watching others and then trying to imitate them. We watch someone riding a bicycle, and we

The speech of demonstration is often fun and lively.

attempt to copy the technique. Cooking lessons, carpentry, calf roping, and calligraphy can be taught with a good demonstration.

There are several ways to create and present a strong demonstration. First, break the process down into smaller units that follow a logical order. A complex gymnastic routine will be easy to understand if each move is taken one at a time. The most intricate pattern—music, lace, dances, macramé, computer programs—can be made clear if its structure is identified and divided into smaller units.

Next, arrange the units in logical order. Determine the appropriate sequence for your topic and group the basic steps into that order. You will probably build from the simple to the complex. For example, when you talk about model airplanes, you might begin by demonstrating assembly of the fuselage, then the wings, and then the supporting struts.

Third, be sure that each step of the demonstration is connected by a clear **transition.** You must show your listeners how the links of your chain are joined together. Watch a cooking show or a demonstration of carpentry or plumbing on television. Each step of the process is clearly linked to the previous one. Professional demonstrators know that showing these connections is the best way to teach someone who does not understand a process enough that they can comprehend it clearly. In class, you might demonstrate a hobby or craft, an experimental procedure, or a design sequence. In a career setting, you may be asked to show others in your workplace how to do a certain procedure or how to accomplish a specific task. For example, you could be a training technician, showing others how to run a blueprint or loading machine or how to operate a computer terminal or a spreadsheet program. In many jobs, you will be called on to make a formal presentation to a group demonstrating one of your company's important procedures.

A significant part of any demonstration presentation usually involves visual aids. Recall that in Chapter 11, several guidelines were presented for the effective use of visual supporting materials. It would be wise to review those guidelines before preparing a speech of demonstration. Even if you know your topic very well, your audience does not, and competent speakers approach a demonstration not from their own expert perspective, but from the point of view of their listeners. Remember to present your demonstration so that everyone in the audience can see it and at a pace that they can follow.

The parts or steps of a demonstration function in your speech outline at the same level as a chart, map, diagram, or photograph. A demonstration is another form

TECHNOLOGY IN COMMUNICATION

Computer Aids

One of the interesting developments in the speech of demonstration is how demonstrations have become more electronically generated. Using an interactive laptop computer and a CD-ROM unit, many presenters now include computer graphics as part of their demonstrations. A lecture on Shakespeare's plays can now include a projected outline of the plot and a diagram of the relationship of the characters, followed by an actual video clip of a production to demonstrate these elements in action.

of visual aid and should be indicated as such on your outline. The guidelines for those visual materials are the same as those for your demonstration. If you have access to a videocamera, it will be beneficial for you to videotape your demonstration first, then watch it from the perspective of an audience member.

Speeches of Exposition

While these speeches certainly may include elements of definition and perhaps of demonstration, they go beyond the limits of these forms to include additional explanation and are somewhat more complex in their subject matter and supporting materials.

If you are trying to explain surfing to your listeners, you might begin with some historical references to the Polynesians. Then you might show a diagram or photograph of a surfboard, demonstrate how to position your feet or hold your body, and then relate some personal experiences or stories about surfing competitions. The purpose of this speech goes beyond definition or demonstration, although it includes elements of both. The goal of a speech of **exposition** is to explain completely some event, idea, or process. These speeches are most successful when you select a topic that is of interest to your audience and when you use a variety of vivid supporting materials.

When you make a **topic selection** for a speech of exposition, keep in mind that the information must be complete. Although you can never say everything about any topic, you can anticipate the major elements that listeners need to know and those that they will most likely want to know. Keeping your thesis sentence to a relatively narrow idea can help you to explore it in depth.

For example, investing in the stock market is too complex a topic for a five-minute speech. But you can divide this general topic and select one aspect of it—municipal bonds or how to invest on a college student's budget. These smaller topics will make it possible for you to present a complete explanation, whereas the general topic will not. In short, your goal of creating understanding can be attained by keeping your topic clearly and narrowly focused and by applying the guidelines discussed in earlier chapters for organizing and supporting speeches.

The speech of exposition may be the most frequently used presentation, so you should be thinking of ways to use definition and demonstration in combination to create a more effective speech. For example, you may wish to make the definition of your topic A in the body of your outline. You could then take some of the methods of definition described above and make those A.1, A.2, and A.3. For the B heading, you might develop a demonstration and show some aspect of your topic. These items become B.1, B.2, and so on. The supporting materials in this section would be mostly visual—maps, photographs, and actual demonstrations. You could then finish the speech with a C heading, which might cover developing the relevance of the topic to your audience and making connections between your explanation of the topic and the experiences or values of your audience. The supporting materials for C.1, C.2, and so on might consist of stories, examples, verbal illustrations, comparisons, contrasts, and perhaps a few more defining examples or even some additional visual aids.

To summarize, the informative speech is one of the most important and most frequent speaking experiences you will encounter. Both in class and on the job, you will need to explain ideas, interests, abilities, and duties—either your own or someone else's. Knowing how to prepare a complete explanation, enhanced by definitions and demonstrations, will enable you to present a well-prepared, clear expository speech.

PATTERNS OF INFORMATIVE SPEAKING

As you know, the goal of an informative speech is to convey information, so the presentation pattern that you select should help the audience to understand your material. This section traces the step-by-step development of an informative speech so that you can see how to construct such a speech yourself. The first three steps are (1) select your topic, (2) compose your thesis sentence, and (3) develop your supporting materials.

Selecting your topic means to review the possible areas you could talk about, judging them on their suitability to the allotted time, to the informative purpose, to the audience, and to you. The topic is usually a general idea that meets the following criteria: It is something you know about and that interests you, something that you can adapt to your listeners' interest and relevance, something you feel comfortable talking about, and something about which there is sufficient, *available* information for you to develop a substantial and worthwhile message. If the topic is too broad in scope, select a subdivision.

Next, compose your thesis sentence. The key to creating a clear thesis sentence is to make it focused, simple, and comprehensive. Your entire speech is guided by your thesis sentence, so it is worth some time and effort to phrase it well. Suppose you have selected investing as your topic, and now it is time to narrow down this general idea. You consider your allotted time and the fact that the audience is composed of people who know very little about sophisticated investment strategies. You know that they have some knowledge of the stock market, and you guess that they would probably like to learn more about this aspect of investment. You create several tentative phrasings and finally settle on this one: "Stock market mutual funds are an easy way for people to begin investing."

Now you can turn to a consideration of an appropriate outline format and begin constructing your speech. Since you are not going to give a speech on the history of the stock market or the location of various parts of the stock exchange

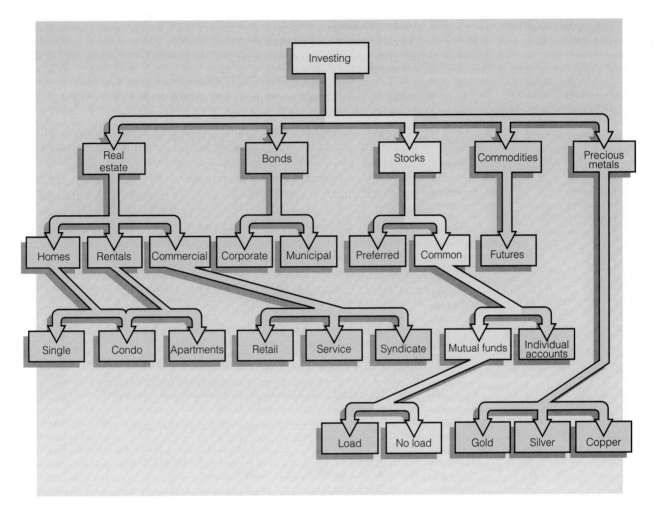

Narrow your topic, select a path, and follow it.

building, you reject both the chronological and spatial patterns and select a topical format instead. Your outline begins to take shape and looks like the following outline:

    I. Introduction
   II. *(thesis sentence)* Stock market mutual funds are an easy way for people to begin investing.
  III. *(body [preview])*
      A. Defining the stock market

Starting with these two items, you can then create a few more major subdivisions:

    I. Introduction
   II. *(thesis sentence)* Stock market mutual funds are an easy way for people to begin investing.

III. *(body [preview])*
   A. Defining the stock market
   B. How the stock market works
   C. How small investors get started

You already know that IV will be your conclusions—a quick review of the main ideas A, B, and C, the thesis, and your introduction. Notice that you do not yet have an introduction. Do not be concerned about that at this point. It will be added later. For now, just save some space for it, and continue to construct your speech.

The next step is to gather your supporting materials. If you follow the suggestions presented earlier, you will visit one or more libraries with a stack of 4" × 6" index cards, you will arrange interviews with a few knowledgeable persons, and you will take an inventory of the books and materials about your topic that you already possess. After you have accumulated a variety of supporting materials, it is time to sort them into groups according to the A, B, or C subdivisions. Any items that do not fit into those categories can be set aside. A possible introduction may reside in that pile. With some work, your outline now looks like this one:

I. *(introduction)* Short story about parents who started a small investment fund for children's college education.
II. *(thesis sentence)* Stock market mutual funds are an easy way for people to begin investing.
III. *(body [preview])*
   A. Defining the stock market
      1. Quotation from *Merriam-Webster Dictionary*
      2. Description from *Investor's Encyclopedia*
      3. Interview with Brenda Hill, local stockbroker
   B. How the stock market works
      1. Visual aid—flowchart of purchase/transaction
      2. Statistics on quantity of daily transactions
      3. Quotation from *Everybody's Business* (textbook)
      4. Graph of Dow Jones averages—ten-year trends
   C. How small investors get started
      1. Types of investments—examples
      2. Yield projection statistics
      3. How college students can benefit
      4. Quotation from Ramon Arguello, investment counselor in town
IV. *(conclusion)* Brief review of A, B, C, thesis sentence, and introduction
V. Bibliography
      1. Source #1
      2. Source #2
      3. Source #3
      4. and so on

Notice that this outline is simple. It states the key ideas and avoids any extraneous items. It does not elaborate on each item but simply indicates it. It provides variety in the supporting materials by beginning with a story and including a definition, three quotations, two statistics, two visual aids, and some examples and descriptions. The speaker makes an effort in the outline to relate to a college audience, so this outline is probably for a speech in a beginning speech class.

Notice that the idea for the speech came out of an abstract and unwieldy topic—investing—and narrowed it down so that it could be discussed in an informative way in five to seven minutes. Notice also that it relies on specific supporting materials to clarify the meaning of the subdivisions of the body. You could take the same topic, and even the same thesis sentence, and create an entirely different speech. You might select another pattern or choose from your store of supporting materials seven or eight alternative items. The preceding example is only that—one example. How you would develop a similar topic depends on your personal perspective, creativity, and associations.

In general, an informative speech can follow a variety of organizational formats, and you should try out a few of them to get a feel for each type. An informative speech does not usually follow a problem–solution or motivational sequence. You are more likely to use a chronological, spatial, or topical pattern in your presentation, as was shown in the example.

This review was designed to take you through the process of creating an informative speech. Try to follow the same steps as you create your own informative presentations. Remember that the basis for good communication is good organization, and the key-word outline is a good way to achieve that organization. Once you have your outline in order, consider it a preliminary draft of your speech. You can always change it, and it is much easier to change an outline than a manuscript. If you find new material that you think is better than the material you selected, just eliminate the old and insert the new. If you change your thinking about the subject, feel free to change the outline—that is,

CRITICAL THINKING IN COMMUNICATION

Structuring the Informative Speech

Notice how your skills in examining ideas in a sequence can be used to help you select an organizational framework. The post hoc fallacy is the one you should keep in mind while arranging your main ideas. The post hoc fallacy means thinking that an event that follows another event must therefore be its result. Do the items that make up your topic follow a *logical* pattern in time, space or structure? If they do, then your ability to apply inductive or deductive reasoning can help you to decide which pattern is most appropriate for your particular speech. Listeners like logic, too. If you create an organizational pattern that flows smoothly, your audience's critical-thinking abilities will be stimulated and will, in turn help your listeners to discover and remember your main ideas. When the time comes to present your speech, the clear pattern that you have organized will help you to remember the correct sequence of items, and it will help the audience to make the transitions from idea to idea with you. Critical thinking applications play an important part in your entire communication.

to rework the order, substitute new supporting materials for old ones, add or delete information, or make any other modifications you like. One of the best resources at your disposal can be time. If you give yourself enough time to create your outline, then put it away for a day or two, and then come back to it, you will gain some perspective on it, and maybe some fresh ideas will help you to improve it. Last-minute preparers do not give themselves this gift, and their speeches are weaker for it.

Once you have gone through your revision to a point at which you are satisfied, it is time to begin practicing your presentation. Select a presentation style—probably extemporaneous—and copy your outline either on a single sheet of paper or on a few (three to seven) note cards. *Limit your notes to the outline format you have already prepared.* Many beginning speakers fall short at this point, and they attempt to write out their presentation on note cards, word for word. Unless the occasion calls for a manuscript speech, limit your notes to your outline. Then put into practice the ideas and guidelines from Chapter 12 to help you achieve clarity and impact in your speech.

EVALUATING INFORMATIVE SPEECHES

In addition to the criteria for evaluating speeches outlined in Chapter 12, you can examine your informative speech from three points of view: (1) the goals involved when you are a listener, (2) the goals you would have as a speech critic, and (3) the larger goals you have as a consumer.

Goals as a Listener

As a listener, you will be seeking particular information from speakers. You will want them to make their ideas clear so that you can understand the point of the presentation. You should be able to restate the speaker's thesis sentence in your own words. You should also be able to recall the main ideas that developed the thesis, and you will often be able to remember some of the more significant supporting materials that the speaker used. Now the people who listen to *your* speeches should be able to do the same. They will evaluate your presentation according to how easy it was for them to accomplish their listening goals. If you put yourself in their place as you create your speech, you will be able to double-check yourself in advance. Any adjustments that you make from the listener's perspective will help to give your speech greater clarity.

Goals as a Critic

To be a good **speech critic,** you need to keep in mind the evaluation criteria presented in Chapter 12: the standards of presentation, ethics, and audience adaptation. Although each of these areas measures a different aspect of the speech, all must be considered in order to carry out a complete evaluation of the quality of the speech. Most untrained audiences tend to focus on only a few of the presentation skills of the speaker—voice, eye contact, appearance, smoothness of delivery. More insightful critics will balance their perceptions of those areas with an attention to organization, support, honesty, completeness, and value to the listeners. That is why your instructor may emphasize certain areas that at first may not seem that important to you or your classmates. Your teacher has been trained to keep all of these factors in mind and to balance them while forming a critique of the speaker and of the speech. The critical feedback that you get from a teacher may be in oral or written form or a combination of the two. Very often, a teacher will focus the oral critique on the positive aspects of the speech and save any commentary on weaknesses or areas needing improvement for a written critique. The major factors that a speech critic will keep in mind are the topic, audience adaptation, form or pattern, organization, time allocation, clarity, transitions, use of supporting materials, use of language, and delivery. Notice that for a speech critic, delivery is only one of several areas to be evaluated.

There are ways to combine all aspects of a speech into a coherent evaluation. For reasons of efficiency, the evaluation criteria are often clustered on an

---

Student Name _____

Topic _____ Date _____

SPEECH EVALUATION
Dr. Zeuschner

Scale: (0-5 points possible per item)

0 = *Missing or done incorrectly*
1-2 = *Meets minimum requirements for university–level work*
3-4 = *Fulfills requirements above university minimum level*
5 = *Substantially beyond expectation for university minimum*

Outline: Overall impression, coherence, form, clarity, neatness ____

Topic: Appropriately adapted to audience, substantial ____

Introduction: Clear, compelling, commanding attention, interesting, relevent, sufficient length ____

Thesis Sentence: To the point, simple, single sentence ____

Transitions: Clear relationship of ideas, smooth flow ____

Body: Logical order, organization, cover the necessary points ____

Support: Quality of supports, evidence, substance ____
Variety, impact of supports (incl. visual aid, if used) ____

Reasoning: Connections and conclusions clearly warranted ____

Ending: Clear, simple review of major ideas, thesis, introduction ____

Bibliography: Sources listed clearly at end of outline ____
Substantial consultation evident ____
Sources utilized in flow of speech ____

Communicative Skills: Vocal quality, nonverbal ____
Direct presentation, non-dependence on notes ____
TOTAL ____
(possible 75)

Evaluation: 30-40 points = *Average*
45-50 points = *Excellent*
55+ points = *Outstanding*

SPEECH CRITICISM FORM

Critic: _____ Speaker: _____

Speech subject: _____

Date of Rehearsal: _____ Place of Rehearsal: _____

Time Spent: _____
Significance of topic and value of ideas:

Adequacy and appropriateness of supporting materials:

Clarity of organization:

Adaptation of content to audience:

Choice and fluency of language:

Use of voice and body in delivery:

Either one of these evaluations forms will help to guide feedback and critique.

evaluation form. Evaluation forms cover major principles of public speaking and allow critics to be specific in their criticism. A professional critique will cover these same areas, although it will probably be in narrative form and many extend to a dozen or more pages. The professional speech communication journals often publish exceptionally well-done pieces of criticism as a way of offering insights into the communication processes of notable speakers. In any case, the two forms shown here differ in areas of emphasis, the second one allowing for more free commentary from the critic. You may use these guides when you are criticizing other speakers or as a tool for self-evaluation. You could also create your own, or perhaps your class has one that everyone can use.

The main value that being a good critic will have for you lies in your ability to tell others and yourself about the *specific* strengths and weaknesses of a speech so that the speech can be improved. Critiques help you specifically to become a better speaker by pinpointing areas where you are already competent or where you demonstrate skillful application. They also help by pointing out to you areas where your speaking skills could be improved. By observing the strengths of others, you learn what techniques are effective and worthy of emulation. By noting the weaknesses of other speakers, you identify speaking behaviors to avoid. In other words, if you can be a good critic of others' speeches, you should be able to look at your own messages more carefully and use your critical insight to improve them.

Goals as a Consumer of Information

Because you consume information daily and in large doses, it pays to be selective about the messages to which you give your time and attention and those that you can reliably dismiss as being of poor quality. One of your lifelong functions will be that of a **consumer of information** in our information society.

IMPROVING COMPETENCY

The Value of Honest Feedback

One of the best ways to improve your competency as a speaker is to use the power of intrapersonal communication. As you recall, the messages you send yourself about yourself are quite capable of motivating and influencing you. How can you give yourself honest feedback about your speaking abilities? Technology can aid you through the use of a videocamera. Try checking one out from your school if you do not have one readily available. Did you find a speech buddy yet? If not, then this is an excellent opportunity to look for one. Have your buddy videotape you, and do the same for your buddy. Then, after you have heard your buddy's comments and suggestions, play back the tape of your speech and look at it in light of the critique. Then try being a critic for yourself, and find out whether it helps to pay attention to the internal monitoring that is your own personal feedback. We are usually our own most severe critics, so be gentle with yourself, but be honest.

You will continue to receive messages constantly; and to some degree, you have already developed a system for evaluating them.

Many people do not evaluate the messages that come their way very carefully but simply accept or reject them on the basis of some automatic response pattern that they have developed. Young children, for example, seem to accept messages uncritically. As teenagers, people typically begin to reject many messages, especially those from parents or other authority figures. Again, this type of rejection may be automatic, based solely on a rejection of authority rather than on an evaluation of the message.

As you go through a typical day, you will be bombarded by informative messages from newspapers, magazines, television, friends, neighbors, teachers, and others. As you evaluate messages in the public domain, remember to look at three areas: their application to you, the trustworthiness of the source, and their demonstration of good communication principles.

Application to you means that any message has some value if you can use it. For example, as you listen to the news, look for connections that you can make to your own circumstances. A broadcast on earthquake preparedness in the area in which you live will connect to your need to prepare your living quarters. At the other extreme, the broadcast may be lengthy, sensational, and attention-getting yet not have any real value for you. Have you ever seen the way some television stations cover a gruesome train wreck? They interview survivors who are frightened and in shock. They ask family members of the fatalities, "How do you feel?" and in general exploit the sensational aspects of the story. This kind of information probably has little value for most listeners except to appeal to their emotions with pictures of other peoples' tragedies. A critical evaluator would ask, "How does this apply to me?" Your answer to this question will give you insight into what the source is trying to accomplish and how well it is reaching its goals. If your listening goals are not being met, you can question the value of continued listening.

A source that is trustworthy merits your attention more than one that is not. Trustworthiness includes having a record and reputation for furnishing truthful information, carrying out reliable reporting, conducting conscientious research, and having supplied previous information that was substantial and related to the interests of the intended audience. If the person or source has a long-standing and well-earned reputation for being accurate, you can use that credibility as an evaluative criterion. *The New York Times,* for example, has a long-standing record for being truthful and accurate in the stories it publishes. Network news broadcasts on radio and television also make substantial efforts to be accurate in their reporting. You probably have friends whom you can reliably trust to give you accurate information because they have always done so in the past. You probably can think of leaders in your community—in clubs, religious organizations, and business or political affairs—who have established reputations for accuracy, so you also view them as trustworthy sources of information.

However, if you do not have the source's record, how can you evaluate the trustworthiness of the source? That question can be answered by the third measure of public communication criticism: use of good communication principles.

Good communication principles include all the factors you have been studying in this section, especially the use of the supporting materials. Does the

Informative speaking means presenting information clearly.

speaker use outside research and cite it during the presentation? Or does the speaker depend solely on self-reports, unnamed experts, or undocumented studies? Does the speaker supply names, dates, titles of publications, and qualifications of authorities cited? Is there any support at all? You may hear someone say, "A recent survey shows conclusively that. . . ." While that statement may very well turn out to a trustworthy support, without a specific citation you have no way to judge its credibility. On the other hand, if the speaker says, "A Gallup poll published last week in *Time* magazine shows conclusively that . . . ," you have a basis for evaluating that support. If the speaker said, "A poll of several neighbors published in a mimeographed flyer proved conclusively that . . . ," you would have another basis for evaluating the information. Check the citations offered.

In addition to verifying the supporting materials, you could use one of the speech evaluation forms and check for good use of other principles. Is the message well organized? Is the thesis clearly stated? How does the message apply to you? You probably will not be carrying a copy of these forms around with you for the rest of your life, so you will need to make a permanent copy in your mind of the major principles involved. You will always remember this system if you apply it regularly—by being a critic of others' speeches and of your own presentations. Just as you are a careful consumer of automobiles, stereo equipment, clothing, appliances, and food products, can you become a careful consumer of information. You want value for your money when it comes to purchasing products, so demand value for your time when listening to information presented in the public forum.

In summation, you can apply your evaluation skills as a listener in the classroom or career setting, as a critic looking for specific strengths or weaknesses, or as an everyday consumer. Each of these roles can, in turn, help you to create better messages. When you listen to a presentation with an open, critical mind, you can then become an objective critic of your own work. While perfection is not a reasonable goal, improvement certainly is. Give yourself praise when you do a good job, and always seek to improve a worthy effort so that it meets the requirements of clarity, substance, and impact.

IMPROVING INFORMATIVE SPEAKING COMPETENCY

The four elements of communication competency—repertoire, selection, implementation, and evaluation—have been implicit in the discussions throughout this chapter. Your repertoire of choices is now expanded by knowing the several approaches that are available to you when you prepare an informative presentation. Guidelines for choosing one or another are now well established, as are the areas to keep in mind in applying any of those choices. Finally, you are now familiar with some detailed methods for evaluating communication choices made by yourself and others.

Among the most important ways for you to improve your communication skills is to learn to make your meaning clear. Be concerned with your choice of words. Review the material on verbal communication if you like, and apply the suggestions given there to the preparation of your informative speech. Keep your vocabulary at a level that is appropriate for the listeners. Think about what they are likely to know already, and what they probably do not yet know, about your topic. Being concrete and specific will help you to achieve clarity. Watch your use of pronouns (she, he, it, they) and be specific when possible—Adele Jones, Robert Gomez, Sandy Point State Park on Highway 41, or Mayor Settle.

Enliven your specific references with vivid descriptions. Color, size, shape, comparison, and contrast will help your audience to create a memorable mental image from your words. "Then I returned home" can be transformed into "After the fire died down, I raced home to tell everyone else about it, but arrived out of breath and too exhausted to speak for several minutes." The latter statement is, to say the least, more interesting, vivid, and memorable for your listeners.

Try to balance your use of exciting language with an effort to be concise. Being concise means to express your thoughts with efficiency, avoiding extra words that do not add information to your ideas. Keep your presentation simple. Your listeners cannot reread your previous sentences as they can in a written essay. If your sentences stretch out and become complex, compound, and lengthy, apply the principle of conciseness in the selection and implementation of your language choices. Check your language use for economy and brevity.

Clear transitions also help an audience to follow your ideas. Connector sentences such as "First we will examine the causes of the war" help your listeners prepare to hear that particular part of your presentation. After each major section, you should link your ideas together with a transition sentence such as "Now that we have looked at the causes of the war, let us examine its effect on the people in the region." This sentence lets your listeners know that you are finished with one major section and are moving to the next one. Of course, you could also say, "Next, the war's effects," but this sentence only announces the change, it does not link the two ideas, nor does it help the audience to move smoothly from one idea to the next. Again, the audience cannot reread what you have just said. Oral style differs from written style in that it requires clear and frequent transitions.

One method to help the audience listen is related to the transition and is called a preview. On the sample outlines you may have noticed the following: "III. *(body [preview])*." As you begin the main part of your speech, it is useful to let the audience know how you will divide the topics stated in your thesis sentence. By giving listeners a preview, you enable them to identify your information by category. Your listeners will prepare themselves mentally to receive three or four units of information from you. Your organizational pattern will also be made clear in advance, and you will have provided a helpful, overall orientation to your presentation. "To explain the effects of the Vietnam war, I will first discuss the causes of the war, then describe some of the effects it has had on the people of the area, and finally talk about several of the major impacts it has had in the United States." This short preview gives your audience a clear pattern of your speech and will help them to pay attention to what you are about to say.

Similar to a preview is an internal summary. When you take a moment in the middle of your speech to summarize the major ideas up to that point, you are doing an **internal summary.** If your speech is longer than eight or ten minutes or contains a very complex sequence of ideas, an occasional internal summary can help your listeners to understand and remember your speech. If you are giving a short, impromptu speech, an internal summary benefits both you and the audience because it gives you a moment to think about where your speech will go next.

Transitions, previews, reviews, and summaries are all methods of improving your informative speaking abilities. If you make frequent use of them, your speech will flow smoothly, and its meaning will be clear. These techniques will help you to remember each section of your speech as you pause mentally and use a transition or a summary to prepare for the next section of your presentation. Get into the habit of employing these tools; they can help you to develop into an effective, informative speaker. If you are not sure when to use them, it is better to have them on hand anyway than to risk leaving them out and losing your audience as you move from one idea to the next. Competent speakers always have these tools in their repertoire of skills. They practice which ones to use and when, and they also regularly evaluate the effectiveness of these methods in their speeches.

SUMMARY

Informative speaking consists of speeches that define, demonstrate, or explain. These three styles can be mixed successfully in a single presentation, yet the goal remains the same: to leave the listeners with a greater understanding of the topic than they had before the presentation. A successful informative presentation has that goal as its main focus.

Methods for organizing informative presentations and for evaluating those presentations were also presented in this chapter. Competency can also be increased by using good supporting materials for interest and clarity and by working on verbal skills, using transitions, being concise, and including previews and summaries.

When evaluating informative speeches, remember to concentrate on the value of the message to the listener, whether you are the listener or the listener is *your audience.* Adopt the perspective of a critic or a day-to-day consumer to help you make that judgment. Apply the principles of good communication to any messages that you send or receive. Informative speaking is a common experience in both classroom and career settings. Being a receiver of information is a lifelong role, so learning to become expert at it is worthwhile. This chapter was designed to start you on that path.

KEY TERMS

definition, *p. 265*
demonstration, *p. 267*
transition, *p. 268*
exposition, *p. 269*

topic selection, *p. 269*
speech critic, *p. 274*
consumer of information, *p. 276*
internal summary, *p. 280*

EXERCISES

1. Imagine that you have been asked to present a speech of definition to your class. What topic could you choose that would be informative to them? What resources would you gather to support it? How would you organize it? Go through the same questions for a speech to demonstrate and a speech of exposition. Has your teacher assigned one of these for you to present next week?

2. Although many televised speeches are designed to be persuasive, some may be informative. Do news broadcasters follow the patterns of organization presented in this chapter? Watch the network news for three consecutive nights, and keep track of which patterns occur most frequently. What about the nature specials or biographies that you see on television? What patterns do they use?

Compare your examples with those of other students in class.

3. As you prepare your informative speech, try at least two different organizing patterns for the same topic. Select the one that "feels" better, and try to explain why it seems to work and the other does not.

4. Seek out a public speaker on your campus, and attend the presentation in person. Keep track of the outline, the pattern of organization, the supporting materials, and the style of presentation. How would you rate this person? What did the speaker do that you would like to emulate in your own presentations? Did the speaker do anything that you think should be avoided?

REFERENCES

Hoar, Nancy. "Genderlect, Powerlect and Politeness." *Women and Communicative Power.* Annandale: Speech Communication Association, 1988.

Lakoff, Robin. "Stylistic Strategies within a Grammar of Style." *Language, Sex and Gender.* Ed. J. Orasanu, M. Slater, and L. L. Adler. New York: Annals of the New York Academy of Sciences, 1979.

Lakoff, R. T. *Talking Power.* New York: Basic Books, 1990.

Tannen, Deborah. *Talking 9 to 5.* New York: Morrow, 1994.

Persuading Others

- Identify the main components of value systems and explain how attitudes change.

- Describe a variety of persuasive speeches and the ways in which they are developed, supported, and presented.

- Present your ideas to influence others.

- Believe that you have something substantial to say and feel confident to say it.

- Develop and present a persuasive speech to your classmates.

- Evaluate and critique the persuasive messages of others.

When you think of the great speakers of the past, you are probably thinking of the great *persuasive* speakers. The speakers who are remembered are those who influenced the events around them. Ancient Greek orations, many of which are still available for us to read today, were often persuasive discourses about the great issues of the day. Collections of these orations feature both pro and con speeches about a single subject.

From the ancient Greek orations to the Iroquois addresses in the Long House, to the abolitionists and suffragettes, to the President's most recent State of the Union speech, public speeches have dealt persuasively with the great issues of their time. Many of these orators often spoke at great length—from thirty minutes to several hours. These speakers followed the guidelines for effective speaking for their time, and many of those guidelines are still appropriate today. Your **persuasive speeches** will join a several-hundred-year-old tradition of carefully prepared communication about significant, contemporary issues. Those many years have produced proven ideas and insights regarding the way people react to messages that are intended to influence them and how a speaker—in this case, you—can take advantage of those insights to produce a message that can successfully persuade your audience to think, feel, or act in a particular way. In addition to the wisdom passed down by a long, rhetorical tradition, modern psychology has provided useful knowledge about how to influence the minds and emotions of other people.

We begin with a definition of persuasion, then follow with an examination of three categories of persuasive messages. A discussion of how we form and modify our attitudes is followed by a description of four types of persuasive speaking. The chapter also presents information on supporting materials, organization, and persuasive language and presentation styles. Finally, we look at ways to evaluate and improve persuasive speaking.

A DEFINITION OF PERSUASION

A message that influences the opinions, attitudes or actions of the receiver is a persuasive message. The definition of a persuasive speech includes the process used to create a message that is intended to influence the listener. Whenever you try to convince someone to eat at your favorite restaurant, vote for your preferred candidate, attend a particular religious service, or buy a compact disc by your favorite group, you are dealing with persuasion. Although each of these messages has *influence* on the audience as a goal, there are three categories of persuasion that are usually identified by the type of influence they address.

FACTS, VALUES, AND POLICIES

Typically, you can create a persuasive speech about one of three main types of concerns. These concerns, or questions, are related to facts, values, and policies.

Facts are usually the concern of historical and legal persuasion. Did Lincoln issue the Emancipation Proclamation for political reasons? Was John Doe mur-

DIVERSITY IN COMMUNICATION

The Evolution of Acceptance

It might seem strange to you, but the ability of ordinary citizens to speak in public on important issues is a relatively new concept. Even in the early history of our country, only white males could participate in important meetings, either as advocates or antagonists. In the late 1800s, women seldom attended meetings, much less spoke at them. At some of the early women's Suffrage conferences, men ran the entire meeting, and at issue was whether to allow such people as Susan B. Anthony or Elizabeth Cady Stanton to speak. Sometimes these women had to sit in a separate section of the auditorium, screened off with a curtain. Even more interesting is the case of Sojourner Truth, a former slave who for years faced the double barrier of being African American and female before finally gaining a large and strong audience of listeners—mostly white males.

Diversity has only recently come to advertising. Before 1960, virtually no people of African, Latino, or Asian ancestry appeared in any television commercials. In 1968, S. I. Hayakawa speculated that it would be revolutionary to include all types of people in commercials, since the companies behind those ads depend on high credibility to make their sales. In some ways, the current increase in the diversity of people in television commercials demonstrates their inclusion in society as a whole.

dered? Was Amelia Earhart a spy? Does that newspaper article libel my reputation? These are questions or propositions of fact.

Values are deeply held beliefs that direct our lives. Do we support public education? Is honesty the best policy? Does a promise of lifelong commitment mean the same thing as marriage? Values represent the area in which some of the most intense and personally involving persuasion takes place.

Finally, questions of **policy** are those that ask what should be done. Should we spend our vacation touring the coast on bicycle, visiting Disney World, or helping to rebuild grandmother's house? Should we take a vacation at all? Should we vote for Candidate X? Should we vote? These actions are the subject of speeches that discuss policies.

Each of these concerns—fact, value, and policy—can be discussed in the same speech. If an education bond issue is to be successful, its proponents need to convince you of the facts, relate the facts to your values to motivate you, and finally, persuade you to act. A political candidate and the makers of a new brand of detergent both follow the same steps in their efforts to persuade you. However, most persuasive speeches are categorized by their ultimate goal, even if they touch on other, ancillary goals or concerns along the way.

To be successful in your attempts at persuasion, you need to address the motivations of your listeners. These motivators are the values and attitudes that are shared by large groups of people. Let us begin with a quick review of those values and attitudes.

Value Systems

In Chapter 7, values and attitudes were presented in relation to self-concept. You probably recall that values comprise a person's primary orientation toward life—the principles by which a person's actions are guided. Your **value system** provides you with a general orientation to life situations. Values tend to remain stable and are less likely to change than are attitudes or beliefs. If they do change, they will probably change very slowly. Therefore values are difficult things to change in a persuasive speech, especially if the speech is a short one. Short speeches are typically given in classrooms, in brief presentations by political candidates, or in television commercials. Instead, these persuaders use the existing values of the audience as a basis for creating a persuasive message. In that way the message can concentrate on an attitude—a smaller unit of belief that is more easily modified if listeners perceive the core value from which it stems to be the same as the core value that is implicit in the message. For example, two candidates for office assume that their listeners value education, so they try to persuade their audience that one of them will do a better job of supporting education.

The question of which candidate will better implement your value system leads to a consideration of attitude toward the two office seekers. If you believe that one will do a better job of acting on your values than the other, your attitude toward that person will be more positive than your attitude toward the other.

ATTITUDE CHANGE THEORY

How do attitudes form? More important in the context of persuasive speeches, how are they changed? These questions are the subject of research by communication scholars who study **attitude change theory.**

Early studies of persuasion and influence included a definition of the concept of attitude. As you know, attitudes are based on values and more specific applications of those values to the events in the world around you. A simple definition provided by researchers in the 1930s is still valid today and is useful in learning more about persuasive speaking. An attitude can be defined as "primarily a way of being 'set' toward or against certain things" (Murphy et al., 1937).

Because attitudes are internal and cannot be seen directly, we rely on reports about attitudes to tell us what they are. These reports may be simple, such as responses to questions and other verbal or nonverbal expressions of them. For example, a person might say, "I don't like Senator Jones's record on educational issues. I think I'll vote for Smith instead." Answers to a questionnaire about likes and dislikes in general and responses to a public opinion poll are also expressions of attitudes.

Attitudes may come from many sources, and many people, especially in the field of psychology, have tried to explain both the development of attitudes and attitude change theory.

Early Approaches

The period before World War II saw the development of several approaches to the study of attitudes. The early work on attitudes followed the work of Pavlov

Sojourner Truth, an illiterate slave, overcame many attitudinal barriers and became a powerful orator.

and his experiments in operant conditioning in which dogs were trained to salivate when they heard a bell ring. The sound of the bell had previously been associated with food, and so the bell became a *conditioned stimulus* for the dogs.

Psychologists then applied Pavlov's findings to humans and speculated that our attitudes might be a result of some repeated association, or conditioning. A similar theory was formulated by B. F. Skinner; but instead of forcing an association to create a conditioned response, a reward was provided every time a correct response was given. Although the work was initially done with rats—teaching them to press a lever to get a food pellet—these findings in *behavior modification* were applied to human behavior. For example, if you expressed a particular opinion as a child and your parents said, "My, what a wonderful child!" or made some other positive response, you may have been reinforced in that opinion. A third approach was taken by Hull, who theorized that both habit and drive worked together to create reinforcement. **Habits** are repeated behaviors; **drives** are needs, such as the need for food, shelter, and the avoidance of pain or injury. As we respond to these needs, we develop predispositions for behaving or believing in certain ways (Hilgard and Bower, 1966).

During World War II, a great deal of attention was focused on the extensive use of propaganda through the use of mass media. Films became a weapon of psychological warfare, and all the countries participating in the war made propaganda films for use in their own countries. They also produced other films for export to persuade people in other countries to be on their side.

The use of training films by the U.S. Army allowed for extensive testing of various types of persuasive messages on the attitudes of soldiers, largely because thousands of them were available to be tested in a fairly controlled setting. Much of this work was connected with Yale psychologist Carl Hovland. His studies concluded that most of the early army training films had little effect on soldiers' attitudes. The government then wanted to discover what kind of messages *would* produce a predictable change of attitude. Hovland found that sometimes an attitude would change after a period of time. This delayed reaction was called *the sleeper effect*. He also noticed differences in attitude change between the presentation of a message that gave only one side of an issue and that of a message that gave mostly one side and a little of the opposing side as well. The researchers discovered that one-sided messages had a positive effect on audiences who already held the particular attitude, but two-sided messages had an effect on people who were initially unfavorable to the message (Hovland et al., 1949).

Later, Hovland and others who were influenced by his work continued to study how attitudes are affected by source credibility and by fear appeals. Briefly, **source credibility** theory says that receivers of information are more likely to be influenced by a source that they find to be credible. Most studies show that immediately after a presentation, audiences are more influenced by highly credible speakers than by speakers who are not so credible. But because of the sleeper effect, the influence of both high- and low-credibility sources begins to even out as time passes.

What constitutes high credibility? Researchers have identified four elements associated with credibility: expertise, dynamism, trustworthiness, and goodwill. These factors exist in the minds of the audience as beliefs. In other words, it is important to your credibility that the audience *believe* that you are an expert, that you are trustworthy, that you have goodwill toward them, and that you are energetic. Sad to say, the phenomenon of source credibility explains why people are taken in by con artists every day. Since we do not have a good, dependable, or absolute way to determine the existence of these qualities in other people, we depend on unreliable criteria such as appearance or whatever people tell us about themselves. Genuine tests of credibility require a little more investigation. These tests were covered in Chapter 12 in the discussion of criteria that are used to evaluate public speeches and in the discussion of ethics and communication.

Source credibility is not a modern concept in persuasive speaking. Early Greek and then Roman rhetoricians wrote extensively about how the speakers of their day could persuade others, and prime among their concerns was source credibility—called *ethos*. **Ethos** is usually translated to mean the speaker's character, and you can see the root of the word *ethics* in that term. Good ethos probably blends together what we call *expertise, trustworthiness,* and *goodwill*. When you talk about someone's reputation, you are probably referring to those qualities as well. Far from being an abstract and intangible idea, a good reputation is a very im-

TECHNOLOGY IN COMMUNICATION

Digitizing Images

With the improvement of sophisticated photograph development techniques, alterations in pictures became possible. Thus with airbrush techniques, some advertisers would insert hidden messages in their ads, messages that were intended to reinforce the persuasive impact of the ad. The development of digitized sound and images now let us remove, insert, or otherwise alter features of the message. On a home computer, you can change someone's eye color pixel by pixel and give your Uncle Fred's new digitized likeness glowing magenta pupils, one orange tooth, or extra ears. "Seeing is believing" is probably on its way out as a truism because of our digitized technology.

portant characteristic for anyone to possess. It either opens up or closes off the potential for communication, depending on the quality of the reputation.

Advertisers depend on creating and using a positive reputation. That is why they hire easily recognizable people who already have a positive reputation to appear in their advertisements. They put actors, sports figures, and celebrities in their ads, having paid them enormous sums of money, hoping that you will be influenced sufficiently by their reputation to transfer it to the product being sold or that the ads will at least catch your attention. Automobile ads constantly tell you how high the product was rated in consumer satisfaction polls or how low it was rated in surveys of automobile repair costs. Lawsuits are filed over defamation of character because a person's reputation, character, or ethos can be demonstrated to have monetary value.

Later, we will discuss how you can develop credibility with your listeners to persuade them. If you want to affect their attitudes, keep in mind that source credibility is a major factor in bringing about that change. Another factor that was extensively studied was the use of fear as a persuader.

Fear Appeals

You probably remember seeing films in driver education classes showing the results of terrible accidents. Perhaps your dentist's office has photographs of rotten teeth, bleeding gums, or deformed jaws on the walls of the waiting room. These are obvious **fear appeals.** Do they work?

In a classic study conducted by Janis and Feshbach, fear appeals were used to create better dental hygiene. Building on the work of Hovland, these researchers knew that an attitude could be modified more easily if the subjects of the study were psychologically aroused during the presentation of the persuasive message (Hovland et al., 1953). The subjects, students at a large high school, attended a mild, medium, or strong fear-related lecture on tooth decay. In general, the most improvement in dental hygiene occurred in subjects who had been exposed to the mild fear appeal. The least effective approach turned out to be the strong fear appeal.

Additional research showed that two-sided messages were stronger in their positive effect on receivers' resistance to later persuasive efforts (Lumsdaine and Janis, 1953). Therefore if you want your audience to resist rebuttals to your presentation by other speakers, you should probably present some of the other side's arguments during your presentation. Another line of research showed that the strength of the fear appeal must be realistically related to the change that is desired. For example, a very simple action, such as brushing your teeth, may be seen as being too simple a way to prevent horrible disfigurement. One strong point of these studies was that the measured attitude change was not just a change of answers on a questionnaire, but an actual change in behavior. Another strong point was that attitude changes seemed to be long-lasting.

In an effort to account for the variations in the results of studies of fear appeals, researchers later identified three factors that work together to make fear appeals change attitudes (Rogers, 1975). These factors are (1) the amount of harmfulness of an event, (2) the likelihood of the event happening to the listener, and (3) how well the action being recommended is likely to work. For example, if a problem does not seem to be very significant or harmful, it is unlikely to cause fear. On the other hand, if the degree of harm seems overly exaggerated, the audience will dismiss the problem. Or an audience may agree that the problem being discussed is bad but feel that it does not apply to them. It is therefore unlikely that they will feel involved enough to modify an existing attitude or behavior. Finally, an audience may find that the problem presented is indeed terrible and believe that there is a chance it will happen to them, yet they do not adopt the solution or action.

It appears that all three elements must be relevant to the audience for fear appeals to work. The current national effort to stop the spread of AIDS is an excellent example of how these elements are used. Almost everyone is convinced that AIDS leads to death, in fact, that it is a direct cause of death. There is no need to concentrate on the first element of fear appeals—harmfulness. It is toward the second element that much of the persuasive effort against AIDS is being directed—that it can happen to anyone. At first this statement was not believed by most people. AIDS was associated with members of the gay community, or perhaps with Haitians, or with a few recipients of blood transfusions, or with drug addicts who share needles. The death of movie star Rock Hudson and the persuasive speaking of Elizabeth Taylor helped to increase discussion and attention related to the disease, but not until basketball great Earvin "Magic" Johnson became infected with the HIV virus were many Americans able to accept the second factor of this appeal to fear—the disease was spreading beyond the groups originally associated with it. The third factor—the effectiveness of the solution to the problem—is still the center of much debate about safe sex, abstinence, or totally monogamous relationships. How have people's attitudes and behavior been affected by persuasive and informative speeches about AIDS? Public opinion and private practices are monitored constantly by health officials, and some positive changes in both opinions and actions are being reported.

If you take a course in persuasion, political communication, or mass media, you are likely to study in detail the work of the investigators named here and many others. Modern psychological investigation has provided extensive information about attitudes and how they are changed. For now, these few elements of attitude change theory can at least help you to think about the messages that you receive daily from advertisers, as well as the messages that you create when you try to persuade others.

TYPES OF PERSUASIVE SPEECHES

There are several ways to approach the various persuasive speaking situations that you may encounter. Four general categories of speech seem to cover most of them. They are (1) speeches to convince, (2) speeches to actuate, (3) speeches to reinforce or inspire, and (4) debates and public argumentation.

Speeches to Convince

When the primary audience reaction that the speaker is trying to obtain concerns the listeners' opinions, then it is likely that the speech that is being given is a speech to convince. No direct action is required of the listeners; their attitude will be the focus of attention. For example, if a speaker tells you that Franklin

Roosevelt was wrong to try to increase the size of the Supreme Court, that Sara Teasdale is a better poet than Emily Dickinson, that abortion is wrong, or that more money should be spent on the space program, you are dealing with a speaker who is trying to convince you of something. Once again, very little, if any, action is required. Later on, you may form your opinion of Roosevelt as a President, buy Dickinson's collected works, put a bumper sticker on your car opposing abortion, or vote for a candidate on the basis of that person's position on supporting funding for NASA. Nevertheless, the immediate goal of the presentation is not to create a sleeper effect in terms of action, but to modify your attitude.

Speakers can certainly discuss controversial issues; and while historical issues do not have any action implications, other issues may. An audience may be convinced that abortion is wrong and then feel justified in asking the speaker, "So, what do you want me to *do* about it?" You may be convinced that NASA needs more money, and it seems logical to ask the speaker-advocate, "How can I help get NASA more funding?" Those questions about action are what change speeches to convince into the next type of speech: speeches to actuate.

Speeches to Actuate

Getting people to do what you want them to do is sometimes difficult. You first need to convince them that the action you propose is the right one for them. The next step, taking action, is the goal of the speech to actuate. Nearly all advertising is geared toward action. It does the Superclean Dishwasher Company little good if you are convinced that the product is good but you do not actually buy it. Advertising can be direct or very subtle, but the intention is clear: to motivate the receivers of the information to engage in some sort of action. On the job, you may hear a speech about getting better safety behavior from employees or more productivity. Clearly, these are persuasive speeches that are designed to actuate. On campus and in your community, you regularly get persuasive messages asking you to vote for a certain issue or candidate. The key word in a speech to actuate is usually *should*. You should work harder, you should vote for Joanne, and you should buy a Superclean Dishwasher.

Speeches to Reinforce or Inspire

These speeches are commonly given to audiences that are already leaning in a favorable direction. A sermon is a good example of such a speech. People seldom come to a religious service to be converted. They usually attend because they already share the religious beliefs of the speaker, and the sermon simply reinforces those beliefs and builds enthusiasm in the congregation. Many public speakers try to make their listeners feel more enthusiastic for one reason or another. One such example is that of the team coach talking before a game. The coach does not need to make the team want to win, but the coach must energize the players so that they will try harder to win. Speakers at most public ceremonies, such as dedications, awards ceremonies, or graduations, use the inspirational model. The speaker's goal in each of these situations is to remind the audience of the values or commitments its members already hold or once held and then get them to become rededicated or reinforced in those values. These

Martin Luther King, Jr.'s inspiring speech "I Have a Dream" reinforced the values of the listeners.

speeches are usually filled with inspirational stories, examples, and testimonies and often appeal more to the emotions of the listeners than to their logic. Audiences, of course, bring their expectations of these inspirational elements with them to the occasion, and good inspirational speakers, being sensitive to these anticipations, tailor their speeches accordingly. A graduation is not the time for a speaker to announce support for a presidential candidate or to push the sale of a favorite sports car. One of the most famous speeches of our era, Martin Luther King, Jr.'s "I Have a Dream," is a stunning speech of inspiration. The thousands of people who marched with Dr. King to the Lincoln Memorial in 1963 already supported the cause of civil rights. They were tired and sometimes impatient, so he reinforced their original commitment with the power of his voice and his words.

Debates and Public Argumentation

A special type of persuasive speaking occurs when two people speak—one for and one against the same issue. These forums, usually called **debates,** feature the opportunity to hear opposing views from supporters of both sides. A public forum can be held on a question of fact, value, or policy. Although it is possible to have more than two sides, interactions featuring multiple positions are usually less satisfying to an audience because of the necessity of keeping fine distinctions among the advocates in mind. For example, every four years, during presidential elections, you may see a televised "debate" with five, six, or seven candidates, each of whom is vying for the party's nomination. Although these forums may be useful for gaining superficial impressions of the candidates, they are less debates than showcases. In fact, the national Speech Communication Association now refers to these events, even when just two people are speaking, as joint appearances by the candidates, not as debates.

Public argumentation can be an important part of community involvement and civic awareness. Presentations can include meetings of the city council or board of supervisors, commissions and government hearings, and programs sponsored by local interest groups. Republican and Democratic party organizations are found in most communities, and other groups, such as environmental action associations, religious organizations, other political parties, civil rights leagues, and many others hold public meetings to address issues and questions of importance to them. These meetings, in addition to being a rich source of information about particular topics, continue the long U.S. tradition of freedom of expression.

One thing that all of the speakers in these speaking situations have in common is a desire to motivate the audience. To get people to agree with them, they need to organize and support their ideas in a way that goes beyond what is required of the informative speaker. On the other hand, both the supporting materials and the organizational patterns used by speakers in public argumentation can be adapted to the persuasive setting.

Developing Motivating Supporting Materials

From before the time of Aristotle, speakers have been concerned with finding the most effective way to reach others with their message. Aristotle called these methods *proofs* and divided them into three main categories: personal proof, which he called *ethos;* emotional proof, known as *pathos;* and logical proof, or *logos*. These categories still represent useful ways of analyzing speeches of persuasion.

Ethos

Ethos, or personal proof, was included in the earlier discussion of source credibility. To create an impact on your listeners, you must tap the four elements of expertise, trustworthiness, dynamism, and goodwill that are within you. You can show yourself to be an expert by actually being one. That means that you can pick topics about which you already know a good deal or about which you can do extensive research. Furthermore, you should have a personal connection to the topic to show the audience that you have both knowledge of, and a genuine concern for, the topic. During the speech, reveal that you have done extensive research and can quote objective sources and established experts. You want your listeners to credit *you* with having the competence to be an expert on the topic. Politicians who visit a disaster site or travel to other countries to get first-hand experience are seeking ethos, or personal proof.

Second, your audience is more likely to be persuaded by your speech if they think you are trustworthy. Once again, the best way to appear trustworthy is to *be* trustworthy. The reputation for honesty and truthfulness that you earned in the past will greatly enhance your credibility with your current audience. As was discussed earlier, professional persuaders in advertising and politics constantly try to give their clients either the appearance or the substance of honesty. Your classmates will have an impression of you from previous communication interactions; and in a formal setting, someone will probably introduce you and will mention your trustworthiness in the past.

Dynamism, the third element of ethos, is the one that is most directly under your immediate control. Audiences generally respond favorably to speakers who are lively, energetic, and upbeat—if, of course, these behaviors are appropriate to the topic and situation. Voice, posture, gesture, and movement—all can contribute

> ## THE STORY OF COMMUNICATION
>
> ### Quintillian's Notion of the Credible Speaker
>
> The Roman rhetorician Marcus Fabius Quintillian lived from about A.D. 35 to A.D. 95 and is most famous for his twelve-volume book *Institutio Oratoria,* in which he set forth his ideas about the expression and presentation of messages and critiqued many of the great writers of classical times. His ideal speaker was someone who was a "good person, speaking well." With this simple phrase, Quintillian summarized the philosophy of many books, including this one. You need to *be* credible, not just act as if you were, and then you need to follow up with a strong presentation. This advice is moving into its third millennium, and it is worth teaching to each new generation.

to an impression of dynamism. You may need to adjust your delivery style to the size of the room, the audience, and the space available, but an interesting presentation will keep an audience interested. The delivery skills discussed in Chapter 12 did not come from some abstract idea about an ideal speaker. They are grounded in research confirming that a good delivery style makes audiences more attentive and receptive to the content of your speech. In persuasive speaking, a delivery that communicates sincerity and dedication to the topic will be received by the audience as part of the persuasive message. More information about persuasive delivery styles follows in this chapter.

Goodwill, the fourth element of ethos, requires that you tailor your message to the needs and for the benefit of your listeners. If you have their best interests at heart, they are likely to be responsive to your speech. You can also demonstrate goodwill as you give your presentation. Are you pleasant? Do you observe social courtesy and everyday norms of behavior? Do you communicate positive regard for your audience? All of these factors will help to create a climate of goodwill during your persuasive message. The advertising that you see on television features warm, family scenes at a fast-food restaurant, a young person calling home to mom, or a major oil company showing how it cares for the animals and plants in the environment. All are attempts to secure the viewer's goodwill.

In addition to developing your credibility through these methods, you can add persuasive force to your messages by using the other two types of proof that Aristotle identified: emotion and logic.

Pathos

Emotion, or **pathos,** helps your listeners to become involved or aroused. Attitude change theory states that getting the listener to identify with or have feeling for the topic creates a persuasive communication climate. Arousing and using your listeners' feelings can be a highly effective way to get them to pay attention to what you are saying and may also motivate many of them to do what you ask. Consider magazine ads that ask you to send money to help poor children. They may show a picture of a sad-eyed child dressed in ragged clothes, and you may feel a response of sympathy. On television, you may see film footage of people in desperate condition in programs that are designed to raise money for worldwide hunger relief. These are examples of emotional proof. However, do not think that sadness and pity are the only emotions that you can use persuasively. Any human emotion can help you get your audience involved in your thesis. Persuaders often used humor, fear, and pride. How do persuaders get you to buy their brand of toothpaste or mouthwash? Fear is usually the motivator. What awful fate awaits you if you have bad breath or dull teeth? Sometimes a funny story or example will make the audience feel good about the topic. Humor, then, can be a persuasive tool, and so can poking fun at something. Political cartoons are an example of using humor to persuade.

Research shows that emotional proof, or pathos, can be very strong in helping to persuade others. Research also indicates that emotion is best used when it is combined with solid reasoning so that your listeners both feel *and* understand your message. One of the best ways to get emotional support into your persuasive messages is to use compelling stories or examples. Remember, they must be short enough to simply illustrate one or two ideas in your speech. You could include a moving or humorous personal experience, a touching example, a humorous anecdote, or a compelling description of an event that relates to your thesis. Some communicators use emotional proof to the exclusion of any other. This technique is effective only in the short run and with an audience that does not respond thoughtfully to messages. The best use of emotion in persuasive speaking is in conjunction with other forms that also help to make the topic memorable and motivating. Most listeners, especially as their level of education and sophistication increases, demand the inclusion of factual information and a logical interpretation of that information before they make any important commitments.

Logos

Emotional supports are powerful, but they must be used with care and only to heighten interest or command attention. They must not replace other forms of proof. **Logos** was Aristotle's term for logic, or reason. While logic certainly includes making connections from a set of facts and drawing logical conclusions from those facts, as used here the term also includes the entire range of logical supporting materials and the reasoning process that brings them together. (See the Critical Thinking in Communication box on the next page.)

Recall that inductive reasoning asks you to find supporting materials that are typical. When you create persuasive messages, select supporting materials that meet this logical test. Have you chosen examples that are representative of other examples that are readily available? Or did you select examples that represent only one side of the issue? If so, you not only violated the rules of induction, you also ignored the psychological research that found that it is more effective to introduce arguments for both sides of an issue rather than one side alone. Good induction also takes into consideration the effects of time and requires that you select supporting materials that are recent. Finally, your supports must be *sufficient* if they are going to help you prove your point.

Applying deductive principles to the selection and use of persuasive supporting materials can be accomplished in several ways. You can adopt a deductive organization for the body of your speech by first presenting and then supporting a general principle in the same way that you would lead off with a major

---

CRITICAL THINKING IN COMMUNICATION

Logical Constructs in the Persuasive Speech

In the chapter on critical thinking, you learned about deduction and induction as logical forms of reasoning. The tests of both truth and validity were used to examine sequences and conclusions. The same processes now apply to material in this chapter as you examine both the facts used in persuasion and the processes used to link those facts together to reach a conclusion. Suggestions drawn from Chapter 4 can now help you to apply those logical elements to your persuasive speaking and listening.

---

premise in a deductive syllogism. Next, the middle part of the speech, the body of the speech, would develop related concepts in the same way that you would phrase minor premises. Finally, a conclusion would constitute the final section of the body of the speech in the same way that a syllogism ends with a conclusion.

You may wish to make causal claims during your speech. Causal claims link events by stating that one event (cause) made another event happen (result). The major shortcomings of causal reasoning involve the fallacies of hasty generalization, whereby a conclusion is drawn too quickly from insufficient support, and of *post hoc,* whereby a statement is in error because it assumes that if one event follows another in time, the first event must be the cause of the second. As an educated persuader, use the principles of critical thinking to help you avoid these reasoning pitfalls. These elements of formal reasoning are a good place to start, but you might also make use of informal types of critical thinking to augment your use of logos.

Informal Reasoning

The best way to recall the earlier discussion of informal reasoning is to think about the Toulmin system presented in Chapter 4. Toulmin examined the reasoning process as people use it to help them reach conclusions. He noted that we take some information (grounds) and connect it to a conclusion (claim) by means of some principle (the warrant). For example, several of your friends like Nana's Ice Cream (grounds), so you conclude that it is probably a good place to go after a movie (claim) because your friends' judgments on such matters are usually right (warrant). In your persuasive speech, you will probably offer grounds to support your claims. In so doing, make certain that you examine the warrants that are operating. For example, if nobody knows your friends or, worse, your friends are known but not trusted, then your grounds will not be connected to your claim in the minds of your audience. Persuasion, and all communication for that matter, happens as a transaction between senders and receivers. Failure on the part of many would-be persuaders to consider the warrants *of the audience* has meant failure to persuade altogether.

Consider your own firmly held core values, such as your religious, moral, ethical, or political values. Others who hold different but also firmly held values are unlikely to be persuaded by your warrants. As illustrated by attitude change theory, you must appeal to the audience on the basis of *their* values, because it is within a person's value system that warrants often develop.

Why do different people reach different claims or conclusions, when presented with the same data? Members of a jury often differ, even after hearing the same information. The famous O. J. Simpson trial demonstrated that listeners from various backgrounds interpreted the same information very differently (Lacayo, 1995). Why? The answer is that they apply different *warrants,* or principles, to their reasoning processes. Make certain that when you develop persuasive messages, you examine the warrants that are operating in your own reasoning processes and assumptions.

For your persuasive message to be effective, you also need to select supporting materials from the items your research has produced. You should have a variety of resources at your disposal, including statistics, short stories, quotations, examples, visual aids, and illustrations. Use the ideas contained in ethos, pathos, and logos to help you select the best and most appropriate materials from the many possible supports. Choose those that will most probably motivate your listeners. A review of the principles of audience analysis in Chapter 11 can also help you to make a connection between your supporting materials and your listeners. A good rule of thumb is to create variety in your supporting materials, both in their probable effect on your listeners and in their type. For example, avoid using too many statistics, quotations, or personal anecdotes. At the same time, make certain that you appeal at one time or another during your speech to your listeners' sense of logic, their emotions, and their impression of your credibility. How much logic? How much emotion? How much credibility? It all depends, as in any speech, on you, your topic, the audience, the occasion, the time limits, and the circumstances. You can be sure, however, that the best speakers include each of these areas in their speeches.

 ## DEVELOPING PERSUASIVE ORGANIZATION

Although you could certainly use any of the organizational patterns discussed earlier to prepare a persuasive speech, those patterns lack the advantage of being specifically designed to persuade. There are several ways to outline your persuasive message, building a case for your thesis and taking your listeners from one idea to the next, creating a strong, motivational speech. First, we look at some logical patterns based on what you already know about critical thinking. Then we examine a special method of preparing persuasive speeches that has been used and tested for over fifty years, called the *motivated sequence*.

Logical Patterns

Perhaps the most common way to organize a persuasive message is to use the problem–solution pattern. This **logical pattern** outlines a problem or problems in a certain area and then urges the listeners to adopt a particular solution. The body of the speech has only two major divisions: A. Problems, followed by B. Solutions. This pattern is easy for a speaker to use and for an audience to follow. The only real difficulties that this pattern involves is that the problem may not be significant or the solution offered may not be practical, may cost too much, or may not solve the problem. Make certain that you use the principles of cause-and-effect reasoning when preparing a problem–solution speech. In addition, test for fallacies of *non sequitur,* especially the *post hoc* fallacy.

If you use a problem–solution format, your outline will look like this:

   I. Introduction *(a compelling story related to problem X)*
  II. Thesis sentence *(You should solve problem X.)*
 III. Body *(preview)*
     A. Identify the problem
       1. Supporting material that defines it
       2. Supporting material that shows its significance
       3. Supporting material that shows its extent
       4. Supporting material that applies to listeners
     B. Solution to the problem
       1. Proposed action step
       2. Justification for the proposed action
       3. Probable consequences or benefits of the proposed action
 IV. Conclusion *(brief review of A, B, thesis sentence, and introduction)*
  V. Sources/bibliography

This type of presentation is commonly used in groups, committees, civic organizations, councils, and clubs and even among roommates. You sense a problem and propose a solution. Everything from cleaning the city streets to cleaning the bathroom that you share with roommates can be organized into a problem–solution format. It is quite clear and direct.

A format that is related to problem–solution is the cause–effect format. If you wanted to convince someone that there is a logical relationship between a sun tan and skin cancer, you would use a cause–effect organizational format. This format resembles the problem–solution format in many ways. The first step in both is the same. However, if you were to consider a historical question—the causes of World War I, for example—you would see that no solution is included in your format. Instead, you would be trying to establish causal links between events. Your logical reasoning would have to be clear, compelling, and free of fallacies for your audience to be convinced of your thesis. Your organizational pattern would look like the problem–solution one, but it would not have a solution or an action step.

Motivated Sequence

Perhaps the most widely studied organizational pattern is the one developed by Alan H. Monroe over sixty years ago (Monroe, 1935). The reason that it has gained such popularity is because it works! Its parts are similar to outline sections you have already studied, but their arrangement is such that it helps to lead your listeners to the desired conclusion. The five steps of the motivated sequence are (1) attention, (2) need, (3) satisfaction, (4) visualization, and (5) action.

The *attention* step is similar to the introduction of any speech outline. Here is where you capture the interest of your listeners and turn it into concern for your topic. To establish a *need,* you indicate a problem that should be solved. The need step can involve a fact—understanding an event or solving a mystery; or a value—reevaluating a position on evolution or on safe sex; or a policy—electing a person to office, buying a particular car, or supporting national health insurance.

Once you have the attention of the audience and have addressed the need involved in your thesis, you move directly to showing your audience the solution—that is, the *satisfaction* step. This step may be fairly short and is often a restatement of your thesis. This is when you ask your listeners to change their minds or take some action. The next step is *visualization,* and here is where you can be somewhat imaginative. Try to get your audience to *see* the consequences of your solution, to *imagine* the benefits they will get if they adopt your thesis. You can also indicate the negative effects of *not* choosing your thesis: the bad things that will happen if they do not adopt your idea. Some speakers do try to introduce both positive and negative visualizations in this step, thereby creating a comparison–contrast form of supporting material.

Finally, you request of your listeners a specific *action.* It is usually a directly focused form of your satisfaction step and may be designed to be inspirational or motivational. "So when you go to the polls tomorrow, remember to put an X next to Jane Doe's name!"

If you were preparing a standard outline for a speech and wanted to put your ideas into a motivated sequence pattern, your quick outline would look like this one:

    I. Attention step *(introduction: story, example)*
   II. Thesis sentence
 III. Body *(preview)*
     A. Need step *(problems, difficulty)*
        1. Supporting material #1
        2. Supporting material #2
        3. Supporting material #3
        4. Additional supporting materials
     B. Satisfaction step
        1. Support for your solution
        2. Details of your plan or idea
     C. Visualization step
        1. Support for the positive effects of your idea

> 2. Support for the negative consequences of rejecting the idea
> D. Action
>   1. Description of steps to take
>   2. Support for acting on the idea
> IV. Conclusion *(brief review of A, B, C, D, thesis sentence, and attention step.)*
> V. Sources/bibliography

By using a persuasive format to organize your speech, combining that outline with strong and appropriate supporting materials, and motivating your listeners through your credibility, the strength and logic of your reasoning, and your appeal to their emotions will create an influential presentation (Gronbeck et al., 1995)

DEVELOPING PERSUASIVE LANGUAGE

Getting people to do what you advocate is a difficult process, but you can improve your chances of success if you put some time and effort into increasing the impact of your language choices. Most effective speakers select their words very carefully.

As in your informative speeches, you want your **persuasive language** to be clear and memorable. One way to create a response in your listeners is to excite their imagination. When you use the motivated sequence in your organizational plan, you will engage their imaginations directly during the visualization step, but you can tap into their imaginative processes throughout a speech using imagery.

Imagery

There are several ways in which language can help you create images or scenes in the minds of your audience. Chapter 6 presents ways in which language affects our thoughts and imagination. One powerful way is by analogy, which is a form of comparison. Analogies are usually divided into two types: figurative and literal. A figurative analogy is the more imaginative because it takes two things that are not alike in the real sense and uses comparison to make one of them more colorful and memorable. A literal analogy takes two real things and compares them. For example, an easy chair is like a recliner in many real ways, and your college is very much like my college in many real ways.

Examples of figurative analogies are much easier to think of just because they are so colorful and memorable. When people speak of our country as a ship of state and compare the President to a captain, they are using figurative analogy to express an idea about how our country is governed or should be governed. Of course, the President is also very different from a captain in many ways, but as with other analogies, there is a point to be made. A company may be compared to a bicycle, with each element of the corporation connected somehow to some part of the bicycle, or a family may be compared to a tree, or a community to a beehive, or the object of your affection "to a summer's day."

You probably recall that the type of comparison that uses the word *like* is a simile and that other comparisons are called *metaphors.* Long, extended, story-length comparisons are labeled *allegories,* and many of our religious teachings come to us in the form of *parables,* another form of metaphor. Each time you see these types of supporting materials, you are helping your message become clear and memorable to your audiences. In the field of communication, recent attention has focused on the use of stories as a way to help researchers and scholars understand how people receive, organize, remember, and respond to communication (Fisher, 1984, 1985).

As a persuader, take advantage of this knowledge and of the tools described here to help you make your ideas memorable and effective. Research conducted at Michigan State University demonstrated that speeches that used analogies had a greater persuasive effect on their listeners than did those that did not use analogies (McCroskey and Combs, 1969).

Colorful and judicious use of adjectives and adverbs can also enhance your speech and the willingness of your audience to get involved in your ideas. Creative use of description to create images can make your ideas live on in your listeners' minds. You might simply describe someone as being tall, or you could elaborate, saying that he "was a giant of a man, towering over the heads of everyone else in the room." The first description does not create a scene in your listeners' minds, whereas the second one creates a vivid image immediately.

Adjectives and adverbs are the descriptors in our language. They can, of course, also help to describe the image that your audience is forming about you and your ideas. Your audience is judgmental and can label you as being outgoing and upbeat or a talkative, overbearing loudmouth. The subject of the description could be the same person, but the imagery creates a very different picture. Did the soccer player walk away from the field slowly, or did she "drag herself along, one aching step at a time, until she finally sank into a heap at the sidelines"? Use the power of language to make your message memorable with images that will remain in your listeners' minds long after you have stopped speaking.

Impact

Another way to create and use persuasive language is to give impact to your message through emphasis, humor, and personal references.

Emphasis means that you alert your audience to important ideas as they emerge by using transitions. A transition might be worded as follows: "This next idea will save you hundreds of dollars on your car repair bills." Notice how the transition calls attention to an important point. The statement "This problem is not limited to our cities, but can be found right here on campus" emphasizes the application of your ideas directly to your immediate audience. Of course, you must limit your use of emphasis, or everything will seem really important. When that happens, your speech never varies from a high pitch, creating a situation that becomes very stressful for the audience.

Humor is another way to give your ideas impact. You may recall that pathos included the use of humor as a persuasive technique. The test of humor, as of all other supporting materials, is that it must be appropriate to the situation. A persuasive speech is often about controversial ideas, and while humor can help the audience relax to receive your message, you must be careful not to offend your listeners and turn them against your thesis. Good humor based on wit, surprise, intelligence, and goodwill can enhance your credibility. On the other hand, if your humor is based on sarcasm, vulgar or off-color material, or mean satire, you can damage or destroy the impact of your message. Sarcasm is usually perceived as pettiness, and vulgarity may offend your listeners. Satire is very hard to do well and may confuse your audience about your real message. Good persuasion does not demean, offend, or confuse your listeners.

Finally, personal references command attention and make a connection between you and your material that the audience can appreciate. Your firsthand experience with a topic can be worked into your presentation so that it enhances your expertise. The story of your sunburn can be a dramatic support for your speech on sunscreens. Your experience of driving a friend to the hospital after he had drunk too much will give impact to your speech on alcohol abuse. These supports can be powerful, so it is wise not to overdo them. The speech should not turn into a monologue about the great tragedies in your life, or you will risk losing your listeners. The topic must remain relevant to your *receivers* throughout your presentation; and if your personal references are directed to a significant idea in your speech, they can add impact to that relevance.

DEVELOPING PERSUASIVE PRESENTATIONS

Your delivery should match your thesis. You should speak about significant, relevant, important issues; and your presentation should reflect these purposes. Do not hesitate to communicate to your listeners that you find the material you are speaking about to be very important. In comparison to your delivery when you give an informative speech, your delivery of a persuasive speech will probably be more serious, formal, and dynamic; will include a greater range of voice variety; and will make use of more pauses. You need not become theatrical, nor employ dramatic gestures, but you should truly reflect the importance of your ideas in a way that is appropriate to the audience and the situation. Watch yourself practice on videotape to get a feeling for the persuasive impact your presentation is making. Is there anything more that you can do to increase your effectiveness? Do you need to tone down your presentation because it is too jarring? Is your speaking rate too fast for your audience to follow as you tell an important and touching story? Are you making use of pauses so that your listeners can get a sense of drama before you present a key idea? Do you sound cheery, upbeat, and bright during your speech on child abuse? Do not forget the test of appropriateness: Do you and your presentation fit the room, the topic, and the audience?

In addition to vocal considerations in speeches of persuasion, keep in mind nonverbal elements. Gestures and facial expressions must be consistent with the ideas expressed. If your movements are too grandiose or if your facial expression is inappropriate, your listeners will be distracted from your thesis and instead will concentrate on your nonverbal behaviors. The impact on the audience should come from your idea, not from your delivery of the idea.

Good organization, supporting materials, and variety in type and function of supports, combined with a presentation on a substantial and worthwhile

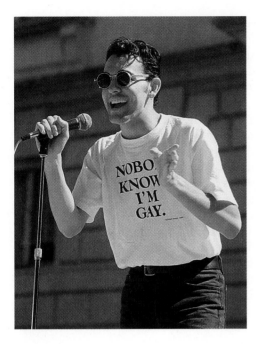

Humor and energy contribute to persuasive presentations.

topic, will create a successful persuasive message. Your speech will gain polish when you add persuasive language and a persuasive delivery.

ADAPTING PERSUASIVE SPEECHES TO YOUR AUDIENCE

Now that you have a variety of persuasive tools from which to select as you prepare your speech, you need to think about the different conditions you may face as you analyze your listeners. Four distinct types of audiences may be present: supportive, interested, apathetic, and hostile.

If you know that your listeners are already likely to be in support of your thesis, then you can treat your speech as one to inspire or reinforce. You may need to give them some of the most recent information so that they feel confident that they are current, and you may find your use of pathos to be important to reenergize their efforts. Perhaps a reminder of some direct action steps that they need to take will finish your presentation.

Suppose your research into your audience reveals that they are interested in the topic but undecided on the issue. You can then compose your presentation to include strong evidence, paying careful attention to expert testimony and statistical supporting materials if appropriate. These people are likely to have some idea of opposing arguments, so take advantage of the attitude change theory research that advises you to include some mention of opposing arguments and a rebuttal to those arguments.

A third condition you may face is apathetic listeners—they are not yet interested and do not care about your issue. Sometimes apathy can be traced to lack of knowledge, so you would spend a significant portion of your time developing the problem. In your outline, main section A in the body should have sufficient supporting materials to show the extent of the problem *and* how that problem directly affects your listeners. If your audience is apathetic because the issue really does not apply to them, seek another topic; you would be violating one of the principles of ethical speaking if you tried to persuade an audience to act on an issue of no importance to them.

Finally, you may face a hostile audience—they are already opposed to your position. Rather than give up, you may be able to reach them if you first spend time developing common ground with these listeners. Using Burke's terminology, seek their *identification* with you and your perspective. Demonstrate the qualities of goodwill and trustworthiness. Once you have created a common ground, proceed with your expertise to connect their interests, concerns, and values with your position.

If you take time to do a considered audience analysis, you stand a better chance of reaching your desired goal in persuasion. Of course, you may face an audience that includes a mixture of all these types, so you may need to combine approaches. Since the hostile group may quit listening first, you might want to begin with common ground materials and end with your reinforcement and inspirational elements. Attention to these considerations will help you to be evaluated positive by your various listeners.

EVALUATING PERSUASIVE SPEECHES

As is true for informative speeches, you can evaluate persuasive speeches from the three perspectives of a listener, a critic, and a consumer. Compared to an informative speech, there are more things to listen to and listen for in a speech of persuasion. Consequently, there are more things to evaluate in persuasive speaking.

Listening Goals

When listening to any speech, the listener evaluates the organization, relevance of the topic, main ideas, and supporting materials. When the speech is persuasive, the listener must also be very demanding in evaluating the logic that is used to connect all of these elements into a motivating message.

As a listener, first try to decide whether the speech is aimed at convincing, inspiring, or moving you to action. Listen carefully for the thesis, because it might not be stated overtly but might merely be implied, as in the case of most advertising and political presentations. A listener should always be concerned about the value of the proposed action *for the listener.* You can be certain that presenters sense some value in the proposed action for themselves, but what motivates them to want *you* to join in? It may be their care and concern for your welfare, that their favorite cause needs more supporters, or that they stand to gain personally or financially from your support. A critical listener uses active listening skills in this situation to sort out ideas, discover the thesis, evaluate information, check the quality of supporting materials, and follow the development of the main ideas to determine whether sections build on each other in a logical manner.

Since persuasive speeches usually involve values and attitudes and are often about controversial subjects, it may be difficult for you to concentrate on your active listening skills. Suppose the speaker is talking about abortion, gun control, the death penalty, college tuition, nuclear power, or any one of a dozen other topics about which people have strong opinions. If the speaker takes a position that is different from yours, you will have to try hard to keep listening with an open mind. It will be difficult to withhold a quick judgment and avoid preparing a rebuttal mentally while the speaker is still talking. It would seem that when you need the skills of active listening the most, you are the least able to use them. Therefore an important listening goal in persuasion presentations is to be very attentive to your own reactions. Suppose that the speaker has selected a controversial topic and the view that is expressed in the speech is exactly like your own. Again, active listening will be difficult because you may spend your listening time cheering the speaker along mentally and forget to activate your listening skills.

You may not be able to be a successful listener every time you listen to a persuasive message, but the *effort* to do so can still help you to evaluate persuasive messages, as both a critic and a consumer. You will be better prepared for both of those roles if your listening practice has been complete and careful.

Critical Goals

As you can see from the items discussed in the section on listening goals, you as a listener need a complete set of criteria to function as a competent critic of any message. The evaluation criteria that are presented in Chapter 12 can help to make you an effective critic of persuasive speeches. Evaluate the speaker's methods, supporting materials, audience elements, and presentation. Examine the logical, emotional, and personal forms of proof that are used in the message, and be especially concerned with the speaker's adaptation (or lack thereof) to a particular audience. Has the speaker taken care to apply the ideas, costs, and benefits of the message to this particular group of listeners? Are the supporting materials directly related to the interests of this group?

Take a close look at how the speaker uses language, transitions, interest, and delivery skills. Can you comprehend the vocabulary? Is it offensive? Does it move you? Does the speech follow a sensible and appropriate pattern that you can identify? The critique forms used in class can help you begin to organize your criticism. Later, you will want to come back to the list of items you use to criticize other presentations and apply them to your own messages.

Criticism involves more than just picking out the flaws and successes of others. The goals of a critic are to explain why and how a presenter does certain things but not others in their speeches, evaluate the success or failure of the presenter's choices, and suggest alternatives.

In any message, there are probably areas of excellence and areas that are in need of improvement. As a critic, you should try to carry out an objective evaluation, using the criteria for judging good speeches in a way that is independent of your personal opinions or biases. For example, you may be opposed to handgun controls but still able to judge a speech that advocates such controls as being well organized and convincingly presented. You can agree or disagree with a thesis and like or dislike a speech. It is challenging to give positive criticism to a speech when you oppose its thesis. It is also a challenge to admit that a speech supporting your favorite cause was not very well presented. However, a critic must be able to do exactly that if such a judgment is warranted by applying objective criteria. However, this does not mean that critics can never express their opinions. Opinions are the topic of the next section on being an effective consumer of persuasive messages.

Consumer Goals

The best consumers hold an informed opinion that they develop by listening carefully, completely, and critically to the great volume of information with which they are bombarded every day. If you have learned how to be an active listener and an objective critic, you are in an excellent position to draw reasonable conclusions and take wise and sensible actions. You will be able to base your decisions on complete information and good judgment. Some people form opinions on the basis of surface impressions or a quick response. As a trained communicator, you can avoid making superficial responses to advertisements and instead seek out complete and reliable points of view. Persuasive speakers will ask you for your time, your money, or your personal support. To be an effective consumer, you should think very carefully before parting with any of those things. Before you consider such a major commitment, evaluate very carefully any persuasive messages, especially those from advertising and politics, for the value they can give you. Professional persuaders have the job of getting you to part with something. Make certain that your job is to be a professional consumer, and insist that presenters, including yourself, maintain high standards of clarity, support, ethics, and honesty in the information that they design to influence you and others.

IMPROVING PERSUASIVE COMMUNICATION COMPETENCY

Unfortunately, there are few controls over the kind and type of persuasive messages to which you are exposed every day, so *you* must become a competent source for controlling the quality of these messages. Being personally competent at persuasion will be valuable to you for the rest of your life as you listen to, react to, and send out persuasive communication.

The first step toward persuasive communication competency is to be aware of the principles and techniques of persuasion. By studying how people can and do change attitudes, you can enlarge your own repertoire of communicative options. Attitude change theory, combined with the wisdom inherited from classical rhetoric and modern presentation techniques, have given you sophisticated, technical skills as well as an appreciation and knowledge of human behavior. This combination of knowledge, choices, and skills enhances your basic competency.

Next, using guidelines reflected by the choices that are available to you, select a topic from among your options. Construct a message based on your analysis of the topic, yourself, the audience, and the occasion. Continue working on your speech until you have constructed a solid piece of communication. The selections you make from among your choices of supporting materials are important because they underscore your personal credibility. Logical reasoning and providing for audience involvement add even more credibility to your presentation. Keep in mind that you have a variety of patterns to use for the organization of your speech, so select one that you think is appropriate for both you and your subject.

Once you have made all of the selections mentioned above, it is time to implement these choices in your actual presentation. Practice giving your speech by using appropriate delivery skills, increasing the impact of your vocabulary, viewing yourself on videotape, and having someone listen to and react to your practice sessions. Be sure to follow the guidelines for time allotment as well.

If you work conscientiously on these guidelines and recommendations, your presentations not only will implement and increase your knowledge about persuasion, but you will also be ready to judge the outcome of your efforts in an evaluation.

Evaluation means that you carry out some self-evaluation as your own best critic. Using the criteria for judging persuasive messages, review your presentation to see how well it measures up to those standards. Did you focus on your own concerns or those of your listeners? Did you select a topic that was significant to them, as well as to you? Were your supporting materials substantial, relevant, recent, well researched, and credited to their sources? Were you able to introduce variety into both the forms of support and their function to establish credibility, logic, and emotional proof? You should have presented a message that is rich in content, clear in meaning, and challenging to the intellect of your audience. Did you do that?

Another way to be evaluated is through the responses of your listeners. Did the audience react favorably? Did you get some direct feedback, either from your listeners or from your instructor? Take into account the evaluation of others, and add it to your own evaluative perceptions to obtain a full, balanced evaluation.

SUMMARY

Your attitudes and values give direction to the way you live your life. The development or changing of listeners' attitudes and the ability to influence their actions are at the heart of persuasion. The theories about how these changes come about are important to know to gain a full understanding of ourselves as communicators—both senders and receivers of messages.

The variety of persuasive messages—speeches to convince, to reinforce, or to move to action—all have a similar goal: to influence the audience. You can choose claims or questions of fact, value, or policy when selecting your topic. As you plan a persuasive message, you must pay careful attention to the types of supporting materials that you select. Apply the principles of critical thinking in choosing evidence to substantiate your main ideas. Does your evidence enhance your personal credibility, demonstrate logical connections, and provide an emotional link between your audience and your topic?

When you are ready to organize your outline, look at different patterns, such as the problem–solution or the motivated sequence patterns. Try organizing your information in a variety of ways until you find one that seems to work best for you, your audience, the setting, and the time allotted for your speech.

Use the ideas discussed above for creating an impact through an enhanced use of language and delivery skills. You can create and maintain listener attention and interest if you apply those suggestions. Follow the steps that you know very well by now of selecting a topic, creating a thesis sentence, organizing the body, selecting effective supporting materials, and creating an interesting introduction and conclusion. These steps parallel the process for preparing an informative speech, but their content and their logical interconnection are specifically directed to the goal of motivating your listeners.

You have also learned how to evaluate a persuasive speech from the perspective of a listener, a critic, and a consumer. Finally, you have seen how you can use those evaluation techniques and apply them to improve your own competency as a persuasive communicator.

KEY TERMS

persuasive speeches, *p. 284*
facts, *p. 284*
values, *p. 285*
policy, *p. 285*
value system, *p. 286*
attitude change theory, *p. 286*
habits, *p. 287*
drives, *p. 287*
source credibility, *p. 289*

ethos, *p. 288, 293*
fear appeals, *p. 289*
debates, *p. 292*
public argumentation, *p. 292*
pathos, *p. 294*
logos, *p. 295*
logical pattern, *p. 298*
persuasive language, *p. 300*

EXERCISES

1. Watch television for one uninterrupted hour to collect data on the types of persuasive appeals that are used in advertising. Collect examples of the following appeals: fear, humor, and pity. Can you identify other appeals? Then make a note of the different values on which television commercials are based. Prepare a three- to five-page report about your hour-long observation and share it with the class.

2. If persuasive speech presentations are given in your class, take critical notes on one of them. Then present a brief critique to the class, based on your evaluation of the speaker's choice of topic as well as the organization, supports, and delivery.

3. Bring several magazine ads to class, and describe how ethos, pathos, and logos operate in maga-

zine advertising. Do some ads always have only one kind of appeal, whereas others use a different appeal? What do you think accounts for these differences?

4. The next time you observe a persuasive speaker in person, notice the adaptations that the speaker employs or misses. For example, does the speaker make reference to the specific situation—time, audience, and location? Is the vocabulary that he or she uses appropriate to the audience? What other specific adaptations do you notice?

5. Present a six- to eight-minute long persuasive speech to your class following the guidelines presented in this chapter.

REFERENCES

Fisher, Walter. "Narration as a Human Communication Paradigm: The Case of Public Moral Argument." *Communication Monographs* 51 (1984), 1.

Fisher, Walter. "The Narrative Paradigm: An Elaboration." *Communication Monographs* 52 (1985), 347.

Gronbeck, B., K. German, D. Ehninger, and A. Monroe. *Principles and Types of Speech Communication*. 12th ed. New York: HarperCollins, 1995.

Hilgard, E. R., and G. H. Bower. *Theories of Learning*. Englewood Cliffs: Prentice-Hall, 1966.

Hovland, C. I., I. L. Janis, and H. H. Kelley. *Communication and Persuasion*. New Haven: Yale University Press, 1953.

Hovland, C. I., A. R. Lumsdaine, and E. D. Sheffield. *Experiments on Mass Communication*. Princeton: Princeton University Press, 1949.

Lacayo, Richard. "An Ugly End to It All." *Time*, 9 Oct. 1995: 30–37.

Lumsdaine, A., and I. Janis. "Resistance to 'Counterpropaganda' Produced by One-Sided and Two-Sided 'Propaganda' Presentations." *Public Opinion Quarterly* 17 (1953).

McCroskey, J. C., and W. H. Combs. "The Effects of the Use of Analogy on Attitude Change and Source Credibility." *Journal of Communication* 19 (1969), 333.

Monroe, Alan H. *Principles and Types of Speech*. Chicago: Scott, Foresman, 1935.

Murphy, G., L. B. Murphy, and T. M. Newcomb. *Experimental Social Psychology*. New York: Harper & Row, 1937.

Rogers, R. W. "A Protection Motivation Theory of Fear Appeals and Attitude Change." *Journal of Psychology*, 91 (1975).

Speaking on Special Occasions

After reading this chapter, you should be able to:

- Describe the times, places, and circumstances where you might have speaking opportunities.

- Understand the methods that you can use to help you speak in a variety of situations.

- Feel capable and willing to present speeches of introduction, commemoration, and thanks, as well as short-notice presentations and oral readings.

- Organize and present a short-notice speech.

- Prepare and present an oral reading.

*I*n addition to the informative and persuasive presentations that you often make in class and on the job, there are special-occasion speeches that require their own preparation guidelines. You might be introducing someone to an audience, and that person will be the featured speaker or guest, not you. You could be asked to speak at a commemorative event, such as a graduation, a recognition ceremony, or a similar occasion. Possibly, *you* are the person being honored, and you need to respond and thank those who are honoring you. In a career setting, you may be asked to present an idea on the spot and will need to deliver an impromptu speech about your project, company, or special interest. Sometimes you will read someone else's words, such as a short story, poem, or religious text. Each of these situations requires good speaking skills, of course, but what follows are some special suggestions to help you get the most out of the experience. Let's start with the speech of introduction.

SPEAKING TO INTRODUCE ANOTHER PERSON

A **speech to introduce** has several requirements. As a member of an organization, you may be asked to introduce a visitor or a guest at a program or event. You may recall your own important occasions, such as your graduation, when someone introduced the main speaker. Keep that experience in mind as you learn about the goals of speeches of introduction.

Goals of the Introduction Speech

Speakers who introduce others usually tell a little about the person and express appreciation for the person's being the main speaker. They may also present the title or theme of the speech. Good speeches of introduction are usually short, and the more the audience already knows about the speaker, the shorter the speech of introduction should be. For example, if you are introducing the head of your company at the annual employee luncheon, all you need to do is make a few goodwill remarks—perhaps some humorous ones, depending on the attitude of the guest of honor. In fact, the official protocol for introducing the President of the United States is, in its entirety, "Ladies and Gentlemen, the President of the United States." That's all, just a single line.

On countless occasions when clubs and other organizations bring in a guest speaker for a program, they will need someone to introduce that person at the appropriate time. It may be the same person who will act as moderator for the event, or it may be a selected person whose sole job will be to introduce the speaker. If that person is you, there are several things you can do to introduce the speaker effectively.

Methods of Organization and Presentation

First, a speech of introduction must focus on the guest speaker, not on you or anything else. Keep the listeners' attention on the person who will be speaking right after you. Place him or her in a favorable and interesting light. If possible, do some research on the person ahead of time. For example, if you have enough time in advance of the speaking date, you can write to the speaker and ask for a biographical sketch. If the person is already well known nationally, you can find detailed information about the person by checking current biographies in the reference room of a library. If possible, arrange interviews with people who know your guest—colleagues, co-workers, or family members—or you might arrange to interview the person directly. Interviews take time to set up. It is also difficult to think of good questions in advance, so an interview may not be possible if you are given your assignment shortly before the event.

If information about the person is not available in printed sources and you have not been given enough notice in advance, there is a limited amount of information that you can get. Suppose that the guest arrives just a few minutes before the speech is to take place. You will not help yourself or your guest by trying to rush through a hurried, last-minute question-and-answer session. Perhaps you can get a few moments alone with the guest, away from others who will also be trying to get the speaker's attention. Or you can talk with the person who invited the speaker originally and find out a little about the speaker. Then you might review the information briefly with your guest, and ask, "Is this all right? Is there anything I should add or take out?" In that way, you save your guest from having to make up an entire introduction for you. Perhaps you can conduct a telephone interview beforehand, or you could arrange to meet the guest and drive the person to the event. In any case, it is your responsibility to do some research in advance of the event, and you may be forced into a very cramped time frame. If you have a few days' notice, do not waste it by waiting until the last minute to prepare your introduction. Speech preparation, any speech preparation, will be enhanced by as much advance work as you can manage to do. Use your time, whatever it is, to your best advantage.

Second, it is very important that you keep your speech concise. Your research may reveal dozens of interesting facts, little-known personality characteristics, or charming stories about the person's early years, school activities, hobbies, adventures, and activities, but do not try to include them all in your speech. Select one or two that are very important or reveal some central aspect of the guest's life or personality. Your goal is to present the person to your audience in a positive and informative way, not to give the main speech. Just include some basic data for the benefit of the audience, and round out that information with one or two anecdotes.

Third, keep your speech short. This advice is easy to follow if the speech is concise. A speech of introduction is rarely more than two or three minutes long, and the better known the person is, the shorter the speech should be. Follow the rules of good speech organization just as you would for any other speech by constructing a clear outline. The introduction will probably begin with a salutation to the audience: "Good morning, everybody. I am happy to welcome all the members of the GoodDay Products engineering division to our annual breakfast." Then move directly to your thesis sentence, which tells your audience the topic of the main speech: "Today I am pleased to introduce our keynote speaker, Chris Masterson, who will be speaking to us about 'Chips and Dips: Variations in the Computer Industry.'" Next, organize the body of the speech in a pattern—probably the *chronological* pattern—and include in the body two or three main headings. The chronological pattern is typical for the speech of introduction and usually includes a brief biography and some notable

You may be asked to introduce someone, present an award, or give a thank-you speech to a group.

achievements. The body ends with a brief description of the person's most recent activities, and the conclusion states the reason that the person was invited to speak at the particular event. Of course, you could try other patterns. A *topical* pattern might include personal information, education, and achievements, but these items still have a chronological aspect. If you provide a few specific supporting materials, such as dates, titles of books or articles the person has written, names of schools attended, and one or two very short anecdotes about significant events in the speaker's life, you will have a complete speech. Then you will be ready to conclude with a transition sentence that helps turn the podium over to the speaker: "Ladies and gentlemen, please join me in welcoming today's guest, Chris Masterson." Because your speech will be very short, it is not necessary to review the thesis sentence as you would in longer speeches.

Make certain that you say the person's name clearly a few times, and if you have a title for the talk, include that as well. However, do not preview the guest's speech or give away any special information that the speaker plans to announce. The audience should remember the speaker, not the person who introduces the speaker. By remembering to focus on the speaker, doing some background research, preparing a concise outline, keeping the speech short, and creating a positive setting with a clearly expressed transition to the guest, you can present a strong speech of introduction.

SPEAKING TO COMMEMORATE A PERSON OR EVENT

Sometimes, rather than introducing someone else who will speak, your purpose is to express appreciation for, or present an award to, someone. There are many similarities between a speech of introduction and a speech of recognition.

Goals of a Commemorative Speech

Like a speech of introduction, a **commemorative speech** must focus on the person or event being recognized, not on the presenter of the speech. The same processes of research can be followed, and solid, specific information—dates, stories, accomplishments—should provide the substance of the speech.

The reason for these events is usually to honor or recognize the outstanding achievements of others and perhaps to present them with prizes or awards. Preparation for these speeches begins like the preparation for speeches of introduction.

Methods of Organization and Presentation

You can gather information and prepare your speech by focusing on why the person is being honored. You have much more speaking time for this speech than for a speech of introduction. You can include more supporting materials and will probably want to include some information about the award itself— when and why it was started, notable previous recipients, or any other information that creates a context for the current ceremony and explains its significance to the audience. This part of your presentation would probably be main heading A on your outline. Heading B would begin with the background of the person currently receiving the award, and section C would briefly describe the current activities and future plans of the recipient. For example, the presentation of the annual motion picture Academy Awards on television usually begins with a short speech explaining the background of the award and how the voting is done. You can provide the same function if you develop section A of your outline as background information. If you have been asked to present an award that is named in honor of someone or is supported by a specific organization, it is appropriate to take a moment and talk about that person or organization and explain their connection to the award. Again, your focus must be on the award and the recipient, not on yourself, your reactions, or your ideas. Use an outline, select a pattern of organization, and practice your speech aloud several times to establish and maintain a dignified tone for the occasion.

> ### *TECHNOLOGY IN COMMUNICATION*
>
> #### One Billion Watching!
>
> Thanks to advances in satellite broadcasting, award shows on television, such as the annual Academy Awards each March, are regularly broadcast to huge audiences. It is estimated that the 1996 telecast went to over one billion viewers worldwide. Imagine preparing a speech to talk to a billion people! And you thought your classroom audiences were a challenge?

Sometimes, as at the Academy Awards, the name of the recipient is kept secret until the very moment that the award is presented. For most occasions, however, the person will already be known to your audience and no purpose is served by keeping the recipient of the award a secret. If you try to keep the recipient's identity a secret, as you begin to list details of the recipient's background, life, achievements, and so on, the audience will be busily telling each other that they have guessed who it is—an audience reaction that takes away from your presentation. Unless there is a serious and compelling reason to build genuine suspense and a purpose for genuine surprise in the speech, you probably should give the award winner's name in the thesis sentence and perhaps several times afterward during the speech.

Another form of commemoration is the speech of praise, which is usually given when someone reaches a milestone, such as when a person retires, leaves an organization after many years of service, or completes a term of office. Another form of this speech is given to honor someone who has died.

If the person is leaving an office or ending employment, you may wish to set a mood focusing on fond remembrances of the past and good wishes for the future. Often, a successful speech of this type mixes humorous stories or examples with a few solemn items. If the person will be missed a great deal, you can say so and acknowledge this feeling but not emphasize it. Your listeners will be sad enough without your dwelling on the sense of loss they will feel when the honoree departs. Keep your remarks positive, or even festive, as a way to balance some of the sadness. Good speeches at retirements will certainly thank the employee for the past, but some humor and positive references to the future will keep the mood upbeat.

If you are speaking to honor someone who has died, use some of the same guidelines that are used in speeches of retirement. A eulogy, the praising of someone who has died, usually demands a solemn tone throughout, although a touch of humor can add a positive note if it is appropriate to the person being honored. Suppose the person being honored by your eulogy was lively, outgoing, and always ready with a joke or a funny story. Using a little bit of that tone in the eulogy would seem appropriate. But always make certain that your comments are appropriate to the person. If the deceased was grumpy and not well liked by others, do not fabricate stories about a lovable person or invent person-

THE STORY OF COMMUNICATION

The Eulogy as Literature

Some of the greatest speeches in human history have been presented as eulogies. In classical Greece, the funeral oration of Pericles provided a model for study; students still study Pericles in public address classes today. You may have already memorized the best-known speech in U.S. history, a speech given at a cemetery to commemorate the soldiers who were buried in Gettysburg, Pennsylvania.

The combination of the solemn occasion, the greatness of the person being memorialized, the talent and skill of the speaker, and the moment in history at which the occasion takes place can come together in a eulogy to produce a lasting work of oratorical literature. An eloquent statement that examines the struggle of a professed atheist who hopes eventually that he is wrong is Robert G. Ingersoll's "At His Brother's Grave." Adlai E. Stevenson's eulogy for Eleanor Roosevelt commemorated her life of service and inspired others to follow her example.

ality traits that did not exist. Search for positive things to say and focus on them, but do not create information just for the sake of your speech. Be positive, but be appropriate. On this occasion, you need to analyze your audience very carefully and keep consideration of their feelings uppermost in your mind as you prepare and present your speech.

Speeches commemorating the dead or someone who is leaving a company or retiring can be sad, but they can also serve to inspire and honor. Because they mark important turning points in our lives, they deserve care and attention in their preparation and presentation. These are not speeches to trust to last-minute inspiration.

SPEAKING TO ACCEPT OR THANK

Sometimes the person being honored at a special event will be you. This exciting, uplifting, and sometimes surprising moment will be another opportunity for you to present a short speech.

Goals of the Acceptance Speech

Thanking people is the other side of giving awards or honors. Should you be the one selected to receive an award or prize, you need to thank the presenters appropriately. You may know about the award in advance of the presentation event, so you can prepare a short **acceptance speech** of a minute or two that is well structured and practiced. The exception to this time limit will be when, in conjunction with getting the award, you are also to be the featured speaker for the occasion. At graduation ceremonies, colleges sometimes confer an award—often an honorary doctoral degree—on the person who will then give the commencement address. The Nobel Prize ceremonies, especially for literature and peace, often feature the recipient's acceptance speech as a main component of the presentation. In this case, the person getting the prize or award has several months in which to prepare a long speech. At other ceremonies, such as the Academy Awards, the potential winners are narrowed down to a list of five, and each one is instructed to prepare a one-minute speech and be ready to give it at a moment's notice. My favorite acceptance speech on this occasion was given by Liza Minelli when she was selected best actress in 1972. Her entire speech was as follows: "Thank you for giving me this award!" which she said after she had walked happily onto the stage, smiling broadly and warmly. Then she strode off stage. Other award winners usually thank people who have been important to their winning the prize or who have been a significant presence in their lives. If the prize is named in honor of someone, mentioning that person adds a nice touch. In expressing thanks for a scholarship, for example, you might want to say, "I am especially appreciative of the Evelyn Johnson family for donating this award, which will help me cover the costs of my tuition next year." Specific comments like these are appropriate if they are kept short and if they relate to the purposes of the award.

All of these speeches—introduction, commemoration, and acceptance—are special forms of speaking, but they have in common the following elements: analyzing the purpose and the audience, adhering to time limits, and observing speaker guidelines. All of these speeches are usually short and often require some special thought about what material to include in the body and what style of delivery is most appropriate to any particular situation.

SPEAKING ON SHORT NOTICE—IMPROMPTU

In both your classroom and, later, your community and career settings, there will be times when you will be called on to "say a few words," yet you will not be given a significant amount of time in which to prepare a speech. You may be asked to speak immediately, in which case your specific preparation time is only a few seconds, or you might be given a few hours' notice, as when a company supervisor tells you in the morning that you will be asked to give a report later that day. Or you could be at a civic meeting and decide to speak on the issue being discussed, so you take a few minutes to jot down some notes. This type of **short-notice speech** is called *impromptu speaking*.

Goals of Impromptu Speaking

The main feature that distinguishes this speech event from others is time. You can have impromptu informative, persuasive, and even entertaining speeches. You can speak to introduce, to thank, to inspire, or to motivate, all on short notice. The important thing to remember is that the impromptu speech is still a speech and has all the elements of a speech if done correctly.

Even without the luxury of time, you still possess many resources that you can use to prepare and present an impromptu speech. The most important resource you have is yourself. You have enormous amounts of information stored in your memory, and the successful impromptu speaker is one who can tap into that reserve of material and pull out specific stories, facts, numbers, dates, examples, and even visual aids to use in an impromptu speech. These speakers are successful because they are able to recall quickly something appropriate to the occasion from a past vacation or newspaper article they once read, a favorite story of their grandparents, or a scene from a movie that is pertinent to their speaking situation. They can think of songs they heard on the radio, magazine articles or college classes that captured their interest, or popular television shows they have enjoyed, and pull out of those experiences a statistic, a quotation, or an example. Effective impromptu speakers are also those who give many impromptu speeches, because the practice they get diving into their memory banks helps them to become better and better at finding and using the materials that are stored there. Regular use of these personal resources makes them more easily accessible.

Additional sources of information for impromptu speeches can be the audience and the occasion. What do you know about your listeners that you can use in your presentation? Do they share a theme, common element, motto, or activity that you can include in your remarks? Perhaps you can recall something about their purpose, history, or previous achievements. Previous speakers may have mentioned items that you can incorporate into your speech and on which you can elaborate to adapt them to your thesis. You can also take a quick look at any program notes, information handouts, or bulletins that have been prepared for the occasion. If you are speaking at a special event, include remarks about the event. If your talk happens to be on a date near a holiday, tie the holiday into your speech. You may be in a special building or city or on a college campus that is notable in terms of your speech. An impromptu speaker must be particularly alert to all aspects of the situation and surroundings to be effective.

One of the most often used skills in speaking is impromptu speaking. Unlike some of your other classes, in which you may have been tempted to study for the final exam and then move on, leaving the material behind you, your speech class teaches you speaking skills that you can apply in nearly every facet of your life for many years to come.

The short-notice speech is based on the same principles of good public speaking as any other speech, so let us review those principles and apply them to an impromptu setting.

Methods of Organization and Presentation

The ideas you learned in Chapters 11 and 12 can be adapted to the impromptu speech quite easily. Focus on a simple thesis sentence, select an organizational format, include specific supporting materials, add a quick introduction and a conclusion, and observe the time limits, either formal or informal, that may be in effect. One of the best methods for achieving success with a short-notice speech is to outline your remarks—a small piece of scratch paper or even the back of a program is quite suitable. You already know that the spoken part of an outline has four parts: the introduction, thesis sentence, body, and conclusion. If you have time to create a bibliography, you are not doing an impromptu speech. Create an outline with space in the body for two to four main ideas and some space under each of those for a few specific supports.

When creating the body of the speech, remember to choose a chronological, topical, logical, or motivational pattern. Variations on the chronological pattern are popular because they are easy for both the speaker and the listeners to remember. As long as the pattern that you select is appropriate to the thesis, the occasion, and the audience, use it. For example, if you were in an American literature class and were suddenly asked to report on your view of the character Jim in *Huckleberry Finn,* you could easily visualize the chronological pattern and divide your answer into "First impressions of Jim," "The river journey," and "Final evaluations." Your presentation would be clear and easy to follow, and you could support each idea with brief examples from the novel. Or you might quickly decide that a good way to analyze Jim's character would be in terms of relationships (topical pattern), in which case you would discuss his interactions with Huck, with other young people, and so on. This analysis is probably more sophisticated and interesting but tougher to do on short notice. However, many successful students approach the writing of essay exams as if they were impromptu speeches, and a relational pattern might occur to you if you were sitting and thinking about your answer during an extended examination period.

If you were at a planning commission meeting in your town and the topic was the approval of a new access road near your house, you might select a persuasive pattern for your impromptu speech. You could cite the inadequacy of the current roads *(problem)* and the better traffic flow that would result from the proposal *(solution)*. If, on the other hand, you were opposed to the road, you could still use a persuasive pattern, but you would present ideas in opposition to its construction. For example, you might use the motivated sequence pattern and begin with a statement about increased traffic being a safety hazard *(problem)*, followed by some specific examples as support. You might then suggest an alternative route for the road *(solution)*. Get your listeners to imagine improved traffic flow and safety from your new idea *(visualization)*, and conclude by urging the rejection of the original idea and the adoption of your idea *(action)*.

In the above examples, several patterns could be used. You could use a chronological pattern for the new road speech or the problem–solution format for discussing the character of Jim. However, there seems to be a rightness to some patterns that warrants their use. Practice in using a variety of these formats will keep them fresh in your mind and available for your use at a moment's notice.

Once you have decided on a thesis, selected an appropriate organizational pattern, and researched some supporting materials, you need a good idea for an attention-getting introduction. Notice that deciding on an introduction is one of the *last* things that you do in preparing for an impromptu speech, just as it is

IMPROVING COMPETENCY

Outlining the Essay as a Speech

Try this technique the next time that you take an essay examination. Before you begin to write, jot down Roman numerals I, II, III, and IV in the left-hand margin in small print, leaving a large space between III and IV. Leave I blank for the moment, and note the main point of your answer in a few key words next to II. Next, try to create two, three, or four major ways to explain your thesis, and put these into some order (topical, chronological, and so on) as A, B, C, under III. In other words, make a thumbnail outline of your answer. It is worth investing a few moments in preparing your answer in this way, because writing down all the key words and ideas right at the beginning will help you to recall details and relationships later. Sometimes fatigue sets in, and an important idea you thought of at the beginning of your writing, and that you intended to include in the middle of your writing, simply gets left out—because you forgot it. Or you may take off on a tangent, and your answer begins to stray from its main idea. Without an outline, you may be connecting ideas, but they may lead down a path away from your main point. Once you make your outline, reread the question. Does your thesis sentence provide a direct response to the question? If so, then begin writing, perhaps using a specific item for your introduction or saving a few lines for your introduction so that you can come back and insert the introduction later. If your outline is not as directly responsive to the question as you might like, you can concentrate on the outline for a few more minutes, perhaps rephrasing the thesis sentence, developing a new organization pattern, or adding a few more facts or other supporting materials. For long answers, a clear, focused, organized essay can be a lifesaver, for both the writer and the reader. Don't forget your quick preview at III and a comprehensive review for your conclusion. Your answers will be easier to write and easier to read.

DIVERSITY IN COMMUNICATION

Folk Tales

One of the richest sources of material you have for gathering support for your impromptu speeches is in folk tales from around the world. These tales are handed down because they contain a clear message based on some moral principle and are told in an appealing, engaging, and memorable form. But do folk tales really fit the bill for good supporting materials? Yes; these tales survive in our heritage because they are clearly told, are easy to remember, and often contain a moral or truth that is universal and transcends time and place. While you may be very familiar with some folk tales, especially those told at home and in school, do not overlook the vast literatures of other cultures. School textbooks have only recently included non-European literature to any great extent. Students in elementary school this year will have much greater exposure to literature from around the world than you did, but you can make up for this loss by visiting a library and checking out the collected folk tales of a variety of cultures. Even better, can you visit someone from a different culture who tells stories? Perhaps you have a relative who is closely linked to a culture that is different from yours and who could share tales with you personally. Many libraries have reading hours that often feature a particular culture, and they would welcome your attendance. By increasing your knowledge of the stories of many cultures, you not only add to your available storehouse of information to be used in impromptu speeches, you also expose yourself to the wisdom of the world's peoples.

often one of the last items in the preparation of other kinds of speeches. Introductions should be interesting and appropriate and should lead up to the thesis sentence. You can use stories or quotations that you like. Folk tales or proverbs can also be included. Fairy tales usually have a moral; if the moral is the same as the point of your thesis, use it. Perhaps your point of view on the new access road is that the benefits of having it are not real, but illusory. A quick reference to the story about the emperor's new clothes will focus everyone's attention on your point. Parables from the Bible, stories of Native Americans, examples from the Koran, and stories about your family are all possibilities for introductory material. Make the length of your introductory story appropriate to your overall time frame, and do not get so involved with the details of the story that you do not have time for the rest of your speech. Ten percent of your total time is a good guideline for introductions. Introductory material should be relevant, clear, appropriate, and short.

When it is time to end your impromptu speech, recall the general principles for ending any speech. Do not generate any new ideas; review quickly the main headings but not the supporting details; repeat your thesis; and conclude by referring back to the introduction. Many times, an impromptu speaker will finish the body of the speech and stop there. Remember that the audience still needs a quick review or restatement of the thesis to have a lasting impression of your ideas. Any speech that is longer than three minutes would probably benefit from a review. If the speech is shorter than that, just state a short, simple conclusion to tie your ideas together.

As was mentioned earlier, all speeches have a time limit, either formally imposed, arising from the audience's tolerance, or from the situation. Since you cannot practice your impromptu ahead of time to get an idea of how long it will take, you will have to be careful to time your speech without practice and without violating the time limit. In some public hearings, speakers are limited to three or perhaps five minutes. Ask someone to give you time signals. Trying to time yourself is difficult because you are already trying to remember to do a dozen other things. People sometimes take off their watch, look at it very carefully, set it down next to their note card outline, and never look at the watch again. Your best strategy is to keep your ideas flowing and try to finish in a little under the time allotted. If you have made your point, clearly supported it, and quickly reviewed it, stop talking. Even if there is a moment or two remaining, resist the temptation to add some new point or a new story. They will be out of sequence and be seen by your listeners as padding. They can also create confusion where once there was clarity. When you are finished with your outline, stop talking.

Even if no absolute time limits are given to you, you need to think about the psychological limits of the situation. At a large public meeting, there may be dozens of people waiting for you to finish so that they can have an opportunity to speak. Be sensitive to these limitations so that your listeners keep listening to you and do not turn their attention away from your content and to the time that you are taking up. If you are in a classroom situation with only ten minutes remaining in the period, be careful of using all the remaining time so that no one else gets a chance or so that the teacher needs to keep the class late to make important announcements. Your going beyond the time limit then creates an impact on the event that follows. For example, the next class may be waiting to get into the room, or the students in your class may be trying to leave and get to their next class on time. If your audience is waiting to go to lunch or catch a bus, even one second over the time allotted will be wasted, and you stand a good chance of turning potential supporters into hostile reactors.

These suggestions for short-notice presentations can be put into practice in a few seconds, if necessary. However, you also need to have your delivery skills on tap to be effective in the impromptu situation. Effective delivery of impromptu speeches begins by practicing the suggestions for overcoming nervousness. Deep breathing and muscle-relaxing techniques will help to keep your mind clear so that access to your storehouse of information will be easier. If you had a chance to sketch a rough outline, go over it, making your handwriting neat, clear, and large, while you practice deep breathing. When you give the speech, use your outline if possible. If a speaker stand or lectern is available, place your outline on it so that it is not noticeable. A well-modulated voice, good eye contact, and natural and appropriate gestures work in an impromptu speech as in any other. You many need to move and turn around to make eye contact with everyone, or you might stand where everyone can easily see you. The volume of your voice must be adjusted to the size of the room. Watch the previous speakers—if there have been any—to see how they adapted, and use any information you gain from observing their presentations to the advantage of your own.

In summary, the short-notice speech should look as much as possible like any other speech that you give. The best way to achieve this goal is to give

Keeping democracy alive and vital means partici- pating as a citizen, often as an impromptu speaker.

impromptu speeches as often as possible. Take opportunities to comment in class, at work, and in public. Each time you do, you are providing yourself with valuable experience for the next time you speak at a moment's notice.

 READING LITERATURE ALOUD

The final area of public speaking on special occasions may involve you in read- ing literature aloud to an audience. Sometimes this reading is part of a cere- mony, such as at many religious functions.

Goals of Oral Interpretation

In her influential text, Charlotte Lee defined oral interpretation as "the art of communicating to an audience a work of literary art in its intellectual, emotional and aesthetic entirety" (Lee, 1971). Thus the goal of an effective reader of liter- ature is to help the listeners understand, feel, and appreciate the work being read. As in most other types of communication, the focus is not on the person doing the reading or speaking, but on the content of the message. You may find opportunities to read aloud at ceremonies, at reading hours in a library, at orga- nizational programs, or to your friends or your children. In fact, research in the area of child development demonstrates that reading aloud to very young chil- dren has a clear, positive effect on their acquisition of language skills.

Oral interpretation uses literature as a way to bring together the author, reader, and audience through shared experiences. You might look through the writings of various authors for an appropriate selection to read. Use your per- sonal experiences and feelings as guides in selecting material to share with an

Reading aloud to children is rewarding to both the reader and the children.

audience. The audience will respond, sometimes by visible and audible feedback, letting you know how your reading is being received.

Oral interpretation brings together the author, reader, and audience through the means of literature (Swanson and Zeuschner, 1983). First, the author writes the material and experiences the emotional impact of creativity. Second, the reader searches among the writings of various authors for the proper selections to read, using personal experiences and feelings as guides in selecting pieces to share with an audience. Finally, there is the audience, who, by visible and audible responses, lets the reader know how a reading is being received. This may sound like a simple thing to do, but to be an effective interpreter of literature, you must find good materials to read, be able to analyze the literature to discover what the author intended, and draw on personal experience to put feeling and meaning into your presentation. Practice reading literature aloud to polish both your interpretive and delivery skills. Study the literature you selected to read, and during your reading, look at the reactions of listeners to help you improve the audience's understanding and appreciation of the reading.

Students who are interested in oral interpretation should read the opinions and ideas of writers in this field as one means of enriching their understanding of what constitutes effective oral reading. You probably can take a course in oral interpretation at your school.

Creative reading is **audience-centered,** in that the "stage" is the audience's imagination. Your responsibility is to use verbal and nonverbal symbols that enable the audience to create appropriate mental images. Using imagination, both the reader in the presentation and the audience members in their participation draw from their life experiences.

Methods of Creation and Presentation

Presenting literature involves trying to keep communication channels with your listeners open; reacting in your mind to the literary situation as an observer of it; and then communicating your reactions, thoughts, and feelings to an audience with a variety of visual, vocal, and nonverbal combinations (Swanson and Zeuschner, 1983).

There is a distinction between acting and oral interpretation. Interpretation is a communicative presentation; acting is communication through representation. You should deliver your material in a manner that is appropriate to a *reading* situation. It is difficult to pinpoint the difference between interpretation and acting, but you should avoid attempting to portray props, actions and characters. You should also avoid the use of gestures that go beyond what is considered appropriate for good public speaking.

The following chart should help you sort out the difference between being an interpreter and being an actor (Zeuschner, 1978).

Criteria	*Acting (Stage-Centered)*	*Interpretation (Audience-Centered)*
1. Who are you?	A character	Yourself
2. Who is telling the story?	Actors	You
3. Where is the scene?	Stage	Imagination
4. What is your relationship to the situation?	Participant	Observer
5. What kind of expression is used?	Representation	Suggestion
6. What is your relationship to the literature?	The actor tries to portray the writer's concepts by actually representing them.	The reader and the listener share as observers of the writer's concepts.

In oral interpretation, the reader's primary intention is to enable the listeners to imagine the situation from the writer's perspective. When an interpreter's actions and gestures distract the attention of the listeners from the material being read, they forfeit the main purpose of the reading. There should always be economy and focus in the art of oral interpretation.

To achieve the response that you desire as an effective oral reader, you should demonstrate the ability to articulate and enunciate properly, and display variety in the pitch and tone of your voice, in your patterns of intonation, and in your rate of speech. To achieve effective communication with the audience, you should also maintain eye contact with audience members, as you would do in any speaking situation.

You might want to begin with an introduction leading into the material to be read. An introduction is strongly recommended in a public performance because it helps to identify the material being read and creates a context for your listeners. Sometimes, as in a religious ceremony, the material may be selected for you, and someone else may write the introduction.

Remember, the reader's job is to present an intelligent interpretation of a significant piece of literature. The choice of that literature, like the choice of a speech topic, should be based on an audience analysis.

When you think about selecting and organizing your material, ask the following questions: Is the material of an appropriate quality and type? Is the material appropriate to your ability? Do you have variety in your material, and do the various selections complement one another or provide an agreeable contrast?

When writing your introductory and transitional comments, think about the following questions. Does the introduction state the purpose of the reading and the material to be read? Does it evoke interest? Do the transitional comments demonstrate your comprehension of the material and lead the audience from one selection to another? Are your introductory and transitional comments presented in an extemporaneous, communicative manner?

As you work on communicating the author's meaning, consider these questions. Does your interpretation project the author's ideas and attitude? Does your interpretation show that you understand the references and the allusions in the material? Are you able to establish a mood that is suitable to the material? Are you using appropriate phrasing, emphasis, subordination, inflection, and articulation?

Finally, as you work on your communication of emotion, consider these questions. Do you make use of vocal and physical imagery? Does your reading take advantage of appropriate sound patterns—alliteration, assonance, onomatopoeia? Do you employ the rhythmic elements of verse form, prose cadence, tempo, or rhyme? Do the elements of pitch, volume, quality, time, stance, posture, gestures, and facial expressions contribute to your communication?

Readers' Theatre

A special type of oral interpretation involves a group ensemble format that is usually called a **readers' theatre.** Its purpose is to give a group the opportunity to present a literary script using their voices and bodies to suggest the intellectual, emotional, and sensory experiences in their presentation of a piece of literature. People who participate in a readers' theatre try to develop the ability to communicate complex ideas and feelings through individual and group manipulations of vocal and physical variables to involve the audience in the literature.

A readers' theatre is usually composed of three or more readers (Lewis, 1991). In a readers' theatre presentation, there are a variety of ways to use eye contact and focus, such as direct eye contact with the audience, on-stage focus, or off-stage focus above the heads of the audience. The focus that is used in a readers' theatre presentation should be determined by the particular treatment of the literature.

There are several varieties of readers' theatre programs, including school productions, religious events, and community readings. Presentations might consist of a thematic collage of various literary selections from one or more authors or an excerpt from, or adaptation of, a single piece of prose, poetry, or drama. Props, costuming, lighting, and music may sometimes be used to enhance the program. However, these extraliterary devices should not dominate the presentation. Groups may also use physical and vocal variables: movement, choral and antiphonal reading, staging, and so on.

The interpreters should convey the meaning of the material and its feeling, imagery, and thought. Monologues, dialogues, choral reading, and other forms may be used to embellish the intellectual and emotional meaning of the script. Group members should probably share equally in the presentation. No one reader should dominate or monopolize the program. The readers are expected to present, through original remarks and interpretive readings, greater insight into the literature than the audience might gain from a silent reading of the script.

Of course, any group wants to know how well its presentation is being received. Readers' theatre groups can evaluate their reading in several ways. The quality of the material can be judged by examining its literary merit. Is the material fresh and interesting? Does it leave the audience with a sense of having participated in a total experience? You can check for balance in the program by making sure that cast members have an equal share in the presentation. Are the roles of cast members of equal importance? Your vocal action, delivery, and style can be evaluated by asking these questions: Did the material allow for suitable vocal variety, and was this provided? Were flow, pacing, and tempo effective? Was any characterization particularly distinct and believable? How well did group members interrelate? Was there consistency of focus on stage, off stage, and with the audience?

You can evaluate the organizational pattern of the script by examining the unity of purpose in the program. In a thematic piece containing various selections, in a collage of one author's work, or in a compilation of prose, poetry, and drama by several authors, was an organizational pattern evident? Finally, you can gauge the overall effect of the program by asking yourself the following questions: Was the program in good taste? Did the program retain the interest of the audience throughout the entire presentation? Did the audience experience a sense of emotional and intellectual fulfillment from the program?

In a readers' theatre program, monologues, dialogues, choral readings, and other oral presentation forms may be used to embellish fully the intellectual and emotional meaning of the script. Reading a full text in oral interpretation or taking a course will give you more ideas and details if you are interested in following through on the material presented here.

Whether you are reading alone or with a group, you will need to select materials if they are not provided for you. How can you find good literature for a reading? In general, you should begin by selecting materials that you understand and enjoy. To a degree, good literature is literature that *you* like and appreciate. It is wise to begin your search for literature in your previous reading and categories of literature that you appreciate. For readings of expository prose, the *Readers' Guide to Periodical Literature* is an excellent source of citations of magazine articles on all kinds of subjects, and it is indexed by topic area. The periodicals that are listed include the *Saturday Review of Literature, Atlantic, Harper's,* the *New Yorker,* and a wide variety of other periodicals. Textbooks and anthologies, particularly those used in English, American, and foreign-language literature courses, provide excellent sources of expository prose readings.

Narrative prose differs from expository prose in that it tells a story. To tell a story, it uses characterization, dialogue, and plot. Narrative prose has more emotional content than does expository prose. It is found in journals, diaries, letters, and, of course, novels and short stories. For summaries of plots of novels, consult *Masterpieces of World Literature in Digest Form,* and you should have no difficulty at all finding anthologies of short stories. Book reviews in newspapers and magazines will give you clues to interesting new novels and stories. Best-seller lists in book stores and magazines also offer good ideas to interested readers.

Poetry is usually represented in major literary anthologies. The *Poetry Index* provides one of the best sources of reference to poetry selections. Most libraries devote entire sections to works written by poets. Books on literary criticism are also useful to students in researching poetry, as well as other forms of literature.

For drama, the *Play Index* is recommended. In addition, collections of the best plays by year are quite popular and can be found in most libraries. Many publishers print paperback copies of one-act plays, and special publishing services offer monthly publications listing new play titles.

A reader recognizes that there are numerous ways to treat any subject, but some ways are more effective than others. You may be fond of certain poems,

CRITICAL THINKING IN COMMUNICATION

Criteria for Selecting Literature

Among other factors, there are three important criteria that you can use to help you evaluate the quality of the literature to be selected for reading.

1. The *universality* of literature means that the idea expressed is potentially interesting to all people because it reflects common experiences. The emotional response that is evoked is one that most readers and listeners have felt at one time or another. Universality does not mean that the material will immediately appeal to all people regardless of their intellectual or cultural backgrounds, but it does mean that the potential is there for any person to relate the piece of writing to a personal or common experience.

2. *Individuality* implies that the writer has a fresh approach to a universal subject. While seeming to be the opposite of universality, individuality means that the idea expressed is handled with a personal touch and does not sound like dozens of other writings on the same theme or subject. The key to individuality in writing may be found in language choice, images, and methods of organization. To decide whether a writer has individuality, you will need to become acquainted with a wide variety of literature.

3. *Suggestion* means that the author has chosen references and words that allow readers to add to or enrich the subject matter from their own background. Suggestion means that the writer has not told everything but has given a sufficiently clear direction for the imagination of readers to follow that they may draw on their own experiences to add meaning and emotional impact to their reading (Cunningham, 1941).

plays, or stories because of your early associations with them. Provided that your early associations are similar to those of the audience, relying on favorite poems, plays, or stories can serve as a useful starting place for creating a program. However, it is a good idea to broaden your horizons and not limit yourself to what you already like. The important thing is to establish criteria for evaluating the literature to be selected for reading. Such criteria ought to help you discover new literature and integrate these discoveries into your personal repertoire.

The factors of universality, individuality, and suggestion are closely related and serve to balance each other in effective writing. The universal idea is drawn from an experience that all people are able to share; the individual method of expressing the idea is different from those used by other authors; and the suggestion of associated ideas and responses points the way for the imagination to follow and allows for continuing enrichment on many levels of meaning (Yorden, 1993). Sometimes these factors are not all present in a selection with equal force, nor is it necessary that they be. But if one of them is missing entirely, it is likely that the literature under consideration is low on quality.

Preparing Materials for Reading

After a piece of literature has been found and selected for a program, the task of preparing the script and excerpting sections to be read is next. The following guidelines can help you to begin this task (Lee and Galati, 1987).

Arouse interest in the reading. Anything you might say that would leave the audience thinking, "This should be interesting," is appropriate. The art here is to tell enough but leave enough out that the listener will want to hear the reading. Establish the correct mood and the proper setting for the particular piece of literature that you have selected. Your introduction should be brief. When you read several different pieces in the same program, introductory remarks may be spaced over the entire reading by making brief statements just before each selection.

Type or neatly write out all introductory remarks, the transitions, and the piece(s) making up the program, and place them in a folder or notebook. Folders and notebooks should be neat and not distracting—that is, not covered with a colorful picture or stickers and not torn or worn out. Type, write, or print materials in bold, easy-to-read letters, using double- or even triple-spaced lines for easy access to the material at a glance while reading. Leave space for marginal comments or markings that will be helpful in projecting emphasis while reading. Never become completely dependent on the folder or notebook. The audience should not even be aware of it.

Excerpting Materials for Reading

Sometimes the material you select will be too long, or you might want to use only parts of it. Proper excerpting is both permissible and essential. The following suggestions regarding excerpting may be helpful to you as you prepare your reading (Lee and Gura, 1987).

Know the time limit, and read your selection(s) several times until you can judge the approximate amount of material that must be excerpted to make the selection fall comfortably within the time limits. Next, read the selection(s) for personal impact. Be able to distinguish the essential descriptions, narrations, and allusions from the nonessential ones. Discussing your decisions about what is or is not essential with someone else can be helpful. Remember that part of your impact is likely to come from the slowly developed moods that an author builds through carefully selected descriptions and allusions, so do not end your excerpt prematurely. Make up sentence bridges between parts. Wherever possible, use the author's own language for your sentence bridges to conform to how the author might have written the transition. Delete the words *he said* and *she said* throughout the selection(s). Perhaps you can add names to distinguish among the characters, but do so only occasionally, not before every line of dialogue. Subplots can be cut, as can minor characters. Cut sections or stanzas from poetry, taking care to preserve the rhythm and cadence of the original piece. On the other hand, use only relevant lines or stanzas if they are being used as essential theme materials.

To be an effective reader, you must review your feelings, attitudes, and moods regarding particular pieces of literature. When practicing, let yourself go a little in terms of expressing emotions. Allow your feelings an opportunity to guide your vocal expressions and physical movements. Practice reading aloud, and practice often. Whenever possible, record yourself reading part or all of a program. Become a good storyteller by developing a once-upon-a-time quality for every reading. Every time you read aloud, project a first-time atmosphere. Your listeners should be captured by the opening moments of every reading. Listen to others, and learn to recognize what captures your own attention to other readers. Effective reading bypasses self-consciousness. Study methods and techniques of voice control. Such study should include attention to breath control (exercises in inhalation and exhalation) and volume and projection (the loudness and direction of the voice). Your voice must be appropriate for the surroundings and the literature. You must also learn to punctuate the literature with your voice and read the selections at an appropriate rate of speed (Lee, 1971).

All of these suggestions, when put into practice, can help to make you a competent reader of literature with a large repertoire of selections and of reading techniques. You will be able to be selective about which materials you use and which reading techniques and skills you use to be more effective in any given situation. You should be able to put these skills into effect if you practice sufficiently. Finally, you will be able to ask and answer evaluative questions to judge your reading and that of others.

SUMMARY

Speaking in special situations can help to increase your overall communication competency. You can see how paying a little attention to the requirements of introducing, thanking, and commemorating or of reading literature thoughtfully and with feeling can enhance your performance in these situations, and create a positive impression of you in the minds of the audience. You have started down the road to competency by learning about the various types of special-occasion speeches. As you analyze their requirements and your own speaking situations, you will be able to select from among them combinations which suit you and your purpose. As you gain opportunities for practice, your skills in implementing your choices will increase. Each of these special-occasion speeches has elements of evaluation that you can apply to round out your increased communication competencies as a speaker for special circumstances.

KEY TERMS

speech to introduce, *p. 310*
commemorative speech, *p. 313*
acceptance speech, *p. 315*
short-notice speech, *p. 316*

oral interpretation, *p. 321*
audience-centered, *p. 322*
readers' theatre, *p. 324*

EXERCISES

1. Watch a speech of introduction either in person or on television, and evaluate it according to the suggestions presented in this chapter. Did the speaker put thought and care into the presentation? If so, how?

2. Interview a member of your class, and pretend that you are going to present that person at an important meeting fifteen years from now when that person is the featured speaker. Prepare a two- to three-minute speech of introduction for your classmate, and ask that person to do the same for you. Present your speeches to the class. For this assignment only, you may invent reasonable information to cover the fifteen-year time period (L. R. Zeuschner, 1995).

3. Attend a meeting of your student government, a hearing on campus, a city or county public forum, or a meeting of a political or special-interest group. Listen carefully, then select an issue about which you have feelings, and present an impromptu speech. Were you able to follow the suggestions for preparation and presentation offered in this chapter?

4. One of the most satisfying ways you will ever spend an hour on a Saturday morning is to volunteer to read stories to children at your local library. If not on a Saturday morning, find out when the library does have a story hour and sign up to be a reader for one time. Then follow the guidelines to select, prepare, and present a story or two. You will probably want to volunteer again once you have done so the first time.

REFERENCES

Cunningham, C. C. *Literature as a Fine Art: Analysis and Interpretation*. New York: Ronald Press, 1941.

Lee, Charlotte I. *Oral Interpretation*. 4th ed. Boston: Houghton Mifflin, 1971.

Lee, C. I., and F. Galati. *Oral Interpretation*. 5th ed. Boston: Houghton Mifflin, 1987.

Lee, C. I., and T. Gura. *Oral Interpretation*. 7th ed. Boston: Houghton Mifflin, 1987.

Lewis, Todd. *Communicating Literature*. Dubuque: Kendall-Hunt, 1991.

Swanson, Don R., and R. B. Zeuschner. *Participating in Collegiate Forensics*. Scottsdale: Gorsuch Scarisbrick, 1983.

Yorden, J. E. *Roles in Interpretation*. 3rd ed. Dubuque: Brown and Benchmark, 1993.

Zeuschner, Linda Rockwell. "Introducing the Speaker Fifteen Years from Now." *GIFTS: Great Ideas For Teaching Speech*. 3rd ed. Ed. R. B. Zeuschner. New York: HarperCollins, 1995.

Zeuschner, R. B., ed. *The Handbook of the Pacific Southwest Collegiate Forensics Association*. Los Angeles: PSCFA, 1978.

Communicating in Careers

After reading this chapter, you should be able to:

- Understand the roles and functions of communication in career settings.

- Describe the influence of norms, roles, and distortions in organizational communication.

- Feel comfortable with your communicator style as it relates to a career situation.

- Apply your skills and knowledge to improve your personal communication competency in any organization.

*E*ach of these three career settings—businesses, organizations, and professions—depends on skill in the application of communication principles to become established, to be maintained, and to grow. Try to imagine a business that does not communicate its existence to the rest of the world, an organization that does not conduct regular meetings, or a profession that does not continually seek out new members. They would soon be out of commission. In spite of the different purposes for their existence, all organizations share some communication characteristics. In many ways, these characteristics are similar to those found in small groups, so some of the concepts that you learned in Chapter 10 will be familiar to you as you see how groups, acting together, create organizations.

A DEFINITION OF ORGANIZATIONAL COMMUNICATION

Organizational communication may be defined as the process of small units acting together to form organizations. Think of an organization as an open system composed of people who create and exchange messages within a network of interdependent relationships to cope with the environment (Goldhaber, 1990). It has been estimated that when you add together all the time you spend at work and in social organizations, religious groups, sports associations, educational institutions, and civic associations, about 90 percent of your time is spent in some sort of an organization (Levinson, 1973). No wonder organizational communication is such a popular field of study.

Within this definition, there are several ways to categorize the study of organizations and their communication. The major approaches to this study are dealt with in the section that follows, in which you can see how elements of the definition are found in each category.

ORGANIZATIONAL BEHAVIOR

Organizations have been studied for many years and these studies tend to be identified with one of three or four general approaches: (1) classical, (2) human relations, (3) social systems, and (4) organizational culture (Goldhaber, 1990). By taking a brief look at each of these categories, you will better understand how communication functions in an organization.

Classical

The **classical approach** is sometimes called the *scientific approach*. It grew out of early attempts to apply principles of scientific investigation to the behaviors and issues involved in the emerging industries of the country. The person who is most often associated with initiating this approach is Frederick Taylor, who was active in his research before World War I. He began what later grew into an entire field of investigation known as *time-and-motion studies*. A worker or a job would be carefully monitored in an attempt to find the maximum level of efficiency for the completion of any given task. For example, Taylor's early major work involved a study of the optimal size shovel that coal yard workers should use. The goal here was to create the most efficient combination of shovel weight and numbers of shovel loads so that a worker could scoop the maximum amount of coal possible in one hour. By combining those factors, Taylor was able to reduce dramatically the number of necessary workers in a coal yard and still maintain the same level of output. Management was pleased, of course, since it then had to pay only 140 workers instead of the previous 400 to 600 workers. Profits increased as expenses went down (Goldhaber, 1990).

You can see immediately that this approach is heavily weighted toward profit/loss and input/output figures. It treats workers and jobs as static, interchangeable, and somewhat mechanistic entities. This view is concerned primarily with physical demands and ignores other factors, such as worker satisfaction or on-the-job training so that workers can move to different jobs. The classical approach enjoyed great popularity for some time (Groves, 1995), and the automobile assembly plant was where it was put into practice with great enthusiasm on the part of management. You might also envision the classical approach in use in a large university or a state department of highways. Thus it has been used in both the private and public sectors. Division of labor, span of control, and hierarchical structure are the areas that are most important to the formal, or classical, approach to organizations. Think of a strong auto company executive making major decisions, then sending them down through a complicated hierarchy of vice-presidents, division managers, area superintendents, section leaders, line supervisors, lead workers, and finally to production workers. Imagine your college as having a top administrator—or, even higher, a board of trustees— several vice-presidents, deans, department heads, and so on, and you will have a picture of a formal organization. One of the reasons that workers are often unhappy and that strife, such as labor–management disputes or campus protests, breaks out periodically may be the impersonal, inflexible structure that dominates the thinking of people at the top of an organization having a classical or formal philosophy.

Human Relations

The **human relations approach** is something of a reaction to the classical approach. In the late 1920s, the shortcomings of the formal approach were apparent in a lack of worker satisfaction and an increase in labor organization to counteract an often impersonal and exploitative treatment of workers. It was hypothesized that unhappy workers might also be less productive and that, conversely, if the work environment could create positive feelings in employees, they might become more productive.

From the results of applying psychological insights into the way people behave in the workplace, it became clear that human reactions and feelings were an important aspect of any organization. This relationship between people's feelings and the functioning of the organization started the human relations approach to organizational communication as a serious study and as a counter to the classical approach.

This approach pays attention to the psychological state of the people in an organization, and the job of management is therefore to try to keep employees happy. More importance is placed on input from workers, and a democratic

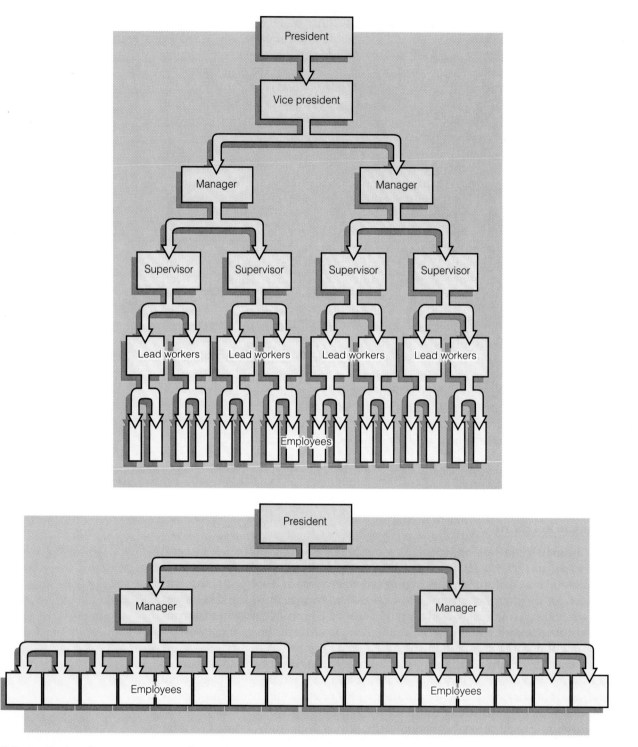

Tall organizations have more concern for supervision and control than do flat organizations.

THE STORY OF COMMUNICATION

The Hawthorne Effect

One especially enlightening and psychologically inspired study was conducted as a research project in 1937 in the Western Electric Company plant in Hawthorne, Illinois, near Chicago. These studies happen to be some of the most famous studies ever conducted on worker psychology. My grandfather was a worker in this plant at that time, so they have always been of interest to me.

Seeking to discover whether worker productivity could be increased (a classic goal) if workers were satisfied with the working conditions, researchers began to raise and lower the amount of heating, ventilation, and lighting in the work areas. One part of the study clearly showed that if the lighting intensity was increased, worker productivity also increased. Then an odd thing happened. The researchers decreased the amount of lighting, and worker productivity *increased*. From this unexpected finding, they concluded that it was not really the lighting that was creating the change, but merely the fact that the workers knew that they were being studied. In other words, they responded to the experiment itself, not to the variations in lighting (Roethlisberger and Dickson, 1939). This response is called the *Hawthorne effect*, or sometimes the *experimenter effect.*

style of leadership is more typical of this type of organization than of a classical organization, which is controlled by an authoritarian leadership style.

Social Systems

The social systems view of organizations emphasizes the interconnections among all parts of the organization. If a change is made in any one place in the structure, that change will have consequences for all other parts as well. The idea that human interactions form a system, like a biological cell system or circulatory system, probably comes from Ludwig von Bertalanffy. He described general systems theory based on a systems model from the physical sciences (von Bertalanffy, 1956, 1962).

Because the organizations with which we deal are populated by humans, the social dimension is an integral part of the structure, and so the system becomes a social system. The means by which we create our society is communication, so the role of communication determines how the system will operate. This fact can be easily illustrated by examining any event and then following the sequence of events that flow from it. For example, your history professor lectured a little longer than usual one afternoon, and because of that, you were three minutes late in arriving at the post office, which had closed before you could mail your water bill. Your tardiness resulted in a 50 percent penalty being added to your next month's bill, which resulted in your roommates' being angry with you. You then paid the penalty, which meant that money was deducted

> ## CRITICAL THINKING IN COMMUNICATION
>
> ### Systems Analysis
>
> The cause–effect logical pattern is at the heart of systems theory, since it attempts to trace any action (effect) in the organization back to some cause. The post hoc fallacy is especially dangerous in systems analysis because a time sequence may make a false cause–effect relationship look like a real one. In reality, most events have a multiplicity of causative agents that interact with each other, so a simplistic application of systems theory may prevent good critical thinking. Trained systems analysts are on the lookout for oversimplifications of causal relationships, so they apply the critical-thinking approach of seeking and testing a variety of causes for either direct or contributory relationships to the events they are studying. Your own critical-thinking skills should be applied in any discussions that you have about your organization's systems.

from your monthly budget, so you could not afford to go out with a very intriguing person from your history class. All events and actions have consequences. A systems approach in business or other types of corporations and organizations therefore requires an extensive, ongoing use of communication networks for constant feedback and adjustment. Without a great deal of shared communication, events and their consequences could spiral out of control. Good management of a system demands that managers have a constant flow of information from all sectors of the organization.

A **systems approach** emphasizes interactions and relationships, not structures, lines of authority, or the psychological well-being of individuals within the system. In a system, all elements must be kept in mind in trying to describe, analyze, or modify any part of the organization. Key places to focus on are where elements of the system connect to each other. If there are problems in the system, those connecting points would be a place to start in looking for solutions to those problems.

You have probably heard of open and closed systems. A closed system is one in which little or no input is allowed from outside the system. An open system is reactive to the environment. It accepts and accounts for input from outside itself and accepts that it, in turn, affects its surroundings. Although a person can pretend that an organization is a closed system, in reality most organizations constantly interact with outside elements and, to one degree or another, must be open to input from areas beyond its control. If you try to imagine a closed system—a space shuttle, for example—you can still find outside elements that may affect its operations, such as changes in sunlight or darkness, possible collisions with particles, or even signals and transmissions from the earth. A *nearly* closed system is possible, and for some purposes you might wish to treat an organization with which you are working as such. However, in reality, all organizations are influenced by, and respond to, elements outside themselves. For that reason, this chapter was introduced with a definition of an open system as being typical of an organization.

Organizational Cultures

Finally, organizations can be looked at from a **cultural perspective.** This trend looks at a system as if it were a society, with norms and roles, a history of heroes and villains, and both expressed and implied values and attitudes. Once established, these norms are generally understood and accepted by individuals in the organization, are often present without being directly spoken of, take time for newcomers to learn, and are slow to change (Putnam and Pacanowsky, 1983).

There are many theories about values and attitudes that help to define any society or culture and that can be easily applied to the study of organizations. You could, for example, take the theory advanced by Schutz that people try to fulfill their needs for affection, inclusion, and control and look to organizations to satisfy those needs. You might also look at Maslow's hierarchy of needs and analyze an organization according to its ability to satisfy an individual's safety, esteem, or self-actualization needs.

Another cultural perspective deals with your view of yourself. Are you

---

TECHNOLOGY IN COMMUNICATION

The E-Mail Revolution

Communication is the key to any social system, and organizations the world over are communicating more and more with such technological advances as voice-mail, electronic mail boxes, fax machines. A few years ago, my department office was one of the first to have a simple answering machine. Now the entire faculty is hooked into e-mail, so a message arrives in the electronic mailbox of the desired person and waits for him or her to retrieve it. The messages can be stored, responded to, passed along, printed, or deleted as desired.

One of the effects of the new e-mail system is to create more rapid responses. Letter or memos that were sent in an envelope through the mail room took two days to deliver, and the messages that were taken by machines or office workers were not always accurate. In addition, it took three parties to respond to the telephone message. Now communication is direct, thus freeing up secretarial time and energy for other tasks.

Furthermore, the use of paper has diminished greatly, and no longer do we hunt for a scrap of paper with someone's name and number. Just check your log, and you have automatic reply capacity along with the time and date the person sent you the message.

With the development of modems for home computers, many organizations are finding that their employees answer mail and conduct work projects from remote locations. Thanks to the Internet and the World Wide Web, you can get and send messages just about anyplace where you can plug a computer into a telephone line.

This technology is not without its shortcomings and can work only if the people with whom you wish to communicate are also plugged into the system (Solomon, 1995). Nevertheless, nearly every organization and the people who work in them are seeing how electronic communication is beginning to affect our organizational lives.

---

self-indulgent or altruistic? Do you think of people as being basically honest and self-motivated, or do you think of humans as being self-centered and lazy by nature? Responses to these questions were the focus of Douglas McGregor's study of company philosophies as embodied by owners' and managers' views of people (McGregor, 1969). Although McGregor felt otherwise, his studies showed that most managers thought about their employees from a pessimistic view of human nature. This pessimistic view has come to be called **Theory X.** An optimistic philosophy about people is called **Theory Y.** Each approach creates a different organizational culture. For example, if managers think that people are basically lazy and need constant supervision, they will, through policies and procedures, establish a climate that might result in their workers' behaving in exactly those ways. Do you recall the notion of self-fulfilling prophecies in Chapter 7? McGregor thought that there might be a link between the way people are treated and the way they behave. So he suggested a positive view that required that managers change their own cultural norms and those of their organizations and that they recognize in workers aspects of self-motivation, a capacity for development and growth, and a willingness and ability to function responsibly. McGregor felt that management must work to create a society within the organization that fosters these values and attitudes and that would include some of the elements suggested by the systems approach: worker participation, attention to the whole person (from a human relations perspective), and the dynamic evolution of the organization from a cultural perspective.

Another communication scholar, Rensis Likert, also studied organizations according to their values and attitudes. He developed a four-part way of analyzing organizations that is similar to McGregor's. Likert's system included the study of leadership, motivation, communication, interaction, decision making, goal setting, control, and performance (Likert, 1961). These aspects of an organization, working together, can also be viewed as places where cultural norms develop. Likert's System 1 is much like McGregor's Theory X, in which a great deal of authority and control is exercised and very little credit is given to the members of the organization for their input. You can imagine a country or society in which the government controls everything, and people lose interest in being self-motivated. The former Soviet Union was thought to be such a country, and indeed its worker productivity was low in comparison to that of other industrialized countries. In our own culture, large numbers of businesses attempt to operate on these principles, and they seem to lack energy and innovation. Likert's System 2 is a little more attentive to workers but is still dominated by a central authority. System 3 moves more toward participation as a cultural norm, and System 4 is about the same as Theory Y, showing great concern for, and involvement of, members of the organization in nearly every aspect of its operation.

Another study of organizations along the lines of cultural norms emerged in the 1980s and is called by its author **Theory Z.** This approach to organizations borrowed heavily from Japanese management practices and is an obvious link of organizations and culture. William Ouchi studied major corporations in Japan and then tried to adapt some of their norms to U.S. businesses. He looked at such factors as lifelong employment, complex evaluation systems, job rotation, slow promotion, and cooperative decision making. Many of these aspects of Theory Z are deeply rooted in Japanese culture.

Some critics of Theory Z contend that the values and attitudes of Japanese culture cannot be transplanted to U.S. organizations and replace U.S. cultural norms. Some areas in which U.S. attitudes are different from Japanese attitudes are a low commitment by employees and management to permanent relationships, a desire to specialize, and the expectation of rapid promotion. Nevertheless, some corporations have attempted to adapt Theory Z practices to their organizations and have met with some success (Ouchi, 1982). This approach operates less in large businesses and industries and more in small, family enterprises in which, for example, "three generations have been serving your dry-cleaning needs." You might also see elements of Theory Z governing clubs and civic or fraternal organizations. If you were a long-term member of an Elks Lodge or a local Friends of the Library, you could establish a long-term relationship, rotate jobs, and experience slow advancement. The famous Rose Parade on New Year's Day in Pasadena, California, is put on by the Tournament of Roses Association, which follows some of the precepts of Theory Z. Members put in years of service doing virtually every job or committee assignment in a slow process of advancement leading eventually to the Queen Selection Committee and perhaps to top leadership posts. Hierarchical churches and even university administrations require similar broad and long-term experience and service of members if they are to be considered for advancement in the hierarchy (Rehder, 1981).

Obviously, a cultural approach to an organization can be complex, but it offers an integrated way of studying all types of organizations, and it helps to account for personal factors, systems elements, and communication behaviors.

ORGANIZATIONAL BEHAVIOR: NORMS AND RULES

From the discussion of an organization as a culture, you can see that the development of norms and rules for behavior is an integral part of any organization. Organizations may have either formal or informal rules and *roles*.

Formal rules are those that are specified, as in a constitution, the bylaws of a club, or a union contract that has been ratified. You may see such rules in printed operating procedures or in employee manuals. You and your roommates might even organize yourselves with a written set of expectations, assignments, and policies. Roles may be specified, such as president, treasurer, social activities coordinator, manager, and so on.

Informal rules are norms of behavior that stem either from the general culture or from patterns of interaction that develop informally within a particular organization. For example, someone in the office may simply take over the job of watering the plants. Someone else may be the one who always breaks the

Employees of any business have both formal and informal communication networks.

> ## *DIVERSITY IN COMMUNICATION*
>
> ### Cultural Patterns in Organizations
>
> **A**s roles develop in an organization, think about the cultural norms from which they have emerged. Is your organization still operating under traditional, gender-based norms by which refreshments are always provided by female members and audiovisual equipment is always set up by males? Are there norms of behavior in the organization that influence the arrival time at meetings or the expectations of an annual party? Do members of ethnic minority groups become leaders? Do conversations change when a minority group member joins in—that is, do people stop telling jokes that feature minorities? Is it acceptable to make sexist or racist comments or tell demeaning stories in the organization's culture, or does the culture, as expressed by the members and trend setters, discourage and provide negative reinforcement for such behavior? As the type of people who assume leadership positions increasingly diversifies in our society, new styles of communication may emerge. For example, cooperative work groups are often the norm in Asian, Latino, and African American cultures in general and among women in particular (Tannen, 1994). With a change from a management corps that is almost exclusively dominated by Anglo men to one that includes diversity, styles of communication may also change and, along with them, the cultural patterns of the organization.

tension at meetings with a funny remark. You might find yourself in the role of mediator between two of your roommates, or you might be one to suggest a new place for lunch at work.

As you go further into the study of organizational communication, you will see that these behaviors are different in different settings but that each organization operates with both formal and informal rules and norms.

UPWARD AND DOWNWARD DISTORTIONS

As communication travels around an organization, it does not remain unaffected by its journey. Some of the interesting discoveries that researchers have made deal with the **upward and downward distortions** of information that seem to occur almost automatically in any large organization.

When messages travel from people near the bottom of a hierarchy toward the top, a censoring and filtering process seems to occur (Haney, 1962). Since no one wants to be the bearer of bad news to powerful people, there is a tendency to stress only the positive side of any information that travels upward through different levels in an organization. What might start out as a complaint from the workers on a loading dock about unsafe and potentially dangerous working conditions is relayed to their supervisor as follows: "While things generally are going OK, the guys on the dock are unhappy about the unsafe condition of the ramps." The manager, when asking the supervisor how things are going on the loading dock, might hear this statement: "Things are generally good—lots of output. But they're working on fixing the ramps to make things even better!" When the vice-president asks the manager about things in that section of the company, that person is told, "The loading dock is doing fine, with a minor repair nearly complete on the ramps." The president is likely to get the following report: "There are new goals and levels of achievement, and production and plant improvements coming from the loading-dock crew." Upward distortion abstracts and summarizes information and typically retains positive messages while softening or eliminating negative ones. Details are omitted, and others are added. Messages are simplified, and perhaps reorganized into a positive-sounding package (Krivonos, 1976).

Downward communication includes messages about goals, company policies, announcements, and instructions, and it also creates the tone or climate of an organization. These messages are subject to distortion for many of the same reasons that upward communication is. There is so much information to disseminate in an organization that ideas and instructions must be abstracted and condensed. In this process, details are left out, and an opportunity for filling in the blanks occurs. A short message from the president may be discussed at length, thought about, and interpreted from dozens of perspectives by people on the receiving end of that information (Tomkins, 1984). If the workers trust their supervisors and managers, the information is less likely to be perceived in a distorted way.

Of course, there is always the danger of too much information flowing down, creating an overload situation in which virtually everything is ignored. In a recent faculty election, the two major competing groups issued a series of statements and counterstatements that they duplicated on paper of various colors and placed in each of the 958 faculty members' mailboxes. It started with one group stating a position on a Monday and a response from the other arriving by Thursday. There was a reaction on the following Monday, a rebuttal on Wednesday, and a retort on Thursday. It seemed as though bulletins were arriving in faculty mailboxes by the hour. Some faculty members would pull out several bulletins at a time, not having had the chance to read even one of them before the next arrived, hot off the press. By the final days of the campaign, virtually everyone was simply pulling the materials out of their boxes and dropping them into the trash. One reaction to message overload is to ignore all messages. So how do organizations cope with all their information and with the normal distortion of messages? One way is to establish correction points throughout the system to respond and adjust to the flow of information. The people who provide such correction points are called *gatekeepers* and *facilitators*. The personnel department at a company often serves as a gatekeeper.

GATEKEEPERS AND FACILITATORS

Just as the names suggest, **gatekeepers** and **facilitators** deal with the flow of information in a system. If a great deal of information is coming in, someone in the organization may act to limit the amount coming to you at any one time. Typically, a secretary will perform this function by screening calls, visitors, and messages. Messages must then get past the "gate" to reach their intended destination. Any person who is in a position to control the flow of information from one place to another is acting as a gatekeeper. As messages flow down, for example, a supervisor may call a meeting or issue a bulletin or a notice that summarizes the proceedings of a managers' meeting. Some information will be allowed to pass through this gate while other items will not. An effective gatekeeper applies judgment in reviewing information and in letting appropriate, important, or necessary information through while using those same criteria to screen out or delay messages that are not vital or timely. One approach to the study of organizations is to analyze its flow of information to look for stoppages, bottlenecks, or breakdowns. Once identified, these problem points can be examined in terms of gatekeeper behavior.

In contrast to the gatekeeper, who screens out or slows down the information flow, a facilitator helps messages to move along in the system. Since feedback is vital to the long-term health of an organization, facilitators help to get feedback by making sure that important information arrives at its appropriate destination. A union steward, for example, may have a regular meeting with a manager who is two or three levels above the workers. The steward thus provides a direct feedback link from the workers to the manager that bypasses several gatekeepers and avoids several possible distortions. The steward can then carry the following message: "The ramps are a hazard and unsafe and must be replaced on the loading dock immediately." This message may be vital to the company. It may help to avoid injury to workers and maintain a constant and safe output from the loading dock. Facilitators provide an important balance to gatekeepers as long as they use the same criteria that gatekeepers do of selecting appropriate and timely information to move along through the system.

Facilitators help to regulate the flow of information in an organization.

Gatekeepers screen messages to prevent information overload.

Both gatekeepers and facilitators are important if they function properly, but both can hurt an organization if they do not. For example, the gatekeeper who allows virtually everything to go through will contribute to overload and will obscure important information by trivial messages. At the other extreme is the gatekeeper who screens out vital information or keeps important details out of circulation, hampering decision making. The facilitator who passes along every piece of gossip or makes major issues out of minor problems also overloads the system and runs the risk of finally being ignored. Facilitators, too, must guard against failure to pass on or push for information that is crucial to the well-being of the system.

As you can see, gatekeepers and facilitators serve twin functions—two sides of the same coin—and they operate in any large system. There may be formal mechanisms, such as grievance representatives or receptionists, or there may be informal roles that develop to provide these functions. In any case, some sort of control over the flow of information in an organization is vital and necessary. These roles, and the people who fill them, are at the heart of any organizational system.

A third direction in which messages travel is sideways. This type of communication is called *horizontal,* and it can include everything from the formal instruction on new procedures that one office worker gives another to the information you get from other students about a teacher they have had and that you are about to have. Horizontal, or lateral, communication is subject to all the problems of both upward and downward distortion because messages are always altered as they travel from source to source. In a common party game or classroom illustration, many people sit in a large circle. A message is then given to one person, who whispers it to the next, and so on around the circle, until the last person is asked to write out the message. The final message is then compared with the original, to which inevitable changes have been made, sometimes creating a humorous result. The information that travels this way may be gossip, rumor, or important details about someone or something, or it may be social or career oriented. Goldhaber reports that horizontal messages usually involve problem solving, coordination, conflict resolution, and rumors (Goldhaber, 1990).

IMPROVING COMPETENCY

Breaking the Rumor Chain

Identify the rumor paths in a group, club, or organization in which you are involved. Spicy tales can be the stuff of coffee break conversation, late-night roommate discussions, or idle office chatter. Resist the temptation to become part of the rumor chain, and see whether by refusing to pass rumors along, you can break the chain. You might simply ask the sender of the message about its source and provide an important feedback link to check out the information. You may find that spreading this type of information gives the people who do it a sense of power and control. Indeed, a facilitator is an important person, but perhaps those who score high on Schutz's measurement of need for control are not the best ones to be in charge of facilitating messages.

PERSONAL, SMALL-GROUP, AND PUBLIC CAREERS

How you fit, or do not fit, into a particular organization will influence how satisfied you are with a career choice. If you like working by yourself, you are not necessarily excluded from working for a large company. There are several careers that will enable you to work in a small office and have limited interactions with others. If you are gregarious and like crowds, even a small company can provide that setting if you are in the right role and at the center of every interaction. You can combine your knowledge about yourself and your personal communication preferences with some understanding of how organizations work to make more informed choices about your career.

APPLYING INTERVIEWING SKILLS

In Chapter 9, you read about some different types of interviews, including the job interview. In addition to the advice and information presented in that chapter, think now about the kinds of information you can seek about an organization during an interview. Given your knowledge about Theory X and Theory Y and your own preferences for a type of organizational culture, you can be on the lookout for information about decision making, leadership, worker involvement, and other distinguishing marks of one type of organization or another. Is a Theory Z company your ideal career setting? Then look for information about average length of employment and opportunities for job rotation. Company stock plans, matching investing programs, or profit-sharing systems that indicate an expectation of a long-term relationship may help you decide to apply to one type of company over another.

If you want to communicate to the interviewer that you are someone who would fit into their organization, think about the message style you use and the appropriateness of the impression you will leave at the end of your interview.

IMPROVING CAREER COMMUNICATION SKILLS

As you think about the topic of organizational communication, you can apply your knowledge of communication on the job and in a college setting. Your repertoire of choices has expanded simply by knowing that managements operate with different styles. Once you can identify a style, you will be able to analyze possible reactions and responses appropriate to that style. You can explain why some organizations are more satisfying to your friends than they are to you. Your expanded knowledge will help you to view your social organizations, associations, and career settings with new perspectives and insights.

Once you have increased your base of understanding, you can then select a communicator style to help you operate better within a given type of organization. Are you in a position to be a gatekeeper or facilitator? Can you use appropriate channels for feedback? Do you want to join an association that offers rapid advancement on a narrow career track, or do you wish to seek out a company with long-term commitments and an opportunity to change jobs and assignments to learn the business? Selection from among these options should be guided by criteria that you have developed from a personal inventory of your strengths, interests, and needs.

Implementing your choices may not always be easy. An organization is a complex network of interdependent relationships, and influencing that network can be a difficult task, For example, you may decide that Company X is just exactly the place where you wish to build your career, but out of four dozen applicants, someone else is selected. You were ready to implement your selection, but the organization did not cooperate. Or you may have an excellent suggestion based on your analysis of a need that your organization has, yet the decision makers fail to adopt it. What you can do is remember the principles you have learned here about organizations and implement as many as you can in your career and personal activities. For example, one of the reasons you are in college is so that you will become an influential person in your community and career. You will not be a line worker in a production facility, but a supervisor, manager, division head, or president. When you arrive at those positions, think about implementing the ideas that you discovered in organizational communication classes and which are appropriate to your career circumstances. Even if you are just the acting assistant night manager of a burger palace, think about how the employees you supervise for three hours a night are motivated, the style or culture of the establishment, and your own personal philosophy of management.

You will be using feedback as part of your evaluation of the choices you make. Feedback about your own performance as a supervisor or manager may be difficult to accept, especially if it is not flattering. It is vital, however, to incorporate feedback into your sense of competence in organizational communication. Be sensitive to subtle signals from others about your style or your impact. Are anonymous suggestions sometimes posted on your telephone? Do others offer ideas that are different from your own? If so, do you engage in active listening to be open and honestly attentive to them? This short chapter on organizational communication can only point out areas of interest or concern. The feedback that you would need to develop your competency in this area could come only from much more extensive study and practice. Take advantage of additional opportunities to acquire more information about organizational communication, and you will greatly increase your repertoire.

SUMMARY

If, as Levinson claims, we spend 90 percent of our time in some sort of organization, the materials in this chapter are important to you for every waking day. Think about organizations as systems that are open to influence and use communication to create a network of interdependencies. As you recall the four approaches to studying organizations—classical, human relations, systems, and culture—think about the usefulness of each approach, and try to apply them to some of your organizations. As you think about styles, cultures, and values, recall some of the principles of small-group communication, especially the ideas concerning leadership. Which styles and types work best in which environments?

Finally, the knowledge that you have gained from this chapter on organizational communication can increase your communication competencies in general by expanding your knowledge base and giving you criteria for selecting among alternatives in organizational communication. You can put those criteria into practice now or as you increase your influence in an organization. Finally, you can respond to feedback, which then helps you to evaluate your choices. As you pursue greater knowledge in this field, the basic principles outlined here will be augmented by refinements and applications showing how complex and important organizational communication is to everyday life.

KEY TERMS

organizational communication, *p. 332*
classical approach, *p. 332*
human relations approach, *p. 333*
systems approach, *p. 336*
cultural perspective, *p. 337*
Theory X, *p. 337*
Theory Y, *p. 337*

Theory Z, *p. 338*
formal rules, *p. 339*
informal rules, *p. 339*
upward and downward distortions, *p. 340*
gatekeepers, *p. 341*
facilitators, *p. 341*

EXERCISES

1. Obtain an organizational chart for your school. Analyze it according to the four approaches defined here. Which best describes the approaches used by your campus? Compare your notes with those of a small group from class to find whether they agree or disagree with your categorization. Be prepared to explain your choices.

2. Keep track of your upward and downward messages for a few days. Do you edit or summarize messages in accordance with the tendency to distort mentioned in this chapter?

3. Identify five key people at work, in a club to which you belong, or at school, and describe their roles in terms of gatekeeping or facilitating a flow of information. Are they effective in their roles? In other words, do they function to assist the organization reach its full potential? What could they do to improve their role behavior?

4. If you had to describe an organization that you know well, such as your college or work place, which style of management—Theory X, Y, or Z—would describe the organization most accurately?

Now find an organization that has a different style, and compare the two. What accounts for the differences between them?

5. Visit a career center, and speak with a counselor about your communication style and possible career options. If the center has some standardized tests related to job satisfaction and personality, arrange to take one of them. What did you discover about your communication style and the organizational culture in which you would most like to work?

REFERENCES

Goldhaber, G. *Organizational Communication.* 5th ed. Dubuque: Wm. C. Brown, 1990.

Groves, Martha. "Opening the Books." *Los Angeles Times* 29 Oct. 1995: D1.

Haney, William. "Serial Communication of Information in Organizations." *Concepts and Issues in Administrative Behavior.* Ed. Sidney Mailick and Edward H. Van Ness. New York: Prentice-Hall, 1962.

Krivonos, Paul. "Distortion of Subordinate to Superior Communication." International Communication Association Meeting. Portland, Oregon. 1976.

Levinson, Harry. "Asinine Attitudes toward Motivation." *Harvard Business Review* 51 (1973), 70–76.

Likert, Rensis. *New Patterns of Management.* New York: McGraw-Hill, 1961.

McGregor, Douglas. "The Human Side of Enterprise." *Human Relations and Organizational Behavior.* Eds. K. Davis and W. Scott. New York: McGraw-Hill, 1969.

Ouchi, W. *Theory Z.* New York: Avon Books, 1982.

Putnam, L., and M. Pacanowsky. *Communication and Organizations: An Interactive Approach.* Newbury Park: Sage, 1983.

Rehder, R. "What American and Japanese Managers Are Learning from Each Other." *Business Horizons* (April 1981).

Roethlisberger, F. J., and W. J. Dickson. *Management and the Worker.* Cambridge: Harvard University Press, 1939.

Solomon, Michael D. "E-Mail Access May Not Live Up to Expectations." *Los Angeles Times* 29 Oct. 1995: D13.

Tannen, D. *Talking from 9 to 5.* New York: Morrow, 1994.

Tomkins, P. K. "The Functions of Human Communication in Organizations." *Handbook of Rhetorical and Communication Theory.* Ed. Carrol Arnold and John Bowers. Boston: Allyn and Bacon, 1984.

von Bertalanffy, Ludwig. "General Systems Theory." *General Systems* 1 (1956).

von Bertalanffy, L. "General Systems Theory." *General Systems* 7 (1962).

Family, Community, and Classroom Communication

After reading this chapter, you should be able to:

- See how communication develops between parents and children.
- Understand the impact of the classroom on the development of communication competency.
- Describe communication's role in creating communities.
- Feel responsible to participate actively in our democracy.
- Work at improving community, classroom, and family competencies.

he ability to communicate effectively in a variety of settings is essential to leading a productive life. This chapter explores three vital areas of communication interaction beyond the school and work settings. The first two sections discuss some of the issues related to communication and family, such as how we learn to communicate as children, and some of the interactions we have in home and school settings. The third section examines your role as a communicator in your community and outlines how you can be a more effective participant in civic life. Since freedom of communication is a defining characteristic of a free people, you will acquire some insights into helping democracy work in your community. Our ability to improve each of these areas is part of the continuing focus on expanding communication competencies. Let us begin with our original small group: the family.

COMMUNICATING IN THE FAMILY

What are the unique features of family communication that make it valuable to study? Part of the answer to that question is found in the definition of family communication. Scholars identify several key components: **"Family communication** is the interaction developed over time by a group of related people who share common living space" (Pearson, 1989). Although the traditional family consisted of a father, mother, and their children, this definition goes beyond that pattern to encompass the variety of family situations found today.

Looking more closely at our definition of family communication, we find that *interaction* means the exchange of verbal and nonverbal messages and comes directly from the definition of communication presented in Chapter 2. The concept that a family's communication interaction *develops* is also significant in that patterns of interaction are initiated, expand, change, grow, and sometimes disintegrate *over time*. Think about your communication with your parents, brothers, sisters, or, if applicable, your own children. When a baby is born, most of the messages are directed at the baby. As the baby matures, she or he begins to send more messages, and these messages become more complex. There may be a time when the messages become strident, such as in early adolescence, as the child creates distance and distinctiveness from his or her parents. There may be a warming and reconciliation as the roles of parent and child become more equalized as the child becomes an adult. These changes require time, and a group living together over time will go through a variety of changes in communication interactions. Being *related* can mean being related biologically; but any long-term relationship certainly qualifies, including those involving adopted children, blended families, communal groups, and extended families. A family may be related by commitment, economic need, living quarters, interdependence, biology, marriage, or a combination of these factors.

Families are an interpersonal system (Galvin and Brommel, 1996) that links members such that what happens to one member affects the entire system. For example, if Maria needs money to help pay her tuition, the rest of the family feels responsible for helping to meet that need, and some members may attempt to increase their wage earning to assist her or may reduce some of their expenditures. A need in one part of the family creates a systemic response from the rest

IMPROVING COMPETENCY

Family Roles and Communication

Next time you are at a family gathering, notice the communication patterns of adult children and their parents. Some people in their thirties and forties become childlike when they are with their parents. Others have established more adult relationships with their parents. Still others, whose parents may be very old or incapacitated, have reversed the roles and are now the "parents," taking care of aging "children." I have a friend who is in her early fifties and still hides from her mother the fact that she smokes. Her mother is seventy-five years old.

of the family. Families function as an open system, meaning that they are subject to events from the outside, and these events have an effect on the whole system. Remember a time when the primary caregiver in your family became ill. That person's functions needed to be taken over by someone else or were left undone during the period of illness. Many plots of novels, movies, and television programs are based on this scenario—people trying to do jobs they are unfamiliar with and failing or succeeding—with comedic or dramatic results.

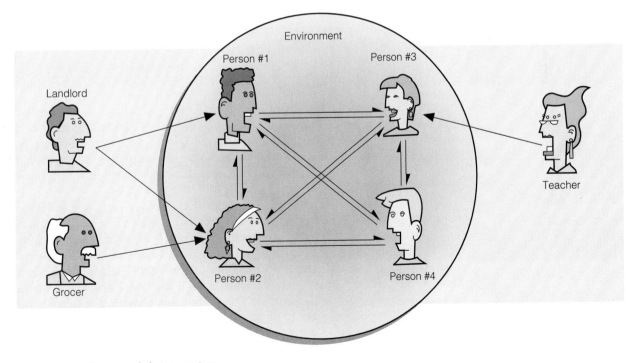

Many factors affect our daily interactions.

> ## DIVERSITY IN COMMUNICATION
>
> ### Gender Issues
>
> Television and movies have often relied on gender roles to create humor. Can you picture scenes of the helpless dad trying to figure out how to run the washing machine or the heroic mom bringing in the harvest? These stereotypes are the subject of many tellings and retellings in our media. They emphasize (in addition to gender-role stereotyping) the systemic nature of a family. Be on the lookout for such story lines as you watch sitcoms or the latest movie. Television series such as *Roseanne*, *NYPD Blue*, *Home Improvement*, *Married with Children*, *Family Matters*, and even *The Simpsons* use gender roles and systemic interaction to create their plots. See how the *system* of a family is often portrayed and taken for granted.

PARENTS AND CHILDREN

The most influential sources for communication development in any human are the primary caregivers, usually the parents. In the broadest sense, parenting and caregiving include the traditional notions of providing food, shelter, and comfort. The responsible parent provides developmental assistance as well, including education, socialization, emotional support, and communication. Once we have a definition of family communication, it becomes important to see how it develops in a family setting. The first step is to look at the acquisition of communication skills by young children.

How Children Acquire Language

You can examine the collection of sounds made by a babbling infant, the first recognizable word, the combining of several words, and the development of a larger vocabulary. You can also study nonverbal factors, which influence meaning, the formation of longer, complete sentences, the application of syntactic rules, and the lifelong process of adding vocabulary and developing a sophisticated use of language.

The field of psycholinguistics examines these facets of language development, and scholars in the field have concluded that children in all cultures pass through the same stages of development (McNeil, 1970). Children learn by imitating the sounds, speech patterns, and nonverbal behaviors of those around them. It is no more difficult for a Thai child to learn the Thai language, for a Xhosa child to learn Xhosa, or for an Uzbeki child to learn Uzbeki than it was for you to learn your native language. The language you speak, the culture you have, the values you hold are all products of your birth circumstances. Change those circumstances, and you change those products. Humans are born with the ability to make the sounds of any language; the clicks and glides of another language are not any more difficult for a child to make than are the sounds that you make (Hopper and Naremore, 1978). What happens very early is that cer-

Each culture sustains itself by communicating its values and history to its children.

tain sounds are reinforced by parents, whereas other sounds are not part of the environment and simply get lost as a child develops. Other people's patterns make just as much sense to them as yours do to you.

How Children Acquire Meaning

It may be possible to separate the accumulation of sounds from the understanding of meanings attached to those sounds, but the easiest way to deal with meaning is as it accompanies sounds, and later, writing. Research shows that we learn to listen, then to speak, then to write. These processes are not completed in childhood and may be refined over a lifetime. When trying to understand the process of meaning, it is helpful to think of the child who is exposed to a family pet and learns to associate the sound "doggie" with the dog. A transfer occurs when a cat comes into view and the child makes the sound "doggie." The child recognizes some of the important characteristics that these animals have in common and uses the same sound to describe the cat. However, as the child's discerning ability improves, he or she learns to call a variety of similar animals by their own sounds, or names. This discriminating ability develops along with the increased ability to attach specific meanings to the words. Remember Chapter 6, in which you read about the semantic development process. Only through repeated exposure to a variety of stimulations can a child develop the richness of meanings needed to function well in a social setting. The family is the setting that provides most of the early stimulation that is the basis for competent communication development.

Reading Aloud to Children.   One of the best ways to provide children with a rich and stimulating communication experience is through reading stories aloud. Anyone who has been around children has heard the request for a story at bedtime, naptime, or quiet time. In addition to providing entertainment, reading stories, such as fairy tales, can teach children about our culture and the common questions we all face in life. In his award-winning book *The Uses of Enchantment,* psychologist Bruno Bettelheim contended, "Today, as in times past, the most important and also the most difficult task in raising a child is helping him to find meaning in life" (Bettelheim, 1977). Bettelheim believed that most children's literature has been made so "safe"—by excluding any mention of death or grave calamity—that it merely entertains and fails to instruct or engage the imagination in a deep and meaningful way.

On the other hand, the story must capture the attention of children so that the message can be absorbed. As writer Margaret Atwood put it, "The aim of the tale may well be able to instruct, but if it does not also delight it will play to empty houses" (Atwood, 1995).

Classical European fairy tales often begin with the death of a parent or a disaster that forces a person to make a choice when confronting the challenges of life. Think of Cinderella or Snow White as examples. The sanitized versions of these stories are ultimately boring because they do not relate to a young person's needs to understand and deal with life's meaning. Bettelheim suggests that parents select stories that transmit important cultural values and help children to recognize and deal with common fears.

Reading stories *aloud* creates a special imaginative moment for both the reader and the listener. Reading aloud also creates a vocal bond between the reader and the listener. By emphasizing the vocal variety that is called for in a story with multiple characters, parents can help their children pay attention to the richness that paralinguistic factors bring to communication. Through reading aloud, you can enrich your children's vocabulary and thus increase their listening comprehension. Reading aloud to children tells them that reading books is important to your family. It is not necessary to be a great actor to be a good storyteller (Bauer, 1977). You need to read with enthusiasm and take delight in sharing literature with children. Even a small amount of practice can yield big rewards in terms of your ability to enjoy and convey a story.

Grandparents are a gift; great-grandparents are a treasure. How so? Simply by reading aloud.

Affecting Self-Concept through Communication.   Storytelling can help children to imagine places and events and help them to gain perspective on their own lives. In addition to the information on family communication discussed in Chapter 7, there are patterns of communication that help or hinder a child's ability to develop a healthy self-concept. Because the family is a system whose members affect all parts of the system, you need to see how each child can affect the overall pattern. There may be expectations, rules, or patterns to a family system that create expectations for a child. The messages that are sent can take the form of "scripts" that each member learns to recognize and play out (James and Jongeward, 1973). Thus when a family sends a message to its children that they are expected to be musical, athletic, or tough, the children may assume that role as part of their self-concept. Especially important are messages about sex roles and attitudes toward food, independence, obedience, and responsibilities. One recent, unhappy example that made news in *People* magazine described how a man from a culture with strict codes regarding obedience became so distraught about his teenage daughter's behavior—talking back, hanging out at the mall with boys and girls—that he killed her. Both the father and the daughter had strong self-concepts. The father acted on his script because the daughter was trying to break away from hers.

We all receive messages based on our families' expectations of our futures. These may range from "Oh, you'll probably be a lawyer" to "Well, girls can't be lawyers, so you'll probably be a secretary until you get married." At early ages, these messages become powerful predictors of how we will behave. Most of us pass along these messages thoughtlessly; that is, we do not examine the assumptions or implications of our automatic messages, we simply pass them along. Is it true that you are destined to become your parents? In many ways, yes. Such a destiny may be fine if you are content with the kind of parenting you received. If you are not, then you need to learn new patterns of behavior so that you first change your own script, then change the one you pass on to your own children. For example, you can create alternative messages, such as "take your daughter to work" days, which help to expand the repertoire of goals, models, and skills for girls who might otherwise feel limited. An expansion of the repertoire is the first step to expanding communication competency.

 ## CLASSROOM COMMUNICATION

The second most important factor in developing communication comes when the child leaves home to attend school. Because we spend six to eight hours a day for nine or ten months a year for twelve to sixteen (or more) years in school, the classroom can become a source of important communication lessons, beyond the subjects taught. As with a family, the classroom can be viewed as a system. Researchers conclude (Clark et al., 1971):

> The classroom must be managed as a complex, ever-changing communication system composed of a multiple of human variables; and these human variables must determine how communication skills can be employed for the clearest, most appropriate communication in a given situation, in class and out. (p. 3)

> ## THE STORY OF COMMUNICATION
>
> ### Family Communication Patterns
>
> One of the great sports broadcasters of our time is Vin Scully. His ease and continuity keep listeners informed and entertained. I once met Scully at an airport, where we stood next to each other while boarding an airplane, and I mentioned how impressed I was by his on-air talent. He replied, "Well, we Irish have always been great storytellers!" It is true that Irish families have a reputation for telling stories, often with several generations sitting around the table. It also may be true that his family, based on their cultural pattern, expected him to be good at telling stories, and like many of us, he lived up to the expectation. To improve your own communication competency, try keeping track of the expectations you received from your family—going to college, getting married, and becoming a professional, are common ones for students in college, but there are many others. Competency begins with self-knowledge.

Since the classroom is a system, it can be approached with all the communication variables that we find in other communication settings. You can examine **classroom communication**—listening, critical thinking, and interpersonal skills, as well as self-concept, small groups, public speaking, and oral reading. Some classrooms have dimensions of organizational communication, and some include work in media and culture as part of their activities (Cooper, 1994). Rather than tackle the entire field, we will focus on the aspects of communication between teachers and pupils that are unique to the classroom.

Between Teachers and Pupils. The most important figure in the classroom is obviously the teacher, owing to the power and authority of the position. This power is useful as long as the students respond to it and the teacher avoids abusing it (McCroskey, 1992). A great deal of research has been done on how teacher variables influence the communication climate of the classroom. For example, if the teacher sets a positive tone, respects the children, and treats them with dignity and tolerance, then the positive attitude becomes part of the pupils' attitude (Cooper and Galvin, 1983). A positive attitude then leaves the room free of barriers to good communication and open to more learning. Behaviors, especially nonverbal communication, that promote closeness help to lower barriers and increase the positive evaluation students give their teachers. The positive evaluation seems to occur at all levels of education and across cultures (McCroskey et al., 1995).

As one researcher pointed out, "Perhaps the single most important step that teachers can take in the classroom is to provide an educational atmosphere of success rather than failure" (Civikly, 1982). A quick example illustrates the effect that teachers have on allowing their students to learn. Consider **wait time**—when a teacher asks a question and waits for a response. How long should a teacher wait for an answer? Do you know that adding a second or two to that time will make an important difference in the learning? In general, teachers wait no more than *one second* for a student's response. Once they get an answer, they wait again, barely *one second* before they start talking (Cooper 1994). Another study reveals that by increasing the average wait time, teachers see improvement in students' use of language and logic, as well as in their attitudes and expectations (Rowe, 1986). When a teacher waits just two or three seconds more, there are more student responses, more questions, more speculation and creative thinking, a greater number of different students getting involved, increased student confidence and achievement, and fewer disciplinary problems. While all students experience these benefits, minority children in particular seem to profit from those few seconds of increased wait time. Teachers find that they increase the intellectual level of their own questions and are better organized when they extend the wait time. Silence may be one of the most overlooked communication strategies for increasing classroom learning.

Between Parents and Teachers.   Perhaps one of the most difficult events in a child's life is when she or he brings a note home from the teacher or when the parent is asked to come in for a conference. Some parents may have had their own unpleasant experiences in school, and they may communicate this tension

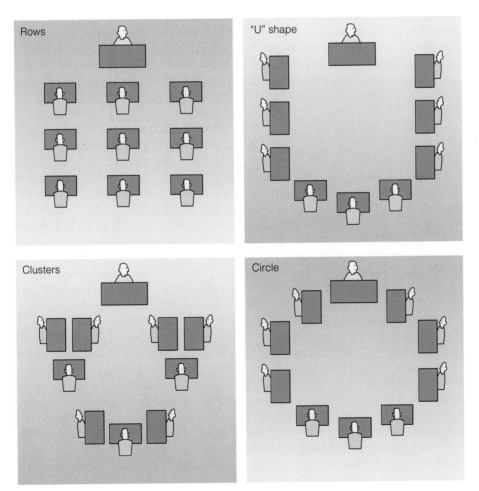

The way a classroom is arranged can affect interaction patterns and communicates different expectations for communication.

CRITICAL THINKING IN COMMUNICATION

Sexism toward Students

A current study by the American Association of University Women confirms that teachers, both male and female, give more time and attention to boys in the classroom than to girls. Teachers wait longer for boys to answer questions. Minority girls seem to be hurt the most, since they typically initiate more interaction with the teacher and yet receive the least amount of attention (Merl, 1992). This teacher attention is a forceful element in the development of critical-thinking skills as well as a positive self-concept. For example, increasing the time a teacher waits for a student's answer results in increased sophistication and complexity of those answers. Critical-thinking skills can be enhanced through positive teacher–student interaction. Even the simple acts of calling on all students who volunteer and increasing wait time by a fraction of a minute develop these skills.

to their children. Others may not have much education, so they may feel intimidated by speaking to the teacher. Still other parents may be so well-educated that they believe that they are more knowledgeable than the teacher and so have little to gain from a conference. All of these attitudes point to potential problems in **parent–teacher communication,** where family communication patterns meet school patterns. Each party in the conversation needs to be aware of the other's circumstances to foster an optimal situation.

For example, parents need to be aware of their children's activities and accomplishments in school. If they visit during open house events and get to know teachers on a regular basis, parents will not find a teacher conference or letter home threatening. However, in many single-parent or blended families and those in which both parents work full-time outside the home, it may be extremely difficult for parents to create this connection to their children's schools. Nevertheless, any opportunity to visit the school, such as athletic events or school programs, can provide that link between parents and teachers that makes the interactions go more smoothly.

Teachers can create a positive communication climate if they know something about the child's home situation before sending a note home or requesting a conference. Does the child have any special circumstances, such as a single-parent situation or a recently blended family? What languages are spoken at home? Which parent is most likely to be contacted? Are there health or financial considerations that affect the child at school? If you were the teacher, you could use your knowledge of systems: You know that an event in one part of the system is likely to affect the rest of the parts. Try to discover what is going on in the system. Then use your communication skills to build a positive atmosphere, listen carefully, and respond completely. If you avoid the traps of abstract language or ambiguity that may result from using "edtalk," you should be able to create clear communication with any teacher.

Both parents and teachers can include active storytelling in the daily or weekly routines. One interesting way to include oral communication is by having students investigate the life stories of others, perhaps an older relative or neighbor. By interviewing others, recreating their stories, and present these to the class, students can improve their interpersonal skills, increase their understanding of cultures, and gain knowledge and skill in oral performance (Stucky, 1995).

With the increased popularity of international student exchanges at all levels of education, some attention needs to be given to the student–student interaction and the cultural varieties that are at work in that exchange. In higher education, for example, nearly half a million international students study annually in the United States. These students report that the single most important element in their development of competency to communicate and to adjust is their ability to talk with U.S. students (Zimmermann, 1995). Students talking to other students can develop a positive communication climate if they are willing to engage each other in conversation and if they can demonstrate some skill and sensitivity to intercultural communication. Many of these skills are discussed in Chapter 19 in the section about intercultural communication.

Improving Adult–Child Communication Competency.   The four basic communication elements also apply to adult–child communication: Increase your repertoire of communication elements, select from that enlarged pool of choices, put your choice into action, and then review the results. You can enlarge your options by learning how children acquire their communication skills and how you can help them to enhance those skills. You can increase your communication with children to include everything from games, discussions, and play to reading aloud from children's literature. You can examine your own family patterns and think how they influence you. Evaluate the patterns you wish to keep and those you wish to modify. To implement any new skills may be difficult. Your communication patterns are deeply connected to your sense of self, family, culture, and perhaps religion. Seeing them as choices is very difficult for most of us because we take them to be the "natural" or "right" way to do things. Feedback is your most useful tool, allowing you to continually evaluate the effectiveness of the choices you make in your behaviors.

COMMUNICATING IN THE COMMUNITY

A community is composed of many groups, including the family and the school. In Chapter 1, the insight that communication builds a community was traced from earliest days to modern times. In contemporary society, one of the disturbing trends is that fewer people are participating in community life. Voter participation is down, attendance at civic meetings is off, and leadership in organizations such as the Girl Scouts is suffering because of parent apathy. Many people cite increased public awareness of wrongdoing on the part of officeholders from the President down to local police officers as one reason for public withdrawal from participation. Others cite the economic pressures of career building, frequent moves to new communities, and enhancement of personal financial prospects as reasons why fewer young people are participating in civic affairs. Whatever the reasons, the loss of our national vitality becomes evident as fewer people—those who exert the greatest pressure—wind up having more influence. It is interesting to note that Ronald Reagan won the presidency with support from about 26 percent of the eligible voters, George Bush became President in 1988 by garnering about 27 percent, and Bill Clinton won in 1992 with about 24 percent. The largest number, about 50 percent, did not vote at all. Clearly, the claim that "majority rules" in this country is a myth.

Participation Means Communication

Your communication skills will be useful to you and your family. But those same skills can be used by someone in a complete dictatorship. What makes you different from the enslaved population of some despotic regime? You have the opportunity to use your communication skills in the public arena to help decide how to run your country.

As you participate in civic life, you will find many opportunities to practice **community communication.** You may be at a public event, perhaps a school board meeting or a local service club. If a new subdivision is planned for the hillside above your home, you may find yourself at the local planning commission or at a city council meeting. In each of these settings, you carry with you certain responsibilities as a free citizen.

Responsibilities as a Listener. In good listening, you must give the sender of any message your attention. In the section on ethics, you learned how the value of information must be heard to be judged. You need to pay attention to discover and evaluate the ideas being presented. But paying attention is only the first step. You must then follow through with the evaluation. The discussion on ethics stressed tolerance for the ideas and opinions of others. That tolerance is still important, but the effective participant will *accept* only ideas that stand up to close evaluation and judgment. Applying the elements of critical thinking can help you to review information and determine what value it has for you as a consumer of information.

Responsibilities as a Speaker. By attending college and taking courses such as this one, you join a group of people with intelligence, education, and communication skills. When you attend a public meeting and have an opinion to express, you should feel comfortable participating. There are many in the audience who would speak out if they knew how, but they are inhibited by their lack of training. Others may speak, but they are unable to focus an idea or express their point clearly. You can approach the situation like any other speech: Think of your thesis, select an organizational pattern, and pick some information to use as supporting material. You may wish to jot down a quick outline and then apply your presentation skills so that your idea is clear and compelling. Remember to speak up, but only when you have something worthwhile to say. That is how responsible communication works in a democracy.

Clubs, Organizations, and Activities. One of the benefits of living in a free society is that you may associate with any group or organization. As a group, you do not need anyone's permission to conduct activities. There are social clubs, service clubs, sports clubs, religious clubs, political clubs, garden clubs, cooking clubs, and culture clubs. These groups are the networks that help us to maintain a sense of connectedness to society. These groups also keep us informed. Ideas can be tried out, and sometimes groups can exert pressure on government. For example, a civic beautification club lobbied the city government to install more trash receptacles around town and even raised money to help buy them. They also lobbied to plant more trees and flowers on public property. In another case, the service clubs got the city to close off the main street for a day to hold a community fair. In addition to their activities, clubs provide a chance to meet people. As was mentioned earlier, some people lack confidence in our institutions. One reason is that people move a great deal more these days than people did in previous generations. Clubs and community organizations give people a way to establish connections in new locations, and many groups have branches all over the country. If you move to a new area, you will have a ready-made group to help you feel acquainted with your new surroundings. By using your communication skills, you can become an active participant in and valuable member of your community.

DEMOCRACY COMMUNICATES

The hallmark of a free country is lots of communication. Every community needs radio and television stations, newspapers, and public meetings to ensure that ideas are not the monopoly of a few, vested interests. A recent trend that is a cause of great concern is that more and more outlets of communication in the United States are controlled by fewer and fewer people. (Mass media are examined in greater detail in the next chapter.) Press conferences, interviews, public appearances, letters to the editor, movies, and television, are all part of the process of **democratic communication.** Even if some of the communication is not to your liking, at least the ideas can be examined and evaluated openly and can be rejected if they are found lacking in important qualities. In a closed society, you never know what ideas are possible because they are stopped before they are ever heard.

Citizen Preparation

An active citizenry begins with the education and involvement of ordinary people. One of the founders of our country, Thomas Jefferson, believed strongly that universal education was the safest way to ensure the survival of democracy. The fact that U.S. citizens can take advantage of state-supported public education is one measure of how well our country tries to prepare its citizens for participation. It is likely that you are required at some point to take a course in U.S. government. Many of you are required to take a class in communication so that you can increase your effectiveness as a participant in civic life. Preparation means gaining the skills and knowledge that are required to have a voice in society. Many high schools and colleges are now recognizing that communication education is an important factor in preparing active participants.

Citizen Participation

Once you have been trained, it is important to put that training to work for you and your community. Edmund Burke, an Irish statesman and orator during the

THE STORY OF COMMUNICATION

"Finally, they came for me . . ."

Especially compelling are the stories and examples of people who fail to use their powers of speech and wind up losing them altogether. After the horrible terror brought about in Nazi Germany, a Lutheran minister named Martin Niemoeller told the judges at the Nuremberg war trials why he and so many other capable speakers did nothing. He said, "At first they came for the communists, and I was against communism, so I did not speak out when their rights were violated. Then they came after the trade unionists, and since I was not a union member, I did not speak out when their rights were violated. Next they came for the students, and I was no longer a student, so I did not speak out. They came after the Jews, and I was not Jewish, so I was silent. They came for the Catholics, but I am a Protestant, so I did not speak out. Finally, they came for me, and there was no one left to speak out."

The process of losing democracy is very simple. Just remain silent.

1700s, once said, "Nobody made a greater mistake than he who did *nothing* because he could only do a *little*." Although it might seem like a small thing to speak at a planning commission hearing or take part in a public debate over the environment, everyone who participates adds to the total communication effort that drives the decisions of our society (refer to The Story of Communication box above). Each person speaking up reaffirms the differences between a democracy and other types of government. Sometimes by speaking up, you provide others with the incentive to join in with their voices.

The skills of public communication must be used, or these skills will be forgotten. There is a story about a group of researchers who typed out the articles in the Bill of Rights, then removed the title. They stood on street corners and asked people whether they would sign a petition supporting these rights. Most people declined, many saying that they "didn't want to get into trouble." Can you imagine where we would be if our forebearers held such an opinion? Our national anthem might still be "God Save the Queen."

Improving Community Communication

The process of improvement can also be simple. Listen, evaluate, respond, and participate. As a consumer of information, listen to others in your community as they call for action, decision, or support. Evaluate their messages on the basis of completeness, honesty and fairness, and consider what proposed ideas mean to you. Respond with a letter to the editor or with a reply at a public meeting. Join clubs, associations, and groups. Find associations that help to build the community, and then put your communication training to work in the organizations you join.

SUMMARY

When you look at the connections between the family, the school, the community, and, in the next chapter, the mass media, you can sense the many ways of learning about communication applies to nearly every aspect of your life. Working for improvement in any of these areas may be a lifetime occupation—a long-term process rather than a quick course to be completed. Nevertheless, you can begin immediately to make improvements in any area of your life that needs work, and these improvements can be a source of accomplishment for you. The competent communicator is skilled in a variety of contexts.

KEY TERMS

family communication, *p. 350*

classroom communication, *p. 356*

wait time, *p. 356*

parent–teacher communication, *p. 358*

community communication, *p. 360*

democratic communication, *p. 361*

EXERCISES

1. Interview your oldest living relative. Ask him or her about early family life—what patterns of interaction were used, who made decisions, what the family did for entertainment. Compare the responses to your experiences. Are there any aspects of your relative's early life that you are missing but would like to get back? Why?

2. Recall an unpleasant interaction that you had in elementary school with an adult, perhaps a teacher. Now contrast that example with a positive one. Compare the two experiences on the basis of the communication variables that were involved: listening, evaluation, feedback. If you could talk to the adult in the first case, what advice would you now have for this person, based on your knowledge of communication?

3. Attend a public meeting in your community for any club. Notice whether the members are eager to greet you and make you feel welcome. Even if you explain that you are just fulfilling a class assignment, you can sense how clubs can be useful in becoming part of a community network. Share your experience with your classmates.

4. Visit the student activities center on campus, and get a listing of clubs. How many are there? How many had you heard of before? How do these clubs make your campus a community?

REFERENCES

Atwood, Margaret. "Not So Grimm: The Staying Power of Fairy Tales." *Los Angeles Times Book Review* 29 Oct. 1995: 11.

Bauer, C. F. *Handbook for Storytellers*. Chicago: American Library Association, 1977.

Bettelheim, Bruno. *The Uses of Enchantment*. New York: Vintage Books, 1977.

Civikly, J. "Self-Concept, Significant Others and Classroom Communication." *Communication in the Classroom*. Ed. L. Barker. Englewood Cliffs: Prentice-Hall, 1982.

Clark, M., E. Erway, and L. Beltzer. *The Learning Encounter*. New York: Random House, 1971. 3.

Cooper, P. *Speech Communication for the Classroom Teacher*. 5th ed. Scottsdale: Gorsuch Scarisbrick, 1994.

Cooper, P., and K. Galvin. *Improving Classroom Communication*. Washington: Dingle Associates, 1983.

Galvin, K., and B. Brommel. *Family Communication: Cohesion and Change*. 4th ed. New York: Harper Collins, 1996.

Hopper, R., and R. J. Naremore. *Children's Speech*. New York: Harper & Row, 1978.

James, M., and D. Jongeward. *Born to Win*. Reading: Addison-Wesley, 1973.

McCroskey, J. *An Introduction to Communication in the Classroom*. Edina: Burgess, 1992.

McCroskey, J., V. P. Richmond, A. Sallinen, J. M. Fayer, and R. A. Barraclough. "A Cross-Cultural and Multi-Behavioral Analysis of the Relationship between Nonverbal Immediacy and Teacher Evaluation." *Communication Education* 44 (Oct. 1995).

McNeil, D. *The Acquisition of Language*. New York: Harper & Row, 1970.

Merl, J. "Schools Badly Shortchange Girls, Researchers Report." *Los Angeles Times* 12 Feb. 1992: 1.

Pearson, J. C. *Communication in the Family*. New York: Harper & Row, 1989.

Rowe, M. B. "Wait Time: Slowing Down May Be a Way of Speeding Up." *Journal of Teacher Education* (Jan./Feb. 1986).

Stucky, N. "Performing Oral History: Storytelling and Pedagogy." *Communication Education* 44 (1995).

Zimmermann, Stephanie. "Perceptions of Intercultural Communication Competence and International Student Adaptation to an American Campus." *Communication Education* 44 (Oct. 1995).

Mass Communication and Society

- Define the role of mass media in democratic societies.
- Understand four approaches or models that are used to describe the attributes of mass communication.
- Define the purposes and functions of mass communication in society.
- Discuss the development of public relations from consumer and career perspectives.
- Improve your competency to consume mass communication wisely.

*A*s you saw in the previous chapter, one of the major systems in a democracy is an active, free press, known as the mass media. The mass media are a good place to continue our studies of social aspects of communication because we use them in our families, schools, and democratic institutions. A definition of mass media focuses the discussion, and then we examine how the media work, how they affect our lives, and how we can help to improve them.

MASS COMMUNICATION DEFINED

As with the other types of communication, mass media contain all the elements for a communication transaction: a context, a sender/source, messages, channels, receivers/decoders, and feedback/interference/noise. In examining the distinction between mass media communication and other types of communication, it helps to look at the root of the word *media*. In Latin, media means *middle*. You can see that meaning at work when you speak of a *mediator* in a dispute, the *median* number in a series, and even the narrow strip of land or concrete in the middle of a busy road: the *median*. What is in the middle in this communication form is some device—something between the source and receiver—that mediates the communication. That something could be electronic, such as a television, radio, computer, or compact disc, or it could be paper, such as a book, magazine, or newspaper. The fact that something comes between the source and the receiver and conveys the message gives us a clue to understanding the rest of the definition. **Mass media** communication therefore means the exchange of messages through some channel of broad diffusion. This exchange involves several elements.

First, the contexts of mass media often are simultaneously private and public. Television comes into your home, and newspapers and magazines may be read in private, yet they are all out there for anyone and everyone to see and consume.

Second, mass media contexts are either immediately timely or historical. They may be reports of current events, or they may be books and manuscripts from past centuries, civilizations, and cultures.

Next, the sources/senders are sometimes large organizations or institutions. Television networks, publishing companies, and lobbying groups that publish newsletters are more complex sources than a single speaker or people in

---

IMPROVING COMPETENCY

The Model of Communication

Select two media sources, and do a quick application. Perhaps you want to use this book and the television as your choices. Describe the elements of communication that are at work in both media. Now select two different forms of media, and repeat the process. Becoming aware of the elements is a basic, constructive step in gaining mastery over the concepts and in understanding the influence of the mass media on all of our lives.

a small group discussion. The messages that they transmit are carried over some sort of intervening channel; and since they are sent to a potentially wide, diverse, and perhaps unknown group of receivers/decoders, they often take on general characteristics. The feedback, if any, may be delayed and indirect. Interference and noise, such as "snow" on television, smeared ink in the magazine, or static on the radio, is common.

HOW MASS COMMUNICATION WORKS

There are many ways to think about mass media and the ways in which they work. These ways of thinking can be called *models,* and as we have become more familiar with the workings of the media, we have developed different models to think about how mass media work.

One-, Two-, and Three-Step Approaches

In early analyses of mass media, people used a simple speaker–audience model. Someone sends a message to the target audience—that is a **one-step approach.** What was missed in the analysis of this approach was the fact that people react to media messages in a delayed manner. Because of the delay, people are affected by more events than just the source. This observation led to the expansion of the one-step view to a more complex model.

The second model held that people were more likely to pay attention to other people whom they respected than to the media source (Lazarfield et al.,

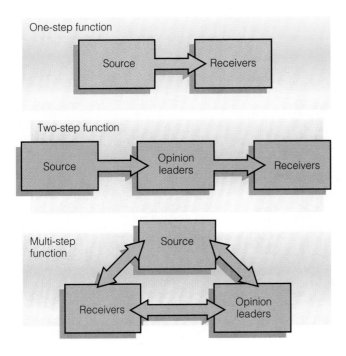

The one-, two-, and three-step models of mass media communication.

1944). This theory, based on reactions of people to the 1940 presidential election, held that opinion leaders functioned in every community and responded to some media messages, and then other people responded to the opinion leaders. However, the **two-step approach** was found to be too simple because people responded both to media and to influential individuals.

The **three-step approach** (or multiple-step) looks at the interaction among receivers, senders, and other receivers. Some of the influential people may be members of the media, such as television anchors Sam Donaldson, Ted Koppel, Larry King, Barbara Walters, and Bernard Shaw. The multiple-step model reminds us of the many transactions that take place—The media affect us, and we, in turn, have an effect on them through our viewing, reading, and writing habits.

Diffusion, Uses, Gratification

In addition to the step approaches, researchers have also perceived the media to have a variety of functions in society. Mass media can work to spread information: the **diffusion** of ideas. The quick spread of clothing, hairstyle, music, and dance trends among young Americans can be attributed to television's ability to diffuse information from coast to coast simultaneously. Likewise, we all know certain things because they appear on every news broadcast and in nearly every major newspaper and news magazine. It was estimated that 600 million people "attended" the 1981 wedding of Prince Charles and Lady Diana Spencer of England through the use of live television. The media are also capable of diffusing information over time, such as books that endure for generations and films from years ago. Each day brings new compact discs featuring "oldies" from the 1940s, 1950s, 1960s, and 1970s. Media forms can preserve events, allowing future generations to experience the sights and sounds that otherwise would not last beyond their real-time existence.

Television reaches virtually every household in the United States.

We use mass media to perform several functions. We need *information,* and we get it from media. Years ago, people depended on each other's memories and abilities to tell stories and convey information. As Chapter 1 points out, the story of humanity is also the story of communication. When humankind learned to speak, people spoke to others, who remembered and passed the information along, often through an honored storyteller. When written symbols for our sounds developed, we were able to improve the accuracy of our messages. Now, with increasing access and use of the Internet/World Wide Web, such information transfer and storage has expanded to include millions of people as new sources of mass communication. From the beginning, information has been at the heart of mass media.

We are also *entertained* by media, and many of the examples in this chapter come from the world of entertainment. You don't usually get your entertainment without paying for it, however. For example, when you buy a book or CD, you pay directly. For the programs you watch on PBS, you pay with your subscriptions or with tax-free donations from major corporations or foundations. For other television and radio entertainment, you pay by viewing advertisements. These advertisements tell us about the persuasive use of mass media. The chapter on persuasion and attitude change discusses how governments try to persuade mass audiences and how products or opinions are sold on the basis of persuasive media messages. Some people believe that the media also dull the audience into a state of inaction. We can become hypnotized by television, turning into passive couch potatoes. The media can also create fame, since everyone who appears on television is exposed to a vast audience. I was once a contestant on a television game show; afterward, I began to receive letters from people who had seen me and were reacting to my comment that my wife and I collect antique records. One woman wrote offering to sell us her collection of 1950s Frank Sinatra and Bing Crosby records. (The records that we collect were usually made before 1920 and are the old Edison cylinders, some dating back to the 1890s.) Other people get notoriety because of horrible crimes or disasters.

The private aspect of media can exert great influence over people who are seeking to gratify needs for companionship and contact. Robert Young, the actor who gained fame as the father in *Father Knows Best,* and later played the physician in *Marcus Welby, MD,* has told of people seeking him out for parenting tips and medical advice. This type of pseudo-relationship comes from the media being used to create groupness—a feeling of being connected to others through the media. Some soap opera fans write to a favorite character, offering advice. During the O. J. Simpson murder trial, hundreds of letters arrived each week to various participants, giving them advice as how to proceed with the case.

Clearly, we use media for a variety of reasons. Whether we are reading about Princess Di's latest problems or watching the news for election results, media pervade our lives.

Gatekeepers and Opinion Leaders

Another way to look at media is by examining how they control the flow of information. As was mentioned above, media come between the source and the receiver. Recall the descriptions of gatekeepers and facilitators in Chapter 16.

Because their ability to transmit information is finite, media producers must make choices about how much and what kind of information to send. In the case of persuasive messages, they select biased information that favors their position. How about a daily newspaper or the evening newscast? They too have real limits on what they send out. They act as gatekeepers, letting some information through and keeping other information out of the flow. As you watch the news on different television stations in a large media market, you can see their decisions in action. One station might devote several minutes to a spectacular fire, showing rescue operations, fire trucks, and flames. Another station might not even mention the story. These decisions are made according to editorial policies, managerial decisions, opportunity for covering the story, and a dozen other factors (perhaps political orientation, advertiser approval, and so on). Editing, selection, and censoring of material are constant components of mass media.

Opinion leaders may be influential people in business, politics, religious, civic, or community groups. They may also be employees of media organizations. One thing is probable: If they are opinion leaders, they are probably communicating their opinions through the media. One of the ways to define opinion leaders is to note their appearances on television and radio and in print. In the multiple-step approach to media, these people play important roles in the transactions between media and receivers. Are they selected for their insight? Intelligence? Creative approaches to the world's problems? Critical thinking skills? Deep knowledge? Or might their pleasant voices, good looks, and energetic personalities be factors? Imagine Abraham Lincoln trying to run for President today. Do you think he would have a chance?

The HUB Model

Another way to look at media was provided by scholars in the 1970s and is called the **HUB model** (Hiebert, Ungurait, and Bohn, 1974). This model can be compared to dropping a stone into water: The ripples radiate outward from a center. This model takes into account most of the important factors that operate in mass media.

The completeness of the HUB model provides a useful way to think about all the stages that messages go through on their way from a source to a receiver. First, the encoding process must be considered at the center of the model. Next, think about the codes we use—our language and nonverbal codes that come from our backgrounds and education and develop in a cultural context. Note the presence of gatekeepers, who act to prevent the flow of information. Then come the mass media, with their special functions, focus, and limitations. You can see a circle of regulators surrounding the media, such as distribution factors, availability, laws, rules, and economic pressures. Filters are the next ring, and they mean somewhat the same here as they did in the chapter on listening. Filters screen out material; you don't have time to read the whole story, so you skim it. You find a musician unfamiliar or offensive, so you tune the music out. Audiences are the next-to-last ring. When you considered audience analysis in the chapters on public speaking, you acted much like a media analyst evaluating the ways to adapt a particular message. Finally, the last ring is the effects, or the outcome discussed in Chapter 2.

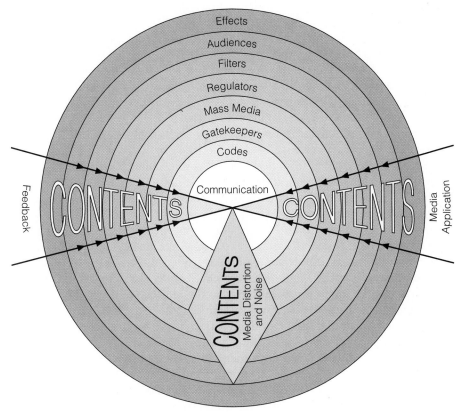

The HUB model.

Some important additions in the HUB model include the media's amplification of a message by the sheer power of dispersion—the message is repeated and received many times. The quality of feedback cuts through the entire model to indicate the importance at each step of the possible responses. Finally, the contents of a message are influenced by the process of transmission itself. Factors such as distortion and noise are mentioned in this part of the model.

All four of these approaches are useful in helping people to understand how media function and affect our lives. They also represent an evolutionary development of our understanding of media. It is easy, after having seen the HUB model, to see how limited the step models are. But when they were first offered, they helped researchers to gain insights. Building on those insights, we have developed the more complete and sophisticated models represented by HUB.

THE IMPACT OF MASS MEDIA ON OUR LIVES

You cannot escape mass media; indeed, some of your everyday decisions are probably influenced by messages coming from the media. The products, services, options, and candidates all come to you through media presentations. Let's look at a few of the areas.

Entertainment

Not only does entertainment come to you through media, but messages about entertainment are also contained in the media. You look at the newspaper or consult a World Wide Web site to decide what movie you want to see. There are television shows and newspaper articles that review movies, and movie ads appear in both media. Fewer families sit at home in the evenings and play musical instruments, work puzzles, read aloud to each other, or play games. For many people, entertainment means watching television. It is estimated that the television set is on for an average of seven hours a day in the typical U.S. home. By the time you graduated from high school, you probably had watched 22,000 hours of television—about double the time you spent in school (Work and Work, 1975). You probably spend about 85 percent of your free time watching television for entertainment.

Sports programming is another major use of media entertainment. Most major newspapers devote at least several pages, if not a whole section, to sports events. It is interesting to note some of the coverage choices made by news editors. For example, most smaller-market newspapers cover local high school sports in depth. Large photo spreads may accompany these stories. Local television in small markets may broadcast live high school football, baseball, and basketball games, while radio covers many of the same events even more thoroughly. Major-market media usually stick to professional and college teams, a local college or university if it is not otherwise covered, and perhaps the state or regional final match between high schools. Certainly, coverage of professional teams is provided for the entertainment value. The Olympic Games are worth hundreds of millions of dollars in advertising revenue for the network that covers them. As in the pseudo-relationship developed by soap opera fans, sports fans also write letters to favorite players, establish long-term and intense loyal-

Mass media allow for mass entertainment.

ties to certain teams, and purchase products displaying their team's logos. The media thrive on such relationships because they provide a steady market as these consumers follow their teams. A media disaster occurred in 1985 when the Kansas City Royals played the St. Louis Cardinals in the World Series. Both cities are smaller major league locations, and both draw fans from two neighboring, low-population states. Media sales time and space declined, especially in major markets. The network sales manager's World Series dream is to have a team from California play a team from New York and to have the series go the maximum number of games before being settled.

The entertainment uses of media also include the print media, books, magazines, newspapers, web site activities on the Internet such as "chat rooms," as well as the sound and sight media, films and recordings. Broadcast media carry concerts, musical events, plays, and films. The popularity of the MTV and VH-1 networks, the on-line services such as America Online, and the millions of computer software games for home use demonstrates the entertainment function of media.

The advent of cable television has allowed television to specialize in much the same manner as magazines. A subscription service can target a segment of the viewing and listening audience and deliver entertainment that is tailored to that group. The percentage of households in the United States that subscribe to cable television has increased dramatically over the past twenty years. In 1975, when HBO first started broadcasting by satellite transmission, the total number of homes it reached was 265,000. Twenty years later, cable television is in more than 60 million homes and reaches over 125 million people (Vivian, 1995).

TECHNOLOGY IN COMMUNICATION

The Satellite Dish

Large satellite dishes became popular in the early 1980s, primarily among people in rural areas where it was too expensive to lay cable and local reception of television was limited or nonexistent. In 1994, RCA and DirecTV began offering a small, 18-inch satellite dish to customers for around $600. Digital sound and pictures were available everywhere directly to your home or recreational vehicle from an orbiting satellite. By 1997, the price dropped to $300. In 1995, services began coming to some homes over telephone lines, using fiber-optic technology to transmit movies and programs to their television sets through telephone equipment. The development and advances of both digital processing of information and the transmission capacities of fiber optics and satellites have enhanced and enlarged our mass media output. In the future, satellite and cable, especially in regard to entertainment, will probably grow in both the variety of programming available and the number of homes served.

Knowledge

It would be a mistake to dismiss media, especially television, on the basis of the entertainment function it serves. Children can learn about the world from watching television programs such as *Sesame Street*. Programs on nature and travel are also examples of television that educates. On a broader level, virtually all television programs communicate something about our culture. Even sitcoms tell about manners, events, styles, or places that may be unfamiliar to viewers. The setting of a series may inform viewers to some extent about that locale. A series may be set in Chicago, Atlanta, or Alaska or in an African

DIVERSITY IN COMMUNICATION

Local Cable Responds to Community Needs

Media outlets were the subject of much interest during the riots in Los Angeles and other cities in late March 1992. After the Rodney King verdict, one local cable company in the riot-torn area of South Central Los Angeles was in danger of being attacked. The station managers talked to the rioters who threatened the building, explaining to the rioters that a popular television program was provided only by this local cable station. Many in the group knew and watched this program, and so they moved on. The diversity of programming that cable provides can directly address the concerns of local communities and can establish rapport and fill a need that more broad-based media cannot.

American family's home, on a rural farm, or in a single-parent family. If your viewing is narrow, however, the range of information will also be narrow. During an informal survey done in 1990 among seventh to tenth grade students at a shopping mall, 100 percent of those interviewed could identify "Downtown" Julie Brown, a host personality on MTV, while virtually no one was able to identify the Vice President of the United States.

Some series spawn clothing styles, music trends, or changes in popular vocabulary. Television programs can educate their viewers in subtle ways by their settings and situations. Viewers create impressions about our culture and its values from situations that are presented in the media.

Opinions and Impressions

Because it's in the news, it must be important—well, important to someone. The media have been accused of telling people what to think. In persuasive message transmissions and in closed societies, this is true. In the United States, media tell us what to think about through the process of gatekeeping. If you have no opinion about the civil strife in Sri Lanka, it may be because that long terrorist war is not covered by most news outlets. It is not that the media form your opinions, but that their selection and presentation of information define the things about which you will form an opinion. It can be important to challenge the media to cover a wider variety of issues. Many alternative newspapers and magazines report stories that the major news outlets will not cover.

Covering an item in a magazine or choosing to put it on the front or back page of a newspaper conveys an impression about the event's importance. The British tabloid press is fond of photographing Queen Elizabeth with the wind blowing off her hat or lifting her dress. Former President Ford was plagued by a media fascination with any small trip or bump; during his term, we saw him, more than once, stumbling on the steps of an airplane staircase, and rubbing his head after a collision with a low doorway. In time, an impression forms from the repeated use of these images.

CRITICAL THINKING IN COMMUNICATION

Testing Media Bias

During elections, especially presidential ones, it is common for politicians and their aides to blame mistakes and problems on the media. There are, undoubtedly, instances of people being misquoted and stories being distorted. What tests of critical thinking could you use to support or deny such claims of bias? Refer to Chapter 4 if you like, and check the standard tests for reliability in supporting any generalization or in drawing either a deductive or inductive conclusion. How many, if any, of these tests do the critics of media coverage pass? How many do the media pass?

Propaganda and Diversion

Finally, media can affect us if they are instruments of **propaganda.** Propaganda is the repeated sending of carefully crafted messages which deliberately distort information to emphasize a predetermined aspect of it. In the section on attitude change theory in Chapter 14, you found that propaganda must be consistent and contain elements of truth to be effective. Some historians and media researchers blame media propaganda for getting us into the war with Spain in 1898 or for creating enough fear and distrust of Americans of Japanese descent that they were hauled off to camps at the start of World War II. Propaganda can be powerful when the media are its agents. Likewise, by following the dictates of corporate sponsors, the media can direct attention toward favored issues and away from those that may be controversial. For example, a survey of magazines regarding their policies on cigarette advertising discovered that magazines that did not accept cigarette advertising were more likely to have news articles about the dangers of tobacco than were magazines that accepted cigarette advertising. Could it be that some publications want us to look in some directions but not others?

Although serious crime as reported by the FBI's national statistics has dropped steadily for several years, public perception is that the amount of crime has increased. Welfare costs actually amount to less than 1 percent of the federal budget but are seen by the general public as a major element of national spending. Crime and welfare abuse make interesting stories. On the other hand, by offering pleasant, funny, upbeat thirty-minute stories on television, are the media using **diversion** to keep us from considering important issues and problems in our lives or in society? It would be difficult to prove such a hypothesis; it is easier to take steps to guard against the possibility that media are being misused.

Mass media in a free society take two things into consideration. The first is the freedom of speech that we have developed in this country; the second is the standard of ethics that should be used by people exercising free speech. Several issues are important here, including the truthfulness of ideas that are presented as fact rather than the expression of opinion, judgment, or redress of grievances. In general, U.S. courts have upheld the free expression of opinions even if they are offensive to everybody else. However, it is illegal to make false claims over

THE STORY OF COMMUNICATION

The Power of the Press

In the early days of this country, the British government recognized the potential power of a critical press. John Peter Zenger (1697–1746) published a small newspaper in New England that was critical of the king's representative, the Governor of New York. Zenger was arrested, and his presses were smashed. In a landmark trial, he was acquitted of the charge of libel and thus helped to set the stage for you to enjoy a press and other media that are free to criticize the government.

the media, especially if those claims are likely to cause harm or create danger to public safety. Perhaps one of the most famous cases involved Justice Oliver Wendell Holmes, Jr., who in 1919 wrote of the "clear and present danger" test for free speech limitations. He wrote the now-famous saying: "The most stringent protection of free speech would not protect a man in falsely shouting 'fire!' in a crowded theater and causing panic." This image is powerful and illustrates clearly the difference between protecting untruthful claims of fact that create danger and claims that are simply controversial opinion.

The other side of the issue was demonstrated in 1985 when the *Chicago Tribune* carried an opinion piece by its architecture critic, who described billionaire Donald Trump's planned 150-story building as "one of the silliest things that anyone could inflict on New York." Trump sued the critic and the paper for libel, but he lost. The opinion may have been subjective and unflattering, but calling something "silly" is nevertheless protected because it's opinion and therefore unlikely to cause anyone any harm or danger. Incidentally, think back to the "fire in a crowded theater" example. What do you suppose the facts of the case were? Do you imagine that someone went to a Saturday afternoon matinee and suddenly jumped up, shouting "Fire!" and causing a panicked rush for the doors in which dozens were injured, trampled, or even killed? While that scene makes for a dramatic picture, it is not even close to the facts of the case. The person on trial in 1919 was on trial for standing on a New York sidewalk, handing out leaflets praising the Russian Bolshevik revolution. Because the metaphor of shouting "Fire!" was so captivating, the argument was made that supporting the Russian revolution was *like* shouting fire, and the leaflet distributor's conviction was upheld. It is doubtful today, with the great variety of political information that we tolerate, that such a person would get our attention for more than a moment, let alone be arrested, tried, convicted, and jailed for being a danger to public safety.

You may be aware of the debate over allowing prayers in the public schools or free speech on the Internet, or the conflicts over the labeling of record albums with obscene lyrics. The issue of freedom of speech and the responsibility to follow ethical guidelines are far from settled. Each year finds new court cases involving the tension between these forces. You will have many opportunities in your life to follow this issue, but the trend has been clear since John Peter

Zenger's times: Our laws have consistently expanded and broadened freedom of speech and have narrowed the limitations that can be placed on that freedom.

PUBLIC RELATIONS

Many students of communication think about careers in the mass media, and public relations is often mentioned as one possibility. There is much interest in, and some confusion over, the use of the term *public relations* and what it means to become a public relations professional.

Public Relations Defined

Public relations may be defined as the communication process by which organizations seek to create positive relationships with individuals and other organizations. Because it is a communication process, you will find in it the elements of the communication model from Chapter 2. There is a source, usually a manager or a public relations officer of an organization. There is a message, encoded and created on the basis of the intent of the message and audience analysis. The channels of transmission are usually those of mass media, so public relations is an aspect of mass media studies. The destination of the messages is the target audience, and feedback occurs if the public relations message succeeds in getting the desired response. Noise is always present, and the entire process takes place within an environment.

Public relations developed early in the 1900s in response to the extremely negative opinion that many people held of business and industry. As you may recall from your U.S. history classes, the late 1800s saw the development of giant industries, railroads, and mining and manufacturing concerns, which, in some cases, led to widespread abuse of workers, poor working conditions, and safety and health hazards for both the workers and the general public. Although not all businesses and industries exploited their workers, there was enough abuse to spur the development of unions. Unions were a way for workers to protect themselves and gain concessions from management concerning working conditions and wages. Management reacted by trying to change its practices and its public image. Some industries hired former newspaper writers and editors to help them communicate their ideas and positions to the public and to elected officials. World War I saw government get into the public relations business when President Woodrow Wilson hired a firm to convince the public that the United States should join in the fighting going on in Europe.

Since that time, public relations has grown and become a permanent fixture in government, business, and industry to the point at which even labor unions have their own public relations campaigns. Perhaps you have seen the television spot in which a woman is explaining to her daughter that they have to sell their house and move because she lost her job making clothing. It seems that too few people are buying American-made clothing to keep her factory open. This advertisement is part of a public relations campaign aimed at creating a positive climate for union workers in the clothing industry. There is a similar campaign by the milk industry to encourage consumers to notice how good milk is by having a variety of celebrities depicted with "milk mustaches."

Types and Functions of Public Relations

Although the goals of public relations might seem similar to those of advertising, there is an important difference. Both advertising and public relations use persuasion to achieve their desired end, but advertising uses a narrowly focused campaign to sell a product or service. Public relations, on the other hand, is aimed, first, internally at helping management to create policies and decisions regarding its business conduct and affairs and, second, at how the organization is perceived both internally and externally. A public relations campaign might focus on nurturing positive feelings among employees toward the company, or it might create a public image of an honest and trustworthy organization. Advertising is directed at increasing sales or services (Leiss et al., 1995). Although advertising and public relations both use elements of mass media, they usually function as separate units within a particular organization.

As was mentioned above, both internal and external elements are involved in an organization's public relations activities. Both of these elements usually follow a four-step process in creating an effective campaign. First, they identify the existing relationship: How are they doing now, who is connected to the organization, and on what terms? For example, a business might analyze its existing customers, or a politician might look at current supporters. Second, the existing relationships must be evaluated. The positive and negative aspects of the existing relationship must be weighed. Third, the public relations campaign creates strategies for improvement or expansion of relationships. The public relations team thinks of new services to offer customers or, in the case of the politician, ways to increase voter contacts. Finally, the organization implements these plans. Public relations professionals design a timetable, develop a budget, and draw up a list of steps, functions, jobs, and assignments. If these steps sound familiar, that's because they are parallel to the communication competencies steps that are mentioned at the end of nearly every chapter in this book. The steps of public relations communication offer another area in which you can apply your knowledge and skills in communication competencies.

Careers and Consumption

The field of public relations has tried over the years to improve its image. Years ago, it was perceived as trying to cover up for misdeeds of industry or politicians, and some people still remember that unsavory beginning. However, the 1950s saw the development and growth of professional standards and organizations in the field. The Public Relations Society of America is one such professional organization, and it created a process by which people can become certified in public relations. Its code of standards lists several aspects, of which three are especially important: (1) Public relations professionals must adhere to truth and accuracy and to generally accepted standards of good taste. (2) They may not engage in any practice that tends to corrupt the integrity of the channels of communication or the process of government. (3) They may not intentionally communicate false or misleading information. These standards are parallel to the statements involving free and responsible speech as well as the standards for ethical communication that are described in the chapters on public speaking. The overlap should serve to underline the relative agreement in our society about honest and ethical communication and the standards that are expected of those who publicly communicate their ideas and opinions (Biagi, 1990).

As a public relations professional, you would be expected to know about the processes of mass media. You would need to be able to engage in extensive audience analysis and formulate plans and ideas for creating and sending accurate messages. In addition, you would be responsible for evaluating the success or failure of your public relations effort. If you're interested in public relations, find out whether your college has a student affiliate group of the national society or offers courses in this area.

As a consumer, you need to recognize public relations as a persuasive campaign, designed to influence your opinion about an individual or organization. You need to apply the standards for being an effective consumer of persuasive communication that were presented at the end of Chapter 14, as well as the ethical standards outlined at the end of the chapters on public speaking (Biagi, 1990). Use your critical-thinking skills to examine the message. Remember to evaluate supporting materials, relevance, and value to you, the consumer.

IMPROVING MASS COMMUNICATION COMPETENCY

The guidelines for improving competency begin with having lots of different media—a form of expanded repertoire. Although we do have an alternative press in this country, relatively few people read alternative publications. In particular, very few students read materials other than what is assigned in classes. A teacher may assign you to read articles on the same subject but from two very different types of newspapers. This kind of assignment is designed to enlarge your *repertoire* of information sources. Most libraries subscribe to a variety of national political and cultural periodicals.

Next, it is vital that as a consumer of information, you *select* a wide information base to help you check for errors or discrepancies. Find sources with strong reputations for accuracy and thoroughness. The ability to access huge amounts of information over the Internet greatly expands your potential database. You might not be able to direct the way a publication presents its information, but you can buy better publications, listen to reliable sources, and change the channel when a program fails to meet your standards.

The tests for ethical and worthwhile information need to be *applied* regularly so that you do not lose the standards by which to judge information. Throughout this chapter, you have been given the advice to listen carefully and thoughtfully, and then to evaluate on the basis of completeness, clarity, honesty, and value to the receiver. You can remind yourself, "What's in it for *them*?" when persuasive messages come to you through the media. In a popular 1995 film, *Legends of the Fall,* there is a scene in which the older son visits his father, accompanied by a dozen supporters who want the son to run for Congress. The father turns to the son and asks, "And what do these gentlemen expect to get in return for their support?" There is a long, uncomfortable pause while the "gentlemen" shift and look away. Good question.

As you *evaluate* your improvement as a consumer of information, you will, in a small way, be providing feedback to the organizations that create the messages.

If you watch only high-quality programming, purchase only high-quality newspapers, and subscribe only to high-quality magazines, the other sources will be forced to change or go out of business—assuming that your habits are shared by thousands of others. You can, of course, try direct feedback. You can write to radio or television stations or to newspaper and magazine editors and take your opinions directly to the source.

SUMMARY

When you look at the connections between the family, the school, the community, and the mass media, you can sense the many ways in which learning about communication can apply to nearly every aspect of your life.

This chapter discusses how mass media operate and examines several perspectives from which they are analyzed. Mass media can be used for information, entertainment, and persuasive purposes. The field of public relations is a form of communication that uses the tools of mass media to affect opinions,

not necessarily behavior. Advertising, on the other hand, aims to affect consumer behavior directly.

Improvement in any of these areas may be a lifetime occupation, a long-term process rather than a quick course to be completed. Nevertheless, you can begin immediately to make improvements in any area of your life that needs work, and these improvements can be a source of accomplishment for you. The competent communicator is skilled in a variety of contexts.

KEY TERMS

mass media, *p. 366*
one-step approach, *p. 367*
two-step approach, *p. 368*
three-step approach, *p. 368*
diffusion, *p. 368*

opinion leaders, *p. 370*
HUB model, *p. 370*
propaganda, *p. 375*
diversion, *p. 375*

EXERCISES

1. Your library probably subscribes to a variety of newspapers. Select two that cover politics. Compare their coverage of the same event, and note the similarities and differences, such as the amount of space devoted to the item, page placement, and language, including quotations, used in the story. What conclusions can you draw from these similarities and differences?

2. Repeat Exercise 1, but this time select newspapers from a different country or those aimed at an ethnic group other than your own. For example, select a British, Canadian, or South African newspaper if you read only English. If you read another language, select a newspaper or magazine in that

language. You could also look at publications that are aimed primarily at African Americans, Latinos, or another ethnic group or any of the religious newspapers, as long as they are not published by and for people with your particular background.

3. Contact a representative of a local public relations firm or someone from your college's public relations or media relations office. What aspects of the job do they find most challenging? Most rewarding? How do they incorporate ethical issues? Are they members of the professional certification association (the Public Relations Society of America)? If your campus has a student chapter, attend one of its meetings.

4. The issue of freedom of speech is ongoing, and such topics as hate speech on campus and censorship of song lyrics seem to be important to many students. Arrange to interview a member of the ACLU, or invite such a person to your class. Find out whether members of your library staff are involved with these issues in their professional associations, and arrange to interview them.

5. Prepare a debate on a freedom of speech issue such as hate speech or pornography. If you follow a parliamentary style, the teams don't have to be even in number, and not everyone has to speak during the debate. Select the side you wish to defend, meet in teams, and conduct outside research on your position. Prepare speeches and positions with your team members. If you are undecided, then you can be the audience/judge. As the audience/judge, prepare a ballot and a critique, explaining the reasons behind your vote. Rules can be simple, such as no interrupting, each side speaking for a set amount of time, and each team having five minutes to cross-examine its opponent.

REFERENCES

Biagi, Shirley. *Media/Impact*. Belmont: Wadsworth, 1990.

Hiebert, Ray, Donald Ungurait, and Thomas Bohn. *Mass Media: An Introduction to Modern Communication*. New York: David McKay, 1974.

Lazarfield, P., B. Berelson, and H. Gaudet. *The People's Choice*. New York: Duell, Sloan and Pierce, 1944.

Leiss, W., S. Kline, and S. Jhally. "Advertising, Consumers and Culture." *Communication in History: Technology, Culture, and Society*. Ed. David Crowley and Paul Heyer. White Plains: Longman, 1995.

Vivian, John. *The Media of Mass Communication*, 2nd ed. Boston: Allyn and Bacon, 1995.

Work, J., and W. Work. *Relating: Everyday Communication*. Boston: Houghton Mifflin, 1975.

Diversity in Communication

- Define intercultural communication, gender and communication, communication and aging, and communication and health.

- Understand the importance of diversity in communication.

- Identify the communication barriers that operate in diversity situations.

- Feel committed to overcoming obstacles to communication in diversity settings.

- Gain confidence in your ability to communicate appropriately in diverse contexts.

- Improve your skills in communicating in a variety of situations.

D iversity in communication includes areas that are not well known in the long history of communication but nevertheless represent emerging topics of great interest in communication research and application. As the field of communication study has expanded to include more and more people of diverse backgrounds, the ideas and issues being studied have also expanded. Like most traditional academic disciplines, the focus was almost exclusively on European traditions until the past few decades. Nearly all of the leaders and researchers were men from this background. Now, our understanding of the complex issues associated with studying communication has been enriched by our enlarged focus and expanded network of scholars.

The communication variables that are involved when people are of different cultures, races, and ethnic groups are perhaps best established at this time in the area of diversity. The dynamics of communication between the sexes has fascinated people for centuries, yet only now is it becoming part of the discipline of communication. When people age, they acquire, develop, and modify their communication patterns, and up until now, we did not explore those patterns beyond a simple child-adult model. It is now known that people continue to grow, change, and develop as long as they live, and those dynamics, as well as their state of health, affect their communication interactions in later life. Each of these areas—culture, gender, age, and health—are defined in this chapter. Some of the major issues that they raise are also discussed so that you will have a sense of where the study of communication today is leading scholars in terms of the future.

INTERCULTURAL COMMUNICATION

Intercultural communication is that which "occurs whenever a message is produced by a member of one culture for consumption by a member of another culture, a message that must be understood" (Samovar and Porter, 1994). Because individuals communicate from a self that is shaped by their experiences, and because experiences exist within a culture, people bring a variety of perspectives and world views to their interactions with others. When there is a significant overlap between one person's experiences and another's, there is likelihood of a shared repertoire; therefore words and other meanings are likely to be similar. However, when experiences differ, as they do in different cultures, then it is likely that repertoires are different, and communication becomes more difficult and less shared.

The term **culture** also needs to be defined, as it can be used in a variety of ways. To some, it may mean upper-class concerns with manners, music, art, and cuisine. To others, it describes the objects and artifacts that are discovered by archaeologists and anthropologists studying ancient civilizations. Charles A. Ellwood, an influential cultural anthropologist of the last generation, wrote a definition of the word *culture* for the *Dictionary of Sociology,* part of which reads as follows: "Culture: a collective name for all behavior patterns socially acquired and socially transmitted by means of symbols" (Fairchild, 1944). The clear emphasis in this definition on communication demonstrates the central place that our symbolic interactions occupy in the creation and continuation of culture.

Whatever a person's background is, there is a universal desire and ability to communicate.

When Kroeber and Kluckhohn (1952) reviewed different perspectives on, and definitions of, culture, they stated the following:

> Culture consists of patterns of and for behavior acquired and transmitted by symbols, constituting the distinctive achievements of human groups, including their embodiments in artifacts; the essential core of culture consists of traditional [historically derived and selected] ideas and especially their attached values.

As you view cultures—your own included—think of the values that are communicated by each culture's symbolic use of objects, behaviors, and utterances. Since values determine behavior, different people behave differently because they perceive and organize their values differently. "Intercultural Communication seeks to understand the values of other people" (Newmark and Asante, 1976). Culture-defining values grow over time, are reinforced by the people who learn and use them, and are transmitted to successive generations in a process that is complex and has communication at its heart.

Importance of Communicating across Cultures

You live in a world that is linked together by commerce, trade, education, the arts, literature, science, and the pressing issues of improving humanity and even saving humanity. Only a short time ago, nations and regions seemed to be autonomous, but we now know that events in formerly remote areas of the world can and do have an impact on our lives, and vice versa. The ozone hole over Antarctica is presumed to have been caused by hydrocarbons and aerosol sprays, mostly from North America and Western Europe. The rapid destruction of the rain forests, which seem almost boundless to their immediate human inhabitants, will decrease the oxygen supply for all of the earth's inhabitants and will deplete the variety of plant and animal life on the planet—*forever*.

What these events have in common is that we and the rest of the world know about them, and we know about them because of advancements in communication via electronic messages. These advances in communication have shrunk the world so that information travels around the globe today much as it used to travel around small villages and towns in the past.

Global Village

What the mass media—especially telephones, radio, the Internet, and television—have done is to make events that take place anywhere the common knowledge of people everywhere. This phenomenon was called "the global village" by media writer Marshall McLuhan, who wrote extensively on the influence of the media on civilization (McLuhan, 1964). One effect of the rapid dissemination of information is that it creates the possibility of neighborliness. However, it is important to realize that having access to information does not guarantee that people will develop understanding, appreciation, or tolerance. Communication scholar Dean Barnlund (1975) sees the problem as follows:

> A greater exchange of people between nations, needed as that may be, carries with it no guarantee of increased cultural empathy; experience in other lands often does little but aggravate existing prejudices. Studying guidebooks or memorizing polite phrases simply fails to explain differences in cultural perspectives. (p. 5)

The challenge that intercultural communication presents is to go beyond intercultural tourism and apply the same skills and commitment to communicating in the intercultural setting as in other settings. The tourist who travels to other countries and reports seeing only Coca-Cola signs is a victim of seeing only what is already familiar. The Coca-Cola signs already have meaning for U.S. tourists, and tourists in general perceive only what they are prepared to receive. Think about the information in Chapter 7 regarding expectations and self-fulfilling prophecies, and you can understand why Barnlund's warning should be taken seriously. If you are *ready* to experience rude Parisians, poor Guatemalans, aloof Londoners, or inscrutably polite Japanese, that is probably what you *will* experience.

Intercultural communication can also apply to our multicultural society, although some researchers in the field make a distinction between *intercultural* and *international* communication. Different groups within the United States share some common characteristics, such as a similar geography, similar laws, similar political and social phenomena, and similar mass media influences. Within this context, however, unique cultural factors remain strong and can be seen in neighborhoods such as Chinatown, Little Italy, the French Quarter, and

IMPROVING COMPETENCY

Intercultural Communication and Media

Pick up a copy of a daily newspaper, and look at the articles that relate to cross-cultural communication. You will find stories about economics (trade or products), stories about entertainment (films, music groups, art), and sports stories about international competitions or sports figures from a variety of cultures. Stories like these in a single issue of a daily newspaper underscore the importance of intercultural communication. Which ones relate most closely to your interests? By looking for intercultural connections in your daily life, you can increase your competencies in intercultural interactions.

hundreds of lesser-known enclaves all over the "national village" in which we live. Thus in the United States, "cultural memberships are pluralistic and overlapping" (Hecht, et al., 1993). When the similarities among people are reduced by travel to different countries, difficulties in communication are compounded. In addition, the constant influx of immigrants to this country further complicates the smooth flow of communication that is necessary to keep people together as one culture.

To sum up, people move all over the globe—sometimes as visitors and sometimes as new residents. This fact creates the sense of having a global community within the borders of this country. Nevertheless, the same principles of intercultural communication apply in both international and national settings. For the purposes of our discussion, we have approached them both with a common theme. In any case, the fact that our lives are brought closer to people who were formerly distant creates in this country the sense of a global village.

Global Economy

A second major reason to study intercultural communication arises from the effect on people of economic pressures. If you remember your U.S. history, you will recall the economic factors that shaped the American revolution against Great Britain. The British government imposed a series of taxes and restrictions on trade; and since the colonies were dependent on commerce with England, they were at the mercy of those laws. One argument that was put forth in support of revolution stated that by becoming independent, the colonies could expand their trade options and create an economy with links to a variety of nations, instead of just one.

The 200 years that followed have seen the creation of a complex global economy, with its national trade and commerce patterns intertwined to a point at which you will indeed see Coca-Cola signs almost everywhere in the world.

In the past fifty years, the economic recovery of Europe and the development of Asian countries have been the most significant and influential events in the world economy. The key role that the Middle East oil economies play in our lives was underscored by the Persian Gulf War of 1991. Moreover, the United States is the largest consumer economy in the world, our relationships with Europe are still strong, and at the same time, we are enjoying increasing interactions with our neighbors in Asia, especially Japan, Korea, and Taiwan. In the near future, China—with nearly one fourth of the world's population—Indonesia, the Philippines, and Malaysia will play larger and larger roles in the economic development of this country.

These countries have unique cultures and systems, cultures that are different from our culture and those of our traditional European partners. The economic well-being of our country will depend on our ability to do business with these emerging economies. Slightly farther into the future, the more recently emerging economies of African and Latin American countries and regions will also become increasingly significant parts of our economy, as exemplified by the NAFTA agreement.

In the past, we may have been able to take the position that we were the world's superior economy and that other countries should cater to our markets. This relationship is changing as other areas, especially a unified Western Europe and a huge economic power in Japan, become centers of influence. What these changes mean for the United States is that we will need to adopt a perspective of equality and partnership with new economies. Part of that process requires the development of literacy in communicating with other cultures. On a personal level, your career options will probably increase if you can master the necessary aspects of intercultural communication.

Given these two forces—the shrinking of communication time and space, and the increase of economic interconnections—it is easy to see the value, importance, and place of intercultural communication in the world of tomorrow.

LEARNING ABOUT OTHER CULTURES

If you are going to avoid the trap of becoming no more than a tourist in other cultures, you need to confront the problem of intercultural communication directly. One way to attain clear intercultural communication is first to become aware of the barriers that prevent you from gaining competence in this area.

Filters and Screens

As you may recall from earlier chapters, there are definite psychological barriers to good listening called **filters and screens.** These are the mechanisms that distort incoming messages. Sometimes this distortion is small and has no appreciable effect on the fidelity of the message as you understand it. At other times, these barriers can actually reverse the meaning, or ignore the content of, an incoming message. When the sender and receiver are from different cultures, these screens operate in an intensified manner. Moreover, there are additional problems that create filters and screens in intercultural communication. They include (1) ethnocentrism, (2) offensive behavior, (3) failure to perceive differences, and (4) culture shock. Each of these problems can create perception barriers to good intercultural communication.

Ethnocentrism.   When you focus on your own culture and automatically evaluate it as being superior to any other culture, you are practicing **ethnocentrism**. Remember the superiority behavior that was mentioned in Chapter 8 as described by Jack Gibb? Ethnocentrism takes this same attitude and puts it in a cultural context.

Many people feel pride in their heritage. Ethnocentrism goes beyond this feeling to a conviction that what they know and do is better than what anyone else knows and does. An ethnocentric person notices differences and points them out constantly, to the detriment of another culture. For example, on a recent trip to the lumber yard near my home, I overheard another customer talking to a sales clerk about an order for several items. The clerk was several feet away and was filling out the order slip. He called, "How many feet of pipe did you want?" The customer answered, "Dos," which in Spanish means "two." One of the other clerks mumbled, "No, none of that here. If you can't speak the language of the country, go back where you came from! We speak only English here!" The customer tried to laugh off the hostile remark and said,

"Hey, I thought you smart fellas were all bilingual." Another clerk then joined the conversation. "If you want two feet of pipe, ask for two feet." A heavy, awkward silence followed. The transaction was completed without further incident, but the damage had already been done. The thin veneer of laughter did little to disguise the clerks' ethnocentrism.

As I thought about the incident, it seemed quite likely that the customer's family had lived in the area many generations longer than the clerk's family, yet this was not thought of as the customer's country because of the dominance of English-only speakers. The clerks' unwillingness to tolerate a second language is a sign of ethnocentrism. Even though the customer had been carrying on a long conversation in fluent English, the clerks bristled at one word of Spanish. Sometimes people fear that they are inferior, so they compensate for that feeling with dominating behavior. Perhaps these clerks resented the fact that the customer could speak two languages and they could not. In any case, the automatic, unthinking belief that your own culture is superior to another simply because it is *your* culture is the essence of ethnocentrism.

Even in classrooms in which the topic is intercultural communication, it may be difficult to think about or discuss issues related to culture, especially race. Students in the United States are often uncomfortable in such situations because we have a social taboo about such discussions in mixed-race settings. We like to think of our society as free and just, and we dislike the thought that it, and ourselves, might have elements of racism (Tatum, 1992).

Offensive Behavior.   Another screen or filter is created when a person engages in inappropriate or offensive behavior. This problem is usually expressed by nonverbal communication and is often unintentional and probably automatic. Behavior that is perfectly acceptable and even expected in one culture may be offensive, rude, or even obscene in others. In many Arab cultures, for example, the left hand is used only for toilet procedures, and to eat with that hand or to touch someone with the left hand is considered crude, gross, and insulting. Many Americans eat finger foods with either hand and give great offense if they continue this practice in Arab cultures. Whistling, eye contact, and certain gestures are just some of the obvious ways in which we can and do violate the rules and expectations of other cultures. With the worldwide distribution of U.S. movies, it is interesting to speculate how other cultures perceive us when they see us behaving in a bizarre fashion in our movies.

In any case, decisions about what to do or say—or even whether it is permissible to speak to someone at all—must be made consciously and knowledgeably if you are to avoid offensive behavior. You may think that a friendly, relaxed informality is just the right approach to take in your behavior, but that attitude comes from an ethnocentric vision about the way you and other people ought to behave.

Failure to Perceive Differences.   Another barrier to intercultural communication is the unwillingness to recognize diversity in acceptable behaviors. The inability to recognize differences means, in broad terms, that we forget that there are large gaps between cultural norms. On a personal level, it means that we treat every member of a culture like every other member and thus fall into a stereotyping pattern. Each level of this inability to perceive differences deserves some explanation.

Failure to recognize differences in broad terms occurs when you assume that there is a similarity among cultures in the goals, motives, values, or attitudes that drive their communication interactions. You may have an idealized vision that we are all the same people in spite of superficial differences in appearance, dress, or food. The singer Sting asked in one of his songs whether the Russians love their children; obviously, they do love their children very much. His point was that we do indeed share similarities with the Russian people. Even so, it is a mistake to assume that these similarities are universal. For example, there are cultures in which children are a burden to be borne, a commodity to be sold or exploited, or even an intrusion not to be tolerated—to the point of abandoning or even killing them once they are born.

It is also true that being born into any particular culture is an accident of birth. Had you been born and reared elsewhere, your cultural background would not be what it is now. Your preference in foods, your language, perhaps your thinking patterns, and certainly your important core values would all be different if your place of birth or your parentage were different (Giles and Johnson, 1981).

On a personal level, you might assume that all members of another culture think, believe, and behave alike. This way of viewing other people is called *stereotyping*. Even if your view is a positive one, it is still a stereotypical view. Are all Japanese polite? Are all Dutch people committed to cleanliness? Are all African American males good at basketball? Are all Norwegians great skiers? These examples of stereotypes may be tied to film images, myths, or any number of other questionable sources, yet many people believe them, and such beliefs result in treating individuals of other cultures as if they were all alike in important respects that have little foundation in reality. In reality, people of other cultures may share some cultural similarities but not others, just as the people in your classroom are similar in some ways but not in others.

By now, you probably realize that other cultures are no more monolithic than your own. There are important differences among various subgroups in any culture. While members of subcultures may share some broad cultural values, white male police officers in Los Angeles are not the same as gay white male civic leaders in nearby West Hollywood. And within *those* two groups, more differences exist. Although you may be able to make some generalizations about other cultures, remember to recognize the differences within them, even when they use the same language and share a broad cultural identity.

Culture Shock.   The last barrier to intercultural communication that we discuss is culture shock. The psychological reaction that you may feel when shifting from one culture to another has come to be known as **culture shock.** The term can be traced to anthropologist Kalvero Oberg. He described four stages that people go through when they experience situations that are very different from those to which they are accustomed. Examples include moving to a new city, traveling to a new country, and becoming part of a new and distinct organization, such as a fraternity or sorority, religious organization, military unit, or corporation (Oberg, 1960).

Stage one is a honeymoon phase, during which the new experience is perceived to be interesting, picturesque, entertaining, and charming. You may notice several superficial differences such as music, food, and clothing, and the exotic or fresh appeal of the new experience keeps you feeling interested and positive. If you are a real tourist, you probably do not stay long enough for this phase to wear off but go on to the next new location or experience. There are people who frequently change jobs, majors, romantic partners, travel plans, clothing styles, foods, diets, or cars so that they never get very far away from the honeymoon stage of culture shock. It is very pleasant to travel and to sample and explore whatever is new, so this pattern is understandable, if ultimately not deeply enriching.

When you stay in a new environment for a while, you move to stage two—the crisis stage—in which the shine wears off and day-to-day realities sink in. In a relationship, you notice annoying habits; in a new country, you find barriers to establishing connections or to learning the language beyond a few polite phrases. Suddenly, your new major includes a class or a professor you dislike. The difficulties and unpleasantness of reality replace the charming and picturesque "honeymoon." However, if you stick with the experience and try to deal with it realistically, you will probably move to the third phase of culture shock: recovery.

In recovery, you learn the systems, procedures, language, or nonverbal behaviors of the new environment so that you can cope with it on the basis of some mastery, competence, and comfort. After about two weeks in London, I began to feel familiar with traveling by "tube," shopping nearly every day for groceries, paying in the correct currency, buying a newspaper, and using some phrases that are unique to English people. I had the advantage of speaking the same basic language and of sharing a great deal with the English in some broad, cultural aspects. In a country that was very different from my own, it would probably have taken me longer to move into the recovery phase.

Finally, the fourth, or adjustment, phase occurs when you feel that you function well and almost automatically in the new culture. You no longer need to make mental conversions of the country's money; you know where services are located and how to use them; you understand some of the rituals or habits that accompany ordinary life, and it is relatively easy for you to accommodate them. A greater enjoyment of the new experience is now possible, and you may regain some of the initial positive regard you had in the honeymoon stage. If you stay long enough on a visit from a big city to a small town, or vice versa, you may become so well acculturated that when you return to your original home, you will again experience culture shock. For some people, it may take several days to readjust, depending on the length of time they were away. Usually, however, since you are in your home culture, your shock wears off faster than the shock that you experienced in the new culture.

Cross-Cultural Communication Competency

Scholars who study intercultural communication have identified eight areas in which you can build competence in an intercultural setting. These eight items are called the BASICS (Behavioral Assessment Scale for Intercultural Competence) of intercultural communication. (Lustig and Koester, 1996).

These eight competencies will help you to adapt to any change in your cultural context. If you were to join a new company, you would soon learn that it is not okay to set your coffee cup on the supervisor's desk (display of respect) but it is okay to seek help directly from the supervisor on a work issue (task role behavior). Perhaps one of the most difficult competencies described by Lusting and Koester is tolerance for ambiguity, since it may require you to put your

TABLE 19.1   The BASICS of Intercultural Competence

Display of respect	The ability to show respect and positive regard for another person.
Orientation to knowledge	The terms people use to explain themselves and the world around them.
Empathy	The capacity to behave as though you understand the world as others do.
Task role behavior	Behaviors that involve the initiation of ideas related to group problem-solving activities.
Relational role behavior	Behaviors associated with interpersonal harmony and mediation.
Interaction management	Skill in regulating conversations.
Tolerance for ambiguity	The ability to react to new and ambiguous situations with little visible discomfort.
Interaction posture	The ability to respond to others in descriptive, nonevaluative, and nonjudgmental ways.

behaviors on hold and observe carefully in a new or unfamiliar situation. Although the BASICS of intercultural communication can be taken as good general guidelines, remember that one of the areas of difficulty is the failure to recognize differences. When applying the BASICS to your own behavior, be on the lookout for variations within each culture (Lustig and Koester, 1996).

There are many steps that you can take to build a repertoire of skills to help you to communicate in cross-cultural situations. In addition to the BASICS approach, you can, of course, try to learn the language of the host culture. Even if that language is a form of your own native language, there will be differences between the two, sometimes important ones, to which you need to pay attention. For example, you might be unfamiliar with the British use of the word *bonnet* for the hood of a car and be perplexed when you are asked to lift your bonnet while topping up at a petrol stop. If you ask for napkins in a grocery store in England, you will be directed to the aisle containing disposable diapers. Remember not to assume that a *similar* language is the *same* language. The writer George Bernard Shaw once described the United States and Great Britain as "two countries divided by a common language." In the case of a clearly different language, you are apt to realize that you don't know the terms and will make an attempt to learn them.

In terms of nonverbal communication, Leathers (1986) gives nine guidelines that you can keep in mind when adjusting to a different culture. You can monitor your behavior by following these suggestions:

- Become familiar with the facial expressions that are typical of the culture. Find out whether the public display of emotions is acceptable and, if so, which type of emotion.
- Learn and follow the rules for the correct form and sequence that are involved in greeting rituals.
- Learn what status distinctions must be observed and how to acknowledge them.

CRITICAL THINKING IN COMMUNICATION

Intercultural Communication in the Classroom

If you took a poll of your classmates regarding some important issues—abortion, capital punishment, public support for education, immigration, taxation, ethics—you would find some agreements and some disagreements. These agreements and disagreements show how people who might share a basic culture still have important differences. The critical thinker recognizes the fallacy of hasty generalization and avoids it in cross-cultural communication. You can then see that even in a single cultural sample, a varying percentage of respondents will support one item but not others. This same principle would hold true if you sampled a population from another culture. So use your critical-thinking skills to help you to minimize stereotyping.

- Determine how much physical contact is allowed, by whom, and in what situations.
- Try to be sensitive to norms regarding how close people stand to each other. Find out what eye behaviors are appropriate, and become familiar with the expectations and rules for touching.
- Follow nonverbal regulators for conversation management, and learn them yourself.
- Identify the culture's most important, general nonverbal behaviors, and modify your own so that you identify and fit in with the values of the culture.
- Learn the specific, nonverbal behaviors that communicate insults, and avoid using them.
- Know the type of clothing and personal artifacts that are and are not compatible with cultural expectations. Gender-related norms of dress can be especially problematic for Americans.

Following these suggestions for verbal and nonverbal adaptations to other cultures will certainly enlarge your repertoire. Then you can follow up by putting into practice the results of your efforts to learn how to communicate when you find yourself in a culture other than your own. You can select new behaviors from your increased store of alternatives and choices. As you implement your knowledge, watch and listen for feedback, and then use that feedback to evaluate your choices or to add more verbal and nonverbal behaviors to your repertoire. All of these factors may then lead to success in meeting your goals or objectives in an intercultural situation (Spitzberg, 1994).

COMMUNICATION AND GENDER

Some communication scholars discuss communication between men and women as a form of cross-cultural communication (Tannen, 1990). The experience of growing up as a male or as a female in any society probably differs, as it certainly does in this society. Writer Deborah Tannen described it this way: "Even if they grow up in the same neighborhood, on the same block, or even in the same house girls and boys grow up in different worlds of words" (Tannen, 1994). You have already been exposed to the issue of gender and communication from watching television programs that offer male and female perspectives on issues or events or even from talking to friends about difficulties you may be experiencing with someone of the opposite sex. Some differences in the way people communicate are due to the relationship per se and are independent of gender differences. However, being male or being female creates some specific communication consequences that are being studied with increasing interest.

Males, Females, and Communication

Gender-related communication is much like cross-cultural communication in that the differences that being male or female create in communication and behaviors are a potential barrier to communication effectiveness (Tannen, 1990). The topic of **gender** and communication refers to the specific communication behaviors that a person uses because of being either male or female. Unlike biological sex, gender-related communication behaviors are not inherited, nor are they caused by chromosome composition. These behaviors are acquired and used by you as a result of your own and others' reactions to your biological sex. Women produce eggs and develop mammary glands, and men have beards and larger larynxes—as a matter of genetic determination. However, saying, "That's a lovely mauve Porsche, isn't it?" rather than saying, "That purple Porsche is classic!" represents a learned behavior of which either gender is capable but in which only one or the other generally engages.

Importance of Gender

Since we are destined to live in a two-gender world, and because many of our most significant interactions will be with people of the opposite gender, it is self-evident that this area of study is important. Add to this idea the finding that women's communication is treated differently—and usually valued less—than men's communication, and you can readily see that a basic inequality exists in our society. This inequality leads to women's relative absence from top positions in virtually every area of academic, business, civic, and political life. Not only is this situation unfair to women, it also costs every society in which it occurs untold amounts of energy because only part of the society's resources are being used. Studying gender and communication can help everyone to understand the realities of gender-related differences in communication instead of perpetuating assumptions about male-female communication. Using knowledge-based reality is a sound approach to making choices in life; acting on untested, albeit popular, myths is not. Knowledge about gender and communication can help you to become aware of unwarranted stereotyping and make it your goal to treat all people as individuals. Although real or meaningful differences between men and women should not be ignored, we should not unnecessarily emphasize those that are either unimportant or untrue (J. Stewart, 1986).

Aspects of Gender

Gender-related differences in language usage can be divided into three general categories (Pearson, 1985): (1) substantive differences, (2) hybrid substance/structure differences, and (3) structural differences. Each of these categories has several elements.

Substantive Differences.   Vocabulary that includes swearing, expressions of hostility, profanity, and expletives is used primarily by men. Women more often use hypercorrection and softening or weakening elements such as intensifiers, hedging, fillers, and qualifiers. In terms of a general vocabulary, women have a larger repertoire of terms, especially adjectives and adverbs (Lakoff, 1975; Crosby and Nyquist, 1977). Therefore women are able to be more precise and descriptive in using words to convey meaning exactly. Women were also found to have more elegant speech than men. However, younger men use more varied and elaborate speech than older men do, so this difference between men and women may be fading (Rich, 1977).

When it comes to expressing hostility and using profanity or expletives, men traditionally seem to use more of this type of language than women. However, one study found that in reality, the two sexes behaved about the same. Nevertheless, both men and women *predicted* that men would engage in stronger profanity than women would (Staley, 1988).

Hypercorrection is the behavior of reminding others about the correct form of expression, usually immediately after they have used an incorrect form. The use of him/her and he/she may be the issue or a verb form such as "If I *were* a millionaire" instead of "If I *was* a millionaire." An American student attending the ballet in London had a hypercorrection experience when the Queen entered unannounced and took her place in the royal box. There was a slight stir in the audience, and the student stood up, turned around, and in a fairly loud voice began to exclaim, "It's her! It's her!" One Londoner finally said sarcastically, "It's her . . . what?" The student, apparently unaware that "she" was correct and "her" was incorrect, simply repeated, "It's *her!*" Whereupon the woman sitting next to the student rescued the situation by saying, "It's . . . her . . . Majesty."

Women's speech also contains more elements that soften, or discount, the message. These elements include intensifiers, hedges, fillers, and qualifiers. The intensifiers *so, very, such* and so on, especially when emphasized and elongated in speech (Lakoff, 1975), are more typical of women's speech than of men's. If men use them, they are likely to be perceived as being effeminate, since women were found to use five to seven times as many of these words as did men (McMillan et al., 1977).

Women also use more words such as *maybe, possibly,* and *somewhat* as a way of making statements sound more tentative. One interesting finding that Pearson (1985) noted showed that children of both sexes showed no differences in their use of qualifiers, but by the time they reached adulthood, the females were clearly employing more qualifying phrases or words. Women are also more likely to use vocal fillers—*okay, um*—especially in mixed-sex situations, giving the impression of uncertainty or hesitation (Hirschman, 1975). As standards change, we may experience a lessening of the differences.

Hybrid Differences. In terms of hybrid differences, Pearson (1985) reviewed several studies and concluded that women and men structure their interactions differently. In conversations, women are more likely to be interrupted by men than men by women. Women seem to be more sensitive to turn taking than men are. Men tend to speak more often and for longer periods of time than women do. Men also tend to control the topics discussed. For example, in a conversation, the items that are introduced by men are usually picked up by women, who follow them along, whereas men do not respond to topics introduced by women. They often either ignore the topics, respond minimally, or shift the topic back to the one they had introduced (Pearson, 1985). Women are more likely to engage in questioning, even when the questions are substitutes for statements, such as saying, "Is it time to be going?" to mean "It's time to go." Women also convert statements into questions by using a tag form: "It's time to go, isn't it?" Tags added to a statement may be perceived as communicating deference, uncertainty, or hesitation—all of which reinforce sex-role stereotypes about decisiveness. One researcher found that **tag questions** may be used by both men and women but that they vary in context. For example, women use tags in mixed-sex conversation to draw out the men, that is, pull them into responding (Thorne, 1981).

Structural Differences. Included in structural differences is the amount of time used to talk in conversations by each sex. In mixed-sex settings, men usually talk more than women, or they talk for an equal amount of time (Thorne, 1981). No study indicated that women talked more than men. In addition, Pearson (1985) reviewed nine research articles, all of which noted the likelihood of men interrupting women in conversation but not the reverse:

> **Interruptions** are generally perceived as attempts at conversational dominance, since they minimize the communicative role of the person being interrupted (Markel et al., 1976).

Researchers have also studied sex-role stereotypes and sex differences in nonverbal communication (L. Stewart, 1986). Body positions, postures, gestures, facial expressions, and vocal characteristics all have sex-role associations. Women are generally better than men at encoding and decoding nonverbal messages, while men use more space in giving nonverbal messages. Both men and women are concerned with appearance; men associate body type with power, and women associate it with thinness. This latter concern may contribute to eating disorders, which are vastly more common among women than men (L. Stewart et al., 1986).

Gender and Communication Competency

Gender and communication concepts have a significant application in a variety of settings. For example, whereas sex-role communication behaviors in same-sex combinations can be fairly straightforward, they become more complex and interesting in mixed-sex couples and in marriage. The attitudes and expectations of the partners affect their communication patterns—for better or worse. You have read about the greater time and attention that are given to boys by classroom teachers of both sexes, and we still have social expectations of sex-appropriate behavior and career expectations of sex-appropriate areas of achievement, though this situation seems to be changing somewhat. Some of these expectations are played out for us in the media, but whether the media set these expectations or simply reflect them is a questionable matter.

When you leave the educational setting and move into career situations, you will find sex-role and gender-linked communication patterns on the job (Tannen, 1994). One study looked at factors that helped women to succeed in business and career settings (Morrison et al., 1990). Six factors were linked to success in this survey of high-achieving business women:

1. Mentoring. Others, often supervisors, offered help, advice, and assistance.
2. Achievement. The women developed a record of accomplishments.
3. Desire. By putting in long hours and working hard, they showed that they were committed to their work and were capable of some personal sacrifice.
4. Management skills. The women demonstrated an ability to motivate people to perform and, at the same time, to earn and keep their trust and respect.
5. Willingness to take risks. They would travel or move as needed to build a career.
6. Assertiveness. The women were decisive, were able to make tough choices, and were willing to stand up for their ideas, projects, or subordinates.

As you read this list developed from a study of successful women executives, you probably noticed that these traits would be valuable to men in business as well. One area that still remains distinctly gender-related, however, may be women's willingness to work together, while men still maintain some territoriality and competitiveness in their careers (Loden, 1990). Women in management can bring a teamwork style to the work setting that stresses cooperation more than competition. In mixed-sex teams, women tend to assume cooperative, assuring, and affirming communication patterns unless there is a structure that decreases or prevents interruptions and moves for dominance, communication behaviors that are more common to men (Sommers and Lawrence, 1992). As gender-related mores change, you need to be aware of the options for change that are open to you as well.

COMMUNICATION, AGE, AND HEALTH

This discussion concerns two emerging areas of study: the effects of age and the effects of health on communication. Both areas are receiving serious and increasing attention from communication researchers, and courses in these subjects are becoming more common.

With age, many people experience changes in identity (Galvin and Brommel, 1996). The study of communication and aging is the study of the effects of chronological age on an individual's message production and perception and corresponding adjustments that others make when sending messages to older people. For example, if an older person's primary definition of a self-concept was a career and that person retires, what happens to self-definition and self-esteem? They change, and changes in self-concept affect message production

As people age, their communication patterns can change.

and perception. Consider a person who has been completely involved in rearing children. When the children grow up and leave, what replaces that person's previous communication patterns? Changes in role and accompanying changes in self-esteem may lead to stress both on the person's intrapersonal communication and on relationships.

Some studies show that when members of a group are about the same age, there is a positive effect on interpersonal and group communication (Zenger and Lawrence, 1989). People who are around the same age probably have more in common with each other than people of widely different ages do, so interaction is facilitated. Growing older can enrich a person's repertoire and make that person an increasingly valuable participant in any interaction. It is not only the fact that people age that is important but that they have had more experiences in a variety of situations (Shaw, 1981). Therefore, while communication among people similar in age might be easier, communication among people of different ages might be more interesting and valuable.

THE STORY OF COMMUNICATION

Grandparents

Do you have a grandparent, or perhaps a great-grandparent, with whom you communicate? If so, you have a real gift. My grandmother used to read aloud to her great-grandchildren (my daughter and son) until just before her death at age 95. She was also fond of telling stories of her experiences as a child and told my children how she had seen the world change so much between 1888 and 1983. "I came up from candlelight, to watch a man walk on the moon" was the expression she used to emphasize how much had transpired in a single lifetime. If grandparents are a gift, great-grandparents are a treasure.

There are difficulties in communication among people of different ages, just as there are in any other communication area. Obstacles that are similar to cross-cultural barriers arise when people are of widely different ages. The so-called generation gap is really a communication gap. Older people generally have different time perceptions from those of younger people, and differences in mobility between the two groups may also be important. Older people are sometimes subjected to stereotyping in the same way that people from other cultures are. In addition, health concerns, such as vision or hearing impairments, affect older people more often than younger people. Let us next consider the effects of health on communication.

Health and Communication

One way to define this area is to say that it is the study of how health variables affect the production, perception, and reception of messages. Researchers describe it as follows: "The study of **health communication** focuses on the interaction of people involved in the health care process and the interpretation and dissemination of health related information" (Ray and Donohew, 1990; Jackson, 1995). It is an interdisciplinary study, pulling together insights from the medical, psychological, sociological, and even political areas to analyze the communicative interactions.

Obvious barriers to communication are presented by people with hearing losses or vision impairments. Mobility difficulties, such as being in a wheelchair, can also have an impact on a person's communication repertoire and skills. In some studies, people's mental health has been shown to be positively affected by solid communication abilities. Research is being done on the effects of the communication of social support, some of which shows that stress, depression, and even cancer can be helped with increased communication and social support (Jackson, 1995).

Differences in physical ability or health may affect communication interactions.

Conversely, when you think of people who lack mental health, you might consider the signs or symptoms of their illness as being communication impairments. If you were assigned the exercise of role-playing a schizophrenic, a manic-depressive, or a paranoiac, how would you portray this person other than through bizarre or unusual communication patterns?

The widespread use of drugs in our society has resulted in some severe cases of communication impairment. The abuse of alcohol and other substances can create both temporary and permanent communication barriers in people that may be difficult to overcome because they are difficult to identify.

Another area of interest to health communication specialists deals with the health care system and how it communicates with its clients. For example, physicians may not always know how to explain, in everyday terms, a condition, treatment, or procedure to their patients. How a hospital communicates with the family of a patient and what kind of public-service messages about health issues are made for radio or television consumption, are also areas of investigation for communication researchers.

In addition to sending unclear or inappropriate messages, people with physical or mental health problems also may *be sent* different kinds of messages. For example, many people automatically talk louder to a person in a wheelchair, even though the person in the chair may not have a hearing impairment. Typically, people who have some obvious disability find others speaking to them in louder tones and using simpler vocabulary. Why do people make these adjustments to their communication behaviors when sending messages to disabled persons? It may be a question of stereotyping, just as it is in cross-cultural communication.

Benefits from Improved Health Communication Competency

Improvements in the interpersonal communication between physicians and patients have the potential to increase both the patient's and physician's satisfaction, to enhance the patient's comprehension of advice and directions, and perhaps even to decrease the number of malpractice suits (Jackson, 1992, 1995). Similarly, with better use of mass media campaigns, knowledge and skill of communication in health-related areas can promote better health, prevent disease, and reach larger groups. Communication scholars are also involved in applying their research to planning, influencing, and evaluating health care policy.

TECHNOLOGY IN COMMUNICATION

Health, Culture, and Media

One of the interesting intersections in the field of communication occurs when advances in health technology meet resistance from people because of cultural barriers. For example, in the 1940s and 1950s, films warning people, especially college students, about the dangers of marijuana were tried as part of a public health campaign. One such film, called *Reefer Madness,* purported that smoking marijuana would lead to virtually instant insanity. The culture and the message were so at odds that this film is now a classic on the "midnight movie" circuit, where audiences roar at the clumsy attempt to use this mass media tool in a public health campaign. The message must be believable to be effective.

Overcoming Communication Barriers Related to Age and Health

The first step in overcoming these barriers is to recognize that age and health do have communication significance for you and that you are likely to alter and adjust your messages on the basis of factors related to age and health.

In an effort to overcome stereotyping, you need to recognize some of the strengths and insights that people of different ages and abilities bring to interactions. You can also examine your attitudes and behaviors toward older people to find out whether they are appropriate. Age and health are linked, and studying their interaction presents interesting prospects for enlarging our knowledge about communication.

SUMMARY

Diversity in communication is an exciting area, but certain problems hamper researchers' ability to acquire knowledge about them. The complexity of interactions will increase as the peoples of the world communicate with each other more easily and frequently. However, your knowledge of how filters and screens operate in daily life can be applied to messages that travel from one cultural background to another. Taking care to monitor both your verbal and nonverbal behaviors, you can go beyond a superficial touring of other cultures and gain insight into yourself as well as others. Culture shock may be one result of interaction with another culture, but now that you are prepared for it, you should be able to get through it to a deeper understanding of yourself and other cultures.

You will also experience the effects of gender on communication for the rest of your life, and research on this subject clearly reveals the power and dominance differences that are displayed by men's and women's communication patterns. Become sensitive to the disparities in communication patterns between men and women and to the inherent waste of potential resources that these disparities cause. Then you can begin to alter your own communication patterns to reflect a greater sharing and use of time with other people and more appreciation of contributions to communication from everyone with whom you interact.

Age and health are becoming important areas of communication research. By exploring the effects and processes of communication interactions related to age and health, researchers learn more about what our lives might be like in the future. This brief discussion serves only as an introduction to this fascinating area of inquiry. By developing an interest in these areas, you too may one day join the complex world of communication interaction as a researcher in age and health.

KEY TERMS

intercultural communication, *p. 384*
culture, *p. 384*
filters and screens, *p. 388*
ethnocentrism, *p. 388*
culture shock, *p. 390*

gender-related communication, *p. 394*
gender, *p. 394*
tag questions, *p. 396*
interruptions, *p. 396*
health communication, *p. 399*

EXERCISES

1. Trace your family history for a few generations, if possible. Then write an imaginative essay about the cultural adjustments members of your family might have had to make as they moved, changed jobs, married, and traveled. Reflect on the cultural adjustments you might have to make during your lifetime.

2. Does a television station in your area broadcast in different languages? Or is there one that broadcasts in English but is targeted to a specific cultural group? If so, watch a selection of programs for a few nights, and observe the cultural communication patterns used by the people on these programs. Watch a soap opera or the evening news. What perspectives are revealed in these programs?

3. Most college campuses have an international club, and it is the perfect place to meet people from different countries and cultures. Attend either a meeting or an activity of such an organization on your campus. If there are many organizations, each aimed at a particular cultural group, visit one or

two of them and record any barriers to effective intercultural communication that you observe. How many of these barriers did you encounter on your visit? Were you a tourist? Would you visit the same group again? Why or why not?

4. Keep track of gender jokes that you hear in person, on television, or on the radio, and look for gender jokes in print. At what traits are these jokes aimed? Does their humor depend on stereotyping? Some live comedy television shows feature male and female stand-up comics who talk a great deal about the opposite sex. Why are their monologues funny?

5. If you are male, observe a conversation between a man and a woman, and keep track of the number of interruptions and the person making them. If you are female, observe a similar conversation, and keep track of the number of tag questions and the person making them. Do your subjects reflect the research findings? Do you, in your conversations with individuals of the opposite sex?

REFERENCES

Barnlund, D. C. *Public and Private Self in Japan and the United States.* Tokyo: Simul Press, 1975. 5.

Crosby, F., and L. Nyquist. "The Female Register: An Empirical Study of Lakoff's Hypotheses." *Language and Society* 6 (1977).

Fairchild, H., ed. *Dictionary of Sociology.* New York, 1944.

Galvin, K. M., and B. J. Brommel. *Family Communication: Cohesion and Change.* 4th ed. New York: HarperCollins, 1996.

Giles, H., and P. Johnson. "The Role of Language in Ethnic Group Relations." *Intergroup Behavior.* Ed. J. Turner and H. Giles. Chicago: University of Chicago Press, 1981.

Hecht, M. L., M. J. Collier, and S. A. Ribeau. *African American Communication.* Newbury Park: Sage, 1993.

Hirschman, Lynette. "Female-Male Differences in Conversational Interaction." *Language and Sex: Difference and Dominance.* Ed. Barrie Thorne and Nancy Henley. Rowley: Newbury House, 1975.

Jackson, Lorraine. "Information Complexity and Medical Communication: The Effect of Technical Language and Amount of Information in a Medical Message." *Health Communication* 4(3) (1992).

Jackson, Lorraine. Personal letter. 31 Jan. 1995.

Kroeber, A. L., and C. Kluckhohn. *Culture: A Critical Review of Concepts and Definitions.* New York: Random House, 1952.

Lakoff, Robin. *Language and Woman's Place.* New York: Harper Colophon Books, 1975.

Leathers, D. G. *Successful Nonverbal Communication.* New York: MacMillan, 1986.

Loden, M. "Feminine Leadership: Or How to Succeed in Business without Being One of the Boys." *Manager's Bookshelf.* Ed. J. Pierce and J. Newstrom. New York: Harper & Row, 1990.

Lustig, Myron, and Jolene Koester. *Intercultural Competence: Interpersonal Communication across Cultures.* 2nd ed. New York: HarperCollins, 1996.

Markel, N., J. Long, and T. Saine. "Sex Effects in Conversational Interaction: Another Look at Male Dominance." *Human Communication Research* 2 (1976), 356.

McLuhan, M. *Understanding Media: The Extensions of Man.* New York: McGraw-Hill, 1964.

McMillan, J. R., A. K. Clifton, D. McGrath, and W. S. Gale. "Women's Language: Uncertainty or Interpersonal Sensitivity and Emotionality?" *Sex Roles* 3 (1977).

Morrison, A., R. White, and E. Van Velsor. "Breaking the Glass Ceiling: Can Women Reach the Top of America's Largest Corporations?" *Manager's Bookshelf.* Ed. J. Pierce and J. Newstrom. New York: Harper & Row, 1990.

Newmark, E., and M. Asante. *Intercultural Communication.* Annandale: Speech Communication Association, 1976.

Oberg, K. "Culture Shock: Adjustment to New Cultural Environments." *Practical Anthropology,* 7 (1960), 177–182.

Pearson, J. *Gender and Communication.* Dubuque: Wm. C. Brown, 1985.

Pearson, J., L. Turner, and W. Todd-Mancillas. *Gender and Communication.* 2nd ed. Dubuque: 1991.

Ray, E. B., and L. Donohew. *Communication and Health: Systems and Applications.* Hillsdale: Erlbaum, 1990.

Rich, Elaine. "Sex-Related Differences in Colour Vocabulary." *Language and Speech* (1977), 404–409.

Samovar, Larry A., and Richard E. Porter. *Intercultural Communication.* 7th ed. Belmont: Wadsworth, 1994.

Shaw, Marvin E. *Group Dynamics: The Psychology of Small Group Behavior.* New York: Academic Press, 1981.

Sommers, E., and S. Lawrence. "Women's Ways of Talking in Teacher-Directed and Student-Directed Peer Response Groups." *Linguistics and Education,* 4 (1992).

Spitzberg, B. "A Model for Intercultural Communication Competence." *Intercultural Communication.* Ed. Larry A. Samovar and Richard E. Porter. 7th ed. Belmont: Wadsworth, 1994.

Staley, Constance C. "The Communicative Power of Women Managers: Doubts, Dilemmas, and Management Development Programs." *Women and Communicative Power: Theory, Research and Practice.* Ed. Carol Ann Valentine and Nancy Hoar. Annandale: Speech Communication Association, 1988.

Stewart, J. Bridges Not Walls. New York: Random House, 1986.

Stewart, L., P. Cooper, and S. Friedley. *Communication between the Sexes: Sex Differences and Sex-Role Stereotypes.* Scottsdale: Gorsuch, Scarisbrick, 1986.

Tannen, D. *You Just Don't Understand.* New York: Ballantine, 1990.

Tannen, D. *Talking from 9 to 5.* New York: Morrow, 1994.

Tatum, Beverly D. "Talking about Race, Leaning about Racism: The Application of Racial Identity Development Theory in the Classroom." *Harvard Educational Review* 62 (1992).

Thorne, B. Speech given at Michigan State University, East Lansing, Mich., 1981.

Turner, J. and H. Giles, eds. *Intergroup Behavior.* Chicago: University of Chicago Press, 1981.

Zenger, T., and B. Lawrence. "Organizational Demography: The Differential Effects of Age and Tenure Distribution on Technical Communication." *Academy of Management Journal* 32 (1989), 353.

Communication and Technology

- Understand how communication creates civilization.

- Explain how major communication events have affected history.

- Appreciate the processes that continue to shape communication development.

- Describe the effects of technology on major communication contexts.

- Feel confident about your ability to participate in communication situations using advanced technology.

C hapter 1 introduced the idea that the story of communication is also the story of human civilization. Whether we were discussing the ancient Africans, the Greeks and Romans, the Incas, or the Chinese, the common thread was how their communication systems created their daily lives, culture, and powers. Because these civilizations were able to invent or adapt new technologies that preserved their messages, we can use our communication abilities and thereby communicate with these long-dead people and learn from them about their lives.

COMMUNICATION TECHNOLOGY DEFINED

Perhaps you should think for a moment about the use of the word *technology*. Current users of the term seem to refer to the most recent advances in mechanics or electronics, but it is important to remember that the simplest tool, at the time it was invented, was the cutting-edge technology of its day. Therefore although you think of high-definition television, satellite transmission of cellular telephone conversations, electric-powered automobiles, or notebook computers as technology, other people at other times experienced paper, iron knives, dugout canoes, or bone needles as their technological advances. We use the term **communication technology** to mean "the body of tools, machines, materials, techniques, and processes used in human interaction for the sending and receiving of messages" (after Barnhart and Barnhart, 1979). Although the study of technology through history could be a fascinating approach, the focus of this chapter is on some of the important influences that our inventions have had on our communication. These influences are discussed in this chapter in the order in which they were introduced in the text. After a review of communication technology and civilization, we look at personal communication and technology in the intrapersonal, interpersonal, interview, and small-group settings. Next, the section on public communication and technology examines the public speaking and career contexts. The section on social communication and technology applies research findings to the areas of family, school, and community communication; mass media and society; and intercultural, gender, age, and health communication. Finally, we, see how communication competencies are affected by technology.

COMMUNICATION TECHNOLOGY AND CIVILIZATION

David Crowley and Paul Heyer, two Canadian scholars who have studied technology, culture and society, tell us (1995), "communication media have their enduring effect through their capacity to organize and reorganize the distribution of information and forms of knowledge in society" (p. 2). Building on the work of Harold Innes, they take the view that each communication technology brings inherent features to the civilizations that invent and use them and thereby affect the social institutions of any culture. For example, with the invention of papyrus (new technology) around 2700 B.C., stone tablets (previous technology) were replaced, leading to profound changes from an absolute monarchy to a more shared, democratic organization (Innes, 1950).

There is evidence that Neanderthals used images about 35,000 years ago and recorded these symbols by carving and engraving. Often, these symbols were notches that might have recorded the count of animals or shapes that parallel the phases of the moon, perhaps done in repeated sequences over several months (Marshack, 1978). This symbol-using behavior was passed down for thousands of years. In Mesopotamia, other symbols emerged as counting devices in the form of small, thimblelike tokens that represented various goods such as sheep or oil and could be stored in a clay ball envelope for later reckoning (Schmandt-Besserat, 1986). Pictographic writing emerged in Asia, Mesopotamia, and Egypt around 5000 B.C. These symbol systems meant that their cultures could now extend communication across time and place. In Chapter 6, we discuss how this notion of *time binding* and *space binding* has been used by Korzybski, Hayakawa, and other general semanticists to explain the impact of communication on civilization and societies.

The Greeks are credited with developing the alphabetical system, which included consonants (derived from the Phoenicians) and vowels. The flexibility of this symbol system gave rise to the flowering of literature and philosophy as one person's thoughts and ideas could be preserved beyond the immediate hearers and could be read, contemplated, and responded to by many others at different times and a variety of places. Have you been assigned to read and write an essay in response to the writing of Plato? If so, you have shared in an assignment that some of Aristotle's students completed for him, some of Quintillian's students in Rome struggled with, Renaissance students in Venice completed for their teachers, someone in Tokyo did last week, and someone in Caracas will start next month.

The technological advances that are represented by the invention of papyrus, parchment, block printing, movable type, radio, television, and electronic microchip circuitry have affected the way in which societies developed. "In addition to the immediate and obvious consequences of these technological shifts, there have been a series of longer-term effects that permeate our lives in sometimes subtle ways" (Crowley and Heyer, 1995, p. 1). For example, the ability of papyrus to be moved more easily than stone meant that orders, messages, reports, and therefore *control* could be expanded by central authorities to wider and larger areas. It also meant that larger numbers of people had to be able to read and write to understand and carry out orders and to provide feedback. Literacy was associated with power from the very first, and power was usually associated with religion, magic, and force of arms, making writing an extension of these sometimes terrifying forces. If you could control the words of the priest, ruler, or general, you became a partner in this power (Diringer, 1948). Communication technology—the development and expansion of these media tools—has been (and is being) used both as an agent to maintain social order and as an agent to create change (Crowley and Heyer, 1995).

The extensive system of roads that the Romans built throughout their farflung empire had the express purpose of allowing messages to travel faster between central and outlying authorities. The technological advances of writing, standardized grammar, horse-drawn durable chariot wheels, and road paving and grading combined into an effective communication network so that messages could travel substantial distances in a matter of days and arrive in exactly the same form as sent. The written word captured the spoken word and sent the "voice" of the emperor or central authority to many people and many locations. Thus control over the huge territory that the Roman armies had conquered was accomplished by the use of what might seem to us today to be fairly simple technologies. The idea that increased sophistication in technology resulted in increased power is clear. It also raised questions about who would have access to this increased control of information and thus increased power. The very same forces that built an empire could also mean that more people would have access to those forces.

Access to Communication Technology

One of the questions that communication technology has raised, from ancient times to today, is who is to be given access to new message resources? In ancient Egypt, only priests were taught to read. In 1996, the **Internet** had over 35 million users in 135 countries, and that number was growing by 10 to 15 percent *monthly* (Carveth and Metz, 1995). From the introduction of the technology of the electronic computer on February 14, 1946, it took a relatively short fifty years for this technology to span the world (Strauss, 1996). In 1996, Congress passed and President Clinton signed a major bill reforming laws governing communication technology. One provision of the law prohibited sending "indecent material" over the Internet on the justification that children have easy access to that medium of communication. Although that section of the law was made void by the courts, it did show how access to information is a continuing concern with every new technology.

In closed societies, communication is always the target of access limitations and controls. When I traveled in the Soviet Union in 1987, for example, I never saw a copy machine. Never. The multiple ones that you and I depend on each day on every floor of the library, in our offices, at club headquarters, and our neighborhood convenience store or copy center were simply nonexistent in that society. I remember asking at a hotel in Saint Petersburg to make a copy of a page from a restaurant menu and having to wait for twenty minutes while a supervisor was found and brought to me. She then explained the forms that I would need to fill out, the justification I would need to provide, the approvals that would be necessary from a variety of authorities, and the days that all of these steps would take—all for something you or I would not give a second thought to.

In the early days of the United States, it was illegal to teach a slave to read or write, and severe punishment awaited any who violated these laws. Girls were often given little education. The ability to read and write meant access to information and less control by others. Some people used religion to circumvent these laws. If slaves or women could justify their desire to read in order to read the Bible, some exceptions were made. But as we saw in Chapter 6, after the Gutenberg Bible spread access to this book to thousands of previously excluded people, debate and challenge to existing authority arose. In the United States, many abolitionists and suffragists began with the Bible as the foundation for their movements. Many of the early African American and female advocates of these causes started their education with religious texts.

Current access to computer technology reflects some of these same elements of restricted access, with men tending to get more and deeper levels of training than women in both educational and career settings (Brunet and Proulx, 1989). On the other hand, with the increasing availability of computers due to ever-decreasing costs, huge increases in access are occurring to link colleges and universities with elementary schools and well-to-do private colleges with inner-city classrooms (Sussman, 1992).

One of the principles of the founding of the United States was the freedom of communication, which is especially prominent in the First Amendment to the Constitution but is found in several other places as well. Each year, new challenges to restrictions on our communication by government are brought forth, often as a result of a new technology that affects a communication medium. All television sets that are manufactured after 1996 must have the "v-chip" installed, which is supposed to enable parents to block certain violent or otherwise objectional programs so that their children do not have access to them. As we discussed in several earlier chapters, one continuing tension in our society concerns the amount of free expression we will tolerate and the amount of restriction on expression we will accept (Cisler, 1990).

This tension is often expressed in legal and religious forums. This chapter is neither forum, but it is important to recognize these questions. They can be examined from an ethical perspective, using some of the ideas that we developed in the section on spoken communication as a guide.

Ethics and Communication Technology

Most immediate questions of ethics and electronic communication can be addressed from the perspective that is used to discuss informative and persuasive speaking. Based on elements drawn from critical thinking to test evidence, this perspective asks you to examine the communication's truthfulness, completeness, care and precision of expression, and value to the receiver. When thinking about the impact of a technological development on a culture or society, we need to think about the potential for expanding each of these dimensions, as well as the possibilities for violating our system of ethics (Forester, 1991).

Truthfulness is the base from which to begin your ethical examination of a new technology. Does this technology help to discover, reveal, preserve, or communicate truth? For example, using a computer-based library search to help write a term paper would seem to add greatly to your ability to discover the best findings and results. By expanding your access to many more sources of information than a conventional library card catalog, you are using technology in an ethical way to help you arrive at accurate information. However, if the same computer network technology can be used by rival political candidates to spread rumors or bits of information out of context about each other, the use of the technology fails the ethical test for truthfulness. Clearly, as in the other forms of communication, it is not the technology solely, but the use of the technology, that determines this evaluation. The tools by themselves have no morals; the users of those tools do (Smitter, 1995).

The test of *completeness* asks you to determine whether the whole truth is being told or only carefully or ignorantly selected bits of information are being presented that distort the ultimate impact of the message. As is pointed out in

Ancient libraries were made possible by advances in communication technology.

the chapter on persuasion, you could easily have a series of information bits, each true by itself, but if key parts are missing, the final impression would be distorted. Technology has made communication more available; has made storage and retrieval of information more permanent, abundant, and accurate; and has made the movement or transfer of information easier, faster, and farther with each development. When paper or parchment made the storage of vast amounts of information possible, we had our first libraries. I once visited the library in the ancient city of Ephesus on the coast of Turkey. There, you can imagine the walls lined with shelves holding the collected writings of Greek civilization to that point in history. Now the entire holdings of that great building could probably be stored on one or two compact discs, and instant retrieval from your CD-ROM would find a document that might have taken a librarian in A.D. 65 at least several minutes to perhaps several hours to locate. Technology has enhanced our ability to be complete in our information gathering and using.

The *care and precision* of expression have also been enhanced as a result of technological advances in communication. When the written alphabet captured the spoken word, problems associated with accurate memory of texts were eliminated. It also meant that some standard rules of grammar were needed to keep meanings clear. When printing spread the written word to vast numbers of people, that technological advance meant that many people could have access to and check on the accuracy of information they previously had to accept without verifying. The videotaped testimony in modern trials can form a powerful record of statements. Many police units use the videocamera to record people undergoing sobriety tests at roadside checkpoints. Often, when shown these tapes, people who were inclined to try to fight the citation give up in the face of such precise communication about their own actions. The impact of the tape showing Rodney King being beaten points up both sides of this advance. The accuracy of the few moments captured on tape was undeniable. The major

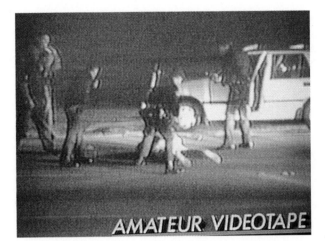

Video technology provides powerful testimony.

counterargument was that the tape was being shown out of context—that a few moments before that segment was recorded, there was violent resistance from Mr. King. But in the absence of videotape, the image that was broadcast over and over on television is the one that endures. The part of the ethical standards involving care and precision does not stand isolated from the standards of truthfulness and completeness.

Finally, the *value* of any technology for the receivers or consumers must be considered. Just as it is probably unethical to try to sell expensive encyclopedias to a family that can barely meet its monthly food bill, so too must any technological advance be evaluated by its impact on the people receiving it. Clearly, communication technology has opened up tremendous volumes of information, but is the information useful (Beadle, 1995)? Also, many ways of relating to each other, our families, our cultures, and our environment have been altered or replaced by technology. Television has been accused of destroying reading (Birkets, 1994), games, and conversation as family activities and causing, with those reductions, a reduction in the ability to relate to each other. On the other hand, communication technology has been used to help foster awareness of social justice issues by exposing people to information about the inequities suffered by others in society and by providing an electronic network to help bring concerned people into action groups (Palmeri, 1995).

Thus ethics and technology are linked in many important ways, and as an ethical communicator, you need to test the communication technology advances in much the same way that you would test a door-to-door encyclopedia sales pitch, or any other message you are asked to consume. These tests also give you a sense of how technology shapes our lives and our cultures. Someone once observed, "First we shape our tools, then our tools shape us." Has your life been shaped by television? The telephone? Your computer? The Internet?

There are studies that point to a whole social system or culture that is formed by users of the Internet (Bolter, 1984). It has become a "virtual community" of "netizens" with emerging customs, rules, and norms. Some of these norms are found in the ways in which a user approaches communication with others. A special form of Internet social rules is called *netiquette* to combine the terms *network* and *etiquette* (rules for behavior in polite society). New words and terms to define these network cultural norms are appearing to help newcomers learn the rules (Raymond, 1993) and become functionally integrated into the culture (Goode and Johnson, 1991).

Thus you have a brief perspective on how technology, especially the technology that is involved most directly with our communication interactions, affects the growth of civilization and an introduction to how questions of access to communication skills and technology are as old as writing itself and as current as the microchip. You have also seen how elements of ethics apply to communication technology. Let us now look at some of the effects technology has had on various communication contexts.

PERSONAL COMMUNICATION AND TECHNOLOGY

Intrapersonal Communication

When you learned about intrapersonal communication, you were asked to examine thinking and the development of the self-concept as they relate to your communication interactions. Already the effect of electronic communication technology on self-esteem, self-perception, self-disclosure, and patterns or styles of thinking can be seen (Gronbeck, 1991). In ancient days, the invention of writing and papyrus made it possible to share one's inner thoughts with people who were far away, thus giving them time to pause and reflect on their responses to those ideas. Much of this reflection focused on the nature of people and their relationships to knowledge, the universe, and each other. These ideas still concern students of philosophy, who still read the thoughts of ancient minds because of the technology ancient writers invented and used.

Self-concept is affected by communication technology. Do you consider yourself a reader? A game player? A hacker? You can use some aspects of computer-mediated technology to create a self and send that self out browsing the Internet. There are hundreds of examples of people creating a personality for the sole purpose of using it as a part of the on-line communication action (Chesebro and Bonsall, 1990). Men have been known to create female personalities, women to masquerade as men, people to change or mask their age, race, income, educational level, looks, and a variety of other personal attributes simply by creating fictional messages about these items. Thus not only have ancient advancements in communication media affected the way individuals and cultures perceive themselves, but each current advance in communication technology also affects the users, often in ways we cannot directly perceive because we are in the middle of the experience (Ong, 1982).

Interpersonal Communication and Technology

One of the great advances in communication technology was the ability to send a letter—a personal correspondence. The interpersonal relationships that were established through this medium for several thousand years continue today. Sometimes you may see a group letter, as when people mail out holiday greetings and enclose a printed review of their family activities for the year. The same

CRITICAL THINKING IN COMMUNICATION

Technology and Logic

Because computers are based on a digital platform, requiring a logical sequence of operations, there has been a tendency to think of them as being completely logical, mathematical, and technical. These elements are traditionally associated with a male, Eurocentric thinking style. However, recent research has revealed a diversity in the applications that programmers and other users of the technology bring to their interactions (Turkle and Papert, 1990). These researchers expand our concept of critical thinking to include a variety of approaches to knowledge, each as a style of thinking, each having validity in its own terms. They acknowledge that the "formal, propositional way of knowing has been recognized traditionally as a standard" (p. 129) but point out that large body of research shows how science, mathematics, and other traditional subjects have all experienced advances through informal, concrete, intuitive, and ad hoc kinds of discoveries. They connect these types and styles of knowing to feminist perspectives about the contributions of "women's ways of knowing" and thus expand our traditional concept of critical-thinking approaches (Turkle and Papert, 1990).

result is the goal of electronically mediated communication. By posting messages on an electronic bulletin board, interpersonal relationships are created, developed, maintained, and terminated. People who are involved in these groups exchange messages, give emotional support, gossip, find friends, lose friends, visit the library, brainstorm, fight, create romances, and find marriage partners or heartbreak (Rheingold, 1992).

In computer-mediated conversations, there may be more equality in participation, since the visual and verbal elements of status or power that help high-status or verbally assertive people dominate face-to-face conversation are eliminated (Perrolle, 1991). Does that mean that interpersonal relationships on the computer are free of such inferences? Not really. Using some of the work done by Mark Knapp that is discussed in Chapter 8 in terms of relationship development and deterioration, we can see that **e-mail** users can reveal their relationship perceptions by the use of formal or informal tone, by inclusions of more or fewer asides or expressions in parentheses, by whether they finish sentences, and so on (Walther, 1992).

You can see that interpersonal relationships have been affected by technology through time, whether it meant writing someone a letter or ignoring them by watching television. You can review the steps of relationship development that Knapp outlined and realize that technological communication can assist or hinder almost any step.

Interviewing and Technology

Question-and-answer interviews are still conducted, for the most part, without great technological applications. The extensions of our voices and presence through the telephone have made the sales interview a nearly constant, daily part of life: Telemarketing is one type of interview in which the technology of telephones has replaced the support of shoe leather. I use technology, in the form of a call-screening answering machine, to eliminate many of these interruptions of my dinner. However, when our university recently hired a new faculty member, we conducted a series of telephone interviews with our top five or six applicants. The budget would not allow bringing all of these people to our campus, so for a very few dollars—probably less than $10 each—we had thirty or forty minutes of conversation with twice the number of people we would have invited to visit in person. The refinement of adding video pictures to the telephone has been available for many years, but the cost factor is only now starting to diminish sufficiently that it will be widely available in a few years. That technological advance will allow us to put visual nonverbal elements back into the conversation.

I once applied for a job on my campus to assist the president. The finalists were selected and scheduled for interviews while I was on a trip to Greece with a group of students. The initial screening was done by telephone by our vice-president, who was also traveling at the time. Therefore, I had my first interview while sitting in hotel room in Athens talking to a vice-president in a hotel in London about a job in California.

Even popular television interview shows have taken the seemingly private conversations of two people and made them accessible to millions of viewers. Some shows, such as those of Jay Leno and Oprah Winfrey, have hundreds of people present in the studio, but others, like those of Larry King and Charlie Rose, really do capture the intimate conversation of just two people talking. Sometimes a third party is invited into the conversation in the form of a viewer call-in element. Recently, "Oprah!" turned to the Internet and went on-line with a feedback element ("Oprah Online!," 1995).

Many prospective job applicants no longer just send in a resumé, as we discussed in Chapter 9, but also include a CD, videotape, or other electronic element to their application. When my son applied to colleges, one sent him a pre-formatted diskette, which he filled out on his home computer and sent back. His data were read into the college mainframe in a matter of moments, and his application status was available to users at dozens of locations on campus. Now some campuses skip the "send it in" phase of the diskette and allow one to apply on-line. A student in high school can sit in a counselor's office, dial into the college system, and respond to a template-formatted series of questions. The student can even transfer transcripts and SAT scores without ever leaving the counselor's office. This advance in communication technology also means that students can learn their admission status within days, or perhaps even minutes.

The interview most often takes place in a sales or job context. You can also see the applications of communication technologies in a variety of personal or entertainment settings.

Small-Group Communication and Technology

One part of our definition of small-group communication indicates that members must be in a face-to-face situation. This requirement ensures that full communication is possible by making the visual nonverbal cues available to all members. Telephone conference stretch this definition, although most of the other parts of the concept are present. With the addition of a video element, you can have a virtual group, and most of the aspects of this setting are sufficiently present to treat such meetings as genuine small-group meetings

One of the first problems that virtual groups on the electronic network face is how to capture the essential nonverbal elements of messages. One group, which has met in this format since 1976, found a way to address that shortcoming by incorporating nonverbal cues in the text (Turoff, 1989). For example, you can use the elements of your keyboard to create pictures called **emoticons.** By using a colon, a dash, and a close parenthesis, you can create a sideways smiling face :-), known as a *smiley*. Sometimes, a sender who wants to convey a humorous tone or softening effect adds the word "smile" to the message. For example, the editor working on this book wrote me a message saying, "Please respond quickly, we know the time is short, but we need that material this week! (smile)" You can have fun with these pictures and other elements, such as a frown :-(or all capitals to simulate YELLING AT SOMEONE. By using these additions, a

The Unofficial Emoticon Directory	
:-)	Your basic smiley. This is used to inflect a sarcastic or joking statement since we can't hear voice inflection over UNIX.
;-)	Winking smiley to accompany a flirtatious and/or sarcastic remark.
:-(	Frowning smiley. Used to show displeasure at something said or to convey a negative feeling.
:-I	Indifferent smiley. Better than a frowning smiley, but not quite as good as a happy smiley.
:->	User just made a really biting sarcastic remark. Worse than a :-).
>:->	User made a really devilish remark.
>;->	Winking smiley and devil combined. Indicates a lewd remark was just made.
Those are some basic ones. . . . Here are a few somewhat less common ones:	
:,(	Crying.
:-T	Keeping a straight face; tight lipped.
:-y	Said with a smile.
:-I	Disgusted/Grim/No Expression.
8-)	Wears glasses.
:-P	Sticking out tongue.
(-:	User is left handed.
%-)	User has been staring at a green screen for fifteen hours straight.

small group of communicators can sense some of the information that is otherwise lost by using the media.

This loss may only be temporary for small-group communication participants on a network that can process **hypertext.** This technological advance allows nonlinear, multimedia images to be included in the conversation. As speed and capacity increase, small-group conferences in the near future will have access to a richer message than today's electronic bulletin boards and message rooms can provide.

Small groups always have been important contexts for communication. We know that Socrates met his students in small groups, often outdoors, where they explored questions and sought answers in an intimate, direct setting. The value of small-group communication has increased with civilization, and we use it in everything from our government decision making to our family conferences. The development of technology has allowed us to rethink our concept of direct communication, and the increasing ability to convey nonverbal messages will also increase the completeness of the messages that we exchange in small groups.

PUBLIC COMMUNICATION AND TECHNOLOGY

Just as personal communication has altered and expanded with technological advances in the past, public communication has also been affected. Two areas, public speaking and career and organizational communication, are subject to the effects of technology, and both altered considerably with the advances of the past.

Public Speaking and Technology

In ancient times, the public speaker was a central person in the life of a community. Sometimes this person was the messenger or town crier, sometimes the revered storyteller, sometimes the influential orator. The technology of writing preservation and transmission made oral transmission less important at times for those who could read; but until literacy became widespread, barely 400 years ago in the West, the written word did not have much direct effect on the general population. The public still depended on the reader of the word, as in religious services and town meetings.

The effect of printing created in the American colonies the elements that led to revolution. But the immediate effect of the public speaker's addressing a crowd and communicating, with all the verbal and nonverbal elements, surpassed that of the more indirect newspapers and pamphlets. The image of our revolution is caught in Patrick Henry's speech more than in John Adams's papers.

Radio broadcasting changed public speaking from a direct medium to an indirect, though still immediate, event. Voices could now be sent to vast audiences in real time, and the listener's imagination, envisioning the speaker or events being described, created a highly engaging communication event (McLuhan, 1964).

The emergence of televised communication has again altered our concept of public speaking. For one thing, the time dimension has become increasingly compressed, and speeches now rarely last more than a few minutes. Ten or fif-

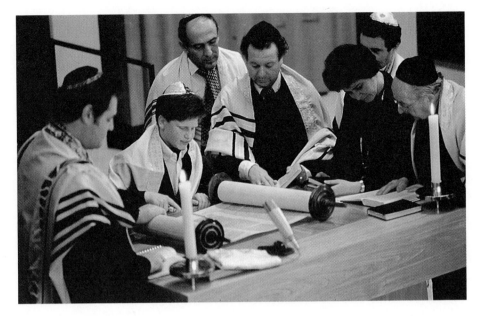

Reading of ancient texts still provides an important link to the past.

teen minutes of a single person speaking is unusual in televised presentations. The concept of audience analysis has also changed (Smitter, 1995), and the more general the aim of the speaker, the greater the tendency to create easily grasped messages and to use immediately effective rhetorical devices. In her important analysis of the effect of technological advances, communication scholar Kathleen Hall Jamieson wrote, in *Eloquence in an Electronic Age,* "No longer are we educating speakers or citizens capable of Aristotelian deliberation" (p. 241). In part, she contended, this is due to a lack of a shared cultural tradition that would allow listeners to recognize and relate to the ideas and images that speakers might use. Instead, public speakers now create an instant context for their listeners through the use of narrative. Usually emotional in tone, these stories tend to dominate the speaking of public figures, so pathos begins to crowd out logos and, to an extent, ethos as means current speakers use to have the desired effect on audiences. Audiences become more tolerant and expectant of a good story, less able to process careful reasoning, and less interested in detailed supporting material (Jamieson, 1988).

Thus the advances of communication technology have changed the way in which audiences respond to public speaking. On a practical level, speakers have also adapted with new technology. A few years ago, a hand-drawn chart or diagram was the typical visual aid. The overhead projector and later slides and video playback monitors brought color, precision, and even sound and action into the public speaker's tool box. The current use of Powerbook technology in business and professional presentations incorporates the elements of computer-driven images and greatly expands the repertoire of the speaker. It may even be that speaking through computer networks or e-mail may be a way for people with severe communication apprehension to break down that barrier. The safety of anonymity and the control over your exact message may embolden otherwise reluctant communicators to get into the conversation (Rheingold, 1992).

Former President Ronald Reagan was often called "The Great Communicator" because he was able to incorporate touching stories into his speeches.

Career Settings and Communication Technology

In addition to the effects of advances in communication technology on the way we apply for jobs, there are also effects on the way we do our jobs. Telecommuting is fast becoming a way in which many Americans "go" to work. Instead of driving long distances and physically staying in a job location, many people in business, finance, law, marketing, sales, publishing, and other areas now stay home and go to the office via the home computer.

For those who work from home or at an office location, communication advances have begun to affect they way they send and receive messages. In Chapter 16 you read about how messages flow upward and downward in an organization and how the direction influences senders to modify their messages. The same phenomena can be seen in e-mail messages as they travel around a company. For example, one study found that people sometimes add their signature to an e-mail message. Since the e-mail already has a sender ID at the top of the message, adding a signature can be seen as a strategy to express status. The study found that signatures were added to 33 percent of the upward-traveling messages and to 13 percent of the lateral messages but to *none* of the downward-traveling messages. "[T]he presence or absence of the signature was analyzed as a paralinguistic reflection of the hierarchical and communication relationships between the mail file sender and the receiver" (Sherblom, 1988, p. 44). Clearly, the new technologies are being used to express human concerns, as in the past.

The impact of new communication technology will be felt in virtually every occupation. In law, for example, each new technology has had to be tested and validated for many years before gaining acceptance. The justice system is built on a system of recognizing precedence—what happened in the past—and is slow, even reluctant, to adopt new technologies (Buchanan, 1995). When "lie detector" (polygraph) machines became available, they triggered much resistance and challenge to their accuracy in court trials. Polygraph evidence is still generally inadmissible in U.S. courts. The admission of videotaped evidence has been followed by the use of CD-ROM in trials such as that of the Menendez brothers, two young men who were accused of murdering their wealthy parents for the insurance money (O'Neil, 1995).

Technology has been present in career settings since the beginning of careers. The first writing developed as a way to record business transactions or keep inventory. Now, whether you have a career in which you use sophisticated programs, engage in desktop publishing, or simply read your mail at your terminal, communication technology will be part of your work world.

SOCIAL COMMUNICATION AND TECHNOLOGY

Each development in communication technology has affected the way in which societies are organized and on the actions of people in those societies. Each of these technologies has built on the face-to-face model in that they bring people together. The advances that we have had over the centuries have tended to make the mediated communication closer and closer to the original, face-to-face interaction (Meyrowitz, 1985). For example, when writing replaced the spoken relayed message, it began to resemble the sender because it was in his or her own handwriting. Even today, your signature is a way to leave your personal, authentic mark on an important communication. When radio and recorded sound were the new technologies, the sender's actual voice was captured, so the listener heard the sender's words in her or his own voice. Obviously, television and video provide the visual element, and fiber optics and holograms will make possible the transmission of three-dimensional images. Let us examine each of the social contexts and discover some of the effects that advancing communication technology has had.

Family, School, and Community Settings

Family communication patterns have been the concern of many people over the years as the impact of new technologies is felt in the family group. The oral tradition of many families, which centered on storytelling or conversation, was threatened by print technology. As more and more people began to read, the focus shifted to private communication, although in some places, reading aloud to other members of the family or friends became a common event. With the advent of radio, many families gathered around the radio for entertainment and news. One of my earliest childhood memories is of waking up on Saturday morning in our pretelevision days and listening to adventure tales on the radio. On Sunday morning, someone read the comic section of the newspaper aloud over the radio, and my brother and I would follow along with the pictures as we lay on the living room floor in our pajamas. Television has unmistakably altered the way in which our families communicate, and much controversy still exists over the possible impact of violence, alternative morals, and other issues on families and children. Recently, many outlets around the country canceled an episode of the popular television program *Friends* because it depicted a lesbian wedding.

Even though we still send soldiers off to war, the way they write home or the way they get mail from family and friends has changed dramatically. When the United States sent troops to Bosnia as part of the United Nations force, many soldiers took along laptop computers. These were connected to cellular telephones, which were capable of direct satellite uplink to folks back home ("How the Troops Will Communicate," 1995).

You are exposed to communication technology every day in your classrooms. Remember that the VCR or Powerbook visual aids that you may see in your classroom are part of a long chain of advances in technology that have brought us from clay tablets in schools to small chalk slates for each child to notetaking on a laptop computer. That journey took about 3,000 years, and the chalk slates were popular in this country until about 100 years ago. The movement from chalk slate classrooms to hypertext and CD-ROM displays has been so swift that no single generation of the past five has been taught only with one technological advance. Films were introduced, and film strips were popular in the era between the world wars. Television, tape recording, and videotape are now being replaced by digital imagery. The questions of access and use still concern educators, especially with the finding that computer use in the classroom is not evenly distributed by gender, causing one educator to look at "research on gender differences in learning styles, software, curriculum and classroom layout . . . to equalize disparity through teacher training" (Nye, 1991, p. 94). On the other hand, one benefit of having a class communicate with each other and the teacher via e-mail has been that the teacher can personalize and adapt to the individual student. Coombs (1993) said, "I found that this interactive computer medium gradually altered my perceptions of the students. . . . I gained a greater realization that different students learn differently and could take time to focus on individual needs."

You can see that using the most recent technology in a classroom has positive and negative associations, although such use now seems widespread, at all levels from elementary to postgraduate education and in nearly every subject (Kuehn, 1994). Some researchers look forward to the multiple benefits of using communication technology, especially in the college setting. Three such benefits for **computer-mediated communication** have been identified as (1) extending learning beyond the classroom through such means as increased instructor availability, demonstrating caring, and including outside experts; (2) balancing

Computers are now found in nearly every school and grade.

power by increasing student responsibility and initiative and sharing control; and (3) increased efficiency through widening access to resources, facilitating quick assignment turnaround, keeping accurate course records, and helping to focus participation (McComb, 1994). It is reasonable to expect many of these benefits to apply to elementary and secondary school settings as well, although we may need to pay careful attention to possible disparities in economic status and home access to computers, as well as differences in gender responses to computers (Levin and Gordon, 1989; Kramer and Lehman, 1990).

In the community, communication technology advances affect the way in which we conduct our political and civic lives. As pointed out in Chapter 1 and earlier in this chapter, the way in which communication changed over the ages had direct bearing on the changes and developments in government and religion. Power began to be distributed to people who had access to information, and control of information took on new challenges for each succeeding age of communication technology advancement. We have moved from systems of a single ruler to a powerful elite of rulers, to a parliament, to a citizen participation democracy, all based on the access to information. Thomas Jefferson noted (Koch and Peden, 1944),

> Were it left to me to decide whether we should have a government without newspapers, or newspapers without a government, I should not hesitate a moment to prefer the latter. But I should mean that every man should receive those newspapers and be capable of reading them. (p. 411)

Clearly, democracy must have both access to information and exercise of that access to function well. One trend noted in Chapter 18 is the decreasing number of college students and other citizens who regularly read a newspaper.

Some scholars point to a shift in our culture from the technology of newspapers to the technology of television as one reason for the decline in readership and for a shift to an image-based election campaign style (Sullivan, 1995). Our sense of community has been altered, now that we no longer meet together in large halls to listen to candidates debate, then talk with our neighbors about what we experienced in common. Instead, we are often alone in our homes, being subjected to brief visual images of candidates. Sometimes the opposition produces these images to create visual arguments that would never be presented orally. Such visual messages are called **argument by composition.** For example, in 1968, a commercial interspersed photos of then Vice-President Hubert Humphrey with other photos of riots in the streets, soldiers under fire in Vietnam, and children living in poverty in Appalachia. The images shifted back and forth, creating a visual link and a visual argument that associated Humphrey with these terrible scenes, implying that he was somehow responsible (Jamieson, 1988).

On the other hand, some advances may well increase information access and enhance citizen democracy. The term **teledemocracy** has been coined to describe such an impact of communicating technology (O'Sullivan, 1995). Some scholars foresee increased civic participation, linking citizens across time and space, increasing opportunity for some who are not able to get out, providing mass feedback and direct responses to questions or issues, and equal access to information (London, 1995). It is clear that the new technologies open up new opportunities for citizens to communicate directly with elected officials and thus feel more connected to the political system (Carveth and Metz, 1995).

All will not be smooth, however. The advances in communication technology indicate that the ethical questions and tests outlined earlier in this chapter need to be applied rigorously and often if we are to be able to depend on the messages that these advances create, especially in the mass media (Sullivan, 1995).

Mass Media and Communication Technology

The most obvious area for looking at communication technology is the mass media. Virtually every example you have read about in this book—from clay to papyrus, chariots, town criers, newspapers, and the Internet—deals with mass media. Certainly, the effects of mass media now reach virtually every home, primarily through television. Because 97 percent of all homes in the United States have at least one television set, this medium is the dominant one for now. At the rate of increase of computer users, however, we will see the great "information superhighway" reaching a similar number in the near future (Gates, 1995).

One disadvantage of advances in communication technology is that fewer and fewer people are making the decisions about what will be part of our media resources. Just a few years ago, there were approximately fifty major corporations that controlled major media outlets in the United States. By 1995, this number had dropped to below twenty, and these same companies were dominant worldwide. It has been predicted that this number will soon be reduced to about six as a result of mergers and takeovers (Bagdikian, 1992). The problem that is associated with the concentration of media into a few hands is a loss of diversity. We may be headed in a direction that will reverse the past 5,000 years to the point at which what we see and know is controlled, once again, by a few "priest" companies. Some scholars worry about the mass homogenization of culture worldwide (Beadle, 1995) and have started using the term **technopoly** to describe this trend. Because many of these companies are based in the United

---

THE STORY OF COMMUNICATION

Bill Gates

When the story of the information revolution caused by the widespread access to computer technology is written, one of the most interesting people discussed will be Bill Gates. As the founder, developer, and owner of Microsoft, Gates was able to take his love for computer games and translate it into programming ideas. As a high school student, he used to spend many hours playing computer animated games; and when the opportunity arose for him to work with and develop software to run sophisticated programs, his interest and background helped him to become the leader in the computer industry. By the time he was thirty-six, his net wealth was in the billions of dollars. Having spent some time reflecting on the changes he had witnessed and to some extent caused, he wrote a book in 1995 speculating on the future of communication through the superhighway of information. He remains upbeat and optimistic about the effects that universal access to information will have, even if he is challenged personally and professionally to keep a leadership role.

States and U.S. consumers are expected to provide most of the profit for these groups, it seems reasonable to foresee a common world culture based on the lowest common denominator of media broadcasting as seen in the United States. Serious students of culture cannot be optimistic. Just as we are losing biodiversity in the rain forest largely because of U.S. consumer-driven demands, so may we lose cultural diversity in response to those same pressures.

Intercultural, Gender, Health, and Age Communications and Technology

Intercultural communication is already experiencing tremendous changes brought about by new communication technologies. This has always been the case. As the ancient empires developed new message systems, they were able to expand their territory and conquer new peoples, often eliminating or absorbing their cultures. With the speed and reach of today's electronic systems, communication technology touches nearly every corner of the world and can do so in moments. Scholars are now attempting to document the effects on culture that such an increase in reach and decrease in time have had (Korzenny and Ting-Toomey, 1992).

The effects of communication technology on gender and communication issues are discussed in previous sections of this chapter and in Chapter 19. These range from greater empowerment with the acquisition of reading and writing skills to the issues of access, control, and even gender identity that are raised by the "curtain/window" quality of computer-mediated communication. The "curtain" effect comes from the sender's ability to mask himself or herself from receivers. The "window" part derives from the ability to look at and be "seen" by hundreds or even thousands of other on-line communicators (Hunkele and Cornwell, 1996). How we balance these aspects of computer-mediated communication, how men and women encode messages, and how we interpret these messages are areas that are ripe for study. For example, in the chat rooms that are popular on the Internet and on-line services, a FAQ (frequently asked question) of newcomers to the room is about their gender. Some reveal information, and some invent information to create a fantasy identity.

Health and age issues are also affected by communication technology. In early times, the ability to send written messages and to store and retrieve information meant great advances in health care. Physicians of the ancient world could read about how their predecessors, who were often from other places, treated various illnesses and conditions. One the most influential books in history has been *Anatomy* by Galen, who lived from about A.D. 130 to 200. Even if not as accurate as later works, these writings formed a significant advance because of the sophisticated communication technology of writing.

In the modern era, you can see the effects of communication technology in everything from the 911 emergency telephone network to computer simulation of surgery as a training tool in medical schools. Some severely handicapped people are able to use a keyboard to communicate to others with messages on screens. For deaf people, the TDY capacity on telephones allows a printout of their messages to parties at the other end of the line. The voice element that has recently developed in computers now gives people who were previously unable to speak an opportunity to have spoken interaction. The world-famous physicist

Professor Stephen Hawking, one of the most brilliant scientists of today, uses computer-mediated communication to present his theories.

Stephen Hawking is one such person. He is the author of *A Brief History of Time* and other influential works yet is unable to use his physical voice, has virtually no ability to move his arms and legs, and moves only with wheelchair assistance. Yet he uses a personal computer to dictate his books and lectures to large audiences with computer-mediated communication (Perrolle, 1991). Because computer networks do not reveal some items, such as race, age, and physical condition, these items may cease to be barriers, since the communicators' prejudices on these topics are not brought into the interaction (Rheingold, 1992).

One especially positive development concerns the ability to use computers to treat and perhaps cure language disabilities, such as dyslexia, which may affect as many as 15 to 25 percent of all children. At the University of California Medical Center in San Francisco, researchers found that dyslexic children process sound recognition at slightly slower than normal rates, especially sounds such as /d/, /t/, and /b/. Therefore, their brains miss coding these sounds into their communication. Researchers found that by using computer-mediated communication, they could slow down speech and then play it to these children. When the brain patterns were established to recognize the sounds and the children became used to hearing and processing them, researchers used a computer to slowly increase the speed, and the brain would adapt and catch up. Most children in this study showed the same amount of improvement in four weeks that had previously been seen only after one or two years ("Giving Language Skills a Boost," 1996).

The effects of communication technology on our interactions as we age have shown results similar to those on health. Some physical limitations that come with age affect our communication abilities. Hearing, for example, typically diminishes with age. The communication technology of ear trumpets led to the invention of hearing aids. Remember that Thomas Edison was trying to

Sometimes, a communication technology invention may find application far beyond the original intention.

help deaf people when he invented the phonograph and thus revolutionized the world of entertainment and education. In addition, current advances in communication technology allow people who might have difficulty in travel because of their age to be connected to lively, ongoing interactions through computer modems. As voice-activated computers become increasingly available, the manual dexterity that is needed to operate a keyboard will become less important, thus opening a communication link for people who may have lost mobility in their hands. Also, some of the bias against older people in communication situations that is noted in Chapter 19 may be mitigated because of the curtain effect of electronic communication (Hunkele and Cronwell, 1996).

Clearly our communication tools have served to expand our personal communication spheres with each age of civilization. All aspects of our communication world have been affected, sometimes gaining significant advantages, sometimes losing unique or interesting cultural elements. Knowing that these advances are always going to be part of our future, the question arises, How can we be prepared for them?

TECHNOLOGY IN COMMUNICATION

A Classical Connection

In the project at the University of California Medical Center in San Francisco, a number of people are working to create games and exercises to help dyslexic children practice listening for the sounds that they previously were missing. Although the lead research was done by neuropsychologist and neuroscientist Paula Tallal of Rutgers University and Michael Merzenich of the University of California, they needed assistance in the development of activities for these children to reinforce the therapy. They turned to the help of research assistants, among them Thomas Jacobson, a recent graduate of the classics program at St. John's College in New Mexico. Although Mr. Jacobson's formal college studies focused on the works of Plato, Erasmus, Descartes, Spinoza, and Shakespeare, he also had a long-standing interest in computer games. His inventiveness and creativity are finding their way into entertaining and useful therapies that may soon help the nearly 7 million children who are struggling with language learning disorders (Maugh, 1996).

COMMUNICATION COMPETENCIES AND TECHNOLOGY

The elements of communication competency that have carried through the entire text also serve as a framework for meeting the future. You can expand your *repertoire* by increasing your familiarity with a variety of emerging technologies. You have probably already done this in the area of entertainment. Most households and even individual students have the popular advances in communication technology immediately available. Do you own a CD player? A VCR? An answering machine? Do you own or have access to a personal computer? Do you have an e-mail address? Do your classes include an element of interactive, on-line communication? Do you use the electronic search mechanism at the library or from your room at home? The more of these elements you become familiar with, the greater your repertoire will be. Taking classes or workshops is a way to focus this increase in your repertoire.

Selecting the most appropriate of these technologies will require you to analyze the purposes and effects you are seeking with your communication. You will need to analyze the intended receiver of your messages. For example, it does little good to have access to e-mail if no one with whom you wish to communicate has it. Also, some messages may be most effective in one medium but not others. Computer scientists are hard at work addressing this question so that they can influence the selection of computer choices and encourage the development of computerization in some directions and avoid other choices (Hakken, 1991).

Your *implementation* of your choices will depend on your skills and training with new technologies, your comfort with and propensity for using a particular medium, and your access to these technologies. Some of these areas depend on your geographical location, your economic status, and the effects of gender and culture, with sometimes surprising results. The massive effort of Apple Computers to have every elementary school child gain access to a computer may overcome some effects of economic limitations. Other studies have shown that women are more likely than men to adopt new technologies in some situations (Vernon-Gerstenfeld, 1989).

The ability to engage in *evaluation* of your communication choices requires the creation of criteria for that evaluation and clear feedback about the results of your implementation. The same criteria that are discussed at many points in previous chapters can be your base here: Were your messages clear? Were they appropriate? Did they have the desired effect? Were they ethically sound? If so, then you are well on your way to being a competent communicator in the electronic age.

A Final Word

The history of humanity can be viewed as the history of our communication advances. The beginning of the book started with that perspective, and you have seen it weave through every chapter, concluding with this review of the major contexts of communication and how some of the thousands of communication technologies over the past millennia have affected the way you communicate today. There is a division of thinking about the effects all these advances have had on us and even greater division about what they will bring to our immediate future (Lanham, 1993). Some see us as shifting our attention away from machine-centered concerns about our computer technology to a more human-centered position as new hardware and software make our technology not only user-friendly, but "user-like" (Hakken, 1991). Others debate the type of culture and people we will become, with technology overpowering people and making us unaware of our history, disconnected from nature, ignorant of deep values and human motives, and focused only on rules and correct solutions to clearly defined problems (Bolter, 1984). Others see the liberating qualities that new technologies make possible and enjoy contemplating a new esthetic culture in which information takes on an artistic dimension as we integrate male and female styles, incorporate collaborative and competitive cultural norms, and increase the ease and access of technology applications (Lockheed, 1985). In all, these areas are touched on in this chapter, and new perspectives and applications to each communication context appear regularly.

SUMMARY

This chapter organized the discussion of communication technology in a way that parallels the rest of the book, for you to be able to focus on the tremendous variety in this area. You have seen how the story of communication is the story of human progress, as each new invention that helped expand our communication abilities also fostered the expansion of civilization. From the early systems for recording grain shipments or livestock inventory, to the instantaneous communication brought about by silicon microchips and the World Wide Web, communication developments have been linked to advances in our knowledge, memory, and transmission of information.

This chapter also stressed the nature of communication: change. With a rate of replacement in computer technology that is nearly fifty percent annually, we see the dramatic nature of that progress. In thousands of less obvious ways, the changing world of communications affects us. The way we use our libraries or write letters or do our shopping have all changed in the past ten years, and will change again in the next ten.

You have learned through this chapter how each of the major communication contexts described in earlier chapters has felt the impact of technology. You can see how interpersonal, small group, and intercultural contexts of communication each has an expanded meaning or application due to advances in communication technology.

Helping you to develop your competency in this area was the final challenge presented in this chapter, and in this book. It is a challenge which is echoed in the competencies you have learned about and developed in prior chapters, but one which also points you to the future. With the entire course behind you at this point, realize the many competencies you have acquired and move toward that future with the confidence that you can continue to grow in your skills and insights. The world of communication study is fascinating, and while this text is just a beginning, it can provide you with a good foundation for future development. Best wishes in your adventure!

KEY TERMS

communication technology, *p. 406*
Internet, *p. 408*
e-mail, *p. 413*

emoticons, *p. 415*
hypertext, *p. 416*
computer-mediated communication, *p. 420*

argument by composition, *p. 421*

teledemocracy, *p. 421*

technopoly, *p. 422*

EXERCISES

1. Establish an Internet account at your school if you do not already have one. Use it to access the holdings of the Library of Congress. Can you find this book listed?

2. Keep track of the number of communication media you use in a single day. Create a timeline for each one, depicting with a bar graph how far back each medium stretches in history. Do you use any old and new ones in combination? If so, which ones and why do you have them working together?

3. If you were to join a conversation group through an on-line service, which topics would interest you? Would you create a modified self in these interactions? If so, what aspects of yourself

would you alter, enhance, or conceal? If you create a fantasy self for the purpose of going on-line, create a Johari Window to indicate which items would be placed in which pane of the window.

4. Take an issue of computer access, such as freedom of speech, gender bias, or cultural effects, and prepare a report for the class on your investigation. Note whether you did any of your research via electronic media.

5. Select one of the studies cited in the chapter references, and find and read the entire article. What issues were addressed, and how did they support their conclusions? Create a brief report for the class on your findings.

REFERENCES

Barnhart, Clarence, and Robert Barnhart. *The World Book Dictionary.* Chicago: Thorndike-Barnhart, 1979.

Beadle, Mary. "Communication in the Global Metropolis: Technopoly and the Fundamentals of Communication." A paper presented at the Speech Communication Association annual meeting, San Antonio, Texas, Nov. 1995.

Birkets, S. *The Gutenberg Elegies: The Fate of Reading in an Electronic Age.* Boston: Faber and Faber, 1994.

Bolter, J. David. *Turning's Man.* Chapel Hill: University of North Carolina Press, 1984.

Brunet, Jean, and Serge Proulx. "Formal Versus Grass-Roots Training: Women, Work and Computers." *Journal of Communication* 39 (1989).

Buchanan, Raymond. "Running from Synthetic Reality: The Court System Confronts Technology." A paper presented at the Speech Communication Association annual meeting, San Antonio, Texas, Nov. 1995.

Carveth, Rod, and J. Metz. "Frederick Jackson Turner and the Democratization of the Electronic Frontier." A paper presented at the Speech Communication Association annual meeting, San Antonio, Texas, Nov. 1995.

Chesebro, James, and Donald Bonsall. *Computer-Mediated Communication: Human Relationships in a Computerized World.* Tuscaloosa: University of Alabama Press, 1990.

Cisler, Steve. "An Essay on the Openness of Networks, Electronic Free Speech, and the Security of Computers." *Online* (Nov. 1990).

Coombs, N. "CMC: The Medium and the Message." *Electronic Journal of Communication* 3 (1993) (SEND EJCV3N2 $COOMBS, COMSERVE@VM. ITS.RPI.EDU).

Crowley, David, and Paul Heyer. eds. *Communication in History: Technology, Culture and Society.* White Plains: Longman, 1995.

Diringer, David. *The Alphabet.* New York: Philosophic Library, 1948.

Forester, Tom. "Computers and Behavior." *Phi Kappa Phi Journal* (Summer 1991).

Gates, Bill. *The Road Ahead.* New York: Viking, 1995.

"Giving Language Skills a Boost." *Science* 271 (Jan. 1996).

Goode, Joanne, and Maggie Johnson. "Putting Out the Flames: The Etiquette and Law of E-Mail." *Online* (November 1991).

Gronbeck, Bruce, T. J. Farrell, and P. A. Soukup, eds. *Media, Consciousness, and Culture.* Newbury Park: Sage, 1991.

Hakken, David. "Culture-Centered Computing: Social Policy and Development of New Information Technology in England and the United States." *Human Organization* 50 (1991).

"How the Troops Will Communicate." *USA Today* 14 Dec. 1995, 6A.

Hunkele, Michele, and Karen Cornwell. "The Cyberspace Curtain: Hidden Gender Issues." *Voices in the Street.* Ed. S. Drucker and G. Gumpert. Cresskill: Hampton Press, 1996.

Innes, Harold. *Empire and Communications.* Toronto: University of Toronto Press, 1950. Reprinted in David Crowley and Paul Heyer, eds. *Communication in History: Technology, Culture and Society.* White Plains: Longman, 1995.

Koch, A. and W. Peden, eds. *The Life and Selected Writings of Thomas Jefferson.* New York: Random House, 1944.

Korzenny, F. and S. Ting-Toomey. *Mass Media Effects Across Cultures.* Newbury Park: Sage, 1992.

Kramer, Pamela, and Sheila Lehman. "Mismeasuring Women: A Critique of Research on Computer Ability and Avoidance." *Signs* (Autumn 1990).

Kuehn, Scott. "Computer-Mediated Communication in Instructional Settings: A Research Agenda." *Communication Education* 43 (April 1994).

Lanham, Richard. *The Electronic Word: Democracy, Technology and the Arts.* Chicago: The University of Chicago Press, 1993.

Levin, Tamar, and Claire Gordon. "Effect of Gender and Computer Experience on Attitudes towards Computers." *Journal of Educational Computing Research* 5 (1989).

London, Scott. "Teledemocracy vs. Deliberative Democracy: A Comparative Look at Two Models of Public Talk." *Interpersonal and Computing Technology: An Electronic Journal for the 21st Century* 3.2 (1995), 33–35.

Marshack, Alexander. "The Art and Symbols of Ice Age Man." 1978. From *Human Nature.* Alexander Marshack. 1978. Reprinted in David Crowley and Paul Heyer, eds. *Communication in History: Technology, Culture and Society.* White Plains: Longman, 1995.

Maugh, Thomas. "High-Tech Hope for Children with Language Disabilities." *Los Angeles Times* 5 Jan. 1996, A1.

McComb, Mary. "Benefits of Computer-Mediated Communication in College Courses." *Communication Education* 43 (April 1994).

McLuhan, Marshall. *Understanding Media: The Extensions of Man.* New York: McGraw-Hill, 1964.

Nye, Emily. "Computers and Gender: Noticing What Perpetuates Inequality." *English Journal* (March 1991), 94–96.

Ong, W. J. *Orality and Literacy: The Technologizing of the Word.* New York: Methuen, 1982.

"Oprah Online!" *People* 27 Nov. 1995.

O'Sullivan, Patrick. "Computer Networks and Political Participation: Santa Monica's Teledemocracy Project." *Journal of Applied Communication Research* 23 (1995).

Palmeri, Anthony. "Fostering Social Justice in an Electronic Age: The Teacher as Public Intellectual." A paper presented at the Speech Communication Association annual meeting, San Antonio, Texas, Nov. 1995.

Perrolle, Judith. "Computer Mediated Conversation." *Phi Kappa Phi Journal* (Summer 1991).

Raymond, Eric, ed. *The New Hacker's Dictionary.* Cambridge: MIT Press, 1993.

Rheingold, Howard. *Virtual Communities.* Reading: Addison-Wesley, 1992.

Schmandt-Besserat, Denise. "The Earliest Precursor of Writing," 1986. From "Tokens: Facts and Interpretations," *Visible Language,* 20, 1986. Reprinted in David Crowley and Paul Heyer. *Communication in History: Technology, Culture and Society.* White Plains: Longman, 1995.

Sherblom, J. "Direction, Function and Signature in Electronic Mail." *Journal of Business Communication* 25 (1988), 39–54.

Smitter, Roger. "Hyperliteracy: Fundamentals of Communication through *The Electronic Word.*" A paper presented at the Speech Communication Association annual meeting, San Antonio, Texas, Nov. 1995.

Strauss, Robert. "When Computers Were Born." *Los Angeles Times* 7 Feb. 1996, E1.

Sullivan, David. "Media and the Epistemological Shift toward Persona Politics." A paper presented to the Speech Communication Association annual meeting. San Antonio, Texas, Nov. 1995.

Sussman, Vic. "Communicating in the New Age." *U.S. News and World Report* 23 Nov. 1992.

Turkle, Sherry, and Seymour Papert. "Epistemological Pluralism: Styles and Voices within the Computer Culture." *Signs: Journal of Women in Culture and Society* 16 (1990), 128–157.

Turoff, Murray. "The Anatomy of a Computer Application Innovation: Computer Mediated Communications (CMC)." *Technological Forecasting and Social Change* 36 (1989).

Vernon-Gerstenfeld, Susan. "Serendipity? Are There Gender Differences in the Adoption of Computers? A Case Study." *Sex Roles* 21 (1989).

Walther, Joseph. "Interpersonal Effects in Computer-Mediated Interaction: A Relational Perspective." *Communication Research* 19 (Feb. 1992).

Speeches for Further Study

PATRICK HENRY

March 23, 1775

Mr. President:

No man thinks more highly than I do of the patriotism, as well as abilities, of the very worthy gentlemen who have just addressed the House. But different men often see the same subject in different lights; and, therefore, I hope it will not be thought disrespectful to those gentlemen if, entertaining as I do opinions of a character very opposite to theirs, I shall speak forth my sentiments freely and without reserve. This is no time for ceremony. The question before the House is one of awful moment to this country. For my own part, I consider it as nothing less than a question of freedom or slavery; and in proportion to the magnitude of the subject ought to be the freedom of the debate. It is only in this way that we can hope to arrive at truth, and fulfill the great responsibility which we hold to God and our country. Should I keep back my opinions at such a time, through fear of giving offense, I should consider myself as guilty of treason towards my country, and of an act of disloyalty toward the Majesty of Heaven, which I revere above all earthly kings.

Mr. President, it is natural to man to indulge in the illusions of hope. We are apt to shut our eyes against a painful truth, and listen to the song of that siren till she transforms us into beasts. Is this the part of wise men, engaged in a great and arduous struggle for liberty? Are we disposed to be of the number of those who, having eyes, see not, and, having ears, hear not, the things which so nearly concern their temporal salvation? For my part, whatever anguish of spirit it may cost, I am willing to know the whole truth; to know the worst, and to provide for it.

I have but one lamp by which my feet are guided, and that is the lamp of experience. I know of no way of judging of the future but by the past. And judging by the past, I wish to know what there has been in the conduct of the British ministry for the last ten years to justify those hopes with which gentlemen have been pleased to solace themselves and the House. Is it that insidious smile with which our petition has been lately received? Trust it not, sir; it will prove a snare to your feet. Suffer not yourselves to be betrayed with a kiss. Ask yourselves how this gracious reception of our petition comports with those warlike preparations which cover our waters and darken our land. Are fleets and armies necessary to a work of love and reconciliation? Have we shown ourselves so unwilling to be reconciled that force must be called in to win back our love? Let us not deceive ourselves, sir. These are the implements of war and subjugation; the last arguments to which kings resort. I ask gentlemen, sir, what means this martial array, if its purpose be not to force us to submission? Can gentlemen assign any other possible motive for it? Has Great Britain any enemy, in this quarter of the world, to call for all this accumulation of navies and armies? No, sir, she has none. They are meant for us: they can be meant for no other. They are sent over to bind and rivet upon us those chains which the British ministry have been so long forging. And what have we to oppose to them? Shall we try argument? Sir, we have been trying that for the last ten years. Have we anything new to offer upon the subject? Nothing. We have held the subject up in every light of which it is capable; but it has been all in vain. Shall we resort to entreaty and humble supplication? What terms shall we find which have not been already exhausted? Let us not, I beseech you, sir, deceive ourselves longer. Sir, we have done everything that could be done to avert the storm which is now coming on. We have petitioned; we have remonstrated; we have supplicated; we have prostrated ourselves before the throne, and have implored its interposition to arrest the tyrannical hands of the ministry and Parliament. Our petitions have been slighted; our remonstrances have produced additional violence and insult; our supplications have been disregarded; and we have been spurned, with contempt, from the foot of the throne! In vain, after these things, may we indulge the fond hope of peace and reconciliation. There is no longer any room for hope. If we wish to be free—if we mean to preserve inviolate those inestimable privileges for which we have been so long contending—if we mean not basely to abandon the noble struggle in which we have been so long engaged, and which we have pledged ourselves never to abandon until the glorious object of our contest shall be obtained—we must fight! I repeat it, sir, we must fight! An appeal to arms and to the God of Hosts is all that is left us!

They tell us, sir, that we are weak; unable to cope with so formidable an adversary. But when shall we be stronger? Will it be the next week, or the next year? Will it be when we are totally disarmed, and when a British guard shall be stationed in every house? Shall we gather strength by irresolution and inaction? Shall we acquire the means of effectual resistance by lying supinely on our backs and hugging the delusive phantom of hope, until our enemies shall have bound us hand and foot? Sir, we are not weak if we make a proper use of those means which the God of nature hath placed in our power. Three millions of people, armed in the holy cause of liberty, and in such a country as that which we possess, are invincible by any force which our enemy can send against us. Besides, sir, we shall not fight our battles alone. There is a just God who presides over the destinies of nations, and who will raise up friends to fight our battles for us. The battle, sir, is not to the strong alone; it is to the vigilant, the active, the brave. Besides, sir, we have no election. If we were base enough to desire it, it is now too late to retire from the contest. There is no retreat but in submission and slavery! Our chains are forged! Their clanking may be heard on the plains of Boston! The war is inevitable—and let it come! I repeat it, sir, let it come.

It is in vain, sir, to extenuate the matter. Gentlemen may cry, Peace, Peace—but there is no peace. The war is actually begun! The next gale that sweeps from the north will bring to our ears the clash of resounding arms! Our brethren are already in the field! Why stand we here idle? What is it that gentlemen wish? What would they have? Is life so dear, or peace so sweet, as to be purchased at the price of chains and slavery? Forbid it, Almighty God! I know not what course others may take; but as for me, give me liberty or give me death!

ELIZABETH CADY STANTON

The First Woman's-Rights Convention, July 19, 1848

We have met here today to discuss our rights and wrongs, civil and political, and not, as some have supposed, to go into the detail of social life alone. We do not propose to petition the legislature to make our husbands just, generous, and courteous, to seat every man at the head of a cradle, and to clothe every woman in male attire. None of these points, however important they may be considered by leading men, will be touched in this convention. As to their costume, the gentlemen need feel no fear of our imitating that, for we think it in violation of every principle of taste, beauty, and dignity; notwithstanding all the contempt cast upon our loose, flowing garments, we still admire the graceful folds, and consider our costume far more artistic than theirs. Many of the nobler sex seem to agree with us in this opinion, for the bishops, priests, judges, barristers, and lord mayors of the first nation on the globe, and the Pope of Rome, with his cardinals, too, all wear the loose flowing robes, thus tacitly acknowledging that the male attire is neither dignified nor imposing. No, we shall not molest you in your philosophical experiments with stocks, pants, high-heeled boots, and Russian belts. Yours be the glory to discover, by personal experience, how long the kneepan can resist the terrible strapping down which you impose, in how short time the well-developed muscles of the throat can be reduced to mere threads by the constant pressure of the stock, how high the heel of a boot must be to make a short man tall, and how tight the Russian belt may be drawn and yet have wind enough left to sustain life.

But we are assembled to protest against a form of government existing without the consent of the governed—to declare our right to be free as man is free, to be represented in the government which we are taxed to support, to have such disgraceful laws as give man the power to chastise and imprison his wife, to take the wages which she earns, the property which she inherits, and, in case of separation, the children of her love; laws which make her the mere dependent on his bounty. It is to protest against such unjust laws as these that we are assembled today, and to have them, if possible, forever erased from our statute books, deeming them a shame and a disgrace to a Christian republic in the nineteenth century. We have met

> To uplift woman's fallen divinity
> Upon an even pedestal with man's.

And, strange as it may seem to many, we now demand our right to vote according to the declaration of the government under which we live. This right no one pretends to deny. We need not prove ourselves equal to Daniel Webster to enjoy this privilege, for the ignorant Irishman in the ditch has all the civil rights he has. We need not prove our muscular power equal to this same Irishman to enjoy this privilege, for the most tiny, weak, ill-shaped stripling of twenty-one has all the civil rights of the Irishman. We have no objection to discuss the question of equality, for we feel that the weight of argument lies wholly with us, but we wish the question of equality kept distinct from the question of rights, for the proof of the one does not determine the truth of the other. All white men in this country have the same rights, however they may differ in mind, body, or estate.

The right is ours. The question now is: how shall we get possession of what rightfully belongs to us? We should not feel so sorely grieved if no man who had not attained the full stature of a Webster, Clay, Van Buren, or Gerrit Smith could claim the right of the elective franchise. But to have drunkards, idiots, horse-racing, rum-selling rowdies, ignorant foreigners, and silly boys fully recognized, while we ourselves are thrust out from all the rights that belong to citizens, it is too grossly insulting to the dignity of woman to be longer quietly submitted to. The right is ours. Have it, we must. Use it, we will. The pens, the tongues, the fortunes, the indomitable wills of many women are already pledged to secure this right. The great truth that no just government can be formed without the consent of the governed we shall echo and re-echo in the ears of the unjust judge, until by continual coming we shall weary him. . . .

There seems now to be a kind of moral stagnation in our midst. Philanthropists have done their utmost to rouse the nation to a sense of its sins. War, slavery, drunkenness, licentiousness, gluttony, have been dragged naked before the people, and all their abominations and deformities fully brought to light, yet with idiotic laugh we hug those monsters to our breasts and rush on to destruction. Our churches are multiplying on all sides, our missionary societies, Sunday schools, and prayer meetings and innumerable charitable and reform organizations are all in operation, but still the tide of vice is swelling, and threatens the destruction of everything, and the battlements of righteousness are weak against the raging elements of sin and death. Verily, the world waits the coming of some new element, some purifying power, some spirit of mercy and love. The voice of woman has been silenced in the state, the church, and the home, but man cannot fulfill his destiny alone, he cannot redeem his race unaided. There are deep and tender chords of sympathy and love in the hearts of the downfallen and oppressed that woman can touch more skillfully than man.

The world has never yet seen a truly great and virtuous nation, because in the degradation of woman the very fountains of life are poisoned at their source. It is vain to look for silver and gold from mines of copper and lead. It is the wise mother that has the wise son. So long as your women are slaves you may throw your colleges and churches to the winds. You can't have scholars and saints so long as your mothers are ground to powder between the upper and nether millstone of tyranny and lust. How seldom, now, is a father's pride gratified, his fond hopes realized, in the budding genius of his son! The wife is degraded, made the mere creature of caprice, and the foolish son is heaviness to his heart. Truly are the sins of the fathers visited upon the children to the third and fourth generation. God, in His wisdom, has so linked the whole human family together that any violence done at one end of the chain is felt throughout its length, and here, too, is the law of restoration, as in woman all have fallen, so in her elevation shall the race be recreated.

"Voices" were the visitors and advisers of Joan of Arc. Do not "voices" come to us daily from the haunts of poverty, sorrow, degradation, and despair, already too long unheeded. Now is the time for the women of this country, if they would save our free institutions, to defend the right, to buckle on the armor that can best resist the keenest weapons of the enemy—contempt and ridicule. The same religious enthusiasm that nerved Joan of Arc to her work nerves us to ours. In every generation God calls some men and women for the utterance of truth, a heroic action, and our work today is the fulfilling of what has long since been foretold by the Prophet—Joel 2:28: "And it shall come to pass afterward, that I will pour out my spirit upon all flesh; and your sons and your daughters shall prophesy." We do not expect our path will be strewn with the flowers of popular applause, but over the thorns of bigotry and prejudice will be our way, and on our banners will beat the dark storm clouds of opposition from those who have entrenched themselves behind the stormy bulwarks of custom and authority, and who have fortified their position by every means, holy and unholy. But we will steadfastly abide the result. Unmoved we will bear it aloft. Undauntedly we will unfurl it to the gale, for we know that the storm cannot rend from it a shred, that the electric flash will but more clearly show to us the glorious words inscribed upon it, "Equality of Rights." . . .

FREDERICK DOUGLASS

July 4, 1854

Fellow citizens, pardon me, allow me to ask, why am I called upon to speak, here today? What have I, or those I represent, to do with your national independence? Are the great principles of political freedom and of natural justice, embodied in that Declaration of Independence, extended to us? and am I, therefore, called upon to bring our humble offering to the national altar, and to confess the benefits and express devout gratitude for the blessings resulting from your independence to us?

Would to God, both for your sakes and ours, that an affirmative answer could be truthfully returned to these questions! Then would my task be light, and my burden easy and delightful. For who is there so cold that a nation's sympathy could not warm him? Who so obdurate and dead to the claims of gratitude that would not thankfully acknowledge such priceless benefits? Who so stolid and selfish that would not give his voice to swell the hallelujahs of a nation's jubilee, when the chains of servitude had been torn from his limbs? I am not that man. In a case like that the dumb might eloquently speak and the "lame man leap as an hart."

But such is not the state of the case. I say it with a sad sense of the disparity between us. I am not included within the pale of this glorious anniversary! Your high independence only reveals the immeasurable distance between us. The blessings in which you, this day, rejoice are not enjoyed in common. The rich inheritance of justice, liberty, prosperity, and independence bequeathed by your fathers is shared by you, not by me. The sunlight that brought light and healing to you has brought stripes and death to me. This Fourth of July is yours, not mine. You may rejoice, I must mourn. To drag a man in fetters into the grand illuminated temple of liberty, and call upon him to join you in joyous anthems, were inhuman mockery and sacrilegious irony. Do you mean, citizens, to mock me by asking me to speak today? If so, there is a parallel to your conduct. And let me warn you that it is dangerous to copy the example of a nation whose crimes, towering up to heaven, were thrown down by the breath of the Almighty, burying that nation in irrevocable ruin! I can today take up the plaintive lament of a peeled and woe-smitten people!

> By the rivers of Babylon, there we sat down. Yea! we wept when we remembered Zion. We hanged our harps upon the willows in the midst thereof. For there, they that carried us away captive, required of us a song; and they who wasted us required of us mirth, saying, Sing us one of the songs of Zion. How can we sing the Lord's song in a strange land? If I forget thee, O Jerusalem, let my right hand forget her cunning. If I do not remember thee, let my tongue cleave to the roof of my mouth.

Fellow citizens, above your national, tumultuous joy, I hear the mournful wail of millions, whose chains, heavy and grievous yesterday, are, today, rendered more intolerable by the jubilee shouts that reach them. If I do forget, if I do not faithfully remember those bleeding children of sorrow this day, "may my right hand forget her cunning, and may my tongue cleave to the roof of my mouth"! To forget them, to pass lightly over their wrongs, and to chime in with the popular theme would be treason most scandalous and shocking, and would make me a reproach before God and the world. My subject, then, fellow citizens, is *American slavery.* I shall see this day and its popular characteristics from the slave's point of view. Standing there identified with the American bondman, making his wrongs mine. I do not hesitate to declare with all my soul that the character and conduct of this nation never looked blacker to me than on this Fourth of July! Whether we turn to the declarations of the past or to the professions of the present, the conduct of the nation seems equally hideous and revolting. America is false to the past, false to the present, and solemnly binds herself to be false to the future. Standing with God and the crushed and bleeding slave on this occasion, I will, in the name of humanity which is outraged, in the name of liberty which is fettered, in the name of the Constitution and the Bible which are disregarded and trampled upon, dare to call in question and to denounce, with all the emphasis I can command, everything that serves to perpetuate slavery—the great sin and shame of America! "I will not equivocate; I will not excuse"; I will use the severest language I can command; and yet not one word shall escape me that any man, whose judgment is not blinded by prejudice, or who is not at heart a slaveholder, shall not confess to be right and just.

But I fancy I hear someone of my audience say, "It is just in this circumstance that you and your brother abolitionists fail to make a favorable impression on the public mind. Would you argue more and denounce less, would you persuade more and rebuke less, your cause would be much more likely to succeed." But, I submit, where all is plain, there is nothing to be argued. What point in the antislavery creed would you have me argue? On what branch of the subject do the people of this country need light? Must I undertake to prove that the slave is a man? That point is conceded already. Nobody doubts it. The slaveholders themselves acknowledge it in the enactment of laws for their government. They acknowledge it when they punish disobedience on the part of the slave. There are seventy-two crimes in the state of Virginia which, if committed by a black man (no matter how ignorant he be), subject him to the punishment of death; while only two of the same crimes will subject a white man to the like punishment. What is this but the acknowledgment that the slave is a moral, intellectual, and responsible being? The manhood of the slave is conceded. It is admitted in the fact that Southern statute books are covered with enactments forbidding, under severe fines and penalties, the teaching of the slave to read or to write. When you can point to any such laws in reference to the beasts of the field, then I may consent to argue the manhood of the slave. When the dogs in your streets, when the fowls of the air, when the cattle on your hills, when the fish of the sea and the reptiles that crawl shall be unable to distinguish the slave from a brute, then will I argue with you that the slave is a man!

For the present, it is enough to affirm the equal manhood of the Negro race. Is it not astonishing that, while we are plowing, planting, and reaping, using all kinds of mechanical tools, erecting houses, constructing bridges, building ships, working in metals of brass, iron, copper, silver, and gold; that, while we are reading, writing, and ciphering, acting as clerks, merchants, and secretaries, having among us lawyers, doctors, ministers, poets, authors, editors, orators, and teachers; that, while we are engaged in all manner of enterprises common to other men, digging gold in California, capturing the whale in the Pacific, feeding sheep and cattle on the hillside, living, moving, acting, thinking, planning, living in families as husbands, wives, and children, and, above all, confessing and worshiping the Christian's God, and looking hopefully for life and immortality beyond the grave, we are called upon to prove that we are men!

Would you have me argue that man is entitled to liberty? that he is the rightful owner of his own body? You have already declared it. Must I argue the wrongfulness of slavery? Is that a question for republicans? Is it to be settled by the rules of logic and argumentation, as a matter beset with great difficulty, involving a doubtful application of the principle of justice, hard to be understood? How should I look today, in the presence of Americans, dividing and subdividing a discourse, to show that men have a natural right to freedom? speaking of it relatively and positively, negatively and affirmatively? To do so would be to make myself ridiculous and to offer an insult to your understanding. There is not a man beneath the canopy of heaven that does not know that slavery is wrong for him.

What, am I to argue that it is wrong to make men brutes, to rob them of their liberty, to work them without wages, to keep them ignorant of their relations to their fellow men, to beat them with sticks, to flay their flesh with the lash, to load their limbs with irons, to hunt them with dogs, to sell them at auction, to sunder their families, to knock out their teeth, to burn their flesh, to starve them into obedience and submission to their masters? Must I argue that a system thus marked with blood, and stained with pollution, is wrong? No! I will not. I have better employment for my time and strength than such arguments would imply.

What, then, remains to be argued? Is it that slavery is not divine; that God did not establish it; that our doctors of divinity are mistaken? There is blasphemy in the thought. That which is inhuman cannot be divine! Who can reason on such a proposition? They that can may; I cannot. The time for such argument is past.

At a time like this, scorching iron, not convincing argument, is needed. O! had I the ability, and could I reach the nation's ear, I would today pour out a fiery stream of biting ridicule, blasting reproach, withering sarcasm, and stern rebuke. For it is not light that is needed, but fire; it is not the gentle shower, but thunder. We need the storm, the whirlwind, and the earthquake. The feeling of the nation must be quickened; the conscience of the nation must be roused; the propriety of the nation must be startled; the hypocrisy, of the nation must be exposed; and its crimes against God and man must be proclaimed and denounced.

What, to the American slave, is your Fourth of July? I answer: a day that reveals to him, more than all other days in the year, the gross injustice and cruelty to which he is the constant victim. To him, your celebration is a sham; your boasted liberty, an unholy license; your national greatness, swelling vanity; your sounds of rejoicing are empty and heartless; your denunciation of tyrants, brass-fronted impudence; your shouts of liberty and equality, hollow mockery; your prayers and hymns, your sermons and thanksgivings, with all your religious parade and solemnity, are, to Him, mere bombast, fraud, deception, impiety, and hypocrisy—a thin veil to cover up crimes which would disgrace a nation of savages. There is not a nation of savages. There is not a nation on the earth guilty of practices more shocking and bloody than are the people of the United States at this very hour.

Go where you may, search where you will, roam through all the monarchies and despotisms of the Old World, travel through South America, search out every abuse, and when you have found the last, lay your facts by the side of the everyday practices of this nation, and you will say with me that, for revolting barbarity and shameless hypocrisy, America reigns without a rival.

ABRAHAM LINCOLN

His Second Inaugural Address, March 4, 1865

Fellow Countrymen:

At this second appearing to take the oath of the presidential office, there is less occasion for an extended address than at the first. Then a statement somewhat in detail of the course to be pursued seemed very fitting and proper; now, at the expiration of four years, during which public declarations have constantly been called forth concerning every point and place of the great contest which still absorbs attention and engrosses the energies of the nation, little that is new could be presented. The progress of our arms, upon which all else chiefly depends, is as well known to the public as to myself. It is, I trust, reasonably satisfactory and encouraging to all. With a high hope for the future, no prediction in that regard is ventured. On the occasion corresponding to this four years ago, all thoughts were anxiously directed to an impending civil war. All dreaded it. All sought to avoid it. While the Inaugural Address was being delivered from this place, devoted altogether to saving the Union without war, the insurgent agents were in the city seeking to destroy it without war—seeking to dissolve the Union, and divide the effects by negotiating. Both parties deprecated war, but one of them would make war rather than let it perish, and war came. One eighth of the whole population were colored slaves, not distributed generally over the Union, but located in the Southern part. These slaves contributed a peculiar and powerful interest. All knew the interest would somehow cause war. To strengthen, perpetuate, and extend this interest was the object for which the insurgents would rend the Union by war, while the government claimed no right to do more than restrict the territorial enlargement of it. Neither party expected the magnitude or duration which it has already attained; neither anticipated that the cause of the conflict might cease even before the conflict itself should cease. Each looked for an easier triumph and a result less fundamental and astonishing. Both read the same Bible and pray to the same God. Each invokes His aid against the other. It may seem strange that any man should dare to ask a just God's assistance in wringing bread from the sweat of other men's faces; but let us judge not, that we be not judged. The prayer of both should not be answered; that of neither has been answered fully, for the Almighty has His own purposes. "Woe unto the world because of offenses, for it must needs be that offense come; but woe unto that man by whom the offense cometh." If we shall suppose American slavery one of those offenses which, in the providence of God, must needs come, but which, having continued through his appointed time, He now wills to remove, and that He gives to both North and South this terrible war, as was due to those by whom the offense came, shall we discern that there is any departure from those divine attributes which believers in the living God always ascribe to Him? Fondly do we hope, fervently do we pray, that this mighty scourge of war may speedily pass away; yet if it be God's will that it continue until the wealth piled by bondsmen by two hundred and fifty years' unrequited toil shall be sunk, and until every drop of blood drawn with the lash shall be paid by another drawn with the sword, as was said three thousand years ago, so still it must be said that the judgments of the Lord are true and righteous altogether.

With malice toward none, with charity for all, with firmness in the right, as God gives us to see the right, let us strive on to finish the work we are in, to bind up the nation's wounds, to care for him who shall have borne the battle, and for his widow and orphans; to do all which may achieve and cherish a just and a lasting peace among ourselves and with all nations.

WINSTON CHURCHILL

The Battle of Britain, June 18, 1940

During the first four years of the last war the Allies experienced nothing but disaster and disappointment. . . . We repeatedly asked ourselves the question, "How are we going to win?" and no one was ever able to answer it with much precision, until at the end, quite suddenly, quite unexpectedly, our terrible foe collapsed before us, and we were so glutted with victory that in our folly we threw it away.

However matters may go in France or with the French government or other French governments, we in this island and in the British Empire will never lose our sense of comradeship with the French people . . . If final victory rewards our toils they shall share the gains—aye, and freedom shall be restored to all. We abate nothing of our just demands; not one jot or tittle do we recede . . . Czechs, Poles, Norwegians, Dutch, Belgians, have joined their causes to our own. All these shall be restored.

What General Weygand called the Battle of France is over. I expect that the Battle of Britain is about to begin. Upon this battle depends the survival of Christian civilization. Upon it depends our own British life, and the long continuity of our institutions and our Empire. The whole fury and might of the enemy must very soon be turned on us. Hitler knows that he will have to break us in this island or lose the war. If we can stand up to him, all Europe may be free and the life of the world may move forward into broad, sunlit uplands. But if we fail, then the whole world, including the United States, including all that we have known and cared for, will sink into the abyss of a new Dark Age, made more sinister, and perhaps more protracted, by the lights of perverted science. Let us therefore brace ourselves to our duties, and so bear ourselves that, if the British Empire and its Commonwealth last for a thousand years, men will say, "This was their finest hour."

FRANKLIN ROOSEVELT

A Declaration of War Against Japan, December 8, 1941

Mr. Vice-President, Mr. Speaker, members of the Senate and the House of Representatives:

Yesterday, December 7, 1941—a date which will live in infamy—the United States of America was suddenly and deliberately attacked by naval and air forces of the Empire of Japan.

The United States was at peace with that nation and, at the solicitation of Japan, was still in conversation with its government and its Emperor, looking toward the maintenance of peace in the Pacific. Indeed, one hour after Japanese air squadrons had commenced bombing in Oahu, the Japanese ambassador to the United States and his colleague delivered to the Secretary of State a formal reply to a recent American message. While this reply stated that it seemed useless to continue the existing diplomatic negotiations, it contained no threat or hint of war or armed attack.

It will be recorded that the distance of Hawaii from Japan makes it obvious that the attack was deliberately planned many days or even weeks ago. During the intervening time the Japanese Government has deliberately sought to deceive the United States by false statements and expressions of hope for continued peace.

The attack yesterday on the Hawaiian Islands has caused severe damage to American naval and military forces. Very many American lives have been lost. In addition American ships have been reported torpedoed on the high seas between San Francisco and Honolulu.

Yesterday the Japanese government also launched an attack against Malaya.

Last night Japanese forces attacked Hong Kong.

Last night Japanese forces attacked Guam.

Last night Japanese forces attacked the Philippine Islands.

Last night the Japanese attacked Wake Island.

This morning the Japanese attacked Midway Island.

Japan has, therefore, undertaken a surprise offensive extending throughout the Pacific area. The facts of yesterday speak for themselves. The people of the United States have already formed their opinions and well understand the implications to the very life and safety of our nation.

As Commander-in-Chief of the Army and Navy, I have directed that all measures be taken for our defense.

Always will we remember the character of the onslaught against us.

No matter how long it may take us to overcome this premeditated invasion, the American people in their righteous might will win through to absolute victory.

I believe I interpret the will of the Congress and of the people when I assert that we will not only defend ourselves to the uttermost but will make very certain that this form of treachery shall never endanger us again.

Hostilities exist. There is no blinking at the fact that our people, our territory, and our interests are in grave danger.

With confidence in our armed forces—with the unbounding determination of our people—we will gain the inevitable triumph—so help us God.

I ask that the Congress declare that since the unprovoked and dastardly attack by Japan on Sunday, December 7th, a state of war has existed between the United States and the Japanese Empire.

WENDY LIEBMANN

The Changing Consumer, January 16, 1992

Picture it. Twentieth century America. It began as an age of immigration. People flocking to these shores from Poland and Russia, from Ireland and England, from Italy and Germany. Sometimes by choice. Often by necessity. Often through no free will of their own. Arriving in their millions, they landed in New York, Galveston, New Orleans, and made their way throughout the country.

They came looking for the American Dream. A chance to work for a living, to earn enough to feed their families, to practice their own religion, hold their own political views—with no fear of persecution. They came to be Americans.

And they were. They assimilated as fast as they could learn the language The immigrant children cast off their foreign ways. They wanted to dress like Americans, look like Americans, eat like Americans, speak like Americans, live like Americans. And so was born the dominant face of 20th century America. And so was born an opportunity—to sell the American Dream to *the* American consumer. One idea to one group of people.

It began with a man named Henry Ford, and a revolutionary concept: mass-producing an affordable product—an automobile—for a universal consumer. As the century evolved, mass marketing became the way of business. Returning from a war that crystallized the American ethos, young, aggressive men and women, eager to succeed, demanded their "chicken in every pot, car in every garage" . . . and a television in every living room.

As a result, brands like Coca-Cola, Levi, Ivory, Revlon, Ford, Gillette, and McDonalds came to define America and Americans—both in this country and throughout the world.

With mass market brands came mass media to spread the word, and mass market retailers to sell the product. In the '50s and '60s it was Sears Roebuck & Co., Montgomery Ward, J.C. Penney, E.J. Korvette, K-Mart, Kroger, A&P, Publix, Winn-Dixie, and Safeway. In the '70s, '80s and '90s, it was Eckerd, Wal-Mart, Walgreens, Drug Emporium, Food Lion, Sam's, The Gap, and Price Club.

Brand-name products in the hundreds and thousands came to be purchased in just about any mass retail store—from the drugstore to the discount store, from the deep-discount drugstore to the warehouse club.

The over-extended distribution of branded merchandise contributed to the blurring of retail channels, and by the 1980s, the "massification" of American business was complete.

Unfortunately, however, it was complete just in time to confront the *"de-massification"* of the American consumer.

Like the Old South of a century ago, the homogeneous America of the 20th century is now gone with the wind. The mass market is dead. The consumer of the 21st century is not one, but many. A kaleidoscope of demographic and psychographic segments, each with distinct, and often mutually exclusive, needs and desires. While 20th century America was a melting pot, 21st century America will be a mosaic.

Picture it. *Twenty-first century* America. It will begin as an age of immigration. People will flock to these shores from Haiti and Cuba, from Mexico and China, from Hong Kong and Uzbekistan. Sometimes by choice. Often by necessity. Often through no free will of their own.

Arriving in their millions, they will land in Los Angeles, Seattle, Miami, and stay just where they land, in a ghetto-like community reminiscent of their homeland.

Like their 20th century counterparts, they will come looking for the American Dream. A chance to work for a living, to earn enough to feed their families, to practice their own religion, and hold their own political views—with no fear of persecution. They will come to be Americans. But different Americans, diverse Americans, maintaining a strong sense of their own heritage and the character of the land from which they came.

They will *not* assimilate as fast as they can learn the language. In fact, English will never be their primary language. They will be proud of their national tongue.

They will not cast off their foreign ways. They will not dress like Americans, eat like Americans, speak like Americans, live like Americans, as those in the 20th century. Instead they will retain the essence of their own distinctive culture.

And so will be born a new face for 21st century America. And so will be born an opportunity—a necessity—to sell a new American Dream to many diverse American consumers. The specialization of American business will arrive to meet the diversification of American consumers.

America in the 21st century will be characterized by its differences, not its similarities. America in the 21st century will be a mosaic of different ethnic groups and cultures that no longer view assimilation as their American Dream.

By the year 2000, nearly one-third of the U.S. population will be nonwhite or Hispanic. By the year 2056, the "average" American will be African, Asian, Hispanic, or Arabic. In California, parts of Florida and Texas, Spanish—not English—will be the predominant language.

But America in the 21st century will be characterized not *only* by its ethnic diversity, but also by the aging of its population.

Picture it. Twenty-first century America. An aging nation. No longer a nation of youth.

By the year 2000, nearly 30 percent of the population will be over 50. No longer young, aggressive men and women eager to succeed, demanding their "chicken in every pot, car in every garage," and a television in every living room.

Instead, they will be older men and women who are determined to, who must—through necessity—stay fit and healthy to live their longer lives.

Wellness will be of great concern. As much because of the fear of the high cost of health care, and how to afford it, as for its psychological rewards.

These will be cautious men and women who understand the value of money, and the need to save it. Men and women who know that price alone is not the issue, but that value for their money is paramount.

Men and women who will not pay more for anything than they believe it is worth. To whom worth and value have a new meaning. No longer confined to the old "price + quality" equation, but expanded to include service, convenience, selection and the overall purchase experience.

Intelligent, experienced—oftimes cynical—men and women who will demand quality information upon which to base their choice of stores and products.

Men and women who will choose a store based on its brand image—its ability to deliver a unique promise, a promise confirmed by the products and service it offers. Men and women who will not accept the promise of health care from a store that sells liquor and tobacco will not accept the promise of everyday low prices from a store that offers weekly sales.

Loyal men and women who know when to value a brand and a store—and when to reject it—when it does not address their specific needs.

And so will be born a mature face of 21st century America. And so will be born an opportunity—to sell a realistic, real, caring American Dream to older and more experienced American consumers.

But America in the 21st century will be characterized *not* only by its ethnic diversity and the aging of its population, but also by a diminishing level of aspirations. What began in 20th century America as an age of immigration, of hope, of new beginnings and boundless aspirations, of streets paved with gold, will be no more.

Picture it. Twenty-first century America. An age of diminishing expectations. A realization that doing better than your parents is no longer guaranteed. That having a job for your entire working life, owning your own home, sending your children to college and retiring to a warm climate at age 65 are no longer assured—even if you are willing to work hard all your life.

An age of adult children living at home. Of two, three and four income families—grandparents, parents and children helping to make ends meet. The necessity of multiple generations living together to share the burden of daily life.

And so will be born a concerned face of 21st century America. And so will be born an opportunity—to sell the American Dream to a consumer who does *not* believe he or she can afford it.

So, how will we market to, and satisfy this consumer of the 21st century, this ethnically diverse, aging consumer with significantly diminished expectations? Certainly for the one-size-fits-all mass marketer of the 20th century, it is an all but impossible task. *The mass market is dead.*

And so *must* be born a new face for retailing in 21st century America. *The mass market is dead*, long live specialty marketing.

Picture it. Twenty-first century America. The retailer will be part of and reflect the community. The store's environment, the products it sells, the employees and the message it evokes will be tailored to the specific nature and needs of the community it serves.

If an Hispanic community, the employees will be Hispanic. The merchandise will be tailored to the color preferences and taste preferences of Hispanic consumers. The signing and advertising will be in Spanish. The promotions will support traditional Spanish holidays and festivals. And manufacturers' sales representatives will come from or be part of that community.

If an older community, the employees will be older. The merchandise and service levels will be tailored to the needs and preferences of older consumers. The store will be designed to make for a comfortable, relaxed shopping trip. A coffee shop (a meeting place), motorized shopping carts, a personal shopper, numbered parking spaces, store-to-car delivery, home delivery 24 hours of the day.

In all, a store's image and credibility will come from its roots within the community—its commitment to that community. Not merely from its success as a well-known "national brand" retailer.

Even today, there exist examples of successful retailers who have begun to practice this 21st century philosophy. Von's Tianguis (tee-an-geese) in California and England's The Body Shop are two examples of specialized, community-oriented retailers.

Tianguis with its tortilleria, instead of a bakery. Stores loaded with chili peppers, cilantro, beans, salsa, Mexican cheeses, over 600 items of product tailored to its predominantly Mexican customers.

And The Body Shop, an environmentally and socially-conscious bath and body store, where store personnel are required to spend several hours per week working for a local charity or social program.

In 21st century America, *value* will be the key to all successful retailing. Picture it. A retailer who emphasizes value of purchase *and* shopping experience above all else. Whether that retailer sells apparel, health and beauty aids, prescription drugs, electronics, toys, sporting goods, stationery or food. Not necessarily the lowest prices in town—but the best value in town.

The customers will know—before entering the store—that they will find exactly what they want and pay no more for it than it is worth—*every day of the week*. In fact, when they leave the store they will believe they got more than they paid for. Sale-driven retailing of the 20th century will be no more.

Twentieth century examples of value-based retailers: Wal-Mart, Toys 'R' Us, Warehouse Clubs, deep-discounters. The first signs of 21st century value-based retailers.

Picture it. A 21st century retailer where *service* is given regardless of the price of the merchandise. Customers will know—before entering the store—that if they need help, they need only ask. Someone will show them where the appropriate merchandise is, answer their questions, offer suggestions and give recommendations—but only if the customer wants it.

Customers will know that if they don't have time to go to the store they have only to call their personal shopper who will take their order, charge it to a credit card and deliver it—free of charge—within 48 hours.

If they want to return or exchange an item today, tomorrow—or six months from now, they need only return to the store to get their money back. No receipt necessary. No questions asked. If too busy, they have only to call the store to arrange a door-to-store pick-up to return the merchandise—free of charge.

Sound familiar? Perhaps a 21st century Wal-Mart store?

Picture it. A 21st century retailer where *selection* of merchandise defines the image, credibility and essence of the store. No longer the same merchandise replicated store after store after store as in the 20th century. Instead a tightly tailored mix defined by the nature of the store and the community in which it operates.

Picture it. An apparel store designed to attract value-conscious, style-conscious consumers. A narrow mix of quality fashion basics in multiple colors and fabrications. No sales. Just everyday great values.

A quick and easy store to shop. A mistake-proof selection. Mix anything with everything for faultless fashion. A constantly changing mix of merchandise to pique the shopper's interest. Need help, just ask and it's there. A different size, a different color, a different fabric. Not in that store. Not in another store. "We'll special order it from our factory." And it will be delivered to your door, within days, free of charge.

Sound familiar? Perhaps a 21st century Gap Store? Picture it. A 21st century retailer where the store is a brand unto itself. A "good health store." Every imaginable product for fitness, beauty and health: vitamins, food supplements, medications, beauty products, weekly health and beauty lectures, a health food bar. Next store a fitness club. "Good health" advisors. Beauty advisors. No cigarettes, no liquor, no soda and no chips!

Sound familiar? Perhaps an Eckerd Store of the 21st century?

The 21st century consumer will not be satisfied with me-too stores and copy-cat products, with empty promises of service and selection, with poor quality and snake-oil mentality, "Come and get it, come and get it. Today only. . . ."

Consumers will shun me-too stores and me-too products and instead expect, demand, credible, innovative products with realistic benefits, tailored to their specific needs.

In the 21st century, consumers will reject new products that are merely knock-offs of existing items. Another brand of two-in-one shampoo and conditioner will not be tolerated. Product innovations that make life easier, more comfortable, are more economical and efficient, that consciously reflect the needs of specific customers will succeed. Quality will be paramount.

Innovation, quality, service and value will be the price of entry to the 21st century. Distinctive, credible messages from a retailer and a manufacturer to its community. Not department stores selling service and selection when they offer none. Not drug stores selling promises of health care and cigarettes at the same time. Not manufacturers promising an innovative new product—the 10th of its kind on the market. Instead marketers who will he accountable for their message, who will guarantee their performance, who will provide affordable quality, who will listen to and respect their customers.

Picture it. Twenty-first century America. An age when the specialization of American business will arrive to meet the diversification of American consumers. An opportunity—a necessity—to sell a new American Dream, an affordable American Dream, a credible American Dream to the mosaic that will be America.

Index